THE ORIGINS OF THE ENGLISH NOVEL, 1600–1740

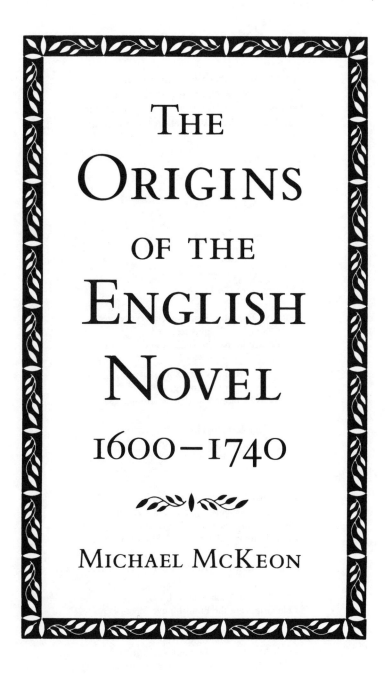

THE
ORIGINS
OF THE
ENGLISH
NOVEL
1600–1740

MICHAEL McKEON

THE JOHNS HOPKINS UNIVERSITY PRESS

Baltimore

This book has been brought to publication
with the generous assistance of
the National Endowment for the Humanities
and the Andrew W. Mellon Foundation.

Originally published, 1987
Third printing, 1988
Johns Hopkins Paperbacks edition, 1988

The Johns Hopkins University Press
701 West 40th Street
Baltimore, Maryland 21211

∞ The paper used in this publication meets the
minimum requirements of American National Standard
for Information Sciences—Permanence of Paper for
Printed Library Materials, ANSI Z39. 48-1984.

LIBRARY OF CONGRESS CATALOGING-IN-PUBLICATION DATA

McKeon, Michael, 1943–
The origins of the English novel, 1600–1740.

Bibliography: p.
Includes index.
1. English fiction—Early modern, 1500–1700—
History and criticism.   2. English fiction—18th century—
History and criticism.   I. Title.
PR841.M3   1987   823'.009   86-18495
ISBN 0-8018-3291-8 (alk. paper)
ISBN 0-8018-3746-4 (pbk.)

To Muriel, Peter, and Richard

Contents

Acknowledgments

I would like to thank the William Andrews Clark Memorial Library, the National Endowment for the Humanities, the American Council of Learned Societies, the Guggenheim Foundation, and Boston University for generous financial aid at various stages in the long life of this project.

Two decades ago, Hugh Amory introduced me to the problems of early modern narrative that, having occupied my thoughts for many years, now finally receive some airing in the following pages. More recently, I have been indebted to a number of people for helping me think more critically about the several dimensions of my argument. Individual chapters benefited from the diverse critical and scholarly powers of Larry Breiner, Bill Cain, Rudi Cardona, Richard Greaves, Gene Green, Jim Iffland, Richard Neugebauer, Max Novak, Ruth Perry, and Ian Watt. More extended sections of the book received valuable readings from Doug Canfield, Jerry Christensen, Timo Gilmore, and Erica Harth. Keith Stavely gave the entire manuscript his painstaking attention during a period when he was hard at work on his own book. Papers based upon parts of this study elicited useful assistance from Barbara Harman, Abdul JanMohamed, Annabel Patterson, and Fritz Ringer. Early and late, I have received much-appreciated readings and encouragement from Fred Jameson, Earl Miner, and Pat Spacks. I am grateful to John Pearson and Penny Moudrianakis—the former for accomplished word processing, the latter for accomplished copyediting—for improvements to the manuscript that go far beyond the mechanical. To my wife, Carolyn Williams, I owe the greatest gift: uncompromising intellectual and un-limited emotional support.

THE ORIGINS OF THE ENGLISH NOVEL, 1600–1740

tinguishing feature of the novel is its "formal realism," "a set of narrative procedures which are so commonly found together in the novel, and so rarely in other literary genres, that they may be regarded as typical of the form itself . . . The lowest common denominator of the novel genre as a whole [is] its formal realism" (32, 34). Watt specifies the novel's distinctive "narrative procedures" with subtlety and precision: the repudiation of traditional plots and figurative eloquence; the particularization of character and background, of naming, temporality, causation, and physical environment (13–30). Yet in isolating its formal features as strictly definitive of the new genre, Watt simultaneously argues their intimate, analogous relation to other developments of the early modern period that extend beyond the realm of literary form.

This "contextual" dimension of the argument he elaborates on several levels. Most immediately, Watt proposes a close analogy between the epistemological premises of formal realism and those of "philosophical realism," the modern tradition of realism inaugurated by Descartes and Locke (11–12 and chap. 1 passim). Less directly but with an insistence that pervades the entire book, Watt is concerned to argue a connection between the rise of the novel and the transformation of the social context of early eighteenth-century England. The philosophical, the novelistic, and the socioeconomic are united during this period in their validation of individual experience, of one or another sort of "individualism," which is manifested in the realm of the social by a number of inseparable phenomena: the development of capitalism and of economic specialization, the spread of a secularized Protestantism, the increasing dominance of "the commercial and industrial classes," and the growth of a reading public (61). Watt associates these phenomena with "the middle class" (e.g., 48, 59, 61), and he thereby encourages us to understand his thesis as a singularly persuasive treatment of a venerable theme: the historical coincidence of the rise of the middle class and the rise of the novel.

The force of Watt's argument has been evident to all readers. To what sorts of criticism has it seemed, in the quarter-century since its publication, most vulnerable? Although commentary has been very extensive, it can be summarized under two related headings.[2] Many critics have pointed out that even though Defoe, Richardson, and Fielding explicitly subvert the idea and ethos of romance, they nonetheless draw upon many of its stock situations and conventions. The general problem of romance in all three novelists is related to the particular problem of spirituality, equally antithetical to the secularizing premises of formal realism, in Defoe. Watt is judicious and illuminating on the ambivalence of Defoe's Calvinist otherworldliness, but in the end he is obliged by his thesis to treat as the function of a mechanical and merely "editorial policy" the spiritualizing presence that overshadows and infiltrates much of Robinson Crusoe's adventures (81). Moreover (an observation that does not so much contradict as complicate Watt's thesis), "romance" continues to suffuse the period itself. The Restoration and the early eighteenth century experienced an enormous outpouring of fiction that, by Watt's and most other standards, must surely be associated with the anti-individualist and idealizing tradition of romance. Finally, there is the corollary problem that even those ancient and medieval forms that define our notion of what "romance" amounts to can be shown to reflect, critics have claimed, some major features of "formal realism."[3]

Watt is well aware of the way that Fielding in particular evades the specifications of formal realism, and he has provided some hints of how his original and more comprehensive theoretical framework for *The Rise of the Novel* would have done Fielding greater justice by treating formal realism as a less dominant formal criterion.[4] But this leaves us in something of a dilemma. For Watt's thesis is attractive in great measure because of the precision with which he associates formal realism with "the novel," and the plausibility with which he ties the rise of the novel to contextual developments that bear a clear analogy to formal realism. If we want Fielding, we must dissipate and weaken the explanatory framework by requiring it to accommodate "romance" elements and the anti-individualist tendencies they imply. If we want the explanatory framework, we must be prepared to exclude much of Fielding from the rise of the novel. In other words, one central problem that Watt's unusually persuasive argument has helped to uncover is that of the persistence of romance, both within the novel and concurrently with its rise. And behind this lurks a yet more fundamental problem, the inadequacy of our theoretical distinction between "novel" and "romance."

My subject to this point has been Watt's vulnerability in delimiting the formal characteristics of the novel. The second major feature of his thesis that has remained problematic concerns the contextual aspect of the argument, the rise of the middle class. Where is the evidence, critics have asked, for the dominance of the middle class in the early eighteenth century? How was it distinguished—by contemporaries and in reality— from the traditional social categories of the aristocracy and gentry, especially as the nobility of early modern England was itself transformed by cultural attitudes and material activities that bear a clear relation to the new "individualism"? What, indeed, are we to make, in this context, of the familiar type of middle-class upstart whose middle-class identity is defined by nothing so much as a self-negating impulse, a will to be assimilated into the aristocracy? On the other hand, what are we to make of the unsettling argument that middle-class individualism originated not in eighteenth- but in thirteenth-century England? So far as the theory of the novel is concerned, the most troublesome figure once again seems to be Fielding. If the formal features of his novels are enmeshed in the romance tradition, form, content, and Fielding's own biography might appear to suggest a sympathy with the social perspective not of an emerging middle class but of a nobility particularized as the "declining gentry." Watt has acknowledged the degree to which the new literary form of the novel not only subverts, but also expresses, social norms that are still traditional in the early eighteenth century.[5] But if this is so, our view of both the middle class and the novel has been seriously obscured. Of course the obscurity is reciprocal; and for our purposes, the real casualty is a highly suggestive theory of the rise of the novel that would correlate two categories, neither of which can be made to have any definitional stability.[6]

But the problem of the persistence of romance and the aristocracy, like that of the preexistence of the novel and the middle class, may be made more tractable simply through the process of reformulation. For it begins to appear that we are dealing with two different versions of the same difficulty, and that what is required is a theory not just of the rise of the novel but of how categories, whether "literary" or "social," exist in history: how they first coalesce by being understood in terms of—as transformations of—other forms that have thus far been taken to define the field of possibility. What sort of guidance does genre theory provide for the pursuit of such an understanding?

2

In recent years the most influential contributions have been made by what might be called the "archetypalist" theory of genre. Archetypalist theory is composed of several not entirely compatible strands of modern thought about myth and the nature of the archaic mind. The term itself is most closely associated with the view of myth as the imitation and repetition of divine models or "archetypes." In the words of Mircea Eliade, the regeneration of the archetype suspends or abolishes time, duration, and history, for "he who reproduces the exemplary gesture . . . finds himself transported into the mythical epoch in which its revelation took place." Through the periodic annulment of time, primitive humanity gives its experience the transcendent and sacred value of a primordial past, which, in the act of re-creation, loses its pastness. Archaic people thus "escape" the disvalued temporality and ongoingness of history, and "live in a continual present" which is coextensive with the presentness of the great, founding acts of cosmic Creation and human origins.[7]

Claude Lévi-Strauss brings to the study of myth the interests of the structural anthropologist rather than those of the student of comparative

religion, but if his work therefore diverges from Eliade's in many respects, he retains a central concern with the separability of history and
mythic archetype, or (his preferred term) "structure." The dichotomy of
structure and history is roughly analogous, in Lévi-Strauss, to that of
form and content. "Content" is variously associated with "history,"
"empirical diversity," and "demographic change." Both the archaic and
the structuralist procedure work by "disregarding" or "bracketing" or
"abstracting from" content so as to isolate the formal—the structural—
continuity that persists despite variations in content. The most celebrated
example of this procedure in the structuralist analysis of myth is Lévi-
Strauss's treatment of the Oedipus myth. By disregarding the variable
content of its many versions, structuralist method reveals the true meaning—the invariant structure of the myth—for the primitive minds that
have made it. This meaning reflects the structuralist procedure, for it
entails the abstraction of a stable formal relationship from the vicissitudes
of historical change, imaginatively "overcoming" a felt contradiction
between experience and belief by demonstrating that both are internally
contradictory in a structurally similar fashion.[8]

So myth is defined by its capacity to disentangle itself—to provide an
"escape"—from history. But myths are in a perpetual state of transformation, and those that stray beyond the archaic conditions of their origins cease to perform this definitive function and therefore cease to be
myths. At this point, with the impossibility of an escape from history,
archetypalist thought encounters the necessity of a theory and a history
of genre. In the formulation of Lévi-Strauss, the birth of genre is a
deteriorative process: "mythic substance allows its internal principles of
organization to seep away," and "structure deteriorates into seriality."
This initial decay of mythic structure consists not in the "expiration" of
form but in its irresistible subjection to outside invaders, and its issue is
"episodic myth," a serial narrative that exudes episodes to fill its short
periods or assimilates them, unconstrained now "by any internal logic,"
from external sources. At the far end of this process are the origins of the
novel:

The past, life and the dream carry along with them dislocated images and
forms, by which the writer is haunted when chance or some other necessity,
contradicting the necessity by which they were once engendered in the actual
order of reality, preserves in them, or rediscovers in them, the contours of
myth. Yet the novelist drifts at random among these floating fragments that
the warmth of history has, as it were, melted off from the ice-pack. He
collects these scattered fragments and re-uses them as they come along, being
at the same time dimly aware that they originate from some other structure,
and that they will become increasingly rare as he is carried along by a current
different from the one which was holding them together. [The novel says]
not only that it was born from the exhaustion of myth, but also that it is

nothing more than an exhausting pursuit of structure, always lagging behind an evolutionary process that it keeps the closest watch on, without being able to rediscover, either within or without, the secret of a forgotten freshness.[9]

This elegiac account of the birth of genre frankly conceives of literary history in normative terms, as the coordination of "historical" evolution with "literary" devolution. Elsewhere Lévi-Strauss's language has a more studied neutrality, and he is concerned to distinguish the emergence of genre into two distinct sorts of literary narrative: the "romantic-novelistic" and the "legendary-historical." The "original formula" of a myth, he says, "degenerates or evolves, as you will, beyond the stage where the distinctive characteristics of the myth are still recognizable." The diplomatic diffidence of this language does not aim to deny that these decisive transformations entail the decay, even the "death," of myth. It "finally exhausts itself—without disappearing, for all of that. Two paths remain open: that of fictional elaboration, and that of reactivation with a view to legitimizing history," paths that follow the general rule of replacing "literal expressions with their metaphorical equivalents" or with "relations of contiguity."[10]

The "exhaustion" of myth, in other words, can also be understood as a strategic redeployment of its "original formula" to different ends. The shift in emphasis is important because it broaches a model of generic change that places literature in a historical relationship to myth without also subjecting it to a normative mythic model—that is, to an archetypalist view that literary form is defined by its resistance to or "escape" from history. If "history" is what happens to "form" to make it deteriorate into "genre," literary history approaches the status not just of a contradictory process but of a contradiction in terms. In Lévi-Strauss's restatement of how myth is transformed into genre, there is at least the suggestion that it is not that history happens to form, but that form happens in history; and that "genre" is the principal category by which we acknowledge the inescapable historicity of form itself.

The life work of Lévi-Strauss has been only very tangentially concerned with the theory of genre and the history of genres. The most influential exponent of archetypalist thought as a means of making literary history intelligible has been Northrop Frye, whose several versions of the basic distinction between "archetype" and "history" express a far more rigorously dichotomizing view of the relationship than appears at least in Lévi-Strauss's most recent restatement. "The imagination," Frye says, "is the constructive power of the mind, the power of building unities out of units . . . What the imagination, left to itself, produces is the rigidly conventionalized." Lest we assume that he cannot mean to hypostatize, like the archaic mind's "escape" from history, an imagination truly separated from the rest of experience, Frye makes clear that he means just that: "In the course of struggling with a world which is separate from itself, the imagination has to adapt its formulaic units to the demands of that world, to produce what Aristotle calls the probable impossibility. The fundamental technique used is what I call displacement, the adjusting of formulaic structures to a roughly credible context."[11]

The implication of this dichotomy is that the human mind, in autonomous isolation and unmodified by empowering circumstance or context, determines the invariable features of literature. These features, called the formal or structural principles of literature, do not change. When we speak of literary change, what we are responding to is the way variable and external "contexts" register their contingency as what we call "content." Content is the relatively accidental product of "the world," and it undergoes incessant change; form is essential and does not:

I call it displacement for many reasons, but one is that fidelity to the credible is a feature of literature that can affect only content . . . The requirements of literary form and plausible content always fight against each other . . '. Literary shape cannot come from life; it comes only from literary tradition, and so ultimately from myth.

In myth we see the structural principles of literature isolated; in realism we see the *same* structural principles (not similar ones) fitting into a context of plausibility.

In every [fictional] mode [the poet] imposes the same kind of mythical form on his content, but makes different adaptations of it.

Myths of gods merge into legends of heroes; legends of heroes merge into plots of tragedies and comedies; plots of tragedies and comedies merge into plots of more or less realistic fiction. But these are changes of social context rather than of literary form, and the constructive principles of story-telling remain constant through them, though of course they adapt to them.[12]

Literary form and plausible content, literary form and social context: as these passages suggest, it is not easy to tell whether Frye's conception of "literature" includes (however distinct they may be) both "form" and "content-context" or consists of form alone. But in either case it is clear that the relation between the two terms is an uncompromisingly dichotomous one. It is clear as well that Frye would concern himself not simply with static literary structures but with literary history. Yet, in an odd way, it is only by focusing on what is quite inessential to literature that we are able even to conceptualize literary change. As soon as we turn to "literature itself"—that is, to form—literary history becomes no more possible than is the "history" of the single invariant structure of the several versions of the Oedipus myth in Lévi-Strauss's analysis. This paradox does not prevent Frye from dividing history into "the five epochs of Western literature," each of which is dominated by one of the five great literary "modes," and he is able to observe as well "that European fiction, during the last fifteen centuries, has steadily moved its center of gravity down the list." "Reading forward in history," he adds, "we may think of our romantic, high mimetic and low mimetic modes as a series of *displaced* myths, *mythoi* or plot-formulas progressively moving over towards the opposite pole of verisimilitude, and then, with irony, beginning to move back" (35, 34, 45).

But what is it that is in motion here? Grammar suggests "the modes of European fiction," but it also implies that these are stages less in a process of transformation than in a static "series" of mythic structures. The differences between the modes—which create the illusion of movement—are differences in degree of displacement from the primary mythic mode. We may line them up next to each other and we may say that one has now "become" another, but we cannot observe them undergoing process. The only element in this scheme that has an integrity sufficiently stable to permit us to speak of it as changing is the essence of literary form or mythic structure, which is so stable as to preclude change altogether. On the other hand, the element into or through which myth is displaced is the indefinitely contingent content, whose very nature is defined by a discontinuity that must prohibit all hypotheses of process. Frye's literary modes, in short, do not really exist in history. Instead they are composed of strictly autonomous elements that, alternatively and always separately, either stand apart from its movement or are somehow indistinguishable from it. So far from enabling a theory of literary history, Frye's modal periodization freezes history into an immobile "literary structure." Any literary history will be obliged to conceive its subject in terms both of identity and of difference, in order to do justice to the inescapable notion that there is something here sufficiently integral to remain discernible as such, yet sufficiently variable to be in flux. But unless these two conditions are seen to be constituted by each other, inseparable (although distinguishable) features of the same subject, they will resolve themselves into antithetical extremes, one associated with "literature" and the other with "history," between which the process of literary history itself will evaporate.

Frye's belief in the unconditional separability of form from content leads him to identify the structural principles of all literature with the "literary archetypes" that he finds isolated and "undisplaced" in archaic myth. But the increasing displacement of archetypal structure in the other modes does not subvert his premise that form and content are separable, for it is the power of the literary critic to "stand back" from these displaced modes (as Lévi-Strauss stands back from the epiphenomenal events and details of the Oedipus versions) so as to perceive the "organizing design" that identifies all literature with the mythic archetypes. Yet "romance," not "myth," is really the crucial term in Frye's archetypalist theory, for he explicitly broadens its meaning to include not simply the romance "mode" but the entire spectrum of more-or-less displaced literature bounded by the extreme poles of "myth" and "naturalism" (140, 136–37). Thus, in the narrow sense, the eighteenth-century novel "was a realistic displacement of romance, and had few structural features peculiar to itself."[13] But in a more general sense, romance represents the basic "tendency . . . to displace myth in a human direction and yet, in contrast to 'realism,' to conventionalize content in an idealized direction" (137).

Frye explains this tendency by way of a hierarchy of figurative devices that, in recalling Lévi-Strauss on the two "paths" taken by the mythic formula once myth itself has been exhausted, also betrays a normative charge that was conspicuously absent in that account: "The central principle of displacement is that what can be metaphorically identified in a myth can only be linked in romance by some form of simile . . . In a myth we can have a sun-god or a tree-god; in a romance we may have a person who is significantly associated with the sun or trees. In more realistic modes the association becomes less significant and more a matter of incidental, even coincidental, imagery" (137). "Displacement" is the secularization term that Frye prefers to Lévi-Strauss's more ostentatiously evaluative "deterioration," but it is clear from this passage that its implications are really no less normative. For myth and its archetypes are here understood to be the central "place" of literary essence and meaning. Because of this, the difference between the immediate identifications of archetypal figures and the relatively mediated associations more common to other modes is a register not only of itself—of the technical differences between distinct rhetorical tropes for signifying— but also of an unequal proximity to the locus of meaning itself.

The normative resonance of the term is of course indispensable to its development in Freudian theory, upon which Frye's usage tacitly depends. For Freud, displacement "is nothing less than the essential portion of the dream-work . . . The consequence of the displacement is that the dream-content no longer resembles the core of the dream-thoughts and that the dream gives no more than a distortion of the dream-wish which exists in the unconscious."[14] By the same token, displacement is (for Frye) the essential portion of literary history, whose function is to distort the archetypal essence of literature by encrusting pure imagination or mind with the events and details of "plausible content." The central problem with such a view of historical change is not, I must stress, that it is transparently tendentious. The normative bias is only the outward sign of what is fundamentally problematic: that historical process itself has been evacuated from the analysis of how a genre comes into being. For if our model of change is distortion, the "new" literary form consists of nothing but the old one, now obscured by layers of epiphenomenal accretion. What we are witness to here is not the transformation of form but its calcification.

Nor does the problem disappear with the inversion of bias—although the exercise can be instructive. The unavoidable tendency of the term "displacement" to skew the literary historical process in a devolutionary direction is most obvious when we consider other signal metaphors that Frye might have borrowed from Freud with equal plausibility—for example, "free association." If literary history is conceived not as the dream work but as the dream analysis, not as distortion but as enlightenment, then the successive stages of literary evolution become just that: an evolution from the darkness of distortion toward semantic light. The archaic mind, no longer the normatively pristine realm of "forgotten freshness" and the collective unconscious, becomes a confused clutter of figurative identifications whose purpose is to mystify consciousness by "displacing" real human relations into imaginary significations. And the course of literary history becomes, accordingly, a process not of displacement but of "emplacement," the progressive "specification" of imaginative forms to the only locus of real meaning, the circumstantial and material reality of human experience. From this perspective archetypalist interpretation, which purports to "stand back" from the particular displacement so as to close the gap between it and the obscured locus of meaning, in fact amounts to the allegorizing imposition of imaginary meanings onto real ones. The demystification is useful and bracing. And as a model of historical process it is rather more promising than the archetypalist one in that it seems more readily to encourage a view of literary change as a genuine interpenetration of "form" and "content." Still, it remains too easy to see these categories instead as mechanical and essentially autonomous functions, enacting now not the distortion but the disclosure of one by the activities of the other.

The idea of literary history as a process of specification or emplacement can be useful in provisional applications, and I will invoke it from time to time in the following chapters. Used less guardedly, it is likely to encounter the sort of criticism that is sometimes lodged against Erich Auerbach's *Mimesis* (1946), that of an "evolutionary" bias toward "realist" modes; or the kind of objection—of a stealthy "persistence" and "preexistence"—that has been directed at *The Rise of the Novel*. Not that Watt's study is evolutionary in the sense of asserting the superiority of the novel to earlier forms. But just as archetypalist theory tends to overemphasize continuity and identity, so its alternative approach tends to exaggerate alterity and difference. Indeed, each approach finds its own partiality mirrored in the other: Auerbach and Watt stand over against Lévi-Strauss and Frye as their antithetical fulfillments. The confrontation suggests what a "total" theory of genre might look like. And the promise, at least, of such a theory is contained in the work of Mikhail Bakhtin.

3

Many critics have been sensitive to the unique status of the novel as the *modern* genre, the newcomer that arrives upon a scene already articulated into conventional generic categories and that proceeds to cannibalize and incorporate bits of other forms—the traditional and canonic genres as well as aberrant, "nonliterary" writings—in order to compose its own conventionality. To some it has seemed that these conditions of origin may even render problematic the status of the novel *as* a genre. Indeed, this sense of the novel's lack of "internal" rules, its resistance to the authority of traditional convention, its self-creation through the negation of other forms—these apprehensions of the novel's generic incoherence are easily assimilable to the archetypalist view of the novel as a deterioration or a displacement of essential form and structure. The argument can of course be distinguished from that tendentious extreme, especially as it directs our attention not to the novel's "loss" of structure but to the historical conditions of early modern Europe that militate against traditional models of structural coherence. Still, the elegiac, archetypalist echo is not easily, or perhaps properly, eradicated.[15]

More than any other critic, however, Bakhtin has treated as positive and even liberating the fact that "the birth and development of the novel as a genre takes place in the full light of the historical day." So far from throwing the generic status of the novel into question, this recognition only invites a revaluation of archetypalist metaphor. The history of the traditional genres is precisely "the life thay have lived as already completed genres, with a hardened and no longer flexible skeleton . . . Studying other genres is analogous to studying dead languages; studying the novel, on the other hand, is like studying languages that are not only alive, but still young."[16] Words like these might encourage us to find in Bakhtin a simple inversion of archetypalist bias; and our expectations are to some degree fulfilled by his characteristic dismissal of all "stylized" and "conventionalized" modes of discourse. In novelistic discourse, on the contrary, "language is transformed from the absolute dogma it had been within the narrow framework of a sealed-off and impermeable monoglossia into a working hypothesis for comprehending and expressing reality" (61).

But there is compelling reason to resist the view of Bakhtin as a simple mirror inversion of Frye. For his very tendentiousness, his very commitment to the superiority of "heteroglossia" and of its self-conscious internalization of dialogic discourse is the indispensable key to his profound sensitivity to the historical existence of genres. The dialogic quality of

novelistic discourse is a microcosmic model for the dialectical relations
that generally subsist between literary genres, the self-reflexive way in
which they are themselves constituted by the parodic reflection, internalization, and negation of other forms:

For any and every straightforward genre, any and every direct discourse—
epic, tragic, lyric, philosophical—may and indeed must itself become the
object of representation, the object of a parodic travestying "mimicry." It is
as if such mimicry rips the word away from its object, disunifies the two,
shows that a given straightforward generic word—epic or tragic—is one-
sided, bounded, incapable of exhausting the object; the process of parodying
forces us to experience those sides of the object that are not otherwise included in a given genre or a given style (55).

By such arguments Bakhtin sophisticates immeasurably the central archetypalist insight of the historical persistence of "myth" or "romance,"
disclosing in generic discourse a dense layering of precursor and survivor
forms that has an implicitly ideological significance: "Language is something that is historically real, a process of heteroglot development, a
process teeming with future and former languages, with prim but mori-
bund aristocrat-languages, with parvenu-languages and with countless
pretenders to the status of language" (356–57).

Bakhtin's responsiveness to the dialectical character of genre formation is rooted equally in his Russian formalism and in his Marxism.
Among the formalists, Viktor Shklovsky's celebrated idea of "defamiliarization" is particularly important because it conceptualizes, as the
touchstone of literary value, the mechanism by which a literary artifact
becomes effectually known only through its estrangement. For
Shklovsky (as to a great extent for Bakhtin), the self-conscious "baring of
the device"—the placement of it against a ground that reveals its status *as*
a device—is fundamentally esteemed over its mere tacit and habitual
functioning. To defamiliarize literary forms is thus also to contextualize
them, by conceiving their status to depend on their relation to the ground
that is constituted by other forms, within what is then plausibly seen as a
"literary system." And even the formalist can be seen to exploit the
temporal potential of defamiliarization: for example, in the argument
that modernist movements like futurism seek to overcome the tendency
of traditional words and works to die—or become "fossilized"—
through familiarity. For "system" and its components are themselves
grounded in history, in the past preexistence and the future persistence of
forms: to contextualize is necessarily to historicize. The generic capacity
of a work is defined both by its intertextual affiliations with some works
and by its intertextual detachment from others. Indeed, the notion of
"parody" is as fruitful as it is to Bakhtin because it conflates these two

movements into a single dialectical gesture of recapitulation and repudiation, imitation and disillusion, continuity and rupture.[17]

Bakhtin's full historicization of these formalist insights would seem to provide the most profound response to the archetypalist view that the generic volatility of the novel is a sign of its ageneric status, its radical poverty of structure. It is not simply that the novel, because of its modernity, is exposed to Lévi-Strauss's deteriorative "warmth of history." For it may also be said that the modernity of the novel uniquely permits us to see in it, as in a laboratory specimen illuminated by "the full light of the historical day," that dialectical process by which all genres have heretofore been constituted. Thus the anomalous character of the novel as a genre is inseparable from its capacity to exemplify the generic norm. The absolute appearance of its anomaly is an illusion that owes (it might be argued) to the impossibility of reading the teeming heteroglossia peculiar to the nonliterate, archaic epochs in which the traditional genres came into being under the "full light" that we are able to train upon our own.

But Bakhtin does not pursue this plausible line of thought that appears so compatible with his historicizing approach to the understanding of genre. And he does not do so because we are not entirely wrong to see in him the mirror inversion of Frye's archetypalism. The crux of the similarity lies in the dual status of Bakhtin's "novel." Like Frye's "romance," it denotes not only the relatively determinate literary form but also the generalized aura and ethos of that form—which entails, in Bakhtin's words, "taking genre not in its formalistic sense, but as a zone and a field of valorized perception, as a mode for representing the world" (28). Rather than permit antecedent genres to manifest in their own, precursory form elements that will become dominant in "the novel," Bakhtin digs an implausible gulf between the "rigid," "fixed," "sealed-off," "straightforward" closure of traditional genres and the "openended" "flexibility" and "indeterminacy" of "the novel" (4, 7, 8, 99, 296). And it is then "the novel," in its suprahistorical capacity, that must serve to denominate its own preexistence.

The dichotomy exaggerates both the reified homogeneity of the old genres, which are made to appear distinct from all process, and the unlimited horizon of the novel, which is the essence of process and differentially depicts reality as "only one of many possible realities." And the effect of the dichotomy is to obscure—as in Frye, but with a normative reversal—historical change itself. For Bakhtin, literary history entails not the "deterioration" of structure or the "displacement" of form, but a revivifying "novelization" that frees genre from its own deadly ossification:

The absolute past, tradition, hierarchical distance played no role in the formation of the novel as a genre . . . In the presence of the novel, all other

genres somehow have a different resonance. A lengthy battle for the novelization of the other genres began, a battle to drag them into a zone of contact
with reality . . . [But] the novelization of other genres does not imply their
subjection to an alien generic canon; on the contrary, novelization implies
their liberation from all that serves as a brake on their unique development.
(37, 38, 39)

With the language of "novelization," the history of literary forms becomes not an incarceration but a liberation from dead form, not displacement but an emplacement within "the zone of reality."

   The reversal of archetypalist theory is by no means absolute; the
profoundly dialectical quality of Bakhtin's thought precludes that it be
so. Thus the traditional genres are conceived not only as impervious
structure that is "dragged" from one zone to another by novelistic process but also as susceptible to their own "unique development," to something like the internalization of process. Indeed, this susceptibility may
be signaled by the real difference between the two chosen metaphors,
"displacement" and "novelization," and their respectively mechanical
and animate suggestiveness. But Bakhtin's dialectical commitment is
most secure on the microlevel, in the description and analysis of novelistic discourse. On the macrolevel of genre history it becomes less dependable—most strikingly in his formalistic and pervasive willingness to
speak as though "novelistic discourse" were not only quite separable
from other discourse but also something like the "authentic" literary
language. This sort of bias has instructive consequences for his more
particular account of the eighteenth-century novel. For whereas Ian
Watt's emphasis on "formal realism" leads him to focus on Defoe and
Richardson and to slight Fielding, Bakhtin's exclusive affirmation of
heteroglossia permits only Fielding, of the three, to qualify as a "characteristic and profound model of novelistic prose" (275; see also 301–2,
308–9, 361–62).

   The divergence of Bakhtin and Watt seems at first glance surprising,
for we might wish to find in their proximity a reassuring confirmation of
our general apprehensions about an "evolutionist" or a "progressive"
tendency. By the same token, it may seem odd to attribute what is here
problematic in Bakhtin's work to his formalism rather than to his Marxism. I think the account is accurate nonetheless, and that in order to make
good the promise of Bakhtin's work to provide something like a "total"
theory of genre we would do well to look to Marx himself.

4

Bakhtin's resolution of "the novel" into its two capacities—the "formalistic" genre and the "mode of representing the world"—may be seen
as the opening gambit of dialectical method, the provisional analysis of

the whole into its parts so as to disclose the antithetical means by which the whole—the category of genre—is constituted. Indeed, he might even be said to share this gambit with Frye, were it not that Frye's extraction of "mode," so far from aiming at provisionality, is a foundational act from which he never looks back. And this is generally true of modern critical discourse. The idea of literary "mode" enjoys some currency as a convenient way of registering the persistence of literary form without being obliged to account for, as it were, the "other half" of its historicity.[18] Conventional treatments of determinate "genre," on the other hand, have done their work if they have correlated a specific form with its immediate facilitating context. In confronting a very similar problem in genre theory, Fredric Jameson has shown how these categories, and the approaches they imply, tend to resolve themselves into a mutual exclusion that argues not the dialectical but the "dual" nature of genre.[19] The current critical use of "mode" and "genre" is the result of twin acts of surgical removal. In fact the present utility of these categories requires that the very fact of their removal be (except for the occasional and lingering twitch of the absent limbs) compassionately forgotten. Marx offers the hope of avoiding surgery altogether: not by prohibiting the methodological act of division, but by making it a systematically provisional component of method.

Let me return for a moment to a much earlier stage in the argument, the hypothetical analogy between the rise of the novel and the rise of the middle class. Although I chose not to pursue it at that point, the analogy (whether or not it is empirically verifiable) tacitly discloses a dimension of the problem of genre theory that is all but invisible when the literary category alone is the focus of attention. For the comprehensive subject of genre theory must be not just the genre as a "conceptual" category, nor yet the process by which that category comes into being, but the relationship between this conceptualization and the quasi-objective category—a class of literary products in the sense in which the members of a social class constitute a quasi-objective category—which both preexists, and is precipitated by, its conceptual formulation. In the introduction to the Grundrisse, Marx discusses the method of political economy in a way that fully acknowledges these two distinct kinds of category, and that I will take as a model for the elaboration of a dialectical theory of genre.[20]

As Marx describes it, the central problem in the method of political economy is one of beginnings. Suppose that we begin with the general category of "production":

Production in general is an abstraction, but a rational abstraction in so far as it really brings out and fixes the common element and thus saves us repetition. Still, this general category, this common element sifted out by comparison, is itself segmented many times over and splits into different determinations. Some determinations belong to all epochs, others only to a few . . . Even

though the most developed languages [for example] have laws and characteristics in common with the least developed, nevertheless, just those things
which determine their development, i.e., the elements which are not general
and common, must be separated out from the determinations valid for production as such, so that in their unity—which arises already from the identity
of the subject, humanity, and of the object, nature—their essential difference
is not forgotten. (85)

Marx's "rational abstraction" bears an evident relationship to the archetypalist categories "form" and "structure," as well as to that "constructive power of the mind, the power of building unities out of units," which
Frye calls "the imagination." But "production in general" is not an unconditional abstraction, and in the argument that follows, Marx both
propounds and exhibits the dialectical method whereby "unity" and
"difference" are kept simultaneously before our eyes.

   This is achieved by two major strategies. First, he argues that the
economic activities of production, consumption, distribution, and exchange exist in dialectical relation to one another. On the one hand,
production would seem to stand apart from the other factors as their
prior and determinant cause. But on the other hand, Marx's acrobatic
argumentation soon persuades us that production is so thoroughly conditioned by (for example) consumption as to be quite inseparable from it.
For consumption entails an imaginative and functional anticipation of
production: it "creates the motive for production; it also creates the
object which is active in production as its determinant aim" (91). So all at
once the factors appear indistinguishable: Marx archly observes that
there is "nothing simpler for a Hegelian than to posit production and
consumption as identical" (93). But the dazzling feats of dialectical synthesis are not an end in themselves. Analysis and synthesis cease to be
partial movements, in fact, only as they are brought into conjunction
with each other. The economic factors stand neither in identical, nor in
dichotomous, but in dialectical relation: production must be understood
both as the generally determinant factor and as, in a more partial and
"one-sided" sense, susceptible to the determinations of the other factors as
well (99). This one-sided sense of production has the real but provisional
truth characteristic of all knowledge that comes by dividing one segment
of human life from its continuum. But the usefulness of such analytic
exercises depends entirely on their success in incorporating within themselves a recognition of their own provisionality.

   An immediate case in point is the second of Marx's strategies for
uncovering the operations of dialectical method. So far he has been jug-
gling the four factors of political economy as though they were abstract
universals. But as his early observations have made clear, this has been a
self-consciously provisional abstraction from the realm of historical experience: for "whenever we speak of production . . . what is meant is

always production at a definite stage of social development" (85). Now Marx corrects for the partiality of this abstraction, showing that the problem of pursuing a dialectical method must always be a historical problem.

Let us suppose, now, that we begin once again with that "rational abstraction" which Marx has called "production in general." What is the relation between this mental abstraction and, not just the several more concrete categories of production, but the concrete material activities that the abstract concept presupposes? What can it mean to say that we "begin" with "production," an imaginative category whose apparent formulation at the moment when we begin the process of understanding belies a long and rich prehistory in the disparately concrete conditions of material production that it now is able, with hindsight, to generalize and enclose? But to conclude from this that the real beginning of our understanding is to be found in this concrete prehistory is not quite right either. For the abstract categories from which understanding now proceeds not only owe their origins to this moment in material development; in a certain sense they are accurately descriptive only of the material conditions under which they now are formulated.

As a rule, the most general abstractions arise only in the midst of the richest possible concrete development, where one thing appears as common to many, to all. Then it ceases to be thinkable in a particular form alone . . . The simplest abstraction, then, which modern economics places at the head of its discussions, and which expresses an immeasurably ancient relation valid in all forms of society, nevertheless achieves practical truth as an abstraction only as a category of the most modern society. (104–5)

At the same time it must be borne in mind that a "simple abstraction" of this sort "by no means begins only at the point where one can speak of it *as such*" (106).

What is the difference between the idea of the "rational abstraction" (*verständige Abstraktion*) with which we began and the idea of the "simple abstraction" (*einfache Abstraktion*) to which we have been led? Marx uses both terms with a gentle irony, for it has turned out that there is nothing very "rational" about the rational abstraction, whereas the "simplicity" of the simple abstraction conceals a considerable historical complexity. Yet it is not entirely misleading to see in the latter category nothing but the former category employed now with a self-conscious recognition of the complex determinacy of its own abstraction. No longer confined to the four economic factors traditional to academic investigation, Marx offers us the clarifying example of the category "labor." "Labour in general," although an ancient mental category, achieves its fulfillment only with Adam Smith, whose "indifference towards any specific kind of labour presupposes a very developed totality of real kinds of labour, of which no single one is any longer predominant . . . Indifference towards specific labours corresponds to a form of society in which individuals can with ease transfer from one labour to another" and in which labour "has ceased to be organically linked with particular individuals in any specific form" (104). Thus "bourgeois labour" does indeed reflect and presuppose rudimentary, precapitalist material conditions. But it can do this only, as it were, retroactively, by virtue of a material development sufficiently advanced to permit the formulation of abstract concepts that comprehend both the rudimentary and advanced states.

The abstractions of capitalism provide the bext example of what is, nevertheless, fundamental to all historical life: the inseparability of diverse social formations within the dialectical continuum of history, and the will of each to regard itself with a "one-sided" partiality, to cut itself off from the continuum. For

since bourgeois society is itself only a contradictory form of development, relations derived from earlier forms will often be found within it only in an entirely stunted form, or even travestied. For example, communal property. Although it is true, therefore, that the categories of bourgeois economics possess a truth for all other forms of society, this is to be taken only with a grain of salt. They can contain them in a developed, or stunted, or caricatured form etc., but always with an essential difference. The so-called historical presentation of development is founded, as a rule, on the fact that the latest form regards the previous ones as steps leading up to itself, and, since it is only rarely and only under quite specific conditions able to criticize itself . . . it always conceives them one-sidedly. (105–6)

The trenchant critique of "evolutionary" and "progressive" partiality with which this passage concludes is only the most striking evidence of Marx's methodological power, his capacity to harness self-criticism as an essential and regulative engine of knowledge. And so his own "historical presentation of development" captures, in its very language, the contradictory movement of oblique replication that is embodied in Bakhtin's principle of parody. But in Marx the principle works unambiguously on the macrolevel of historiography, experimentally exposing all process to the antithetically normative standards of "development" and "caricature." This systematic frustration of the tendency toward "one-sidedness" in historical knowledge is the outward sign of an effort to grasp process "as such," by disclosing in the fact of difference an articulation sufficiently subtle—the entire range of nuance enclosed by the poles of development and caricature—to mediate the gap between difference and identity. Marx's historical dialectic requires us to envision not two distinct categories impinging on each other but a single category comprehended in its temporal multiplicity: the simple abstraction.

By now it will be clear that the title of this study is to be taken, as Marx would say, only with a grain of salt. Or rather, speaking of the "origins" of the novel must be understood to entail the disarming "simplicity" of describing its emergence as a simple abstraction. The origins of the English novel occur at the end point of a long history of "novelistic usage"—at the moment when this usage has become sufficiently complex to permit a generalizing "indifference" to the specificity of usages and an abstraction of the category whose integrity is presupposed by that indifference. This is what Louis Althusser means when, in explicating the introduction to the *Grundrisse,* he says that "Marxism establishes in principle the recognition of the givenness of the complex structure of any concrete 'object,' a structure which governs both the development of the object and the development of the theoretical practice which produces the knowledge of it. There is no longer any original essence, only an ever-pre-givenness, however far knowledge delves into its past."[21] To begin at the beginning therefore requires that we begin at the end. By the middle of the eighteenth century, the stabilizing of terminology—the increasing acceptance of "the novel" as a canonic term, so that contemporaries can "speak of it *as such*"—signals the stability of the conceptual category and of the class of literary products that it encloses. My procedure in this study will be to work back from that point of origin to disclose the immediate history of its "pre-givenness."

But to thus account for the origins of the novel in the eighteenth century—for its emergence as a simple abstraction—will also entail acknowledging the emergence of romance as a simple abstraction in the preceding two centuries. The reasons for this relatively close historical conjunction need not be rehearsed at this introductory stage of my argument, but it will come as no surprise that the two phenomena are related in terms both of the history of genres and (the separation is provisional) of material history. A dialectical theory of genre, so far from rejecting the archetypalist insight into the relationship of "romance" and "the novel," would aim instead to make it truly comprehensible by grounding it in the history of literary and material forms. The problematic persistence of "romance" and "the aristocracy," with which I began this discussion, is comprehensible in part as the necessary continuity of those forms on which the decisively different forms of modernity are yet dependent for their dialectical negation. But the persistence of the traditional categories is also an optical illusion, since the categories themselves, and the crucial "traditionality" that determines our sense of their persistence, are conceptual products of the same several centuries in which "the novel" and "the middle class" come into being. Although possessed of a more highly articulated "pre-givenness," the categories "romance" and "the aristocracy" are broadly contemporary with the categories that "replace" them.

5

Modern criticism's sensitivity to the "contractual" and "institutional" capacity of literary genres implicitly attributes to them an explanatory function that is both epistemological and social. Genres provide a conceptual framework for the mediation (if not the "solution") of intractable problems, a method for rendering such problems intelligible. The ideological status of genre, like that of all conceptual categories, lies in its explanatory and problem-"solving" capacities. And generic form itself, the dense network of a conventionality that is both elastic and profoundly regulative, is the prior and most tacitly powerful mechanism of the explanatory method of genre. Genres fill a need for which no adequate alternative method exists. And when they change, it is as part of a change both in the need they exist to fill and in the means that exist for its fulfillment.

In the following pages I will argue that the problems associated with the thesis of the rise of the novel in the early modern period may be overcome by reconceiving that thesis according to the assumptions of a dialectical theory of genre. "The novel" must be understood as what Marx calls a "simple abstraction," a deceptively monolithic category that encloses a complex historical process. It attains its modern, "institutional" stability and coherence at this time because of its unrivaled power both to formulate, and to explain, a set of problems that are central to early modern experience. These may be understood as problems of categorial instability, which the novel, originating to resolve, also inevitably reflects. The first sort of instability with which the novel is concerned has to do with generic categories; the second, with social categories. The instability of generic categories registers an epistemological crisis, a major cultural transition in attitudes toward how to tell the truth in narrative. For convenience, I will call the set of problems associated with this epistemological crisis "questions of truth." The instability of social categories registers a cultural crisis in attitudes toward how the external social order is related to the internal, moral state of its members. For convenience, I will call the set of problems associated with this social and ethical crisis "questions of virtue." Questions of truth and questions of virtue concern different realms of human experience, and they are likely to be raised in very different contexts. Yet in one central respect they are closely analogous. Both pose problems of signification: What kind of authority or evidence is required of narrative to permit it to signify truth to its readers? What kind of social existence or behavior signifies an individual's virtue to others?

The instability of generic and social categories in the period from 1600 to 1740 is symptomatic of a change in attitudes about how truth and virtue are most authentically signified. But the novel comes into existence in order to mediate this change in attitudes, and it therefore is not surprising that it should seem a contradictory amalgam of inconsistent elements. In fact, the crucial period of the novel's origins is best understood according to a dynamic model of conflict that occurs, for questions of truth as well as virtue, in several stages. Let me simplify and summarize this conflict as it is conducted within the arena of the emergent novel and as it is described, more exhaustively, in the following pages.

At the beginning of the period of our concern, the reigning narrative epistemology involves a dependence on received authorities and a priori traditions; I will call this posture "romance idealism." In the seventeenth century it is challenged and refuted by an empirical epistemology that derives from many sources, and this I will call "naive empiricism." But this negation of romance, having embarked on a journey for which it has no maps, at certain points loses its way. And it becomes vulnerable, in turn, to a countercritique that has been generated by its own over-enthusiasm. I will call this countercritique "extreme skepticism." In refuting its empiricist progenitor, I will argue, extreme skepticism inevitably recapitulates some features of the romance idealism which it is equally committed to opposing. For questions of virtue, the terms alter, but the two-stage pattern of reversal is very much the same as for questions of truth. We begin with a relatively stratified social order supported by a reigning world view that I will call "aristocratic ideology." Spurred by social change, this ideology is attacked and subverted by its prime antagonist, "progressive ideology." But at a certain point, progressive ideology gives birth to its own critique, which is both more radical than itself, and harks back to the common, aristocratic enemy. I will call this countercritique "conservative ideology." Even this brief summary may help to revise the idea that the persistence of romance and of the aristocracy is a problematic feature of the origins of the novel that needs to be, not explained, but explained away. For the traditional categories do not really "persist" into the realm of the modern as an alien intrusion from without. Now truly abstracted and constituted *as* categories, they are incorporated within the very process of the emergent genre and are vitally functional in the finely articulated mechanism by which it establishes its own domain.

One value of this approach to the origins of the English novel is that it fully accounts for the well-known complexity of the genre at the moment that it attains its institutional and canonic identity: its capacity, that is, to comprehend not only Richardson but also Fielding. This is the clearest sign of the new genre's triumph as an explanatory and problem-solving mode, its powerful adaptability in mediating questions of truth and virtue from opposed points of view. But the approach is valuable as well for the way it emphasizes a less recognized complexity of the new genre, its foundation in the analogical structure of questions of truth and virtue. Of course, in an important respect this analogy between epistemological and socioethical problems helps to sophisticate and to retrieve the familiar correlation between the rise of the novel and the rise of the middle class. Like "the novel," "the middle class" is one of those simple abstractions whose early modern origins mask a considerable preexistence. And like "the novel," "the middle class" (and the category "class" as such) filled an explanatory need for which there had been no satisfactory alternative.

For the purposes of this study, however, the most striking dimension of the analogy lies not outside the novel, between literary and social formations, but within it. In its preoccupation with questions of virtue, I will argue, the emerging novel internalizes the emergence of the middle class and the concerns that it exists to mediate. Indeed, one crucial explanatory function of the new genre is to demonstrate that questions of truth and questions of virtue become more tractable when seen as analogous versions of each other. And the coherence of the analogy can be seen in the correlative logic by which, in a movement that only culminates with Richardson and Fielding, the formal posture of naive empiricism tends to accompany a substantive stance of progressive ideology, and extreme skepticism is reflected in an analogous, conservative ideology. This insight—the deep and fruitful analogy between questions of truth and questions of virtue—is the enabling foundation of the novel. And the genre of the novel can be understood comprehensively as an early modern cultural instrument designed to confront, on the level of narrative form and content, both intellectual and social crisis simultaneously. The novel emerges into public consciousness when this conflation can be made with complete confidence. The conflict then comes to be embodied in a controversy between Richardson and Fielding—writers who are understood to represent coherent, autonomous, and alternative methods for doing the same thing.

Parts One and Two of this study will be concerned with the arena of conflict, with the broad range of texts and contexts in which questions of truth and virtue are experimentally engaged. Part Three will be devoted to more extended readings of several narratives that are commonly seen as central, in one way or another, to the origins of the English novel.

I

QUESTIONS OF TRUTH

— One —

The Destabilization of Generic Categories

Modern studies of seventeenth-century prose fiction used to suffer from
a particularly virulent form of taxonomic disease. Its signs could be seen
in the way the effort to discriminate and classify the several genres, an
essential if preliminary first step, stealthily tended to become an end in
itself. Typologies of fiction, romance, history, and novel are posited, take
root, sprout subcategories, and quickly send out feelers that intersect
with one another to create strange, hybrid forms whose very existence
finally must vitiate the discriminatory function of the original taxonomy.[1] It is easy enough to see why this happens. The common understanding that the novel "rose" around 1740 provides a *terminus ad quem*
which appears to organize all that follows within the ample boundaries of
the great modern form, but which also requires that what precedes this
founding act will resemble chaos. And this impression receives some
support from the way contemporaries talk about their prose fiction, for it
is only around the middle of the eighteenth century that "the novel"
becomes the dominant and standard term. Until then we are confronted
with a much more complicated usage, about which three generalizations
may be made. First, seventeenth- and early eighteenth-century writers
often use the terms "romance," "history," and "novel" with an evident
interchangeability that must bewilder and frustrate all modern expectations. But second, alongside this confusion we can perceive a growing
impulse to make the dyad "romance/history" stand for an all-but-abso-
lute dichotomy between opposed ways of knowing the world. Yet finally, the easy confidence of this opposition is itself opposed by the will to
assert the similarities, as well as the differences, between history and

romance. The first phenomenon is easily exemplified in the space of a few pages. The second and third are the subject of the major part of my first three chapters, and they define one of two crucial movements—the posing of "questions of truth"—in the origins of the English novel.

I

"ROMANCE" AS A SIMPLE ABSTRACTION

A convenient source for the study of contemporary attitudes toward the classification of literary genres may be found in publishers' booklists. In 1672 the bookseller John Starkey advertised his list of publications by printing a catalog of books divided into the following six categories: Divinity; Physick; Law; History; Poetry and Plays; and Miscellanies (i.e., "miscellaneous"). Under the heading "history" he includes Suetonius, Rabelais, the "Novels" of Quevedo, biographies, travel narratives—and the collection at whose end the catalog itself is printed: *The Annals of Love, Containing Select Histories of the Amours of divers Princes Courts, Pleasantly Related.* By modern standards, the most pressing problem with this mode of classification is the absence of any will to distinguish consistently between "history" and "literature," between "fact" and "fiction." Robert Clavell's periodical catalogs of books printed after the Great Fire of London reveal a similar readiness to categorize "romances" and "novels" along with what we would be more likely to agree are "histories." So, too, William Thackeray's 1689 trade list divides his chapbooks into "small godly books," "small merry books," "double-books," and "histories," including in the latter category a miscellaneous assortment of chivalric romance redactions and other sorts of narrative. Francis Kirkman, an author and translator as well as a bookseller, prefaced his translation of *Don Bellianis of Greece* with a discussion and list of two sorts of "histories." The first list is composed largely of late popularizations of twelfth- and thirteenth-century romances, including *Don Bellianis* itself. The second category is "another sort of Historyes, which are called *Romances*," and it contains similar works along with several of the French "heroic romances," whose composition had begun to wane only in the last few years. Elsewhere Kirkman calls another late-medieval popularization a "history," observing that "we have several books of this nature in *English*, viz. *Novels*, but they are all translations."[2]

But if only this sort of generic "confusion" was evident during the later seventeenth century, there would be considerably less reason to be interested in it. There coexists with this bewildering laxity of labels, however, a more familiar and reassuring impulse. The book catalog of William London, for example, obligingly separates "History" from "Romances, Poems and Playes." In fact these two opposed tendencies can even be found in the same writer. In the inaugural issue of *The Gen-*

tleman's Journal, Peter Motteux announces that his periodical will concentrate on the reporting of "news" similar to that printed in "our *Gazettes*," a category which turns out to comprise not only accounts of current political events and intellectual fashions but also poetry and short "novels." Yet several numbers later, Motteux is concerned on the contrary to distinguish "news" from novels, odes, songs, philosophy, and other disparate sorts of discourse.[3] What is most significant about Restoration usage, in other words, is precisely the fact that it is not entirely foreign to us. Our acute sense of inconsistency derives from the encounter not only with generic chaos but also with attempts to discriminate the "factual" from the "fictional" in a way that is recognizably "modern." It was during the course of the seventeenth century that much of the labor involved in this discrimination was expended, and it was evidently an act of epistemological as well as generic definition. By the time "the novel" was beginning to be accepted as the canonic term for prose fiction in the modern age, the epistemological transformation that is vital to its constitution as a genre had proceeded very far. Long before this terminological triumph, the battle was being fought not in the name of the novel but first of all in that of "true history." The sometimes easy acceptance of "romance" under the heading of "history" in late seventeenth-century booklists therefore must not be allowed to mask the concurrent confrontation between two divergent views of how to tell the truth in narrative.

The usage of booksellers might easily be multiplied, but the more telling instances are those that reflect the status of "romance" not only as a distinct generic, but also as a broadly epistemological, category whose meaning is overwhelmingly trivializing or pejorative. According to John Nalson, for example, "History without Truth or with a mixture of Falsehood, degenerates into Romance." Thomas Shadwell praised a fellow playwright for avoiding the anachronisms common in the French historical drama: yet "even our *English* Authors are too much given to make true History (in their Plays) Romantick and impossible." And Aphra Behn's Belvira tells her lover, Frankwit, that "Women enjoy'd, are like Romances read, or Raree-shows once seen, meer tricks of the slight of hand." The generic term has an irresistible epistemological extension. Joseph Glanvill observed that in sleep "we Dream, see Visions, converse with *Chimaera's,* the one half of our lives is a *Romance, a* fiction." On the eve of Charles II's Restoration, Marchamont Nedham refuted the notion that royal clemency would be shown to republicans by remarking that " 'tis a Romance . . . to think that Revenge can sleep, but like a Dog, to wake at Will." By an easy transference, credulity in the auditor is mendacity in the speaker. Thus Dryden's Mrs. Millisent protests pertly: "This is a Romance,—I'le not believe a word on't.—" Thus the satirical figure Poor Robin is said to have "had an excellent Talent in the Mystery

of Romancing, call'd by the Antients *The Art of Lying*." And the fact that
this understanding is really more modern than "ancient" is suggested,
finally, by Samuel Butler's remark that "a little Philosophy will serve to
Qualify a Romancer (which is oftener taken to signify a Lier then in any
other Sense)."[4]

Yet it is relevant, even necessary, to inquire into the status of "the
mystery of romancing" among the ancients before proceeding to document the early modern revolution in epistemology. The inquiry is
needed to test and to substantiate my central assumption that the novel is
an early modern phenomenon. For if, as I would argue, "romance" is one
of those "simple abstractions" of which Marx speaks, and if it "achieves
practical truth as an abstraction only as a category of the most modern
society"—that is, at the dawn of the modern world—it also "expresses
an immeasurably ancient relation valid in all forms of society." And if the
early modern epistemological revolution is the decisive stage in the origins of the English novel, it is not for all that the origin of the conceptual
category of which "the novel" is the most concrete embodiment. In the
following sections I will consider two earlier periods whose innovations
are suggestively analogous to those of the period that is my central
concern, and that therefore can be seen to "contain them in a developed,
or stunted, or caricatured form, but always with an essential difference."[5]
My organizing interest here will be in attitudes toward how to tell the
truth in narrative. My tacit but recurrent questions will be: How do
people conceive the relationship between "fact" and "fiction," between
"history" and "literature" ("myth," "romance," "poetry")? To what
degree is the narrative of history itself subjected to a rationalizing periodization? What is the influence on narrative epistemology of empirical
strategies of abstraction and objectification in natural and legal studies?
What are the epistemological consequences of alternative modes of narrative "technology"—of orality, literacy, and typography? The rapidity
with which I review vast tracts of learning and controversy in the periods
of the "precursor revolutions" may perhaps be excused by space
limitations.

2

PRECURSOR REVOLUTIONS: THE GREEK ENLIGHTENMENT

In the last few decades, an anthropological interest in the comparative
study of literate and nonliterate cultures has been concentrated on the
field of classical scholarship in such a way as to stimulate new thought
about an old subject, the nature of the Greek Enlightenment. The "poetic" qualities of all nonliterate communication derive from its mnemonic
and preservative function. In such a culture, according to Eric Havelock,

"the problem confronting memory is to remember a host of what we would call 'facts' or 'data' which in separation cannot be remembered. Therefore one fact must be connected with its predecessor; therefore it must be framed in such a way as to recall its predecessor; therefore, while itself a 'new' fact, it must nevertheless resemble its predecessor, as an echo resembles its original." In accord with this "inhibition against new invention," separate items of information are preserved by being experienced as inseparable, as part of a larger, self-adjusting continuum of knowledge. These special demands of what Havelock has called, with conscious paradox, "the oral documentation of a non-literate culture," obviously entail attitudes toward notions of "originality," "factuality," and even "historicity" that are very different from those of a literate culture. Because they admit of none of the independent tests of verification on which our ideas of historical authority depend, the authoritative linearity of oral lineages is deceptive. In fact the genealogies in use among oral peoples stabilize knowledge by changing over time. "The social element in remembering results in the genealogies being transmuted in the course of being transmitted . . . Myth and history merge into one: the elements in the cultural heritage which cease to have a contemporary relevance tend to be soon forgotten or transformed."[6]

Writing "reifies" memory. The physical preservation of knowledge produces not only documents and archives but also the conditions for the "objective" comparison of data, even the inclination to regard knowledge as a collection of discrete "objects." The connection between the invention of the Greek alphabet around 700 B.C. and the Greek Enlightenment two or three centuries later has seemed a suggestive one to scholars, not just because the classical flowering was literate in form, but because those intellectual qualities that we most associate with its remarkably innovative character—rationality, critical skepticism, abstraction, logic, objectivity, historicity—are also those that we have learned to associate with the experience of the transition from an oral to a literate culture. But at this point two important caveats must be registered. First, the correlation of the Enlightenment with the literacy revolution need not entail the argument that the latter provides the great and single "explanation" of the former. Second, the experience of the literacy revolution is by no means as simple as the instantaneous "transition" from one state to another. The celebrated "Homeric problem" is bound up with the impression that the Homeric poems seem to be the product neither of oral nor of literate composition but of both.[7] The two modes have been shown to overlap in diverse settings and periods. This is obvious enough in the long "cultural lag" between the invention of the alphabet and the classical flowering at the end of the fifth century, a period in which cultural literacy must be seen as potential rather than actual, and in which the alphabet was applied primarily to works "previously com-

posed according to oral rules of memorization. That is why Greek literature is predominantly poetic, to the death of Euripides."[8]

The tension between oral and literate modes, and between the habits
of mind which they tend to entail, can be felt throughout the range of
classical Greek culture. The genealogies of the gods that compose
Hesiod's *Theogony* recall those of the Homeric poems, yet they also seem
like records that have been abstracted, in a very un-Homeric fashion,
from the larger contexts of storytelling. And Hesiod explicitly evinces a
critical attitude toward chronology and historical veracity that certainly is
absent in Homer. By the sixth century, Hecataeus, Xenophanes, Her-
aclitus, and others had begun to formulate a rationalist critique of Homeric myth according to distinctions between historical truth and fiction.[9] If Herodotus is "the father of history," there is good reason to
associate the classical emergence of the category "history" as a simple
abstraction with the rigorous tests for veracity employed by Thucydides.
But the example he set had virtually no followers in the historiography of
Greek and Roman antiquity, which generally elevated rhetorical criteria
over what we would call the demands of historical accuracy.[10] Moreover
Thucydides entirely agrees with Herodotus in preferring the oral testimony of eyewitnesses to the evidence of written documentation.[11] That
Thucydides follows the standards of an oral culture would seem to be
suggested also by scholars who have argued that the impulse toward
"scientific" historiography is subverted, in him, by the pervasive influence of the tragic *mythos*.[12] But if, as is claimed, *The Peloponnesian War*
adheres to the Aristotelian definition of tragedy, it is no less expressive of
a literate viewpoint for that. Aristotle's revolutionary simple abstraction
"poetry" is as much the twin of his Thucydidean "history" as its antithesis, for both reflect in different ways the striking linearity and objectivity
that are so characteristic of literate narrative as distinguished from oral
myth. If there is an oral remnant in Aristotle's view of tragedy, it is to be
found not in his abstracted conception of *mythos* but in the idea of *catharsis,* which confirms the formal excellence of the well-made plot by the
nonliterate, performative criterion of audience effect.[13] What is truly
revolutionary about Aristotle's *Poetics,* the abstraction of "poetry" from
its mythic substratum, had no greater currency in classical antiquity than
did the abstracted "history" of Thucydides.[14] The full exploitation of
both ideas will not occur until the European Enlightenment.

Formulated midway between these two experiments in abstraction,
Platonic philosophy is the central achievement of the Greek Enlightenment both in the obvious sense and insofar as it most dramatically enacts
the confrontation between oral and literate modes of cognition. In the
Phaedrus, Socrates compares favorably the oral discourse of dialectic with
the reifying abstractions of the written word, which encourages its users
to call "things to remembrance no longer from within themselves, but

by means of external marks." And to Dionysius, Plato remarked that "what are now called his [i.e., Plato's] are the work of a Socrates grown embellished and modernized." On the other hand, the import of the brief dialogue that frames the *Theaetetus* is that had not Euclides taken careful notes on the bygone dialectical encounter that it records, correcting his failing memory against that of Socrates, we would not now have the opportunity to sample its wisdom in any form.[15] So the Platonic dialogues seem to constitute both a reified displacement and a preservative "emplacement" of Socratic dialectic. But according to Havelock, we are wrong to view even dialectic as "pure" oral discourse. By asking the speaker to repeat himself and to reformulate his meaning, Socratic method works to separate the knower from the known, rationalizing consciousness by waking it from its "dream language and stimulating it to think abstractly." From this perspective we may envision even Socrates as a demystifier of myth, much as Freud is a demystifier of dreams. Dialectic becomes the "scientific" method by which the laconic and deceptive parataxis of unselfconscious thought is given hypotactic clarity through being emplaced within the denser and more exhaustive detail of the speaker's own specifications.[16]

We call Plato's figures "myths" because we sense in them that dialectical motive of the archaic mind to tell a proleptic story so as somehow to reach an originating realm of ends that is inaccessible by more direct means. As Socrates says in his preamble to the myth of the charioteer in the *Phaedrus,* to describe the nature of the soul "would be a long tale to tell, and most assuredly a god alone could tell it, but what it resembles, that a man might tell in briefer compass."[17] And this—the use of resemblances to attain reality—is of course also the subject of the myth of the charioteer, which recounts the struggles of the soul to escape its human contingency and to regain, by *anamnesis* or remembering, its divine place of origin. Yet the very fixity that myth obtains, not only through Platonic inscription, but also through Socratic narration, may incapacitate it for the instrumental, recollective function that it is meant to serve. Havelock contends that the Socratic abstraction of the autonomous psyche—the individualized subject of the charioteer myth—is "the counterpart of the rejection of the oral culture."[18] In a similar fashion, the self-consciously framed beauty and integrity of the myth itself fixes and controls it in a way that is foreign to the oral experience of myth.

"Myth" is succeeded by "romance" in the archetypalist scheme of cultural devolution,[19] and there is some logic in treating the unstable productions of newly literate Greek culture—Socratic "myth," Thucydidean history, Sophoclean tragedy—as versions of romance narrative, relatively self-sufficient and emplaced objectifications of oral culture. But the tentativeness and instability of the emplacement require emphasis. Aristotle cites *Oedipus the King* more often than any other drama, not only because in retelling the myth Sophocles has radically rationalized it into a linear movement from beginning to middle to end, but also because the unity of the plot consists in the way it permits a subversive reversal and discovery to arise "naturally" from its ostensibly progressive structure.[20] Yet the pattern of "reversal" is far more pervasive than Aristotle suggests. Among the episodes of the drama that conduct us from the beginning to the end of the dramatic action, there is the particular class of "flashback" episodes which achieve that general end by conveying information about events that occurred before the beginning of the dramatic action. And what is most remarkable about these retrogressive flashbacks for present purposes is that the order of their revelation in the ongoing sequence of dramatic events comes near to being a precise reversal of their chronological order as historical events: the more Oedipus progresses into the future, the more he is driven, ever deeper, into the past. The experience is that of "romance," the closest postarchaic equivalent of the mythic "abolition" of time and history. What is experienced as the unity of a "continual present" by the archaic mind is emplaced, by the newly historical consciousness of the Greek Enlightenment, as a historical rupture between movement "forward" and movement "back."

Toward the end of classical antiquity and concurrent with the composition of those works that posterity has learned to call the "Greek romances," Apuleius gave to the Socratic "psyche" its most celebrated romance objectification.[21] Modern scholars of ancient narrative, disarmingly relaxed in their use of generic terminology, have been inclined to locate "the origins of the Greek novel" in the conjunction between the popular traditions of oral narrative and the increasing literacy of the Hellenistic period.[22] And much of the prose narrative of late antiquity reflects, in its casual and discontinuous commitment to a general idea of historical truth, the legacy of a "literacy revolution" that helped to establish the idea, but by no means the ascendancy, of the standard of "historicity." The anachronistic term "romance" is as good as any to collect together these varied and highly influential narratives: the pirates and shipwrecks of Heliodorus's *Aethiopica*, Xenophon's *An Ephesian Tale*, and Chariton's *Chaereas and Callirhoe*; the skeptical travel voyages of Lucian's *True History*; even the unnatural *Natural History* of Pliny the Elder, which founds a long line of sober investigations into what is "strange but true."[23]

3

PRECURSOR REVOLUTIONS:
THE TWELFTH-CENTURY RENAISSANCE

The historiographical concern that is shared by the great monotheistic religions is linked to their common dependence on the historical authenticity of sacred traditions and texts as the central means by which their validity is established. Far more thoroughly than the Greek euhemerizers, the Hebrew prophets denounced and demythologized the archaic mind. Abstracted from a proliferating immanence in natural locations, God is situated instead in history—or rather, is felt to leave his mark upon the history he has made by punctuating it with discontinuities. These gaps paradoxically define history's objectivity and linearity. It is God who periodically intrudes upon and confirms the ongoingness of history, not humanity that "abolishes" it by recapitulating the archetypal events. These events, insusceptible to ritual repetition in the total, archaic sense of that notion, are subject instead to empirical verification. The paratactic and mysterious disorder of Old Testament narrative alludes to an order that waits, in the interstices of history itself, for the eventual unfolding of time, but also for the incidental light that is cast by textual interpretation and historical documentation. The biblical writers themselves value narrative continuity, canonicity, and the exactness of sources.[24] "*Mythoi,* or just stories, were what other religions had: what Christians had were *logoi,* true stories."[25] And from a very early stage in the Christian era, the defense of the faith against rivals consisted in claiming the historicity of Christ and documenting the authenticity of the gospel narratives.[26]

But the radical historicity of Hebraic religion was not entirely carried over by Christianity. According to Gershom Scholem, "What appeared to the Christians as a deeper apprehension of the external realm appeared to the Jew as its liquidation and as a flight which sought to escape verification of the Messianic claim within its most empirical categories by means of a non-existent pure inwardness." In the pursuit of this ambivalently external and inward realm, Christian thought redirected the Socratic emplacement of myth in "romance" to the central problem of Christian epistemology, the mediation of spiritual truths by temporal and corporeal means. In the following self-reflexive story of Augustine, the romance wanderers themselves risk the sort of emplacement—the vehicle turned tenor—their story teaches should be both sought and shunned:

To enjoy something is to cling to it with love for its own sake. To use something, however, is to employ it in obtaining that which you love . . . Suppose we were wanderers who could not live in blessedness except at home, miserable in our wandering and desiring to end it and return to our native country. We would need vehicles for land and sea which could be used to help us to reach our homeland, which is to be enjoyed. But if the amenities of the journey and the motion of the vehicles itself delighted us, and we were led to enjoy those things which we should use, we should not wish to end our journey quickly, and, entangled in a perverse sweetness, we should be alienated from our country, whose sweetness would make us blessed.[27]

The exquisite balance of Augustine's romance is recapitulated, in large, by the complicated attitudes that surround pilgrimages, saints' lives, and their documentation during the Middle Ages. In the *peregrinationes* that are contemporary with Augustine, the highly circumstantial account of the holy sites and of objects seen along the way serves an idea of "historical truth" that has to do with the authenticity not so much of these particular places as of the sacred histories their description and veneration evokes.[28] The circumstantiality of pilgrimage narratives and saints' lives is analogous to the concretion of the relics of the saints, authenticating sacred truth by a visual and palpable embodiment of it.[29] But medieval commentators are fully alive to the dangerously seductive sweetness of pilgrimage as tenor, not vehicle, as something to be enjoyed for its own sake rather than used to greater ends.[30] In the later Middle Ages, the activity of pilgrimage blends easily and insidiously with the pleasures and the *curiositas* of the growing tourist trade. The immensely popular *Mandeville's Travels,* which is contemporary with works (*The Canterbury Tales, Piers Plowman*) that both criticize and reflect this inclination to literalize and secularize the activity of pilgrimage, is heavily indebted to the turgid and factual guidebooks to the Holy Lands and to the longer "itineraries" of nominally pious travels.[31]

This tension in pilgrimage narrative and saints' lives is of course part of the general tendency of Christian thought, that remarkably stable edifice, toward a contradictory instability. In the classic formulation of Johan Huizinga, "Every thought seeks expression in an image, but in this image it solidifies and becomes rigid. By this tendency to embodiment in visible forms all holy concepts are constantly exposed to the danger of hardening into mere externalism . . . If, on the one hand, all details of ordinary life may be raised to a sacred level, on the other hand, all that is holy sinks to the commonplace, by the fact of being blended with everyday life." The tension may be felt in the way the technique of Christian typology has been expounded by one of its most celebrated interpreters. In *Mimesis,* Erich Auerbach juxtaposes typology with the narrative methods of classical antiquity in a way that emphasizes its paratactic distraction of the reader or listener from the temporal connections and the sensory substance of the narrative line. But in his article "Figura," typology is contrasted instead with Christian allegory, and here the concrete historicity of typological plotting, the sense of Christian history itself as the temporalized and unified unfolding of human salvation, stands out.[32]

The thesis of a twelfth-century renaissance identifies this period, in particular, with an acceleration of the empirical and historicizing impulse. The thesis was first formulated to describe a cultural flowering whose centerpiece was the revival of classical learning, especially that of the natural sciences and philosophy.[33] More recently it has been associated also with a general and pronounced increase in literacy and in the use of literate modes. According to M. T. Clanchy, "Printing succeeded because a literate public already existed; that public originated in the twelfth and thirteenth centuries." As in the Greek Enlightenment, the literacy revolution of twelfth-century Europe has been seen to have a profound epistemological significance. It is not just that literacy is a precondition for and consequence of the revival of ancient texts. It also encourages the growth of "empirical attitudes" that suffuse all medieval thought, encouraging (for example) a more skeptical approach to the authenticity of saints' relics and a more rationalistic interpretation of the figurative status of the Eucharist.[34]

Perhaps the most striking evidence of the growth and effects of literacy lies in the field of law. It is in post-Conquest England, says Clanchy, that royal writs become central in property litigations, and writing becomes the normal mode of conducting legal business. These developments are intimately related to the contemporary rationalization of the idea of judicial trial. According to Howard Bloch, the feudal system of ordeal, which is justified by the assumption that divine will and righteousness are immanent in human affairs, is now replaced by inquest, testimony, witnesses, documentary evidence, and the possibility of appeal—strictly human mechanisms that bespeak a commitment to the faithful re-creation of past events in their historical factuality. Of course oral and customary modes persist alongside literate and written modes for centuries afterward, and in some cases (as in the continuing preference for oral over documented witness) even prevail. Even so, Bloch would see the replacement of ordeal by inquest as part of the general "tendency toward legitimization of the concept of individualism," a term that alludes to an influential, if sometimes controversial, reformulation of the thesis of a twelfth-century renaissance.[35] Understanding the term to refer to the possession of the "autonomous, independent, and indigenous rights" of the citizen, Walter Ullmann has situated the emergence of "the individual" in the thirteenth century, and he associates this change with a general alteration in "historiography." Colin Morris has both broadened the phenomenon and pushed back its emergence, locating the flowering of "autobiography" in the twelfth century.[36] But the argument for a critical skepticism in twelfth-century historiography has not been strongly advanced.[37] One potential source of evidence is the putative readiness of the age to conceive itself as a period, distinct both from the recent past (a perception facilitated, in England, by the rupture of the Conquest) and from the classical antiquity that even now was undergoing a "revival." Yet the fundamental impulse in these retrospections on historical difference seems less like the will to periodize than like the need to establish continuity, to reassert a sameness. And if the schematically periodized history of salvation is now, for the first time, broadly accommodated to the present period and to its political realities, salvationist history remains fundamentally a scheme that is ordained for humanity, not constructed by it.[38]

The canonical truth of Scripture is still, in the twelfth century, the unique standard of spiritual and historical truth against which all other writings are understood by definition to be relatively less veracious. The vera, the "facts," of a history are relevant but subordinate to its veritas, or "truth," and in cases of apparent conflict the pure abstraction is superior to the concrete attribute. As in late antiquity, "history" is conceived as a subcategory of grammar or rhetoric, and the rhetorical criteria of "historicity" are able to be fulfilled by disparate modes of discourse.[39] It has been customary to see twelfth-century romance as a development away from the historical orientation of the epic and the chanson de geste. But just as the "historical" and the "literary" are not clearly discriminated in the heroic chanson, so medieval romance tends to see itself as a species of historical truth and to claim its "historicity" by methods that cannot be distinguished from those of the chanson de geste or the chronicle. In fact "estoire is the earliest recognizable designation for romance; as such the word is connected with the origins of romance in medieval historiography, and particularly in family history."[40] "Romance" does indeed "arise" around the twelfth century, and one sign of this is the gradual emergence of the term itself as accepted usage. But its formulation as a distinct mode of discourse does not clearly depend either on a special affiliation with, or on a special repudiation of, the historical.

If "history" was conceived during the Middle Ages as a branch of rhetoric, its principal trope was that of the lineage. And this holds for romance as well, the truth of whose "matter," like that of all discourse, owed to the fact that it was inherited. To be sure, the matters of France, Britain, and Rome were accorded different degrees of authority. The Arthurian matière de Bretagne had the most dubious roots. The genealogy established at the fall of Troy, on the other hand, provided a national lineage not only for the followers of Aeneas but also, through Priam, for the barbarian tribes that roamed and settled the rest of Europe. And the standard authorities on the Trojan origins, in chronicle and romance, are not Homer and Virgil but Dares of Phrygia and Dictys of Crete, who are understood to be more dependable because they are eyewitnesses to the events.[41] The author of the fourteenth-century *Gest Hystoriale*, for example—variously described by modern commentators as an "alliterative romance," a "historical romance," and a "chronicle"—adheres to his own more recent sources in insisting on the foundation of truth provided by Dares and Dictys. And the longest Middle English version of the twelfth-century Old French *Partenopeu de Blois*, although filled with supernatural marvels, devotes its first 503 lines to the authority of the Trojan lineage and to the hero's subsequent genealogy.[42]

At the beginning of his *Cligés*, Chrétien de Troyes enhances the authentications of the Trojan lineage by informing it with the literate and documentary authority of the manuscript in which we "ceste estoire trovons escrite." Chrétien's romances make it especially clear how the literacy revival reinforces (and in some cases even seems to supplant) the authenticating trope of the lineage by that of the objectifying powers of the written object. In *Erec et Enide*, for example, the wonderful account of Erec's robe ("Quatre fees l'avoient fet . . .") is painstakingly buttressed by the authority of "el livre" of Macrobius. And in the prologue, Chrétien boasts of his power to permanently fix in the memory this story that court *jongleurs* have been in the habit of mutilating and corrupting.[43] Other romances, contemporary with those of Chrétien, exploit the power of transcription to objectify and authenticate their own oral conception, sometimes explicitly relying on the legitimating forms of the legal inquest to achieve this end.[44] Struck by the interplay in twelfth-century romance between the tropes of objectification and the dominance of otherworldly and subjective idealism, some critics have argued the "modernity" of its narrative stance, finding there a perceptual relativity and a radically "individualistic" epistemology that self-consciously and definitively undercut all secure notions of "reality" and "meaning."[45] Certainly the basic skepticism that is entailed in the adducing of documentary sources can easily extend into a more searching skepticism about the reliability of documentation itself: both attitudes are evident in Chaucer's allusions to his several authorities for the story of the Trojan War. But what looks to us like a very modern "indeterminacy," bred of skepticism sufficiently extreme to question the complacent orthodoxy of empiricism, may instead reflect a state of mind, decidedly prior to the establishment of any such orthodoxy, in which the powerful ideas of "objective" and "historical" truth are yet insufficiently dominant even to be sharply distinguished from their putative antithesis. The indeterminacy of medieval romance, in other words, is fully characteristic of the form as it exists at a stage well before those familiar, antiempiricist associations have crystallized around it, a development that may be taken to signify the necessary precondition for the emergence of the modern conception of "indeterminacy" itself into intelligibility.[46]

The "authentication" of medieval narrative is achieved through a variety of conventions, which can provide it with a foundation that is felt to be somehow "empirical" in a sense far looser than any modern conception of that term—for example, through the authenticating frame of the dream vision. The aura of the marvellous inhabits "historical" and "romance" narrative indistinguishably, coexisting with—indeed, coalescing against—the air of historical and circumstantial truth.[47] In twelfth-century romance, the supernatural marvels of Christian-influenced narratives—saints' lives, Mary stories, the *chanson de geste*—were reinforced by the Celtic magic of the matter of Britain. The result of this confluence is the discontinuous plot and "unmotivated" episode of romance narrative, whose "authenticity" sometimes seems to consist, like that of biblical parataxis, in the tacit intrusion of the otherworldly.[48] Of course the analysis of romance narrative structure is far more complicated than this observation would suggest, and scholars are by no means in agreement on the meaning, or the historical relationship, of repetition, bipartition, interlacing, dilation, Chrétien's *conjointure,* and the like.[49] Yet it may be possible to generalize that the implicit structural aim of all romance of this period is a kind of "qualitative" completeness, an elaboration or omission of episode and detail not on the authority of what is required by the empirical nature of the subject but according to an invisible principle, rhetorical or theological, the intuition of whose authoritative workings is necessary to render complete that which only appears partial.

The qualitative standard of completeness in romance narrative commits it less fully to linear continuity and representation than its considerable affiliations with "history" would suggest. By the same token, we may sense the relevance of this standard to epistemological concerns in the later Middle Ages that have little to do with the ongoingness of narrative as such—for example, to the *fin amor* of troubadour poetry and the courtly love that animates so much of twelfth-century romance. To be "true" to another is a mode not of empirical veracity but of human connection coordinated by suprahuman principal or essence. The "trouth" of feudal fealty, loyalty, and service, of divine *caritas* and human charity, feeds the chivalric devotion of the romance knight and gives to it the aura of a commitment that is indistinguishably epistemological and ontological.

Like "romance love," the striking importance of naming in romance may be associated with "telling the truth" by means that are rooted in the empirical but empowered by an essentialist authority. The power of names is their power to signify lineage: not only the genealogical essence of family, but also the etymological mystery that lies at the heart of words themselves. Thus the linearity of lineage conducts us, as in archaic or Christian cognition, to the possession of essential truths, which are contained by the name through a species of contiguous magic or symbolic embodiment. When Chrétien's Erec defeats his opponent he tells him what service he would impose: " 'Et ton non revoel ge savoir.' / Lors li dist cil, ou voelle ou non: / 'Sire, Ydiers, li filz Nut, ai non.' "[50]

If romance names are the outward embodiment of an inner or essential truth, romance character development tends to proceed by discontinuous leaps between states of being—by "rebirths"—and to be signified by the successive divulgence or alteration of name. But the power of knowing a name is fundamentally changed under conditions of literacy. Just as the significance of the verbal oath of fealty must be diminished by the increased currency of documentary proofs, so the power of the articulated name must have waned when, in thirteenth-century England, even serfs were required to have a seal or *signum* for the personal authentication of documents. Mikhail Bakhtin observes a similar correlation in the realm of narrative form: "The absence of internal conclusiveness and exhaustiveness creates a sharp increase in demands for an *external* and *formal* completedness and exhaustiveness, especially in regard to plotline."[51] The more the mediation of essential truth is objectified and concretized, the more narrative epistemology is implicated in a shift from qualitative to quantitative standards of completeness. The major locus of this crucial shift is the early modern period.

4
HISTORICISM AND THE HISTORICAL REVOLUTION

In the history of Western thought, the innovations of the Greek Enlightenment and the twelfth-century Renaissance with respect to the ideas that came to be embodied by the term "romance" are of course monumental. Yet it is only in the early modern period that the category attains the status of a simple abstraction, in definitive opposition to the notion of "true history." The conditions that are responsible for this development, I will argue, are closely analogous to, yet in their combined effect decisively different from, those that were most important in the precursor revolutions.

The fundamental significance of early modern thought in the history of historiography is that it enters into an identification with the past whose very power and insistence paradoxically announce the implacable fact of difference. With the Renaissance revival of learning, "the classical past was looked upon, for the first time, as a totality cut off from the present; and, therefore, as an ideal to be longed for instead of a reality to be both utilized and feared."[52] Erwin Panofsky is generally representative in distinguishing the Renaissance from earlier "renascences" as a difference in degree that amounts to a difference in kind. What is crucial here is the periodizing perspective, and so modern scholars reflexively acknowledge the Renaissance consciousness of period by celebrating the

Renaissance as, in turn, the crucial period in the history of historiography. By the seventeenth century, the paradoxical nature of this periodizing perspective is evident in the way the Renaissance reverence for antiquity has bifurcated into the quarrel of the ancients and the moderns.

The voyages of discovery contributed to what might be seen as the spatial equivalent of the Renaissance consciousness of period. The analogy was especially compelling for English people preoccupied with the problem of how to understand just what difference had been made by the Norman Conquest. Of the ancient Britons, John Aubrey speculated: "They were two or three degrees, I suppose, less savage than the Americans." Sir Henry Spelman remarked that Saxon laws "may seem an Utopia to us present; strange and uncouth: yet can there be no period assigned, wherein either the frame of those Laws was abolished, or this of ours entertained; but as Day and Night creep insensibly, one upon the other, so also hath this Alteration grown upon us insensibly." Traditional attitudes toward the past helped domesticate the new discoveries to the familiar. Travelers and ethnologists easily accommodated exotic peoples of the New World as they might those of classical antiquity, by similitudes. But since the absence of the Christian faith already was accepted as a known fact of difference in the latter peoples, the otherness of alien exotics could be comfortably assimilated on the model of ancient paganism as well. Millennarians hoped that the native Americans would prove to be the Ten Lost Tribes of Israel. Yet the co-optive force of European curiosity also harbored, in its very intensity, an intimation of the inaccessibility of what it sought to know. Signified by the spatial fact of oceanic distance, this inaccessibility might be represented by the Old World's temporally shrouded nostalgia for the innocent savagery of the New, or by what Margaret Hodgen calls the "negative formula," which consists precisely in the self-conscious failure to discover any mediating cultural similitudes.[53]

In terms of the periodizing perspective, at least, the distinction between the Renaissance and the Reformation is not very significant. The humanist discrediting of the Donation of Constantine severed the continuity not only of the Roman Empire but also of the Roman Catholic Church. The early opponents of reform expressed a fundamental truth in condemning the vernacular translation of Scripture as "the new learning."[54] Once under way, in fact, the Reformation was experienced as an epochal historical rupture far more definitively than the Renaissance need be—especially in countries like England, where the political and institutional marks of reform were deep and pervasive. This is one reason for the revival of apocalyptic historiography in Reformation thought, and it is probably in ecclesiastical rather than in humanist contexts—with reference to the period between the Church Fathers and the Protestant divines—that the term "the Middle Ages" was first employed.[55] Spurred by the humanist revival, the reformers argued the apostolic antiquity and "primitiveness" of the Church, whose pristine purity they would salvage from the Middle Age corruptions of the Roman Catholic. Both old and new, Protestant purity so outstripped all previous reform movements in its will to distinguish itself from recent corruptions that it inevitably detached itself from the distant and normative past as well.

The periodizing perspective leads in two very different directions, whose obscure but profound connectedness may be intimated by the fact that in modern usage they both have been designated "historicism."[56] In the first view, the differentiation of history into periods encourages an optimistic ambition to construct the positive laws of universal history. In the second, it promotes the more chastened belief that every historical period is singular and perhaps unknowable from without. Each view reflects a partial aspect of what we might call comprehensively a "scientific" mode of understanding. And there is a very general logic in the expectation that they will form a temporal progression, the "extreme skepticism" of the second view succeeding the "naive empiricism" of the first, even if the two views are also likely to coexist in any more specific context of study.

What is the relationship between the periodizing perspective of the Renaissance and the "historical revolution" of the late sixteenth and early seventeenth centuries? One inevitable response to this question is to subsume the latter period under the former as its terminal manifestation.[57] But in early modern England the question is particularly vexed by the dominance of a mode of thought that militates against the periodizing perspective itself. The "common-law interpretation of English history," as it has been called by J. G. A. Pocock, bears striking evidence of the persistence of nonliterate modes of thought under scribal and even typographical conditions. The cornerstone of this commanding edifice of English legal thought was the identification of law with unwritten custom. In Pocock's words, "The common lawyers, holding that law was custom, came to believe that the common law, and with it the constitution, had always been exactly what they were now, that they were immemorial: not merely that they were very old, or that they were the work of remote and mythical legislators, but that they were immemorial in the precise legal sense of dating from time beyond memory—beyond, in this case, the earliest historical record that could be found. This is the doctrine or myth of the ancient constitution." In sixteenth-century France, the authority of Roman—of civil and canon—law provided a comparative backdrop against which French legal humanists were able to descry the outlines of a non-Roman French feudal law. English law, apparently free of this subjection to Roman authority, was in effect de-

nied the liberating basis of comparison offered by the Roman model, and
it remained subservient to the notion of an immemorial past and of an
uninterrupted historical tradition.[58]

But the significance, and the dominance, of the common-law influence on English historiography can be exaggerated. For one thing, the
understanding of the law as ancient custom or *jus non scriptum* also had the
general effect, as many historians have observed, of encouraging and
sponsoring primary historical research.[59] The belated English "rediscovery of feudalism" in the seventeenth century emerged from the research
of several members of the Society of Antiquaries, which was heir to the
Elizabethan Society and to the tacit and energizing insight that the idea of
"ancient custom" might imply not only stasis but adaptive change.[60] No
doubt it is true that the ahistorical potential of the common law's identification of law and custom—its tendency to conflate past with present
rather than to periodize—was greatly aggravated by the growing political crisis of the early seventeenth century, which led Sir Edward Coke
and his followers to argue the sovereignty of Parliament through the
existence of the "ancient constitution" time out of mind. But the heat of
controversy also encouraged the explosion of the common-law myth.
This assumption would be plausible even with respect to antiquarian
rediscoverers of feudalism like Sir Henry Spelman. But it is obviously
true of the radically historicizing legal reformers of the Interregnum, and
of Robert Brady's royalist extension of Spelman's work under the auspices of the Exclusion Crisis after the Restoration. Indeed, the first Society of Antiquaries met with royal disfavor and was suppressed because its
research into the "ancient liberties" of the Anglo-Saxons fostered the
distinctly controversial idea that the Norman Conquest had broken the
continuity of custom, and that feudal tenures and the rule of the English
monarchy were alien impositions upon English liberties.[61] This view,
which was revived by the Levellers after civil war broke out in the 1640s,
amounted to the discovery of feudalism, as it were, "from the other
end"—as a discrete period by virtue of being discontinuous with what
had come before—and it, too, contributed to the abolition of feudal
tenures in 1646.

Because the Stuarts claimed descent from Arthur, political controversy also encouraged the antiquarian demystification of Arthurian legend.
But the discrediting of the matter of Britain, of "the British History" as
promulgated by Geoffrey of Monmouth, must be seen more generally as
a long-term project of Renaissance skepticism.[62] And as such it testifies
even more clearly to the fact that the English "common-law mind" did
not preclude the will to discriminate the "mythical" from the "historical"
that characterizes contemporaneous French legal humanism. It is in England, after all, that the scientific revolution had its deepest rooting. The
application of "empirical method" to the study not only of nature but

also of history had profound implications for the idea of "romance" in seventeenth-century English culture, and I will take these up in the following chapter. For the present it is necessary only to observe how fully the notion of "scientific" inquiry suffused contemporary historical research. In the antiquarians of the later part of the century it encouraged the archaeological study of "objects," of non- or quasi-literary artifacts like charters, coins, inscriptions, and statues, and it became a common activity to assemble and preserve great collections of cultural as well as natural "curiosities." But documents are also objects. Empirical attitudes in the study of history and the practice of law helped stimulate an unprecedented dedication to the collection of records, and validated both the first-hand "evidence of the senses"—eye- and earwitness report—and the "objective" testimony of documentary objects.[63]

The critical difference between these early modern developments and earlier, similar ones that I have discussed may be sensed in the way the seventeenth-century scientific movement seems both to renew and to fulfill its empirical precursors. The same must be said of the print revolution, whose widespread cultural significance has recently been reformulated, with exhaustive ingenuity, in the work of Elizabeth Eisenstein. According to this argument, the very conception of an "objective" history owes a great deal to print technology. By permanently preserving and reproducing what could be no more than transient productions in oral and even scribal culture, print stabilized culture itself and the past in particular as a realm of experience henceforth susceptible to objective study: that is, as a collection of objects. Print made common first the very notion of competing accounts of the same event and then the norm of "objective" research and understanding through the systematic collection, comparison, categorization, collation, editing, and indexing of documentary objects. Print "abstracted" scribal culture as scribal literacy had abstracted oral culture. The archaeological preference for nonliterary antiquities, which we see developing in the later seventeenth century, reflects not a flight from the abstraction of script and print but a heightened commitment to it, to the sort of authoritative and "objective" knowledge that can be gained only from the study of that which time cannot efface. Thus Joseph Addison's Philander observes that "a cabinet of medals is a body of history." Coinage "was a kind of Printing, before the art was invented." But coins "tell their story much quicker" than books, and more dependably than writing; for "a coin is in no danger of having its characters altered by copiers and transcribers."[64]

In the tangible objectivity of texts, print provided the sort of "basis of comparison" that the presence of Roman law afforded the French legal humanists, but far more definitively and inescapably because physically implicated in the very activities of perception and study. For Eisenstein it is the preservative powers of print that achieved the permanent periodization of classical antiquity and that qualitatively distinguish the Renaissance from earlier revivals of learning. Here, as elsewhere, her argument has a crucial doubleness. It is not only that typography augmented immeasurably the human capacity for a rational and objective understanding of the past. It also helped confirm objective analysis itself as a normative value; it encouraged people to see, and to want to see, the past "as such"; it disclosed not only the lineal continuum of universal chronology but also the possibility of empirically demonstrable periodizations; it permitted to develop a sense both of an accumulated and ongoing tradition and of that tradition's vulnerability to skeptical criticism and to subversion. Finally, print and its uses promoted criteria of judgment that are appropriate to discrete and empirically apprehensible "things"—singularity, formal coherence, self-consistency—and a test of veracity that accords with the process of typographical reproduction itself: the exact replication of objects or events in their external and quantitative dimensions. So in this analysis, print helped condition not only the "scientific" turn in historical studies but also the scientific revolution itself. And the scientific revolution represents not the birth of "empirical attitudes" but the result of two historically inseparable but distinguishable phenomena: the unprecedented validation of empirical attitudes, and the unprecedented opportunity to facilitate those attitudes through a fundamental transformation in the production and management of knowledge.[65]

The third great revolution in early modern thought that Eisenstein's work enrolls under the aegis of typography is the Protestant Reformation, and this connection was a commonplace even for the people of the seventeenth century. Consider Andrew Marvell's ironically denunciatory apostrophe to "The Press (that *villanous* Engine) invented much about the same time with the Reformation, that hath done more mischief to the Discipline of our Church, than all the Doctrine can make amends for." Marvell's contrast of Protestant publication with priestly (both Catholic and Anglican) censorship and authority is confirmed by the modern view of Reformation Protestantism as preeminently the religion of the book— of the Bible, but also of doctrines and practices that more subtly and pervasively express the values of typographical objectivity and historicity. Against the collective and hierarchical authority of the apostolic succession, the Reformation set the documentary objectivity of God's Book and the immediate historicity of the individual reading experience. In fact, in the words of William Haller, "this was what the reformers put in place of the Mass as the decisive high point of spiritual experience— instead of participation in the sacrament of the real presence on one's knees in church, they put encounter with the Holy Spirit in the familiar language of men on the printed page of the sacred text." Once again, the Reformation did not invent the Christian preoccupation with historical and textual authentication. But the conjunction of this traditional concern with the medium of print qualitatively transformed the bookishness of Christianity and made Protestantism the heretical revolt against the Church which became "permanent," and hence a new orthodoxy.[66] The intimate relationship between Protestant thought and early modern empirical, historicizing habits of mind—to which I will return more particularly in later chapters—reveals the variety of channels by which epistemological revolution is accessible, so that institutional avenues in one national culture (French civil and canon law) are balanced by those of others (the English Reformation).

5
THE CLAIM TO HISTORICITY

Eisenstein's involvement of literary, historical, religious, and scientific revolution within the great mechanism of typography is so omnivorous that it stands vulnerable to certain kinds of criticism.[67] Even so, her powerful thesis has a fundamental importance for the later history of romance and for the origins of the novel. During its first two centuries print produced much of the "new" learning, but it reproduced a great deal of the old as well. Eisenstein observes that in this respect, print culture supplanted scribal culture by duplicating it in greater abundance than ever before. The "discovery," even the "invention," of feudalism was at least in part a result of this reproductive process, which first gave to what have become the familiar and distinctive features of "medieval" culture a certain typographical fixity.[68] It is at this time, and largely through the mass-produced publication of editions, compilations, redactions, continuations, and translations of medieval manuscripts, that "romance" is abstracted into existence as an objectified corpus and attains the status of what Marx would call a "simple abstraction." If ancient Greek culture is predominantly "poetic" long after the invention of the alphabet,[69] medieval romance paradoxically is at the height of its dominance and influence in the early modern period; and this is so because it is only then that it can be spoken of "as such."

So print helps transform romance into a self-conscious canon. But it also helps "periodize" romance as a "medieval" production, as that which the present age—the framing counterpart of the classical past—defines itself against. Medieval romance, in which the antecedents of our "history" and "romance" coexist in fluid suspension, becomes "medieval romance," the product of an earlier period and increasingly the locus of strictly "romance" elements that have been separated out from the documentary objectivity of "history" and of print, the technology to which it therefore owes (at least in part) both its birth and its instantaneous obsolescence. In this respect it may be useful to think of early modern "romance" as an "antithetical" simple abstraction, since its categorial constitution renders it serviceable in the negative definition of "the novel," the "thetical" simple abstraction that soon will be posited through the dialectical negation of romance. Of course the early modern dichotomization of "history" and "romance" is greatly overdetermined. Print contributes to and reinforces an "objective" standard of truth which is also, especially in narrative, a "historical" standard of truth, of historicity: Did it happen, and how did it happen? And the verifying potential of print is so powerful that the historicity of the act of publication itself could seem to supplant, and to affirm, the historicity of that information which print putatively exists only to mediate. Now, we might expect that once romances began to be published, this magical act would transform and "objectify" them as well. What militates against this is the fact that the idea of romance is itself in the process of a transformation which, fed by many sources, makes the typographical objectification of romance a contradiction in terms and the sign of a woefully naive reader. "But in your reading have a great care in the choice of your Authors," advises one moderately skeptical commentator. "For some I have known (otherwise ingenious enough) apt to believe idle Romances, and Poetical Fictions, for Historical Varieties [i.e., verities] . . . What Impressions Books of that nature have made upon some much studious in them, is sufficiently known, who will believe no otherwise but that they are true, and for this only reason, *Because they are Printed*." One notorious instance of such naive reading is that of Don Quixote.[70]

In the seventeenth century the standard defense against the charge of "newness" was still the claim to be renewing or reforming the old. But the unprecedented (and unavoidable) experience of preserving the old in permanent, printed records enforced a sensitivity to, and an acceptance of, the undeniable newness that distinguished the present from the past. This transformation in attitudes toward the new is reflected in the seventeenth-century development of "news" as a significant if ambiguous conceptual category, and of journalism as a popular if eclectic professional activity. In one sense there is nothing new about "news," since the sermon had traditionally performed the function of news dissemination. But "the replacement of pulpit by press" was far more than a simple change in medium, and contemporaries knew that quite apart from the question of their "news content," the difference between the oral delivery and the printed publication of sermons was considerable.[71]

Printed "news" first flourishes, in the later sixteenth century, not as a serial publication (the newsletter, the newspaper) but in the form of printed ballads. Sold throughout the following century by itinerant chapmen like Shakespeare's Autolycus, news ballads recall the unnatural natural history tradition in their naive dedication to the wonderful and the incredible. But the claim to historicity has now become far more elaborate, exploiting especially the techniques of authentication by firsthand and documentary witness that have developed during the late medieval and early modern periods.[72] As a result, the increasing validation of empirical modes of truth actualizes the latent tension between the claim to truth and the nature of the material whose truth is claimed. In Shakespeare and some other usages, the effect is humorously but decisively to subvert the claim to historicity. But in many of the ballads themselves there is no evidence at all of an ironic intent, and the old claim that a story is "strange but true" subtly modulates into something more like the paradoxical formula "strange, therefore true." The fact of "strangeness" or "newness" ceases, that is, to be a liability to empirical truth-telling, and becomes instead an attestation in its support.[73] As we will see, the printed ballad is only one of the contexts in which this unstable reversal can be seen in seventeenth-century discourse. At its most striking, the formula "strange, therefore true" amounts to the insistence that the very appearance of the incredible itself has the status of a claim to historicity.

6

NAIVE EMPIRICISM AND EXTREME SKEPTICISM

The news ballad provides ample evidence that by the seventeenth century the claim to historicity has attained general acceptance as an important convention in "popular" as well as "elite" narrative culture.[74] During the middle decades of the century, the narration of news begins to detach itself from the ballad form and to take on the aspect of a distinct discursive entity. The combination of revolutionary politics and a succession of governments whose left-wing Protestantism ensured a relative freedom of the press led to an unparalleled efflorescence of news reporting. The effect of this outpouring was double. On the one hand, it helped validate the new as worthy of attention and to associate news with the historical authenticity of printed documents. On the other hand, the experience of comparing highly partisan and divergent "true accounts" of the same events induced a considerable skepticism regarding the ostentatious claims to historicity which had already become quite conventional. Indeed, as the instance of Shakespeare suggests, the skeptical reaction to "naive empiricism" in news reporting predates considerably the outbreak of the English Revolution. During the 1630s, Richard Brathwaite attacked the news reporter's shameless use of the claim to historicity and its authenticating devices: "To make his reports more credible (or which he and his stationer onely aymes at) more vendible, in the relation of every occurrent: he renders you the day of the moneth; and to approve himselfe a scholler, he annexeth these Latine parcells, or parcell-gilt sentences, *veteri stylo, novo stylo*." For Brathwaite, the "newness" of the newsmongers argues not truth but false invention, and he calls their work "novels" in order to disparage them in this spirit. Ben Jonson devoted an entire play to providing a mirror "wherein the age may see her owne folly, or hunger and thirst after publish'd pamphlets of *Newes,* set out euery Saturday, but made all at home, & no syllable of truth in them." Like Brathwaite, he associates the typographical reproduction of "news" with counterfeit coinage and the production of commodities.[75]

To some critics it was clear that the news problem was really the problem of freedom of the press. "My intention in this Paper," says a writer of 1642, "is no otherwise but to describe the *abuse of Printing, in publishing every Pamphlet that comes to their presse.*" Now "they begin to go beyond the Sea for new Newes . . . they have infused into their noddles variety of very rare Letters, consisting of more then true wonders wrought by our Party against the Rebels; great overthrowes, and strange myracles by the Rebels, wrought against the Protestants, and such like." "History" was the common, normative term against which to define the false historicity of invented news reports. Another writer ruefully observes that "however Poets have got an ill name, I had rather beleeve in the supplement of *Lucan,* then the relation of the battell at *Newbury.*" John Cleveland discredits the news reporter in similar terms: "To call him an Historian, is to Knight a Man-drake . . . He is the *Cadet* of a Pamphleteere, the *Pedee* [i.e., footboy] of a Romancer. He is the *Embrio* of a History . . . In summe, a *Diurnall-maker* is the antemark of an Historian." Elsewhere Cleveland, a resolute Cavalier, calls the newspapers of London radicals "the *Round-heads Legend,* the *Rebels Romance,* stories of a larger size than the eares of their *Sect,* able to strangle the belief of a *Solifidian.*" Thus the rebel news reporters, invalidated as romancers and constantly engaged in the invention and discovery of imaginary plots, are "the *Quixots* of this age [who] fight with *Windmils* of their own heads."[76]

In the charges and countercharges that liven the battle over news reporting during the revolutionary years can be discerned the outlines of a pattern that will emerge with increasing clarity in varied contexts over the next few decades. The pattern marks the climax of the early modern revolution in narrative epistemology, and it is of fundamental importance in the origins of the English novel: the naive empiricism of the claim to historicity purports to document the authentic truth; the extreme skepticism of the opposing party demystifies this claim as mere "romance." But this basic formulation of the pattern belies its dialectical fluidity, for what looks like an "extreme critique" from one perspective reveals itself as a "naive claim" from another. This fluidity is due to the crucial fact that both postures, which are versions of the antithetical offshoots of Renaissance "historicism,"[77] are fundamentally skeptical and have much in common. "Naive empiricism" is no less opposed to the falsifications of "romance" invention than is "extreme skepticism": in fact it is the earnest energy of the naive empiricist critique of falsehood that renders it vulnerable to the countercritique of extreme skepticism.

Yet despite the similarities of these two postures and the artificiality of designating them thus as though they were self-consciously articulated categories, there is some use in looking more closely at the characteristically dialectical nature of their relationship.

This dialectic can be seen in John Rushworth's preface to his influential collection of Interregnum documents, a project that we quickly learn to associate with the naive antiquarian collecting of "objects," but that we first encounter as a highly skeptical denunciation of journalistic romancing. Among the generation that lived through the late troubles, Rushworth says,

some durst write the Truth; whilst other mens Fancies were more busie then their Hands, forging Relations, building and battering Castles in the Air; publishing Speeches as spoken in Parliament, which were never spoken there; printing Declarations, which were never passed; relating Battels which were never fought, and Victories which were never obtained; dispersing Letters which were never writ by the Authors . . . Such practices, and the experience I had thereof, and the impossibility for any man in After-ages to ground a true History, by relying on the Printed Pamphlets in ourdays [*sic*], which passed the Press whilst it was without controul, obliged me to all the pains and charge I have been at for many years together, to make a great *Collection;* and whilst things were fresh in memory, to separate Truth from Falshood, things real from things fictitious or imaginary.

So Rushworth's skepticism about the possibility of writing a "true history" turns out to be a rather limited demurral, and only by way of prologue to his own naive claims to historicity. He was "an Eye and Ear-witness of the greatest Transactions . . . I pretend onely in this Work to a bare Narrative of matter of Fact, digested in order of time . . . I use the Language of that Time of which I write . . . [and] if I speak of any transactions which I my self did not see or hear I do so with all the caution imaginable . . . I have esteemed the most unaffected and familiar Stile the best."[78]

But what finally justifies our view of Rushworth as a "naive empiricist" is the way in which he, in turn, is criticized by his opponent. Like Rushworth, John Nalson skeptically attacks the bias and prejudice of his antagonist (in this case Rushworth himself). But unlike him, Nalson resists the naive claim to historicity in his own self-presentation, aiming instead at an alternative method of historical skepticism: "I must confess, in the following Discourse I have not tied my self strictly to the Rules of a Bare Collector, but indulged my self in the Liberty of an Historian, to tie up the loose and scattered Papers with the Circumstances, Causes, and Consequences of them."[79] If Nalson's interpretive "liberty" with the shape and structure of his narrative calls to mind the "qualitative" standard of completeness common in twelfth-century romance, Rushworth's punctilious regard for bare "matter of fact" and the linear "order of time" subjects his narration to a far more quantitative standard. Yet Nalson has not abandoned the goal of critical and skeptical history, as his title makes clear. He has abandoned the naive claim to historicity, without fully articulating how his alternative historical method will achieve the great and common end of defining itself against "romance" as well.

Extreme skepticism levels the charge of stealthy romancing even at the style of naive empiricism. I have already cited Richard Brathwaite's irritation at the circumstantial, authenticating details that tend to accompany the claim to historicity in news reports. In Sir Richard Steele's urbane critique, the relationship between naive journalism and the old romance is both epistemological and stylistic. Echoing Cleveland, Steele remarks "that the News-Papers of this Island are as pernicious to weak Heads in *England,* as ever Books of Chivalry to *Spain.*" The effort to appear both new and true produces a copious discontinuity that is oddly reminiscent of romance circumlocution: "My Contemporaries the Novelists have, for the better spinning out Paragraphs, and working down to the End of their Columns, a most happy Art in saying and unsaying, giving Hints of Intelligence, and Interpretations of indifferent Actions, to the great Disturbance of the Brains of ordinary Readers." In one unusual exception to this rule, "the matter was told so distinctly" that it seemed "there was no News in it; this Paper differing from the rest as an History from a Romance. The Tautology, the Contradictions, the Doubts, the Wants of Confirmations, are what keep up imaginary Entertainments in empty Heads."[80]

So by the end of the seventeenth century the idea of news already carries a double epistemological charge: the credible claim of objective historicity, and the claim demystified as a "romance" convention in disguise. Of course the contemporary status of "news" is more complicated than that. Manuscript newsletters continue to circulate throughout the century, frustrating our easy association of news with typographical objectivity. Whether written or printed, moreover, news reports continue to be transmitted and received orally by many people.[81] Thus news reporting retains its ties to nontypographical modes and to the relatively nonhistoricist epistemologies with which they are associated. Nor is it plausible to make these spirited disputes over the truth-value of news, or the legislative history of journalism in its formative stages, bear the full weight of the origins of the novel, as some critics have maintained.[82] Nevertheless the news controversy of the seventeenth century provides us with an important and circumscribed arena in which the patterned interplay of "naive empiricism" and "extreme skepticism" can be seen to coalesce out of the swirling clouds of early modern historical and scientific thought. The following pages will provide other examples.

In the end printing may well have abstracted—"petrified" or "fossilized," in the words of two recent historians—the tradition of oral creation. But the vital interaction of oral and printed modes persisted at least through the seventeenth century, most obviously in the case of broadside songs and ballads. Print not only replaced orality; over the short term it also stimulated and perpetuated oral culture, perhaps even coloring its productions with the objectivizing attitudes of typography.[83] Over the long term, print also occasioned a greater literacy revolution than any that had occurred in scribal culture. The "rise of the reading public" in early modern England has long been thought to have influenced the rise of the novel. To what degree does current knowledge warrant this supposition? The extent of the literacy revolution in the period of our concern, its relation to the rise of the reading public, and the role of a new readership in conditioning the rise of the new genre are matters on which there is great interest and little definitive evidence.[84] The crucial fact is typography itself, and the gradual emergence of a print culture. These developments are easily summarized.

By the close of the seventeenth century England had become a major producer of paper, type, and various kinds of publication, a development that could not have occurred without the abolition of protectionist printing legislation. By the middle of the eighteenth, licensing laws had been replaced by copyright laws; the commodification of the book market as a mass-production industry had become organized around the mediating figure of the bookseller; and the idea that a writer should get paid for his work was gaining currency on the strength of the perception that there was a growing mass of consumers willing to foot the bill.[85] On the other hand, these new consumers of print were also produced by print—most obviously by the early modern "educational revolution," which received a great stimulus from the invention of the press and played the central role in raising the levels of literacy in England. But in the origins of the novel, as elsewhere, it is worth pursuing the insight that "consumption creates the motive for production; it also creates the object which is active in production as its determinant aim."[86]

Problems arise, however, in the attempt to specify more finely the nature, or even the size, of that reading public whose consumption of the novel helped determine its production. Only one kind of literacy, and that quite ambiguous in its implications, is directly measurable by existing records at this time: the ability to write a signature. By this measure, the increase in literacy in the century from 1650 to 1750 is real, but irregular and not very explosive.[87] Do these figures provide evidence of the rise of the reading public? Although the ability to sign is manifestly not the same as the ability to write, reading skills in any case were likely to have been much more widely spread than writing skills during this period, especially among the lower orders. But what level—or, more crucially, what habits—of reading can be inferred from the figures?[88] If the more subjective apprehensions of contemporaries are any guide, women and servants of both sexes were devoting much of their time in the early eighteenth century to reading "novels" and "romances." But if there is good evidence that the opportunity for such leisure activity existed, there is little to confirm that it was actually used for that purpose. From Dante on, the fear that women's morals will be corrupted by reading romances is quite conventional, and its articulation at this time may provide evidence less of the rise of the reading public than of the persistence of anxiety about women.[89]

It is certainly true that by the end of the seventeenth century and quite apart from newspaper publication, the necessary institutional mechanisms exist for a marked increase in the reading of narrative by the lower orders. Already by the 1660s, the production of cheap chapbooks had outstripped ballad production, and the distribution networks of chapmen and chapwomen, who used inns as distribution centers, spread throughout the entire country. In the last quarter of the century, moreover, new and reprinted books began to be issued serially in fascicles, which common people could buy for pennies.[90] On the one hand, the currency of chapbook redactions toward the end of the seventeenth century suggests that the division between "popular" and "elite" culture has already taken place. On the other hand, the fact that eighteenth-century prose fiction seems to undergo surprisingly little revision for the chapbook format might be taken to indicate the upward assimilation of humble readers and the consolidation of a relatively homogeneous "middle class" reading public. Yet on the evidence of subscription lists, at least, a very large proportion of the readership of Defoe, the *Spectator,* and other "middle class" publications belongs to the nobility and gentry.[91] In the end, the problems associated with demonstrating the rise of a middle-class reading public are no more amenable to quantitative evidence than are those connected with the rise of the novel. For even if a wealth of precise empirical data on reading behavior were available, we would still be faced with the definitional problem of deciding the identity of "the middle class."[92] Under these circumstances it is perhaps better simply to embrace, as a basic premise, the dialectical relation of production and consumption as a constitutive force in the origins of the English novel. Both authors and readers, we may assume, were profoundly affected by the epistemological revolution whose intricate and far-reaching ramifications it is the purpose of these chapters to document.

7

ROMANCE, ANTIROMANCE, TRUE HISTORY

Like other Renaissance revivals, the rediscovery of Aristotle's *Poetics* was a consequence of the historicist dedication to distinguishing the present from the past. But it was a peculiarly apposite revival, since it conferred on modern culture the critical distinction between "poetry" and "history" which had been one fruit of that far more ancient period of modernity. The history of Aristotle's influence in this respect is complex and uneven. Many Renaissance writers affirmed the general notion of the autonomy of "poetry," but many more did not, and we must look to the later eighteenth century for the real ascendancy of this idea. Some, like Tasso, responded to the Aristotelian doctrine of "imitation" by elaborating a notion of poetic verisimilitude that was distinct from factual historicity. But what about imitative prose narrative? The problem is not only that Aristotle was silent on the subject but also that in the Renaissance it was quite customary to think of "history" as a prose form. Of course Aristotle had formulated a poetics that might include imitative prose, and he criticized the common tendency to define poets "not by reason of the imitative nature of their work, but indiscriminately by reason of the metre they write in." Nevertheless most of his early commentators saw verse as a necessary condition of poetry: paradoxically, the very authority of Aristotle's historicizing differentiation of "history" from "poetry" militated against the admission of any prose form as "poetic." The tendency can be seen in the following reply to Tasso: "Imitation is the genus of poetry, narration that of history. The former has the verisimilar for its subject, the latter the truth. The first is made in verse, the second by its nature in prose."[93]

To formulate the problem of the origins of the novel in terms of how one dominant prose form "became" another is really to ask how romance responded to the early modern historicist revolution. In seventeenth-century prose narrative, verisimilitude and the claim to historicity are incompatible and competitive expressions of that revolution. Verisimilitude will prevail, but only in the long run and only as the reformulated doctrine of "realism." In the short run and throughout the critical period of the origins of the English novel, the claim to historicity is dominant. And when it is refuted, the terms are less likely to be those of Aristotelian verisimilitude than those of extreme skepticism. In fact it is mainly through the uncompromisingly acerbic mediations of extreme skepticism that the doctrine of realism slowly becomes acceptable, and then authoritative, in modern thought.[94] The claim to historicity and its more extreme negation of "romance" are preferable, at first, for obvious reasons: they are a far more direct and immediate reflection of empirical and skeptical epistemology. Of course the claim to historicity is no less a rhetorical trope than verisimilitude; the difference is that it is not rationalized as such. "It is no argument to me," says Meric Casaubon, "that a thing is true, because it is possible; no, nor because probable: nay, it is certain, that many lyes and falshoods are founded upon this very thing, *probability*." Père le Moyne rejected the medieval notion that history is a subcategory of grammar or rhetoric, for "how can you reconcile Truth, the soul of History and the goal of the Historian, with verisimilitude, the form of Oration and the aim of the Orator . . . ?" No doubt it is easy for a historian to use rhetorical flourishes and eloquence, says the Duchess of Newcastle, but these are, "at the best, but pleasant Romances," and amount to "telling Romansical Falshoods for Historical Truths."[95]

But the claim to historicity by no means excluded the doctrine of verisimilitude in seventeenth-century prose narrative, especially in France. In his celebrated history of romance, Daniel Huet regarded "nothing to be properly *Romance* but Fictions of Love Adventures . . . I call them Fictions, to discriminate them from True Histories; and I add, of Love Adventures, because Love ought to be the Principal Subject of *Romance*."[96] Huet is speaking of the *romans* that flourished during the earlier part of the century, which contemporary English people were content to call "romances," and posterity, the "French heroic romance." This efflorescence appears odd if we suppose that the Renaissance assault on the idea of romance should have brought an instant end to their composition. The fact that it did not means less that the assault was insubstantial than that it was to some degree internalized by romance as self-criticism. Thus the French heroic romance characteristically justifies itself by reference to the doctrine of *vraisemblance,* associating its fiction-ality with a quasi-Aristotelian "probability."[97] *Vraisemblance* has a wide appeal in these romances, and sometimes its incompatibility with the claim to historicity strictly conceived is simply ignored. It is a common insinuation, for example, that a work is both *vraisemblable* and a *roman à clef* that alludes to real people. Moreover, the French romance will some-times go so far as to proclaim heartily its own divergence, in select scenes, from well-known instances of what it calls "romance" im-probability (which, we are obliged to notice, nonetheless crop up fre-quently elsewhere in the text). Generally speaking, seventeenth-century writers were able to overlook the incompatibility of Aristotelian proba-bility and the claim to historicity as much as they did because they tended to read the *Poetics* through the spectacles of empirical epistemology.[98]

After 1660, the French heroic romance is supplanted by the *nouvelle* and by other pseudohistorical forms in which the claim to historicity is more dominant and elaborate. Copiously published in English, these *romans à clef,* "secret histories" and memoirs, and *chroniques scandaleuses* generally purport to be about not simply real happenings but great events in the lives of eminent personages. The heavy aura of state secrecy and imperative diplomatic subterfuge, generally abetted by the English translators, then permits statements of obscurity, skepticism, and out-right censorship or denial to achieve, antithetically, the validation of the narrative in question.[99] This kind of authenticating device bears a re-semblance to the "strange, therefore true" formula of the modernized unnatural natural history. which the competition between *vraisemblance* and the claim to historicity helped make explicit. According to Marie d'Aulnoy, the frequent conflict between strict truth and probability has tempted her more than once to aim at the latter by deleting from her travel accounts all "the strange Stories you will find therein . . . [For] I do not doubt but there will be some, who will accuse me of hyperbolizing, and composing Romances." Needless to say, the temptation has been resisted. "In a word: I write nothing but what I have seen, or heard from Persons of unquestionable Credit; And therefore shall conclude with assuring you, That you have here no Novel, or Story, devised at pleasure; but an Exact and most True Account of what I met with in my Travels."[100]

In the passage from the "heroic romance" to the "secret memoir" one has the sense of crossing an invisible and indeterminate divide. We have seen that seventeenth-century romance defends itself against assault in part by becoming modestly historicized, by becoming "antiromance." Are the French secret histories and travels to be seen as self-consciously defended romances, or as naive empiricist critiques of romance? Posed abstractly, the problem is insoluble. But the response of contemporaries may encourage us to understand these works within the dialectical framework that has become familiar from controversial discussions of the truth value of "news." In the following passage, Pierre Bayle moves from the particular example of Marie d'Aulnoy to the general case of works like hers by means of the method I have associated with the posture of extreme skepticism; that is, by invalidating the "true history" of naive empiricism, calling it instead nothing more than the "new romance."

It is a pity the public cannot be persuaded that she deserves much credit. It has prevailed, as a general opinion, that her works are a mixture of fictions and truths, half romance, and half history; and there is no other way to distinguish fiction from true matter of fact, but by comparing her's with other books. It is an inconvenience which daily gets ground by the liberty that is taken to publish the secret amours, the secret history, &c. of such and such lords famous in History. Booksellers and authors do all they can to make it believed that these secret Histories have been taken from private manuscripts: they very well know, that love-intrigues, and such like adventures, please more when they are believed to be real, than when they are thought to be mere fables. From hence it is, that the new romances keep as far off as possible from the romantic way: but by this means true history is made extreamly obscure; and I believe the civil powers will at last be forced to give these new romancers their option; either to write pure history, or pure romance; or at least to use crotchets to separate the one from the other, truth from fiction.[101]

In fact, once romance begins to incorporate antiromance elements, it enters into a transformative process that itself appears to recapitulate the

double critique that is fundamentally characteristic of early modern epistemological revolution: first, of romance by naive empiricism; and then,
of both by extreme skepticism. The reason romance can now seem to
contain this complex movement within itself is that it has become a
simple abstraction. Because twelfth-century romance had maintained
both "romance" and "historical" elements in suspension, the early modern autocritique of romance falsehood also entails a critique of what is
now separated out as a false historicity. The phenomenon is somewhat
older than the Renaissance. *Amadis of Gaul,* the epitome of chivalric
extravagance for early modern skeptics, itself contains considerable antiromance sentiment. And when the fourteenth-century reworking of
earlier redactions was itself revised and expanded at the end of the fifteenth century, the author's general skepticism about such antique narratives is concentrated not just on their incredibility but on the pointedly
"historical" pretensions of "feigned histories in which marvellously unnatural things are to be found, which very rightly ought to be deemed
fakes." The new Book Five of the present project then becomes a self-
consciously parodic case in point, "validated" by a ludicrous version of
the topos of the discovered manuscript: it "came to light in a stone tomb
discovered underground below a hermitage near Constantinople and was
brought to this part of Spain by a Hungarian merchant, being inscribed
on parchment so old that only with great difficulty were those who knew
the language able to read it."[102]

This kind of epistemological self-consciousness is central to the Renaissance *romanzo,* most of all to the *Orlando Furioso* (1516, 1521, 1532),
whose self-reflexive critique of romance fictiveness also criticizes, along
the way, the casual pretense to historical truth that is one of the traditional
romance methods of self-authentication. In fact the parody of the discovered manuscript topos is a very common technique by which Renaissance romance tries to adapt to epistemological revolution and to keep
itself honest, and it can be found even in the French heroic romance.[103]
Modern scholars usually treat the romance parody of the discovered
manuscript topos as a critique of the claim to historicity. But it is better
understood instead as an implicit instance of that claim, the most conventional means by which "modern" romance becomes conscious and skeptical of its own customary conflation of "history" and "romance." The
point is of some importance. In a scribal culture, the retrieval of early
manuscripts provides a protection against errors introduced by copyists,
a protection that is outmoded by typographical reproduction.[104] The
topos of the discovered manuscript makes an appeal to the past that is
based upon the normative values of antiquity, linear continuity, and
succession, and it possesses, itself, a long and illustrious lineage as a
means of establishing narrative authority. But naive empiricism and the
claim to historicity reflect the periodizing perspective of early modern

historicism, which goes very far (as we have seen) toward demystifying the appeal to the past. In its most pronounced form, the difference was conceived as nothing less than that between the investment of faith in a remote truth attested to by external authorities, and the immediate authentication of an empirically apprehensible truth that is present for all to see. Thus Samuel Butler satirizes the antiquary as he who "devours an old Manuscript with greater Relish than Worms and Moths do, and, though there be nothing in it, values it above any Thing printed, which he accounts but a Novelty."[105]

So the parody of the discovered manuscript topos is in the general spirit of the claim to historicity rather than in the spirit of its critique. Contemporaries were able to make its central point with clarity and conciseness: "A Romance, or an Imposture, may be as ancient and more ancient than a true History, this is nothing to the purpose." And they were even able to reconstruct the topos so that it could uphold the authority not of antiquity at all, but of documentary historicity. This can be seen in the way the "translator" of a popular collection of letters deals with the problem of whether we are to expect of them "a *Romance* or a *real History*." For the letters are authenticated not by their age—they came to light as "a great heap of Papers; which seem'd more spoil'd by Dust than time"—but by their circumstantial contemporaneity and by the tests of critical historiography. Here only the outer shell of the topos remains; its conception of "historical authority" has been completely transformed.[106]

But if the argument from antiquity and the claim to historicity represent theoretically opposed positions in early modern thought, the complex history of narrative conventions at this time affords some notable instances of their alliance. This is most true in the negative case, as the parody of the one may seem to lay the grounds for the parody of the other, a phenomenon that occurs most strikingly in the headlong development of the antiromance after Ariosto. The great example, of course, is *Don Quixote* (1605, 1615), where the discovered manuscript topos is obscurely implicated in the progress of the narrative itself from naive empiricism to extreme skepticism.[107] From Spain the antiromance momentum quickly passes to France, and in the work of Charles Sorel, as in that of his master, Cervantes, we see fulfilled the inevitable tendency of antiromance to challenge its incorporation by romance, renounce the function of internal self-criticism, and constitute an autonomous and antithetical form. As the very title of his work proclaims, Sorel's commitment to true history entails the reciprocal and explicit repudiation of romance, for "*Romances* contain nothing but *Fictions*, whereas this must be thought a *true* History." "You learn out of *History*," says Sorel's Clarimond, "things that you may alleadg [*sic*] for authorities; but of a *Romance* there's no fruit at all."

Yet although the dominant thrust of this antiromance is to deflate the Quixotic credulity of Lysis and of the pastoral romance, beliefs held dear by the credulous reader of "true histories" are not entirely secure from disenchantment either. The book ends with the author stretching his devices of authentication well beyond comfortable limits, informing us that it had been his "design to tell you of the divers fortunes of the Shepherd *Lysis,* according to the notes I had of them from *Philiris* and *Clarimond,* who it seems [however] had not the leisure to put them into order." But readers may not be fully convinced by this sort of evidence in any case, and Sorel supposes that some may even be tempted to travel to Brie so as to see the famous Lysis in the flesh. The trip would be pointless, for "what know they whether I have not related a fable to them instead of a true History; or that I have not, to disguise things, and not discover the persons I have spoken of, as indeed I have, call'd them by other then their ordinary names, and mistaken *Brie* for some other Province?"[108] Sorel's implication—that empirical validation may be of no easier access than the idealist bases of romance truth—is the fundamental insight of extreme skepticism; which is not to say that it is quite the same thing. In antiromance, the familiar pattern of reversal still has the air of working itself out within the general ambit of romance. After all, Sorel's target is not the hard-nosed and autonomous brand of "historicity" that is espoused by naive empiricism, but the milder claims and the postures of *vraisemblance* that modern romance has extruded around itself like a self-protective carapace.[109] Nevertheless the pattern of reversal bears a general resemblance to what we have seen elsewhere. Once the problem of belief is raised with sufficient insistence, "romance" tends toward the status of "antiromance," and "antiromance" tends in turn to become also "antihistory." But the logic of this second reversal may then seem at least to raise the question of an unwanted return of romance.

If Paul Scarron's play with the truths of romance and "true history" is milder than Sorel's,[110] Antoine Furetière's technique is to deny so minutely and strenuously the indebtedness of his "true History" to the well-known romance tropes ("inventions that have been presented in so many formes, and so often turned and patched they can no longer be made use of") that he finds he has no conventions at all with which to proceed, and "can, therefore, tell you no more of this Story." Here we will find no lord's squire or lover's confidante, no riot of weddings at the conclusion, no long and intricate interpolations "tacked together with Romantick Thred," but simply "this most faithful Relation, to which I only give form, without any alteration of the matter." But of course the nature and very existence of "matter" is a function of conventional "form," as Furetière himself has assured us. In fact the story does get related, and in fact it is preceded by an "Epistle" that disarmingly identifies what is to come as both history and "Romance."[111]

What becomes of the genre of romance across the Channel? It is a widespread misconception among literary scholars that when English writers of the later seventeenth and early eighteenth centuries attack "romance," they refer specifically and exclusively to the French heroic romance of the early seventeenth century. Certainly the French romance came in for its share of criticism. But it was in no sense the "very type" of romance for these writers, whose assault on the romance tradition is really quite continuous with that of the English humanists on medieval romance.[112] As we have seen, the French romances were translated and given an English audience of some indeterminate size. They also inspired the creation of a small number of English imitations. The patriarch of these English heroic romances, John Barclay's *Argenis* (Latin, 1621; English, 1625), is obviously indebted also to the older tradition of Spenser and Sidney for its dominant attitude toward the notion of historical truth. Barclay's aim is less verisimilitude than the aura of political allegory that already is a part of the *Arcadia* and *The Faerie Queene* (1590, 1596) and that later *romans à clef* will sharpen into something closer to what I have called the claim to historicity. Thus one of Barclay's translators includes a "Clavis" and warns the reader against taking this work "as an idle Romance, in which there were no other fruit conteined, but fantasticall tales." And the author himself, calling this a "new kind of writing," remarks that "he shall erre, as well, that will haue it all to be a true relation of things really done, as he that takes it to be wholly fained."[113]

Language like this seems to hover between the traditional, Augustinian strategy of mediating an essential truth by contingent means, and the historicist identification of truth with historical truth. It is confusing because the reader is encouraged to associate "history" both with the fruit and with the chaff that should be used but not enjoyed, handled but not eaten. This uncertainty persists in the several English romances that were printed around the time of the Restoration, and it mixes there with the alternative mode of being responsible to "history" that consists in the doctrine of verisimilitude. Roger Boyle and George Mackenzie draw upon both Aristotle and the Aristotelian Sidney to argue that romance "Probability" "may be as Instructive as, if not more than," historical truth. "Besides, Romances tell us what may be, whereas true Historyes tell us what is, or has bin." On the other hand, Boyle sees fit to boast of having included two "True Historyes" in his romance, and both writers elaborate their versions of the metaphor of the epistemological fruit and chaff.[114]

After the Restoration, English booksellers entered upon the no-doubt profitable venture of printing collections of short, largely foreign narratives.[115] These collections reflect the sort of epistemological eclecticism that I have been arguing is generally characteristic of the romance attempt to internalize a modestly historicizing self-critique. Some of the works they contain make a pronounced claim to historicity through the posture of autobiographical memoir, secret history, or authenticated document.[116] One collection validates the truth of its tales by including a table of historical sources for them, quickly modulating into verisimilitude then with the remark, "I have augmented the History" with exchanges which, "if they are not what they really spake, they are at least what they might."[117] But most of these narratives either orchestrate the collision between "history" and "romance" so listlessly as to assert very little,[118] or evince no formal self-consciousness whatsoever.

When English writers undertake the secret history or memoir, they tend to rehearse the same, contradictory range of skeptical postures as do their French practitioners. To be sure, it was possible to present such works with a relatively simple and straightforward claim to historicity.[119] But the practice of (Mary) Delarivière Manley is perhaps more representative. In the speculative preface to the first part of one of her secret histories, Manley clearly distinguishes between "a True History" (which must cleave to historical factuality) and the work of "he that composes a History to his Fancy" (which instead is responsible to "the Probability of Truth"). Both "Little *Histories* of this Kind have taken [the] Place of *Romances*," Manley adds, but she is silent here on the crucial question of which kind her own little history purports to be. The preface to the second part opens by emphasizing the documentary historicity of the work: echoing her title page, Manley claims to have translated it from the "Original Manuscript" in the Vatican library. Almost immediately, however, this degenerates into a heavily parodic use of the discovered manuscript topos: "the Manuscript is so Ancient that 'tis suppos'd to be Writ by *Cain* in the Land of *Nod*." Manley's deflation of the topos supposedly serves to refute the view that her work, a transparent and scandalous *roman à clef*, is "a Modern History, and related to several Affairs Transacted near Home." But of course it really serves to do nothing of the kind. As Manley remarks, her heroine is so unprepossessing that this "alone is sufficient to perswade me this Story is all a Romantick *Tale of a Tub*, tho' some People, I cannot tell from what Grounds, are positive there is some Truth in it." The inflamed reader may be excused for concluding, both despite and because of these denials, that the "romance" is also a "history." Its truth is that not of strict historicity but of the historical fruit which stands revealed once we have stripped away the mediating chaff of "romance."[120]

In France it is Pierre Bayle who programmatically invalidates the secret history and memoir as the new romance. In England it is once again Sir Richard Steele; but here the disease is diagnosed as a specifically French import. Several months before his critique of English news reporters, Mr. Tatler proposes to discuss some merry gentlemen of the French nation, who have written very advantageous histories of their exploits in war, love, and politics, under the title of Memoirs. I am afraid I shall find several of these gentlemen tardy, because I hear of them in no writings, but their own. To read the narrative of one of these authors, you would fancy that there was not an action in a whole campaign which he did not contrive or execute; yet, if you consult the history or gazettes of those times, you do not find him so much as at the head of a party from one end of the summer to the other. But it is the way of these great men, when they lie behind their lines, and are in a time of inaction, as they call it, to pass away their time in writing their exploits. By this means, several who are either unknown or despised in the present age, will be famous in the next, unless a sudden stop be put to such pernicious practices. There are others of that gay people, who, as I am informed, will live half a year together in a garret, and write a history of their intrigues in the Court of France . . . The most immediate remedy that I can apply to prevent this growing evil, is, That I do hereby give notice to all booksellers and translators whatsoever, that the word Memoir is French for a novel; and to require of them that they sell and translate it accordingly.[121]

The reversal implicit in Steele's argument was available by other means as well. In England as in France, "antiromance" learned to liberate itself to some degree from its romance enclosure and to deflate not only romance but also history. For example, it is easy enough to identify the complacent claim to historicity in *A Tale of a Tub* (1704) as one of those modernist practices that Swift attacks in the idiosyncratic narrator whom he impersonates. Halfway through his digressive and irregular discourse, the author returns once more to the tale proper, ostentatiously noting where he had left his principals and underscoring in the process his manipulative control of the narrative. To this he adds: "However, I shall by no means forget my Character of an Historian, to follow the Truth, step by step, whatever happens, or where-ever it may lead me." Yet in the context of our present concerns it is important to recall that Swift's *Tale* is not only an antihistory but also—and first of all—an antiromance. For the story of the three brothers is itself a romance fairy tale whose allegorical essence is "shut up within the Vehicles of Types and Fables."[122] And if Swift is contemptuous of the naive empiricist method of locating meaning on the narrative surface, he is no happier with the brutal excavation of truth through laborious and proleptic interpretation. His dismay at superficial and deep reading alike is one version of the central problem of the *Tale,* the untenable choice between being a fool and being a knave. It is also one instance of the omnivorous skepticism that may be set in motion by the antiromance impulse. For a more explicit and comprehensive exploitation of narrative possibilities, however, we may turn briefly to William Congreve's *Incognita* (1692).

Congreve's famous "Preface" reiterates the familiar complaint that the "miraculous" and "impossible" pleasures of romance always must fade as the reader realizes "that 'tis all a lye." The alternative to the lies of romance Congreve calls not "true history" but "the novel," and its hallmark is less strict historicity than probability, the representation of events "which not being so distant from our belief bring also the pleasure nearer us." This emphasis may be taken to reflect Congreve's indebtedness to the French antiromance, and it encourages in us the expectation also of a corollary, antihistorical reversal aimed at the relatively muted and self-protective sort of historicism that is characteristic of modern romance itself. Certainly the first reversal is achieved in the style of the French antiromance, by parodic impersonation. Like Sorel's extravagant shepherd, Congreve's personages are figures out of an idealizing romance, satirized most of all for an indefatigable credulousness that economically evokes also the gullibility of the average romance reader. The heartsick lovers Aurelian and Hippolito, constantly duped by their own tendentious desires, at one point argue "themselves into a belief, that fortune had befriended them with a better plot, than their regular thinking could have contriv'd. So soon had they convinced themselves, in what they were willing to believe." At the end of a long account of Aurelian's *précieuse* fantasy of his beloved's face, Congreve remarks: "And a thousand other things his transport represented to him, which none but lovers who have experience of such visions will believe." And the Quixotic delusions of Congreve's heroes, although primarily amatory, are occasionally military, as when they mistake a ceremonial chivalric joust ("only design'd for shew and form") for the real thing.[123]

The satiric point here is clear enough, but Congreve also lards his narrative with devices of authentication which assert the documentary truth of what he is telling us. He gives us private letters "word for word"; he presents himself as an earwitness to many of the events he recounts, at the least through the firsthand testimony of Aurelian himself; and where this degree of authentication is not available, he scrupulously announces: " 'Tis strange now, but all accounts agree, that . . ." As in the French works he follows, Congreve's very insistence on his role as the neutral and transparent recorder of what has happened—the very antithesis of those visionary, creative romancers who are his heroes—leads him to protest the truth and plausibility of his narrative so energetically as to raise our suspicions rather than quell them. "I would not have the reader now be impertinent," he says, "and look upon this to be force, or a whim of the author's, that a woman should proceed so far in the approbation of a man whom she never saw, that it is impossible, therefore ridiculous to suppose it." Our growing sense that this may indeed be the "force of the author" comes not, of course, from the implausibility of the event itself but from earnest and distracting authorial intrusions like this one. And by the end of the story we find ourselves awash in romance discoveries

and implausible resolutions that can only be attributed to the manipulative way in which the story has been told. In such an atmosphere,
Congreve's laborious efforts to ascertain what is "probable" at the very
local level appear at best impertinent.[124]

Lest we miss the potential parallel between his romancing personages
and ourselves, Congreve takes advantage of a critical interview between
the doting Aurelian and his beloved to drive the parallel home: "For I
would caution the reader by the bye, not to believe every word which she
told him, nor that admirable sorrow which she counterfeited to be accurately true. It was indeed truth . . . cunningly intermingled with fiction," a partial account of a plot whereby she had temporarily "concealed" herself, "as the reader shall understand ere long: For we have
another discovery to make to him, if he have not found it out of himself
already." So Congreve the grave recorder of events is unmasked as Congreve the creative articulator of plots and counterplots, disguises and
discoveries. The antiromance impulse is completed by its "antihistorical" corollary movement, which effectively punctures both the
claim to historicity and the pretense to verisimilitude. There is a pleasing
symmetry in the fact that several decades after its publication, *Incognita*
was claimed to be really a *roman à clef* waiting for the death of its eminent
principals to be definitively decyphered.[125] A bookseller's opportunistic
ploy to promote sales, the claim reverses the narrative's antihistorical
impulse once more, subjecting all to the omnivorous empiricist appetite
for "real events" that Congreve's parodic impersonation ironically had
whetted.

Despite its availability through Aristotle and Aristotelian sources, the
idea of probability as a positive and stable standard of narrative truth
remains only moderately attractive to seventeenth-century English writers. In Congreve's amused subversion of verisimilitude there is the
groundwork for a view of probability as a kind of "aesthetic" truth,
aware of its own fictionality and detoxified of crude empiricist illusion.
The major obstacle to this relatively immediate approach to the idea of
the aesthetic in England is the extraordinary power of empirical thought
itself.

The complex development of the romance genre, its resolution into
"romance" and "historical" elements, each of which is subjected to internal critique, provides a striking model of generic change. But the epistemological origins of the English novel cannot be understood in generic
terms alone. More crucial still is the status of "romance" as a general
epistemological category, and the more comprehensive and decisive dialectic in which it figures. The key to this dialectic—to the double reversal of romance idealism by naive empiricism and of both by extreme

skepticism—is the dynamic energy of the historicist revolution which is the subject of this chapter and the moving force behind the transformation of "romance" into a simple abstraction. At the heart of this revolution, at least in seventeenth-century England, is the scientific movement. In the following chapter, the contest between "romance" and "true history" will remain my major concern, but now as it serves to articulate and organize the early modern crisis of secularization.

— *Two* —

The Evidence of the Senses:
Secularization and Epistemological Crisis

I

THE CONTRADICTORY UNITY OF THE NEW PHILOSOPHY

The idea of secularization is a paradoxical one. Its progressive and optimistic promise is of a faithful accommodation or translation of the
sacred to a profane world, of the past to the present, whereby an essential matter is understood to be preserved within an altered form. But
secularization may also be a process of mistranslation in which reformation amounts to deformation, purification to corruption—in which to
know and experience what has been given is felt to be a crude act of
"comprehension," a swallowing up of sacred truth by a secular reduction of it. This paradox haunts seventeenth-century England on every
level of thought and activity; it is inseparable even from Francis Bacon's
supremely sanguine accounts of the "new philosophy" of empirical
method.

Although Bacon's method of "true induction" starts "directly from
the simple sensuous perception," its dependence on what he calls "the
evidence of the sense" is corrected by "experiments fit and apposite,
wherein the sense decides touching the experiment only, and the experiment touching the point in nature and the thing itself." Properly managed, the problem also entails a solution: "For certain it is that the senses
deceive, but then at the same time they supply the means of discovering
their own errors." By these means the new philosophy "may discover
and explain in the motion itself, not what is accordant with the phenomena, but what is found in nature herself, and is actually and really
true." We are not wrong to hear in Bacon's formulation a reminder of
Christian epistemology and the problem of mediating spiritual truths by

corporeal means. The truth of nature is a material truth, but Bacon is
concerned to show how the materialist interpretation of nature conducts
us to the truth of the spirit:

For I am building in the human understanding a true model of the world,
such as it is in fact, not such as a man's own reason would have it to be . . .
[But] there is a great difference between the Idols of the human mind and the
Ideas of the divine. That is to say, between certain empty dogmas and the true
signatures and marks set upon the works of creation as they are found in
nature . . . The former are nothing more than arbitrary abstractions; the
latter are the creator's own stamp upon creation, impressed and defined in
matter by true and exquisite lines. Truth, therefore, and utility are here the
very same things.[1]

The familiar view of nature as "God's other book" permits Bacon to
retain the notion of the universe as a great sign system, and to conceive of
the scientist as one who reads in material reality the contingent signifiers
of God's great signifieds. Yet the prohibition of "the idols of the human
mind" is so comprehensive that it can seem to enforce less a relationship
of signification than one of decorous segregation. Bacon attacks the sort
of philosophy that, corrupted "by superstition and an admixture of
theology," is "fanciful and tumid and half-poetical." "From this un-
wholesome mixture of things human and divine there arises not only a
fantastic philosophy but also a heretical religion. Very meet it is therefore
that we be sober-minded, and give to faith that only which is faith's."[2]
    Once the human and the divine are thus approached as separable
realms of knowledge, the role of natural phenomena as instrumental
signifiers is likely to become little more than a respectful trope. All the
exhilaration of positive discovery lies with natural philosophy, which is
encouraged increasingly to disdain its traditional function as "merely a
passage and bridge to something else," and to embrace the effective status
of an autonomous end in itself, the signifier turned signified. The felt
immanence of spirit in matter loses its conviction; the relationship between spiritual and material study ceases to be one of hierarchical super-
ordination and becomes one of analogy. This change may be sensed,
perhaps, in the careless ease with which Bacon employs the model of
divine authority as though it were a rhetorical figure. He observes, for
example, that "the true method of experience" operates systematically
"even as it was not without order and method that the divine word
operated on the created mass." "Again, discoveries are as it were new
creations, and imitations of God's works." And in the end, the analogy
itself becomes overbalanced. The familiar language of spiritual events
finds its highest function to rest in signifying the more present reality of
material success, so that by patient diligence the new philosopher learns

how to correct "the depraved and deep-rooted habits of his mind," enacting in little the triumph of the scientific movement as a whole in "the removing of despair and the raising of hope through the dismissal or rectification of the errors of past time." Where Bacon's analogy falters, of course, is in the unremarked discrepancy between the spiritual salvation of fallen humanity through divine mediation, and a secular salvation that is indebted to nothing but human industry and self-sufficiency: "Only let the human race recover that right over nature which belongs to it by divine bequest, and let power be given it." In developing an image of himself as a latter-day prophet of the new faith, "sowing in the meantime for future ages the seeds of a purer truth," Bacon permits us to watch the very process by which the pious secularization of divine creation may reverse itself and become the human appropriation of creativity.[3]

The separation of human from divine knowledge in Bacon is strictly parallel to his division of the new and the old learning into "two dispensations of knowledge . . . not hostile or alien to each other" yet manifestly unequal in their potential for enlightenment. What he makes of the wisdom of the ancients is suggested by his interpretive procedure in the work which bears that name, an essay that subjects pagan myth to the same sort of disingenuous demystification which he more tacitly exerts on the spiritual component of God's book of nature. To be sure, he admits, many regard "the fables of the poets" as mere child's toys. "It may be that my reverence for the primitive time carries me too far, but the truth is that in some of these fables . . . I find a conformity and connexion with the thing signified, so close and so evident that one cannot help believing such a signification to have been designed and meditated from the first, and purposely shadowed out." "The thing signified" by these pagan narratives is not Christian truth but the material truth of nature: thus the story of Pan is that of nature itself; Proteus is secularized as matter; and the love represented by Cupid is *the natural motion of the atom.*" What the Church Fathers do explicitly to pagan wisdom, Bacon does, by the silent comprehension of it within his natural significations, to Christian truth as well.[4]

As these accommodations of ancient to modern and divine to human learning would suggest, the conceptual force of the new philosophy is such that it requires of Bacon a new division of knowledge. He protests his "affection and good will towards the received sciences," and he goes so far as to base his principal categories of all human learning—history, poesy, and philosophy—upon the standard divisions of faculty psychology. Beyond this, however, there is little in Bacon's division of knowledge to comfort tradition. Like natural history, civil history should aspire to the rank of an objective, value-free study, "simply narrating the fact historically with but slight intermixture of private judgment." And it is

clear that this represents the single guiding standard of veracity for
Bacon, since he adopts Aristotle's historicizing distinction between history and poetry but reverses their respective truth values. Poesy is understood as "nothing else than feigned history or fables," and the distinction
between poetic and historical truth modulates into one between lesser
and greater truth, "feigned history" and "true history."[5]

Like Renaissance historicism, the Baconian scientific program contains two contrary movements. An optimistic faith in the power of empirical method to discover natural essences points in one direction; a wary
skepticism of the evidence of the senses and its mediating capacity points
in quite another. And what Bacon's rhetorical genius was able to hold
together becomes separated out into controversy once the new philosophy becomes institutionalized under the auspices of the Royal Society.
True, post-Baconian inquiry also elaborated a scientific standard of probability distinct from the conflict defined by these contrary movements;
but the conflict maintained an important presence during the Restoration
period. For his most optimistic heirs (as for Bacon himself), "natural
history" represents the ideal of narrative perspicuity, the means by which
the truths of nature will obtain an unimpeded mediation. And the negative standard to which natural history is opposed is very often the credulous mystifications of "romance," especially when associated with the
discredited authority of the ancients.[6]

2

"NATURAL HISTORY" AS A NARRATIVE MODEL

According to the Royal Society's first historian, its Fellows have been
scrupulous in recording the most trivial natural phenomena, a procedure
"visibly neglected by the *Antients*. The *Histories of Pliny, Aristotle, Solinus,
Aelian,* abounding more with pretty Tales, and fine monstrous Stories;
than sober, and fruitful Relations. [This] is not the true following of
Nature . . . It is like *Romances*, in respect of *True History;* which, by
multiplying varieties of extraordinary Events, and surprizing circumstances, makes that seem dull, and tasteless." So the entire tradition of the
unnatural natural history is now to be discharged as "romance." Thanks
to the exertions of the new philosophers, "every man is unshaken at those
Tales, at which his Ancestors trembled: The cours of things goes quietly
along, in its own true channel of *Natural Causes* and *Effects*." To Joseph
Glanvill, one of the most promising features of the Royal Society's labors
is their collective and communal character, for "the *Histories of Nature* we
have *hitherto* had, have been but an *heap* and *amassment* of *Truth* and
Falshood, vulgar Tales and *Romantick* Accounts; and 'tis not in the power of
particular unassociated Endeavours to afford us *better*." As for the piecemeal
accretions of the old Ptolemaic system, "what a *Romance* is the story of

those impossible *concamerations, Interfections, Involutions,* and feign'd *Rotations* of *solid Orbs?* All substituted to salve the credit of a broken ill-contrived *Systeme.*"[7]

The problem with these antitheses between ancient and modern, romance and true history, is that they are engendered by a sophisticated critical and comparative historiography which cannot long be satisfied with their easy simplicity. For one thing, some of the ancients only appeared to be romancers to those of inadequate understanding. Thus the physics of Archimedes, although possible enough, "sound no better to common Ears, then those of *Amadis de Gaule,* and the *Knight* of the *Sun.*" And by the same token, ignorant attacks upon the Royal Society today are "as if those that doated on the *Tales* of the *Fabulous Age,* should clamour against *Herodotus* and *Thucydides* as idle *Romancers.*" The danger of speculative comparisons like these is that they tend to relativize absolute notions of "history" and "romance," showing them to be matters of degree and dependent upon one's comparative context. Moreover, a corollary of such insights is that many moderns, too, are capable of romance credulity and imposture. Noting the paucity of evidence to support ancient accounts of giants, Thomas Molyneux remarks that "till some such evidence be produced, we may look upon all the stories of those extravagantly Gigantick men, to be little better than the Fables of the Poets of old, or the Whims and Romances of some modern Credulous and Inventive men." And in the view of John Spencer, "the ancient *Grecian* Historians and more Modern Legendaries studied only to make their Relations miraculous enough." Perhaps those moderns "are not severe enough to value truth, and therefore will scarce relate any matter (especially if going a little off from common and quotidian) but it shall look big, and borrow somewhat of a Romance." Might this criticism be made even of the Fellows of the Royal Society?[8]

It all depends, of course, on your perspective. What we are able to demonstrate as true would have seemed incredible to our ancestors: "To have talk'd of a *new Earth* to have been discovered, had been a *Romance* to *Antiquity.*" The Royal Society "*really* are what former Ages could contrive but in *wish* and *Romances.*" Moreover, the enthusiasm of Glanvill and Thomas Sprat leads both to speak of those "glorious Undertakers" of the new philosophy as the new, "illustrious Heroes" of the modern age, greater than those of epic and romance, "generous Vertuoso's, who dwell in an higher Region then other Mortals." This heady flirtation with the fanciful idealism of romance seems odd coming from sober empiricists; it expresses the disorienting experience of historical relativity with respect both to past dogmas and to future possibilities, which begin now to appear limitless. This is Glanvill on the promise of the telescope: "What success and informations we may expect from the *Advancements* of this *Instrument,* it would perhaps appear *Romantick* and *ridiculous* to say;

As, no doubt, to have talk'd of the *spots* in the *Sun,* and vast *inequalities* in the *surface* of the *Moon,* and those other *Telescopical certainties,* before the *Invention* of that *Glass,* would have been thought *phantastick* and *absurd."* From the investigations of the Royal Society "we may hopefully expect a considerable *inlargement* of the *History* of *Nature,* without which," Glanvill adds nervously, "our *Hypotheseis* [*sic*] are but *Dreams* and *Romances,* and our *Science* meer *conjecture* and *opinion.*"9

Skeptical moderns as well as underdeveloped ancients, in other words, may appear quite justified in taking much of the work of the Society with a grain of salt, at least at present. This recognition encourages Sprat to make the following, definitive formulation:

When my *Reader* shall behold this large number of *Relations;* perhaps he will think, that too many of them seem to be incredulous stories, and that if the *Royal Society* shall much busie themselves, about such wonderful, and uncertain *events,* they will fall into that mistake, of which I have already accus'd some of the *Antients,* of framing *Romances,* instead of solid *Histories* of Nature. But . . . it is certain that many things, which now seem *miraculous,* would not be so, if once we come to be fully acquainted with their *compositions,* and *operations* . . . In this there is a neer resemblance between *Natural* and *civil History.* In the *Civil,* that way of *Romance* is to be exploded, which heightens all the characters, and actions of men, beyond all shadow of *probability:* yet this does not hinder, but the great, and eminent *virtues* of extraordinary men of all Ages, may be related, and propos'd to our example. The same is to be affirm'd of *Natural History.* To make that only to consist of strange, and delightful Tales, is to render it nothing else but *vain,* and ridiculous *Knight-Errantry.* Yet we may avoid that extreme, and still leave room, to consider the singular, and irregular *effects,* and to imitate the unexpected, and monstrous *excesses,* which *Nature* does sometimes practise in her *works.* The first may be only compar'd to the Fables of *Amadis,* and the Seven Champions: the other to the real *Histories* of *Alexander, Hannibal, Scipio,* or *Caesar:* in which though many of their Actions may at first surprize us; yet there is nothing that exceeds the *Truth* of *Life,* and that may not serve for our *instruction,* or *imitation.*10

Sprat's formulation is definitive not in resolving the contradictions that have begun to appear in apologies for the Royal Society but in displaying them with eloquence. Interestingly enough, his language suggests that the ultimate triumph of scientific standards of probability over those of certainty may be related to the ultimate triumph of literary standards of verisimilitude over the claim to historicity. At present, however, the standard of probability has the more limited and paradoxical end of facilitating that claim. We have already encountered this paradox in other contexts. Faced with the fact that the new philosophy's narratives may seem very hard to credit, Sprat uses the comparison between natural and civil history to distinguish in the former two different sorts of improbability. The first is like that of the old romances, and it is a reliable sign of falsehood. But the second is like that of the "real histories" of antiquity, an incredibility that surprisingly bespeaks the presence of truth. This is the renovated rationale for the unnatural natural history, the formula "strange, therefore true," according to which the very appearance of unlikelihood acquires the status of a claim to historicity. And it is here that the exception of some of the ancients from modern condemnation proves crucial. For it permits the historicizing insight that what seems strange to one age may be revealed as true to its inheritors.[11]

The defensiveness of Sprat and Glanvill was not unoccasioned. To Henry Stubbe, the early scourge of the Royal Society, its most egregious errors consist in telling romances not about natural history as such, but about the inadequacy of ancient learning in general and of Aristotle in particular. At this rate, he remarks, we will soon be "reduced to that pass, as to believe the story of *Tom Thumb,* and all the *Legends* or *falsifications of History,* which the *Papists* obtrude upon us!"[12] Stubbe frequently calls the new philosophers "novellists." Against their progressive view of intellectual history he opposes a conservative view based on his belief that the novelists are guilty of both suppressing and plagiarizing ancient wisdom: "Most that the *Novellists* have done, is to find out *new reasons* for an *antient practice* . . . 'Tis their usual practice to vouch those things for *new discoveries* which we very well *knew before* . . . We are running on as fast as we can to this condition of *ignorance,* and shall be so inured to *Historical* untruths, *magisterially* imposed upon us, and disused from inquiring into *them,* as to *beleeve any thing.*"[13]

The critique of the Royal Society's "true historians" as romancing "novellists" intent on falsifying ancient history might lead us to regard Stubbe as a dogmatic proponent of the ancients and unalterably hostile to the new philosophy. But this is no more true of Stubbe than it is of other skeptical critics we have encountered, like Richard Steele and Pierre Bayle. In fact, Stubbe was a rather forward-looking physician whose announced "Aristotelianism" did not preclude acknowledging the triumphs of modern science. And some of the same contradictory twists taken by the thought of the Society's devotees can be seen also in those who, like Stubbe, were opposed to it. In Glanvill's rapt speculation, for example, we have already had a taste of how the new philosophers tended to extol the nearly mystical powers of the new instrument of empiricism, the telescope. Critics like Stubbe, although themselves committed to the premises of empirical method, were driven by such outbursts to explore the limits of scientific observation, to suggest not only that telescopes are not "as certain as our Eyes" but also that even "if they were as certain as our eyes . . . yet the employing of that only sense would never assure us of what we see." This sort of criticism is fully representative of the posture of extreme skepticism, for it directs us backward as well as

forward: toward the Christian attack upon the proud belief in the sufficiency of merely physical vision, and to the ongoing sophistication of
modern ideas about contextual and perceptual relativity. Elsewhere
Stubbe tells of a friend who shares his skepticism about the new astrono-
my. Having spoken

of the Celestial *Phaenomena*, how differently they were represented by *sundry
men*, he was more prone to suspect their *dioptrick Tubes*, than *their integrity:* He
thought our Eyes were *Telescopes* of God *Almighty's* making, and the model
by which the others were regulated and amended: and that any man who
regarded the *daily Occurrents in vision*, could never believe it possible, that any
certainty could be derived from *Telescopes* . . . He added, that *our senses* and
the *daily objects* we converse with on earth, did *prejudicate* rather then qualifie
us for *these speculations:* that we might easily observe what *mistakes* arise from
the contemplation of *resemblances*.[14]

That the critique of the new telescopical faith might be made from the
modern perspective of empirical science itself is confirmed by Samuel
Butler's satire about the mistaking of a mouse trapped in a telescope for
an elephant on the moon. Before the error is discovered one of the
enthusiastic virtuosi exclaims:

> Let us cautiously contrive,
> To draw an exact Narrative
> Of what we every one can swear,
> Our Eyes themselves have seen appear;
> That, when we publish the Account,
> We all may take our Oaths upon't.

And the moral of the satire is

> *That those who greedily pursue*
> *Things wonderful, instead of true;*
> *That in their Speculations chuse*
> *To make Discoveries strange News;*
> *And Nat'ral History a Gazette*
> *Of Tales stupendous, and far-fet;*
> *Hold no Truth worthy to be known,*
> *That is not huge, and over-grown,*
> *And explicate Appearances,*
> *Not as they are, but as they please,*
> *In vain strive Nature to suborn,*
> *And, for their Pains, are paid with Scorn.*

The extreme skepticism of Butler's poem confirms, by close association,
the naive empiricist affinity of several modes of discourse that we have
encountered thus far: scientific observation, documentary publication,

legal validation, and news reportage. And its moral—that the "strange, therefore true" of the new natural histories is no more true than the old romance—Butler echoes elsewhere in his character of the virtuoso, who next to rarities "loves strange natural Histories; and as those, that read Romances, though they know them to be Fictions, are as much affected as if they were true, so is he, and will make hard Shift to tempt himself to believe them first to be possible, and then he's sure to believe them to be true."[15]

3

"RELIGION VERSUS SCIENCE"

AND THE PROBLEM OF MEDIATION

Despite the internal contradictions of empirical method, upholders of the Christian alternative to the evidence of the senses were obliged to wage a thoroughly reactive battle against its forces. The difficulty of the fight may be seen in the masterful polemics of Galileo, Bacon's contemporary, against the Scripture-wielding enemies of heliocentrism. All early proponents of the new philosophy maintained, with Bacon, the unity of truth and its final identity with Christian revelation. But the ostensibly accommodating assumption that truth is one had the effect of facilitating, as in Galileo, the stealthy substitution of physical for intellectual and spiritual proofs as the overarching standard for what might still be embraced as truth inviolate.

"The holy Bible can never speak with untruth," Galileo writes to the Grand Duchess Christina—"whenever its true meaning is understood. But I believe nobody will deny that it is often very abstruse, and may say things which are quite different from what its bare words signify." Now, "the holy Bible and the phenomena of nature proceed alike from the divine Word." But in the reading of the book of nature, Galileo continues, exegetical difficulties are less, because the obscurities occasioned by the linguistic accommodation of God's Word to all Scripture readers are absent, nature caring not "a whit whether her abstruse reasons and methods of operations are understandable to men." For this reason, "in discussions of physical problems we ought to begin not from the authority of scriptural passages, but from sense-experiences and necessary demonstrations." To Paolo Antonio Foscarini, Galileo writes: "To me, the surest and swiftest way to prove that the position of Copernicus is not contrary to Scripture would be to give a host of proofs that it is true and that the contrary cannot be maintained at all; thus, since no two truths can contradict one another, this and the Bible must be perfectly harmonious." In those questions where human reason and science are impotent—"for example, whether the stars are animate"—"it is necessary in

piety to comply absolutely with the strict sense of Scripture." But "first
we are to make certain of the fact, which will reveal to us the true senses
of the Bible . . . for two truths can never contradict each other." By this
means, science becomes both the newest and the most authoritative—
because empirical—method of scriptural exegesis, of determining biblical truth.[16]

So the great war between religion and science was not, in reality, a
very straightforward confrontation. Galileo's referral of questions of
religious truth to prior factual tests was welcomed, in the latter half of the
century, not only by scientists but also by theologians.[17] Many pious
contemporaries experienced the relation between religion and science as a
constructive encounter because it seemed a potential solution to what I
have called the problem of mediation. Daniel Defoe gives this age-old
dilemma of Christian faith and pedagogy a succinct formulation: "We
can Form no Idea of any Thing that we know not and have not seen, but
in the Form of something that we have seen. How then can we form an
Idea of God or Heaven, in any Form but of something which we have
seen or known?" John Milton's version is characteristically confident that
the problem is really a solution: "But because our understanding cannot
in this body found it selfe but on sensible things, nor arrive so cleerly to
the knowledge of God and things invisible, as by orderly conning over
the visible and inferior creature, the same method is necessarily to be
follow'd in all discreet teaching." In the traditional methodology of biblical hermeneutics, the solution was accessible through the doctrine of
condescension or accommodation, whereby the approximation of divinity through material figures was understood to accord with God's
own intent. And for many Christians, the lived equivalent of this self-
conscious exegetical assumption was the dialectical experience of immanence, of the ongoing presence of divinity in the things of this world.[18]

What is peculiar to the early modern period is neither an apprehension
of the problem of mediation nor a confidence of its solution, but an
unprecedented intensification of both. The tacit dialectic of matter and
spirit is opened out, with a greater or lesser degree of skepticism, into an
explicit and strenuously argued dualism. Of course this is only another
way of characterizing the paradoxical nature of secularization crisis. Ad-
vocating material registers of truth, optimistic new philosophers earnestly anticipated fundamental advances in the passage from here to there,
from corrupted humanity to a comprehension of the divine. But to those
more skeptical than they, the new freedom only threatened the deformation of the spirit. "What *irreligion* can there be in applying some *Scripture-
expressions* to *Naturall things?*" asks Thomas Sprat. "Why are not the *one*
rather *exalted* and *purified,* then the other defiled by such applications?"
But Henry Stubbe testily replies that this kind of "*Holy Raillery*" hath

given occasion to most prophane Burlesque," that it is a materializing exercise in accommodation which does indeed defile what it would exalt. Exchanges like this one tend to confirm that controversies about the materialism of the new philosophy and controversies about the application of biblical figures are part of the same, more general crisis. "Science" and "religion," moving swiftly toward their modern separation, at this moment stand united in their concern with matters of signification. Ostensibly preoccupied with divergent realms of human experience, the scientific revolution and the Protestant Reformation converge on the common ground marked out by the problem of mediation.[19]

Recent work has done much to revise the old misconceptions and prejudices about Puritan iconoclasm. The central phenomenon is not a hostility to "art" but a suspicion of traditional methods of mediating truth that also pervades much of early modern culture.[20] The purifying tendency in Puritanism, the reforming impulse of the Reformation expressed (among other things) the will to cleanse the Christian signifying system of false and congesting mediators that were felt to obscure the immanence of spirit in matter. But the repudiation of false mediators is a negative gesture that implies its positive counterpart, the discovery of more immediate and self-authenticating paths to the realm of the spirit. Rejecting what they took to be the corrupting idols of Roman Catholic devotion, the Reformers embraced instead what Bacon called "the ideas of the divine," the language of Scripture. The parallel with the Baconian program is not adventitious. The reliance of Protestant thought on the figurative language of the Bible as the one true sense and "literal" Word of God is profoundly analogous to the new philosophical argument that in nature's book was to be found the register and signature of divine intent. Contemporaries certainly understood that the exegetical commitment to "one sense of Scripture, the literal sense," was informed by a commitment to the evidence of the senses. Thus Robert Ferguson believed that "Logicall and Metaphysicall Terms are of all others, the most inept to declare [divine mysteries] in; nor are there any so accommodated to display and unveil them, as Metaphorical expressions . . . to illustrate them by things sensible and of ocular knowledg."[21]

The Protestant use of rhetorical figures entails a mediation that all but lays claim to immediacy. In the teachings of the Reformers, the spiritual signification of a figure is so fully implicated in its facilitating signifier that what appear to be two senses must be conceived as one. According to William Whitaker, "When we proceed from the sign to the thing signified, we bring no new sense, but only bring out into the light what was before concealed in the sign . . . For although this sense be spiritual, yet it is not a different one, but really literal." The spiritual is almost seamlessly enclosed within the literal sense. In William Perkins's explication, the boundary between the "literal" and the "spiritual," the "historical" and the "mystical," is inscribed and effaced in a single movement: "It may be said, that the historie of Abrahams familie here propounded, hath beside his proper and literall sense, a spiritual or mysticall sense. I answer, they are not two senses, but two parts of one full and intire sense. For not onely the bare historie, but also that which is therby signified, is the full sense of the h[oly] G[host]."[22]

The language of Scripture provides a model for the dialectical immanence of the spirit within the letter which in Protestant thought applies also to the world at large. Protestantism elevated typology as the authoritative method of exegesis, enfolding within its literal and historical integrity all admissible dimensions of textual meaning. At the same time, it intensified the concrete historicity of typological thought by extending its reference to include not only Old Testament but contemporary and individual "history," the immediately accessible material of local political conflict or private emotional upheaval. Like Bacon's natural "matter," history is seen to be "impressed and defined" by "the creator's own stamp." The celebrated "plain speaking" of Puritan "mechanick preaching" therefore consisted not in any paucity of figures but in a richness of reference to the plain things of this world, whose very proximity seemed to facilitate a spiritual pedagogy. To "spiritualize" or to "improve" a homely figure—a common occupation or an everyday object—involved the teasing out of its familiar, plain utility the spiritual application it enwrapped. Thus John Flavell promised the seamen for whom he wrote, "to clothe spiritual matters in your own dialect and phrases, that they might be the more intelligible to you."[23]

So Protestant iconoclasm was really quite compatible with the making of images rightly conceived. Moreover Protestantism was the religion of the book, of the documentary object: its proverbial elevation of the printed Word over the graven image only made reformed religion more compatible with a "visual epistemology" that associated knowing with the empirical act of seeing.[24] By these several means, Protestant belief became so intertwined with the evidence of the senses that in the end the truth of Scripture itself seemed to require vindication as the truth of "true history." Over the course of the seventeenth century the venerable physical metaphor "revelation," mediating the inexpressible gift of spiritual understanding and faith, seems to struggle to assert its literal primacy as people increasingly take vision—what is seen with one's own eyes—as the only sound basis of knowledge. At its most emphatic, this conviction will be expressed in the claim that miracles have not ceased and that their persistence may be objectively documented and verified. And as Galileo's defense foretells, the revealed Word of God now also becomes subjected to the skeptical scrutiny of empirical norms of "revelation."

4
THE LITERALIZING OF REVELATION

In England, if not in Roman Catholic Italy, the vulnerability of Scripture itself was paradoxically a clear consequence of Protestant and typographical bibliolatry. The unbridled controversies of the revolutionary decades helped inculcate not only a respect for the documentary historicity of books but also a skeptical awareness that even history books are, after all, only the productions of fallible human beings. "If the King conquer," says the Leveller Richard Overton, "the Parliament will be Traytours to posterity by Cronicle; for who writ the Histories of Anabaptists but their Enemies?" For this reason the Presbyterian Richard Baxter could give "but halting credit" to histories of the medieval Albigenses and Waldenses, "who have left us none of their own writings in which they speak for themselves." "As long as men have liberty to examine and contradict one another, one may partly conjecture by comparing their words on which side the truth is like to lie. But when great men write history . . . which no man dare contradict, believe it but as you are constrained." And as a skeptical royalist observed, "Stories [i.e., histories] of former Ages are no other, then certain kinds of Romances to succeeding posterity; since they have no testimony for them but mens probable opinions; seeing the Historical part almost of all countrys is subject to be questioned." Now, the Word of God might seem to stand apart from this concern. Samuel Mather's account of the typological historicity of Scripture, for example, would appear to afford it an unassailable authority: "There is an historical Verity in all those typical Histories of the Old Testament. They are not bare Allegories, or parabolical Poems . . . but they are a true Narrative of things really existent and acted in the world, and are literally and historically to be understood." But Scripture too was penned by human hands, and it could not be kept from the rational process of "examining" and "comparing" which Baxter describes. "Even of the mysteries of the Gospel," he remarks, "I must needs say with Mr. Richard Hooker, *Eccl. Polit.*, that whatever men may pretend, the subjective certainty cannot go beyond the objective evidence."[25]

Thus the inevitable designation of Scripture as "history" simultaneously celebrated it by the highest standards and opened it to the most damaging of assaults—to being called bad history, or even mere history. The Digger Gerrard Winstanley accused university scholars of wishing to perpetuate the monopoly on interpretation: "You say you have the just Copies of [the prophets' and apostles'] writings; you doe not know but as your Fathers have told you; which may be as well false as true, if you have no better ground then tradition . . . *How can these Scriptures be called the everlasting Gospel, seeing it is torne in peeces daily amongst your selves, by*

various translations, inferences and conclusions . . . ?" And he praises those
who "believe nothing but what they see reason for." Rather than the
Word of God, concludes the Quaker Samuel Fisher, the Bible is "a bulk
of heterogeneous writings, compiled together by men taking what they
could find of the several sorts of writings that are therein,
and . . . crowding them into a canon, or standard for the trial of all
spirits, doctrines, truths; and by them alone." And the Ranter Lawrence
Clarkson found "so much contradiction" in the Bible that "I had no faith
in it at all, no more than a history."[26]

The immediate cause served by these various invalidations of Scripture was not freethinking but the elevation of the spirit over the letter, the
internalization of the Word. As William Dell put it, "The believer is the
only book in which God now writes his New Testament." But the
difference was not always easy to discern. After the Restoration, writers
in the dissenting tradition used the stock repudiation of Scripture according to the standards of objective truth and historicity to characterize not
believing saints but sinners and atheists. Spiritually afflicted, the Baptist
John Bunyan asked himself whether "the holy Scriptures were not rather
a Fable and cunning Story, then the holy and pure Word of God." And
Bunyan's Mr. Badman demands: "How do you know them to be the
Word of God? how do you know that these sayings are true?" Defoe
remarks of a similar sort of person, "The Bible they say is a good History
in most Parts, but the Story of our Saviour they look upon as a meer
Novel." The young hero of a French imaginary voyage is at first so
skeptical of Scripture that he is seen as a "libertine" or "unbeliever": "To
speak the truth, the first time that I gave it a Reading, which was dis-
patch'd in a very little time, I took it for an ill-concerted Romance, to
which however I gave the Name of Sacred Stories. The Book of *Genesis*
seem'd to me to be meer Fiction." Yet another writer compared the
plausibility of biblical citations in political controversy to that of "a tale of
Tom Thumb, or Guy of Warwick."[27]

Thus the historicizing of the Bible was sufficiently volatile, and was
fed by sources sufficiently diverse, to blur fundamentally the distinction
between piety and atheism. Most Protestants would have endorsed the
epistemological assumptions of George Swinnock's concern for the
common people of England: "And how can they know God's will that
cannot read it?" But for some sectarians, the logical solution was to
escape altogether the documentary fetishism of Protestant bibliolatry by
condemning reading and writing themselves as "artificial devices" "invented by men," not to be confused with "spiritual worship." Yet the
attack on literate norms of epistemology was also an important strategy
of Roman Catholic apologetics, which argued the instability of any religious authority that was contained by a book and therefore dependent
upon the fallibilities of copiers, printers, translators, and grammarians.

In 1687, an Anglican apostate to popery found "so many mistakes, and so many errours in the beginning of *Genesis,* that [he concluded] that the *Jewish* Religion is little else than a forgery, and that it has but small evidence of a Revelation from God Almighty."[28] The great work in this Catholic counterattack is Father Richard Simon's *Critical History of the Old Testament,* which was translated into English in 1682 and whose central position John Dryden summarizes in *Religio Laici* (1682) on the way to refuting it. Father Simon's argument is a highly elaborated version of the epistemological reversal achieved by extreme skeptics who argued that "true history" was really nothing more than the new romance. Yet his ostensibly pious critique was so devastating that more than one reader questioned his credentials as a believing Christian.

Dryden's major tactic in 1682 consists in continuing to train the weapons of empirical and historical criticism against the skeptics by whom they have been unscrupulously usurped:

> If *written words* from time are not secur'd,
> How can we think have *oral Sounds* endur'd?

The best "evidence of a Revelation from God Almighty," in other words, is indeed historical evidence, and on these grounds the imperfect transmission of scriptural documents is preferable at least to the oral tradition of popery. But *Religio Laici* also acknowledges, perhaps more searchingly than the aim of refuting dissenters would require, the inexorably democratizing and relativizing force of the critical, reforming spirit from which its own Anglicanism is inseparable. And five years later Dryden announces his conversion to Catholicism in a self-consciously parabolic and "mysterious writ" that does not so much reject the argument of documentary authentication as subordinate it to a less material notion of revelation:

> For what my senses can themselves perceive
> I need no revelation to believe.[29]

The famous drama of Dryden's apostasy represents one man's complicated response to the experience of secularization: formal secession from a movement that seemed to have generated the forces of its own destruction. The more common response during the Restoration was to persist in the purification of faith and the mediation of the spirit using the only instruments that seemed serviceable, the skeptical tools of historical criticism and empirical method. The several shadings of liberal Anglicanism, latitudinarianism, and natural theology are all informed by this general purpose. Sometimes the results were decidedly odd. In 1690, John Craig fixed the time of the Second Coming of Christ by using Newtonian mechanics to calculate algebraically the rate of increase in the "velocity of suspicion" of the Gospels—that is, the increase in "the faculty through which the mind is driven, as though through a particular space of time, to see the contradictory sides of an historical account." The rate of the growth of disbelief in the Gospels is important to Craig because he takes Christ's words in Luke 18:8 to imply that "so little . . . will be the probability of his story at the coming of Christ that he doubts whether he will find anyone who will give faith to this history concerning himself." To find the date of the Second Coming, then, we need only know how long it will take for the probability of the Gospels to vanish. This calculation gives us 3150 A.D., a date which is as advanced as it is because of the documentary nature of the Gospels. Indeed "the probability of the history of Christ vanished at the end of the eighth century, insofar as that history depends on only oral tradition."[30]

Curious attempts like Craig's must have been, if anything, encouraged by John Locke's development of the Baconian-Galilean argument concerning the unity of truth and the relation between the realms of faith and empirical knowledge. The compatibility of these "distinct provinces" Locke affirms by calling reason "*natural revelation,* whereby the eternal Father of light and fountain of all knowledge, communicates to mankind that portion of truth which he has laid within the reach of their natural faculties: [whereas] *revelation* is *natural reason enlarged* by a new set of discoveries communicated by God immediately; which reason vouches the truth of, by the testimony and proofs it gives that they came from God." By the terms of this epistemology, the authority of divine revelation is both incontestable and negligible. For "though faith be founded on the testimony of God (who cannot lie) revealing any proposition to us: yet we cannot have an assurance of the truth of its being a divine revelation greater than our own [natural] knowledge." Those who believe in a revelation that is not supported by empirical evidence Locke calls "enthusiasts": "If they say they know it to be true, because it is a revelation from God, the reason is good: but then it will be demanded how they know it to be a revelation from God." The truth of revelation, then, requires authentication by the truth of empirical knowledge, and "faith can never convince us of anything that contradicts our knowledge." Only those things that are beyond the powers of our natural faculties (Locke's example is not Galileo's question of stellar animism but the prophecy of a future life) are "the proper matter of faith." Reason remains "our last judge and guide in everything," for without the independent tests of empirical knowledge we are unable to distinguish truth as such: "there would be left no difference between truth and falsehood, no measures of credible and incredible in the world." By this means, Locke's indivisible "truth" is overseen by a standard of objective truth whose first premise is the empiricist credo that the instrument of verification can and must be separated from the object verified.[31]

What Locke identifies as the tautology that results from the lack of an independent measure of truth is what I have called the dialectical experience of immanence. He associates it with the "inner light" of enthusiasts, whose "persuasions are right, because they are strong in them. For, when what they say is stripped of the metaphor of seeing and feeling, this is all it amounts to." Now, within the context of our inquiry into the tacit "literalization" of divine revelation during this period, Locke's confident demystification of "inner light" as a merely figurative, hence nugatory, species of illumination is more than striking. For him, the traditional visual metaphor works not to mediate the primary truth of the spirit but to falsely dignify merely subjective persuasions by clothing them in the objective garb of immediate sense impressions. "What I see, I know to be so, by the evidence of the thing itself; what I believe, I take to be so upon the testimony of another." In order to do justice to the truth of revelation, then, what is required is a literalization of the metaphor that consists not at all in recognizing that revelation conducts us to an immaterial truth but in subjecting revelation to material tests of veracity. By these standards we would expect the truth of Scripture to fare rather badly in Locke's hands. Yet in fact he treats "the revelation in the written word of God" rather summarily and surprisingly as an "unerring rule" equal in its authority to reason itself or to the "visible signs" once vouchsafed by God in the form of miracles.[32]

A more wholesale critique of Scripture by the strict rules of empirical evidence was left to the heir of the critical historians, radical sectarians, and liberal Anglicans, the deist movement. Writers like Anthony Collins, Locke's friend and disciple, insisted that the debate on the authority of Scripture be conducted within "the arena of fact claims" and on the assumption that "statements if they are logically coherent refer to true or actual states of affairs which we know." With the deist controversy, "an exegetical or hermeneutical argument about determining the meaning of certain narrative texts has become an argument about the status of the fact claims apparently made in them . . . The meaning of words, particularly in statements of descriptive prediction, is so completely derived from sense experience of the external world that meaning turns out to be identical with verifiability or with likelihood based on past observation."[33]

The force of arguments against the truth of Scripture that were based on principles such as these is most palpable in the writings of those who tried to defend against them. In 1729, the deist Thomas Woolston attacked the Anglican position on the authenticity of biblical miracles. Thomas Sherlock's refutation so readily accepts the empirical and evidential terms of the deist attack that its controlling fiction is that of a court of law, and its standard of judgment is not the sacred Word of God but documentary historicity. Some interested gentlemen of the Inns of Court undertake to use their professional skills in a mock trial whose aim is to test the truth of the Resurrection according to strict rules of evidence. One hundred years after the zenith of the "common-law mentality," Woolston's advocate easily rejects the authentication of miracles on the basis of the antiquity of the Christian faith and of our "possession" of it: "Prescription cannot run against Reason and Common Sense." And his opponent's willingness to forgo this argument at the outset confirms how far the naive empiricist claim to historicity is from the appeal to the authority of antiquity: "I'll wave all Advantage from the Antiquity of the Resurrection, and the general Reception the Belief of it has found in the World; and am content to consider it as a Fact which happen'd but last Year." The heart of the matter, both men agree, is rather the dependability of the testimony of the witnesses to the Resurrection—that is, of the apostolic reports contained in the New Testament. After considerable discussion of the circumstantial details of those reports, the Anglican advocate plays his trump card: "the Evidence of the Spirit . . . of Wisdom and Power, which was given to the Apostles, to enable them to confirm their Testimony by Signs and Wonders, and mighty Works." Woolston's advocate objects that this amounts to a leap of faith beyond the accepted grounds of "Matter of Fact" and "Evidence of Sense," but his opponent makes the neatly Lockean response that he uses the miracles here not as a supernatural "proof" of the fact of the Resurrection but as an independent measure of the veracity of its witnesses. Since their testimony is buttressed by these matters of fact which themselves are confirmed by the evidence of the senses, the credibility of the apostles is proved and the case is closed.[34]

Sherlock's fiction is noteworthy not only insofar as the aggressively empirical form of the argument sits oddly with the substance of what it ultimately seeks to mediate—spiritual truth—but also in its willingness to abandon skepticism, like Dryden in *Religio Laici,* while still ahead of the game. The obvious question that remains unasked here is, How trustworthy is the reported "evidence of the sense" of the miracles themselves? Faced with "the new Errors . . . of a Deist, or Sceptick, or Free-Thinker," the exemplary father figure in one of Defoe's manuals of improvement sanguinely assures his son that we can "answer them in their own Way" by confuting their "reason" through our "facts," for "Reason may be doubted and question'd, but Facts are Matters of Evidence, and undeniable." The son agrees: "Nay, Sir, though they will not allow Scripture Doctrine, they cannot deny Scripture-History; they cannot deny the Facts related in Scripture, nor can they bring any Evidence against the Fidelity of the Relations, or of the Relator." But of course this is just what deists could and did do. In his capacity as an Anglican clergyman, Jonathan Swift was directly confronted by the profoundly unsettling questions of the deists. Yet Swift resisted the hopeful logic of naive empiricism and its conflation of revelation with sense impressions, referring his congregation instead to the venerable Pauline creed: "*Faith,* says the Apostle, *is the Evidence of Things not seen.*" The only apparent alternative to Swift's resolute refusal is the extreme skepticism of a David Hume, who pleasantly and insidiously demonstrates what Swift would leave unsaid.[35]

5

APPARITION NARRATIVES

The empirical critique and defense of biblical narrative during this period bespeaks a preoccupation with a crucial dilemma. In the words of Hans Frei, "Does 'the essence' of Christianity depend on maintaining that the veracity of a historical fact is indispensable for the salvation of mankind?" Frei's formulation permits us to see that it is not enough to treat the "questions of truth" which are our present concern as significant of a revolution *in* epistemology. For what is most important about this revolution is that it entails a transformation from metaphysics and theology *to* epistemology. Henceforth the process of coming to a knowledge of truth will be understood according to a tacitly assumed metaphor of visual sense perception, so that knowing something will consist in having it "in mind," and knowing it well will require that we refine the capacity of our ideas for the accurate, inner representation of external objects. Thus, the psychology of the knower, and of his sources, will become paramount. But the empirical premise in narrative does not simply come into conflict with spiritual pedagogy. The rhetorical stance of the claim to historicity is also the most extreme development of "philosophy teaching by example" and in a profound respect is the logical culmination of the long tradition that used figures, fables, allegories, and exempla to mediate spiritual truth. Now, a general reliance on the evidence of the senses for the teaching of moral truth at this time was not of course obliged always to go quite so far as the claim to historicity. This may be seen in the predominance of casuistry during the seventeenth century. Casuistical argument frames moral pedagogy within highly circumstantial dialogues and stories, "cases" of conscience that, however concrete, do not as a rule assert their factuality. And George Starr has convincingly pointed out the relevance of these ethically oriented narratives to the rise of novelistic narrative. Nevertheless, the enormously powerful pull of the claim to historicity is very obvious in the testimony of the preceding pages: often enough it is only by way of such a claim that Scripture can be apprehensible as true, and thereby morally redemptive. To be saved by a transcendent Truth requires the increasingly separable and prior act of being empirically convinced of it.[36]

Nor was it only the New Testament reporters of sacred events who were being held to the strict rules of evidence in the decades after 1660. So too were contemporary English narrators of supernatural "news" of various sorts. John Spencer observed that "some of these Relations are delivered with such circumstances of time, place, words spoken, Events succeeding . . . as secure them (as much as can be expected) from all suspicion of deceit of sight or imagination in the Attestors." Many readers may have been inclined to discount the historicity of those accounts of strange happenings that had an obviously partisan purpose. But there were many such apparition narratives whose most concrete political end was to rebut freethinkers and atheists by showing that divine revelation is still being manifested, quite literally, before our eyes. Such narratives self-consciously addressed an audience whose stringent epistemological standards are well summarized by Meric Casaubon. It is necessary, he observes,

in the relation of strange things, whether *natural* or *supernatural,* to know the temper of the *relator,* if it can be known: and what interest he had, or might probably be supposed to have had, in the relation, to have it believed. Again, whether he profess to have seen it himself, or take it upon the credit of others: and whether a man by his profession, in a capacity probable, to judge of the truth of those things, to which he doth bear witness . . . So that a man had need, if possible, to know somewhat of the temper of his Historian, before he knew what to think of his relations; such especially, as have somewhat of *incredibleness* in them.[37]

Because the explicit and overriding aim of the apparition narratives of the Restoration is to proclaim the reality of the spiritual world in a materialistic age that has come to doubt it, these narratives assert the truth in the terms that are now the most persuasive, and derive their techniques of authentication from the very stronghold of skepticism which it is their purpose to refute. Their unvarying purpose is stated in the language of documentary historicity: "to *Record Providences,*" to "publish them to the World," to "provide the strong Evidence God has been pleas'd to give . . . to his own Being." In the preface to his own collection of apparition narratives, Richard Baxter gives the most plausible rationale for what is perhaps an unrationalizable procedure:

But I found that my Faith of Supernatural Revelation, must be more than a *Believing Man,* and that if it had not a firm Foundation, and rooting, even *sure Evidence* of *Veracity, Surely Apprehended,* it was not like to do those great works that Faith had to do . . . Apparitions, and other sensible manifestations of the certain existence of Spirits of themselves Invisible, was a means that might do much with such as are prone to judge by Sense.[38]

The connection between the apparition narratives and the new philosophy is in some cases quite explicit. John Dunton, for example, addresses his collection to "the Pious Virtuosi." Another important collector is Joseph Glanvill, apologist for the Royal Society. Glanvill's special interest is the phenomenon of witchcraft, which, "being *matter* of *fact,* is onely capable of the evidence of *authority* and *sense* . . . Now the credit of matters of Fact depends much upon the Relatours, who, if they cannot be deceived themselves nor supposed any ways interested to impose upon others, ought to be credited. For upon these circumstances, all humane Faith is grounded, and matter of Fact is not capable of any proof besides, but that of immediate sensible evidence." If we are reminded by this of the deist subordination of faith to the means of its empirical verification, Glanvill's piety is not to be doubted, for he chastises those more skeptical than he by reminding us that only Satan benefits from the belief "that the stories of *Witches, Apparitions,* and indeed every thing that brings tidings of another world, are but *melancholick Dreams,* and *pious Romances.*" The devil's party consists of those thoroughgoing freethinkers "that can believe all *Histories* are *Romances.*"[39] And it is the capacity of people like Glanvill for a modified skepticism that gives to these collections, as to many other literary products of the period, that characteristic instability which to a later age appears decisively ironic or contradictory. His method is, to say the least, arresting. The great and tireless argument of a supernatural reality is maintained within a succession of narrative frames and articulated there by a complex pattern of circumstantial and authenticating details—names, places, dates, events, eye- and earwitnesses, attentiveness to stylistic "sincerity," confirmations of good character, denials of special bias—all of which subserve the crucial claim to a natural existence; that is, to historicity.

Daniel Defoe's contributions to the form, if more polished in particulars, adhere closely to this pattern. In the "Preface" to *The Storm,* "the terrible Blasts of this Tempest" provide him with an occasion for a Pascalian wager on the reasonableness and prudence of a belief in God: for "a Man cannot answer it to Common Arguments, the Law of Numbers, and the Rules of Proportion are against him . . . No man will lay such a Wager, where he may lose, but cannot win." The rationalism of this stance dictates an utter scrupulousness concerning the historicity of his reporting. Accordingly the balance of Defoe's "Preface" is devoted to a conscientious discussion of the different degrees of authority that may be attributed to his various sources. And the tract itself collects highly circumstantial eyewitness accounts, authentic even in their preservation of stylistic infelicities, which are punctuated by the collector's fulfillment of his promise that "in many Cases I shall act the Divine, and draw necessary practical Inferences." Defoe's account of Mrs. Veal's ghost is a masterful compression of *The Storm*'s technique into the space of a few pages. In its first two sentences, the "Preface" fashions a chain of six links, eye- and earwitnesses who testify to one another's reasonableness, gentility, intelligence, sobriety, understanding, discernment, impartiality, honesty, virtue, and piety. The body of the tract elaborates these judgments against the skepticism of other, easily discredited figures, and tells the uncanny story of Mrs. Veal's appearance with the neutral circumstantiality of a police blotter and the earnest plausibility of a sympathetic but open-minded observer, who at the end acknowledges that "this thing has very much affected me, and I am as well satisfied as I am of the best grounded matter of fact."[40] John Dunton's *Christians Gazette* in general maintains a sharper bifurcation between objective reportage and spiritual application. It is mainly noteworthy for its explicit association of the objectification of divine providence with the reporting of the news, and for the circumstantial intimacy of some of its devices of authentication.

On reflection it is only to be expected that the paradoxical formula "strange, therefore true" should be compatible with the contradictory posture of the apparition narratives. The point is simply made by our acknowledgment that God can do anything, which is of course the central argument of these collections: what looks like romance is really providential factuality. Defoe puts it somewhat more circumspectly:

I confess here is room for abundance of Romance, because the Subject may be safer extended than in any other case, no Story being capable to be crowded with such Circumstances, but Infinite Power, which is all along concern'd with us in every Relation, is suppos'd capable of making true.

Yet we shall no where so Trespass upon Fact, as to oblige Infinite Power to the shewing more Miracles than it intended.

As we might expect, however, Glanvill's more rigorous empiricism will not permit arguments from providence to infiltrate the formal verification mechanism even of a discourse whose substance is fully providential in nature. The result is a very clear rationalization of the "strange, therefore true" formula on strictly psychological grounds, which demonstrates the fundamental priority, for this epistemology, of the claim to historicity in explicit opposition to the effect of verisimilitude:

The more *absurd* and *unaccountable* these actions [of witches] seem, the greater *confirmations* are they to me of the *truth* of those *Relations,* and the reality of what the *Objectors* would destroy. For these circumstances being exceedingly *unlikely,* judging by the measures of common belief, 'tis the greater probability that they are not *fictitious:* For the contrivers of *Fictions* . . . [try] to make them look as *like truth* as possible . . . None but a fool or madman would relate, with a purpose of having it believed, that he saw in *Ireland Men* with *hoofs* on their *heads,* and *eyes* in their *breasts;* or if any should be so ridiculously vain, as to be serious in such an *incredible Romance,* it cannot be supposed that all *Travellers* that come into those parts after him should tell the same story.[41]

By arguments like this one, Glanvill shows himself to be an authentic heir of Galileo, who believed that "first we are to make certain of the fact, which will reveal to us the true sense of the Bible." For despite the supernatural ends of his treatise, divine providence is finally, for Glanvill, an immensely compelling but empty truth, in perpetual need of objective "fact" to fill it with substance.

Like Bacon's new method of empirical investigation, these documentary narratives of supernatural apparitions are fueled by an exhilarating faith in the powers of material phenomena to mediate the truths of divine creation. From this perspective, their secularizing enterprise will seem a faithful and preservative accommodation of the sacred to a world steeped in profanity, and its success will be attributable to the fact that it speaks to skepticism and atheism in the only language they will understand. This language—the evidence of the senses, the literalizing of revelation, the claim to historicity—is the crucial and prior means by which the one great end of Christian pedagogy—the inculcation of faith in God—may be served in the modern world. But the structural instability of all secularizing efforts is aggravated, in the seventeenth century, by an exceptional disparity between means and end. In Bacon's thought, the hierarchical relation of material signifier and spiritual signified may be felt to modulate into respectful analogy, and this in turn threatens at times to transform itself into an antithetical signifying relationship in which the priority of sense experience is felt to have not simply a pedagogic but an ontological force. And from this alternative perspective, the materialist language of empiricism does not so much mediate sacred truth as comprehend it within its own triumphant epistemology, while the claim to historicity is revealed to be not a sophisticated weapon against atheism but its supremely powerful ally.

When we speak of an epistemological "revolution" in early modern England, we point to a categorial instability so acute that the condition of conceptual fluidity and process which characterizes all culture to some degree demands to be acknowledged by a special term. The secularization controversies of the seventeenth century are sparked by a complex and contradictory state of historicism. Fed by diverse and intersecting sources, the momentum of historical consciousness soon becomes self-generated, carrying individuals and groups through the implacable progression of skeptical thought from positivistic objectivity to solipsistic subjectivity, a progression in which each participant disembarks from the vertiginous ride at the personal point of diminishing returns. In this context, "skepticism" can be only a relative term. The preceding discussion has shown us a diversity of such choices, each of which, owing to the indefinite potentialities of the progression, is both internally unstable and capable of destabilizing all other choices. From this condition results a proliferation of epistemological reversals that seem to imitate, in particularized miniature, the continual oscillation that is built into the original and inconceivable relation of spirit to matter. Thus romance becomes antiromance and then antihistory; the "true histories" of the Royal Society are historicized into the "strangeness" of romance; the empirical validation of Scripture as true history reverses into the skeptical depreciation of it as bad or mere history—that is, as romance; the empirical verification of sacred revelation renders it literal; and the historical criticism practiced, to different ends, by sectarian saints, liberal Anglicans, Roman Catholic apologists, and freethinking atheists renders them indistinguishable from one another.

Yet at the same time, the heat of public controversy may harden these liquid experiments in self-subversion into oppositional stances. Thus Cleveland and Steele defame the news-reporting "novellists" as the new Quixotes, while Bayle and Steele condemn the fashionable French historians, and Stubbe and Butler denounce the "novellists" of the Royal Society, as the new romancers. Confrontations like these are the means by which culture institutionalizes itself, making tractable and even serviceable the sheer fluidity of historical process. What they yield is a simplified model of conflict from which the contingencies of indefinite potentiality have been extracted. In effect, such a model brings into being the field of available options by schematizing them, by delimiting the alternative postures that are accessible to participants in that culture. In the present case, the conflict that begins now to emerge from public controversy is first intelligible in sequential terms. The empiricism of "true history" opposes the discredited idealism of romance, but it thereby generates a countervailing, extreme skepticism, which in turn discredits true history as a species of naive empiricism or "new romance." Once in motion, however, the sequence of action and reaction becomes a cycle: the existence of each opposed stance becomes essential for the ongoing, negative definition of its antithesis.

This model of conflict defines the terms in which the crucial "questions of truth" are debated in the Restoration and the early eighteenth century, and the epistemological boundaries within which "the novel" as we know it coalesces during that period. It is a conflict between two different species of "history," respectively hopeful and dubious about the attainment of narrative truth. "Romance" now pejoratively designates all idealist fiction, including religious claims to spirituality which reflect the pride of human sufficiency by being inadequately tied to rational and material evidences. "Enthusiasm" quickly becomes the preferred term for such pride at this time, and its proximity to the discredited notion of romance can be seen clearly in one of Defoe's improving familial conversations. The father asks his children, "Pray what do you mean by a *Romance,* and whence do you derive the Word *Romantick?*" His son defines romance as "a formal made Story in Print, raised out of the Invention of the Author, and put upon the World to cheat the Readers, in the Shape or Appearance of Historical Truth." The daughter adds that "to talk of Things above our Reach, with a Supposition that we were sufficient to the Discourse, is to talk Romantick." What is striking about these complementary definitions is the implication that "romantic" mediation fails to reach spiritual things because it is insufficiently historical, that "the Invention of the Author" is to be condemned not so much for emulating divine authorship as for claiming (but lacking) historicity. It is a moment of epochal transition. The religious critique of romance blends into its secular and historicizing critique, and the conflation is all but seamless.

Approving of both replies, the father proceeds to elaborate a false but suggestive etymology for the word. Because they lacked real miracles, Roman Catholic priests quickly learned to fabricate and disseminate stories of "imaginary Wonder" which, registered in the books, or "*Legenda,*" of the Vatican, gave to any "Collection of Lyes" the generic name "*Roman Legend.*" "Hence, I derive the Word Romance, (*viz.*) from the Practice of the *Romanists,* in imposing Lyes and Fables upon the World; and I believe . . . that Popery is a *Romantick Religion.*"[42] But as we have seen, Defoe's association of romance with the proud inventions of popish religiosity does not in the least imply that "history," either the less or the more skeptical sort, is allotted a strictly secular role. In the arguments and narratives that I have discussed in this chapter, the assertion of historical truth aims to serve the end of inculcating Christian faith. In the early novels it will seek to aid the cause of teaching moral truth.

Thus far my account of epistemological change has been guided by the dominating, antithetical influence of the genre—and the epistemology—of romance. In the following and final chapter on questions of truth, the idea of romance will continue to have a central importance. But it is time now to suggest how some of the more particularized "literary" forms of seventeenth-century narrative, whose general importance in the origins of the novel has long been accepted, are infiltrated by the appeal to the evidence of the senses and by the model of conflict which organizes competing claims to historical truth. As we might anticipate, these familiar forms—the saint's life, spiritual autobiography, the picaresque, criminal biography, and the travel narrative—focus the broad-based experimentation with revolutionary notions of how to tell the truth in narrative upon the particular problem of how to tell the true story of an individual human life.

— *Three* —

Histories of the Individual

As often as not, the Restoration reports of the historicity of supernatural apparitions—accounts of witches or the devil, cases of divine deliverance and judgment—are obliged by the very nature of their concern to relate the providential history of a particular individual. In this endeavor the reporters might have drawn upon several familiar narrative models— especially those of the saint's life and the *de casibus* tradition of the fall of princes—whose sharply bifurcated structure provided the most common paradigm for the medieval treatment of tragedy. Like the reports of apparitions, these traditional narratives tell the story of real human lives suffused with the otherworldly. And though their subordination of the material to the spiritual is far more secure than that found in the volatile narratives produced by the early modern secularization crisis, it is possible to observe in them as well the emergence of the claim to historicity as a formal feature at once vital and problematic to the mediation of spiritual truth.

The following discussion will cover a great deal of narrative territory, but it will be guided throughout by the recurrence, and by the constant equilibration, of a formal tension between what might be called the individual life and the overarching pattern. To recount the individual life "traditionally" entails the location of it within a controlling pattern that is characteristically manifested by discontinuous and unrationalizable— "vertical"—intrusions into the "horizontal" movement of individual history. But the increasing validation of naive empiricism and historicity in this period fundamentally destabilizes this relationship and challenges the older criteria for capturing transcendent truth by making new, more quantitative demands for full and faithful detail. Spiritual biography and autobiography, the picaresque, criminal biography, the travel narrative—in different ways, all of these formative seventeenth-century subgenres reflect the instability of narrative structures whose responsiveness to demands for the conventions of historicity is unregulated by any sense of the rules and limits of those conventions. At the same time, we will see how the tension between individual life and overarching pattern which unites these subgenres is radically reformulated in the confrontation between the "true history" of naive empiricism and its more skeptical critique, a conflict within whose framework the emergent novel begins to stabilize itself.

I

FROM SAINT'S LIFE TO SPIRITUAL BIOGRAPHY

Two well-known lives of the early Tudor period are those of Roman Catholic casualties to Henry VIII's revolt against papal authority. Composed only in the 1550s, with Mary's accession and the temporary return of Catholicism, the lives of Cardinal Wolsey and Sir Thomas More depict the preordained pattern of rise and fall and are superintended by a watchful God whose works are not easily distinguished from the dispassionate mutabilities of Fortune. George Cavendish in particular punctuates his narration of Wolsey's worldly progress with moralizing intrusions as if from above, which both foretell and imitate the mastery of natural life by supernatural decree. But Cavendish also shows a healthy respect for the objectivity and historicity of his human sources—especially for his own worth as a close eyewitness to the events of Wolsey's career. And he promises us a historical circumstantiality more particular and individualized than that traditionally provided by "historiographers of chronicles of princes."[1]

Five years after Cavendish made his modest claims to historicity, John Foxe published his great work in Protestant hagiography, the central aim of which was to document the lives of those martyred by the very sovereign whose reign had encouraged the sympathetic accounts of Wolsey and More.[2] Foxe's book is imbued with a sense of history quite as providential as that of the Roman Catholic writers, although here the great plot, repeated again and again, is not the fall of the mighty but the trial and triumph of God's chosen people. Many of these are also common people, who, assured of election, calmly confute the authority of their social superiors in the plain language of Scripture. Equally remarkable in Foxe's work, however, is the way in which the Protestant reliance on the documentary objectivity of God's Book is internalized within Foxe's own editorial procedures. It is not just that he consults an extraordinarily broad range of documents, but that he brings to this a critical and comparative rigor, a self-conscious devotion to the pursuit of truth in all its exhaustive contingency and detail, that is worthy of a skeptical new philosopher. In the most arresting of these accounts, the scrupulous historicity of Foxe's narration seems able to point the mundane circumstantiality of common lives so as to disclose an inhabiting pattern of spiritual truth at their center—early sin and licentiousness, for example, followed by a wonderful reform and conversion to God's Word, serene defiance of ungodly persecution, and the transcendent triumph of martyrdom.[3]

Foxe can achieve these effects of mediation because he carefully avoids the claim to historicity with respect to events that do not readily admit of a natural explanation. Yet the impulse toward exhaustive documentation is a strong one. Thus he relegates to an appendix an eyewitness account of one who escapes Marian incarceration when a voice instructs him to depart and his prison walls crumble around him. "Albeit I am loth to insert any thing in this book which may seem incredible or strange to ordinary working for quarrelling adversaries," Foxe says, the story is so well attested that "I thought . . . for the incredible strangeness thereof, neither to place this story in the body of these Acts and Monuments, and yet in some out-corner of the book not utterly to pass it untouched, for the reader to consider it, and to credit it as he seeth cause."[4]

Foxe's decision to include this story brings into relief the technical problems that are associated with what I have called the "quantitative" standard of completeness in narrative. Selectivity of narration is built into the very nature of Christian or romance truth—the truth, that is, of an overarching pattern. But because his credibility relies so heavily also on an air of quantitative exhaustiveness, Foxe opens himself to the skeptical criticism that he has not been full enough in his reports, that his unavoidably selective documentation subverts the very historicity (all the facts) that he purportedly would establish. Thus in a special version of the reversal that is by now familiar, "history" risks the charge of recapitulating the absurdities of "romance." And this is more or less the complaint that one "master Harding" levels at Foxe concerning the alleged martyrdom of three women and an unborn child in Guernsey. Having at first called this "Pitiful History" a wholesale "fable," Harding then refines his critique by arguing the falsity of the story on the grounds that Foxe has omitted or obscured details from which we might infer that the victims themselves are morally culpable. The fact that we hear nothing from "the historiographer" about the father of the child (so implies the accusation) argues the child's illegitimacy; the fact that the mother did not plead pregnancy in order to save her child only compounds the guilt. Can this really be the suffering of one of God's saints?[5]

Foxe's withering refutation easily dispenses with his antagonist, but not without raising a series of questions about how to tell the truth in narrative which, seeking to be rhetorical, instead convey the uneasy impression of being, in the present context, unanswerable:

As though that historiographers, being occupied in setting forth the persecution of God's people suffering death from religion and doctrine of Christ, were bound, or had nothing else to do but play the sumner, and to bring forth who were husbands to their wives, and fathers to their children; which new-found law of history, [was] never required before, nor observed of any story-writers . . . To express every minute of matter in every story occurrent, what story-writer in all the world is able to perform it? . . . Although it might be done, what reasonable reader would require it? . . . what if it were not remembered of the author? what if it were to him not known? what if it were of purpose omitted, as a matter not material to the purpose? . . . And shall it then by and by be imputed to shame and blame, whatsoever in every narration is not expressed?

But it is Foxe himself who has created the legalistic demand for fully factual testimony, which he now vainly demeans in comparison with the quest for a higher sort of truth, that of the patent persecution of God's people. Hitherto inseparable, the two kinds of truth suddenly are to be severed. Once it has been invoked, however, the standard of fidelity to an empirically accessible reality cannot be relaxed at convenience. If the overarching truth of these Protestant saints' lives rests at all on the demonstration of their factual truth, problems of how to achieve quantitative completeness and how to justify factual selectiveness may be dismissed only at peril. For there will always be skeptical readers like master Harding to observe that the moral import of an individual life, and hence the great pattern it is narrated to exemplify, depend upon our conviction that we are receiving a truth undiminished by the telling.[6]

The dilemma of quantitative completeness seems recognizable as one particular path taken by the problem of mediation as it becomes increasingly problematic under the auspices of empirical epistemology. But it is really only after the period of our major concern that this dilemma begins to be confronted directly. Once the claim to historicity is systematically acknowledged to be not an absolute but a relative claim, once writers and readers are obliged to address themselves seriously to the question of how much documentation, what sort of detail, is needed to satisfy the demands of "true history," competing theories of "realism" in the modern sense of the term are firmly in the ascendant. But for this to transpire, the quality of being history-like must become separable from the fact of being history and acquire a validity of its own.[7] True history must cease to find its justification in the mediation of "other" truths, whether spiritual or moral, because it will by then have achieved their internalization; at which point it will also cease to need to call itself "true history." Until that extreme point of secularization, the dilemma of quantitative completeness will continue to be broached, but the questions it raises will not be susceptible to solution.

The crucial dynamic in Foxe and in the development of "spiritual biography" during the succeeding century is that between the scrupulously documented individual life and the overarching pattern. Between 1650 and 1683, Samuel Clarke, perhaps Foxe's most prolific heir, collected and published scores of Puritan lives, culled often enough from funeral sermons whose very mode of discourse dictated the application to spiritual ends. Once abstracted from this context, the lives of the Puritan saints were that much more likely to be justified according to the claim to historicity, as in Richard Baxter's defense of Clarke's last collection: "And the true History of exemplary Lives, is a pleasant and profitable recreation to young persons . . . O how much better work is it, than Cards, Dice, Revels, Stage-Plays, Romances or idle Chat . . . Some Enemies deride him for Writing Lives with no more Art: But I take that to be his Commendation; He did not make the Histories, but take them made by faithful acquaintance of the dead . . . To have made Stories himself had been unworthy a Historian."[8] Although Clarke did not include unlearned sectarians like John Bunyan in his collections of "eminent" Puritans, Bunyan's own *Life and Death of Mr. Badman* (1680) is manifestly part of the tradition Clarke helped solidify. To be sure, "Mr. Badman" is a fiction, but he is a self-consciously exemplary one who Bunyan is at great pains to assert is a composite figure of real sins and sinners:

All which are things either fully known by me, or being eye and ear-witness thereto, or that I have received from such hands, whose relation as to this, I am bound to believe. And that the Reader may know them from other things and passages herein contained, I have pointed at them in the Margent, as with a finger thus: ☞

And the narrative is filled with other exemplary "true stories," "as true as remarkable," associated with real names or attested by "a sober and credible person." "But I would, if it had been the will of God, that neither I nor any body else, could tell you more of these Stories: True stories, that are neither *Lye,* nor *Romance.*"[9]

Bunyan's words remind us of how the claim to historicity might be popular even among Puritans whose piety would appear quite untouched by the optimistic epistemology of liberal religion and the new philosophy. To claim historicity for one's story is not only to assert the evidence of the human senses but also to deny the presence of human fabrication. "He did not make the histories," says Baxter, "but take them made," and the ultimate maker of history, as of the Book of Nature, is God himself.

Creatura non potest creare is an Augustinian maxim to which Puritan iconoclasm gave new life. By disavowing human authorship, the claim to historicity achieved, at least hypothetically, both a traditional and a modernizing purpose. It could chasten the materialist sufficiency of the creature and honor the divine spirit of the Creator, even as it also celebrated the materialist standards of critical history. Something like this economy can be seen even in a new philosopher's attempt to revive a pre-Protestant saint's life. When Robert Boyle undertook to retell the martyrdom of Theodora, he aimed to write a true Christian history that would avoid on both accounts the pitfalls of romance. The main obstacle to his project, however, is the paucity of original documentation and the need for "a far greater number of Circumstances . . . to make up so maim'd a story tolerably compleat." To willfully "enlarge this Story . . . into a somewhat voluminous Romance," to "transform a piece of Martyrology into a Romance" by turning "a Martyr into a Nymph or an Amazon," would offend equally against the scruples of a Christian and of a historian, whose "True Examples do arm and fortify the mind far more efficaciously, than Imaginary or Fictitious ones can do," and who therefore is denied "the liberty to feig[n] surprizing adventures." In the end Boyle solves the problem by compromising slightly what both "the subject of the story exacted, and the truth requir'd in History would warrant." On the authority of "Grave and Judicious Historians" he forsakes a strict historicity and permits himself a sparing and pious invention of events and dialogue that are "not improbable in the nature of the thing."[10]

One of the formal advantages of spiritual autobiography is its capacity to maintain the basic biographical dynamic between individual life and overarching pattern through a more subtle narrative balance between present action and retrospective narration. The balance is registered as a structural interplay between the sinful present of the Character and the repentant retrospection of the Narrator, who, incorporating God's omniscience, knows how the story will end.[11] This interplay lends itself, of course, to a very traditional sort of Christian pedagogy. As the plot unfolds horizontally, the dangerous gap between Character and Narrator gradually diminishes through vertical narrative intrusions, until the two finally are one, the latter consciousness having subsumed the former in what might be seen as the narrative equivalent of atonement. Indeed, the instrumental dangerousness of the unrepentant Character is evidently one more instance of the fundamental problem entailed in the mediation of spirit by matter, since it is only by playing out the treacherous drama of depravity that the heart learns its susceptibility to salvation. Milton's famous argument in *Areopagitica* (1644) restates the problem of mediation in terms that have an obvious relevance to this scenario:

Good and evill we know in the field of this World grow up together almost
inseparably . . . And perhaps this is that doom which *Adam* fell into of knowing good and evill, that is to say of knowing good by evill . . . Assuredly we
bring not innocence into the world, we bring impurity much rather: that
which purifies us is triall, and triall is by what is contrary . . . Therefore the
knowledge and survay of vice is in this world . . . necessary to the constituting of human vertue, and the scanning of error to the confirmation of truth.[12]

In spiritual autobiography, the maintenance of historicity is so indistinguishably a matter of both objective and subjective veracity that the
straightforward claim to historicity, as we have encountered it elsewhere,
is less likely or pertinent there than are its attendant devices of authentication, most of all the documentation of the self in its most circumstantial
detail. When Ralph Thoresby first went up to London, his father sent
him a typical directive: "I would have you, in a little book, which you
may either buy or make of two or three sheets of paper, take a little
journal of any thing remarkable every day, principally as to yourself." As
Henry Newcome describes it in his own little book, the authenticity of
the documentary object is so powerful that it seems almost to attain the
status not of a means to an end but of an end in itself: "The truth is Xtian's
note bookes [are] more faithfull registers y^n y^r hearts; & [it is] easier for y^e
devill to blot out a good resolution out [*sic*] of our mindes y^n out of our
bookes."[13] Of course the piety of Newcome's purpose is clear enough.
But passages like these suggest how, even in the absence of explicit claims
to historicity, the dynamic drama of individual regeneration might be felt
to betray itself. For the origin of most spiritual autobiographies in the
daily journal or diary meant that no retrospective pattern was initially
available in the saint's own experience before he sat down to pursue
Milton's "survey of vice" and "scanning of error." The authentic voice of
the Narrator had to be discovered, the Spirit had to be incorporated, in
the very process of making daily entries, an accumulation of discontinuous historical facts which, with the grace of God, would generate its
own chastening and countervailing order. If it did not, the spiritual
autobiography would be stillborn, mere autobiography because insusceptible of spiritualization.

2

FROM PICARESQUE TO CRIMINAL BIOGRAPHY

The picaresque tradition provided early modern Europe with its most
compelling model of how, under the laboratory conditions of narrative
form, to indulge and manipulate the experimental disjunction between
unregenerate Character and spiritualizing Narrator, individual life and
overarching pattern. *La vida de Lazarillo de Tormes* (1554) originated in
those humanist and Counter-Reformation movements that refracted, in

Catholic countries, the Protestant anti-idealism to which the contemporaneous saints' lives of Foxe were indebted. But as in spiritual autobiography, the historicizing epistemology is conveyed in picaresque less through the claim to historicity than through minute attention to the individualistic will of a hero determined to resist the discipline of external authority. In this institutionalized resistance the *pícaro* goes beyond the unregeneracy of the Puritan saint, and his delinquency is, at least in *Lazarillo*, as much an affront to civil and positive as to divine law. Yet it is only with Alemán's *Guzmán de Alfarache* (1599, 1604) that the genre of the picaresque becomes self-conscious, retrospectively celebrating and reviving *Lazarillo* as the founding and authorizing text of a tradition. It is of some interest for our present subject to speculate on the reasons for this lag.[14]

In *Lazarillo*, the dangerous autonomy of the Character is expressed by means of a protagonist whose discontinuity with his moralizing Narrator is minimal simply because the narrative function has for the most part been internalized at the outset. Lazaro, scourge of authority, is also the authoritatively satirical scourge of all moral hypocrisy he encounters. Because of this proximity between his lived experience and its determinant moral pattern, Lazaro's life is conceived as a reflexive act of self-creation, an "autodidacticism" far more radical than that common in spiritual autobiography, where the self-constituting, conversional impulse, however vital, has its clear and ultimate source in divine creativity. The canonizing influence of Alemán's *Guzmán* may be due in part to its conception of the *pícaro* as a dynamic tension between Character and Narrator much in the manner of the spiritual autobiography, a conception that dramatizes the secularization crisis of the seventeenth century more insistently than does Lazaro's autodidacticism, in which the war against self-sufficiency would appear already to have been lost. In any case, the problematic interplay between the truth of present action and that of retrospective narration in *Guzmán,* as well as in succeeding works of the Spanish picaresque, is a central concern of modern criticism, especially insofar as the sharp disjunction of the two voices creates a state of moral ambiguity or appears to require an ironic interpretation of narrative hypocrisy.[15]

The Spanish picaresque began to be directly influential in England after the 1570s and the first English translation of *Lazarillo*. If Thomas Nashe's *The Unfortunate Traveller* (1594) is clearly the best-known, if imperfect, English representative of Lazaro's autodidactic mode, it is not so easy to determine the immediate heirs of *Guzmán's* more sustained narrative interplay. This is largely because close considerations of influence can be of little use in placing a formal phenomenon which, as I have suggested, is rooted not just in the picaresque tradition but in the bifurcated narrative structure of Christian storytelling at large. What is achieved by the picaresque, and by the several sorts of Protestant narrative that flourish in England after the Restoration, is a responsiveness to the factuality of individual life so intense that the dominance of overarching pattern is felt, in varying ways, to be quite problematic. The picaresque interplay between the two levels of narrative consciousness may be felt unequivocally to persist in the English translation of Alemán, James Mabbe's *The Rogue* (1622). And as Mabbe's title reminds us, it is within the English form of criminal or "rogue" biography that we might expect to find the richest native development of that characteristic narrative tension which reflects equally the bold experiments of the picaresque and the risky undertakings of spiritual biography and autobiography.[16]

In the criminal biographies that flourished after the Restoration, epistemological instability becomes acute. The tension between a linear, ongoing present and vertical acts of retrospection is complicated by an explicit claim to historicity which reflects the same contradictions that are evident in its use by the contemporaneous "apparition narratives" of Glanvill, Defoe, and the rest. As arguments in the traditional mode of Christian pedagogy, criminal biographies ostentatiously survey vice and scan error to a religious and providential end that is, if anything, overdetermined: the protagonist both repents and is justly punished for his sins, while the reader learns to emulate the former *exemplum* just as surely as he will shun the causes of the latter. Thus the self-sufficiency of autodidacticism is taken up and detoxified, at crucial points, by the normative didacticism of authority—at least in theory. But coexisting with this scenario are the conditions for its reversal. The delinquent folk hero, whether Spanish *pícaro* or Tyburn highwayman, is compelling enough in his pursuit of freedom to suggest that the common way of "error" may in fact be the road of individual truth. This suggestion would be merely blasphemous and therefore generally unthinkable were it not for a decisive complication. "Authority" in the criminal biography, much more thoroughly than in the picaresque narrative, is an ambiguous conflation of divine and positive law, so that the unarguable will of God is burdened with the weight of what in other contexts might well be recognized as its antithesis, its deforming secularization. It would not be surprising if readers of narratives and spectators at executions alike were distracted at least momentarily by the complacency of an identification—between God and the magistrate, divine decree and its human accommodation—which recent history had rendered extremely problematic.[17]

One formal manifestation of this ambiguity can be seen in the foundation on which historicity is customarily claimed in criminal biography. In these contexts, "true history" is taken to issue first of all from the objective documentation provided by the state apparatus, especially trial transcripts and the official reports of government functionaries. In basing

their insistent claim to a fully historical truth on the authority of the
established order,[18] the biographers replicate the instability of the apparition narratives, in which a materialist epistemology is given the task of
demonstrating a truth that is ultimately spiritual, while state authority
shuttles uneasily between human and divine, fully comfortable with
neither. Of course, state documentation is not the only basis for claiming
historicity in criminal biography. As we have seen in spiritual autobiography, one evidence of the autonomous authenticity of the individual life is its capacity to generate its own personal documentation.
Most often the biographies include the speeches and reflections of the
eponymous protagonist. But sometimes the documentation of the self is
made public in a more dramatically undomesticated form, as in the
"memoirs" of Thomas Dangerfield, which are presented to the public as
having the purity of raw data, of historicity itself, a private journal not yet
spiritualized: "The Entire Life of This *Hero* is Reserv'd for a Better Pen,
and Leisure: The Intent of These Papers being only to Pick up, and to
Furnish Fresh Matter toward the Just History of his Adventures." The
memoirs themselves consist of what is purported to be Dangerfield's
own chronological list of his daily "adventures," short journal entries
that are coordinated with his daily financial "receits" and "expenses," an
accounting that is suggestively reminiscent of the acts of "spiritual book-
keeping" so common in spiritual autobiography. In this rematerialization
of that self-conscious spiritualization, Dangerfield is briefly characterized
by the editor as both a noble hero and a villain. And the ambivalence of
this view is reinforced by the fact (never alluded to in these memoirs) that
this is the famous Dangerfield who was responsible for the baroque
reversals of the "Meal Tub Plot" in 1679, a Protestant hero-criminal who
had appeared, until his circuitous revelations were complete, to be instead a popish one.[19]

Most often, however, criminal biographies of the Restoration assert
their historicity (whether or not their subjects have had a real existence) in
the assorted terms that have become familiar from other productions of
the period; convenient examples can be found in the anonymous work of
the prolific Richard Head.[20] The richest vein to be mined by actual
biographers was the career of Mary Carleton, who was hanged at Tyburn
in 1673 and who occasioned the appearance, in the ten years preceding
her death, of twenty-five distinct publications. Mary's major antagonist,
her husband, John, was apparently a con man not far inferior to Mary
herself. Both Carletons made important contributions to the pamphlet
war, and their earnest claims to historicity reflect on the level of narrative
form the substantive dispute over who bore the principal guilt of dissimulation. Thus in one of her works Mary pointedly distinguishes herself from "Sir *John Mandevile*," questions her ability to persuade readers
"who have no faith for any thing they see not," prints letters verbatim,

and narrates her climactic legal vindication through the documentary reproduction of the indictment, the list of jurors, the trial testimony, her own recapitulatory statement, and the judge's instructions on the rules of evidence, all "according to the exactest copy."[21]

Mary's power derives not from state authority but from personal authenticity, and as long as she is telling her own story she resembles a self-constructed heroine more than an official example of the unregenerate. In the hands of her husband and her biographers, however, the story of Mary Carleton is quite easily criminalized, and her claim to historicity is reduced to the crafty subterfuge of a romancer. Thus John tells us that he first received her personal history complaisantly, as "a pretty Romance," but soon learned to detest her "innumerable cursed fictions." And her biographer Francis Kirkman disarmingly confides that "if I should promise to give you a true account of her whole life I should deceive you, for how can truth be discovered of her who was wholly composed of falsehood? But that I might not err from the truth in what I shall relate to you, I have took some pains to gain intelligence." Having issued this caveat, Kirkman feels free to indulge to the full his own impulse to claim historicity, cite witnesses, and manifest his trustworthiness by repeatedly observing, as John Foxe had done a hundred years earlier, the impossibility of achieving narrative completeness.[22]

Although one of their celebrants boasts that buccaneers far exceed in courage "our common *English* Highway-men," in terms of narrative epistemology the lives of famous pirates are simply nautical versions of criminal biography.[23] They often entail, that is, a characteristic tension between the historicizing truth of the individual life and a countervailing movement of moralizing and repentance. Defoe's collection of pirate narratives is overseen by claims to eyewitness historicity and by the testimony of sober "Sea-faring Men," and the story of Captain Avery begins by carefully distinguishing itself from "Romantick Reports of his Greatness." Another collection, perceived in its original state to be "a spurious Relation," has been critically examined by "Eye-witnesses of those Pyratical Expeditions" who "were pleased to correct, purge and reform it of many Abuses and Mistakes" and fit it for "the most impartial View and Scrutiny."[24]

3

FROM CHRISTIAN PILGRIMAGE TO SCIENTIFIC TRAVEL

The seventeenth century was heir to an ancient and habitual association of travel narratives with tall tales and of travelers with liars. At the beginning of the century one writer recalled the "general Proverb, that Travellers may tell Romances or untruths by authority." Yet a hundred or so years later, another could remark that "novels" have been replaced in fashion by "amusements of more use and improvement—I mean history and travels with which the relation of probable feigned stories can by no means stand in competition." As we shall see, this was not at all the universal view on the credibility of travel narratives in the early eighteenth century. Yet the seventeenth century marks a critical stage of transition. Already by the later Middle Ages, of course, the pilgrimage narrative and its devotion to the overarching pattern of salvation had made a decisive accommodation to the individual life of the secular traveler. What nonetheless gave to this wayfaring curiosity a new, utilitarian tenacity was its alliance with the new philosophy.[25]

It is not simply that concerted efforts at "discovery" have now become an acceptable occupation. The official and titulary purpose of the Royal Society was "for the Improvement of Natural Knowledge," a mandate which its first historian took to empower a vast communications network dedicated to the accumulation of intellectual commodities. According to Thomas Sprat, "They have begun to settle a *correspondence* through all *Countreys;* and have taken such order, that in short time, there will scarce a Ship come up the *Thames,* that does not make some return of *Experiments,* as well as of *Merchandize* . . . [Merchants] have contributed their *labours:* they have help'd their *correspondence:* they have employ'd their *Factors* abroad, to answer their *Inquiries;* they have laid out in all Countries for *observations.*"[26] The conflation of scientific and mercantile "improvement" in the ambitions of the Society gave to foreign travel the energized excitement of a flourishing industry. Its institutional encouragement of the enterprise of travel was by no means responsible, in itself, for the popularity of travel narratives after the Restoration. No single factor could account for the sheer proliferation not only of actual journeys, nor even of their published accounts, but of an entire spectrum of printed, first-person narratives, some recognizably "true," some apparently or obviously fabricated, and all preoccupied with the question of their own historicity and how it might be authenticated. But the Society's instructions on how to keep the daily travel journals on which, in some fashion, the narratives themselves were to be based provide a remarkable instance of how critical and theoretical discourse develops alongside, and in relation to, the development of literary discourse. This in turn helps explain why the epistemology of the travel narrative during this period so richly repays study, and I will devote a disproportionate amount of attention to it in the following pages.

The "literary" interests of the early Society are of course well known. The dedication of the new philosophy to the reform of prose style is the most immediate and most celebrated of its influences on the literary culture of seventeenth-century England. After the Restoration this effort was concentrated in the writings of apologists for, and Fellows of, the Royal Society. Yet it is only concerning the creation of one particular literary form, the travel narrative, that the Society descended to specific directives about the new mode of composition. The self-conscious particularity of these directives distinguishes them from earlier instructions to travelers and explorers, whose precedent they follow. But what is most distinctive about this critical theory, the quality of its concern with the relationship between psychology, persuasion, and stylistic technique, emerges from the intercourse between "official" sponsorship and the responses of travelers and interested commentators. The immediate success of the campaign itself may be assessed by the number of traveler's reports, reflecting the directives, that were sent to and printed in the *Philosophical Transactions of the Royal Society* throughout the Restoration. It was also in the first numbers of the *Transactions* that the campaign originated. In the following pages I will briefly review the directives themselves, and then discuss the accounts and reports that seek in many different ways to elaborate and to practice the fledgling theory of travel narrative.[27]

The general terms of the project will be familiar from other inquiries into questions of truth during this period. Traditional travel narratives often "are more concern'd for Panegyricks of the amaenities of the place, than will well sort with the true and modest relations of their Neighbours . . . But in our designed *Natural History* we have more need of severe, full and punctuall Truth, than of Romances or Panegyricks." Robert Hooke, the first Curator of Experiments for the Royal Society, outlined the conditions that would have to be rectified in the fulfillment of this need:

The want of sufficient Instructions (to Seamen and Travellers) to shew them what is pertinent and considerable, to be observ'd in their Voyages and Abodes, and how to make their Observations and keep Registers or Accounts of them . . . The want of fit Persons both to Promote and Disperse such Instructions to Persons fitted to engage, and careful to Collect Returns; and Compose them into Histories . . . The want of some easie Way to have all such Printed: First singly, and afterwards divers of them together.

As Hooke proceeds to observe, the first deficiency has already been addressed: with respect to seamen, by the mathematician Lawrence Rooke of Gresham College; with respect to general travelers, by the celebrated mechanist and chemist Robert Boyle. In the first number of the *Transactions* appear Rooke's directions concerning instruments and techniques for making quantitative calculations about maritime and meteorological phenomena. To these directions on how to read nature in the most objective sense of the term are added, several numbers later, Boyle's instructions on the composition of "a good natural History," which divide up the field of observation more or less according to the four elements, listing the likely phenomena to be encountered under each head, along with the rational and experimental methods by which they may be interrogated. In 1692, Boyle's "heads," as well as other relevant passages from the *Transactions,* are reprinted and expanded by an anonymous author whose major innovation is to include questions to ask oneself when traveling in particular locales, from Turkey to Greenland.[28]

If these are the basic guidelines by which the circumstantial factuality of nature is to be elicited, more particular suggestions are made concerning how, in Hooke's words, to collect these returns, "and compose them into histories." The object of the directions to seamen, we are told, is "the better to capacitate them for making such observations abroad, as may be pertinent and suitable for their purpose; of which the said Seamen should be desired to keep an exact *Diary,* delivering at their return a fair Copy thereof . . . to be perused by the *R. Society.*" After reprinting Rooke's directions, the editors of a four-volume collection of travel narratives expand on the importance of the relationship between the immediate diary and its subsequent transformation into narrative: "Let [travelers] therefore always have a Table-Book at hand to set down every thing worth remembering, and then at night more methodically transcribe the Notes they have taken in the day . . . It is not amiss, if it may be to [*sic*], view all Rarities in the company of other Strangers, because many together are apt to remark more than one alone can do." This documentary procedure seems generally to have been known and approved by travelers. William Dampier's narrative "is composed of a mixt Relation of Places, and Actions, in the same order of time in which they occurred: for which end I kept a Journal of every days Observations." And of John Braithwaite's narrative an anonymous commentator says, "The Reader will observe that it is written in a natural, easy and intelligible Style, and taken from the very Words of his own Journals, that collected the Occurrences of each Day."[29]

This division of the compositional process into two stages, those of journal and narrative, may seem to recall the autobiographical separation and interplay between ongoing action and retrospective narration, materialistic Character and spiritualizing Narrator. What is significant here, however, is that both levels of narrative consciousness are concerned only to enhance the documentary historicity of the account, and the author is explicitly enjoined to forgo the moral judgments of an overarching narrative voice. Precisely because it is firsthand and immediate, the truth of the Character may be taken as authentic. The work of the Narrator is only to render this truth more stylistically accessible and "methodical," at the most to perform the editorial function of, in Hooke's words, "separating what is pertinent from what is not so, and to be Rejected." By this account the selection might even be performed by another person.[30]

Thus in theory, at least, the narrative overlay in travel accounts is not at all concerned to engender a tension between competing voices, a mood of moral introspection which in other forms facilitates the subsumption of Character by Narrator in what I have suggested is an act of narrative atonement. (In practice, as we will see, even those travel narratives that claim a vigorous historicity are not exempt from this countervailing impulse; at the least the very existence of two versions of the same events is likely to aggravate the dilemma of quantitative completeness.) This is not to say that the instructions of the Royal Society discourage authorial self-consciousness, even introspection. It is simply to argue that the authority and criteria for this self-examination derive not from the over-arching truth of a great Author but from the principles of a materialist epistemology, and that the truth of this epistemology is available not through the renunciation, but through the exploitation, of merely sen-suous human powers.

To some degree, in fact, it is our very freedom from overarching conceptual schemes (as Francis Bacon never tired of arguing) which liberates our subjective faculties for the acquisition of truth. Thus, in Sprat's view, the plain style of the new philosophy's "records" is paral-leled by the simplicity and humility of its recorders, a new breed of philosopher not "skill'd in all *Divine* and *human* things" but "plain, diligent, and laborious observers: such, who, though they bring not much knowledg, yet bring their hands, and their eyes uncorrupted: such as have not their Brains infected by false Images." Enabled to master the new knowledge by his lack of the old, the scientific recorder is an individual happily severed from tradition. Like that of the Protestant "mechanick preacher," his plainness is at once a rhetorical and cultural attribute. Although equipped only with the basic physical accessories of universal, unheroic humanity, he is distinguished by those private virtues of honesty, sincerity, naturalness, and integrity that guarantee the per-spicuous observation and documentation of truth. For the travel narrator, the great task of introspection is first to disclose and to activate these private virtues in himself, and then to communicate them to his reader. Thus, if the end of atonement in spiritual autobiography is attained through the saint's justification by divine grace, in the theory of travel narrative its radical secularization would seem to consist in the traveler-protagonist's personal validation through the attainment of the reader's conviction. This is not, however, a calculated act of persuasion. One of the many traditions from which the scientific recorder has been severed is that of rhetoric. His truth is that of strict historicity as opposed to that of verisimilitude, and the "plainness" of the plain style connotes the artlessness both of transparency and of untutored roughness and irreg-ularity. Montaigne believed "a plain ignorant Fellow . . . more likely to tell the Truth" in a travel narrative, for the better educated "cannot forbear a little to alter the Story; they never represent things to you simply as they are, but rather as they appear'd to them, or as they would have them appear to you . . . and the better to induce your Faith, are willing to help out the Business with something more than is really true, of their own Invention." The fundamental trope of this antirhetorical style is the self-reflexive insistence on its own documentary candor, as well as on the historicity of the narrative it transparently mediates.[31]

4
THE EMPIRICAL STYLE BECOMES PROBLEMATIC

The convention of the patently disingenuous claim to historicity has existed at least since Lucian's *True History*. Even so, "imaginary voyages" printed during the Restoration and early eighteenth century are likely to deal with the question of historical truth in a manner peculiar to an age for which that question has become momentous. The contemporary editors of texts originally composed in an earlier era, for example, are apologetic in the current mode even about works that have been conventionally understood to be allegorical or fabulous. Thus Joseph Hall's *Mundus Alter et Idem* (1609) is translated, at the end of the century, as Quevedo's *Travels,* "A Novel" whose allegorical method is defensively associated with that of "*Sacred Writ*" as opposed to that of "*Romance*." And the early eighteenth-century editor of the late-medieval *Mandeville's Travels* buttresses his tepid vindication of "the Author" for having taken "strange Stories out of what will now be called Romances" with an earnest display of critical scholarship regarding previous editions (thereby tacitly attesting at least to the "objectivity" of the object before us). Imaginary voyages that are original to the Restoration period, like that of Joshua Barnes, often evince an even sharper awareness that the very fancifulness of their travels is in conflict with an ascendant and alien epistemology. A strikingly explicit example of this is an imaginary voyage "to the World of Cartesius," which invokes the model of Lucian and whose spurious protestations of historicity bear a complex (but unarticulated) relationship to its attack upon the materialist philosophy of Descartes.[32]

But the influence of empirical thought on this ancient form is clearest, perhaps, in what might aptly be called the "naturalization" of imaginary voyages during this period. By the end of the seventeenth century, their supernatural element has declined so drastically that a major problem for modern scholars is the determination of whether or not their claims to historicity are to be taken seriously—that is, whether or not "imaginary voyages" may actually have occurred.[33] So one paradoxical effect of the early modern epistemological revolution is, by sufficiently discrediting the very idea of imaginary voyages, to obscure rather than sharpen the distinction between narratives of "real" and of "imaginary" travels. This can be seen in the fact that the editors of one of the larger collections of travel narratives of the time, Awnsham and John Churchill, sometimes are taken in by the adept deployment of the historicizing conventions in what later research has shown to be fictitious accounts. But the fluidity of the boundary between "real" and "imaginary" travels is also evident as a tendency of the former to engender a parodic model for the latter. As travel writers doggedly pursue to its end the logic of naive empiricism, they extend its earnest conventions to the point at which they begin to reflect a subversive image of themselves. From here it is a short step to the imaginary voyage, whose didactic aim, customarily satiric to some degree, is likely to entail now, among other things, the pointed parody of naive empiricism itself.

Like the individual narratives to which I also will refer in the following pages, the Churchills' editorial commentary reveals both the currency and the volatility of the critical theory that was sponsored by the Royal Society. The demand for quantitative completeness in narrative was, of course, entirely consistent with Baconian method and the ideal of "natural history," which encouraged, as Michael Hunter points out, "indiscriminate collecting of information relevant to no particular hypothesis." On the difficult subject of quantitative completeness the Churchills tell us simply that they have omitted no details, in order not to "assume the Liberty of prescribing to the Publick how much of an Author they should read, nor determine which figures are useful, and which superfluous." Many of the authors themselves approach the problem no more directly than through the dense circumstantiality of their accounts; but there are exceptions. William Dampier tells us that he has included small details of "particular Traverses" and "Concomitant Circumstances . . . that I would not prejudice the truth and sincerity of my Relation." Edward Cooke is adamant on the accuracy and completeness of his journal, which "was exactly kept all the Time we were Aboard" and whose "Strictness of Truth" can be "attested by the whole Company of the Ship *Dutchess*." But the narrative is another matter. Readers of the first volume have objected to Cooke's stated omission of details on winds and weather, and the second volume contains the testy defense that "to swell a Volume with what could neither be of Use, nor afford Entertainment, would have been altogether superfluous."[34]

But it is not really this simple to draw the line between the obligatory and the excrescent, as Cooke finds with the story of Alexander Selkirk. In Volume One he is quite taciturn about the discovery of the famous castaway on Juan Fernandes Island. Here, much more, his readers have clamored for details, and although Cooke willingly obliges them in Volume Two, he is uneasy about indulging "this Propension . . . to look for something very extraordinary in any Accident that happens out of the common Course." What about the other two men who were shipwrecked on the same island? Should more be told of them as well?

The definitive documentation of "true history" begins to seem no more rule bound than the arbitrary elaborations of "romance." Cooke's confident allusion to that dichotomy to justify what he will include in the second telling of Selkirk's story conceals his puzzlement as to just how to rationalize a certain degree of selectivity by the absolute standards of naive empiricism:

It would be no difficult Matter to embellish a Narrative with many Romantick Incidents, to please the unthinking Part of Mankind, who swallow every Thing an artful Writer thinks fit to impose upon their Credulity, without any Regard to Truth or Probability. The judicious are not taken with such Trifles; their End in Reading, is Information; and they easily distinguish between Reality and Fiction. We shall therefore give the Reader as much as may satisfy a reasonable Curiosity, concerning this Man, without deviating into Invention.

Nevertheless, Cooke's procedure here makes clear that truly documentary narrative may contract and expand to suit the needs of readers and yet be "true," and he concludes his enlarged version of Selkirk with the equivocal assurance that it is "the whole material Truth, and sufficient on such an Account."[35]

Of course there are certain kinds of selection that seem to require no justification at all, simply because the excised details do not deserve the status of "factuality." The translator of a travel narrative composed by a Spanish Jesuit observes that it contains much religious material that runs counter to our expectations of "a Book of Travels . . . and such things as are usual in Books of this Nature." Consequently he omits or modifies the "religious Narrations" and knits up the loose ends. But despite the Royal Society's instructions, there is nothing more fluid during these decades than the expectations readers bring to "a book of travels." Of one narrative in their collection the Churchills observe ingenuously: "This is a Pilgrimage to the *Holy Land,* and therefore writ in a Religious Stile . . . and is a good Guide for such as desire to travel into those parts." But the skeptical critique of religious credulity could also sharpen the traditional, spiritualist assault on the naive sufficiency of a devotion to merely physical relics and travels. Thus the wise old guide in a contemporary pilgrimage allegory spends much of his time in the guise of a critical historian, deriding pilgrims' superstitious faith in Thomas à Becket's snotty handkerchief and all such "sottish tales" of miracles and sacred sites. "We need not be at the trouble to abuse" these lying legends, he says, "for they make Invectives against themselves, and carry their own Satyrs in their bosome." As for holy pilgrimages, he too is in passage to the site of the body of Christ; but "I poor Soul verily believed all this while that he had been in the Heavens, in the *Jerusalem* which is above: whither I and my Companion are travelling as fast as we can." So the modern tools of skeptical criticism can shore up rather than subvert the temple of faith, and one implication of such an argument might be that there is little to distinguish the materialist credulity of naive Christian pilgrims from that of naive scientific travelers. When Edward Coxere, a merchant seaman, composed his travels around 1690, he found it natural to punctuate his quite circumstantial history with allusions to providence and with intrusive "religious narrations" that culminate in his conversion to Quaker belief. From the perspective of the overarching pattern, the standard of quantitative completeness might itself seem an excrescence.[36]

What are the most common means by which the claim to historicity is deployed in travel narrative? As we might expect, considerable respect is shown for "original documentation." "And indeed nothing can be described more authentick," say the Churchills of the *Life* of Christopher Columbus, "if we will give Credit to Original Papers, and those from so good a hand as the Admiral himself and his own Son." Yet their respect is not unlimited, so that Hakluyt (and to a lesser degree Purchas) is criticized for filling his work with "such a multitude of Articles, Charters, Privileges, Letters, Relations, and other things" whose documentary authenticity cannot disguise their essential insignificance. It is a generally accepted principle that the credibility of a travel account is enhanced by the confirmation of other travelers, but a far more important principle is the superiority of eyewitness to hearsay testimony, however reputable the source.[37] Thus Fernandez Navarette concludes his commendation of eyewitness experience as the basis of all species of reports by telling us that he therefore "resolv'd not to make account in this work of any thing but what I have seen, read, and has gone through my hands." For similar reasons the Churchills are able to allow that even the travel narrative of a Portuguese Jesuit "no doubt is very authentick, as deliver'd by an Eye-witness, who was a Person of Probity. Other things relating to the Unicorn, Rhinoceros, Bird of Paradise, Pelican and Phenix, he writes upon hearsay, which deserve not the same Credit."[38] But as this allusion to "probity" makes clear, the emphasis upon eyewitness experience puts a heavy premium on the psychology of the author. Thoughtful readers will reflect that the claim to historicity is only as strong as the character of its claimant, and therefore much need be said about the "integrity," the "sincerity," and the "modesty" of travel writers. Nor (to adjust slightly the angle of introspection) should they be thought capable of having any practical interest in, or emotional bias toward, the fabrication of untruths.[39]

There is a rhetorical problem here similar to that involved in claiming not just verisimilitude but historicity. The very attempt to disclose one's integrity sometimes reveals only the futility of the effort: " 'tis not so much my Concern to be reputed sincere, as 'tis really to be so." The presence of good character is no more self-evident than is the fact of veracity. Neither is demonstrated by what Locke would call "something extrinsical to the persuasions themselves"; both are, from the point of view of the reader, hearsay reports mediated to him through narrative style.[40] And since the search for immediate evidence is illusory, attention paid to asserting personal integrity is often redirected toward suggesting that good character may be discerned within the very instrument of mediation, within the shape of the style itself. This may entail nothing more concrete than the observation that a general "Air of Truth" suffuses the whole. More likely, the air of truth will be associated with that negative capability which Sprat attributes to the humble and untutored "recorder" of the new philosophy and which manifests itself in a transparent style: "This Narrative has nothing of Art or Language, being left by an ignorant Sailor, who, as he confesses, was in no better a Post than Gunner's Mate, and that to a *Greenland* Fisher; and therefore the Reader can expect no more than bare matter of Fact, deliver'd in a homely Stile, which it was not fit to alter, lest it might breed a Jealousy that something had been chang'd more than the bare Language."[41] Here plainness of style seems almost a precondition for the documentary authenticity— the truth—of the text. In other accounts, the conventional apology for a plain style may be quickly transformed into an aggressive critique of linguistic decoration as incompatible with truth.[42]

At its most unreflective, this devotion to stylistic perspicuity as itself an evidence of historicity exemplifies the familiar credulousness of naive empiricism. The Churchills, for example, do not emerge from the consideration of narrative style and its epistemological implications with their customary skepticism quite intact. To be sure, they are able to discard some "Romantick" accounts according to experiential canons of credibility that have nothing to do with style, just as they can discount the evidence of a self-incriminating style if more material evidence seems to argue the author's credibility. What is most impressive is their willingness, on at least one occasion, to give harder evidence priority over even a style whose qualities would seem to confirm the truth of the narration: "This Author wrote in a commendable Stile; but his History is of no credit, being full of false Relations, as is made out by all other Authors that write of those Parts." At such moments the comparative method of critical scholarship seems to demonstrate its uncompromising rigor. But what are we to make of the Churchills' neutral observation that another writer "relates some Love Intrigues he had with *Moorish* Women, as also very strange Metamorphoses of Men and other Creatures turn'd into Stone. The Relation is plain and without artifice"?[43]

The temptation to an ironic reading is a response, here as elsewhere, to a sudden suspension of skepticism on the part of the authors which to us seems arbitrary. Like the "sottish tales" of Christian devotion, naive travel accounts appear now to "make invectives against themselves, and carry their own satires in their bosom." Critical method all at once looks like nothing more than a set of unfamiliar conventions by which the old, familiar ones have been replaced. And despite arguments to the contrary, the claim to historicity appears committed, at least momentarily, to the truth-value not of things but of words, so that if a narrative observes the proper conventions, it demonstrates its own veracity. This kind of lapse in plausibility must be ascribed not to the conventionality of these narratives but to the imprecision of the theory, and hence the instability of the rules, that govern the deployment of their conventions. The effect of disingenuousness or duplicity results at least in part from the uncertainty of authors and readers alike about just what is required to establish narrative truth. And this is a problem that is felt equally by writers who are "sincere" in seeking to tell a "true history" and by those who are not, since in both cases the question of truth is accessible (although most contemporaries would not have seen it this way) only in terms of the choice between competing conventions. The kinds of problems I have been illustrating in "real" travel narratives also arise, that is, in imaginary ones. In fact there is often very little distance between imaginary voyages that undertake, with some self-consciousness, the parody of naive empiricism and those that claim historicity with earnest and undisciplined exuberance.

Two good examples of the former sort concern voyages to *Terra Australis Incognita;* both are by Frenchmen, and one of them is plausible enough to have received a commendation from the skeptical Churchills.[44] Simon Berington's imaginary voyage provides an instance of the latter sort, for although the story of Gaudentio di Lucca's travels is obviously utopian and its claim to historicity quite wonderful in its extremity, there is no evidence here of parodic intent. Berington's subtitle alone makes clear that the elaborate metastory of authentication will seriously threaten the priority of the travel narrative itself, especially since it applies to the question of narrative truth that ultimate juridical test of veracity, interrogation of the narrator by the Inquisition.[45] From the publisher we hear the labyrinthine story of his receipt of the manuscript, in which the central figure is Signor Rhedi, Librarian at the Cathedral of San Marco, who is quoted in support of di Lucca's character. From the Dominican Master of the Inquisition at Bologna we next hear, in a letter to Rhedi, how the inquisitors have been thoroughly convinced of the truth of di Lucca's "strange Account, which he deliver'd with such an Air of Steadiness, as scarce left any room to doubt of the Truth of it"; he encloses the *Memoirs* themselves for Rhedi's collection, subscribing "F. Alisio de St. Ivorio . . . Bologna, July, 20. 1721."[46] And from di Lucca himself we hear the history of his travels, punctuated by the interrogatories of the inquisitors and by Rhedi's footnotes attesting to the truth of various circumstantial details. Thus, although the plot of the metastory clearly concerns the trial and vindication of its central Character, it is equally clear that he is tested not according to a spiritual standard of truth but by the strict criteria of factuality and historicity. And yet the periodic interruptions of an overarching Narrative voice are by no means absent. Instead they have assumed the secularized form of intrusive questions, posed by an ecclesiastical court, which elicit the very contents of the narrator's true history; and of intrusive annotations, subjoined by a professional keeper of documents, which establish the documentary objectivity of that history as the edited text which now claims our attention.

No mode of discourse is more likely to avail itself of the "strange, therefore true" paradox than the travel narrative, one of whose cardinal conventions is to expect the unexpected.[47] And many of the travel narratives of this period have recourse to this most daring, and most dangerous, claim to historicity. Vairasse d'Allais has his publisher remark that

the Histories of *Peru, Mexico, China,* &c. were at first taken for Romances by many, but time has shewed since that they are verities not to be doubted of.

It is an idle humour in any of us to despise or reject strange Discoveries . . . If any thing is here related of this Country or People seemingly beyond all possibility, we must know, that as this People have the advantage of living in the earthly Paradise, they have knowledges of Nature and natural Effects, which look like Miracles.

As this argument implies, the relativizing effects of travel need not lead us to conclude that nature itself is relative to climate and custom. On the contrary (as another writer suggests), "Nature performs its operations in all parts of the World, according to its primitive Fundamental Laws . . . The Monsters of *Africa* or the *Indies,* are no more surprising to the Inhabitants of these parts, than the Beasts that are commonly seen and bred among us are to the Europeans." Rather, it is our own capacity for knowledge that is relative to our concrete physical circumstances and opportunities. "We have taken for Fables what the Poets or the Ancients have told us of the first Inhabitants of the World," remarks a third, yet the natives of America answer well to those descriptions. "They who never saw more than their own Village, never imagin that Steeples are of any other fashion than their own . . . For of those things which we do not see, we know nothing but by the Report of others. Now Men have not reported to us all things for want of having been upon the Places." But then to dismiss as "romance" what has not yet been seen or reported, or if reported, not yet read, is (says a fourth) beyond foolishness.[48]

These self-defensive efforts by authors of voyages both "real" and "imaginary" find persuasive parallels in the more exotic of Aphra Behn's imaginary "true histories." The well-known claim to historicity that

opens *Oroonoko; or, The Royal Slave. A True History* (1688) is echoed,
more succinctly, at the beginning of *The Fair Jilt . . .* (1696): "I do not
pretend here to entertain you with a feign'd story, or any thing piec'd
together with *Romantick* Accidents; but every Circumstance, to a Tittle,
is Truth. To a great part of the Main, I my self was an Eye witness; and
what I did not see, I was confirm'd of by Actors in the Intrigue, holy
Men, of the Order of St. *Francis.*"[49] Frequent narrative intrusions of this
sort occur throughout Behn's third-person Surinam histories, but no
tension exists in her dual role as narrator and character, because both roles
are dedicated to the single end of physically witnessing, and thereby
authenticating, a central character whose personal history is distinct from
her own. This authenticating end is also served by Behn's rendition of the
"strange, therefore true" formula with reference to *Oroonoko:* "The
Royal Slave I had the Honour to know in my Travels to the other
World . . . If there be any thing that seems Romantick, I beseech your
Lordship [Lord Maitland] to consider, these Countries do, in all things,
so far differ from ours, that they produce inconceivable Wonders; at least,
they appear so to us, New and Strange."[50]

The potential risks involved in this method of claiming historicity are
fully actualized in Behn's travel narratives, whose naive empiricism betrays no parodic intent. If, in Vairasse d'Allais's "earthly paradise," natural effects are said at least to "look like miracles," Behn audaciously and
unapologetically idealizes her Surinam as a prelapsarian Eden; the royal
slave on whose historicity she elsewhere insists is made to fantasize about
his beloved in the familiar figures and heightened language of romance;
and the lovers, after a separation in the Old World, are reunited in the
New with all the miraculousness of a romance discovery (see 2–3, 14, 43–
44, 48–49). In the face of such incongruity, we might be tempted to
suppose for writers like Behn an especially opportunistic "critical theory": only call your travel narrative a true history, and its historical truth
will thereby be empowered to survive the most patent romance fictionalizing. The comparison with a highly self-conscious antiromance like
Incognita is instructive, for Behn shares with Congreve the energizing
antiromance impulse and the will to pursue questions of truth into the
plot itself; yet the pursuit stops short of extreme skepticism even though
the logic of that movement into self-parody feels at times quite
implacable.

Behn values the Surinam Indians for their natural simplicity, and she
derives from their example the precept "that simple Nature . . . better
instructs the World, than all the Inventions of Man." (3). But she also
knows that natural simplicity is an invitation to imposture, as one of her
kinsmen discovers when the natives seek to deify him for the powers
of his magnifying glass: "It were not difficult to establish any unknown
or extravagant Religion among them, and to impose any Notions or

Fictions upon 'em" (56). In passages like these, Behn is torn between her admiration for the natural receptiveness of credulity and the artful protections of skepticism, and in Oroonoko she creates a hero who embodies these antithetical qualities in recognizably Restoration guise. Schooled in an aristocratic doctrine that enjoins implicit faith in the word of others, Oroonoko falls easy victim to the routine duplicity of the English captain by whom he is enslaved: "And *Oroonoko,* whose Honour was such as he never had violated a Word in his life himself, much less a solemn Asseveration, believ'd in an instant what this Man said" (34–35). But he can also play the freethinker and make a "Jest" of the gullible "Faith" that Christians have in "our Notions of the Trinity" (46). When Oroonoko learns definitively that "there was no Faith in the White Men, or the Gods they ador'd," he is even obliged to embrace the decadence of literacy and documentary objectivity, resolving "never to credit one Word they spoke" and requiring that all pledges henceforth "should be ratify'd by their Hands in Writing" (66). But something is lost in this rueful conversion to Western skepticism, and Oroonoko's history soon after comes to its violent close in an apotheosis of desperate revenge and self-sacrifice.

The unstable compound that Oroonoko's character exists to mediate is most suggestively expressed by an earlier episode, in which his "great Curiosity" is so piqued by the incredible phenomenon of the South American "Numb-eel" that "for Experiment-sake" he grasps one of them and almost drowns himself (53). Here the blend of skepticism and credulity is conveyed by an engaging, if momentary, glimpse of Oroonoko as gentleman virtuoso of the Royal Society, and it is this same cultural type that his creator enacts in her own epistemological instability. Naive empiricism and the claim to historicity partake both of the skeptical denunciation of "all the inventions of man" and of the credulous faith that human inventions may thus be replaced by immediate perception and experience. As the ready idolatry of the Indians seems to show, however, neither does the absence of skepticism guarantee the absence of invention, which will always intervene in whatever shapes are conditioned by the particular cultural tribe to which we belong. For Behn this is the point at which skepticism becomes self-defeating, for it denies her the capacity to tell the truth; and she never is moved, like Congreve, to disclose the manipulative power of the author "to impose any notions or fictions upon" the reader.[51] Because the parallel between credulous Indians and credulous readers never breaks the surface of narrative self-consciousness, Behn may perhaps be assured that our simple and receptive faith is rewarded not by imposture but by the truth of what really happened. The hope is that antiromance, the negation of the negation, will thus fulfill itself as the true history of travel narrative. The risk is that for skeptical readers it will simply seem the "new romance."

THE EMERGENCE OF EXTREME SKEPTICISM

So the straightforward demystification of historicizing travel narrative as
the new romance only makes explicit a tendency that is already plain in
the naive claim to historicity itself. The dubious reader of a typically
authenticated Restoration travel narrative confuted the pamphlet's overheated claims by coolly writing on its title page, "By a new fashion'd
Romancer." And fifty years later, John Macky linked the epistemological
critique of French voyages to that of French memoirs: "The French are
certainly the unfittest People . . . to write Descriptions of Countries; for
if they don't mix something Romantic in their accounts, it is thought flat
and insipid and does not go down with them. As most of their modern
Memoirs, like their Novels, are but a new way of Romancing, since *Don
Quixote* laughed Scuderys old way out of countenance; so their Voyages
and Journeys are much the same."[52]

The false modesty of the plain style and its attendant pretensions was
highly vulnerable both to direct attack and to parody. Henry Stubbe, for
example, could not be persuaded to accept the Royal Society's apparently
implicit faith that the simplicity of the writer is a guarantee of his credibility: "That there are more parts of the *world* discovered and sailed unto
then in *Aristotles* time, I grant. But what certainty shall we have of
Narratives picked up from *negligent,* or *un-accurate Merchants* and *Seamen?*"[53] François Misson provides an amusing example of the more
indirect, parodic subversion of the plain style. After extensive wanderings in exile, Misson, a Huguenot, settled in London in 1707 and immediately published the travels of Francis Leguat, an account of an imaginary voyage whose management of the conventions of the claim to
historicity is yet sophisticated enough to have convinced its most recent
editor of its scientific importance. But at one point in his preface Misson
breaks his fiction long enough to impugn the cant reduction of truth and
substance to mere rhetoric. "Leguat's" friends have prevailed on him to
write up his travels, "naming to me a great number of false Voyages, and
some of them ill enough related, which however went off . . . Wretched
Romances, and ill contriv'd Fables, find a Vent; why may not my true
Romance have as favourable a fate? I expect the Critical Reader shou'd say
here, there's a manner of expressing things." And at this point Misson
begins to impersonate the response of a fatuous devotee of those new,
"wretched romances":

There's a manner of expressing things: A Story well told, is read with Pleasure, tho' 'tis even a little Romantick or Trivial in its self. People are now
more earnest than ever for perfection of Language. As for Example, the little
Nothings of the Abbot of *Choisy* in the *Voyage* to *Siam,* have an incomparable
Grace in them, and please much more than many other things made of more

precious Materials. *We cast Anchor: We made ready to Sail. The Wind took Courage. Robin is dead. We said Mass. We Vomited.* Tho' they are poor Words any where else, yet in his Book, which is half compos'd of them, they are Sentences, and the worth of them is not to be told . . . You are in the wrong to imagine your History [the imagined reader continues], tho' true, singular, nay even moral, and as political as you please, can enter into Comparison with a Book that is well Written.[54]

The parodic maneuvers of extreme skepticism are not commonly found in the documents of Protestant piety. Over the long term, the literalization of pilgrimage allegory was, if anything, facilitated by the individualizing and historicizing tendencies of the Protestant Reformation. The Puritan requirement of self-documentation applied to seamen as much as to anyone, and instructions on how to spiritually "improve" sea voyages can resemble closely those of the Royal Society on how to improve them scientifically.[55] But as we have seen, the Christian critique of human sufficiency could also be toughened, rather than corrupted, by skepticism. Among Christian mariners it is the particular achievement of William Okeley to have used the claim to historicity and the empirical standard of truth without being used by it. Deftly alternating between idealist and materialist denigrations of "romance," Okeley manages (in Augustine's words) to "use" historical truth without "enjoying" it, to teach his readers how to make it work for Christian faith, and how to disdain it when it will not. The result is an unlikely but effective compound, the extreme skepticism of the Christian.[56]

Some authors, Okeley knows, believe their readers will accept nothing "below *prodigy* and *miracle . . . gorgons, harpies, centaurs, and enchanted islands . . .* They first form ideas of *ingenious romances* in their own heads, and then obtrude them upon the world for *historical verities*" (sig. B1ʳ). Others write what "we mis-call *histories*": violent and bloody accounts of battle, delivered "with as much confidence and exactness in every *minute circumstance,* as if . . . they had . . . hovered, like *Victory with her doubtful wings,* over both the armies, where they might securely take notes of all that was said or done, in *Shelton's Brachygraphy* [*sic*]" (ii).[57] The present reader need fear no such romance impostures, and Okeley soon provides the familiar assurances that the journey he will narrate "is known to many, and has been sifted and scann'd by such eyes and ears as are not guilty of easy credulity" (xii).

Given this preparation, it is rather surprising to find now that Okeley has in mind higher notions of truth than the historical, that in the last analysis, "romance" attaints narratives that lack not empirical, but providential, truth. As he says disarmingly, the reader "shall meet with nothing *in fact* but what is *precisely true;* what of *wonderment* he may encounter, was of *God's own working,* not of *man's inventing.*" The only distinction that matters is that "between those *romances,* which are the issues of *fine*

wits, and the *serious grave contrivances* of divine providence" (ii). Perhaps
even this studied effect might have been achieved by a skillful historian of
supernatural apparitions. What distinguishes Okeley is his capacity to tell
us plainly when "the history of apparitions" becomes a contradiction in
terms: "But now the *reader's great danger* lies in running over some of
God's works, and yet not seeing *God in his works* . . . The common observer, whose thoughts are terminated by *his eye,* and *his eye* with the
visible heavens . . . loseth quite their *main design,* which is to conduct and
argue our thoughts up to *a first cause*" (iii). Diametrically at odds now
with the Royal Society's view of how to "improve" natural knowledge,
Okeley proceeds to a list of counter-"directions" for one who would read
travel narratives not factually but correctly (iii). These consist mostly of
standard exegetical guides and pious exhortations to faith. But later on he
also makes the shrewd insinuation that there is a plain style plainer than
that concocted for the accurate description of physical reality and horizontal travels: "How many of those who speak the language of the sea,"
asks Okeley, "yet have found her billows deaf to their cries and prayers,
and their stately ships made the scorn of winds, and the reproach of
waves, when we, who had none of their ships, and little of their skill,
have had experience of those Providences to which they have been strangers[?]" (50).

Okeley's strength lies in his judicious skill in assimilating the standards of empirical truth to those of the overarching Christian pattern,
within which any empiricism but an instrumental and temporary one
assumes its true colors as the latest version of human vanity. By this
maneuver the battle lines are redrawn: religious faith and romance become not allies but antagonists. The Christian truth of the spirit, leagued
with a knowing sense of historical truth, is ranged against the great
enemy, the romance illusions of naive empiricism. Okeley's balance in
this maneuver is sure but exceedingly delicate, and a basically secular
mode of extreme skepticism is far more common than the Christian. It is
fair to say that the most acute and comprehensive critique of the new
romance of travel narratives is made by the third earl of Shaftesbury. His
attack should be read at length, if not in full.

We moderns, Shaftesbury says,

care not how *Gothick* or *Barbarous* our Models are; what ill-design'd or mon-
strous Figure we view; or what false Proportions we trace, or see describ'd in
History, Romance, or Fiction. And thus our *Eye* and *Ear* is lost. Our Relish or
Taste must of necessity grow barbarous, whilst *Barbarian* Customs, *Savage*
Manners, *Indian* Wars, and Wonders of the *Terra Incognita,* employ our leisure
Hours, and are the chief Materials to furnish out a Library.

These are in our present Days, what *Books of Chivalry* were, in those of our
Forefathers. I know not what *Faith* our valiant Ancestors may have had in the
Storys of their Giants, their Dragons, and St. GEORGE's. But for our *Faith*

indeed, as well as our *Taste,* in this other way of reading; I must confess I can't consider it, without Astonishment.

It must certainly be something else than In*credulity,* which fashions the Taste and Judgment of many Gentlemen, whom we hear censur'd as *Atheists,* for attempting to philosophize after a newer manner than any known of late . . . Historys of *Incas* or *Iroquois,* written by Fryers and Missionarys, Pirates and Renegades, Sea-Captains and trusty Travellers, pass for authentick Records, and are *canonical,* with the *Virtuoso's* of this sort. The *Christian* Miracles may not so well satisfy 'em; they dwell with the highest Contentment on the Prodigys of *Moorish* and *Pagan* Countrys. They have far more Pleasure in hearing the monstrous Accounts of monstrous Men, and Manners; than the politest and best Narrations of the Affairs, the Governments, and Lives of the wisest and most polish'd People.

'Tis the same *Taste* which makes us prefer a *Turkish* History to a *Grecian,* or a *Roman;* an ARIOSTO to a VIRGIL; and a Romance, or Novel, to an *Iliad.* We have no regard to the Character or Genius of our *Author:* nor are so far curious, as to observe how able he is in the Judgment of *Facts,* or how ingenious in the Texture of his *Lyes.* For *Facts* unably related, tho with the greatest Sincerity, and good Faith, may prove the worst sort of Deceit: and mere *Lyes,* judiciously compos'd, can teach us the Truth of Things, beyond any other manner . . . Yet so enchanted we are with the *Travelling Memoirs* of any casual Adventurer; that be his Character, or Genius, what it will, we have no sooner turn'd over a Page or two, than we begin to interest our-selves highly in his Affairs. No sooner has he taken Shipping at the Mouth of the *Thames,* or sent his Baggage before him to *Gravesend,* or *Buoy in the Nore,* than strait our Attention is earnestly taken up. If in order to his more distant Travels, he takes some Part of EUROPE in his way; we can with patience hear of Inns and Ordinarys, Passage-Boats and Ferrys, foul and fair Weather; with all the Particulars of the Author's Diet, Habit of Body, his personal Dangers and Mischances, on Land, and Sea. And thus, full of Desire and Hope, we accompany him, till he enters on his great Scene of Action, and begins by the Description of some *enormous Fish,* or *Beast.* From monstrous *Brutes* he proceeds to yet more *monstrous Men.* For in this Race of Authors, *he* is ever compleatest, and of the first Rank, who is able to speak of things the most *unnatural* and *monstrous.*[58]

Shaftesbury's diatribe does much to concentrate our view of the posture of extreme skepticism. Like the critics of "novellistic" newspapers, memoirs, and natural histories who have been discussed in earlier chapters, Shaftesbury contends that the lure of the claim to historicity in these narratives is comparable to the enchantments of chivalric romance in a former age. And like those critics, he identifies this as a new brand of "faith," no less credulous for being concerned with anthropological rather than chivalric or Christian marvels, or for being held by modern virtuosos who are known to be skeptics and rumored to be atheists. Once again, finally, we see the familiar reversal whereby the skeptics are rendered gullible by those more skeptical than they.

6

TOWARD REALISM, THE AESTHETIC, AND HUMAN CREATIVITY

The evidence of this chapter—not only the "official" promulgation of rules for the composition of travel narratives but also the unofficial commentary that quickly surrounds the subject—contradicts the general view that the practical origins of the novel were unsupported by any self-conscious critical theory, stylistics, or "poetics."[59] In fact, the conceptual bases of naive empiricism and extreme skepticism are explicitly elaborated at the same time that they are experimentally put into practice. Theory develops in dialectical relation to genre as a supplementary discourse of detached commentary that is yet inseparable, in its own development, from the corollary process of genre formation. The fact that travel narrative provides the richest example of the interplay of critical theory and practice during this period may be due to its enthusiastic sponsorship by an institution and movement that were intensely interested in epistemology and method. But the development of other contemporary forms—spiritual autobiography, the familiar letter—also was accompanied by self-conscious "theory."[60] And if the resulting discourse sounds to the modern ear less "literary" than does the theory of travel narrative, this is perhaps because it is even more convinced of the profoundly functional importance of its concerns—for salvation, for socialization—than is that of the fledgling new science.

The early modern theory of the travel narrative clearly recapitulates the familiar pattern of epistemological double reversal, and it thereby helps crystallize what is misleading about the exclusive identification of novelistic discourse with the indirect discourse of self-conscious and parodic impersonation. For Mikhail Bakhtin's argument accounts for only one of the two major postures whose interaction constitutes the epistemological origins of the novel. And in neglecting the relatively direct mode of critique entailed in naive empiricism, it also neglects the more comprehensively dialectical character of those origins.[61] In one sense it is easy to understand this partiality. The critical indirection of extreme skepticism has a subtle and suggestive power that seems very different from the earnest and sometimes plodding didacticism of naive empiricism. But it is a mistake to view extreme skepticism as a higher stage in the evolution of the novel—not only a negation but a correction of naive empiricism and the authentic "fulfillment" of novelistic discourse. For extreme skepticism is itself a highly vulnerable posture: the fundamental opposition to romance idealism that it shares with—and derives from—naive empiricism is rendered quite equivocal by the simultaneous opposition to naive empiricism itself. How tenuous must be that secret sanctuary of truth, distinct both from romance and from too confident a historicity, which is defined by the metacritical act of double negation?

By arguing the inescapability of romance in true history, extreme skepticism appears also to pursue a far more radical conclusion, the unavailability of narrative truth as such. That this conclusion would be generally unacceptable to contemporaries is especially clear in "Christian skeptics" like William Okeley. For here the partial indebtedness of the extreme skeptical critique of true history to the traditional, religious critique of human sufficiency is unmistakable, and the critical negation necessarily entails the correlative positing of an absolute truth accessible to the mediations of figurative and parabolic narrative. But the narrative truth more typically posited by extreme skepticism is a secularized category that is distinct from the idealism both of Christianity and of romance, and it is bereft of any alternative model. As a result, extreme skepticism can easily seem not the final, teleological triumph of the revolt against romance idealism that was crudely engendered by naive empiricism, but the untenably negative midpoint between these two opposed positions, in constant danger of becoming each of them by turns. If naive historicity is too sanguine about its own powers of negating romance fiction, its critique is too skeptical about that possibility, and the parodic impersonation of the romance of true history risks being nothing more, in the end, than an allusive and playful affirmation of both.

For these reasons extreme skepticism is impelled by its own quandary to experiment with the notion that the inevitable presence of "romance" need not entail prevarication. And so the standard of truth by which Shaftesbury would correct the empirical reliance on brute factuality is a more generalized and universalized "truth of things," a gentle secularization of Christian truth which may be taught by "judicious lies" (or material figures) as well as by facts. The Aristotelian separation of history and poetry, the factual and the probable, the singular and the universal, is a revolutionary doctrine of great antiquity that lay like a time bomb in the cultural unconscious of the West until its "discovery" by Renaissance modernity.[62] Shaftesbury's experimental standard of universal truth in literature is thus both old and new, predating the Christian truth of the spirit yet returning, along with the new "spirituality" of literature itself, when Christian faith enters into its centuries-long abatement.

In the later eighteenth century, the rejuvenated Aristotelian notion of the universal truth of poetry will aid in the formulation of the modern belief in the autonomous realm of the aesthetic. And although thoroughly indebted to empirical epistemology, most of all for its argument that the several realms of knowledge are separable from each other, the belief in the autonomous aesthetic could gain ascendancy only when the coarser and more material vestiges of empirical thought—especially the claim to historicity—had been ejected by the body of knowledge which in modern thought is designated as the last and lonely refuge of transcendant spirit, the sphere of artistic experience. Doctrines of literary realism, which rise from the ruins of the claim to historicity, reformulate the problem of mediation for a world in which spirituality has ceased to represent another realm to which human materiality has only difficult and gratuitous access, and has become instead the capacity of human creativity itself. Realism gathers up and sophisticates the scattered threads of verisimilitude and probability that Renaissance writers had teased out of the *Poetics*. It validates literary creation for being not history but history-like, "true" to the only external reality that still makes a difference, but also sufficiently apart from it (hence "probable" and "universal") to be true to itself as well. The idea of realism exists to concede the accountability of art to a prior reality, without seeming to compromise the uniquely modern belief that such reality as it is answerable to already is internalized in art itself as a demystified species of spirituality.

Yet in writers of exceptional acuity, the autonomous aesthetic and the idea of realism can be seen to be lurking in the logic not only of extreme skepticism but even of naive empiricism. This can be said of the work of Daniel Defoe, who doggedly pursued the problem of the false claim to historicity for the better part of two decades. How can an author sincerely believe that he is telling the truth if he knows that he has invented the story to whose historicity he earnestly attests? In 1704, Defoe's rejection of the idea that such a contradictory device can mediate us to truth is unequivocal. Indeed, he "should stand convicted of a double Imposture, to forge a Story, and then preach Repentance to the Reader from a Crime greater than that I would have him repent of: endeavouring by a Lye to correct the Reader's Vices, and sin against Truth to bring the Reader off from sinning against Sence."[63] Yet the standard of historical truth, and the conviction of its rhetorical efficacy, are so powerful in Defoe's mind that he continues thereafter to make and to justify the false claim to historicity, although with ambivalence and accompanied by a variety of uneasy extenuations.

Shortly after the publication of *Robinson Crusoe* and in partial response to charges that its claim to historicity brands it a "Romance" and a "Lie," Defoe briefly speculates about the relation between history and narrative historicity in a way that makes suggestive inroads into the dilemma of quantitative completeness. Let us grant that a story is "in its Substance true." Yet how easy it is "to relate real Stories with innumerable Omissions and Additions: I mean, Stories which have a real Existence in Fact, but which by the barbarous Way of relating, become as romantick and false, as if they had no real Original."[64] The problem is endemic to the activity of reporting, for "nothing is more common, than to have two

Men tell the same Story quite differing one from another, yet both of them Eye-witnesses to the Fact related" (113). From this meditation on the relativity of narrative historicity it may seem a short step to the view that the claim to historicity means to assert not brute factuality—an unattainable ideal—but a relative fidelity of narration. And from this perspective, the relation between "true history" and "romance" will lose its significance as an absolute dichotomy, to be replaced by that distinction between the fact of being history, and the quality of being to a greater or lesser degree history-like, on which modern theories of realistic fiction are based. Of course the step is really an enormous one, and Defoe is not willing to take it. Instead he insists that however inescapable it may be, "this supplying a Story by Invention . . . is a sort of Lying that makes a great Hole in the Heart" (113).

The step cannot be taken because it would appear to deny the responsibility of narrative to a standard of truth that is separate from and higher than its own inventions. If stories cannot claim their historicity, they are romances, and cannot be taken seriously by writer or reader; they will not be "improvable" and they will fail to effect any moral and spiritual improvement. So instead of pursuing his innovative line of thought, Defoe falls back upon a more traditional defense, supported by the familiar arguments of casuistry and exegetical improvement, which seems to preserve the promise of a successful mediation. The invention of stories may be "a sort of lying," but *Robinson Crusoe* "is quite a different Case, and is always Distinguisht from this other Jesting with Truth . . . It is design'd and effectually turn'd for instructive and upright Ends, and has its Moral justly apply'd" (115–16). In other words, the use of fables is justified by the "moral and religious Improvement" they are able to mediate (sig. A6^r). In arguing this point, Defoe is content to call his own narrative "an allusive allogorick History," a category that includes biblical parables and *The Pilgrim's Progress* (115, 116). But are these "cases" really comparable to that of a false claim to historicity like *Robinson Crusoe's*?[65] Is it not one thing to say that the presence of a moral justifies telling a story that does not advertise its factual untruth, and quite another to say that it exculpates the teller who has made a point of claiming explicitly that his invented story is factually true? Is this not the very definition of "romance"? But perhaps the application of the moral constitutes a retraction of the lie, an admission that the "true history" is really a "fable" or an "allegory." Yet this dissolves the charge of romance from one direction only to reconstitute it from another, for we are still left with narrative that is factually untrue. Perhaps all romances can be justified in this way, as eminently conducive to truth so long as they tack on (as they tend in some fashion to do) an improving moral sometime before they are through. But if this is so, the crucial pedagogic distinction between true history and romance has evaporated before our eyes, and the claim to historicity, whether "true" or "false," stands revealed not only as an arbitrary convention but as one of very limited purpose.

Defoe's attempts to formulate a coherent theory that will comfortably accommodate the false claim to historicity lead in circles very similar to those just described in summary form.[66] They are frustrating discussions because as Defoe works to vindicate the false claim, there is an inevitable slippage in the meaning of the terms that are central to his inquiry. Meanings shift in order to avoid confronting logical contradiction, for conviction must inevitably fail if "true history"is required to include false claims to true history. Defoe's response to this impasse is mixed. In these discursive writings its resolution seems to involve both the vindication, and the repudiation, of the false claim to historicity as a path toward truth. In his "histories" of individual lives, the claim persists along with the emphasis upon the end of moral and spiritual improvement.[67] When the claim is least insistent, Defoe goes so far as to assert that improvement may proceed equally well with or without the historicity of the narrative.[68] And yet, so far from having become a vestigial remnant in these works, the posture of historicity suffuses even those in which the prefatory claim is made only diffidently, in the form of the framing editorial fiction and its circumstantial details of documentation. In these later works, the dilemma of quantitative completeness appears less problematic to Defoe, and he will sometimes even announce the impunity with which he has emended vicious details, the better to serve the end of improvement. Moreover, he defends those instances of vice that still remain, not (as we might expect) by arguing that true history contains vice as well as virtue, but by recapitulating, sometimes testily, the Miltonic advocacy of the survey of vice and the scanning of error.[69] Yet again it is only within the continuing fiction of an original and authentic document edited by another hand that his apparent documentary laxity can have any meaning. In short, it is as though Defoe now feels the need to restrain the presumptuous historicity of the individual protagonists he has invented by announcing the priority and self-sufficiency of moral improvement and its overarching pattern. Even so, the reader may well sense that the historicity of his characters has been quietly preserved within the circumstantiality both of their lives and of the way in which their lives are presented to us.

The persistence of the claim to historicity—the difficulty of overcoming the false claim and the surprising coexistence that it can achieve with the ongoing appeal to the overarching pattern—can be explained at least in part if we recall that to claim historicity for one's story is not only to assert the evidence of the human senses but also to disavow the pride of human fabrication. It is God who wrote the history of the world; assuming the status of a historian therefore reconciles the author to his own inventiveness by subsuming it under that of the Author. By these terms even the false claim to historicity may be experienced as a gesture of humility. In fact it is of some interest to note the surprising alliance between the Protestant and the empirical distrust of traditional modes of mediation, which for a while threw up a joint bulwark against the inexorable validation of human creativity in early modern culture. Of course in many ways the idea of a scientific opposition to creativity is not only unexpected but insupportable. And the late-medieval emergence of analogies between divine creativity and artistic "creation" is surely related to the first efforts to devise a system both of patents for scientific invention and of copyrights for literary authorship.[70] Nevertheless the affinity between Protestant and secular attitudes at this time is, as Max Weber's celebrated thesis has argued, as rich as it is contradictory.[71]

For these reasons it seems fair to say that the ascendancy of the claim to historicity was overdetermined by the historical conjunction of two antipathetic "systems," which imposed upon literary productions analogous demands that they be disowned or fetishized. The claim enacts a fetishism first of all in the ritual and Christian sense of the term. It issues from the culminating conflict between idealist and materialist, theist and humanist, standards, and is a negative response to the rhetorical question, "Can a *human* creation be true?" But in a second and more decisive movement, the claim to historicity enacts an empirical and capitalist fetishism, reflecting the nascent tension between what a later age would call humanist and scientific, subjectivist and objectivist, standards. And here the equally rhetorical question to which the claim responds is, "Can a human *creation* have value?" From this perspective, the author who asserts the historical truth of his narrative validates it by alienating it from himself, thereby stamping it as a documentary object whose value depends upon its autonomy, its separability from himself.[72]

One effect of the vulgar belief that the seventeenth-century distrust of figurative expression is a strictly "Puritan" phenomenon is to conceal the hostility to human creation that lies at the heart of empirical-capitalist thought itself, and that achieves its first and crudest manifestation in the claim to historicity. Very soon this hostility will be mediated and disguised by a more subtle mechanism, which reconciles the modern cult of human creativity with a profound and self-subsistent process of alienation. This is the posttypographical notion that an idea does not really belong to you until you alienate it through publication.[73] Before the existence of patents and copyrights, the value of ideas was preserved by the maintenance of secrecy and by strictly private and elitist consumption. But once ideas can be owned, their value lies in disowning them by making them public—not only in the economic sense of the creation of surplus value, but also in the sense that the very meaning of conceptual ownership depends upon the knowledge of others of your ownership, upon their capacity to know your ideas without also being able to extract material profit from them.

Thus capitalism learns to embrace creativity by discovering its alienability. The reconciliation of Protestant thought to human creativity is finally more absolute than this, but it has a comparable indirection that is characteristic of the secularization process itself. One convenient guide to this process is the change in the use of the idea of divine providence. The entrance of the otherworldly into human affairs is of course a common belief in Christian culture. In story it is registered most often (as we have seen) by plot discontinuities and by narrative intrusions that announce the uncompromising intent of God's overarching pattern.[74] And the insistent invocation of providence in the works of this period might seem to imply, as some critics have argued, a view of the age as one of pervasive and abiding Christian belief.[75] But as I have implied with respect to the Restoration apparition narratives, the very vigor of providential argument, the polemical urgency and extremity of its presentation, signifies not faith but a crisis of faith. Indeed, it is the nature of such a crisis to evoke not only a straightforward skepticism, but also a contradictory effort to employ the tools of skepticism—the claim to historicity—to justify what hitherto might have been "taken on faith" and tacitly assumed to be true.

But it is possible to go further than this, for the currency of the doctrine of providence may itself be seen as the contradictory sign of secularization crisis. Only with the Reformation did theology undertake to correlate so closely the everyday contingencies of this world with an active and intelligible divine justice.[76] Ostensibly (and sincerely) an acknowledgment of God's unknowable power, the doctrine of providence also expresses the will to accommodate divinity to a plan more accessible to human rationality. In fact, the impulse to detect God's immediate and tangible effects might be thought to convey not only a conviction of, but also an uncertainty about, his presence. But such an argument becomes fully plausible only when the doctrine of providence becomes concentrated, as it were, into the doctrine of poetic justice. First formulated during the Restoration, the doctrine of poetic justice has recently been described as a "mirroring of God's justice in literary form" and therefore as a sign of widespread belief in providential justice.[77] But it is more likely that the artistic convention of poetic justice will become important for a culture in which divine justice is felt to be in jeopardy. For whether or not its practitioners conceive it in these terms, poetic justice operates most profoundly not as a representation of the divine but as a replacement of it. Indeed, this is one perspective from which to understand the unacceptability, to a Christian culture, of the Aristotelian conception of poetry. As Francis Bacon wrote, "Because true history propoundeth the successes and issues of actions not so agreeable to the merits of virtue and vice, therefore poesy feigns them more just in retribution, and more according to revealed providence."[78]

To observe that people of the Restoration felt the need to improve on providence is not in itself to distinguish them from their predecessors. For most Christians in all periods have permitted themselves to recognize that what is noteworthy about providence is that it *cannot* be relied on to be just—at least not in this world. "The world is so vile a thing," wrote Samuel Butler, "that Providence commonly makes Fooles, and Knaves happy, and good men miserable in it, to let us know, there is no great Difference between Happiness and misery here." According to a contemporary of Butler,

Affliction (if properly such) is an argument of Divine Affection; and they that miss of troubles temporal, may doubt of happiness eternal . . . And to me there is not a stronger Argument [than earthly injustice] . . . for a general Day of Judgement, and Recompence in a World to come . . . For if Goodness ought to be rewarded, and Vice punished, as all allow, then there must be a time allotted in which it shall receive this reward.

What is therefore unusual about the Restoration is that it should have elaborated this special method—poetic justice—of compensating for the deficiencies of providential justice, rather than having continued to rely on the traditional and orthodox method of the afterlife. As D. P. Walker has shown, it was during this same period that the reality of hell and its "vindictive" justice began to be questioned openly and explicitly. The relevance of the doctrine of poetic justice to an unmindfulness of God's great and final system of equity was clear enough to Samuel Richardson, at least by the time he was engaged in the defense not of Pamela's rewarded virtue but of Clarissa's more saintly sacrifice:

And after all, what is the *poetical justice* so much contended for by some, as the generality of writers have managed it, but another sort of dispensation than that with which God, by Revelation, teaches us, He has thought fit to exercise mankind; whom placing here only in a state of probation, he hath so intermingled good and evil, as to necessitate us to look forward to a more equal dispensation of both.[79]

So there is good reason to see these years as a critical period in which the orthodox spirituality of an equitable afterlife was being replaced by the aesthetic spirituality of an equitable denouement. At the end of the seventeenth century, Jeremy Collier's notorious attack on the immorality of the stage provoked from its many defenders the Aristotelian doctrine of *catharsis*: drama raises the vicious and antisocial passions only in order to purge and quell them by art. One hundred years later, thoughtful readers of the novel of sensibility suspected that this might be the function of art with respect to the virtues as well. For "in these writings our sensibility is strongly called forth without any possibility of exerting

itself in virtuous action, and those emotions, which we shall never feel
again with equal force, are wasted without advantage . . . We must not
fancy ourselves charitable, when we are only pleasing our imagination."
According to another reader, "In the enthusiasm of sentiment there is
much the same danger as in the enthusiasm of religion, of substituting
certain impulses and feelings of what may be called a visionary kind, in
the place of real practical duties." Yet another remarked, "I am afraid lest
the same eye which is so prone to give its tributary tear to the well-told
history of fancied woe, should be able to look upon real misery without
emotion, because its tale is told without plot, incident, or ornament."[80]
In these apprehensions lie the seeds of the Brechtian insight that art in the
modern period seeks to replace not only religious spirituality but responsible action. With the triumph of "aesthetic truth" over naive empiricism,
literary fictions are able to have value without laying claim to being
"real," and the end of literature has become not teaching goodness but
being "good" in itself.

In the early modern "aestheticizing of the spirit"—in the assumption
by art of those tasks which traditionally were undertaken by religious
belief and experience—the idea of the drama has a special role. The self-
conscious analogy between individual author and overarching Author in
writers like Congreve and Fielding probably owes some of its force to the
theatrical experience of both men, and to their familiarity with the common, and increasingly volatile, figure of the human dramatist as an
improving divinity.[81] But if art can be said to "replace" religion in the
mediation of spirituality during this period, narrative may also be said to
replace dramatic form as the preeminent literary mode—that is, as the
primary means by which that artistic mediation is accomplished. How
does this perspective on the origins of the novel illuminate its epistemological foundations?[82]

Modern critics know, as Restoration critics often did not, that the rigid
"unities of time and place" play no part in Aristotle's conception of
dramatic unity. But the modern persistence of the term "neoclassicism"
to describe the broad doctrine of which "the rules" are the most notorious component may prevent us from realizing that the emergence of the
rules, like that of poetic justice, represents not so much a renewal of
traditional standards and beliefs as the onset of crisis and the ingenuous
experimentation (although contemporaries thought differently) with
new modes of thought. The insistence on the preservation of the two
unities in Restoration dramatic theory and practice should be seen as a
formal analogue of the naive claim to historicity in Restoration narrative.
In some ways even more extreme in their devotion to literalistic notions
of credibility, the unities of time and place entail the ideal of a precise
correspondence between the circumstantial conditions of the events that
are fictionally depicted and those that govern their actual depiction. And

to understand both the unities and the claim to historicity, we must look not to classical authority but to the empirical revolution in epistemology. Thus Congreve, evincing the cautious opposition to romance flights characteristic of the extreme skeptic, is able to validate his narrative activity in *Incognita* by drawing attention to his maintenance not of historicity but of the unities.[83]

But in the very articulation of drama's superiority to narrative—"there is no possibility of giving that life to the writing or repetition of a story which it has in the action"—Congreve also intimates one reason for its relative decline. For in an age that far more thoroughly and definitively than ever before identifies truth with the evidence of the senses, the unmediated access to "life" itself that dramatic presentation promises to provide us is much too vulnerable to disconfirmation. Aristotle himself had cautioned that certain things are best left to narrative: epic "affords more opening for the improbable, the chief factor in the marvellous, because in it the agents are not visibly before one. The scene of the pursuit of Hector would be ridiculous on the stage . . . but in the poem the absurdity is overlooked." But in echoing and elaborating on these ancient words, Dryden's Lisideius reflects a preoccupation with matters of visual demonstration and empirically based belief that is recognizably modern:

For what is more ridiculous than to represent an army with a drum and five men behind it, all which the hero of the other side is to drive in before him; or to see a duel fought, and one slain with two or three thrusts of the foils, which we know are so blunted that we might give a man an hour to kill another in good earnest with them . . . The words of a good writer, which describe it lively, will make a deeper impression of belief in us than all the actor can persuade us to when he seems to fall dead before us . . . When we see death represented, we are convinced it is but fiction; but when we hear it related, our eyes (the strongest witnesses) are wanting, which might have undeceived us.[84]

Thus the fundamental capacity of oral presentation for self-authentication—the fact of physical presence—at a crucial historical moment becomes also the ground of its susceptibility to invalidation. Printed narrative, by contrast, substitutes for this vulnerable sort of presence the incontestable factuality, the typographical "fetish," of documentary objecthood.

The argument of Lisideius impels Neander toward the rudimentary formulation of a psychology of artistic response, which later on will be developed more fully by Samuel Johnson. In making this counterargument, both Johnson and Dryden's Neander discredit the two unities and affirm, although in different ways, the essentially "imaginative" nature of the artistic experience.[85] This is very far, however, from a general repudiation of empirical standards. On the contrary, it is only by virtue of a complete and implicit assent to the empirical notion of truth as the evidence of the senses that modern culture became sufficiently tolerant of artful fictions to pass beyond the bare recognition of their incredibility and to conceive the possibility of their validation in other terms. The discrimination of two kinds of truth is once again both old and new, both Aristotelian and uniquely modern. And once again the modern, autonomous realm of the spirit enjoins a secularized sort of belief—not in an ineffably greater power that lies beyond us, but in the actuality of the fictive; in Coleridge's words, "that willing suspension of disbelief for the moment, which constitutes poetic faith."[86] In this way the ongoing materialization of truth in modern times encounters a mild recalcitrance. For if the aesthetic realm is to undertake the role once performed by religion, it must be permitted to practice its own, admittedly more gentle, forms of magic, its ritualization not of life but of art. Yet, although aesthetic spirituality or "poetic faith" thus provided drama with a solution to the problem that had occasioned its replacement by narrative, the novel, once established, maintained its domination of the field by incorporating that solution within its own conception of truth as realism.

II

QUESTIONS OF VIRTUE

— *Four* —

The Destabilization of Social Categories

ARISTOCRATIC IDEOLOGY

The traditional terms of social distinction in early modern England—
"degree," "estate," "order," "rank"—are variously based on an idea of
status derived from the personal possession, or nonpossession, of honor.
And honor is a quality that points, through the crucial mediation of
repute, both outward and inward. On the one hand, it is a function of
ancestry and lineage; less obligatory, but likely to confirm the primary
facts of ancestry, are other external circumstances like wealth and political power. On the other hand, honor is an essential and inward property
of its possessor, that which the conditional or extrinsic signifiers of honor
exist to signify. In this respect, honor is equivalent to an internal element
of "virtue." The notion of honor as a unity of outward circumstance and
inward essence is the most fundamental justification for the hierarchical
stratification of society by status, and it is so fundamental as to be largely
tacit. What it asserts is that the social order is not circumstantial and
arbitrary, but corresponds to and expresses an analogous, intrinsic moral
order. This assumption lies at the heart of what in the following pages I
will be calling "aristocratic ideology."[1]

According to aristocratic ideology, honor as virtue is an inherited
characteristic. On Aristotle's authority, "Those who are sprung from
better ancestors are likely to be better men, for nobility is excellence of
race." James I claimed that "virtue followeth oftest Noble bloud. The
worthines of their antecessours craveth a reverent regard to be had unto
them." Moreover, external appearance itself seemed to substantiate the
notion that honor is truly intrinsic, an inherited trait in the biological as

well as the genealogical sense of the term, for the privileged also tended to be physically more distinguished—taller, heavier, better developed—than the rest of society. As (Mary) Delarivière Manley observed, "It is easie to judge why Persons of Quality have generally more Penetration, Vivacity and Spirit, than those of a meaner Rank: For . . . good Nourishment, and the Juice of Nice Meats, which mixes with the Blood, and other Humours of the Body, subtilizes them, and renders them more proper for the Functions of Nature." This circumstance was reinforced by sumptuary legislation that sought to regulate the extravagance with which the different social degrees might clothe their bodies. As Sir Thomas Elyot sensibly remarked, "We be men and nat aungels, wherfore we knowe nothinge but by outwarde significations. Honour, wherto reuerence pertayneth, is . . . the rewarde of vertue, whiche honour is but the estimation of people, which estimacion is nat euery where perceyued, but by some exterior signe . . . or excellencie in vesture." A more formal means to this end was the heraldic system of recording genealogies by the blazoning of arms, a medieval practice given new life in the fifteenth and sixteenth centuries with the institution of the College of Heralds and their periodic visitations. Edmund Bolton called armor and blazon "the marks by which gentlemen are known, first from the ignoble and then one from the other." And William London asked, "How shall greatness and Nobility of birth be distinguished and snacht from the pretences of ignoble persons without this?"[2]

Now, any status hierarchy that is based on a principle of direct genealogical descent must confront the facts of demography, which militate against the belief in the purity of the blood line that is implicit in aristocratic ideology. A patrilineal system of inheritance like that traditional to English culture cannot generate a male line that will be continuous and self-sufficient over time, for demographical constraints ensure that in a stationary population, forty percent of all families will fail to produce a male heir. Attrition in the direct male line is therefore a complication that aristocratic ideology is obliged to accommodate, and it does so by several means of "patriline repair": more distant male relatives may be assimilated to the line as "surrogate heirs," and the husbands of female members of the line may even be absorbed into it, a process facilitated by a change of name. Related institutional and legal fictions might be used to resolve inconsistencies in the status hierarchy, the causes of which are not strictly demographic but which tend to occur from time to time even in the most stable societies—like the rise of the extraordinary to great wealth or political power. Thus the royal grant or sale of fictitious genealogies and titles of nobility to ignoble families reasserted the integrity of honor by reuniting status with wealth and power. We have already seen, with respect to questions of truth, that the transmutation of lineage is accomplished most effortlessly in the absence of written documentation. Nevertheless, social fictions like these played a vital role in stabilizing medieval scribal culture as well, where their tacit efficacy depended also on a judicious resistance to overuse. And it is instructive to compare these social conventions to the intellectual and literary conventions with which they were contemporary. The commonplace of "true nobility," for example, when used in moderation, also served to buttress the laws of correspondence by allowing for their lapses, since it gave sanction to the rise of the humble to worldly eminence by understanding that rise to be an expression of a singular ability and virtue. The alteration of names in romance marks both a radical discontinuity and a more just signification. And the romance convention of discovered parentage mediates the threat of noncorrespondence by problematically isolating physical beauty and true nobility apart from inherited nobility, only to reconfirm the wholeness of honor at the end of the story.[3]

In the following chapters I will argue that the gradual discrediting of aristocratic honor, the resolution of its tacit unity into the problematic relation of rank and virtue, birth and worth, was accompanied by the accelerated mobilization of social, intellectual, legal, and institutional fictions whose increasingly ostentatious use signaled their incapacity to serve the ideological ends for which they were designed. Some of these fictions became outmoded; others were transmuted, through their own acceleration, into servants of other ideologies. In a similar fashion, I will argue, the novel emerged in early modern England as a new literary fiction designed to engage the social and ethical problems the established literary fictions could no longer mediate—which is to say, both represent and conceal—with conviction. But at this point it is no longer sufficient to refer so easily to "romance conventions" and "aristocratic ideology" as though they were straightforward and unchanging in nature. The origins of the novel and of its associated ideologies must be seen as the culmination of an extended preexistence, and their truly innovative status will become intelligible only against a backdrop that highlights both the continuity and the differences of what came before. What is the ideological character of the narrative fictions the novel replaces? What social conditions do the novel's precursors exist to explain, and how are we to understand the precursory relationship between these phenomena and the origins of the novel? As with questions of truth, once again I must apologize to specialists for the speed and superficiality of this survey.

2

PRECURSOR REVOLUTIONS: THE GREEK ENLIGHTENMENT

According to its most celebrated modern exponent, the stability of non-literate culture reflects a method of classification in which nature and culture are conceived as analogous but separate systems coexisting without interpenetration. Natural species and social groups are seen as "two systems of differences": the crucial analogy is drawn not between particular elements of either system but between formal relationships of difference within each system. By this means "social groups are distinguished from one another but they retain their solidarity as parts of the same whole." Nature is able to stabilize culture, "to serve as a system of reference for the interpretation and rectification of the changes taking place in" social groups. If the analogy were made more directly, this stability would be sacrificed, for it "would no longer be that clan 1 differs from clan 2 as for instance the eagle differs from the bear but rather that clan 1 is like the eagle and clan 2 like the bear." Thus intermixed with cultural elements, the natural system would lose the essential separateness required to reflect back a perpetual and unchanging differential.[4]

In Lévi-Strauss's analysis, the social rule of exogamy reinforces the solidarity of social groups which results from this method of classification, because it binds them together by their differences. Endogamy, by contrast, reinforces the unity of single groups at the expense of greater social solidarity. It enjoins groups to define themselves by particular natural images regarded as hereditary rather than by their relation to other groups. And it disables exogamous exchange by fueling the temptation to think of the sisters and daughters of other groups as of another "species." Myth serves the same ends as does the rule of exogamy. Lévi-Strauss's best-known demonstration of this is his interpretation of the Oedipus myth as the imaginative overcoming of the contradiction between the experience of human birth and the theory of autochthony. The myth "solves" this problem by establishing a differential analogy between experience (or social kinship) and theory (or natural cosmology). Each system confirms the other by being internally contradictory in the same way: the destabilizing effects of the primary contradiction are avoided, and the contradiction within the social system is validated by reference to that within the natural. We need not be fully convinced by this ingenious analysis of the Oedipus myth to appreciate its capacity to suggest the homogeneity of narrative and social fictions within the greater unity of nonliterate cognition.[5]

The coming of literacy is only one of the factors that destabilizes nonliterate culture; others are demographic change and social mobility. Already in the Homeric era, the conflict between Agamemnon and Achilles reflects the tension between the inherited honor of the *aristoi* ("the best"), which is taken to entail first of all the warrior virtue of success in combat, and the more individualized honor of *aretē,* the mark of demonstrated military achievement. Beginning in the eighth century B.C., there emerges a different sort of "aristocracy," the *eupatridai* (or "wellborn"), whose honor is attached much more exclusively to landed wealth. With coinage and the spread of commerce, the phenomenon of "new wealth" aggravates these already established tensions between divergent types of elevated status. "Wealth has thrown lineage into confusion," says the sixth-century poet Theognis of Megara. "We will not take wealth in exchange for our *aretē.*" Yet, "for the multitude of mankind there is only one virtue: / Money." The transient tyrannies of this period were usually led by wealthy parvenus whose economic reforms sought to win the support of the poor against the traditional nobility. In Athens, bitter conflict between the *eupatridai* and the peasant farmers of Attica culminated in the reduction of the latter to the status of slaves or share-croppers, and, on the eve of civil war, in the radical reforms of Solon, Pisistratus, and Cleisthenes. Through Solon's reforms, income alone, not birth, became the legal basis for political participation. One result was a great increase in upward mobility and a successful stabilization of status inconsistency through the validation of new wealth by greater political power and honors. Of course the Solonic reforms also helped weaken the ties of kinship and family. The individual citizen became the recognized legal unit; loyalties to lineage were slowly complicated by commitments to the polis or the deme. Yet the attitudes and structures of Athenian democracy coexisted with the institution of slavery, an implacable fate which, according to Moses Finley, "no man, woman, or child regardless of status or wealth, could be sure to escape in case of war or some other unpredictable and uncontrollable emergency."[6]

One register of these momentous social changes is found in the fifth-century, Sophoclean transformation of the Oedipus myth. In formulating the paradigm of the romance convention of discovered parentage—what Freud would call the "family romance"—*Oedipus the King* transposes the terms of the contradiction between nature and culture and thereby ensures that it will be insoluble. The stability of the natural system of species is replaced by the "natural" ties of kinship and the blood line. The "cultural" system comes to be represented, in turn, by the mobile individuality of one of its single elements; conflict cannot be resolved, because the two coordinate systems are not analogous but intermixed and inseparable. Even by representing the latter "system," Sophocles gives credence to a mode of asserting human origin and identity which plays no part in nonliterate cognition, the criterion of autonomous and individual worth. Doubly deceived about his origins, Oedipus at first has no reason to fear the imaginary, Corinthian kinship; then tries to escape it; but finally is driven to renounce not only its particular

legitimacy but the authority of lineage itself to validate worth. To be the
"child of Fortune" alone is, for him, to be indebted to no one, and he now
displays the false humility of one who owes his "honor" only to himself:

> Keep up
> your heart, Jocasta. Though I'm proved a slave,
> thrice slave, and though my mother is thrice slave,
> you'll not be shown to be of lowly lineage.
>
> . . . .
>
> Perhaps she is ashamed of my low birth,
> for she has all a woman's high-flown pride.
> But I account myself a child of Fortune,
> beneficent Fortune, and I shall not be
> dishonoured.

In the myth, nature stabilizes culture; in the drama, the "nature" of
divine oracle can only punish cultural aberrancy, and the fantasy that
Oedipus will be found a slave bespeaks not only his antigenealogical
impudence but a real possibility in Greek social experience which aptly
expresses the terrible consequence of Oedipus's flight from his fated
lineage. Yet Sophocles also balances us on the great divide defined by the
jointly Delphic and Socratic injunction to "know thyself," the divide
between what Nietzsche calls the premoral and the moral periods of
humanity, between the valuation of an action according to its "consequences" or external effects and the valuation of that same action according to its "origins" or internal intentions. Although we are invited to
sympathize with Oedipus's ignorance as a mark of his innocence, we are
more firmly enjoined to condemn the Socratic will to self-knowledge for
what it is—a plague upon Oedipus's people—and to weigh the justice of
his fate by reference not to his inner state but to the havoc he has wreaked.
And the status inconsistency that Sophocles' fiction exists to mediate is
only incidentally the disruptive rise of "new men" like Oedipus, but
comprehensively the death of the gods and the destruction of the kinship
system.[7]

In other fictions of the Greek Enlightenment, less tangibly attuned
than that of Sophocles to what is being lost, mobility and individual
ambition are likely to seem a force for stabilizing mutability as well as for
aggravating it. Plato provides a highly self-conscious example of such a
fiction, a "myth" of social lineage, in the *Republic*. Soon after formulating the initial hypothesis of a model commonwealth in which the workings of justice may be rendered visible, it occurs to Socrates that the
republic will function most smoothly if a kind of natural division of labor
is permitted to flourish. Each person should be allowed to do "the one
thing for which he is naturally fitted." The first task will be to select out
those "guardians" of the republic who will have a "native aptitude" in the

art of war. The next task will be to subdivide, again according to natural aptitude, the caste of guardians into rulers and auxiliaries. Each selection process will be followed by intensive social reinforcement. Socrates' aim here is to anchor the cultural distinctions of caste division on what he regards as natural differences in aptitude, but for this very reason he now announces the need for a "convenient fiction" of the sort the poets used to tell, one that will be believed by the entire community. It is in fact a myth of autochthonous origins: "I shall try to convince . . . the whole community, that all that nurture and education which we gave them was only something they seemed to experience as it were in a dream. In reality they were the whole time down inside the earth, being moulded and fostered . . . and at last, when they were complete, the earth sent them up from her womb into the light of day." The heart of the myth is its Hesiodic allegory of metals. The several natural castes are determined by the sort of metal—gold, silver, iron, or brass—the gods have mixed in their respective memberships, but these will not necessarily correspond to family lineages. The painful consequences of this crucial fact will be enjoined upon the rulers as fully as upon the lower castes: "If a child of their own is born with an alloy of iron or brass, they must, without the smallest pity, assign him the station proper to his nature and thrust him out among the craftsmen or the farmers."[8]

In the guise of an archaic chthonic myth, Socrates has fashioned a stealthy demystification of archaic culture. "Nature" does not stabilize the "culture" of lineage and kinship relations; on the contrary, it programmatically destabilizes those relationships in service to a revolutionary criterion of natural aptitude that may be autonomous of, even in conflict with, the natural ties of kinship. His convenient fiction, turning the materials of myth against themselves, supports a meritocratic social program whose claim to naturalness is grounded not in a parallel order of nature, nor in the "nature" of kin relations, but in a notion of inborn individual merit. Such a notion is socially unacceptable; hence the need for the social fiction. The general purpose of Plato's republic is to articulate an idea of justice that envisions each part's exercise of its natural function or "virtue" within an ordered whole. Specified to the realm of the social whole, this doctrine envisions a revolutionary method of stabilizing status inconsistency by accommodating external to internal, position to capacity. The "functional" notion of virtue as the natural aptitude for doing what one therefore does can easily be turned around and used to justify an existing social stratification, and some version of this was common enough in medieval political theory; but the Platonic formulation has a rather different import.[9]

So once lineage is abstracted from its limited and instrumental role in the kinship systems of nonliterate culture, it becomes an ambiguous quantity, elevated to a preeminent authority but also vulnerable, under changing social conditions, to a powerful current of subversion. The ancient Greek association of aristocratic honor with military "virtue" persists in the etymological connection between Roman *virtus* and specifically male achievement. In Roman antiquity the past is sacred, most of all the legendary event of the founding of Rome itself. *Auctoritas* is the right and capacity to "augment" (*augere*) the foundations, and it is obtained by lineal descent and transmission, according to Hannah Arendt, "from those who had laid the foundations for all things to come, the ancestors, whom the Romans therefore called the *maiores*." Consequently *auctoritas* is also an attribute of the elder or the aristocrat, inherited and consecrated by historical tradition. In reality the aristocratic *nobiles* of the republic were a hybrid governing elite born of a constitutional compromise in the fifth and fourth centuries B.C. which had countered the growing status inconsistency of parvenu plebeians by giving them a substantial share in patrician powers. Yet the resulting patriarchal oligarchy, consecrated in turn by tradition and *mos maiorum,* by the second century ruled Rome with all the authority of the Ciceronian maxim that "what is done by precedent is done by right." But public office was not entirely inaccessible to the merely meritorious, as the upward mobility of the most famous *novus homo,* Cicero himself, makes clear. Because the exclusive validation of the power of the *nobiles* by the attribution of *auctoritas* left to Cicero the demonstration of mere *virtus* through *fortuna,* he learned to challenge aristocratic ideology by dividing the moral authority of nobility from its conventional, aristocratic usage, and to argue that admission to the Senate should depend upon "industria ac virtus." Cicero's legitimation of the *virtus* of the *novus homo* was soon echoed by Seneca's *Epistula XLIV,* the *locus classicus* of the argument that justice commends the rise of "true nobility" to social eminence. And although Cicero was by no means a unique case during the republican period, the *novus homo exemplum* nonetheless had a paradoxically stabilizing effect similar to that exerted, as I have already remarked, by the commonplace of true nobility.[10]

The ambivalent relationship between the *novus homo exemplum* and the *auctoritas* of tradition is inscribed in the complex attitude, both pious and emulous, of Roman civilization itself toward its Greek ancestry. The greatest poetic achievement of Roman antiquity narrates Rome's foundation, and offers the example of itself, as a *translatio* of empire and the arts westward from Greece to Rome. The wanderings of Aeneas parallel the precedent quest of the Greek hero Odysseus, beginning in the conclusion of the *Iliad* and in the future founder's defeat by the military superiority of the Greeks. But Virgil's submission to Hellenic preeminence in the *Aeneid* is one of those virtuous acts of piety that turn out, like his hero's careful preservation of the household gods, to augment a definitively Roman authority and to proclaim to posterity a strictly Roman glory.

In the "Greek romances" there is a comparable concern with the physical and social mobility of the individual, which scholars have connected with the volatility of Hellenistic social relations. These very disparate narratives also share an Ovidian preoccupation with the metamorphoses of love, so that travel, love, and social change are ingeniously intertwined as though to suggest their interchangeability as emblematic experiences of mutability. As Madeleine de Scudéry observed in a later age of romance, "The Sea is the Scene most proper to make great changes in, and . . . some have named it the Theater of inconstancie." But not only are voyages of extraordinary vicissitude—disguise, shipwreck, imprisonment, capture by pirates and brigands, enslavement—precipitated and complicated by love in the Greek romances. The transformative powers of love are also explicitly compared to these more externalized metamorphoses.[11]

In Longus's tale, Daphnis and Chloe, abandoned as infants on a country estate, are suckled by goat and sheep and adopted by goatherd and shepherd, who suspect their elevated birth but raise them as rustics, the suggestion of theriomorphy thus serving as a figure for the status inconsistency of their pastoral descent. Eros, the winged boy, both torments and protects the children, whose love for each other so far survives the several complications of the story that it facilitates the eventual discovery of their true parentage and the removal of all apparent obstacles to their marriage. Around the time of the Greek romances, Apuleius was telling the Latin tale of Cupid and Psyche, a princess so beautiful that mortals neglect the sacred rites of Venus to worship her instead. Incensed at this upstart mortal, Venus orders Cupid to transport Psyche downward, to inflame her with love for the most debased and monstrous of humankind. Apollo also predicts that she will marry a destructive beast, feared even by the gods, and her despairing parents abandon her on a mountaintop. But Cupid himself is the monster: he transports her to his palace and anonymously impregnates her there to the extreme envy of Psyche's sisters, who rightly suspect that the theriomorphic descent is really a theomorphic elevation. Throughout the tale, Apuleius uses the spice of social emulation in this way to season the physical and supernatural transformations that compose the plot of a story which readers also know concerns the awesome powers of love over the soul. Thus the anger of Venus at Psyche, enacted through her imposition of a series of seemingly impossible labors, is also expressed as an apprehension at "unequal marriages" and a deep resentment that her "family-tree" and "rank will suffer from this wedding with a mortal." But Jove intercedes, Psyche is elevated to immortality with a draught of ambrosia, and love becomes not an agent of mutability but a principle of consistency.[12]

Two features of these romances seem especially noteworthy in the present context. First, in sacrificing the stabilizing separation of nature from culture that Lévi-Strauss associates with mythic narrative, their plots also gain the use of a flexible and extended chain of natural-cultural signifiers for transformation (theomorphy, theriomorphy, physical mobility, disguise, love, marriage, social mobility) whose links can themselves be transformed into each other, so that divinization may be specified to an amatory ascent, and love may be emplaced as the upward mobility of the meritorious. But second, the crucial links in this transformational chain have a paradoxical potential, for they are able not only to overcome the condition of instability and inconsistency but also to aggravate it.

3

PRECURSOR REVOLUTIONS:
THE TWELFTH-CENTURY RENAISSANCE

An instructive parallel can be drawn between the literate techniques of the Greek romances and the demystifying mode of ancient Hebrew culture. The experience of ceaseless physical mobility intensified the Jewish association of moral authority with the state of being "deracinated rather than autochthonic." The Hebrew insistence on paternity and lineage demythologizes the nonliterate myths of autochthony, replacing one mode of stability with a historicized substitute. By the same token, instability acquires a genealogical definition: Original Sin is the sin of the father. Yet in one important respect the Christian Gospel works directly against this Jewish inheritance, opposing the kinship affiliations of both nonliterate and Jewish culture by encouraging the spiritualizing replacement of all kinship ties, including the paternal. "For whosoever shall do the will of my Father which is in heaven," said Jesus, "the same is my brother, and sister, and mother." "And every one that hath forsaken houses, or brethren, or sisters, or father, or mother, or wife, or children, or lands, for my name's sake, shall receive an hundredfold, and shall inherit everlasting life." And the antifamilial implications of the Gospel message were massively reinforced by the early Church's strict prohibition of marriage degrees and by other methods of frustrating familial inheritance. In another respect, however, the Christian story strengthened the family romance and its fundamental if ambiguous grounding in the kinship system. Jesus is a child of lowest descent, born in a place almost theriomorphic in its humility, his disciples are drawn from the common people, and his end is that of a degraded beast or criminal. But he is also a romance foundling whose real parentage is incidentally discovered by marks and signs and who ascends at the end to reassume his proper place beside his father (even as the mildness of his reign also promises to cancel the harshness of his father's lineage).[13]

Among the social factors that contribute to the rise of romance after the first Christian millennium, the most important is the feudalization of European culture. Because feudal services to the lord were seen as indivisible in nature, partible methods of inheritance were deemed unacceptable for the passing on of the fief, and male primogeniture, which found no place in Roman law or Germanic custom, soon became very common. On the Continent the feudal nobility amounted to a paradoxical "new aristocracy." Elevated and ennobled for tenurial services as much as for birth, these noblemen were situated at the head of a line whose principles of strict and stable descent, demographically unfulfillable, only institutionalized a stealthy social mobility. The dominant direction of mobility was downward. Over time, royal support of the great feudal magnates deepened the gulf between them and the lower nobility, eroding the ability of these *hoblereaux* or squireens to survive independently of the great ones from whom they in turn held land in fief. In the case of these declining nobles, blood was severed from wealth and tenurial status. In the case of the younger sons of the new aristocracy, blood was dismissed even more flagrantly by disinheritance consequent upon the rule of primogeniture. Discouraged from marrying by paternal fears of dissipating the estate through marriage jointures (or dowries), these *juventes* underwent an unnaturally extended adolescence, riding in turbulent and errant bands in search of adventure or a rich heiress by means of whom to reattain their lost status. But the demographic vulnerability of the new aristocracy, and for a while its very "newness," also left it open to the upward mobility of commoners ambitious enough to rise, as *ministeriales,* through diverse kinds of service—land or rent enfeoffment, knight service or mercenary warfare, even the leadership of pilgrimages and popular religious movements. Like the *juventes,* these *ministeriales* also looked to marriage as an avenue of advancement, and their great numbers tightened the twelfth-century marriage markets. Finally, this broad pattern of status inconsistency must be placed in the unstable context of the feudal state and its long-term tensions: between feudal relations and kin relations, between the parcelized sovereignties of the feudal nobility and the centralizing tendencies of the monarchy, between feudal service and "civic" service to the state.[14]

As many scholars have shown, it is plausible to see the social purpose of the courtly fictions of the twelfth century as the mediation and explanation of these several instances of status inconsistency. The most direct celebration of the new aristocracy occurs not in chivalric romance at all but in epics of the new man like *The Cid,* whose eponymous hero, born to a minor landowner, rises to the greatest heights through service to King Alfonso and royal intermarriage. Thus worth is conjoined with birth, and honor is made integral: "See how his honor increases, he who in a happy hour was born, for the Kings of Spain are now among his kinsmen!" Romance tends to entail a more mediated form of social explanation. Arthurian romance, for example, can be seen to reflect back to the new aristocracy a flattering image of itself as, in an increasingly pacific culture, the embodiment of the old military virtues of the *aristoi* yet enfeoffed to a passive monarch who is unconcerned to extend his own power. On the other hand, Arthur's court also addresses the situation of the *hoblereaux*: problematically, by stressing the gap between the antiquated ethos of a warrior caste dedicated to trial by arms, and more rationalized forms of justice and service; and idealistically, by transforming the degrading search for material livelihood into a noble quest consistent with a noble birth.[15]

Scholars interested in the social significance of chivalric romance agree that its development of themes of love and adventure represents a clear movement away from the concrete and collective violence of the *chanson de geste*, but they tend to differ on the meaning of this movement. Robert Hanning emphasizes the "individualism" of the form founded by Chrétien de Troyes, its positive implication that individual experience, self-awareness, and internal states of fulfillment are central to human life. R. Howard Bloch instead describes the individualizing and spiritualizing tendencies of courtly love and romance fictions as a "displacement" of physical conflict, and the locution more effectively reminds us that twelfth-century "individualism" is a preeminently social strategy. The intense but metaphorical violence of the love relationship, and then of its internalized *psychomachia*, depicts and effaces the literal violence of baronial relations that is now being acculturated into varying forms of engagement and service to the feudal state. Hanning observes that our modern, "individual-centered" bias leads us to value most, in the *Song of Roland*, the personally based conflicts; but it may be that our reading of *Yvain*, as well, is skewed by an individualism largely imported from without. We even individualize the traditional titles of Chrétien's romances, and speak of *Yvain*, not *Le Chevalier au Lion;* of *Lancelot*, not *Le Chevalier de la Charrete;* of *Perceval*, not *Le conte du graal.* My point may be aided by a comparison with the social strategies of the medieval Church, which Jack Goody has done much to clarify. In encouraging "affective" familial attitudes, the Church may justly be seen to anticipate what received wisdom regards as a peculiarly Protestant tendency. But it would be misleading to cite these attitudes as positive evidence of "individualist" values within the Catholic Church, for the larger purpose they reflect and support is not the validation of the individual but the promotion of Church interests through the subversion of kinship solidarity.[16]

Perhaps it makes better sense to see twelfth-century romance not as the expression and legitimation of individualist values but as a method of investigating the substance of status categories at a time of pressing status inconsistency. It is a technique designed to anatomize "aristocratic honor" into its constituent parts without acknowledging that such a labor is needed—indeed, without acknowledging that its parts are truly separable. The focus on love in the courtly fictions of romance and the lyric is particularly useful to this indirection because it amounts to a strategic concentration on an exceptionally mediatory link in what I have described as the chain of signifiers for natural-cultural transformation. Situated at a midpoint in this chain, the figure of love permits easy passage in both directions, so that presenting problems of inconsistency may be understood allusively along a spectrum of varied kinds of trans-formation. Thus if, in direct comparison with the *chanson de geste,* the focus on love service seems to displace physical conflict, with respect to other possible signifiers it specifies and emplaces problems of status inconsistency within the social domain of sexual courtship, marriage, and the social ambitions of twelfth-century *juventes* and *ministeriales.* The point is not that the marriages (or for that matter the adultery) envisioned in chivalric romance and troubadour poetry can be seen as a faithful mirror of what really occurred but that the literary fictions provide an idealized image of the real connection between sexual alliance and social mobility. The same connection is visible in Andreas Capellanus's ex-treme preoccupation with socially mixed matches; in his nervous di-alogues, courtly love tends to reinforce our sense of the inconsistency between *plebeia, nobilis,* and *nobilior,* even as it seeks to overcome it as the great equalizer.[17]

So love service concretizes a pervasive sense of disparity in status, a yearning to overcome that disparity, and (although formulaically hope-less about the winning of reward and favor) even the means to achieve such an end. But it also entails a profoundly palliating spiritualization of upwardly mobile ambitions and of the arduous material services required to fulfill them. In troubadour poetry, love, tourneys, and chivalric battle can operate as interchangeable signifiers. In *Yvain,* the knight of the lion champions the younger daughter of the lord of the Black Thorn against her older sister, whose unjust engrossment of their father's entire inheri-tance transforms Arthur's court of chivalry into a court of property law, and its knights into protobureaucratic functionaries. Most of all, *fin amor* justifies the attainment of place by the ascription of internal merit. It designates a true nobility and an aristocracy of worth, whose demon-strated possession of the *cor gentil*—love ennobles and makes one do great things—alleviates the incongruity of entry into the aristocracy of birth until time and custom have effaced all record of it. And in this respect courtly love speaks to the anxieties of even the established feudal nobility, whose aristocratic status first derived not necessarily from birth but from tenurial place.

But the power of love to win a consistency of status is inseparable from

its negative power to institutionalize inconstancy, to disrupt and destabilize, to transform downward. This ambivalence of love, first elaborated in the Platonic dialogues, in medieval courtly fictions can mobilize a
broad range of natural and cultural figures for the aggravation of instability. When Laudine renounces Yvain's love he descends into madness
and animality: he flees to the forest and transforms himself into a beast,
stripping himself naked and living on raw meat. Only after this degradation does he meet and save the lion, whose humble blend of nature and
civility becomes his model, and whose name he assumes in signification
of his reintegration and upward ascent through the perseverance of service to Laudine. At the crucial moment, it is the assumed name of the lion
by which Yvain is made known to her and readmitted back into her
presence; only then may the theriomorphic disguises be dispensed with.
Episodes like these make clear how effectively romance love works to
signify not an explicitly and decisively "social" meaning but a transformational chain of meanings in which the social specification plays an
allusively important part in the stabilizing or destabilizing project.[18]

The ambivalence of love, and the delicate balance of the courtly fictions it animates, provide a key to the form in which the antiromance
impulse becomes discernible within romance. Some critics would discover self-parody even in the twelfth-century flowering. "There is no
such line of division between Ariosto and Chrestien de Troyes," says W.
P. Ker, "as there is between Chrestien and the primitive epic" and the
chanson de geste. The very extremity of courtly idealism and its spiritualizing function, seemingly justified by the extremity of the social experience it seeks to engage, can be felt to reinforce rather than overcome the
fatal sense of disparity. At such moments the courtly fiction becomes
counterproductive; internal honor is separated out from external honor,
true nobility from aristocratic nobility. It is easy to exaggerate the failure
of aristocratic ideology to maintain virtue and honor in fluid suspension
at this time. Nevertheless critics are generally agreed that the separation—or the coexistence of romance and "counterromance" impulses—
is most frequently encountered in English literary culture. Courtly fictions were not native to England, and although easily naturalized, they
never attained an entirely secure rooting. What is the social basis for this
phenomenon?[19]

The most immediate and obvious explanation is that feudal institutions, like courtly fictions, were to a major degree experienced as a
foreign import. In England something resembling the Norman system
of services predated 1066; nevertheless the socioeconomic consequences
of the Conquest were enormous, since the disruptive effects of Norman
feudalization were intensified by the demographic factor of mass migra-
tion. It is not only that divisible inheritances were largely replaced by the
patrilineal principles of primogeniture, nor even that the predominant

criterion of birth was inconsistent with the new criterion of tenurial service and landholding. Within two decades the Anglo-Saxon earls and thanes were physically and almost entirely displaced by an alien aristocracy, and the heterogeneous peasantry was conglomerated within the single category "serf." But if the Conquest helped make feudal institutions seem an imposition from without, they were not for all that a discredited fiction. In fact the political absoluteness of the imposition may have made it more easily accepted, for the universality of the system of feudal tenures in England left no powerful competing system with which it might be compared, as was the case on the Continent. And the rule of primogeniture, slowly extended from military to other tenures, soon became common law. So the obvious explanation of English differentness may not take us very far.[20]

Recently Alan Macfarlane pursued this question of differentness by renewing the notion of a medieval "individualism" and extending it to English culture in particular. His argument is two-pronged: English individualism is the result of an extreme application of the rule of primogeniture combined with the peculiarly English legal system of private ownership of land by individuals. But he is not entirely clear on the relative importance or mutual necessity of these two factors. And since the former in any case remains to be demonstrated, Macfarlane makes the legal right of individual ownership (whatever real landowners actually did with their land) bear the weight of the argument. But there is then something perverse in attempting to derive large-scale cultural beliefs worthy of an "ism" from the fact of a de jure capacity, as Macfarlane does when he claims that "since at least the thirteenth century England has been a country where the individual has been more important than the group" and the majority of ordinary people (his concern is with smaller landowners) have been "rampant individualists." What is persuasive about this argument is its requirement that we recognize, as in the literary origins that are my major concern, how fully new forms are grounded in discernible strains of thought and behavior that preexist those forms, and yet do not constitute them.[21]

It is evident that early English romance reflects the inconsistency attendant upon the creation of a new feudal nobility as an effect both of the Norman rupture and of impartible inheritance practices. The Anglo-Norman "ancestral romances" were written ostensibly to naturalize and legitimate the foreign invaders by elaborating for them a factitious legend of English origins, including at some point the obligatory period of exile abroad. But they also reflect the real pain of familial mobility and disruption that was endured by the newcomers. In the *Estoire de Waldef,* the convention of discovered parentage founders on the grief of one separation too many. When Waldef's sons, returned home, depart once more for the Continent, his wife bitterly declares: "They belong to a foreign

kingdom: they were never true sons of ours, but are foreigners who have
come into this country . . . Let them go to the Devil." In the most
famous of these ancestral romances, Guy of Warwick is the son of an
Anglo-Saxon gentleman who, downwardly mobile, now serves as the
steward of a lord. Guy falls in love with the heiress of this lord and
through superhuman love service wins both her hand and an earldom,
only to become in the end a humble palmer, exchanging worldly for
heavenly service and one sort of upward mobility for another. In the
Anglo-Norman *Amis and Amiloun,* the incommensurability of *amor* and
caritas is expressed more ambiguously in a proleptic alternation between
distinct modes of signifying the dangerous inconsistency of a love
match—social rank, wealth, divine decree, disguise, disease—and in
distinct versions the narrative is alternately feudal romance and Christian
hagiography.[22]

According to Thomas Warton, many romances began as legends of
devotion and only later took on chivalric accretions. "So reciprocal, or
rather so convertible, was the pious and the military character, that even
some of the APOSTLES had their romance." The relative inhospitality of
England to courtly fictions may perhaps be understood as an un-
willingness to indulge the all-powerful convertibility of the love signifier
that is so central to the courtly fictions of the Continent. The chain of
figures for signifying states of transformation and instability is not itself
opened to question; rather the dominance of love within that chain is. In
these Anglo-Norman narratives we sense an impatience with the attribution of immanent spiritual significance to merely worldly change, a wish
to take a more frankly homiletic stance, that may be characteristic of
English romance in general. A related but quite different impatience with
the signifying powers of love is felt in the tendency of English romance to
emphasize the problems of social advancement over those of sexual fulfillment, from which they are conventionally inseparable. This emphasis
is obvious enough in the somewhat later rebel romances, which turn on
themes of unjust disinheritance and the status inconsistency bred of primogeniture. The eponymous hero of *Gamelyn,* for example, is a younger
son disinherited by a treacherous older brother who has broken his oath
to their dying father. Of course rebel romances are by no means peculiarly English. But the emphasis is also seen in twelfth-century English
romances like *Horn* and *Havelok,* in which problems of love are felt to be a
subset of the controlling problem of disinheritance and status inconsistency. In these romances, a young prince is alienated and exiled to a land
where, despite intermittent manifestations of royalty, no one recognizes
his elevated status. Long victimized by a usurper, the hero finally ascends
to his place of inheritance and birth through deeds that confirm its consistency with his internal worth.

The English impatience with courtly fictions, then, is a critique that extends in opposite directions. On the one hand, it requires that the putative idealism of courtly love be made honest—which is to say, thoroughgoingly Christian; and it must therefore be seen in the context of the neoplatonic critique of carnal love, the *stilnovist* spiritualization of *fin amor,* and the Spenserian development of the "allegory of love." On the other hand, the English impatience calls not for a purification but for a demystification of courtly fictions, and it is motivated by the wish to disclose the material reality of the ideal superstructure, to specify the signifiers of instability to the realm of the social.[23]

The greatest proponents of this English romance as counterromance, Chaucer and the *Gawain* poet, belong to a later age than that of the Conquest and its immediate aftermath. Two fourteenth-century developments, the Peasants' Revolt and the establishment of a hereditary peerage, are especially relevant to the social themes I am pursuing. The essence of John Ball's perfidy was to apply to the present the question a pious hierarchy was so accustomed to asking of the past:

> Whanne Adam dalfe and Eve span,
> Who was thanne a gentil man?

Like the convention of true nobility, Ball's question had the potential both to conserve and—for a brief time—to endanger social stratification. When the English peerage became hereditary, nobility was to that degree severed from tenurial service, and so far personalized that only the male heir was ennobled by the creation (unlike the custom of the French *noblesse*). The ideal of aristocracy was thus further complicated: the old, pre-Conquest association with familial birth as distinct from tenurial service was reinforced, but rendered arbitrary by the narrow patrilineal restriction. And this can only have aggravated intrafamilial status inconsistency and the emulous suspicion that aristocratic rank signified a rather superficial species of "nobility."[24]

The literary fictions of this period promote a comparable instability, although with a more self-conscious purpose. *Sir Gawain and the Green Knight* is only the best of several "Gawain stories" in which a normative standard of natural or commoner justice challenges the hypocrisy of aristocratic culture by testing it according to its own courtly ideals. An entire spectrum of counterromance is defined within the space of *The Knight's Tale, The Tale of Sir Thopas, The Franklin's Tale, The Wife of Bath's Tale,* and *The Miller's Tale. The Canterbury Tales* themselves can be seen as a general satire on the functional stratification of estates; their author is supremely aware of the fictionality of social categories and of the social fluidity concealed within the assimilative appropriation of courtly terminology and behavior by upwardly mobile "new men." Chaucer's impatience with courtly fictions amounts not so much to a critique of love as to a deidealization of it. In narrative strategy this could be expressed by the relegation of love to a relatively subsidiary role in the chain of signifiers for transformation, one figure among several of comparable value. This movement of specification or emplacement is of course very important for the origins of the novel; but the locus of emplacement in fourteenth-century romance is not always immediately the realm of the social. In *William of Palerne,* for example, the disinheritance, social leveling, and eventual restoration of the prince are dominant concerns, and the psychosexual mutabilities of love are not even the most important engines that contribute to this movement. More suggestive in the mediation of social transformation is a complex and recurrent interchange of signifiers—theriomorphy, animal skins, aristocratic clothing—that concretely evoke an extended chain of natural-cultural metamorphoses even as they focus final attention on the specifically social links of that chain.[25]

This focus, the specification to the realm of the social, is the increasing preoccupation of late-medieval popular English romance. It involves not a flight from love themes but a concentration on their most socially significant feature, the end in marriage—especially as it is facilitated and justified by a show of amatory constancy. The ballad the "Lord of Learne" is in the general tradition of *Horn* and *Havelok:* alienated from his inheritance, an exiled boy is victimized by an evil steward and forced to serve as a stable groom until he wins the love of the daughter of the duke of France. Yet, although his nobility is evident to all who see the boy, he regains his lost status not by discovering his parentage (a fact that fades into the background) but by marrying his lady, whose own virtue is insisted upon in her utter constancy—"Ile neuer marry more but thee!"—to one who at least appears to be a commoner. In another sixteenth-century ballad, "The Nutt browne mayd" pursues her outlaw beloved into the forest, reminding him that "of anceytrye / a Barrons daughter I bee, / & you haue proued how [I] haue loued / a squier of a Low degree." To test her constancy her lover protests this gross inconsistency, adding that he also has another love. But when even this fails to dissuade the maid and her virtue is confirmed, he carelessly remarks, "Thus you haue woone the Erle of westmoreland sonne, / & not a banished man."[26]

The emphasis on constancy in these ballads intensifies the convention of true nobility, in effect underscoring its apparent presence in the man by forcefully attending to the conviction of the woman. And for this reason the anxiety of status inconsistency is intensified as well; it is as though we were being prepared, by the assurance of a correspondence in virtue, to accept a match that might institutionalize an inconsistency of rank. But constancy is also conventionally a female virtue, related to chastity in having the genealogical significance of ensuring the continuity of the male line (I will have more to say about this later). So the preoccupation with female constancy may aim to reassure us, however illogically, that the absence of noble rank need not mean the absence of aristocratic honor. This reading is strengthened by the example of two related fifteenth-century narratives that extend the tendency of these by celebrating what are genuine ascents into the aristocracy by upwardly mobile commoners. Here the unification of internal and external nobility, unattainable through any final disclosure of elevated birth, is achieved instead through marriage as the frank reward for services. These are of course to some degree tenurial and love services, but in both of these works there is evidence of a movement that becomes increasingly important in the origins of the novel, the specification of service to the arena of the private, postfeudal household—the "domestication" of service. But once again, the social ascent of the male "domestic" is softened by an insistence on the motif of female constancy and its allusive assurance of gentility.

Warmly courted by Lord Phenix, Lady Arundel informs him that she is already in love with Thomas of Potte, "a servinge man of a small degree." The men are soon engaged in chivalric contest, Thomas backed by his own lord. After trading blows Lord Phenix gives over; but the real trial is of Lady Arundel, who is made to believe that Thomas has been killed in order to test her resolve. She passes the test, Lord Phenix good-humoredly agrees to support Thomas's cause, and Lord Arundel announces that "of all my Land Thomas a Pott shall be my heyre." His daughter points the moral to her ladies:

> . . . looke you never change your old loue for a new,
> nor neuer change for no pouertye;
> ffor I had a louer true of mine owne,
> a seruing man of a small degree;
> ffrom Thomas a Pott Ile turne his name,
> & the Lord of Arrundale hee shall bee.[27]

The most notable features of "Thomas of Potte" are deepened in *The Squyr of Lowe Degre*. Its hero serves the king of Hungary as marshal, but loves the king's daughter and is highly conscious of the status inconsistency that precludes their love and marriage:

> That I were ryche of golde and fe,
> That I might wedde that lady fre!
> . . . .
> Or elles come of so gentyl kynne,
> The ladyes love that I myght wynne.
> . . . .
> Or els so bolde in chyvalry,
> As Syr Gawayne, or Sir Guy . . .

Devoid of birth and wealth, the squire follows his model, Guy of Warwick, into chivalric service, thereby complying with the explicit instructions of his beloved, who now declares her love for him but knows it
must be justified to her father. Yet the King of Hungary seems quite
untroubled by the inconsistency of the proposed match:

> For I have sene that many a page
> Have become men by mariage;
>
> . . . .
>
> And eche man in his degre
> Become a lorde of royalte,
> By fortune and by other grace,
> By herytage and by purchace . . .

Instead the King is preoccupied with the apparently distinct question of
his daughter's constancy. He posts a guard to ensure that the squire does
not "betraye" her, and he engineers a fight between the squire and a rival
which ends with his daughter's being mistakenly convinced of her lover's
death. The squire secretly departs and returns from his chivalric adventures. The lady, still unconsolable, at last is informed by her father that
her lover is alive and will succeed him to the throne:

> A trewe[r] lover than ye are one
> Was never [yet of] fleshe ne bone;
> And but he be as true to thee,
> God let him never thryve ne thee.

The story bears an odd relationship to the spiritualizations of twelfth-
century romance. Far more pragmatically specified to the social domain
of status inconsistency, it still displaces the anxiety of aristocratic ideology onto the concern with female "integrity," a relatively moderate
displacement that brings us close to the origins of the novel. What is yet
required is a more direct engagement with the problematic integrity that
lies at the heart of aristocratic ideology itself, the fiction of an integral
"honor."[28]

4
PROGRESSIVE IDEOLOGY AND THE TRANSVALUATION OF HONOR

Evidence on many fronts suggests that the early modern period marked a
critical turning point in the efficacy not only of romance but also of the
social institutions with which we are likely to associate it, a point at
which they began systematically to attest not to the concord but to the
discord of internals and externals, of virtue, status, wealth, and power.
Indeed, the very life span of some of these social institutions suggests that
they are to be seen not as the traditional tools of stability but as signs of a

crisis of confidence. The Heralds' Visitations began no earlier than 1529; the last one was in 1686. Sumptuary legislation commenced only in 1337 and ended, for want of approval by the House of Commons, in several abortive attempts of the early seventeenth century. Edward Waterhouse knew that the tale told by these dates was the fatal difference between tacit consensus and explicit injunction: our ancestors distinguished between their social stations by their "Garb, Equipage, Dyet, Housholdstuff, Clothes, [and] Education of Children . . . not by sumptuary Laws, or Magistratique sanction, but by common agreement, and general understanding." A related case in point is the action for *scandalum magnatum,* a legal recourse by which peers of the realm were empowered to vindicate their honor against the slander of their inferiors. It is clear enough that such actions reinforced social distinctions between the nobility and the rest. But the fact that they increased in the late sixteenth and the seventeenth centuries, peaking under Charles II, suggests that they also registered an increasingly defensive awareness that social hierarchy was under assault. [29]

As with the providential argument, that is, we are often obliged to understand the very force with which traditional authority is asserted as one telling sign of its weakness. The sheer volume of argument for the maintenance of status hierarchy in the sixteenth century, especially in the context of hot controversy over the meaning of nobility, bespeaks a nagging uncertainty. Only in that century did the English begin to debate the legal and social significance of the institution of primogeniture. The perpetual citation of Ulysses' memorable degree speech by modern scholars as proof of the stability of the "Elizabethan world picture" depends for its plausibility on our overlooking the fact that it comes in the context of a ferociously demystifying assault on aristocratic ideals and order. In those moments when the delicate workings of intellectual and institutional convention, strained to their limits, seem all at once to proclaim what they would enjoin, we see the mechanisms of historical change laid bare. This pattern can be seen very clearly in the phenomenon that Lawrence Stone felicitously calls the "inflation of honors" under the early Stuarts. [30]

"So elaborate a convention" as the sale of honors, Stone remarks, "will only function satisfactorily if too much strain is not placed upon it." Honors became decisively inflated when unprecedented new wealth and rapid changes in landownership, along with the need for revenues to which no political strings had been tied, persuaded James I and Charles I to transform, through overuse, a stabilizing device into an instrument of social instability. Under Elizabeth it was still possible to see the sale of honors as a sign "whereby it should appeare that vertue flourisheth among us." Writing much later under Cromwell's rule, Sir Edward Walker was not alone in thinking that James's sale of honors had helped foment the late rebellion against monarchy: "For as the Proceedings of former Princes in the wary dispensing of Honours supported the Royal Dignity; so the multiplication of Titles, and the exposing of them to Persons of no publick Merit in their Families or Fortunes, hath weakned and abused it . . . It may be doubted whether [this] were not one of the Beginnings of general Discontents, especially among Persons of great Extraction." Stone's metaphor underscores the central tension between monetary and honorific criteria, which, always implicit in the sale of honors, now becomes a glaring contradiction for contemporaries, conceivable through a variety of figures. According to Walker, the inflation of honors "took off from the Respect due to Nobility, and introduced a parity in Conversation . . . the Curtain being drawn they were discovered to be Men that heretofore were reverenced as Angels." "Now for any man therefore to purchase honour without some worthy action foregoing," thought Thomas Scott, was to be possessed of nothing but "*Parchment honour.*" One ground for the impeachment of the Duke of Buckingham in 1626, according to his enemies, was his instigation of "the trade and commerce of honor . . . He was the first that defiled this virgin of honor so publickly." Buckingham's accusers were conscious that the sale of honors "introduceth a strange confusion, mingling the meaner with the more pure and refined metal." An action for *scandalum magnatum* was brought in 1638 to redress an insult aimed at the crest of one of Charles I's newly created barons. And in 1657, an award of £500 to the Earl of Leicester in recompense for the defamation of his more authentically venerable honor nevertheless provoked counsel for the defendant to wonder "how it is that noble men are so greedy of damages degenerating so much from the excellencies of their ancestors, whose aim have been only by way of indictment to repair their honours, not to improve their purses."[31]

The controversy that was generated by the inflation of honors under the early Stuarts brings into relief the fundamental analogy between questions of truth and questions of virtue as contemporaries themselves were beginning to divine it. If "aristocratic honor" is analogous to "romance" in the epistemological realm, "honor as virtue" occupies the place of "true history." In 1604 a herald lamented that "without a doubt he that buyeth his knighthood looseth the honour of knighthood, and it greveth me beyond all measure that I have cause to speake my mynd of this, for it is piteous to see either the vanity or the pride or the arrogancy or the insolency of this tyme, when so many do desyre the reward of true honour and vertue, and so fewe apply themselves to deserve it." Years later Samuel Butler observed, in the characteristically hardened accents of post-Restoration invective, that "when a Prince confer's Honor on those, that do not Deserve it, He throw's it away out of his own Stock . . . Though a Prince be sayd to be the Fountaine of Honor, it is easily exhausted, when he let's it run lavishly, without Care, and Consideration, like a Coronation-Cunduit to intoxicate the Rabble, and Run in the Canell." The inflation of honors helped fuel the critique of aristocratic ideology that I will call "progressive ideology," a critical posture that bears an analogous relation to naive empiricism. As Butler remarks in his most famous work,

> Nor does it follow, 'cause a *Herauld*
> Can make a Gentleman, scarce a Year old,
> To be descended of a Race,
> Of ancient *Kings,* in a small Space;
> That we should all Opinions hold
> *Authentic,* that we can make old.

For progressive ideology, the experience of disenchantment with titles of nobility, so far from entailing a sense of elegiac loss (as in the case of the Jacobean herald), might seem the necessary prelude to the replacement of the old and outworn fictions by the new truth. Francis Bacon knew that he might have buttressed his novel ideas on natural philosophy with the authority of the ancients, "and so gained for them both support and honour, as men of no family devise for themselves by the good help of genealogies the nobility of a descent from some ancient stock. But for my part, relying on the evidence and truth of things, I reject all forms of fiction and imposture . . . For new discoveries must be sought from the light of nature, not fetched back out of the darkness of antiquity."[32]

A rather different example of the sort of institutional crisis—and response—that helped precipitate the growth of progressive ideology concerns not the first but the second half of the seventeenth century. During this period England experienced a demographic crisis that reduced the general population so sharply that the peak of 1656 was not surpassed until 1721. England's landed elite shared fully in this crisis. The marked decline in male births made the middle years of the century a "watershed" in their inheritance patterns. The norm of direct male descent was challenged severely, and the threat to patrilineal principles could only be met by an extreme intensification of the strategies of patriline repair. Indirect male inheritance increased proportionately, some of it through distant relatives. Greater recourse was had to surrogate heirship and to the attendant device of name-changing. Name-substitution and name-hyphenation commenced in the 1680s; by about 1690 it had become a general obligation that the husband of a daughter or niece through whom the seat passed adopt the family name and become, in the language of land law, a "fictive tail male."[33]

The demographic crisis of the late seventeenth century coincides with the invention of a legal device that rationalized and reformed the English system of inheritance, the "strict settlement." Scholarly debate on the aims and effects of this device has been intense in the last few years. To some the clear significance of the settlement is that it reinforced primogeniture and patrilineal principles by stabilizing the landed estate, limiting the life tenant's powers of alienation and thereby ensuring the descent of the entail in the male heir. But others argue that the guaranteed provisions for daughters and younger sons which the settlement facilitated were its most important aim and the intergenerational transfer of land its desired effect, and thus that the settlement should be seen as a sign that patrilineal principles were on the wane. What may be said at this point is that these disputes testify to the contradictory nature of the institution itself. By attending this closely and explicitly to the mediation of distinct family interests, the strict settlement only emphasized their divergence, separating out elements which, by the less scrupulous and self-conscious consensus of aristocratic ideology, were less problematically comprehended within the general category of "family." The strict settlement helped make the perennial and implicit tension between male owner and male heir, and between patrilineal and kindred interests, an active one; and so it both reinforced patrilineal principles and undermined them.[34]

Patriline repair and the ambivalent gestures of the strict settlement must have contributed to mounting skepticism about the purity of aristocratic blood and the continuity of aristocratic lineages. Daniel Defoe took great pleasure in pointing out the "Mixtures" in the blood of the nobility and the "Gaps in your most Illustrious Successions," beginning with the Norman Conquest:

> Thus from a Mixture of all Kinds began,
> That Het'rogeneous Thing, *An Englishman:*
> ·
> The Wonder which remains is at our Pride,
> To value that which all wise men deride.
> For *Englishmen* to boast of Generation,
> Cancels their Knowledge, and lampoons the Nation.
> A *True-Born Englishman*'s a Contradiction,
> In Speech an Irony, in Fact a Fiction.

Here it is Defoe's critical historicism that links his progressive ideology to his naive empiricism. Elsewhere it is his new-philosophical ridicule of the aristocratic notion that honor is biologically inherited, "as if there were some differing Species in the very Fluids of Nature . . . or some *Animalculae* of a differing and more vigorous kind." To treat the nobleman "as if he were a different Species from the rest of Mankind" is to make "an Idol" of him.[35]

As we might expect, moreover, the progressive attack on aristocratic honor made allusive and suggestive use of the empiricist attack on "romance." According to Richard Allestree, "A *man of Honour* is now understood only to be one that can start and maintain a Quarrel . . . But this new notion of Honour proclaims . . . [that] he passes for a Phlegmatick fool, whose bloud boils not at the first glimpse of an Affront," and it has "introduced such a multitude of ridiculous Punctilio's, that the next Age will be in danger of receiving the Fable of *Don Quixot* for Authentick History." Bernard Mandeville thought that men who are both virtuous and courageous "are rarely to be met with, but in Legends and Romances, the Writers of both which I take to have been the greatest Enemies to Truth and sober Sense the World has ever produc'd . . . The most effectual Method to breed Men of Honour, is to inspire them with lofty and romantick Sentiments concerning the Excellency of their Nature, and the superlative Merit there is in being a Man of Honour." For honor

is only to be met with in People of the better sort, as some Oranges have kernels, and others not, tho' the outside be the same. In great Families it is like the Gout, generally counted Hereditary, and all Lords Children are born with it. In some that never felt any thing of it, it is acquired by Conversation and Reading, (especially of Romances) in others by Preferment; but there is nothing that encourages the Growth of it more than a Sword, and upon the first wearing of one, some People have felt considerable Shutes of it in Four and twenty Hours.

Intending at first to "examine into this Chimaerical groundless Humour" of dueling, Sir Richard Steele is brought up short by the realization that he will thereby offend so many "Men of Honour" as to be undertaking "a Work worthy an invulnerable Hero in Romance, rather than a private Gentleman with a single Rapier."[36]

In the broadest terms, the transvaluation of honor that culminates in the seventeenth century is a process of separation and detachment comparable to that undergone by the compound unit "history-romance" during the same period. "Honor" now fails to unite internals and externals. Progressive ideology requires that it resolve itself into virtue on the one hand and aristocratic rank on the other, a discrimination that repudiates the automatic aristocratic signification of internals by externals. As Butler put it, the degenerate nobleman "is like a Word, that by ill Custom and Mistake has utterly lost the Sense of that, from which it was derived, and now signifies quite contrary." By the end of the century the argument of true nobility has ceased definitively to work as the stabilizer of aristocratic nobility—the exception that proves the rule—and come to represent instead an alternative system of social ethics. "Nor should I speak a syllable against Honours being Hereditary," said William Sprigge, "could the valour, Religion, and prudence of Ancestors be as easily intail'd on a line or family, as their Honours and Riches . . . Could they transmit their vertues as well as names unto their posterity, I should willingly become the Advocate of such a Nobility." But "the vertue descends not with the titles," Defoe insisted, and "the man is but the shaddow of a gentleman, without the substance . . . If he has not the virtue which is the merit, how can he be call'd noble? What remains to the miserable skeleton of a nobleman?"

> What is't to us, what Ancestors we had?
> If Good, what better? or what worse, if Bad?
> Examples are for Imitation set,
> Yet all men follow Virtue with Regret.
>
> . . . .
>
> For Fame of Families is all a Cheat,
> *'Tis Personal Virtue only makes us great.*

Over the course of the seventeenth century, the predominant meaning of the word "honor" as a term of denotation shifts from "title of rank" to "goodness of character." "The Gentleman is to be represented as he really is," says Defoe, "I mean as a Person of Merit and Worth; a Man of Honour, Virtue, Sense, Integrity, Honesty, and Religion, without which he is Nothing at all . . . And why should he not be taken as Nature shows him? Why should he not be accepted for what he is, and not for what he is not?" In the traditional sense of the term, as a quality susceptible of inheritance, honor is no more credible than the fictions of romance. It is "upon this imaginary honour" that anachronistic gentlemen "elate their minds to the uttmost extravagance, [and] value themselves as exalted in birth above the rest of the world." "Honour in this Figurative Sense," Mandeville concludes, "is a Chimera without Truth or Being."[37]

And what of gentlewomen? The common wisdom in early modern England is that in marriages between partners of unequal status, the woman derives her rank from that of the man and not the man from that of the woman. And the implication of this understanding for the question of to what degree aristocratic women are possessed of what I have been calling aristocratic honor—that is, very little—would seem to be confirmed by the peculiarly English custom of obliterating the wife's maiden name upon marriage. It is because of this custom that name-changing by surrogate heirs was necessary, for the blood linkage on the female side had to be reflected, in a patrilineal culture, by a nominal linkage on the male side. Now, this in turn would seem to constitute an exception to the common wisdom, since the surrogate heir clearly derives his rank from that of his wife; however, the exception might likely be rationalized as a derivation of rank (and honor) *through* the female conduit, but *from* the male reservoir. This kind of rationale would be generally consistent in any case with the anthropological account of marriage as a male gift transaction. By this account, the incest taboo prohibits unions within the group so as to promote exogamous marriage and alliance, the exchange of women aimed at the establishment of kinship relations between men.[38]

In the English kinship system, one of the most important kinds of relation between men is the transmission of property by the direct descent of patrilineage. For this reason the English system stresses, as strongly as the prohibition of incest, the injunction of female chastity (or constancy, in its moralized enlargement). This injunction was overdetermined: patrilineal culture required chastity so as to ensure the direct transmission of the inheritance; Christian culture required it not only as a moral virtue but also to encourage, over all competing kinship ties, the "spiritual" kinship of the Church and its enrichment as alternative beneficiary. As a contemporary critic of Samuel Richardson put it, there are two species of chastity, "political" and "religious." The influence of the first derives from the fact that "in all societies there are families, inheritances, and distinctions of ranks and orders. To keep these separate and distinct, to prevent them from falling into confusion . . . the chastity and continence of women are absolutely and indispensably necessary." Religious chastity was first "recommended and enforced" by Jesus Christ and his disciples. But the institutional consequences of strict continence "were pernicious to the publick good, they discouraged marriage, and established that ecclesiastical tyranny, under which all Europe groaned before the reformation and the resurrection of letters." For these reasons Protestant countries have modified the strict rule to the recommendation of "conjugal fidelity and continence before marriage."[39]

Because of this overdetermination, the "political" or genealogical explanation of the rule of female chastity has not always been so obvious. Protests against the double standard that are grounded in the Christian formulation often express mystification that men should be exempted from a supposedly universal moral injunction. After the Reformation, however, the dominance of the Christian rationale is moderated, and the genealogical rationale comes more clearly into view. True, the idea of male chastity is more strenuously defended in Protestant debate; but it also becomes more popular over the course of the seventeenth century as an inherently ludicrous subject. At the same time, people begin to be aware of an intrasexual "double standard"—the fact that female chastity is required far more insistently of gentlewomen than of those lower down the social scale, where the transmission of property is less at issue and partible inheritance predominates over the impartible principles of primogeniture that are observed by the gentle.[40]

Only in the early modern period, when the genealogical foundation of female chastity becomes more evident, does it also become habitual to designate chastity as the female species of "honor," and the frequency of that designation seems to increase over the course of the seventeenth century. But the development of this usage has further significance, beyond this basic correlation, for the elaboration of progressive ideology. For as the progressive critique forces the detachment of "honor as virtue" from male aristocratic honor, it simultaneously encourages its relocation within not only commoners but women, who increasingly come to be viewed not just as the conduit but as the repository of an honor that has been alienated from a corrupt male aristocracy. In narrative this can be seen (I will argue) in the way the late-medieval preoccupation with the constancy of gentlewomen, in love with real or apparent commoners, gives way to a fascination with the constancy of common women, pursued by corrupt aristocrats. Of course the equation of chastity with honor, and honor with virtue, could seem like nothing more than a depreciatory reduction of women, even to contemporaries; thus Samuel Butler's indignation that "virtue, as it is commonly understood in women, signify's nothing else but Chastity, and Honor only not being whores: As if that Sex were capable of no other morality, but a mere Negative Continence." But the equation admits also of another reading, as Mary Astell implies: "As the World now goes, I am apt to think, that a Husband is in no desirable Situation; his Honour is in his Wife's keeping." In associating female virtue with chastity, the eighteenth century is commonly thought to mark a low point of careless patriarchal cynicism. But it may be more accurate to see that association in the context of the progressive critique of patrilineal honor, a critique in which women, besieged by discredited aristocratic honor, come to embody the locus and refuge of honor as virtue.[41]

A final factor is obviously relevant to this argument. In the later seventeenth century, illegitimate and quasi–illegitimate births (in which the parents marry after conception but before birth) comprise about twelve percent of all first births in England. One hundred years later the figure has jumped to an astonishing fifty percent, half of which are fully illegitimate. The figure is not quite as extraordinary as it seems; at least the illegitimacy and prenuptial pregnancy ratio is rising in direct proportion to the rise in general nuptiality and fertility. Even so, general nuptiality is increasing at a slower rate than are illegitimate births. And we are no doubt justified in seeing this shift as overwhelming evidence of a relaxation of attitudes toward the rule of female chastity—although we cannot assume that it reflects the "political" any more than the "religious" component of the rule, especially since the majority of the population belongs to social groups too humble to be maximally vulnerable to the genealogical injunction. The evidence in this shift of an assault on genealogical standards of legitimacy is more univocal if we focus our attention on the rising toleration of bastardy it evinces. Moreover, as with the virtuous heroine of early modern narrative, it is within the context of progressive ideology, and in implicit criticism of aristocratic ideology, that the bastard as hero assumes his full significance.[42]

5
THE RISE OF THE GENTRY

From evidence like this it is easy to understand why much of the difficulty in describing early modern social change has been terminological and definitional in nature. The "rise of the gentry controversy," which originated in the attempt to provide a socioeconomic explanation for the English Revolution and came to dominate historiographical attention during the middle decades of this century, is a case in point. Historians concerned to argue the rise or fall of "the gentry" soon found themselves face to face with the prior question: Who are the gentry? The inconsistency of seventeenth-century usage reflects the lived complexity of historical experience, which resists analytic categorization. I have already alluded to the fact that toward the end of the Middle Ages, the peerage was separated from the rest of the nobility by the creation of the ranks of duke, marquess, viscount, and baron, a "greater nobility" that is sharply distinguished from the "lesser" by being hereditary in title and by entailing the legal right to sit in the House of Lords. And on this precedent, "greater" and "lesser" nobility might be understood to express the difference between "peers" or "aristocracy," and "gentry." But for many contemporaries, the "gentry" were a part of the "aristocracy," which was equivalent to the "nobility." Yet in heraldic language, "noble" meant those of the rank of "gentleman" or above; the distinction between the gentle and the ungentle was clearly the basic social division in early modern England, and it was easy for contemporary writers to conflate gentility with gentry and to treat the latter as a general and inclusive category more or less synonymous with "nobility." By the same token, modern historians who contributed to the gentry controversy became increasingly sensitive to the dangers involved both in mixing categories variously based upon legal, heraldic, social, and economic criteria and in distinguishing them too easily.[43]

But categorial confusion was central to the gentry controversy because it raised not simply the problem of how the identity of one group is conceptualized in relation to that of other groups but also the problem of how to conceive of groups as they exist and change over time. The temporal factor is, of course, crucial to R. H. Tawney's thesis of a "rise" of the gentry to socioeconomic, and then to political, power. Tawney's argument was attacked as tautological by critics who showed that, quite apart from the difficulty of making a static definition of gentry, the thesis defined all upward movement affecting all other groups as swelling the ranks of the gentry alone. In the words of H. R. Trevor-Roper, Tawney's "gentry consists both of the gentry who remained gentry throughout the period, and of those men who began as gentry and ended as peers, and of those who began as merchants, yeomen, or anything else, and ended as gentry." In place of the rise of the gentry, Trevor-Roper advanced the antithetical thesis of a lesser or "mere" gentry, whose declining fortunes in the century before the English Revolution were said to explain the same political phenomena that Tawney's rising gentry had failed to. But Trevor-Roper's own weapons could be turned against him. As Christopher Hill observed, a *lesser* gentry is not automatically assimilable to a *declining* gentry, for "the lesser gentry included those who had successfully risen from the yeomanry." Are the "mere" gentry to be understood both as declining gentry and as rising yeomanry?[44]

So the instability of social categories in early modern England is evident both in contemporary discourse and in that modern discourse which seeks to situate contemporary experience within the distancing and stabilizing framework of historical explanation. Moreover there is a suggestive analogy between these problems in the method of social history and those literary historical problems which are central to Part One of this study: At what point, by what standards, and with what classificatory consequences should apparent categorial change be understood as such? However, the distinctive features of the literary and the social developments ensure that the way in which these common problems are raised and engaged will reflect considerable local differences. One crucial dilemma that can, with hindsight, be seen at the heart of the gentry controversy was this: Should social mobility be taken to alter the group identity of those undergoing movement and to swell the ranks of the group toward which movement is directed, or do the socially mobile bring their former group identity with them to their new locale? For the sake of simplicity these might be called, respectively, the "absorption" and the "retention" models of social mobility. The gentry controversy began in close accord with the assumptions of the retention model. And although it did not end in a clear victory either for the absorption model or for its implicit conclusion—that the gentry failed to rise—some of the most telling arguments along the way pointed in that direction. Moreover, in the wake of the gentry controversy, the hypothesis of the rise of the gentry has been replaced by the more confident orthodoxy of the persistence of the aristocracy, a view that perpetuates the basic assumptions of the absorption model in other terms. In this real and important sense, the gentry controversy is still with us. In the following pages I will briefly substantiate these remarks, and I will argue the necessity of treating the two models not as alternatives but as partial—and partially valid—constituents of a more comprehensive approach to the problem of social instability in this period. Only by such an approach, I think, will the social origins of the English novel become intelligible.

When Tawney first undertook to argue the rise of the gentry, he had in mind something closely assimilable to the older hypothesis of a rise of the middle class. In his own contribution to the gentry controversy, J. H. Hexter took Tawney to task for the "taxonomic illusion" consequent on distinguishing the gentry from the peerage as a rising middle class versus a declining aristocratic class. The distinction between gentry and peerage, Hexter observed, is not economic but legal. "Economically gentry and peerage were of the *same* class—the class that ordinarily drew the larger part of its income from the exploitation of proprietary rights in land." Now, the crucial factor in Hexter's criterion of class definition would appear to be the physical, even geographical, character of the property from which income is derived—in this instance, land. And this is confirmed elsewhere by his strict equation of the middle class with the bourgeoisie in the literal sense of the term—with the mercantile, financial, and industrial enterprise of the cities. According to these standards, rural gentry and urban merchants by definition belong to different "classes." So by the same token, when the seventeenth-century merchant bought land, Hexter argued, he ceased to be "one of the middle class" because he ceased to behave according to middle-class values, instead "sacrificing profit to purchase prestige." Thus the upward mobility of members of the "middle class" really weakened that class while buttressing the "landed aristocracy," into which they were "absorbed." In his most important contribution to the gentry controversy, Lawrence Stone advanced an absorption model similar to Hexter's. The upward mobility consequent on the Tudor sale of church and crown lands, Stone argued, must be seen not as a definitive elevation but as an absorptive assimilation attributable to the structural resilience of the English landowning class, which was able "to absorb new families of different social origin and convert them" to its own values, those of the landed gentleman. Indeed, the temporary eclipse of the peerage helps make Tawney's thesis seem more plausible than it really is: "The rise of the gentry is to some extent— though certainly not entirely—an optical illusion, resulting from this weakness of the aristocracy [i.e., the peerage]."[45]

Yet it is clear from Tawney's original argument that his view of the gentry as a coherent social group that retains its identity as it rises depends fundamentally on criteria of social elevation which have to do not with the location and status of economic production (as in Hexter's argument) but with its methods and success. By these standards, the rising gentry were "rural entrepreneurs" whose innovative methods of land improvement and investment had little in common with the estate management practiced by "rural rentiers"—conservative landowners—

many of whom were aristocrats. But the methods by which these rural, "middle-class gentry" thrived are very similar to those employed by successful urban merchants, "with whom indeed they formed but a single social class." This approach does not dismiss the status-conscious behavior of those urban and "rural entrepreneurs" who evinced their desire for cultural assimilation by purchasing country houses. It reinterprets such behavior as definitive not of fundamental group identity but of one stylistic choice within the larger boundaries of that identity, distinguishing what might be called an "assimilationist" from a "separatist" or even a "supersessionist" attitude toward the reigning, aristocratic values of status. What is fundamentally definitive of group identity, in this view, is not the culturally encoded patterns of consumption which regulate a social system stratified according to "status" but the economics of production by which a social system based upon the standard of "class" is organized. And from this perspective, Hexter's charge that Tawney has committed a categorial error by confusing legal and class criteria may fairly be turned back upon Hexter himself. For despite the aim to discriminate *class* affiliations, his attentiveness to the definitive differences between land and trade, between country and city, more directly bespeaks a sensitivity to *status* discriminants.[46]

6

FROM STATUS TO CLASS

The difference between these two perspectives on the meaning of social mobility—between Tawney's "class" orientation and Hexter's "status" orientation—is fundamentally one of principle. But if neither can be refuted by the terms of the other, it is important to acknowledge also the potential for coexistence. Even Max Weber's account of "status" and "class" as theoretical ideal types declines the language of mutual exclusion: "In contrast to the purely economically determined 'class situation' we wish to designate as 'status situation' every typical component of the life fate of men that is determined by a specific, positive or negative, social estimation of *honor*. This honor . . . can be knit to a class situation: class distinctions are linked in the most varied ways with status distinctions." Within the historical context of early modern social change, the interrelation of status and class criteria appears to be inevitable; and yet for this very reason it is not hard to see why the gentry controversy became polarized in terms of this distinction. For it is precisely during this period that the traditional, qualitative criteria of honorific status were being definitively infiltrated by the quantitative criteria of socioeconomic class. This act of infiltration both recalls, and exceeds, the sometimes strained equilibrium of social values that is familiar from earlier periods, because now (as I have argued) the resilient power of "honor" to extend its tacit sway over the range of personal identity is lost, and the tension is no longer sustained but broken. Class criteria gradually "replace" status criteria: which is to say not that the regard for status is obliterated but that it is subsumed under and accommodated to the more dominant and insistent regard for financial income and occupational identity. Only Thomas Hobbes gives the lie to this generalization, his mind so tenaciously and corrosively quantifying as to argue not a gradual replacement but an instantaneous takeover:

The *Value*, or WORTH of a man, is as of all other things, his Price; that is to say, so much as would be given for the use of his Power: and therefore is not absolute; but a thing dependant on the need and judgement of another . . . The manifestation of the Value we set on one another, is that which is commonly called Honouring, and Dishonouring . . . *Honourable* is whatsoever possession, action, or quality, is an argument and signe of Power. To be descended from conspicuous Parents, is Honourable; because they the more easily attain the aydes, and friends of their Ancestors. On the contrary, to be descended from obscure Parentage, is Dishonourable.

The astonishing Hobbesian analysis provides, as so often, a negative register marking the extreme position to which, however inherent in the logic of its movement, early modern thought did not attain. It also helps us see that the importance, and the misconstruction, of Tawney's original thesis of a "rural entrepreneur" stem from his rather too tacit recognition that the "rise of the middle class" is inseparable from the rise of a class orientation toward social relations.[47]

Another way of saying this is to suggest that in the early modern period, the idea of "class" takes on the character of what Marx calls a "simple abstraction," a conceptualization whose experiential referent has a prehistory that is rich enough both to permit, and to require, the abstraction and the dominance of the general category itself. This conceptual dominance signals a corresponding emergence on the plane of material activity. The traditional dominance of status categories, and the mechanism whereby discrepancies of wealth and power were equilibrated under the aegis of birth and rank, presided over a feudal system of economic relations which dominated and dissipated the force of capitalist practices by subsuming their efficacy within its own. It is often argued that "capitalism" and "the middle class" have existed in England since the twelfth or thirteenth century. But this collapses the historical process which the idea of the simple abstraction exists to articulate: that is, the continuum between the isolated existence of attitudes and activities within a context that channels and contains them, and the full exploitation of those elements as the vital constituents of their context, as that which renders it systematic.[48]

The historical relationship that is made visible by the idea of the simple abstraction may also be clarified by reference to a point that has been emphasized in recent Marxist theory, the duality of Marx's own use of the category "class." On the one hand, Marx employs "class" as an abstract term to describe a kind of socioeconomic relation and conflict that is generally characteristic of all human societies. On the other hand, the category describes a very particular historical reality, that of modern industrial capitalism, whose particularity is registered by the fact that it directly experiences itself in the terms of class—by the fact, that is, of class-consciousness. This dual usage should be seen to express not a logical but a historical contradiction, evincing the kind of dialectical unity that is contained within the development of the simple abstraction. True, the period that concerns us does not witness the flowering of middle-class consciousness. But it would be a mistake to insist too precisely on the fact of such consciousness as the *sine qua non* of the class orientation. The tendency to do so can be associated with a second common argument, both opposed and analogous to the first, which holds that the middle class arrives in England only with nineteenth-century full industrialization. Some proponents of this argument also adhere, not surprisingly, to the absorption model of social mobility so far as the early modern period is concerned, overestimating the resilience of the status orientation and overlooking the most obvious, terminological signs of change. For the consistent usage of the term "class," like that of "the novel," marks not the tentative inception, but the active dominance, of the category. And although it does not appear to provide a truly secure basis for the comprehensive classification of people until the beginning of the nineteenth century, the socioeconomic terminology of "class" begins to be used before the middle of the eighteenth.[49]

Thus it may be instructive to view the gentry controversy as the consequence of too exclusive a fidelity either to a "traditional" or to a "modern" principle of social categorization, with reference to a period that is distinguished by their complete and destabilizing interpenetration. The problem for the social historian is not simply how to remain intellectually responsive to the two different orientations but how to deploy a descriptive language that works simultaneously on two different fronts. For on the one hand, the empirical assessment of social movement depends entirely on a definition of group identity dictated by the traditional but imprecise system of social stratification according to qualitative status. But on the other hand, this traditional system, and therefore the integrity of the groups whose existence it acknowledged, were undergoing a profoundly destabilizing assault by the more quantitative social values associated with a class orientation. But the problems besetting the modern historian are very similar to, and may be illuminated by, those that faced seventeenth-century commentators. In fact, as the historical logic of my argument suggests, it is during this period, under the influence of the developing class orientation, that we begin to see rudimentary efforts at the sort of quantitative social description which has become standard among modern social historians. Early efforts in the field of "political arithmetic" provide some striking examples.

Gregory King's celebrated population table of the 1690s ostensibly aims to give a continuous financial, and therefore quantitative, progression from the top to the bottom of English society. But he is obliged to work with both honorific and occupational categories. King's solution to this problem of inconsistency is straightforward enough. His table observes the hierarchy of status titles at its upper extreme, having recourse to more pragmatically oriented headings as we proceed through those toward the bottom who are without honor. In the middle of the table, however, he runs into trouble. For one thing, certain status groups show a higher income than others to which by status criteria they are subservient (e.g., "merchants" compared with "gentlemen," "freeholders" compared with "clergymen"). Even more, it becomes necessary at some points to intermix occupational with status categories (e.g., "lawyers" with "gentlemen"). And in all these ambiguous cases King allows status criteria to determine the order of his listings, even though the crucial standard of average yearly income should reverse the order. In other words, King's abiding respect for the traditional status hierarchy momentarily overrules his modernizing aim to create a hierarchy of incomes. Our interest in King's ambivalence is increased by the knowledge that after 1677 he was by profession a herald, and that in his table he paradoxically adopted the revolutionary method of statistics to serve what was in general an anachronistic view of the English social order. Over half a century later, Joseph Massie used King's well-known table as a model on which to base his comparison of the amounts of sugar consumed in England by different social groups. But although he carried over King's six traditional categories of elevated status to the top of his own table, they repose there aloof and untouched, a kind of honorific gesture that has nothing to do with the real work of economic discrimination, for which Massie uses completely different categories in the rest of his table. It is as though status categories persist here as a vestigial remnant of a mode of thought which, however useless in the definitive description of contemporary English people by class, still appears quite indispensable.[50]

A different sort of perspective on the problems that arise in trying to describe early modern social structure can be found in the way contemporaries address the problematic relationship between land and trade. The incompatibility of land and trade according to traditional status criteria reflects the likelihood that the inevitable minor discrepancies in the general coextension of birth, land, wealth, and power could easily be rectified by unobtrusive adjustments. Indeed, the absorption model of social mobility is a cultural attitude that reinforces the techniques by which traditional societies efface the evidence of instability and change. But a conjunction of factors in the early modern period conspired to frustrate these stabilizing mechanisms by making the discrepancy of mercantile wealth too great to be ignored—not only an increase in the volume and conspicuousness of merchant wealth but also an increase in controversy over the disinheritance of younger sons and their consequent apprenticeship in trade. Modern historians have drawn attention to per-suasive evidence, in conduct books and social commentary, that the belief in the incompatibility of land and trade was weakened by these develop-ments. But they have also tried to test this "literary" evidence against empirical findings on the rate of interpenetration of landed and trading families by the movement from trade into land, the movement from land into trade, and by intermarriage. The results of this research seem both to confirm the increasing compatibility of land and trade and to challenge it with evidence that in the end actually supports the more general thesis of an ascendant class orientation. For to the considerable extent that it is a real phenomenon, the failure of landed and trading families to intermix during the seventeenth and early eighteenth centuries seems attributable not to traditional status sanctions but to the growing acceptability of trade as an autonomous and self-sufficient social identity in its own right, a "status" group happily severed from the status criteria of birth, land, and the country seat.[51]

But the most telling evidence of a large-scale shift in attitudes lies in the way the very terms of conflict are altered toward the end of the seventeenth century. For after the Restoration it is not the traditional if destabilized opposition between "land" and "trade," but the newly con-ceptualized antithesis between the "landed interest" and the "monied interest," that gradually gains acceptance as the definitive articulation of social conflict. The monied interest was understood to embody the new, quantifying forces of public credit created by the "financial revolution" of the 1690s, whose principal achievement was the establishment of the Bank of England and the National Debt. Members of the landed interest were understood to be distinguished from those of the monied interest not by the status criteria of landownership or the possession of a country seat but by the quite specialized requirement that they live entirely on income from rents. And they defined themselves against all those— including urban merchants and improving "rural entrepreneurs"—who prospered by raising money through the credit mechanism of financial investment.[52] The new terminology, in other words, expresses the de-gree to which the traditional separation of land and trade *within* a status orientation and according to status criteria of gentility and land-ownership has been transformed for contemporaries into a conflict *be-*

tween status and class orientations, cutting across the older categories of land and trade.

7
THE PERSISTENCE OF THE ARISTOCRACY

Despite the success of the gentry controversy in raising difficult questions about the perils of social description at a time of profound categorial instability, in its wake the reigning analysis of early eighteenth-century social structure presents a disarmingly settled picture. The orthodox view of the period is one of political, social, and economic stability. The previous century's unprecedented rate of social mobility has declined, the temporary "crisis of the aristocracy" has abated, and the Whig oligarchy, in close alliance with the landed aristocracy and the monied interest, has begun its hegemonic rule.[53] At the stabilizing center of this rule, it is thought, is the aristocracy. In a real sense, the argument of the rise of an "entrepreneurial" and "middle class" gentry has been replaced by a thesis of the persistence of the aristocracy.

J. G. A. Pocock, in particular, has tried to account for the singular character and strength of the eighteenth-century ruling alliance by suggesting that the entire early modern period be seen as a "single sequence" of "aristocratic orders." Thus, if the "Tudor aristocracy" was (as Stone has established) declining between 1570 and 1640, the "Whig aristocracy" (on J. H. Plumb's authority) was created between 1660 and 1730. At the same time, however, Pocock recognizes that Plumb has spoken of the growth of Whig "oligarchy," not Whig "aristocracy," and he observes that the "Whig aristocratic order" of the eighteenth century lacked any "feudal character" and "was a recent outgrowth of mercantile and patronage politics." Now, it is undeniable that many great landowners in the eighteenth century possessed aristocratic title (just as many others no doubt had gentry status). Nevertheless we may get closer to the heart of this extraordinary alliance if we stress not its "aristocratic" character but the way in which capitalist or "middle class" values have transformed the aristocracy: how individualistic and class criteria are eating away, as it were from within, at a social structure whose external shell still seems roughly assimilable to the status model. As Christopher Hill has said, "By the end of the [seventeenth] century, participating in or benefiting from England's greatest capitalist industry, its money invested in the Bank of England, the peerage was sociologically a very different class from the hangers-on of James I's Court." The analogy with the antiromance turn taken by late-medieval romance is instructive: it was through the wholesale adoption of "antiaristocratic" elements that the aristocracy persisted in early modern England, and the persistence of the category signifies the tenacious strength of status attitudes more than the ascendancy of a discretely definable social body. Of course the analogy is imperfect; yet it is fair to say that the emergence of the language of "class" in the social realm acknowledges something like what is marked, in the literary realm, by the canonization of "the novel."[54]

Like Hexter, Pocock favors a strict identification of the middle class with a commercial bourgeoisie. This encourages him to be skeptical about the thesis of a rise of the gentry—which then would seem to argue the rise of the bourgeoisie—even though he knows Tawney was arguing the rise not of mercantile but of capitalist activity. This reduction of the capitalist to the mercantile market also helps justify Pocock's emphasis on the socially meaningful persistence of the status category "aristocracy," since by stressing the incapacity of an illusory mercantile ascendancy to explain large-scale early modern social change, it seems to substantiate his belief that class-based categories are only inappropriately applied to that period.[55] But in fact both merchants and aristocratic landowners are permeated by the values of a class orientation by the early eighteenth century. And if an earlier generation was inclined to associate the "rise" of capitalism either with medieval mercantile activity or with the industrial revolution of the later-eighteenth and the nineteenth centuries, historians today are closer to agreement that the most significant phase in the early development of English capitalism took place in the sixteenth- and seventeenth-century countryside. "In Machiavelli's Italy," C. B. Macpherson says, "the moneyed men had been the bearers of capitalism; in Harrington's England the gentry were even more important in that role than were the merchants and financiers." Techniques of capitalist "improvement" were exploited first by aristocratic and gentle landowners. By 1699, seventy-one percent of England was already under enclosure, mainly owing to the private agreement of these "possessive individualists" rather than an act of Parliament. If the device of the strict settlement helped shore up aristocratic patrilineage, it simultaneously secured the family estate for long-term capital investment. As proponents of the landed interest knew well, the greater landowners of early eighteenth-century England were inextricably tied to the investment system fostered by the monied interest. Rural and urban enterprise were inseparable parts of a unified capitalist development.[56]

For these reasons it must be said that the understanding of early modern social change in terms of a "single sequence of aristocratic orders" relies too heavily on an absorption model. Like twelfth-century romance, it dulls the felt need for an anatomy of "the aristocracy" with the muffling assurance of an ostensible persistence, but now with reference to a social context that is far more volatile. The creation of the English peerage, the "defeudalization" of the late-medieval nobility, the massive redistribution of land consequent on the English Reformation—these developments had a combined and interactive force that might well seem to argue the need for a new term of social ascendancy. Yet it is also worthwhile to reflect that "aristocracy" itself is an English word of no great antiquity. "Aristocratic ideology" names the impulse, operative in a wide diversity of cultures, to conceal the perennial alterations in ruling elites by naturalizing those elites as a static unity of status and virtue, the ongoing "rule of the best." In fact, one sign that the persuasive power of aristocratic ideology has been diminished is its increased explicitness and urgency under the challenge of alternative ideologies. The vigor of the aristocratic rationale, that is, bears something like an inverse relation to the efficacy of its ideology.[57]

In a certain sense, then, "aristocracy" is itself the new term, the "antithetical" simple abstraction, needed to announce the emergence of a new social organization, an announcement which is reciprocal to that accomplished two centuries later by the "thetical" language of class. The idea of aristocracy is decisively conceptualized at this time over against the articulation of progressive ideology, and its paradoxical function is to mediate the persistence of a category whose impermanence is signaled by the very fact that only now need it be conceptualized as such. This is not to suggest, however, that status values—like deference and paternalistic care—that we commonly associate with aristocratic social relations lose their force in the early modern period. On the contrary, they undergo the more elaborate sort of "theatricalization" that is likely to occur whenever social convention is raised to the level of self-conscious practice.[58]

8
THE FORMATION OF CONSERVATIVE IDEOLOGY

If the idea of aristocracy is indebted to the assaults of progressive ideology for its definitive conceptualization, the ostensible persistence of the aristocracy also owes much of its plausibility to the body of belief I will call "conservative ideology." But the relationship between conservative and aristocratic ideology is far from simple. The conservative Jonathan Swift, for example, is capable of a demystification of aristocratic honor that is fully as bracing as Defoe's. Writing of the Earl of Oxford's "Superiour Capacities," Swift pauses to observe that "as his own Birth was Illustrious, being descended from the Heirs generall of the Veres and the Mortimers, so he seemed to value that accidentall Advantage in himself and others more than it could pretend to deserve." Considerably less generous on the general theme of the arbitrary nature of genealogy and rank, Swift frankly declares that "the Lords degenerate by Luxury Idleness etc. and the Crown is always forced to govern by new Men. I think Titles should fall with Estates." His basic premise, like Defoe's, would seem to be that whatever portion of virtue or merit is inborn or "natural" is certainly not genealogically linked, and that nurture is in any case crucial for its flourishing. Indeed, if there is such a thing as a "natural" inheritance in such things, its effect may be seen more clearly in the frequent extinction of aristocratic lines. For the Great Physician has prescribed, Swift says, a "Remedy in the Order of Nature; so many great Families coming to an End by the Sloth, Luxury, and abandoned Lusts, which enervated their Breed through every Succession, producing gradually a more effeminate Race, wholly unfit for Propagation."[59]

One of the signs of its distance from progressive ideology, however, is the degree to which conservative ideology complicates its attitude toward the common, aristocratic enemy. Quite willing to exercise it himself, Swift nonetheless abuses "that pernicious Talent so much affected, of discovering a Contempt for *Birth, Family,* and *ancient Nobility.*" The argument is subtly pragmatic. "Suppose there be nothing but *Opinion* in the Difference of Blood; every Body knows, that *Authority* is very much founded on *Opinion.* But surely, that Difference is not wholly imaginary." Swift's point is that elevated birth affords opportunities for education, travel, and companionship which are otherwise not available, and that these will give the edge to the noble youth, whose native "*Genius*" may be no greater than that of the commoner. And he concludes that "ancient and honorable Birth . . . whether it be of real or imaginary Value, hath been held in Veneration by all wise, polite States, both Ancient and Modern." So the case to be made for aristocratic birth, fiercely rejected as an essentialist proposition, is readmitted on instrumental grounds. It is not that noble blood signifies internal merit but that it opens doors, that it entails external privileges that are separable from nobility of blood as such and that, properly exploited, will aid in merit's nurture. Charles Davenant's posture is very similar to this. He grants quite candidly that there is no intrinsic connection between aristocratic titles and "virtue and abilities"; yet if our concern is how we might best be governed, an important prudential question remains:

Who with most safety are to be relied on, they whose fortunes are made, or they who are to make their fortunes? They who have a satiety of titles, or they whose ambition may prompt them to attempt any thing to advance themselves? . . . He who has a large estate will not consent to have the laws subverted, which are his firmest security; for where the sword governs, lands at best are held but under a precarious title . . . But they who come into a government with a design to build a family, and make a fortune; who are to get all, and can lose nothing . . . such men are indeed the proper instruments for introducing arbitrary power.[60]

The defense of a noble lineage not for its intrinsic value but for what Swift calls its "imaginary value" is suggestively comparable to the rationale by which extreme skepticism returns to the notional veracity of romance. If progressive ideology is broadly parallel, in the social sphere, to naive empiricism in the epistemological, conservative ideology bears an analogous relationship to extreme skepticism. And this in turn would suggest that conservative ideology takes its fundamental character from its reactive negation of progressive ideology. In the realm of public discourse this profound negation can be heard in the "landed" opposition to the newly emergent "monied interest," to which I have already referred. And for a brief time under Queen Anne, the ascendancy of the Tory party seemed to promise to conservative ideology a powerful administrative outlet. But especially after the Jacobite Rising of 1715, the landed interest was increasingly identified with the body of lesser or "backwoods" gentry whose conservative anticapitalism threw them into that contradictory and largely powerless association with the urban poor which has been called "Tory radicalism."[61] And even during their brief period of power, the Tories' defense of aristocratic values was palpably impaired by the fact that they themselves were inevitable participants in the epidemic disenchantment with aristocratic ideology.

But even though conservative ideology failed to attain an effective political base in the early eighteenth century, its cultural influence was deep and pervasive. And it is on this level that the opposition between progressive and conservative ideology is most significant. Like the relationship between naive empiricism and extreme skepticism, the dialectical antithesis of progressive and conservative ideology emerges over time from the inchoate disorder of categorial instability, as a method of organizing sheer fluidity into a schematic model whose function is not to resolve conflict but to render it intelligible. Linked in their common opposition to aristocratic ideology, progressive and conservative ideology acquire an oppositional coherence as rival interpretations of the current crisis of status inconsistency—of its causes as well as its likely remedies. Their rationalized conflict serves to mediate the profound gulf between status and class orientations until the incorporation of status by class criteria has advanced far enough to provide a new and relatively stable standard of group identity for the modern era. In the accomplishment of this cultural revolution, the origins of the novel play a central role.

9
UNDERSTANDING STATUS INCONSISTENCY

Looking back upon the disruptive consequences of the early Stuart inflation of honors, Sir Edward Walker observed: "Every one is so partial to himself as to conclude he is neglected, if another he conceives either his equal or below him in Merit, Family, or Estate obtain [honor] before

him. So that the Advancement of one is the Discontent of another."
Almost a century later, the Earl of Bolingbroke applied the same principle to disparities in money as well: "There is imaginary as well as real
poverty. He who thought himself rich before, may begin to think himself
poor, when he compares his wealth, and the expense he is able to make,
with those men whom he hath been used to esteem, and perhaps justly,
far inferior to himself in all respects . . . Thus may contraries unite in
their effect, and poverty and wealth combine to facilitate the means and
the progress of corruption." Those attuned to the plight of younger sons
knew that comparison with other people was not the only source of such
discontents; they might also be produced by the inconstancy of one
man's fortunes over time. Thus William Sprigge criticized "the shortness
of that policy, that taking away the Preferments . . . yet never reduced
the means whereby men are qualified for an expectation, and prompted
to an ambition of them . . . Knowledge makes men proud and factious,
especially when they concern their fortunes and employments, are not
correspondent to the grandure of their birth and education." A fellow
advocate of the cause of younger sons simply remarked, "It is happier
never to have been in plenty, then after it to fall into want." David Hume
provides a summary of these insights: "Every thing in this world is
judg'd by comparison. What is an immense fortune for a private gentleman is beggary for a prince. A peasant wou'd think himself happy in
what cannot afford necessaries for a gentleman. When a man has either
been accustom'd to a more splendid way of living, or thinks himself
intitled to it by his birth and quality, every thing below is disagreeable
and even shameful."[62]

These widely scattered observations testify to the sensitivity of contemporaries to what modern social psychology and reference-group theory have called the state of "relative deprivation." The essence of the
theory is, in the words of Walter G. Runciman, the truism that "people's
attitudes, aspirations, and grievances largely depend on the frame of
reference within which they are conceived." It is through the internalization of norms and values that individual identification with a group
occurs, but the range of group attitudes to which an individual may refer
himself is not likely, except in simplified hypothesis, to correspond precisely to the groups of which he is in ostensible and more objective terms
a "member." By this understanding, "social stability" must always entail
a dynamic state of categorial "instability." Or rather it is a term we apply
to situations in which the perpetual tension of multiple and competing
group reference is maintained in such a way as to preclude—not change,
but change that manifests itself as such rather than as part of a larger,
equilibrated whole. "Relative deprivation" attempts to account for the
state of mind of one for whom there is a disparity between present
experience and the expectations created by reference-group identifica-

tion. As Robert K. Merton and Alice S. Rossi observe, the crucial word here is "relative." It is not simply objective loss, but the relation between expectations and (subjectively perceived) objective conditions, that results in the sense of deprivation. So "relative reward" is equally important to reference-group theory.[63]

Especially when it is encouraged to attend not only to the basic comparative factor of multiple reference to others, but also to the complications entailed in comparisons over time, the theory of reference groups acquires a utility similar, in the study of social change, to that of a dialectical theory of literary genre. Both appreciate the force of subjective assessment in the determination of what may then be lived as a fixed order, and both are likely to evolve at times when the literary and social orders have been destabilized by the very awareness of this determinant subjective force. But although reference-group theory has been criticized for attributing to psychological motivations a determinant priority over objective conditions in the explanation of human behavior, such motives may in turn be shown to have determinant material preconditions. The theory insists, that is, not on the inefficacy of material and structural causes, but on the dialectical nature of causation, and on the utility of attending to the particular ways in which the objectivity of categories is mediated by subjectivity.[64]

In the contemporary formulations of relative deprivation that I have quoted there is a diversity of attitude that runs the gamut from Hume's cheerful implacability to Sprigge's pained complaint. Common to all, however, is the experience of discovering that insight is the child of disenchantment, born in the sacrifice of a tacit faith in the consistency of things: of personal identity; of expectations and achievements; of power, wealth, and social rank. The experience of status inconsistency is psychologically and socially subversive, and reference-group theory has therefore seemed to be especially important for the theory of revolution. In place of the hypothesis of the rise of this group or the decline of that, reference-group theory suggests that the very fluidity and indeterminacy of social categories is a crucial precondition for revolutionary behavior. Revolution occurs under social conditions of status inconsistency, and revolutionaries are those in whom these conditions have been most completely internalized as a psychological state. But the sensitivity of reference-group theory to the subjective factor also argues the extension of "revolutionary behavior" to a diverse range of cultural activities, using political revolution as a paradigm for "illegal activity" (perhaps entailing "symbolic violence") within any other realm, including the literary. According to this model, literature is (to adapt the famous maxim of Clausewitz) politics by other means.[65]

The social significance of the English novel at the time of its origins lies in its ability to mediate—to represent as well as contain—the revolutionary clash between status and class orientations and the attendant crisis of status inconsistency. The novel gives form to the fluidity of crisis by organizing it into a conflict of competing interpretations. Progressive ideology ascribes the state of crisis to the social injustice inherent in aristocratic rule, whose arbitrary assignment of rewards to the well-born institutionalized the division of status and virtue as a tradition. Progressive ideology would overcome this crisis by means of the destruction of genealogical inequities, thereby liberating merit to reestablish status consistency by winning its just deserts. Conservative ideology, also mindful of aristocratic injustice, is yet more mindful of its modern replacement by progressive ideology and the rise of the "new aristocracy" of the undeserving. This is the crisis that truly confronts the modern world; but if conservative ideology is supremely confident in its negation of the progressive view, it is less certain of the terms in which the reign of status consistency—the alternative to both progressive and aristocratic injustice—might be posited.

The dialectical antithesis between progressive and conservative ideology comprehends those "questions of virtue" which the novel came into existence to propound. The antithesis was established over the course of the seventeenth century in an intersecting pattern of political, religious, and socioeconomic debates whose language and preoccupations suffuse much of the early novel itself. The following chapter will be devoted to these debates. With the hindsight of modern scholarship we can identify in them the several strands of belief that would soon converge, under the auspices of a developing class orientation, in the fully articulated ideology of capitalism. For seventeenth-century English people, the shared element in these diverse beliefs would necessarily have been much harder to name; but the notion of "reform" may be as good a candidate as any. Using the term in its widest sense, I will argue that early modern reform movements mediated capitalist ideology before its maturity in a way that is becoming increasingly familiar in this study; that is, their tendency to destabilize social categories emerged over time and, often, out of a more obvious propensity to do just the opposite—to reinforce traditional lines of social stratification.

This contradictory impulse has always been discernible in the history of the middle class and of middle-class consciousness, in its combination of two antithetical tendencies: to imitate and become absorbed within the aristocracy, and to criticize and supplant not only aristocracy but status orientation itself. Indeed, it is perhaps the assimilationist and the supersessionist strains of middle-class ideology that define its very nature. Not yet (if ever) embodied within a delimited social class, middle-class ideology slowly suffused different segments of the reigning status groups and gained its first expression through a network of beliefs that were themselves in the process of a critical mutation. The contradictory impulse in reform movements—what I have spoken of as a mechanism of "reversal"—also recalls the doubleness of secularization which preoccupied my concern with questions of truth. Responding to a degree of mutability in all spheres which at least appeared unprecedented, early modern English people set out to reform their world—to return it to its order—with a practical and innovating ingenuity that surely was without precedent. For those who were skeptical of the effort, the necessary questions were obvious enough: "For who ever saw so many discontented persons: so many yrked with their owne degrees: so fewe contented with their owne calling: and such number desirous, & greedie of change, & novelties? Who ever heard tel of so many reformers, or rather deformers of estates and Common weales . . . ?" And yet it is precisely in the hopeful space between reformation and deformation that capitalist ideology was conceived.[66]

— Five —

Absolutism and Capitalist Ideology:
The Volatility of Reform

The notorious difficulty of defining the transition from "feudalism" to "capitalism" reflects the instability of these terms as representatives of distinct modes of distributing social, economic, and political power. One pole of the debate is exemplified by Christopher Hill's ingenious and provocative assertion that "the end of the Middle Ages" in government, agrarian relations, external trade and foreign policy, internal trade and industry, finance, and government borrowing can be located in a momentous succession of seventeenth-century acts of legislation. The most symbolically resonant of these several acts is the 1646 abolition of feudal tenures and the Court of Wards: henceforth ownership is absolute and no longer a condition of feudal fealty and service, and great landowners are able to manage, exploit, and consolidate—to "improve"—their estates free of contractual duties to the king. At the other pole of the debate is the argument, recently advanced by Alan Macfarlane, that because individual ownership has been absolute in England at least since the thirteenth century, English "feudalism" is an illusion, and its "discovery" by historicizing seventeenth-century English scholars amounts to a false periodization of what the common lawyers were right to see as an unbroken continuity.[1]

Within the territory enclosed by these antithetical arguments, historians have tended to agree on the reality of a long-term transition from "feudalism" to "capitalism," and on the need for a special vocabulary by which to account for late-medieval practices that seem at once to derive their impetus from unmistakably feudal forms and to serve quite different institutional ends. "Fiscal feudalism," for example, is a term invented to describe the Tudor and early Stuart policy that sought to transform certain feudal incidents—wardship, purveyance, ship money, and the creation of honors—from relationships of service to techniques for increasing the revenues of the national monarch. Another instance of this sort of historiographical strategy is the idea of "bastard feudalism," which loosely describes a contractual system of political-military retainership, common in the fifteenth century, that was based upon a freely negotiated indenture rather than on land tenure or personal relation. Historians may disagree on whether "bastard" is the proper term to denote this historical hybrid, suggesting as it may a "degeneration" rather than a "refinement" of earlier feudal custom, but the need for some such syncretic designation is generally accepted. Nor has the need been met only from, as it were, the earlier end of the "transition from feudalism to capitalism." Thus Max Weber refers to the mercantilist economic policies of the early modern state as "irrational capitalism" to distinguish their state orientation from the fully differentiated and market-oriented entrepreneurialism of "rational capitalism."[2]

"Absolutism," the category that has been most generally accepted to bridge the gap between "late feudalism" and "early capitalism," alludes to several related historical movements. In contemporary usage, an "absolute monarch" was one whose power was unrestricted by external forces—that is, by pope or emperor. In modern usage, "absolutism" is more likely to suggest first the liberation of the monarch from internal, baronial constraints. Each sense of the term reinforces the general view of the period it designates as that in which the foundation of the modern nation-state was laid. But the formation of the absolutist state was not simply a matter of aggrandizing monarchal power at the expense of baronial influence. Within the framework of that state, the feudal relation of monarch and baron was transformed into the bureaucratic and administrative relation of royalty and nobility, the supreme head of state and its loyal servants. So although some historians would deny England a stage of absolutism because it lacked an absolute prince, the early strength of Parliament relative to the Continental estates systems has also been cited to exemplify an integral participation of nobility and gentry characteristic of the centralized power of the absolutist state.[3]

The innovation in power sharing was economic as well as political. The progressive consolidation of absolute private property by the nobility helped counterbalance the decline of its military authority and of the territorial jurisdictions that had been peculiar to the feudal system. Daniel Defoe acknowledges the connection between the "absolutism" of royal power and that of landed property when he explains that since the abolition of feudal tenures, the English gentry hold and inherit "their lands *in capite,* absolutely and by entail . . . All the knight's service and vassalage is abolish'd, they are as absolutely possess'd of their mannours and freehold as a prince is of his crown." The dynamic tension that animates absolutism, and that is expressed in the tension between royal will and noble privilege, is the impulse to dissolve the limitations imposed by feudal social relations without also dissolving the implicit sanctions of feudal hierarchy. The impulse is unfulfillable. As J. H. Hexter has observed, "Absolutist theory wrenched the idea of hierarchy from its context in the nature of things and made it a matter of the prince's will." This enabling act of absolutist reform gave birth and momentum to successive acts, which both extended and subverted it. The movement is seen in the flowering of absolutist doctrines of royal sovereignty around the end of the Tudor period, and in their transmission and use over the course of the following century. For from this broad vantage point, the emergence of such doctrines can be seen to signal not the culminating triumph of absolute princely authority but the beginning of a process whereby the confident exercise of royal power becomes a more general model for the way in which diverse human exertions aim to reform society to alternative ideals. The movement therefore also provides an initial perspective on the development of progressive ideology.[4]

I
THE ABSOLUTE PRINCE ABSOLUTIZED

The ambition of absolutist theory is to give to the authority bestowed upon the sovereign from without the illusory aura of self-generation. Absolutist doctrines like the divine right of kings and the patriarchal theory of political obligation exalt the will of the sovereign by deriving his power from an elevated source in such a way as to stress the present reality of authority while deemphasizing the reciprocal reality of subordination to another power which is implied in the very fact of derivation. And although they are ultimately rooted in the soil of early Christian and Old Testament culture, these doctrines owe their particular formulation to the critical conditions of late-Tudor and early Stuart rule. It is also around this time that the notion of the *arcana imperii,* or "mysteries of state," is liberated from its derivative subservience to the enabling tradition of the *arcana ecclesiae* and begins to nourish the absolutist conception of the "deified" state. The complex provenance of the conception bespeaks the subtlety with which it invests political with transcendent power. As Ernst H. Kantorowicz has explained, "Christian doctrine, by transferring the political notion of *polis* to the other world and by expanding it at the same time to a *regnum coelorum,* not only faithfully stored and preserved the political ideas of the ancient world, as so often it did, but also prepared new ideas for the time when the secular world began to recover its former peculiar values."[5]

Both the utility, and the hazards, of absolutist doctrine are evident in what befell the fiction of the king's two bodies under Stuart rule. The fiction had served the cause of Tudor absolutism by distinguishing the "natural" body of the king (vulnerable, like those of his subjects, to decay and death) from the sempiternal, "political" body of kingship as such, which marked the great divide between him and all others. In a certain sense the fiction provided a corporate version of the aristocratic dualism of "honor." For the "political" principle of continuous succession is an external register of genealogical status that comprehends and confirms the innate virtue of the "natural" man; and the theoretical distinction between the two bodies argues their virtual inseparability by effectively incorporating the political authority within the natural man we see before us. By 1642, hostilities between sovereign and subjects had reached the point of no return. Yet, so far from repudiating the fiction of the king's two bodies, Parliament used it to justify the claim that, in the words of Peter Heylyn, it might "destroy Charles Stuart, without hurting the king." By means of this reversal, Parliament argued in effect that the essential "virtue" of royal sovereignty inheres in the supranatural capacity of continuous succession, and that the status conferred upon Charles's body natural, because it was now seen to be inconsistent with his merit, might be withdrawn. On May 26, 1642, Lords and Commons insisted that "treason is not treason as it is against [the king] as a man, but as a man that is a king, and as he hath relation to the kingdom, and stands as a person entrusted with the kingdom and discharging that trust." A day later they declared that their actions in Parliament had "*the stamp of Royal Authority, although His Majesty . . . do in his own Person oppose or interrupt the same.*" By rationalizing the king's access to absolute power, absolutist doctrine had most importantly rationalized access to absolute power as such. The parliamentary assumption of an unconditional "royal authority" only extended the lesson taught by the king's assumption of an unconditional "political" authority. So in the end the absolutist assertion of the royal will provided the king's subjects with a crude but effective model for justifying the most extraordinary "reform" of the era—the killing of the king. As Anthony Ascham observed, "They who fight to free themselves from an absolute power, are by that obliged for the time to take upon them the absolutest."[6]

Of course this striking and apparently innovative reversal must be set in context. For several decades the opponents of royal prerogative had been elaborating their own version of the "body political" through the common-law argument of the "ancient constitution" and Parliament's immemorial existence. The breakthrough of 1642 is no doubt indebted to these developments; and yet as our earlier inquiry into the seventeenth-century historical revolution makes clear, the common-law apotheosis of historical succession as immemorial continuity marks not a high point in the reverence for antiquity but something akin to its demise. The real breakthrough to a conception of absolute, self-justified authority would come when the criterion of historical succession itself was cast aside: when, as Christopher Hill has observed, the tumultuous debates of the 1640s briefly redirected attention from "the recovery of rights which used to exist to the pursuit of rights because they *ought* to exist."[7]

In 1642 Charles himself inopportunely provides his opponents with a less radical model of sovereignty—as a coordinate act of lawmaking by king, Lords, and Commons—that will yet subvert his own absolutist ambitions. But in the same address he also acknowledges, with considerable eloquence, the problem of absolutism itself, the inexorable logic by which "all great changes . . . almost infallibly beget yet greater changes," and the authorization of absolute power soon acquires its own devolutionary momentum. Against this nightmare vision of the loss of all degree, the king sets the abiding reverence, customarily deemphasized by absolutist argument, for genealogical tradition as upheld by the royal succession. If, Charles warns, the House of Commons is ceded the power it seeks,

so new a power will undoubtedly intoxicate persons who were not born to it, and beget not only divisions among them as equals, but in them contempt of us, as become an equal to them . . . till . . . at last the common people . . . discover this *arcanum imperii,* that all this was done by them, but not for them, and grow weary of journey-work, and set up for themselves, call parity and independence liberty, devour that estate which had devoured the rest, destroy all rights and proprieties, all distinctions of families and merit, and by this means this splendid and excellently distinguished form of government end in a dark, equal chaos of confusion, and the long line of our many noble ancestors in a Jack Cade or a Wat Tyler.[8]

Some of the king's apprehensions were quite unwarranted—for example, the fear of an economic leveling and the destruction of property rights. The parliamentary abolition of feudal tenures was carefully confined to greater landowners, and after the Putney Debates, those who shared a material interest in halting the work of social reformation closed ranks against those who had grown "weary of journey-work" and wished to "set up for themselves." But if what Hill has called the "revolt within the Revolution" failed to materialize, it was at least fully conceptualized by the radical thinkers of the revolutionary years. If the absolute ownership and heritability of private property was strengthened during this period, belief in the inheritance of nobility (as we have seen) was not. Charles's death, and the problem of how to engage people's loyalty to a Commonwealth, challenged so fundamentally the ingrained association of political authority with genealogical inheritance as to provoke intense debate—the Engagement Controversy of 1649–50—over the increasingly tenuous relation between lineage, political right, and temporal power. The abolition of the monarchy in 1649 was accompanied by the abolition of the House of Lords, an act of erasure that confirmed Charles's fears for "distinctions of families" almost as definitively as did the antiaristocratic sentiments that were spoken and written during the 1640s and 1650s. When the Stuart monarchy was restored in 1660, Charles II dated his reign from the end of his father's, sanguinely restoring to royal sovereignty the legitimating principle of uninterrupted succession. But the expendability of even the fiction of inherited authority was made unmistakably clear after his death by the terms in which the Glorious Revolution was rationalized.[9]

The pressing need to legitimate the deposition of James Stuart and the accession of the Hanoverians, despite the utter disruption of the royal succession which attended these acts, obliged the most mainstream of contemporary English people to make indifference to genealogical inheritance an explicit article of the theory of English kingship. Yet with a characteristic sleight of hand, the transformation was achieved within the absolutist spirit of divine right and the king's two bodies. For Anglican divines were able (at least to their own satisfaction) to substitute for "absolute divine right" "the divine right of providence," which now might be acknowledged to govern all ways in which a prince could succeed to a throne. In the somewhat querulous words of William Sherlock, Dean of St. Paul's, "It is all but Providence still, and I desire to know why the Providence of an [hereditary] Entail is more Sacred and Obligatory than any other Act of Providence, which gives a Setled possession of the Throne?" For Edward Stillingfleet a real, but not fateful, distinction was to be made: "A King *de jure* is one, who comes in by lineal Descent, as next Heir, and whose Right is Owned and Recognized by the Estates of the Realm. A King *de facto* is one, who comes in by Consent of the Nation, but not by Virtue of an immediate Hereditary Right." Stillingfleet believed the crucial question was "whether Allegiance be not due where the Rights of Sovereignty are plac'd, by an extraordinary Act of Providence, and the concurrent Consent of the Nation." In 1701 the Act of Settlement made official the repudiation of immediate hereditary right by declaring Roman Catholics "uncapable to inherit . . . the crown and government of this realm" and by excluding fifty-seven prospective heirs in favor of the Hanoverians.[10]

Now, the clear alternative to hereditary right might seem to be personal merit, and some contributors to the debate did in fact try to solve the problem of the Hanoverian settlement in the terms of progressive ideology. One clergyman wrote that the choice of William of Orange, in compliance with the will of the majority, rested "altogether upon his Personal Merit, in rescuing the Kingdom from Popery and Slavery . . . So that, although he had been quite a stranger to the Royal Blood, the matter would have passed the same way." Of course most observers felt the need for a more accommodating rationale of William's succession. But the distance between the two stances is in any case not very great— comparable as it is, on the public scale of the theory of kingship, to the difference between an assimilationist and a supersessionist posture among upwardly mobile private individuals. At the very least, it is now the pragmatic achievement of popular consent and settled possession that confer merit, dictate status, and permit us the inference of sacred right. The a priori validation that comes with genealogical inheritance has been replaced by the present fact of a successful accession to a position of authority. This reversal cannot fail to recall analogous turns taken in debates on questions of truth: the replacement of the discovered manu- script topos, for example, by the empirical authentications of the claim to historicity, or the use of the doctrine of providence to reconcile divine with human creativity. What is most striking in the present context is the way contemporaries have learned, over the course of the century, to employ the absolutist language of royal sovereignty to justify the discon- tinuity, the willed rupture, of the royal lineage. The absolute power of the prince to order hierarchy has become detachable from his own authority and can be used to reorder even princely hierarchy. Reasons of state are lodged not with the prince but with this burgeoning entity, the state; and therefore also with its loyal servants.[11]

2
SWORD AND ROBE

Renaissance humanism undertook to reform the accepted model of the education of the nobility so as to promote the great end of service to the prince and to the state. This program to some degree only extends the late-medieval ideal of chivalric service to the Christian community and to a state conceived dynastically as the patrimony of the monarch. But it depends as much, at least in England, on the development of indigenous strains of political nationalism and civic service. As the feudal functions of the nobility declined, the growth of the ideal of aristocratic service to the state both acknowledged the ascendancy of royal absolutism and, by underscoring the continuing political importance of the nobility, de- fended against it. Renaissance writings on the education of the gentleman assumed that aristocratic service was less a privilege owed to status than a civic responsibility, which might be filled, if necessary, by ungentle but accomplished parvenus. But if the insistence on the notion of "true nobility" in these writings sought to admonish the nobility for a proud reliance on birth to the neglect of worth, it also aimed to promulgate among them a new, civic conception of gentility and honor that would constitute a refinement of, not an alternative to, genealogical nobility.[12]

However, civic service was also a controversial ideal in the Renaissance absolutist state, because it could be felt to challenge the ideal of feudal service in a cultural setting still bound by many ties to the institutions and ethos of feudalism. It is true that the dissociation of the nobility from a fundamentally military function occurred earlier in England than elsewhere in Europe. What Lawrence Stone has called the "royal monopoly on violence," which characterizes the modern, centralized state, was established under the Tudors: the great bands of armed retainers were reduced and baronial jurisdiction over territorial empires was destroyed; officeholding and service at the national court became more common aristocratic activities. Even the acquisition of aristocratic honor was in a sense "nationalized" during this period, tamed and systematized under the aegis of the royal "fount" of honor. But the very extent of these reforms hastened a reaction against them. Arthur Ferguson has even suggested that to contemporaries, the Renaissance "recovery of chivalric literature constituted a 'rebirth' considerably more impressive than the 'rebirth' of classical culture then also taking place." That the future belonged to the humanist, rather than to the feudal, revival is confirmed by the fact that sixteenth-century treatises on gentility show a decided preference for "letters" over "arms" as the fittest occupation for the gentleman. Yet because the pressure of social change now gave to the old question of "arms versus letters" a new urgency, a strong and ideologically tinged advocacy of "arms" developed as well, especially in romances, where the common, derogatory term for the alternative to knight-errant or knight-at-arms is "carpet knight"—he who shuns chivalry in favor of courting princes and ladies. The degree to which the crisis of the aristocracy in seventeenth-century France was shaped by these particular ideological forces is suggested by the fact that there the current terms for "old" and "new" aristocracy were *noblesse d'épée* and *noblesse de robe*.[13]

With variations peculiar to each locale, ideological conflict between "sword" and "robe" nobility is widespread in the absolutist states of early modern Europe. It organizes into a culturally intelligible split the destabilizing transformation the European aristocracies were undergoing at this time. The works of Castiglione and Machiavelli provide our most profound account of this process because although they are fully attuned to crucial cultural demarcators like "arms versus letters," their deepest concern is to tap the dynamic indeterminacy of absolute state power itself.

Although the animating aim of *The Book of the Courtier* (1528) is to stabilize the role of the new robe nobility, its central experience is one of controlled ambivalence. Stable, systematic relationships of hierarchical subordination—signifiers to signifieds, means to ends—are constructed so as to permit external and elevated authority to be experimentally subjected to a subversive impulse that is at once vertiginous and liberat-

ing. The discussion of whether the perfect courtier should be nobly
born—does birth signify worth, or only good fortune?—is a case in
point.[14] Another is the account of the courtier's language and literary
accomplishments, in which esteem for Latin and for the preservation of
the ancient and vernacular classics by means of imitation is thoroughly
infiltrated by a historicizing awareness that the present is unique and that
no rules are as powerful as time, corruption, and the rule of usage (Preface, 3–6; I, 52–64). Considerations like these lead inevitably to *The
Courtier*'s central question: is the perfect courtier "good and worthy of
praise . . . simply and in himself," or "in regard to the end to which he is
directed" (IV, 288)? Castiglione bends his will to define the greater end
subserved by the courtier's perfection. Surely he must serve the court
lady through the love he has for her. But the twelfth-century tradition of
the art of love has become by now a semiology so complex, ambiguous,
and deceitful, the lady's favor so refined, inaccessible, and sadistic, that
love service comes to seem a perversely paradoxical enterprise (III, 267–
82).[15]

And with this the ground is cleared for Ottaviano Fregoso's climactic
argument that "to bring or help one's prince toward what is right and to
frighten him away from what is wrong are the true fruit of Courtiership"
(IV, 290). Yet the very need of the prince for intellectual and moral
guidance—his ignorance, corruption, self-deceit, arrogance, and a thousand other vices—force the objection that "the Courtier, through whose
instruction the prince is to become so excellent, would have to be more
excellent than the prince . . . In order to set this Courtier above the
Court Lady and make him exceed the bounds that she can attain, signor
Ottaviano has also set the Courtier above the prince" (IV, 327–28).
Means have become ends: the perfection of the courtier elevates him
above both figures whom he putatively exists to serve. It is at this point
that Bembo's long, neoplatonic recapitulation of courtly love intervenes
to provide true closure for the treatise. And whatever ostensible rationale
for the ending, its effect is to reconstruct a system of absolute hierarchy
and service which cannot be dismantled, because it is built upon the
authority of God himself. If birth in the real world of sixteenth-century
Urbino cannot be depended upon to reflect worth, nevertheless "outward beauty is a true sign of inner goodness" (IV, 342), and the final
perfection of the courtier is understood to be that of self-transcendence.
Yet it is difficult not to respond to an energy, greater than that of Bembo's
anachronistic divine frenzy, which emanates from the autonomous figure
of the courtier himself and which expresses the self-creative power of the
principle of service now internalized within his own person.

The title *The Prince* (1532) is in a sense deceptive, for the case of the
hereditary prince is of little concern to Machiavelli, precisely because
"ancestral usages" make his social elevation, and the maintenance of it,

relatively secure.[16] By the same token, the rule of ecclesiastical prin-
cipalities lies outside the province of this treatise because it is "upheld by
higher causes" (XI, 41–44). Divine right and hereditary prescription are
external sources of absolute power, whereas Machiavelli would make
absolutism honest by stripping away the authorizations of hierarchy to
pursue its deepest logic, the profession and exercise of power as a secular,
present-centered, and self-authorized activity. So the protagonists of *The
Prince* are really variations on the "new prince" (Agathocles, Francesco
Sforza, Cesare Borgia), and the treatise's intended audience includes the
English parliamentarians of 1642, Oliver Cromwell, and the proponents
of William of Orange—all those who have abandoned the hereditary (if
not quite the providential) argument in their rationalization of power. As
often as not, new princes are "those who rise from private citizens," and
so in counseling the new prince, Machiavelli is really counseling the
"new man" writ large, those whose upwardly mobile aspirations are
unusually, even audaciously, ambitious (VII, 23–24).

   The quality needed for such a rise, so far from being tied to the anchor
of genealogical status, is by definition the self-generated and transporta-
ble ability to succeed. *Virtù* is already in part a secularization term, an
amoral psychological category for denoting human will and energy. But
as the negative, polarizing case of the tyrant Agathocles makes clear,
Machiavelli finds the term useful because, like "providence," it also bears
an ethical charge whose tacit effect is, under most circumstances, to
validate success as the reward for "virtue." In this normative sense *virtù* is
also, like *polis,* a resecularization term that recurs to the old Roman *virtus*
and connotes the civic virtues of the independent, uncorruptible, arms-
bearing citizen. But if a man like Agathocles obliges us to divide *virtù* into
"virtue" and "ability" (VIII, 31–32), in normal parlance the former quality is implicitly subsumed within the latter as a kind of vestigial but still
essential organ of ethical equilibrium. Like Francis Bacon, Machiavelli
would separate "is" from "ought" and "give to faith that only which is
faith's," but both men also want to exploit the language of that other
realm in order at least to insinuate a radical reversal in our ways of
thinking about spiritual and moral value. Thus Machiavelli also anticipates the latitudinarian and Mandevillian discovery that "private vices"
may conduce to "public benefits," that "some things which seem virtues
would, if followed, lead to one's ruin, and some others which appear
vices result in one's greater security and wellbeing" (XV, 56–57).[17]

   In a similar fashion Machiavelli's *fortuna,* although normally more
fully secularized than the latitudinarian "providence," is also an epigone
of the ancient Roman goddess, and at times the term is used interchange-
ably with "God" and "Heaven" (XXV, 91–94).[18] But since Machiavelli's
perpetual advice to the prince is that he must (to the degree that this is
possible) learn to adapt himself to the mutabilities of *fortuna,* these innu-

endos of otherness make such adaptation intelligible as a paradigmatic instance of the absolutist dynamic: as the internalization of absolute authority by merely human, even common, power. Thus as Andrew Marvell was to discern and Oliver Cromwell to exemplify, the special man of merit renders academic what in "traditional" terms would seem a fundamental difference—between *fortuna* and *virtù*, between God's election of singular men and the human internalization of divinity: "It certainly is the course of Fortune, when she wishes to effect some great result, to select for her instrument a man of such spirit and ability [*virtù*] that he will recognize the opportunity which is afforded him" (*Discourses*, II, xxix, 382). For the Renaissance Florentine, the great example of such a figure is the "newly risen man" whom Machiavelli exhorts to liberate Italy from the barbarians (XXVI, 94–98).

Partial elements of Machiavelli's absolute prince and Castiglione's omnicompetent courtier color both terms of the loose cultural antithesis of "sword" and "robe" as it undergoes successive refinements in the English experience. Generally speaking, the Machiavellian model reinforces in the sword mentality the increasingly antiquated virtues of armed independence, and in the robe mentality the modern virtues of opportunistic self-advancement, whereas the spirit of Castiglione informs both with the ambivalence—whether military-chivalric or bureaucratic—of the self-sufficient servant. But it must also be said that the English version of the antithesis is itself in flux over the course of the seventeenth century, acquiring a temporary stability at the end of it that has moved quite far from any simple opposition of "old" and "new" nobility.

On the eve of the English Revolution, the split into "country" and "court" interests expressed the resistance of those who conceived themselves to be the natural rulers of the countryside to the growth of absolutist state bureaucracy and centralization—to officeholding, the sale and inheritance of offices, and burgeoning techniques of indirect taxation—in which those who represented the court interest were primarily implicated and invested. The revolution and its aftermath both reinforced and complicated the symbolic meaning of this opposition. For one thing, the social complexion of officeholding became more diverse during the Interregnum. "Robe" service not only defined a more progressive social type for the nobility; it also included more and more people of ignoble status. Yet the growing possibility of a governmental career open to talents was even more strikingly registered during these years in the traditional, "sword" realm of military service. In the ranks of the Royalist army, to be sure, the figure of the Cavalier was perpetuating an anachronistic model of personal honor and fealty to the feudal overlord, adumbrated by a pseudoreligious worship of the national monarch. Sundered, by war and primogeniture, from their authority as the natural rulers of the countryside, possessing neither land nor an army career, many younger Cavaliers had become the victims of social dislocation and were reduced to ridiculing the older generation as "the female gentry of the smock." But the social fluidity that disrupted the feudal assumptions of the Royalist army was to become an organizing principle of the New Model Army of the republic.[19]

In 1643 Oliver Cromwell declared:

I had rather have a plain russet-coated captain that knows what he fights for, and loves what he knows, than that which you call a gentleman and is nothing else . . . It had been well that men of honour and birth had entered into these employments, but why do they not appear? Who would have hindered them? But seeing it was necessary the work must go on, better plain men than none, but best to have men patient of wants, faithful and conscientious in the employment.

By prohibiting peers from exercising their traditional military commands, the Self-Denying Ordinance of 1645 helped establish in the New Model Army a chain of command that was independent of the old feudal relations of personal loyalty. Thus one feature of the republican (unlike the royal) monopoly on violence was a de-aristocratized hierarchy in which the ungentle might rise according to their deserts. Along with the rogues, vagabonds, beggars, and Protestant sectaries who comprised the growing category of "masterless men" in the mid-seventeenth century, Christopher Hill includes the soldiers of the New Model Army. But distributive justice and the extension of power to the rank and file were not the only expressions of military absolutism under the republic. The period following the Putney Debates saw the gradual assumption of the power of Parliament—itself de-aristocratized in 1649—by the generals of the army, and its new commander-in-chief's accession to absolute "protectorship" as a kind of symbolic and national representation of the upward rise of the deserving, anonymous multitude. As Marvell knew, part of Cromwell's *virtù* lay in his capacity to mediate genealogical and pragmatic models of sovereignty: "He seems a king by long succession born, / And yet the same to be a king does scorn."[20]

In 1661, the Earl of Clarendon recalled the late Commonwealth as a time when "all ages, sexes, and degrees, all professions and trades, would become reformers, when the common people of England would represent the commons of England . . . The confounding [of] the commons of England, which is a noble representative, with the common people of England, was the first ingredient into that accursed dose, which intoxicated the brains of men with that imagination of a commonwealth." After the Restoration, command of the militia was taken from (in Clarendon's words) "persons of no degree or quality," and restored to "the government of the nobility and principal gentry throughout the kingdom." As Hill has observed, "One lasting legacy of the Interregnum was

a hatred of standing armies among the men of property." This hatred fed
the country interest after 1660 by highlighting military bureaucracy as
one component in the general corruption of ancient liberties and feudal
bonds by the modern absolutist state. The lesson of the Interregnum, it
appeared, was that absolute power, once concentrated in a single ruler,
will inevitably devolve to those who least deserve it, the unpropertied.
But the lesson was contradictory, for it also taught, along with a fierce
opposition to the state power of Whig oligarchy and its parvenu servants,
an equally fierce loyalty to the state power of Jacobite absolutism and its
dream of absolute sovereignty uncorrupted by devolution. By the end of
the century, the country interest had come very close to both the "landed
interest," which so vehemently opposed the reforming methods of capitalist investment and "improvement," and the body of social attitudes I
have called conservative ideology. By the same token, a discontinuous
but discernible tradition can be traced from the court interest that flourished before 1642 to the "monied interest" and the progressive ideology
that flourished after 1688.[21]

But any attempt to account for the crystallization of ideological conflict in the early eighteenth century by reference to matters of strictly
political service and reform leaves too much out. For one thing, there was
the influence of the scientific movement. At the very time that civic
humanists were elevating state service over noble blood and the chivalric
ideal as the only authentic criterion of gentility, new philosophers were
denigrating diplomacy as an outdated and unadventurous mode of service by which to augment the honor of the nobility. "For tis a *greater
credit*," Joseph Glanvill says, "to know the *wayes of captivating Nature,*
and making her *subserve* our *purposes* and *designments;* then to have *learnt*
all the *intrigues* of *Policy,* and the *Cabals* of *States* and *Kingdoms;* yea, then
to *triumph* in the head of *victorious Troops* over *conquer'd Empires.*" Thomas
Sprat observes that since nowadays English military prowess, being
naval, depends on the valor of common seamen, the English nobility are
free to pursue their interests in natural studies. Of course the Baconian
program for the reform of knowledge envisioned a vast collective procedure and a profound public return on the investment. Nevertheless
these remarks betray a characteristically individualistic enthusiasm for
the pleasures and ends of serving science; and Henry Stubbe flatly accused the mechanical education sponsored by the Royal Society of "de-
bauching our *Nobility* [and] *Gentry*" from studying to serve prince and
church. Moreover, contemporaries recognized the connection between
the quantifying premises of the empirical sciences and those of the
monied interest, and they were prepared to draw ideological conclusions
from that conjunction. More important even than scientific service and
reform, however, was the capitalist revolution itself. For in the problems
raised by the early modern experience of individual and national eco-

nomic intercourse, the centrifugal pull toward the validation of self-generated activity which I have identified at the heart of absolutist reform can be seen with unparalleled clarity. As Max Weber was the first and most persuasive to argue, these problems are inseparable from the Protestant Reformation.[22]

3
PROTESTANTS AND CAPITALISTS

The most significant reform achieved by Tudor absolutism was the English Reformation. From the Act of Supremacy to what is sometimes called the Puritan Revolution, the Reformation also provides a bird's-eye view of absolutist reform as a dynamic and destabilizing internalization of authority. "The overthrow of papal authority by Henry VIII thus looks forward to the civil war and the execution of Charles I. The royal supremacy yielded place to the sovereignty of Parliament, and that to demands for the sovereignty of the people." Yet in the realm of faith, the Reformation was not a revolt at all, but a humble resubmission of human depravity to the unchallengable will of a stern and righteous God. The Protestant, and especially the English, Reformation was informed by the tension arising from these several competing and incompatible versions of "reformation."[23]

Henry VIII's frank subordination of church to state was truer to the Lutheran than to the Calvinist spirit of reform. In Luther's program, ecclesiastical and priestly mediation would be replaced by that of the absolutist state, and he thought the established system of social subordination vital to the control of human license. The reading of the Gospel as a plan of social reconstruction, in particular, held no appeal for him. To derive from Christ's love for the humble and from his egalitarian redemption of rich and poor alike a call for social reform was to mistake a spiritual for a material promise. But in Calvin's thought there is a more problematic relationship between the old order of political-legal coercion and the new order of the liberated Christian conscience. Because the reigning social hierarchy is, like the Fall, an attempt to usurp God's order, Calvin can say that "each time men who have been raised to high estate are beaten down, and conversely, each time those who were scorned are honoured, this does not happen without reason." For the time being, the old order must continue to be accorded a provisional authority, but meanwhile the Church will institutionalize the standards of the new, representing a sphere independent of social and political tradition and providing that tradition no automatic sanctity.[24]

Like Calvin, the Elizabethan Puritans understood the new order represented by the Church to encourage vocational activity outside it, as a special realm of Christian freedom in which the coming of God's kingdom might be prepared for. This was true especially of economic behavior, which Calvin tended to emphasize both figuratively and literally as that which the new order must transform. So within the realm of political theory, Calvinist and early Puritan teaching liberated economic activity from state control. At the same time, however, both Luther and Calvin reaffirmed as moral law the medieval church's strict prohibitions against individualistic economic enterprise, and much recent work has confirmed that mainstream Puritan writings before 1640 generally and explicitly express opposition to social mobility, usury, monopolies, and unrestrained profit-seeking. Moreover, certain Calvinist doctrines that are crucial to these matters, especially Calvin's treatment of the vocation or "calling," exerted a profound influence on Church of England attitudes. It was in fact the immediately political implications of the Calvinist premise—the volatile differentiation of new from old order, church from state—that the established church repudiated and that Puritans, in their reform of Reformation, increasingly embraced. Consequently, when a political order based on Puritan principles ceased to be (depending on one's sympathies) a possibility or a threat after 1660, the similarities between Puritan and Anglican belief, especially as to the wide-ranging social implications of Calvinist doctrine, began to grow more visible. [25]

Max Weber's celebrated thesis of a causal relationship between the "Protestant ethic" and the "spirit of capitalism" turns upon Protestant soteriology and the attitude toward earthly works. In the partial minds of the Protestant reformers, the Roman Catholic belief in justification by works encouraged a complacent hypocrisy by assuring the sinner that he might always compensate for particular sins through the performance of good works, thereby proving his personal righteousness and earning God's grace despite his sins. Against this belief in the efficacy of works the reformers set the doctrines of predestination and justification by faith. Grace is a free gift of Christ's own righteousness, imputed to particular saints by the divine will. Those whom God has chosen for deliverance owe their election not in the least to their own exertions but to the grace of God, the gratuitousness of whose choice (at least according to the standards of human merit) is evidenced by the fact that it is predestined. [26]

In these attitudes we recognize one expression of that pervasive Protestant disdain for mediation by external signs and powers—for, paradoxically, the efficacy of human "reform"—which we encountered in the consideration of questions of truth. Jesus had clearly denied the capacity of outward, material achievements to win or even to signify the state of inner grace. In a vehement reaffirmation of this Gospel doctrine of "status inconsistency," Protestant thought extended the denial to all "works" whatsoever. But as with questions of truth, the social implications of this denial were unpredictable. On the one hand, viewing sin as an inherited characteristic so ineluctable that no virtuous behavior could expunge it was, as Christopher Hill observes, "well suited to a society based on inherited status." In the words of the Calvinist Samuel Hieron, "The kingdom of heaven is a reward of inheritance." This "breaketh the neck of all merit . . . If heaven were the hire of servants, or the booty of purchasers, it were something to the purpose; but being the reward of sons . . . there is no colour of desert." But on the other hand, if merit as virtuous behavior counts for nothing, virtue as imputed righteousness is all-important. Not only merit but genealogical aristocracy—*all* the distinctions of this world—are consigned to insignificance by the leveling doctrines of universal depravity and gratuitous grace. "If the only real aristocracy was the aristocracy created by God," remarks William Haller, "nothing really counted but character and inner worth."[27]

So because the doctrine of election, like the emerging class orientation, cut across the old categories of prescribed status, Calvinist Protestantism helped transform the argument of true nobility in the seventeenth century from a traditionalist commonplace into a subversive doctrine. Since true nobility rests with the saints, claimed Edmund Calamy, "a king may cause a man to be called 'noble,' but he cannot make a man 'truly noble.' " And Thomas Edwards opposed the inheritance of political office on the grounds that "it is not the birth, but the new birth, that makes men truly noble." As this language of rebirth suggests, divine election could be conceived not simply as a negation, but as an alternative line, of inheritance—an "aristocracy of grace." In fact, among Puritan writers it was not uncommon to frame the conversion experience according to the aristocratic romance convention of revealed noble parentage. Thus Thomas Hooker suggested that "we are alive as a child taken out of one family and translated into another, even so we are taken out of the houshold of Sathan, and inserted into the family of God; yea into the mysticall body of *Christ*." In a related fashion, Cromwell borrowed the idea of armorial bearings to propose a version of nobility that equally challenged the aristocratic: "May not this character, this stamp [of God] bear equal poise with any hereditary interest that could furnish, or hath furnished, in the common law or elsewhere, matter of dispute and trial of learning?"[28]

But the doctrines of predestination and justification by faith could never have occasioned the Weber thesis by themselves, because the utter passivity to which they relegate the saint, although theoretically subversive of the hierarchical order in which the aristocrat enjoys his equally unearned privilege, is antithetical to any notion of social activism or worldly industry. These impulses enter the "Protestant ethic" through Calvin's reinterpretation of the calling as a "strenuous and exacting enterprise" in discipline—moral discipline, self-discipline, labor discipline—

whose purpose is the glorification of God and the sanctification of the world. In the words of R. H. Tawney, "What is required of the Puritan is not individual meritorious acts, but a holy life—a system in which every element is grouped round a central idea, the service of God." Discipline in the calling made of the private sinner a public saint. "Private persons are self-centered like clods of the earth," said John Ward, "but public persons are turned into other men, and have a public spirit."[29]

If Calvinist election argued a new aristocracy alternative to that of birth, Calvinist discipline dictated a mode of service and reform that bore some similarity to the political activism of the new aristocracy of the robe. Already in the early seventeenth century, gentlemen's conduct books reflect a reforming aim to reconcile gentility with virtue under the aegis of the "true nobility" argument. In the words of Denis Greenville, "So far is Christian Vertue from being Incompatible with true Gentility, that to speak properly, and strictly, a Man cannot be a compleat Gentleman who is utterly void thereof." As Michael Walzer has argued of the revolutionary decades, the "honor" of the new aristocratic gentleman became at least analogous to the "conscience" of the Puritan saint, "and in the amalgamation of sainthood and gentility can be seen that reinforcement of self-esteem and confidence which made possible (and which was expressed in) the diligently 'reforming' activity of the pious magistrate."[30]

That Protestant sainthood should have been conceived in terms not only of an internal state but also of a mode of activity is due to Lutheran as well as Calvinist teaching. For although Luther's call for a priesthood of all believers and Scripture readers repudiates the corrupt mediators of God's will—the priestly hierarchy, papal tradition—it does not so much obviate the problem of mediation as shift responsibility from external and impersonal authorities onto the individual conscience and the community of saints. Predestination and the doctrine of faith make the question "Am I one of the elect?" a dilemma that can be resolved only by what Weber calls "the doctrine of proof," a method by which the saint may obtain from himself and his peers the certainty of salvation which he disdains to receive from his betters. Calvinist discipline provides such a method. "Good works are not a way of attaining salvation, but they are indispensable as a proof that salvation has been attained." "They are the technical means, not of purchasing salvation, but of getting rid of the fear of damnation."[31]

The doctrine of proof helps us see how the important analogy between Calvinist discipline and robe service is also an unequal one. For one thing, the service exacted of the saint finds its ultimate confirmation in the will not of the absolute prince but of the absolute Lord. The idea of a godly, not a princely, service mobilized a spirit of reform whose temporal limits did not necessarily coincide with the limits of the temporal power. The fate of Charles I provides the most glaring example of this truth; years later Mary Astell makes an arresting application of it by observing that " 'tis certainly no Arrogance in a Woman to conclude, that she was made for the Service of GOD, and that this is her End. Because GOD made all Things for Himself, and a rational Mind is too noble a Being to be made for the Sake and Service of any Creature. The Service she at any Time becomes oblig'd to pay to a Man, is only a Business by the Bye, just as it may be any Man's Business and Duty to keep Hogs." Moreover, just as the behavior entailed in Calvinist discipline includes far more than the relatively public-oriented duties of state service, so the criterion of its adequate performance rests ultimately not with an external and objectified authority but with a subtly subjective amalgam of private and community assessment. Calvinist discipline translates the volatility of absolutist reform downward and inward, into the realm of daily private experience.[32]

At least after the defeat of the relatively authoritarian Presbyterian system in the 1640s, Calvinist Protestantism encouraged a dynamic interdependence of individual conscience and community judgment that was a genuine alternative to passive dependence on absolute ecclesiastical authority. But in the momentum generated by that process it also made problematic the relatively internalized and subjectivized forces it ostensibly empowered. In the view of the great Anglican theologian Richard Hooker, there is no "gospel-like behavior" which might serve to tell us who are among the elect, "neither doth God thus bind us to dive into men's consciences, nor can their fraud and deceit (against God) hurt any man but themselves." But for those whose will and confidence are strong, certainty of salvation might become a sufficient if circular proof of it. As in the parallel case of questions of truth, the substitution of relatively "objective" and individualized standards of empirical proof for a tacit faith in external authority only shifts the danger of an arbitrary "absolutism" to the sphere of subjectivity. "Men emancipated themselves from priests," says Hill, "but not from . . . the priest internalized in their own consciences." Haller has made explicit this aspect of the analogy between questions of truth and questions of virtue:

As in later times men were taught to follow with patient observation the least workings of natural law in the external universe, men in the Puritan age were taught to follow by intense introspection the working of the law of predestination within their own souls. Theoretically, there was nothing they could do but watch . . . [But] with the most anxious curiosity, they looked into their own most secret thoughts for signs that the grace of God was at its work of regeneration, and what they so urgently looked for they naturally saw.

But the discrediting of external authority, whether Aristotelian or Roman Catholic, only makes more self-conscious and problematic the
question of how—on what grounds—we give credit to what we are
willing to accept.[33]

For these reasons, "What is a gentleman?" and "What is a saint?" may
be seen as related expressions of status anxiety in seventeenth-century
England. The Calvinist internalization of grace bears some relation to the
process by which "honor" ceased, over the course of the century, to
denote an objective and morally significant "title of rank" and came to
mean instead "goodness of character" and reputation. In the absence of
the once-authoritative guides—tacit social sanction, priestly absolu-
tion—nobility and salvation became problematic categories whose stabilization required not just the inner conviction of the individual but
community accreditation, a validating social consensus by which the
reputation of the individual and the coherence of the category itself were
constituted. As Walzer points out, "The activity of the gentleman acquired a new precision at the same time as his person became more
difficult to define. The same can be said of the saint." So the psychological fluidity that is characteristic of Calvinist doctrine is inseparable from
the sociological fluidity that is characteristic of the period in general. As a
response to status inconsistency, Puritanism produced two antithetical
ideal types of behavior. Those confident of their election had, in effect,
internalized Christ's imputed righteousness and were free to exercise
their virtue in such a way that their upward mobility of the spirit would
be reinforced by reforming zeal and worldly success. Those who could
not shrug off the burden of anxiety and doubt remained with the masses
of the unregenerate at the bottom of the spiritual hierarchy, consumed by
the unyielding problem of self-control and self-mastery.[34]

The susceptibility of Calvinist psychology to the self-fulfilling prophecy of success may help explain why Lutherans accused the Calvinist
system of discipline of reverting to the doctrine of salvation by works.
For the saint who was convinced of his election, the materialized achievements of a godly discipline came to signify the prior and unearned "signified" of spiritual justification. As in all instances of the problem of
mediation, the relationship between signifier and signified took on a
certain volatility. Calvin himself had been fond of using economic metaphors to express the spiritual discipline of sainthood. In the pedagogy of
"spiritualization" that flourished after the Restoration, the "signifying"
powers of the humblest of callings were emphasized by metaphorically
spiritualizing the trades in question. "Earthly callings must needs be
spiritualized," observes Richard B. Schlatter of these writings. "The
purpose of all this teaching on the subject of calling was to bring religion
into the world . . . [But] it is sometimes difficult to remember which of
the things compared is the more important. Was it grace or manure

which was honoured by the simile? The very language of preachers, intended to spiritualize commerce, tended to commercialize the spirit." With perhaps too much ingenuity, John Collinges observed to his humble readers that "he that believeth will and must work, but every one that worketh doth not believe . . . I always thought it a good rule for all Christians, to believe as much as if Works had no influence upon his Salvation, and to work as much as if Heaven were to be earned by meer Working." Moreover, the tendency to transform the outward signifiers of merit into self-validating and self-sufficient signifieds was reinforced by the common advice that even the unregenerate—those denied all possibility of salvation—should at least behave as "visible saints" and preserve outward appearances.[35]

As in the realm of questions of truth, the impulse toward reversal—toward accepting the outward for the inward, the letter for the spirit—can be seen as the paradoxical result of an urge to retain, for its formal utility, an evaluative standard whose substantive efficacy has been forcefully rejected. The naive claim to historicity, it will be recalled, was responsible for generating its own epistemological negation, which attacked the credibility not only of romance but of the "new romance" of empiricist method. In a similar fashion, the critique of Calvinist sufficiency drew strength from the perception that it only perpetuated, in stealthy form, the theology of works of Roman Catholicism. Thus, the great misfortune of Jack, the allegorical Calvinist in Swift's *A Tale of a Tub* (1704), is that a fundamental resemblance to his brother Peter, the Roman Catholic, "thwarted all his Projects of Separation, and left so near a Similitude between them, as frequently deceived the very Disciples and Followers of both." Jack is only the greatest modern practitioner of the "mechanical operation of the spirit," the exhalation of bodily vapors and fluids which are piously taken to signify not matter but spirit, not the effusions of the human body but the gift of God's grace. The central object of Swift's satire is a confusion of levels—both linguistic and behavioral—that results from the attribution to the "objective" reality of divine election what is in fact a subjective exercise in self-praise. The Restoration and the early eighteenth-century reaction against religious "enthusiasm" represents a counterrevolution, generated by the Calvinist revolution itself, which repudiates what are taken to be its excesses even as it shares with that revolution certain Protestant premises concerning the doctrinaire absolutism of papist methods for distinguishing the vicious from the virtuous, the damned from the saved. And the "incredibility" of enthusiasm is understood by its detractors to be simultaneously an epistemological and an ethical vulnerability.[36]

Weber's concern with the soteriology of the Protestant ethic was concentrated on the most "material" level of Calvinist discipline, that of labor discipline, where "works" come closest to meaning "work" in the modern sense of the term. By encouraging material success as a sign of spiritual salvation, Weber maintained, the practical habits of labor discipline—industry, thrift, asceticism, rationalization, even acquisitiveness—were influential in encouraging the habits of capitalist enterprise as well. If this amounted to a process of secularization, however, Weber was inclined to treat it as a positive one that preserved and revitalized religious motivation by redefining its scope within the modern world. More recent commentators have stressed also the secularizing reversal that is implicit even in Weber's title, the way in which the Protestant Reformation inaugurated a long-term deformation, a "capitalizing" on the spirituality it aimed to recover. And over the long term, the Protestant emphasis on the internalization of the authority to determine who is saved could not fail to be fundamentally subversive. In disputes about political sovereignty, the gradual replacement of divine right by human autonomy could be achieved without challenging the notion of political theory itself; but in religious thought this replacement amounts to a contradiction in terms.[37]

The delicate rapprochement between Protestant and capitalist reformation in seventeenth-century England proceeded on several fronts. As in centuries past, religious leaders sought to promulgate a standard of fair dealing which would establish the ethical limits of business enterprise. To the question, "May not a man aim at riches by his calling?" Richard Steele replied: "An End is *subordinate,* or *ultimate;* a *next* end, or a *last* end. You may design to get an Estate, but not meerly for your own sake, but chiefly for God's sake." But the inherent difficulty of such a project was aggravated by two tendencies in Protestant thought. The consequences of the first tendency—to regard material ambition as labor discipline and labor discipline as of unlimited value in the sanctification of the world—can be seen in the Reverend Joseph Lee's spirited defense of enclosures: "It is a very strange principle and unheard-of paradox that nothing can be done to God's glory which tends to men's profit. Do not tradesmen in following their vocations aim at their own advantage, do none of them glorify God thereby?" The second tendency is seen in the peculiarly Calvinist inclination to authorize, as the ethical test of personal behavior, the interested conscience of the person in question, whose intuitive casuistry might always claim a more immediate authenticity than the limits set by any external prescription. Richard Baxter's great work of casuistry, for example, tends to formulate principles of behavior according to the familiar, absolutist requirement of service to an end greater than self-interest, but it does so in such a way that only the subjective self is empowered to judge if those principles are being upheld: "It is not lawful for any one to seek Riches or Trade abroad or at home, principally for the Love of Riches, to raise himself and family to fulness, prosperity or dignity; though all this may be desired when it is a Means to Gods service, and honour, and the publick good, and is desired principally as such a Means."[38]

Many moralists agreed on the general rule of thumb that the limit on profits to be sought in individual transactions, and on the amount of wealth to be accumulated over the course of a career, was set by the satisfaction of necessities and the maintenance of a subsistence standard of living. And one way of accommodating this rule to the authority of individual conscience without thereby authorizing an absolutism of the self was to invoke the complementary rule of charity. "He that sells his commodity as dear . . . as he can," says John Bunyan, "seeks himself, and himself only; (*but charity seeketh not her own, nor her own only:*)." According to John Cook, "The rule of charity is, that one mans superfluity should give place to another mans conveniency, his conveniency to anothers necessity, his lesser necessities to anothers extreamer necessities, and so the mechanicall poore to relieve the mendicant poor in their extreamer need, and this is but the Dictate of the Law of Nature." After the Restoration, however, the most common method of guarding against unlimited self-interest in these matters ceased to be the rule of charity (which after all still depended on personal conscience), and became instead the "impersonal" rule of the market. According to Steele, "The market-price is generally the surest rule, for it is presumed to be more indifferent than the appetites of men." Thus the danger of individual acquisitiveness began to justify a mechanism of limits—the marketplace—whose very nature was defined by the limitless indulgence of human appetites. As an anonymous author expressed it, "Cupidity hath taken the place of charity, and effecteth it after a manner which we cannot enough admire . . . What charity will run to the Indies for medicines, stoop to the meanest employments, and not refuse the basest and most painful offices? Cupidity will perform all this without grudging." By the end of the century, the role of necessity as a limit on accumulation also had fallen by the wayside.[39]

It is of course over the long term that the relationship between Protestant reform and capitalist ideology is most evident. From this perspective it appears relatively simple to pass from the Calvinist belief that labor discipline signifies a prior and unearned election, to the capitalist conviction, supportive of progressive ideology, that worldly success and upward mobility are the signs of moral character. And from here it seems another short step to the absolute autonomy of material achievement. But the Puritan movement also generated, from two different directions, a powerful critique of the Protestant ethic and its complicity with progressive ideology.

Andrew Marvell's relatively traditionalistic critique is based on the recognition that the Protestant ethic and the spirit of capitalism have in common the unscrupulous internalization of limits. Of England's greatest commercial rival, the United Provinces of the Netherlands, he complained:

> Hence Amsterdam, Turk-Christian-Pagan-Jew,
> Staple of sects and mint of schism grew,
> That bank of conscience, where not one so strange
> Opinion but finds credit, and exchange.

Marvell sees that commercial enterprise and Protestant ethics alike require a systematic dependence on reputational credit and toleration of conscientious choice, which, with the erosion of mercantilism and justification by faith, must be accorded an absolute priority. As with the notion of "honor," it is not "credit" itself, but a complex transformation in the way credit has traditionally been accorded and withheld, that now relativizes and endangers it as a system of tacit, unquestioned knowledge. But the Puritan war on the Protestant ethic was also waged by taking the internalizing and subjectivizing subversion of limits farther than the ethic itself found comfortable. And the ultimate effect of this mode of thought was to dissolve the signifying power of worldly success itself, to discover, in its constitution by individual psychology and communal accreditation, the fact of its evanescence. Radical sectarians like the communist Gerrard Winstanley pursued the logic of Protestant reform so tenaciously as to challenge the authority not only of the Protestant ethic but of all externalized and objectified ethical criteria—sin, heaven, judgment, God himself. Passing tumultuously through the secularization process that would take their culture several centuries to experience, these sectarians by-passed the stage of capitalist ideology altogether. So if Calvinist Protestantism gave a vital impetus to the growth of progressive ideology, it also fed, through the distinct modes of Marvell and Winstanley, a vital counterstrain that would contribute to the emergence of conservative ideology.[40]

After the Restoration, Marvell's association of freedom of trade with freedom of conscience quickly became a commonplace. Although the affinity between Puritan belief and commercial success had already been obvious to many English people, the transformation of Puritanism into Nonconformity in 1662, which entailed the legal denial of liberty of conscience to left-wing Protestantism, encouraged it to stress that affinity as a centerpiece of the argument that religious toleration was vital to the interests of the English state. Thus the repressive politics of the Restoration Settlement helped reinforce the phenomenon that in Weber's analysis had originated as an internally generated product of Calvinist doctrine. At the same time, the reestablishment of the Church of England in 1660 relieved Anglicans of the polarizing threat of a Puritan Commonwealth and encouraged them to embrace more openly those social implications of Reformation teaching which had always been central to Anglicanism, or which had by now been suffused throughout English culture by the radical solvent of Puritan activism. Already under Tudor absolutism an elaborate system of poor laws had been institutionalized as a point of public policy, even though the characteristically Protestant assumption was that the burden of relief would fall not on the state but on the godly consciences of wealthy individuals. And the Societies for the Reformation of Manners that flourished after the Glorious Revolution were rooted equally in Puritan and in Anglican piety. Moreover, both popular and learned proponents of the restored Church of England were emphatic in their insistence that work and worldly enterprise were religious duties.[41]

After 1660, the Church of England produced that strain of "natural religion" or "latitudinarianism" which in its own way also justified, as Schlatter has pointed out, "the marriage of self-interest and virtue .... Thus Anglican and Nonconformist, starting from different bases, met at the journey's end." As dissenting clergy "spiritualized" the humble callings of their congregations, liberal Anglican divines reconciled moral law with social reality by "Christianizing" the market society of Restoration England. So latitudinarian Anglicanism aided in the legitimation of that antiaristocratic ideology of the career open to talents to which Puritan thought also had been vitally important—teaching, in the words of Margaret C. Jacob, that "so probable is the success of the virtuous that their prosperity is an even higher sign of God's providence than is the order inherent in nature." Or as Sir Humphrey Mackworth put it, "*Good men do generally fare better, even in this life, than the bad.*" Among these latitudinarians were the clergy who rationalized the replacement of the divine right of royal genealogical succession by an ex post facto providential sanctification of "settled possession." Here we see the same principle translated downward, from questions of state sovereignty to questions of individual virtue. And as before, what may look to us like an adventitious exercise in "Machiavellian" opportunism was generally entered into, we cannot doubt, in the hopeful spirit of an earnest accommodation of old ideals to new circumstances. At the same time, we must be careful to attend to the contemporary charge—a critique of Anglican self-indulgence analogous to that of Puritan "enthusiasm"—that the easy invocation of providence only prostituted it to worldly success, "making it a Sanctifier of any successful Mischief or Murder, of any Side, of contrary Parties, and to patronize Mens worst Imperfections."[42]

The new—especially the Newtonian—philosophy played an integral part in the liberal Anglican vision of the providential system. As Bacon had prophesied, the accumulated evidence of the senses now revealed an intricate and self-regulating natural order that seemed to be coextensive with God's spiritual order. From this it appeared that the social order, as well, most nearly approximated the providential design when it enjoyed

an absolute freedom and self-sufficiency. Over the long term it was the
role of providence that proved least essential to this equation, for as Jacob
observes, "The most historically significant contribution of the latitudinarians lies in their ability to synthesize the operations of a market
society and the workings of nature in such a way as to render the market
society natural." In the end, Calvin's separation of the two orders seems
to have prepared not for the ascendancy of the Church but (like the
separations effected by Bacon, Galileo, and Locke) for the absolutist rule
of secularism. Interest, said Richard Allestree in 1667, "is the great *Idol* to
which the world bows . . . We sacrilegiously entitle our profit to all the
Prerogatives of a Creator, give it an absolute unlimited dominion over us,
allow it to prescribe us all our measures of good and evil; to rule not only
our *Reason* but our *Passions* too . . . Divinity has long since been made the
handmaid of Policy, and Religion's modelled by conveniencies of
State."[43]

That the piety and fervor of Protestant reformation should have aided
in the development of an ideology in which human self-sufficiency renders God strictly superfluous is only the most strikingly paradoxical
instance of the general truth that once set in motion, absolutist reform
reforms absolutely. The vitality of the Weber thesis controversy derives
from this essential incongruity, from the clarity with which Weber's
argument forces us to acknowledge the contradictory movement that
inhabits the heart of historical change. Even if all the subtle threads of
seventeenth-century thought could be unraveled, in the end we would
still feel obliged to demand: Who are these optimistic entrepreneurs of
the spirit that confront us at the turn of the century? Are they capitalists
because God knows they are not Protestant saints, or are they saints
because they themselves are convinced of it? Having embraced an anti-
Protestant materialism that is in part the consequence of their own spiritual discipline, are they to be understood as hypocritical Protestants, or
as lapsed Protestants and the negation of their former selves—not Protestants but capitalists? On a certain level, the Weber thesis is no more
subject to demonstration than is Tawney's thesis of the rise of the gentry,
because it involves us in categorial problems that are solvable not by
empirical but by definitional efforts.[44]

4
EVALUATING HUMAN APPETITES

So the roots of capitalist ideology lie deep within the great absolutist
movement of religious reform, whose originating impulse had been to
turn state policy to the task of extricating spiritual ends from their modern entanglement in material and secular values. In the ostensibly more
secular realm of economic reform we can detect a similar pattern of

dialectical reversal. The economic policy most closely associated with the period of absolutism is state protectionism or mercantilism. From the modern perspective, mercantilist regulation appears antithetical to capitalist free enterprise, an antiquated expression of a commercial and "industrial feudalism." But if absolutism is understood as a dynamic mediation of feudalism and capitalism, state control of the economy becomes intelligible as one stage in a long process in which the power to modify the heavenly laws of mutability and to reform the environment is vouchsafed to increasingly autonomous and individualized human agency. From this perspective, mercantilism is also (in Weber's words) "irrational capitalism," a primitive phase of laissez faire—institutional rather than individual control—instead of its antithesis. In the sixteenth and early seventeenth centuries, monopolies and a strong centralized government were important for the protection of new industries and fledgling merchant capital. The point at which the freedom provided by state protection began to feel like constraint represents not so much a radical watershed between two discrete systems as a further internalization of the principle of reform. A late-Restoration pamphleteer used the evocative language of epic and romance to describe this transition. Restraint of trade was common in the early days, "when Navigation was judged a Mystery next to that of the Black Art and such as would venture their Persons and Estates into the New World, as they termed new found Countries, Heroes equal to Alexander and Caesar." But "as Trade and Commerce became familiar in the World, the Wisdome of Government made the Privileges of Trade universal to their Subjects." In literary as well as economic experience, the early modern process of reform required that mobility, circulation, and exchange lose the otherness of black magic, that they be reconceived as a natural human activity. In the sphere of economic policy, protectionism was the first stage in this long-term reversal. [45]

The landed attack on the monied interest in the early eighteenth century did not provide the initial impetus for the formation of capitalist ideology; it was a culminating reaction against a mode of argument that had been long in the making. Capitalist ideology entails, most fundamentally, the attribution of value to capitalist activity: minimally, as valuable to ends greater than itself and as significant of virtue; perhaps as valuable in its own right; finally, even as value-creating. At the same time that religious rationales were being used to justify capitalist practices in some of these terms, writers on economic policy were learning to advance a similar position within a discursive context that was increasingly free of religious argument. Of course the separation is artificial; and what was required in both discourses was the positing of an absolute power, beyond human scope, whose extraordinary and paradoxical capacity it was to turn individual human limitations to good ends. In Calvinist doctrine this is the divine power of Christ's imputed righteousness, which miraculously justifies the elect despite their natural depravity. The need for recourse to such a power is still evident in the famous, quasi-providential figure of speech Adam Smith uses to explain that the capitalist "intends only his own gain, and he is in this, as in many other cases, led by an invisible hand to promote an end which was no part of his intention." Smith's relatively secularized paradox was well known to the seventeenth century, especially as it served to justify (in the words of Lewes Roberts) "the judicious merchant, whose labour is to profit himself, yet in all his actions doth therewith benefit his king, country and fellow subjects." In fact, seventeenth-century English people did much of the work required to replace the notion of an absolute divine order with one of an equally absolute natural order of economic relations—the market system—which was separable from social contingencies and intelligible according to its own, autonomous laws of operation.[46]

This naturalizing of the economic order was necessary for the defeat of absolutist policies of state protectionism: only permit the system to obey its *own* laws and all will be well. But individual capitalist activity also came to be validated in its own right, and for this to occur it was necessary that absolute authority be humanly internalized, that not just the capitalist system, but the capitalist motive, be naturalized. Of course, Christian thought had been quite clear on the naturalness of the capitalist motive—but only because human nature itself was depraved, hence drawn to the appetitive sins of avarice, cupidity, covetousness, and the like. In fact, early anticapitalists saw "the market" as itself an imaginary projection of endless human appetite upon the world at large. Thus Thomas Scott attacked all—old and new nobility, "Improuers of our Land," rack-renters, monopolists, impropriators—who "study to doe such acts, and invent such projects, as may vndo the publique for their priuate and inordinate desires," who "liue in this world as *in a market,* [and] *imagine there is nothing else for them to doe, but to buy and sell, and that the only end of their creation and being was to gather riches, by all meanes possible.*" And John Denham looked down from Coopers Hill on the City of London, wrapped

> in a thicker cloud
> Of businesse, then of smoake, where men like Ants
> Toyle to prevent imaginarie wants;
> Yet all in vaine, increasing with their store,
> Their vast desires, but make their wants the more.
> As food to unsound bodies, though it please
> The Appetite, feeds only the disease . . .

So what is involved here is also a revolution in the idea of natural law. What early modern thought achieved was, in a sense, the "neutralization" of human nature. "From a moral rule imposed upon man from without," says J. A. W. Gunn, "natural law came to be a mere description of actual human behavior." But what is human behavior if not appetitive? By the seventeenth century, R. H. Tawney observes, "'Nature' had come to connote, not divine ordinance, but human appetites, and natural rights were invoked by the individualism of the age as a reason why self-interest should be given free play." But as my earlier discussion suggests, the choice between divine and natural, religious and secular, causes is not likely to be a meaningful one to those caught up in the secularization process. Thus, at the end of the century the Anglican divine Thomas Taylor could argue that "where an Appetite is universally rooted in the Nature of any kind of Beings, we can attribute so general an Effect to nothing but the Maker of those beings."[47]

As Joyce Appleby has shown, throughout the seventeenth century, writers on economic matters argued that the motive of material self-improvement, of gain and profit, was a universal, ineradicable, and therefore legitimate principle of human nature. That human nature had its own laws was itself a factor in the validation of material self-interest, whose very predictability now appeared to the empiricist reformers of the age as a mark in its favor. The consequent reversal paradoxically gave to human passions themselves, in conjunction with the greater laws of the economic system, a positive role in the stabilization of mutability. According to Appleby, "The undeniable subjectivity of desire had been turned into an objective and measurable force by assuming a constancy in human beings' market behavior." This rehabilitation of desire depended to some degree on the willingness of seventeenth-century writers to discriminate among the passions, to imagine employing the relative innocuousness of (for example) avarice to countervail what were seen as the major and most destructive appetites. At the same time, the category of "interest" was refined in such a way as to mediate the two traditional categories of human motivation. In the words of Albert Hirschman, "Interest was seen to partake in effect of the better nature of each, as the passion of self-love upgraded and contained by reason, and as reason given direction and force by that passion. The resulting hybrid form of human action was considered exempt from both the destructiveness of passion and the ineffectuality of reason."[48]

It has been the perpetual endeavor of politicians, announced Bernard Mandeville, to convince the people "that it was more beneficial for every body to conquer than indulge his Appetites, and much better to mind the Publick than what seem'd his private Interest." Given the extent to which the justification of selfishness had proceeded by 1700, we can see that the immediate impact of Mandevillian thought was due not so much to the novelty of his thesis as to his ambition to bring the fact of this volatile reversal to the level of public consciousness, to repeat it at will. The maxim that private vices lead to public benefits points ambiguously in two directions. As an optimistic exercise in moral and social reform, Mandeville's demonstration that what we call virtue is really vanity, that selflessness is self-service, aims to demystify and humanize virtue so as to reclaim it from the aristocrats and saints and make it the property of real people engaged in the daily pursuits of modern life. Nothing can explode so effectively the apriorist fiction that birth is worth as showing that private "worth" is an inseparable function of the public consequences of human actions. (Here we can sense the affinity between Mandeville and the latitudinarian defenders of William's "settled possession.") Self-oriented activity is not the privilege of those few whose lineage justifies it. The very fount of modern honor, it is of absolute value because all that we value depends on it. It creates values, and this is the criterion of virtue. But even to put the argument in its progressive form mobilizes its radically conservative negation. If the modern wisdom is to subsume virtue under vice, then virtue has fled the modern world; the only alternative to the traditional and tacit acceptance of aristocratic authority is no authority at all.[49]

The crystallization of conflict between progressive and conservative ideology owed a great deal to the ferment generated by the gradual recognition that human appetite was in some real sense value-creating: by the discovery, that is, of exchange value. In reality the indulgence of imaginary wants appeared to produce not only more wants but also the means to their satisfaction. Once freed from the limitations imposed by traditional moral sanction, human nature seemed naturally disposed to establish equivalences between intrinsically disparate commodities, and thence to increase their value by market circulation and exchange. William Petty thought the most important consideration in political economy was "how to make a Par and Equation between Lands and Labour, so as to express the Value of any thing by either alone." The key to this equation seemed to be money, which Anthony Ascham called "an invention onely for the more expedite permutation of things," and which he thought facilitated, in the endless circulation of commodities, a strange new form of human community: "Instead of Community therefore we now have commerce, which *Commercium* is nothing else but *Communio mercium*." A notable example of the modern community of money was the new category the "monied interest," which made a par between the traditional antagonists "land" and "trade" on the basis of their common engagement in market activity.[50]

As the expansion of that activity generated wants and wealth whose existence had not been known before, proponents of the monied interest learned not just to accept but to acclaim the "imaginary" foundation of the market in human appetite. The elasticity of demand began to appear unlimited and absolute: value was nothing more than the imaginative power of individual producers and consumers. "Things have no value in themselves," claimed Nicholas Barbon; "it is opinion and fashion brings them into use and gives them a value." "The Wants of the Mind are infinite, Man naturally Aspires, and as his Mind is elevated, his Senses grow more refined, and more capable of Delight; his Desires are inlarged, and his Wants increased with his Wishes, which is for everything that is rare, can gratifie his Senses, adorn his Body, and promote the Ease, Pleasure, and Pomp of Life." With the validation of the profit motive came the necessary acknowledgment that all profit-making rested upon the psychological assessment of subjective motive; thus the imaginative significance of financial terms like "trust" and "credit," which convey the secularized mechanism of a bond that alludes not to a higher spiritual power but to its own, materialistic suasion. As Christopher Hill has observed, "The supernatural sanction backing the oath of loyalty and the judicial oath—God the supreme overlord—was succeeded in capitalist society by the discovery that it paid a man to make his word his bond because of the rise in social importance of credit, reputation, respectability." Like the Protestant preoccupation with the credit of the community, the overriding concern with reputation among commercial pamphleteers of the Restoration was (in Appleby's words) a "utilitarian conception of honor." For as one of them insisted, "Tradesmen live upon credit, buy much upon trust," and "as they buy upon credit, so they must sell upon trust." "Credit," said another, "is the sinew of conversation, and nourisher of correspondency, the great manager of affairs."[51]

5

PROGRESSIVE IDEOLOGY AND CONSERVATIVE IDEOLOGY

Although tied to the monied interest by their profound appreciation of the market's protean capacity to reward industrious virtue, proponents of progressive ideology were likely to feel uneasy with the insubstantiality of its subjective foundation. Daniel Defoe, sharply critical of that "imaginary honour" which possesses the minds of aristocratic gentlemen, was at least ambivalent about "the Power of Imagination" that rules the modern world of exchange value. He personified Trade as a highly excitable and sometimes enthusiastic victim of "the Storms and Vapours of Human Fancy, operated by exotick Projects." And Credit he depicted as the younger sister of Money, a pert, inconstant, and "absolute" lady whose utter modishness cannot obscure the possibility of a pedigree. For "her Name in our Language is call'd CREDIT, in some Countries Honour." Both figures are female: women retain that association with the volatility of exchange (or of *fortuna*) which they possess under older, patrilineal assumptions. And Defoe seems inclined to wonder if the tantalizing creations of the market have any more lasting substance than those aristocratic fictions which the modern world has learned to discredit—to wonder, that is, if the monied mode of achievement has any greater validity than the old, aristocratic mode known by a different name. In other contexts, however, Defoe warns the nobility that if they live off retail credit they will be tempted to live beyond their means, which will lead in the end to the denial to them of "Credit" and to their "loss of Honour." This image gives to "honor" and "credit" a more neutral synonymity, and elsewhere Defoe is able to treat credit so positively as to make it the essential lubricant of the Great Chain of Being. Our difficulty in deciding Defoe's stance concerning the relation between capitalist credit and aristocratic honor reflects a real uncertainty on his part about some of the more disquieting features of the world of exchange value of which he was, in general, an enthusiastic supporter. The analogy with his posture on questions of truth is worth noting, for there, too, the basic solidity of Defoe's naive empiricism becomes vulnerable to doubts about the false claim to historicity, in which the stability of moral ends is undermined by the "imaginary" status of pedagogic means.[52]

Defoe's discomfort with the subjectivity of exchange value affords us a glimpse of progressive ideology hesitating on the edge of a conservative reversal. Charles Davenant exemplifies the closely contiguous phenomenon of a fundamentally conservative proponent tentatively engaged in the progressive experiment of validating the new modes of monied achievement by an older model of state service. Davenant compares financial credit to "that fame and reputation which men obtain by wisdom in governing state affairs." However "fantastical" it may appear to be, good repute is the reward we give to those who deserve it. So although the statesman may temporarily lose his reputation, it "will be regained, where there is shining worth, and a real stock of merit. In the same manner, Credit, though it may be for a while obscured, and labour under some difficulties, yet it may, in some measure, recover, where there is a safe and good foundation at the bottom." When the system is working as it should, then, the credit of the financial community is the insubstantial sign of what is nonetheless a deserved and substantive merit. Most often, however, conservatives subjected the principles of the monied men and the rationales for absolute capitalist activity—the public benefits of self-service, the naturalness of subjective desire, the value-creating capacities of exchange—to the sort of critique that Defoe takes up but as quickly puts down again.[53]

Willing to acknowledge the "imaginary value" of aristocratic lineage and honor, Jonathan Swift nonetheless turns his most withering scorn of the imaginary upon the monied men, who in advertising their freedom from the tyranny and delusions of aristocratic ideology only recapitulate its worst excesses. The romance mystifications of genealogical and heraldic terminology were bad enough; but "through the Continuance and Cunning of *Stock-Jobbers*," Swift wrote, "there hath been brought in such a Complication of Knavery and Couzenage, such a Mystery of Iniquity, and such an unintelligible *Jargon* of Terms to involve it in, as were never known in any other Age or Country of the World." Swift portrayed the inflated value of stock in the South Sea Company as a species of "Magick" worked by a coven of "Witch" bankers, and when the bubble burst in 1720 he wrote:

> Conceive the whole Enchantment broke,
> The Witches left in open Air,
> With Pow'r no more than other Folk,
> Expos'd with all their Magick Ware.

Swift strongly supported the Property Qualifications Act of 1711, which sought to restrict parliamentary membership to landowners, because it would ensure that "our Properties lie no more at Mercy of those who have none themselves, or at least only what is transient or imaginary." Explaining the fate of the landed interest in recent years, the Earl of Bolingbroke expressed the belief that "a new Interest has been created out of their fortunes, and a sort of property which was not known twenty years ago, is now increased to be almost equal to the terra firma of our island." The vicissitudes of the market and public credit seemed to confirm these convictions, yet by a grotesque inversion, Swift said, "the Wealth of the Nation, that used to be reckoned by the Value of Land, is now computed by the Rise and Fall of Stocks."[54]

For conservative ideology, the monied interest was inseparable from progressive ideology, a peculiarly flagrant expression of its general will to institutionalize a brutal social injustice, unsoftened now by any useful fictions of inherited authority. The old distinctions in wearing apparel, for example, had at least provided for the differences in people's social degree an ostensible and substantive register; "there seeming now," to Richard Allestree, "no other *measure* than the utmost extent of their *money* or *credit;* the later [*sic*] whereof is often so stretcht, that it not only cracks itself, but by an unhappy Contagion, breaks those it deals with." Perhaps aristocratic ideology unavoidably favors certain families over others in a way which, by the strict standards of inborn merit, must be accounted arbitrary. But Swift was convinced that the War of the Spanish Succession had been prosecuted by the Duke of Marlborough (born John Churchill) designedly "to raise the Wealth and Grandeur of a particular Family; [and] to enrich Usurers and Stock-jobbers." If aristocratic ideology might be reduced to the quantitative proposition that the best man was he who possessed the longest lineage, the progressive alternative was that he who had the most money was the best man. Obscured by the righteous rhetoric of industry, discipline, and personal achievement was the amoral reality of the new order, a quantification of virtue so absolute and deforming as to deserve the name "corruption." Swift's passionate resistance to the English imposition of Mr. Wood's half-pence on the Irish common people brings together all of the most hated features of the progressive phenomenon: the alliance of governmental and monied corruption in the exercise of absolute colonialist power; the preferment of the undeserving upstart, the monetary "Projector" Wood, *a mean ordinary Man*"; and the plague of debased coinage, a literalization of monied corruption so repugnant that it can be overcome only, says Swift's drapier, by the utter refusal to participate in the creation of exchange value: "For my own Part . . . I intend to Truck with my Neighbours the *Butchers,* and *Bakers,* and *Brewers,* and the rest, *Goods for Goods.*"[55]

At the center of the assault on progressive ideology was the perception of this great inconsistency: money and power without merit. And for Swift, among others, the paradigm case was Sir Robert Walpole:

> oppressing true merit exalting the base
> and selling his Country to purchase his peace
> a Jobber of Stocks by retailing false news
> a prater at Court in the Stile of the Stews

But although the absence of virtue thus defines the nature of the incongruity, the absence of gentle status remains a conventional signification of degeneracy. We can see this emphasis in Swift's contempt for Wood's meanness, which jars with his sympathetic impersonation of a common drapier in a way that is entirely characteristic of his contradictory "Tory radicalism." We can hear it in Bolingbroke's contempt for those absolute robe nobles, "who, born to serve and obey, have been bred to command even government itself," and in his account of a future Britain "oppressed by a few upstarts in power; often by the meanest, always by the worst of their fellow-subjects; by men, who owe their elevation and riches neither to merit nor birth, but to the favor of weak princes, and to the spoils of their country, beggared by their rapine." And it is on this basis that Bolingbroke made his impassioned plea to gentlemen of large estates to resist "the Incroachments of *Stock-jobbers,* or *beggarly Tools of Power,* who are sent amongst you, without any Recommendation of Merit or Virtue, to supplant you in the Esteem of your Tenants, Neighbours and Dependants." By the same token, Davenant's Whig *agent provocateur* instructs his aide to "detract from, and asperse all the Men of Quality of whom there is any appearance that either their high Birth, or their great Fortunes, or their Abilities in Matters of Government should recommend 'em to the future Administration of Affairs."[56]

So if conservative writers denounce progressive values for defects that ironically echo those of aristocratic degeneracy, their language also reveals a latent uncertainty about the coherence of their own course. In opposing the monied interest, landed proponents were ineluctably drawn to a real, if understated, dependence on the aristocratic values they themselves were unwilling to embrace openly—and in any case were castigating the monied men for perpetuating in a cruder form. To Swift and those who shared his views, the solidity of the landed estate and the personal relations it sustained seemed to offer the best model to counterpose to the unreality of exchange value and the limitless indulgence of human appetite. One problem with this stance, however, was that it was very difficult to separate the idea of land as exclusively value-creating from other, genealogical, elements of aristocratic ideology to which it had been welded by force of long habit. Moreover, by 1700 the attempt to isolate a pristine enclave of noncapitalist land use—"the landed interest"—from the omnivorous economics of the marketplace was not without a certain quixotic futility. In fact, the dilemma of incorporation by the enemy entirely suffused the experience of the Tory radicals, and it was essential to the dangerous quality of paranoid volatility, which gave to the best of their writings a distinctive brilliance. It may be most accurate to see the conservative ideology of the early eighteenth century not as the negation of capitalist ideology but as the expression of a wish to halt the implacable juggernaut of capitalist reform at a stage that preserved, at least for property owners of a certain political and social persuasion, the best of both worlds. Swift articulated what might be seen as the constitutional equivalent of this desire to freeze the process of reform when he complained, with as much poignancy as indignation, that the nobility and gentry had supported the Glorious Revolution and its "Breaches in the Succession of the Crown . . . without Intention of drawing such a Practice into Precedent." After 1688, however, the strict inheritance of monarchal virtue was a bankrupt aristocratic fiction which all but the Jacobites were obliged to repudiate with force; thus Swift himself assured Alexander Pope that "I always declared my self against a Popish Successor to the Crown, whatever Title he might have by proximity of blood." But if lineal descent thus could provide a foundation for virtue no more substantial than that afforded by the despised exchange value, where might one turn for a genuine alternative?[57]

As I intimated in the preceding chapter, the problem was solved, after a fashion, by the indirect defense of aristocratic honor, the divinity of kingship, and related beliefs not precisely as articles of faith but on the grounds of their social instrumentality and usefulness. By the standards of reason and experience, the self-consciously "imaginary value" of such conviction was the key that unlocked its "real" value: not the truth of the belief but the utility of having it. Later on in the century the argument would be sophisticated by Samuel Johnson's acute, protosociological awareness of "acting a part in the great system of society":

But, Sir, as subordination is very necessary for society, and contentions for superiority very dangerous, mankind, that is to say, all civilised nations, have settled it upon a plain invariable principle. A man is born to hereditary rank; or his being appointed to certain offices, gives him a certain rank. Subordination tends greatly to human happiness . . . Thus, Sir, there would be a perpetual struggle for precedence, were there no fixed invariable rules for the distinction of rank, which creates no jealousy, as it is allowed to be accidental.

A direct line extends from the Augustan conservatives to Edmund Burke's lament for the "pleasing illusions" born of the age of chivalry and consumed in the flames of the French Revolution.[58]

But Johnson's rationale betrayed a pragmatic detachment from its object of knowledge that was rather too austere for Bolingbroke, whose true ambition was somehow to imbue instrumental belief with the kind of authority that is reserved for tacit knowledge. This is most evident in the nostalgic attempt to reconstruct, out of an idealized antiquity that had been demystified a generation earlier by Bolingbroke's Tory predecessors, an authoritative model of absolute kingship. Bolingbroke's patriot king—"the most powerful of all reformers; for he is himself a sort of standing miracle" whose very appearance must command assent—would return us to a time when aristocratic nobility, so far from being subject either to belief or to skepticism, was simply the outward sign of "true nobility." Bolingbroke associated this innate authority with the patriarchal *auctoritas* of Roman antiquity before the rise of the undeserving "*Novi Homines*"; but the ideal seemed locatable at several points in the English past as well. In response to one such retrospect, a journalistic supporter of Walpole exclaimed: "What heroic tales are here! more idle and romantic than those of Gargantua." But Bolingbroke was content to be thought a romancer properly understood, perhaps believing that an artfully reconstructed faith was better than no faith at all. In this frame of mind he observed "that the *Good of his Country,* and the *true Interest* of his Prince ought to be the principal Views of every *great Man;* which, as romantick as they may seem, were not altogether unfashionable Topicks in the good old days of Queen *Elizabeth.*" In praise of his honored patron, Swift also used the equivocal language of "romance" to denominate the status consistency of the truly "great man":

> Those mighty Epithets, Learn'd, Good, and Great,
> Which we ne'er join'd before, but in Romances meet,
> We find in you at last united grown.

Nevertheless it is the curse of modernity to have divided personality from prescribed status, and to have condemned the former endlessly to seek from the latter what it is no longer able to fulfill. Thus James Harrington, an important influence on the Bolingbroke circle, attributed to the rulers of his ideal commonwealth an implicit excellence which he called "an *auctoritas patrum,* the authority of the fathers." Yet this Roman model of aristocracy was useful to Harrington for its assurance of a "natural aristocracy" that would rule, he is careful to note, "not by hereditary right, nor in regard of the greatness of their estates only . . . but by election for their excellent parts." The rule of the absolute prince was gradually being usurped by the rule of the private individual and his absolute right to choose his leaders and dispose of his property according to the dictates of his natural appetites.[59]

I have now come to the end of my account of the social conditions, both conceptual and behavioral, of early modern England in which the wide dispersal of questions of virtue coalesced as the conflict between progressive and conservative ideology. In the following chapter I will turn to the narrative representation of this conflict. Why should these ideological patterns have been susceptible to narrative formulation in particular? What kinds of stories did people tell in order to propound most effectively their questions of virtue? How are these stories related to the narrative structures that are most useful in posing questions of truth?

— Six —

Stories of Virtue

I

NOVELISTIC NARRATIVE AS HISTORICAL EXPLANATION

The progressive critique of aristocratic ideology demystifies prescribed honor as an imaginary value, explaining virtue as a quality that is not prescribed by status but demonstrated by achievement. Sparked by the vitality of this critique, a conservative countercritique shares the anti-aristocratic animus against prescription, but rejects also the argument from achievement as nothing other than the modern version of imaginary value, distinguished only by the frank crudity of its corruption. For the foundations of real value and virtue, this countercritique looks back to the tacit authority of aristocratic cultures, to the authoritative aura somehow dissociated from the skeptical and damning estimate of its justification. The degree to which these conflicting postures represent abstractions from actual discourse is clear from the way in which even the hard-nosed polemics of men like Defoe and Swift are complicated by ambivalence. Nonetheless it is precisely the capacity of intellectual structures to be abstracted from the dense undergrowth of thought that permits them to enter into the ongoing process of antagonistic and mutually defining interrelation.

Why should narrative, in particular, be suitable for the representation of these opposed ideologies? Questions of virtue have an inherently narrative focus because they are concerned with genealogical succession and individual progress, with how human capacity is manifested in and through time. Before the origins of the novel these questions were mediated by the aristocratic ideology of romance, a narrative model that provided a persuasive account of private and public history alike. The romance model did not fall into immediate disuse during the seventeenth century; in fact the Stuart monarchy found it quite serviceable in the representation of the royal succession. When Prince Charles and the Duke of Buckingham went in disguise to Spain to woo the Spanish infanta, James I called them his "sweete boyes, and dear ventrouse knights, worthie to be putte in a new romanse." And later Charles commissioned Rubens to discover, in the besieged maiden and her dragon-slaying champion, St. George, the visages of Henrietta Maria and himself. The ideological function of romance narrative became even clearer once the Stuart house entered its mid-century crisis. Two years after the beheading of his father, Charles Stuart was decisively defeated by Oliver Cromwell at the Battle of Worcester, and for the next few weeks the young prince wandered the countryside in disguise, eventually making his way to the relative safety of the Continent. Imitation of the romance model appears to direct the activity not only of the several historical narratives of this episode but even of the historical actors themselves. In order to escape, Charles conceals his royal nobility by dressing first as a "Country-Fellow" and then as a "Serveing-man" and a "Woodcutter." The telltale whiteness of his skin he obscures with coarse gray stockings, and with a distillation of walnut rind familiar to all romance readers as the preferred cosmetic of temporary downward mobility. In the most celebrated incident, Charles takes refuge in the impenetrable branches of a spreading oak tree, evading parliamentary soldiers by recapitulating the romance descent of arboreal metamorphosis. But despite these expedients, more than once his true identity is suspected and discovered by loyal subjects—"majestie beeing soe naturall unto him," according to one commentator, "that even when he said nothing, did nothing, his very lookes . . . were enough to betray him." And this too—the inexpungeability of aristocratic nobility—is a venerable romance convention.[1]

Of course to some degree the historical narratives reflect actual circumstance: disguise was imperative, and the danger of discovery was very real. But the romance conventions also impose upon circumstance a politic interpretation: Charles is the true sovereign; the difficulty of disguise only confirms the internal nobility whose usual signifiers—the external trappings of aristocratic nobility—have been obliterated by misfortune. The romance shape of the story even alludes to events beyond its reach. When nobility of birth is cut loose from its worldly moorings—as in the case of the suppositious foundling or the errant knight—we know that its inborn worth will be recognized in time and finally restored to its rightful seat of authority. So Charles's descent into oblivion foretells the eventual revelation of name, the discovery of parentage that will restore him to the throne of England. At the core of aristocratic ideology is the conviction that a stable social order is a dependable guide to the greater moral order, and in a patrilineal culture based upon degrees of status, social order is a function of genealogy. Most succinctly, birth is a sign of worth. The romance of Charles at Worcester abets this ideological formula by dividing worth from the signs of birth and showing it to be nonetheless unmistakable.

But if the romance of Charles's escape received a particular vindication in the Restoration of 1660, its more general outlook on social experience did not. This can be felt, I think, in the very insistence of these remarkable historical narratives on their conventional romance underpinnings. Aristocratic ideology works most effectively when, as in the courtly fictions of the twelfth century, its status as a normative reading of social reality remains implicit and pervasive. Here, however, the allusive representation of reality is relatively explicit and immediate. It has a force bred of the sense of being under attack: not only by the mortal enemies of Stuart monarchy but also by alternative models for explaining contemporary events. Certainly the events themselves seemed to encourage a different sort of plot and different culture heroes. If Charles was indeed restored to his aristocratic patrimony, the killing of the king had dealt a resounding blow to the royal succession, and the ensuing triumphs of Cromwell and William of Orange eloquently argued the superiority of industrious valor to mere lineage. The regicide and these triumphs bear an obvious and important relevance to the discovery that the modern condition of status inconsistency was not susceptible to the traditional mediations of aristocratic ideology and romance; but it is equally obvious that these events could not in themselves have provided the alternative models of progressive and conservative narrative.

Yet, in a more profound way, the attempt to understand and explain the meaning of recent history—the very battlefield, after all, on which the vulnerability of the aristocratic rationale was being demonstrated—does indeed provide contemporaries with the crucial models of novelistic narrative. To speak, as I have done, of the novel as an "emplacement" or a specification of traditional forms refers, among other things, to its embodiment of the impulse to explain the mutability of human affairs in social and historical rather than metaphysical terms. Traditional accounts of such vicissitudes—familial cycles, ancestral romances, mirrors of princes—limit the scope of inquiry into their nature and causes by emblematizing their subjects, thereby treating the static fact of mutability as itself an unsurpassable explanation. During the early modern period, the fact of mutability—and even its Christian specification to the condition of sinfulness—loses much of its explanatory power. The experience of instability and mobility ceases to be translated so automatically to the fact of mutability, and is increasingly identified and addressed instead as a sociohistorical condition of status inconsistency that is susceptible to more specific analysis and explanation. Very often this explanatory analysis will entail a specification of a complex set of circumstances on the "macrohistorical" level, a synecdochic operation that consists in reducing or concentrating it into a simpler, "microhistorical" narrative structure. And on occasion we can even watch contemporaries laboring to explain large, public macrohistories by quite self-consciously distilling them into the smaller, more accessible, private microhistories of individual and familial life that are to us recognizably "novelistic."[2]

Among the epochal events of the recent past, contemporaries learned to recur to certain critical ones that seemed to have altered the nature of social relations in a decisive fashion, and by this means they organized historical experience into competing accounts of how, why, and even when status, wealth, and power came to be divided from one another. In this way, the implicit "answer" to questions of virtue can be involved within the very shape of the story that propounds them, and narratives about private individuals can retain this explanatory function and resonance by alluding, in the way their plots proceed, to the abstracted rationale of which they provide one example. But at this point it will be useful to clarify what I mean by narrative specification and concentration by looking at several diverse attempts of seventeenth-century writers to explain one particular recent historical phenomenon: the "mutability" engendered by Tudor absolutism.

Like many commentators, Sir Henry Spelman thought the dissolution of the monasteries and the sale of church lands the crucial ingredient in the Tudor recipe for social change. By approving the parliamentary bill authorizing this policy, Spelman says, the temporal lords who were present at the time communicated the "honour" of God "to lazy and vulgar persons." Because not only they but "the whole body of the baronage is since that fallen so much from their ancient lustre, magnitude, and estimation," he concludes that "God, to requite them, hath taken the ancient honours of nobility, and communicated them to the meanest of the people, to shopkeepers, taverners, tailors, tradesmen, burghers, brewers, and graziers." Spelman's narrative is discontinuous, punctuated by a vertical intrusion that explains the fall of the ancient nobility as an analogous and ironic recompense for their guilt in the fall of the church rather than as the linear consequence of other human acts. But if narrative explanation therefore is not fully specified, the basic materials for its specification—the rise of one group and the fall of another—are present. Sir Edward Walker's version of the story retains the aura of divine retribution without its explicit invocation. Here it is families of the nobility themselves that were enriched by the dissolution of the monasteries—but to no lasting end: and "the Greatness and Splendour of the Church being thus destroyed . . . in their places some Men of obscure Beginnings came into Action, and were advanced to Titles of Honour." For Thomas Fuller, the dissolution marks a great watershed after which it becomes all too easy to mistake recently elevated commoners for old gentility. At the end of Henry VIII's reign most of the gentry, "notwithstanding their specious claim to Antiquity, will be found to be but of one Descent, low enough in themselves, did they not stand on the vantage ground, heightened on the Rubbish of the Ruines of Monasteries." Encompassing a broader range of Tudor policies, Jonathan Swift and Daniel Defoe agree in attributing to them the decline of the ancient nobility and the rise of commoners. But they are at odds in the way they color the stories they tell, which is after all vital to the explanatory power of those stories. While Swift associates the social changes he narrates with a devolutionary leap "into the Depths of Popularity," Defoe's attention is caught by the spectacle of the "Purse proud Gentry" and the "frugal Manufacturers" whose industry buys them out.[3]

However diverse they may appear to be, all of these examples are rudimentary narratives carved from the chaos of the previous century so as to render its meaning more intelligible. Moreover, all of them are concerned, from one or another angle, with the decline of the nobility and gentry and the rise of commoners. Now, the further the explanatory aim is pursued, the more these rudimentary macronarratives will be specified to the shape and circumstantiality of familial and personal microhistories. This is in effect the general operating procedure of John Foxe's *Acts and Monuments,* which tells the microstories of private individuals with a homely detail that is still saturated with the paradigmatic aura of Reformation history at large. Over and over the battle between a corrupt nobility and industrious commoners is conflated with the battle between the Roman hierarchy and God's saints; for in the ecclesiastical as in the social realm, the struggle was easily conceived as one of internal and authentic merit against the external and discredited authority of genealogy and hierarchy—that is, of Church tradition and priestly mediation. The first part of "The Story of Roger Holland," for example, is the tale of an idle and licentious apprentice who dances, fences, riots, wantons, and gambles away his master's money at dice. But in the nick of time Roger is turned to reading the Bible and to industrious business enterprise. Henceforth everything is altered. He returns home, converts his parents to the gospel, receives a second stake from his father, and soon prospers as a merchant tailor. It is only now that Roger is called up before his papist inquisitor. And now he manifests, through a spirited resistance and serene martyrdom, that spiritual grace which has already been apparent in his labor discipline and his wordly success. Roger's triumph has been double: not only that of Protestant faith over Roman Catholic works but also the social justice of merit rewarded triumphing over a corrupt ethics of prescribed social status. The conflation of progressive with Calvinist ideology enables Foxe to concentrate the macrohistorical Protestant apocalypse into the contingent specificity of an industrious apprentice tale so that its absolute explanatory power reinforces the thrust of social explanation at the micronarrative level.[4]

The human immediacy of Foxe's *Book of Martyrs* reminds us that a sophisticated model of narrative concentration was already available to contemporaries in the tendency of Protestant typology to make specific the great pattern of Christian history within the realms of contemporary and individual history. When Andrew Marvell tells the history of his patron's house at Nun Appleton, the microplot of the ancestral Fairfacian courtship is suffused with the resonance of Protestant macropolitics. At its climax, the Cromwellian hero William Fairfax wins his "blooming virgin" from the artful nuns who have vainly sought to corrupt her virtue, a triumph of Protestant merit over the long enchantment of Roman Catholic artifice which magically coincides with the dissolution of the monasteries and the passage of the house, until now a Cistercian priory, into safe hands:

> Thenceforth (as when the enchantment ends,
> The castle vanishes or rends)
> The wasting cloister with the rest
> Was in one instant dispossessed.
>
> At the demolishing, this seat
> To Fairfax fell as by escheat.[5]

These examples make it clear that at least from the Protestant perspective, Reformation history—the revolt against the discredited papal patriarch—lent itself very easily to a progressive explanation. But with enough ingenuity it was also possible to concentrate those great events into a conservative narrative. In Swift's version, the history of the Reformation is concentrated into the domestic adventures of three brothers adrift in Restoration London. Or in Swift's words, they "writ, and raillyed, and rhymed, and sung, and said, and said nothing; they drank, and fought, and whor'd, and slept, and swore, and took snuff." Within the enclosed space of this micronarrative, Swift uses a very ingenious method for assimilating the genealogical inequities of Roman Catholic tradition and hierarchy to those of aristocratic ideology. He figures the Church as that brother who deceitfully imposes the rule of primogeniture on the other two, even though all are the issue of a single birth. The Reformation itself is represented by Peter's ejection of the supposedly "younger" sons, Martin and Jack, from the ancestral house. The dissolution of the monasteries is compressed into Martin's industrious attempts to simplify his clothing, an inheritance from his father's will whose ornate corruptions Martin soon learns to correct with a more

studied moderation. Now, up to this point, Swift's micronarrative seems
to conform readily enough to what I have been calling a progressive
concentration. But the most ostentatious and industrious reformer is of
course not Martin the Anglican but Jack the Calvinist. And Jack fits
perfectly the conservative model of the opportunistic upstart who
stealthily circles back to the traditional corruptions even as he loudly rails
against them. Swift's critique of the Calvinist saint as a progressive
upstart permits us to glimpse the ethical center of conservative ideology,
an utter contempt for the self-interested indulgence of appetite that is
hypocritically concealed behind the rectitude of moral reform. Anglican
moderation turns out to be strictly analogous to conservative ideology, a
temperate revolt against a thoroughly discredited past which yet knows
to retain, with a wise indulgence, what cannot be removed without
fundamental damage to the fabric.[6]

2

HISTORICAL MODELS FOR PROGRESSIVE NARRATIVES

So far I have used the single great instance of Tudor reform to show how
the effort to come to terms with—to explain—the vicissitudes of recent
history led contemporaries to construct miniature narratives that are
collectively a clear alternative to narrative explanations based upon the
romance model or the mutability topos. It is time now to leave the Tudor
context in order to show more comprehensively how the differences
between progressive and conservative narratives reflect a difference in the
way social history is being read and interpreted.

   The figure of the younger son is central both to the progressive and to
the conservative imagination. The rule of primogeniture seemed to
many to suggest that the genealogical distinctions of aristocratic ideology had force even at the intrafamilial level. The younger brother in
Aphra Behn's play of that name announces in the first scene, "I'm a
Cadet, that Out-cast of my Family, and born to that curse of an old *English*
Custom." And the more that custom came under attack, the less defensi-
ble appeared a notion of natural inheritance that treated only the first-
born as fully natured. As William Sprigge observed, "The younger Son
is apt to think himself sprung from as Noble a stock, from the loyns of as
good a Gentleman as his elder Brother, and therefore cannot but wonder,
why fortune and the Law should make so great a difference between them
that lay in the same wombe, that are formed of the same lumpe; why Law
or Custome should deny them an estate, whom nature hath given discretion to know how to manage it." Thus primogeniture institutionalized
status inconsistency. At earlier times this potentially disruptive instance
of mutability had been partially mediated, for aristocratic ideology, by
the romance convention of discovered parentage, which simultaneously

confirmed both the nobility of dispossessed younger sons and the ultimate justice of aristocratic culture. But by the seventeenth century, the
discrediting of the social convention had severely impaired the efficacy of
its literary counterpart. This is clear from Sprigge's irritable identification of primogeniture with a myth of the birth of the hero whose explicit
dependence on vertical intrusions constitutes its own refutation. Would it
not be more charitable, he asks, "to expose or drown these latter
births . . . then thus to expose them like so many little *Moses*'s in Arks of
Bulrushes to a Sea of poverty and misery, from whence they may never
expect reprieve, unless some miraculous Providence (like *Pharoahs*
daughters) chance rescue them into her Court and favour?"[7]

Of course disinherited sons might live to show that they themselves
embodied the will of the father more truly than he who had inherited the
title. Shakespeare's Orlando warns us of such an outcome when he repeatedly insists to his older brother that "the spirit of my father . . . is
within me": "You have trained me like a peasant, obscuring and hiding
from me all gentleman-like qualities. The spirit of my father grows
strong in me, and I will no longer endure it." But this sort of triumph,
rather than seeming a demonstration of the aristocratic truth that noble
blood always shows itself in the end, by the seventeenth century was
more likely to be read as a vindication of individual merit within a system
of which the best that could be said was that its inherent injustice gave a
spur to industry. Thomas Wilson, himself a younger son, was obliged to
confess that primogeniture "makes us industrious to apply ourselves to
letters or to armes, whereby many times we become my master elder
brothers' masters, or at least their betters in honour and reputacion, while
he lyves att home like a mome and knowes the sound of no other bell but
his own." Sprigge agreed that at least until recently, a younger son could
"by the wings of his own industry or merits, have raised himselfe to as
high a pitch of honour and fairer fortunes, then those of his elder Brothers birth-right; so that to be the first-born was scarce a priviledge."[8]

In other words, the stories of successful younger sons of the nobility
tended to be accommodated, despite the gentle blood, to the progressive
plot-model of the career open to talents. (Later I will turn to the stories of
those younger sons who failed.) To be sure, one potent justification for
this progressive plot was the essentially assimilationist desire to renovate
old families fallen into corruption. Edmund Bolton advised gentlemen
that apprenticeship was "a vocation simply honest, and may proue a stay
to posteritie, and give credit to their names, when licentious and corrupted eldest sonnes haue sold their birth-rights away." Edward Waterhouse
praised the honest "Callings" of younger sons as "revivals of decayed
greatness unto its pristine vigour," and Defoe asked, "How often do
these younger sons come to buy the elder sons estates, and restore the
family, when the elder, and head of the house, proving rakish and extrav-

agant, has wasted his patrimony . . . ?" And in a world where the mercantile success of younger sons fit so clearly into a more general pattern
of the perpetual circulation and exchange not only of professions but of
status groups, it was tempting to go even further and to round out this
relatively simple model of how status inconsistency might be overcome.
Thus, according to John Corbet, younger sons of "ancient Gentry" become wealthy "Citizens"; these "New Men" retain a gentility of behavior and are successful enough to eventually establish new "Gentile Families." As Defoe succinctly expressed this circular plot, "Thus Tradesmen
become Gentlemen, by Gentlemen becoming Tradesmen." From this
dizzying perspective, the difference between "restorations" and "original
raisings" might seem to fade into unimportance: Bolton's advice to humble fathers, the same as his advice to gentlemen, was to "put your children to be *Apprentises,* that so as God may blesse their iust, true, and
vertuous industrie, they may found a new family, and both raise them-
selues and theirs to the precious and glittering title of Gentlemen."9

But there were problems with this temptation to make linear plots
circular. One great advantage of telling stories about status inconsistency
was that narrative imposed solutions upon problems of social categorization by locating them in time. Stories transformed the static conflict of
incompatible social identities into a potentially intelligible relation of
events on a continuum of change. A narrative whose events are interchangeable, however, has the temporality not of historical process but of
mutability, and it thereby forfeits the capacity for making intelligible
explanations. By arranging events in a certain linear order, progressive
narrative automatically invests personality with the distinct moral
qualities that are implied in the condition of being either in decline or on
the rise. These qualities imply, in turn, an explanatory rationale whose
force is unmistakable. On one side are the extravagant and licentious
older sons of nobility, sunk in decay and corruption; on the other, the
industrious and virtuous younger sons or tradesmen, hard at work in
their honest and quasi-Calvinist callings. The odor of the Protestant ethic
can infiltrate the atmosphere of progressive narrative even when it is
explicitly enjoined. In memorializing Henry Ashurst, for example, Richard Baxter assures his auditors that "it is not so low a matter, as great
birth, or riches, or any other wordly honour, which I am to remember of
our deceased friend . . . But yet as a touch of the History of his life, is fit
to go before his exemplary Character . . . I shall premise a little first of
his Parentage." Like Roger Holland a native of Lancashire, but unlike
him the youngest son of a gentleman, Ashurst is bound apprentice to a
London master. But unlike many dissolute apprentices, Henry spends
his father's annuity on "good Books: Not Play-books or Romances and
idle Tales." And although the master himself goes bankrupt, Henry
borrows money and sets up for himself so prudently that he is soon a very

successful tradesman, which he remains until his death. Baxter makes it clear that not "worldly gain" but "Charity was his Life and business." In fact he owed his estate to his honesty in trading—no doubt in part because he thereby gained the credit of the trading community, but also because "God strangely kept those men that he trusted from breaking [i.e., going bankrupt]."[10]

Despite the force of the Protestant ethic, however, the ideological line could not be drawn with absolute precision; the very fluidity of social conditions determined that the distinction between meritorious success and its absence, between virtue and corruption, would cut across status lines. When Defoe undertakes to teach a lesson to improvident gentry, he imagines two gentlemen of equal income, one of whom lives a life of responsibility and prudence, the other of whom "lives an unhappy mortified Life"; and this, he concludes, "is an Abridgement of the Difference, between . . . the Rise and Decay of Families." The first gentleman, it should be noted, is "a Man of Honour" because he has the wisdom to be "a Mony'd Man." Elsewhere Defoe sympathetically conjures up "a Gentleman of Good Birth and Fortune" whom he proceeds to put through innumerable financial difficulties, only to interject at last that " 'tis too long and too Sad a Story to rip up at this time, to offer at particulars, and to tell what Terrible Extremes, these things have reduc'd some extraordinary Families in *England*." In narratives like these, commoners and tradesmen play at most the secondary and relatively neutral role of engrossing the estates of their luxurious and bankrupt betters. The progressive plots in which they figure as more active protagonists are those which explicitly concern what Bolton calls "founding a new family." And once again Defoe is our most convenient guide to the variations that occur within this basic movement.[11]

On the one hand, status inconsistency may be overcome by the genuine assimilation of the upwardly mobile: "We see the tradesmen of *England,* as they grow wealthy, coming every day to the Herald's office, to search for the Coats of Arms of their ancestors, in order to paint them upon their coaches, and engrave them upon their furniture, or carve them upon the pediments of their new houses; and how often do we see them trace the registers of their families up to the prime nobility, or the most antient gentry of the kingdom?" Here the progressive rise to new status turns out to entail the retrospective renovation of past status: the romance convention of discovered parentage is found secreted within the antiromance movement. However, the emphasis is upon the validation not of genealogical nobility but of "true" nobility, as Defoe goes on to make clear, since the discovery of gentle birth is no more than an expendable aid to assimilation: "In this search we find them often qualified to raise new families, if they do not descend from old; as was said of a certain tradesman of *London,* that if he could not find the antient race of Gentlemen, from which he came, he would begin a new race, who should be as good Gentlemen as any that went before them." Thus if "the first money getting wretch, who amass'd the estate" lacks the breeding we associate with the gentle-born, his son will be truly a gentleman, "and that not upon the money onely." So through socialization—their own, but also that of the community by which they are accredited—such families "in a succession or two are receiv'd as effectually, and are as essentially gentlemen, as any of the antient houses were before them," "and are accepted among gentlemen as effectually as if the blood of twenty generations was running in their veins." Writing from the indignant perspective of aristocratic ideology a half-century earlier, Richard Brathwaite casts a very different light on a very similar scenario. Some

Mushroom surreptitious Peers . . . more beholden to their Titles of Honour by Accident then Antiquity . . . had been found . . . in the publick streets, fields, and garden-alleys, and afterwards highly advanced in these times of distraction, for their service . . . And they would boast that their House, though built up only to the first story, would appear more glorious to the eye of Posterity, then ancient high Structures grounded on shrinking foundations; and that theirs would stand, when those vast piles of declining Nobility should sink. [12]

At this point in the construction of progressive narrative, we find ourselves in transition between stories of assimilation and stories of supersession. By what criteria of gentility will this "new race," born of historical discontinuity, be "good Gentlemen"? The traditional gentry will be so shamed by this "modern gentry," by this "new Class truly qualify'd to inherit the Title," Defoe says, that they will either be reformed or "be hiss't off of the stage of life, be dissown'd for meer ignorance, and be no more rank't among the gentry: a happy time, which I have good reason to think is not very farr off." Of course, in this optimistic projection, what qualifies the new gentry "to inherit the title" is not genealogy at all (which signifies nothing) but that which the old gentry, through their obstinate ignorance, lack: temperance, frugality, honesty, prudence, "the practise of all morall vertues." When these are wanting, "or degenerated or corrupted in a Gentleman, he sinks out of the Rank, [and] ceases to be any more a Gentleman." So the new gentry supersede not only the old gentry but also the old conception of gentility; the new conception consists of virtue and is evidenced now most clearly (although by no means exclusively) in efficient estate management. When Bernard Mandeville observes that the noble ancestors of the great are in reality most likely to have been "uxorious Fools, silly Bigots, noted Poltroons or debauch'd Whoremasters," the romance discovery of elevated parentage is turned on its head. And from this progressive perspective of extreme demystification, the preferred method for overcom-

ing status inconsistency is not assimilation but supersession—the replacement of all the outworn fictions of status orientation by the
emergent criteria of class. As Defoe remarks, "Many of our trading
gentlemen at this time refuse to be Ennobled, scorn being knighted, and
content themselves with being known to be rated among the richest
Commoners in the nation." So the strictest logic of progressive ideology
would dictate a plot that repudiates the venerable plot of lineage itself.
With the new race must come a new way of conceiving the existence of
virtue over time.[13]

In bald outline, then, this is the pattern of progressive narratives and of
their explanatory function. By specifying mutability to the concrete
realm of social stratification and mobility, progressive plots explain it in
terms of the status inconsistency and social injustice that are inherent
features of aristocratic culture. And by representing the downward mobility of unworthy nobility and gentry and the upward mobility of industrious and deserving commoners, progressive plots simultaneously
overcome that inconsistency. But of course the most significant examples
of progressive narrative are a good deal more complicated than this
would suggest. It is possible to abstract a "bald outline" of any complicated intellectual structure, but ideology would not serve the purpose for
which it is formulated were it simple and unproblematic. The purpose of
ideology is to mediate apparently intractable human problems so as to
make them not simple but intelligible, to provide an explanation of
reality whose plausibility will depend on the degree to which it appears
to do justice to the reality it explains. There is therefore an inherent
tension in the explanatory function of ideology: between this will to
engage what is problematic in its subject, and the will to naturalize, to
efface the evidence of the problematic through the very act of engagement. I will conclude my discussion of progressive narrative with an
early example in which, because the naturalizing capacity of the progressive rationale is still rudimentary, this tension can be seen with unusual clarity.

One reason for the enormous popularity of Thomas Deloney's stories
of upwardly mobile apprentices is the frank ingenuity with which he
acknowledges the complications of this basic movement by seeking to
cover his tracks even as he makes them. In the very first chapter of *Jack of
Newbery* (1597), Deloney's hero rises from apprentice to master weaver
by marrying his master's widow. The marriage establishes the pattern,
which holds for Jack's entire career, of the passive protagonist who is so
far from seeming to turn his industry to self-interested ends that he
always appears to be rewarded for his virtue but not through it, preferred
by a superior power rather than elevated by his own exertions. And the
rest of the narrative may fairly be seen as a fabric in which are interwoven
the varied strands by which Deloney both proclaims, and effaces the

evidence of, the elevation of the humble. The proclamations may even
consist in the open admission that to some this mobility looks more like
the problem than the solution of status inconsistency. In Jack's own case,
for example, his former fellow servants are troubled not only by the
quickness of his rise but also by the degree to which he has rationalized
his work habits. The problem is dealt with on three different fronts.
First, Jack's fellows are willing to focus on the meritorious rather than the
antisocial features of his diligence. Second, Jack's own view of his rise,
deeply deferential, is simply that he has been preferred "by Gods providence, and your Dames favour." Finally, the problems created by the
social specificity of the opening marriage episode are soon vitiated by
making the marriage a fabliau setting for the timeless battle of the sexes—
by displacing social conflict, that is, onto a traditional and harmless form
of sexual conflict. [14]

Once Jack himself has risen he repeats this pattern with others. The
widow soon dies, and in the portrayal of Jack's second marriage, to a
servant, as itself an act of expansive largess—we watch the fantastic
ceremony through the wondering eyes of Jack's new parents-in-law, who
see him as a paternalistic overlord—we find the evidence of his own full
assimilation. Yet Jack's rise is not thereby rendered invisible, for he pointedly makes his own conspicuous consumption a lesson to Nan on how
she, too, must learn to live her new status so that the neighbors soon will
learn to accept it (25–26, 64–67). Jack teaches a similar lesson to Randoll
Pert, a drapier fallen on hard times whom Jack sets up again with a
munificent gift that metamorphoses Pert's rags into "a faire sute of appar-
ell"; soon he grows very wealthy, becomes sheriff, and repays Jack's debt
(68–71). Thus clothes make the man: Randoll (like Nan) is enabled,
through Jack's syncretic blend of patriarchal care and capitalist magic, to
become what he potentially was, and the new clothing turns out to be not
a disguise but, like Nan's French hood, an enabling identity.

The logic behind this kind of syncretism becomes clearer once Deloney begins to exploit the historical setting of his story, emplacing Jack's
private micronarrative within the analogous, macrohistorical context of
Tudor absolutism. Within this context, Jack assumes his fundamental
social role as a commoner of enormous wealth, a commercial and industrial employer who is also, as the primary advocate of the interests of the
clothing industry to the court of Henry VIII, a servant of the absolute
state. His principal antagonist is the king's Lord Chancellor, Cardinal
Wolsey, who sponsors an interdiction on the cloth trade and a tax to be
levied on clothiers. Deloney has two major strategies for validating the
clothing interest while at the same time defusing the hostility attached to
the pursuit of commercial self-interest and the ostentatious enrichment
of mere commoners. On the one hand, Jack undertakes "to serve my
Prince and Country" with all the bastard-feudal trappings of a late-

medieval baron, taking the field in full armor at the head of a personal army of 150 retainers (27–29). The anachronistic impersonation is coextensive with an even more self-conscious piece of social theater in which Jack assumes the role of the Prince of Ants in defense of the "poore labouring people" against "the idle Butterflies," "sworne enemies" of the industrious ants and parasitic "upon the labours of other men" (32–34). The head of the "butterflies" is Cardinal Wolsey, whom Deloney makes the type of the upstart robe noble. Here is the truly audacious and destructive social group in Tudor England, negatively defined against the integrity both of the virtuous and productive common people, and of the virtuous sword nobility with whom Jack has drolly identified himself. Potential hostility against the upwardly-mobile is thus deflected from clothiers onto courtiers, at the same time serving those economic interests on which Jack's further mobility will depend.[15]

But the social theater of Jack's status as one of the *noblesse d'épée* remains only that. For if he were to assimilate too fully, by a rise in social rank, he would forfeit the progressive aim that is at the heart of Deloney's narrative, the legitimation of a humble social group in its own terms. So Jack "meekely refuse[s]" Henry's offer of a knighthood and rehearses the self-deprecating claim that "Gentleman I am none, nor the sonne of a Gentleman, but a poore Clothier, whose lands are his Loomes, having no other Rents but what I get from the backes of little sheepe" (28, 43–44). By thus advertising his insignificance according to the land-associated criteria of status, Jack implicitly seeks an alternative language of positive, class criteria which cannot yet be articulated except by negation. Of course the problem is also that by refusing the assimilation to status, Jack refuses as well the only available social mechanism for overcoming the status inconsistency that has been created by his great wealth. And so that wealth is simply effaced by his preferred epithet, "poor clothier." A much more effective solution—Deloney's second major strategy for validating the clothing interest—exploits Wolsey's position not as upstart robe noble but as corrupt Roman Catholic. And it borrows from the more fully formulated value system of Protestant ideology an experimental model for legitimating the clothiers which stealthily anticipates capitalist ideology and a supersessionist progressivism in its appeal.

The solution occurs in the context of a crisis in the clothing industry caused by the interdiction of trade. Jack's appeal to the king frankly acknowledges the real difference between "rich" and "poore" clothiers— that is, between employers and laborers—by way of explaining the mechanism of the crisis. But if they are divided in wealth, the clothiers are united in virtuous service to the public interest. The real divisiveness comes from the self-interest of corrupt courtiers who are responsive only to bribes (50–51). This appeal to the public interest is far removed from the capitalist rationalization of self-interest, but now the moral resonance of Reformation politics helps deepen the argument. The time of the story is the early 1520s, when Henry VIII was still the pope's Defender of the Roman Catholic Faith, and Deloney has the cardinal obsequiously allude to this condition and even suggest that Jack is "infected with *Luthers* spirit." But of course those who read the narrative in 1597 had experienced the reversals subsequently wrought by the absolutist process, and knew that Luther, and therefore Jack, were heroic defenders of freedom from unjust authority. Jack himself completes the masterful conflation of Wolsey's several species of corruption—his truckling popery, his courtiership, and his pretense to gentle status—with the quip that "if my Lord Cardinalls father had beene no hastier in killing of Calves, then hee is in dispatching of poor mens sutes, I doubt he had never worne a Myter" (53). Jack's reflected Protestant virtue invests his socioeconomic identity with the supersessionist integrity of one who disdains the corruptions of status assimilation. Absolute state authority is confronted by the free individual in his double guise: as proponent of Protestant liberties and as spokesman for the economic belief "that the Marchants should freely traffique one with another" (52). And just as the heresy of the 1520s was the orthodoxy of the 1590s, so this orthodoxy bore within itself, for readers a hundred years later, the premonition of a triumph by the absolutism of economic self-interest over the reigning absolutism in church and state.

3

HISTORICAL MODELS FOR CONSERVATIVE NARRATIVES

I began my discussion of progressive plots by observing that the success stories of disinherited younger sons of the nobility were easily assimilated to that model. But what of younger sons who failed? For them the status inconsistency entailed in the rule of primogeniture threatened to become not a temporary social injustice remediable by the confident exercise of virtue but a permanent condition. Sergeant Yelverton, a relatively successful younger son (he was elected speaker of the House of Commons in 1597), was nevertheless pessimistic about his future: "My estate is nothing correspondent for the maintenance of this dignity . . . the keeping of us all being a great impoverishing of my estate and the daily living of us all nothing but my daily industry." The status anxiety of another younger son takes the more intimate form of an identity crisis, for he has "been brought to beleeue, that by being a Prentise, I lose my birth right, and the right of my blood both by father, and mother, which is to be a Gentlemen [*sic*], which I had rather dye, then to endure." Given the nature of their plight, younger sons who had fallen on hard times were likely to be at least as sensitive to the arbitrariness of aristocratic ideology as were those who believed that their industry had succeeded even though their genealogy had let them down. In Sir John Vanbrugh's play, Tom Fashion, younger brother of Sir Novelty Fashion, Lord Foppington, complains: " 'Sdeath and furies! Why was that coxcomb thrust into the world before me?" "But if Merit were to be the Standard of Worldly Happiness," asked Stephen Penton, "what great desert is there in being born Eldest Son and Heir to several Thousands a Year, when sometimes it falls out, that the Person is hardly able to Answer Two or Three the easiest Questions in the World wisely enough to save himself from being Begg'd."[16]

William Sprigge is considerably more acerbic:

What's the Reason so many of the best Names and Families throughout the Realm lie stinking in the streets covered with rags and vermine, but that for a fond and idle fansie of keeping up the name and family, the whole Inheritance is intayl'd on the first-born, and nothing but poverty and misery on all the rest of the bloud and kindred, as if it were lesse discredit to have many beggars, then not to have one Gallant that is able to fly a Hawk, and keep up the cry of Hounds belonging to the Family? What madnesse is it, that on the account of Primogeniture, the whole Estate should be swept away by one who perhaps is fitter to wear long coats and a fools cap, then manage an Estate . . . ?

In Sprigge's eloquent analysis, the great end of the mid-seventeenth-century revolution against monarchy had been to extirpate the ancient and inequitable system of aristocracy which depended upon it. And in 1659 the bitter irony was that this optimistic spirit of social reform had only strengthened the absolutist enemy by (as it were) concentrating and modernizing it. Sprigge asks: "Was it for our interest to put down one Court and King, to set them up in every great Gentlemens Family? Was it for our advantage to throw down the ancient Nobility, whose greatness was balanced by a jealous Monarch, to set up a more numerous of a modern stamp, without any ballance? Are they the less formidable for waving invidious Titles, or will they not be our Masters if they be our Landlords?" In this view, the effect of destroying the venerable institutions of aristocratic culture is not to impede, but to unfetter and unmask, its exercise of power. The old aristocracy seems to have been both transformed into, and replaced by, the new: Sprigge's critique of aristocratic rule modulates from images of luxurious incompetence to ones of tyrannical exploitation, and the modern nobility begins to assume some of the features of the "Whig aristocracy" and monied men of the coming age. Thus he is outraged that citizens now employ "the children of the Nobility to be their servants . . . so much hath wealth gotten the start of Birth, Education, and Virtue," and he asks, "Will virtue be in any reputation, while riches are in such esteem?"[17]

In the sinuous workings of Sprigge's mind we have an unusually lucid instance of how conservative ideology emerges from a negation of the progressive ideology with which it shares a common, antiaristocratic ground. For a man like Defoe, the new nobility (whether or not it assimilates itself to the forms and fictions of the old) vindicates itself by learning to manage money and thereby to found new families. But for Sprigge, the increasingly exclusive emphasis on naked wealth is only the modern version of aristocratic corruption, the modern world's preferred form of status inconsistency. Yet if the conservative animus against modernity seems inevitably to imply nostalgia for an earlier time of social justice, such a utopia can scarcely be located in any Golden Age of aristocratic rule. Sprigge and other younger sons looked back instead to "primitive" systems of partible inheritance, remnants of which might still be seen in customary practices like the Kentish "gavelkind." Such practices were better able to mediate the complex and contradictory values of conservative ideology, since they appealed both to an anti-aristocratic egalitarianism and to a longing for the customary sanction that once gave to aristocratic culture itself (it was thought) a tacit authority. Within a more circumscribed chronology, however, Sprigge identified the years preceding and embracing the English Revolution as the period most decisively responsible for the transformation of social relations that plagued the present. He thought the dissolution of the monasteries had deprived younger sons of a crucial professional outlet; yet since the method of educating them had remained unchanged, the result was relative deprivation and the making of potential revolutionaries. Clarendon shared Sprigge's conservatism but attributed the revolution instead to the upstart rising gentry. At the outbreak of hostilities in Somerset, "there were a people of an inferior degree, who, by good husbandry, clothing, and other thriving arts, had gotten very great fortunes, and, by degrees getting themselves into the gentlemen's estates, were angry that they found not themselves in the same esteem and reputation with those whose estates they had . . . These from the beginning were fast friends to the Parliament." Sir John Oglander thought that the physical toll of warfare itself precipitated social change rather than the other way around, for between 1641 and 1646, "most of the ancient gentry were either extinct or undone . . . so that none of them could appear again as gentlemen. Death, plunder, sales and sequestrations sent them to another world or beggar's bush," and "base men" took their place. Swift concurred that the reason "New-men" have, by and large, conducted the affairs of government since the Restoration is that "the Noblest Blood of England having been shed in the grand Rebellion, many great Families became extinct, or supported only by Minors. When the King was restored, very few of those Lords remained," and Swift argued that that is when our "corrupt Method" of educating the nobility was instituted.[18]

As these observations suggest, the progressive explanation of critical social change was likely to focus especially on the historical macronarrative of Tudor absolutism, while the conservative reaction was more inclined to concentrate on the more recent history of the seventeenth century. But although the English Revolution seemed an important watershed in shaping the modern social topography, for later conservative ideologists the most important event of the century was the Glorious Revolution and its attendant innovations in finance. Of course corruption was in some sense congenital to aristocratic rule, and it had been greatly aggravated by the venalities of the early decades of the century; but 1688 was the point of peripeteia. According to Swift's account,

A Set of Upstarts, who had little or no part in the *Revolution,* but valued themselves by their Noise and pretended Zeal when the Work was over, were got into Credit at Court, by the Merit of becoming Undertakers and Projectors of Loans and Funds: These, finding that the Gentlemen of Estates were not willing to come into their Measures, fell upon those new Schemes of raising Mony, in order to create a Mony'd-Interest, that might in time vie with the Landed, and of which they hoped to be at the Head.

As in the progressive plot, but with a very different evaluative emphasis, the rise of the upstarts coincided with the decline of their betters. In 1702 one of the latter complained that the monied men grow rich at the Exchequer and Exchange while "we continually drudge to pay their great and heavy interests . . . Some of these Gent[leme]n not many years ago were scarce able to keep a pad nag and a drab coat, and now a Gent[lema]n of £5,000 p.ann. is not a fit companion for their greatness." The consequence of these mushroom fortunes, thought Bolingbroke, was "that the landed men are become poor and dispirited. They either abandon all thoughts of the Public, turn arrant farmers, and improve the estates they have left; or else they seek to repair their shattered fortunes by listing at Court, or under the heads of partys. In the meanwhile those men are become their masters, who formerly would with joy have become their servants."[19]

Years later Swift recalled: "I ever abominated that scheme of politicks, (now about thirty years old) of setting up a mony'd Interest in opposition to the landed. For I conceived there could not be a truer maxim in our government than this, That the possessors of the soil are the best judges of what is for the advantage of the kingdom." The conservative imagination of a challenge to innocent land by corrupting money was easily accommodated to a mode of Horatian pastoralism which facilitated the analogical conversion of the macronarrative of recent history to the microplots of private lives. We observe Swift in the process of making such a conversion when, in the course of an attack upon financial credit, he refers to the fall of the Whig ministry in 1710: "For my own part, when I saw this false Credit sink, upon the Change of the Ministry, I was singular enough to conceive it a good Omen. It seemed, as if the young extravagant Heir had got a new Steward, and was resolved to look into his Estate before things grew desperate, which made the Usurers forbear feeding him with Money, as they used to do." In this example of narrative concentration, the macronarrative of a change in the political climate is converted into a micronarrative of the improvement of the estate. An indulgent monarchy is figured as a luxurious young nobleman who, against all expectations, had reformed himself, retained a prudent steward to manage his land, and shrugged off the corrupting influence of City monied men. Swift's hopes for the English monarchy were not sustained for very long. But the figure of the country gentleman, chastened and made wise by modern corruption, is a familiar type in contemporary literature and political thought, and as a normative model it bespeaks a wary sort of conservatism that values the traditional virtues of a landed nobility, somehow shorn of its stupid and credulous vanity. To Bolingbroke, Swift sent a common variant on this conservative story of rural retirement, which he was content to call a "romance." Here the actual process of concentration has already been incorporated within the protagonist as a condition of character, for he is a public figure—a state servant—whose private rustication is itself the sign of his virtue: "But, if I were to frame a romance of a great minister's life, he should begin it as Aristippus has done; then be sent into exile, and employ his leisure in writing the memoirs of his own administration; then be recalled, invited to resume his share of power, act as far as was decent; at last, retire to the country, and be a pattern of hospitality, politeness, wisdom, and virtue."[20]

These micronarratives are noteworthy not only for their relationship to the macronarrative of recent history but also for their upward turn, which goes against the more dominant conservative view of 1688 and its aftermath as a movement of devolution and decay. In fact the transformation of linear into circular movement is a feature of conservative much more than of progressive plotting. In narrative treatments of the English Revolution, this tendency can be attributed in part to the apparent circularity of the events themselves. Thus James Heath depicted the revolution as a revolving globe that eventually returned to its apogee those gentry who at first had been carried in the opposite direction. But the circular return of a happy ending did not require actual events for its justification, as is evident in conservative transformations of the general phenomenon of upward mobility. In John Earle's character of "An Upstart Knight," for example, the knight's father buys the land and the son buys the title, but "in summe, he's but a clod of his owne earth . . . And commonly his race is quickly runne, and his Childrens Children, though they scape hanging, returne to the place from whence they came." And

Swift, observing that "God, who worketh Good out of Evil, acting only by the ordinary Cause and Rule of Nature, permits this continual Circulation of human Things for his own unsearchable Ends," describes a similar cycle of vulgar aspiration, concluding that "the Dunghil having raised a huge Mushroom of short Duration, is now spread to enrich other Mens Lands." The circularity of Swift's history of the Reformation translates this plot structure into its doctrinal equivalent: Calvinist modernity recapitulates the Roman Catholic sins it undertook to reform—a pattern which itself imitates the fundamental conservative critique of progressive ideology as an ironic return to aristocratic injustice.[21]

Although specified to the realms of social mobility and human agency, these circles cannot fail to remind us of the "traditional" narratives of mutability. And as Swift's half-earnest language of unsearchability suggests, the circular turn in conservative plots may seem (as in progressive plots) to sacrifice in explanatory specificity what it gains in symmetry. But there is good reason why this apparent trade-off should be fundamentally more compatible with conservative than with progressive explanation. The premise of the progressive narrative is the status inconsistency of aristocratic rule, founded as it is in the arbitrary criterion of genealogy, and its major movement is likely to lead us toward resolution and the establishment of social justice. But the major movement of the conservative narrative consists in a retrograde series of disenchantments with all putative resolutions. In more traditional narrative, such a movement would prepare for the final recourse to mutability and divine unreadability. In conservative plots it is more likely to generate a desire for the return of an earlier order whose vulnerability has now by one means or another become more resistant to skeptical reduction. For this reason the transformation of linear to circular movement in conservative plots can work to recoup rather than preclude the explanatory power of narrative. Swift's extravagant young heir, shrugging off the bad influence of City usurers, promises to become in his later years the type of the reformed country gentleman who knows best the Horatian wisdom of rural retirement because he returns to it after disastrous encounters with its alternatives. Thus the well-known eighteenth-century circuit from the country to London and back to the country represented a hopeful resolution of what conservative ideology perceived as a national crisis of moral and social decay. But the retirement, so far from expressing a naive faith in the purity and sufficiency of the old forms, depends for its success on the chastened knowledge of human imperfection which only the experience of mobility, circulation, and exchange could have afforded. Indeed, at a certain point in the development of conservative narrative, this pattern of circular retirement will undergo a subtle modulation— from a movement that is primarily spatiotemporal to one that is pri-

marily formal and aesthetic—and the utopian project of conservative
ideology will find what is perhaps its most satisfactory fulfillment, not at
all in the realm of social activity, but in that of epistemology.[22]

So the pastoral circuit is one form in which conservative ideology has
recourse to narrative for the representation and explanation of social
dynamics, without resigning itself to a story of sheer devolution. Another important narrative strategy is to focus not on the poignant fall of
the deserving, but on the fraudulence and depravity—and sometimes the
eventual failure—of those who rise. And here, too, private narrative may
be generated by a concentration of the historical macroplot. This is what
Charles Davenant does, for example, in his brief autobiography of Mr.
Double, which takes shape in a dialogue with his friend Mr. Whiglove.
Whiglove observes that "this has been a happy Revolution" for his friend,
for "Matters are well mended with you of late Years."

> *Double*. They are so, Thanks to my Industry. I am now worth Fifty thou-
> sand Pound, and 14 years ago I had not Shoes to my Feet.
> *Whiglove*. This is a strange and sudden Rise.
> *Double*. Alas! 'tis nothing, I can name you fifty of our Friends who have
> got much better Fortunes since the Revolution, and from as poor Beginnings.

Double then proceeds to give his friend "a short Narrative of my whole
Life," which turns out to be the story of a bad apprentice whose vice is
not idleness but too much industry. First bound to a London shoemaker,
Double cheats his way into a succession of places until the pretense of
having secretly facilitated William's takeover in 1688 helps make his
fortune. At various stages he is exposed as a fraud and an impostor, but he
brazens his way into a position of eminence among the monied men. The
story of the bad apprentice ends with its application: "You have the
History of my Life, but it may serve as a Looking-Glass in which most of
the Modern Whigs may see their own Faces . . . Did they rise by Virtue
or Merit? No more than my self." Davenant's moral insists upon the
convertibility of his private tale of the insidiously industrious shoemaker
to the public sociopolitical history of the times, and it thereby capitalizes
on the compressed power of the tale to deflate the progressive ideology
that justifies the modern phenomenon of upward mobility. Davenant
concentrates the watchwords of this ideology—the career open to talents, worldly success as the reward of virtue—within the cant notion of
progressive "industry," and thereby transforms that notion into a synonym for opportunistic and hypocritical self-aggrandizement.[23]

In some respects Davenant's conversion of history to story reminds us
of (Mary) Delarivière Manley's allegorical "looking-glasses" for modern
Whigs, which attained such popularity during the first decades of the
eighteenth century. Swift, it will be recalled, believed in 1710 that the War
of the Spanish Succession was fought "to raise the Wealth and Grandeur

of a particular Family." But by then Manley's secret histories had already inflated this insight into scandalous narrative reflections on the Marlboroughs and a host of others as well. The main target of the first of these works is Sarah (or Zarah) Churchill, "whom Fortune had cut out purely for the Service of her own Interest, without any Regard to the strict Rules of Honour or Virtue." On the eve of the overthrow of James II, king of "Albigion," Princess Albania (Princess, later Queen, Anne) is convinced that Hippolito (Marlborough) "should have more Honour than to betray his Prince." And Zarah, with a cynical opportunism reminiscent of Mr. Double, replies, "Well, Madam . . . if you depend upon Honour, I hope you never expect to succeed to the Crown of *Albigion*." Concerned "to establish the Interest of her Family firm as well as that of her own," Zarah, although "of obscure Parents," begins by capturing the "Well Born" Hippolito in marriage, and soon the people stand "gazing with Admiration to behold their sudden Rise." Once the princess becomes queen, Zarah fully triumphs, for "*Albania* took the Crown from her own Head to put it on *Zarah's*. This great Rise of hers, and her Power at Court, gain'd her the Title of Queen *Zarah*." "Favourites" have taken the place of "statesmen," a symptom of corruption reflected in the nation at large, where "*Soldiers* turn'd *Usurers* in their *Tents,* and *Salors* in their *Cabbins;* the *Merchant* went no more Abroad for Gain, but Traded safer with the Government." And the people "saw to their Sorrow Men of Vicious and Corrupt Lives and Conversations, without one good Action to recommend them, rais'd in a Trice from Slaves, to be Governours of Provinces, from Poor, to be Rich and Powerful, from Base and Unknown, to be Noble, and Chief of the State; honour'd for their Merit, that is to say, their V——y, because they were *Zarazians,* and Zarah got by their Service."[24]

In the *New Atalantis,* a longer and more diffuse work, it is not so much Sarah as Marlborough who is attacked. The work is narrated, in dialogue form, by Astraea (who has made a tentative and exploratory return to earth), Virtue, and Intelligence; the latter introduces the others and us to Marlborough as Count Fortunatus, who has been "rais'd . . . from a meer Gentleman, to that Dignity." Having heard a portion of his story, Virtue remarks, "What a pity 'tis, that a Person of his graceful Appearance should make no Application at all to *Virtue!*" But as his name suggests, he has had no need for virtue, since "*Fortune* has been his *Deity,* and entirely propitious to him." This is, of course, the Machiavellian fortune that is successfully exploited by the corrupted man of *virtù;* in fact it is the limitless passion for "fortune" that has enabled Marlborough to rise: "In short, he is Excessive in nothing, but his love of *Riches* . . . *Money* is the only means to carry on successively the greatest Enterprize . . . Either to conceal'd *Ambition,* or native *Covetousness,* we must attribute his unbounded, unwearied Desire of *Wealth*."[25]

But although conservative narrative fully flourishes only in the wake of the Hanoverian Settlement and in reaction to the rise of the Whiggish monied men, there are a few important precedents—narratives that not only predate this period but also concentrate the social crisis of an earlier epoch. Perhaps the most imaginative of these is Thomas Deloney's story of upward mobility gone sour.

Thomas of Reading (1600)[26] is set in a twelfth-century England that is overlaid—with some plausibility—with the cultural conflicts of six-teenth-century absolutism: the struggles between baronage and mon-archy, the centralization of power in the hands of the king, and the uncertain role in this transition of "new men" who are disaffected with the old aristocratic dispensation and increasingly committed to protec-tionist legislation and absolute ownership. The new men who are central to the narrative possess the highly ambiguous "newness" of younger sons: Deloney associates the clothing trade of his eponymous "sixe worthy yeomen" with "the younger sons of Knights and Gentlemen, to whom their Fathers would leave no lands," and two of the six are explicitly said to be of ancient lineage (85, 118). Combining the services of twelfth-century *ministeriales* and sixteenth-century robe nobility, Thomas Cole and his fellow clothiers hold office under Henry I and provide soldiers for his wars.[27] In exchange the king solicits their opinion on how best he might further the interests of the clothing trade, and to this end he standardizes the cloth measure throughout England and makes the theft of cloth a capital offense (99–101, 116, 133). But the alliance of king and wealthy commoners goes deeper than that. Deloney is at pains to remind us that tradition accords Henry I the honor of having instituted the high court of Parliament, which by the sixteenth century, at least, might begin to appear an institution of "the Commons" (83, 117). The joint business of government, he tells the clothiers, is to "maintain the profit of the Commons" as well as that of "the whole Common-wealth" (99). Their most profound tie, however, lies in the fact that the king is also a younger son. Henry assumed the throne while his older brother, Robert, Duke of Normandy, was on the Crusades, and he soon became convinced that "although hee was Heire to *England* by birth, yet I am King by possession." Against Robert's return Henry "sought by all meanes possible to winne the good will of his Nobilitie, and to get the favor of the Commons by curtesie . . . thereby the better to strengthen himselfe against his brother." To this self-interested end the commoners are likely to prove more serviceable than the nobility, for many of these support Robert's right, and "all his favourers I must account my foes, and will serve them as I did the ungratefull Earle of *Shrewsbury,* whose lands I have seized, and banisht his body" (85, 86).

Thomas of Reading is remarkable for the consistency with which it alternates between the adventures of the clothiers and the tragic love plot of Margaret and Duke Robert. From a certain perspective the difference seems paradigmatic. Narrated with a highly euphuistic formality, Margaret's story is the tragic romance of a noblewoman who is made the plaything of mutability. Obliged to forsake her "birth and parentage," she enters domestic service with one of the clothiers, pretending humble parentage but betrayed by the tell-tale whiteness of her skin (94–98). "The amorous Duke," "pierct" by Margaret's beauty, entreats her to become "a Lady of high reputation, [rather] then a servant of simple degree." But before the revelation of her parentage can rectify the inconsistency of their stations, Robert is apprehended by his brother and disempowered by blinding. Constant in their love if not in their fortunes, the lovers take leave of each other, Margaret to renounce all worldly status by entering a monastery and by "match[ing] my selfe" not with Duke Robert but with "Lord Jesus" (118, 127–29, 153–55).

Yet it is principally to the lovers, rather than to Deloney, that we owe the romance metaphysics of this love plot. Especially in Margaret's mind, life is a perpetual subjugation to fortune's inconstancy, and the most important means by which its mutability is signified is love, which promises to overcome inconsistency but in the end can only reinforce it. But despite Margaret's reading, Deloney himself has emplaced this love plot within the narrative of twelfth-century politics, specifying its causation to the concrete realms of political strategy and social change. The entanglement of the two plots, their implication in each other, goes far deeper than the fact of their alternating narration. It is not only that Robert's "fate" is controlled by his brother. Margaret's founding experience of mutability, her social leveling, depends upon the fact that her father is the earl of Shrewsbury, one of Robert's supporters whom Henry has therefore expropriated and sent into exile, leaving his kin to "wander up and downe the countrie like forlorne people" (87). To read the story of Margaret and Robert within this explanatory historical context (as the alternating narration obliges us to do with heightened self-consciousness) is to witness the defamiliarizing accommodation of recognizably romance material to the generic hybrid of conservative narrative. The accommodation is very economical. For since the shared status as successful younger sons provides the basis for the alliance of king and clothiers, so far from inhabiting a distinct realm of experience, the love plot evokes just those emotions that are proper to a story about the brutal revenge of the new men against aristocratic primogeniture. The social dislocations of Tudor England are concentrated, by Deloney, into the microplot of one twelfth-century family's status inconsistency. And despite Margaret's words, we have been told enough to know that it is not the mutability of "fortune" that "setteth up tyrants, beateth downe

Kings," but a historically particular compact of social forces that suspend their own considerable differences to engage the common enemy (94).

Of course the relative autonomy of the love plot also deflects these proper emotions from their proper objects—a tentativeness which may be attributed to the precocity of conservative narrative at this time, and especially of its insight into the alliance between monarchy and the commercial interest. But at all those points where Deloney's two plots reflect upon each other, there is real doubt whether "virtue" is to be associated with the absolutist industry and ambition of the younger sons. When Henry justifies hanging people, without trial, for crimes against property by observing that "the corrupt world is growne more bold in all wickednesse," it is difficult not to recall his cynical theft of the crown and to hear these as the words of a supreme opportunist who is willing to buy political support in order to achieve his ambitions. It is significant, moreover, that the observation comes in response to a Northern clothier's harsh remark about the lesser punishment for theft: "What the dule care they for boaring their eyne, sea lang as they mae gae groping up and downe the Country like fause lizar lownes, begging and craking?" (101). For the remark both recalls the forlorn wanderings of persecuted aristocratic families and foreshadows the blinding of the rightful heir to the throne—so that the cruel injustice of the new men toward the old nobility throws the latter into an alliance of social victimization with the comparably persecuted poor. If the idea of "corruption" plays an active role in defining the value system of this narrative, it does so by attaching to the passion for profit. *Thomas of Reading* is anxious to establish the limits of, rather than to rationalize (as in *Jack of Newbery*), individual acquisitiveness. The remarkably neutral tone of the narrator (as distinct from that of his characters) modulates only twice into downright disapproval: of the "wicked" hostess who murders Thomas Cole out of pure "covetousnes"; and of Thomas Dove's former servant, a "smooth-fac'd *Judas*" whose hunger for back wages leads him to deliver his ruined master into the arms of the debtor's bailiff (133, 138, 151). That the celebrated nightmare aura which envelops Cole's murder is indeed reminiscent, as critics have observed, of *Macbeth* depends on our intuition that this, too, is a scene not just of terrible but of guilty foreboding.[28] Deloney's premonitions of disaster parallel Cole's own misgivings: "In conscience, my wealth is too much for a cupple to possesse, and what is our Religion without charity? And to whom more to be shewen, then to decayed housholders?" (135).

In this subtle but intrusive fashion, Cole's repentance of unlimited acquisition helps identify him as the victim of that passion even as it animates, beyond the control of his own penitence, the hearts of his covetous murderers. Cole manages to expiate his acquisitive sins in the nick of time by willing £200 to Dove, but before this act of resurrection can take effect, Dove, as well, must be assailed by accusations. This time the clothier's servants, not his conscience, are the accusers, and despite their wickedness, we must admit they have a point. For they reject out of hand Dove's easy attribution of his financial ruin to the fickleness of fortune and friends, insisting that it be specified instead to the corrupting profit motive by which Dove himself has been pleased to live during his prosperity. The master reproaches his servants with paternalistic righteousness: "From paltrie boies, I brought you up to mans state, and have, to my great cost, taught you a trade, whereby you may live like men. And in requitall of all my courtesie, cost and good will, will you now on a sudden forsake me?" But the apprentices, like Davenant's Mr. Double, have learned too well the mentality of industriousness: "Because you tooke us up poore, doth it therefore follow, that we must be your slaves? We are young men, and for our part, we are no further to regard your profit, then it may stand with our preferment . . . If you taught us our trade, and brought us up from boies to men, you had our service for it . . . But if you be poore, you may thanke your selfe, being a just scourge for your prodigalitie" (149–50). This is the cruel lesson of the clothiers to poor beggars and thieves, now turned back on one of their own. If the story of Margaret and Duke Robert enacts the unjust revenge of the upstarts on their betters, some conservative justice is obtained in these final scenes through the ironic spectacle of the new men hoist with their own petard, the ungovernable passion of self-service.

But of course Dove is reprieved from prison by Cole's posthumous bail, which persuades the rest of the clothiers to chip in so that Dove can "begin the world anew: and by this meanes (together with the blessing of God) he grew into greater credit then ever he was before" (152). The parenthetical qualification is consistent with the sense of piety that suffuses all the final episodes of *Thomas of Reading,* which does not so much Christianize the narrative as lodge a rudimentary conservative insistence on the supremacy of some standard of virtue that not only lies beyond, but is opposed to, self-service. The narration of Margaret's story alternates with the stories of Cole's and Dove's conversions from possessive individualism, and her own decision to "begin the world anew" stands as the model and yardstick for measuring the clothiers' far more uncertain attempts to attain virtue. The narrative ends in a riot of charity and almsgiving by all the clothiers, in support of monasteries (Margaret's among them) as well as the poor (155). In the atmosphere of *Jack of Newbery* we would have no doubt that these acts somehow vindicate their virtue; here, it is not at all clear that status inconsistency has been rectified, rather than aggravated, by the success of the new men and the younger sons.

4
IDEOLOGICAL IMPLICATIONS OF GENERIC MODELS

My central aim thus far has been to show that in the formation of novel-istic narrative, the most important narrative model was not another "lit-erary" genre at all, but historical experience itself. Of course, the distinction is artificial: literary models both structure the way history is experienced and in turn take their "own" shape from that experience. The Spanish picaresque, for example, bequeathed to seventeenth-cen-tury English writers an influential literary form that seemed peculiarly responsive to the crisis of status inconsistency that was felt in different ways throughout early modern Europe.[29]

The eponymous antihero of *La vida de Lazarillo de Tormes* begins his life in the unstable and supremely mobile condition of an orphan, ripe for the discovery of aristocratic parentage but also for self-creation. Early on in his autobiography, Lazaro identifies himself with those who manifest their virtue through "force and industry" rather than with those who inherit noble estates, and he has only contempt for the impoverished *hidalgo* whose obsession with his "honor" overrides all practical consid-erations. Yet in *Lazarillo* the critique of aristocratic ideology is far strong-er than the positive ideology of the new man. In fact, the close relation that this founding picaresque narrative bears to progressive ideology is, if anything, one of satiric inversion. Lazaro parodies the career of the truly noble by cynically demonstrating that rogues can get ahead. Whereas true nobility treatises, according to R. W. Truman, "are concerned with its being praiseworthy to rise in society by the exercise of virtue . . . Lazaro is concerned with its being a virtue simply to rise." Although the traditional order does indeed uphold an arbitrary social injustice, Lazaro's rise does nothing to correct status inconsistency, because it is equally arbitrary, the reward of one whose socialization in adversity is the surest guarantee that his character will be corrupt. In other words, the dominant ideology of *Lazarillo,* and of the rogue narratives that fall directly under its influence, is not progressive but conservative. More-over, it diverges from the conservative as we have come to understand it principally in that it lacks any utopian vision, however remote or contra-dictory, of an alternative. It could be argued that in sixteenth-century Spain, pastoral provides such a vision, that pastoral and picaresque are the antithetical and complementary parts of the literary totality of con-servative ideology—respectively the "alternative" and the "opposi-tional" negations of modern corruption which in other cultures conser-vative ideology deploys as one. Yet when, as in *Guzmán de Alfarache,* the picaro begins to evince a moral standard that is clearly distinguishable from that of his surroundings, Spanish picaresque begins to influence the creation not of fully conservative, but of fundamentally progressive, narratives.[30]

It is not hard to find among conservative ideologists a parodic inversion of progressive values that is clearly indebted to the models of picaresque and criminal biography. Several times Mr. Double refers to himself as a "rogue," and elsewhere Davenant suggestively describes the sort of opportunist whom absolute princes rely on to promote their ends as "a pushing man of a bold spirit, a ready wit, a fluent tongue, obscure and low in the world . . . A man of a wretched beginning, never heard of before, when he sees himself lifted up high, seldom thinks of the laws, impeachments, and the ax." Defoe was intrigued by the parallel between the "little Rogues," who live off highway robbery, and the "great ones," whose criminal specialty is political fraud and commodity exchange. Of course he also found it easy to celebrate highwaymen—and pirates, their international equivalents—as upwardly mobile heroes in the progressive mode. Defoe's Capt. Misson, "a younger Brother of a good Family" with education "equal to his Birth," becomes a "New fashioned Pyrate" rather than new-fashioned gentry and transforms his ship into an egalitarian utopia. Another writer was even able to turn a negative image of the criminal to progressive ends, by making it subvert aristocratic expectations. The family memorials of Gervase Holles begin with a scornful comparison between the assimilationist impulse to acquire false genealogies and the invention of imaginary voyages:

There is nothing appears to me more ridiculous or more nearly allied to a vulgar spirit then what I meet wth in most gentlemen of England, namely a vaine affectation to fly beyond the moone and to credit themselves (as they thinke) wth long and fictitious pedigrees. How many have wee that will confidently tell you their sirnames flourished even in the Saxon times, though the understanding antiquary knowes that they can have no record to justify it . . . This commonly proceedes from poverty of worth w[ch] perswades them to fill wth wordes what they want in virtue.

Himself an "understanding antiquary" with a firm belief in the objectivity of historical documentation, Holles also believes, evidently, in the capacity of virtue to show itself in the absence of a long genealogy. His own lineage is rife with discontinuity, and he is proud of his descent from a merchant. As though to provide a negative vindication of this supersessionist progressivism, he tells the story of Francis Holles, the only surviving representative of the first branch of the family, a young orphan who is reduced, when Gervase first encounters him in the 1620s, to begging for his bread in the streets of London. It is in fact the first Earl of Clare, a noble kinsman of Gervase, who discovers young Francis "as he was playing in the street one day amongst poore boyes." Because he is on his way to Parliament, his lordship has a servant take the boy to his house to await his return. Francis is dressed "in a leather patcht hose and doublet," and the other servants, "not knowing him," set him the task of turning a spit in the kitchen. It is "in this posture and aequipage" that Gervase now sees him; and although he, too, does not "know" the boy, it is as though his birth shines through the deceptive exterior, for "seeing a pritty boy at that employment (indeed he had a very good face and a pure complexion) I asked his name."[31]

The romance convention of inexpungeable nobility is persuasively accompanied by the mutability topos—"Wee shall hardly finde in any family a greater example of fortune's mutability"—for Francis is even now the "cheife" of the Earl of Clare, and his great-grandfather had possessed a vast revenue and a band of seventy retainers. And if this were the romance that the author's self-conscious language would suggest, it would end here, with the boy being elevated to a position befitting his elevated status. In fact the earl does clothe him "handsomely," teach him French, and make him his own page. But the resocialization both works too well and does not go far enough, and Francis quickly displays the effects of relative deprivation: "It is observable how soone the alteration of his condition altered his spirit for he was growne in a very short space a very proud and haughty boy; and understanding what he might have beene he began to looke with contempt upon the other gentlemen his fellow servantes: a sad presage to his future proofe and successe" (35).

It does not take long for this narrative foreshadowing to be fulfilled. Dissatisfied with the boy's progress, the earl seeks the author's opinion on how he might be provided for more justly. Gervase counsels not aristocratic externals but the nurture of internal virtues, for which he has a ready model in his own Protestant industry: "I should like a merchant best, as a calling both generous and in w^{ch} (if it pleased God to blesse his endeavours) he might the likeliest recover an estate as his ancestor had done before him." But the plan fails—partly because of the earl's own frugality and partly because Francis himself does not fit the scenario. Unwilling to stake him to a merchant's career, Clare binds the boy apprentice to a jeweler, with whom he lives for some years "till at length, debauched by a neighbour apprentice, they watched their opportunity when their masters and mistresses were gone out of London in a long vacation, robbed their trunkes, and ran away, and for these 17 yeares hath not beene seen that I could heare of; most likely dead." So the romance discovery of noble parentage ends in the picaresque flight of the criminal; pedigrees are one thing, and virtue, it seems, is quite another (35–36).

The story of Francis Holles suggests how the ideologically significant shape of microhistorical narrative might be refined by intergeneric imitation and parody. Within this process, the romance model is by no means limited to the negative function of parodic inversion. True, the use of romance in novelistic narrative is characteristically framed by the self-conscious sense of its instrumentality *as* romance, marking the space between it and something else. But the space can bespeak a positive ambition somehow to specify the romance model to the unpropitious setting of modern life, and this ambition can animate even the protagonists of progressive narrative. An especially powerful example of this is provided by the notorious Mary Carleton, who was herself the most accomplished of her many biographers. The most inclusive of the tracts that Carleton published in her own defense begins her story at the beginning. The daughter of a German lawyer and diplomat who was known "for his long and ancient descent from an honourable Family" named Van Wolway, Mary hotly denies "that vile and impertinent falshood, that I am of a most sordid and base extraction in this Kingdom, no better then the Daughter of a Fidler at *Canterbury*."[32] She admits that "I am not so honourably descended as I insinuated to the Catch-dolt my Father in Law," who had shared the general misunderstanding that Mary was a German princess. But she vindicates her impersonation of nobility by the fact of having done it so persuasively, and adds that "Ambition and Affection of Greatness to good and just purposes was always esteemed and accounted laudable and praiseworthy, and the sign and character of a vertuous mind" (36, 37–38 [mispaginated 46]). Thus Mary's ostentatious respect for patrilineal descent is clearly the esteem of the social assimilationist, whose most fundamental confidence is in the authority of her own merit.

But circumstance is not as obliging to her ambition as it might be. Orphaned before she is three years old, Mary becomes a ward of the Church, which hopes to make her a nun and to engross her estate. The male power of patrilineal descent becomes negligible in the hands of a "gentlewoman"; Mary evades the nunnery, "blindly wishe[s] I were . . . a man," and eventually resolves to set out for England (10, 12–13, 16, 30, 32). Long a reader of romances, she now seeks to naturalize her mobility by reflecting that "I am not single, or the first woman, that hath put her self upon such hazards, or pilgrimages . . . I might as well have given lustre to a Romance as any any any of those supposed *Heroina's*." But the very attempt to assert the plausibility of this role even in "Modern and very late Times" seems to argue the opposite, for her single exemplum is an anonymous "Princess" who "is the onely Lady Errant in the World." Not only is her model unique; not only does she bear the enabling social status we know Mary lacks; but she is described in an epithet that makes us realize that what Mary really seeks is the freedom of the knight-errant, the sort of mobility that even in romance is enjoyed only by men (23, 32, 34).

But even though established narrative forms cannot provide precedents that would satisfy the full extent of Mary's ambition for mobility, she is inventive enough without them. On her arrival in London she stays at the inn of a Mr. King, who is so impressed by her apparent wealth and status that he lights upon the time-honored plot to "secure my estate . . . by a speedy and secret marriage." In accord with the "received principle of Justice" that *"to deceive the deceiver is no deceit,"* Mary resolves to "counterplot." She is introduced to a Mr. Carleton and his son John (in fact a scrivener who is Mrs. King's brother), and what now ensues is a mutual confidence game (45–46 [mispaginated 38]). John, obsessed with the prospect of feeding the envy of courtiers by becoming a "Private Subject" married to a "Forraign Princess," hires a coach, styles himself "Lord," and presses his suit with great impetuousness and extremely conspicuous consumption. Mary, believing (as she tells us) "that he was some landed, honorable and wealthy man," sustains her own skillful impersonation of rich nobility (51–52, 58, 63, 67). And in pursuing this course, she in effect simultaneously adopts the picaresque role (which comes quite naturally to John) of the male fortune hunter who attains upward mobility by acquiring the estate of a rich heiress.

But again the narrative model proves defective, for it is in the nature of such a plot that there be only one male upstart. Something has to give. Soon after the marriage, much high living, and Mr. Carleton's repeated attempts to induce Mary to transfer her property to his son, it becomes clear that her fortune, which has been expected from Germany for some time, is not going to arrive. What does arrive, however, is a letter that calls her "an absolute Cheat" (70–71). And now the limits of Mary's impersonation of male power become clear, for legal recourse lies with the Carletons. (Later on she claims that German women enjoy greater legal rights than the English, but she also says that "were it not for the modesty of my sex, the bonds of which I will not be provoked to transgress, I would get satisfaction" [126–28].) Charged with bigamy, Mary is conveyed to Newgate for arraignment. But despite the downward course her story has taken, the trial—whose proceedings she provides in documentary detail—vindicates "my Honour and Reputation," and she is acquitted. The story ends with Mary, although conscious of her husband's dishonorable treatment of her and of his disregard for his own honor, ready to receive him in good faith. But the signs are not good, and she now attributes to him a rather more doubtful, picaresque version of the romance mobility she had earlier sought for herself, for she suspects that he aims to enact "the second part of this *Gusman*-story, [to] knight-errant it abroad" so as to entrap another woman in marriage (73, 104, 106, 122, 131, 138).

Although (or perhaps because) it is replete with claims to historicity, there is good reason to doubt the truth of Mary Carleton's narrative self-representation. In several of the score of publications that document the Carleton affair, an unusually insistent connection is made between claims of truthfulness in narration and claims of status and virtue. John Carleton's several narrations of the events, although they do not differ as much from Mary's in factual respects as one might expect, still put an entirely different interpretation on the story. And in the estimate of her modern biographers, whatever John's deceptions, Mary invented the entire story of her origins, since she was indeed a commoner born in Canterbury as well as a multiple bigamist. But the question of factuality is of no concern to the present inquiry. Mary Carleton's autobiography is an extraordinary instance of progressive plotting most of all at the boundary between her real and her constructed lives. It shows her in the process of industriously making herself into a gentlewoman (if not a princess) using the forms and conventions of the genres she knows, but with an awareness that these conventions are not fully adequate to the radical reparations of status inconsistency she has in mind. Their inadequacy consists, finally, not in the archaism of aristocratic honor and romance errantry—even these might be imaginatively specified to present reality—but in the fact that they vouchsafe mobility and power not to her but to men. This is the specification that would be most difficult to achieve, and it may make sense to see her bigamy and her fortune-hunting as, like her literary models, alternative but insufficient means to her end.[33]

"Blindly wishing she were a man" early on, Mary ends her narrative by refuting a number of slanders, among them that "*I* was seen in mans apparel, with a Sword and Feather, in designe to do mischief to some body" (132). The progressive dilemma of how to obtain the worldly reward of virtue without noble status is overlaid, for Mary, by the analogous but far more insuperable problem of female empowerment in an overwhelmingly patrilineal and patriarchal culture. Her autobiographical self-defenses have a persuasive power of which her husband is incapable. Yet she is constrained to remind the "Ladies and Gentlewomen" of England to whom they are addressed that "our Ancestors" instituted orders of knighthood whereby to "defend Innocent Ladies," and she adds conciliatorily that "I do not mention these Stories, to reflect upon any of the English Gallants, for not Taking part in my Cause." Mary's impulse toward unconditional self-defense, toward some radical internalization of neochivalric force and freedom, is continually checked by the threat to her sense of self that such a course would entail. Thus her passionate desire to "get satisfaction" is blocked by "the modesty of my sex, the bonds of which I will not be provoked to transgress." And so the experimental transgression of boundaries—social, sexual, generic—becomes the self-conscious subject of a progressive story that itself aims to extend without transgressing the limits of feminine ambition. Eight years after her acquittal from the charge of bigamy, Mary was transported to Jamaica on charges of theft. But she returned in 1673, was again convicted of theft, and this time died on the gallows. Now her life assumed the reassuring form of the criminal biography, and the tracts that were published in 1673 appropriated and recapitulated her career according to the part-cautionary, part-satiric demands of conservative ideology. Like Davenant's Mr. Double, she became the very epitome of fraud and imposture.[34]

One of the more cautionary of Mary Carleton's biographers was Francis Kirkman, who in the year of her death also published his own extraordinary autobiography. Kirkman's work is framed by several prefaces and a postscript which, approaching ever closer to the very moment of writing, enact an ambivalent vacillation between two historically distinct modes of narrative explanation. On the one hand, Kirkman tells us, we are all on fortune's wheel. Even Dick Whittington rose through luck, not industrious virtue, and the enclosed autobiography is (as its title announces) a sad story of perpetual misfortune, its moral a passive resignation to the whims of mutability. On the other hand there is the muted recognition that Kirkman's troubles may have been caused not by bad luck but by bad character. Here the model is not romance mutability but the confessional mechanism of spiritual autobiography and the *Guzmán*-strain of picaresque narrative, for Kirkman believes recent improvements in his business affairs "to be the effects of my repentance in this Treatise." And if the complaint of unluckiness asserts the meaninglessness of social mobility, the confessional voice seems to propound, with great optimism, the progressive faith that commercial success is an immediate register of spiritual commitment. But then it all depends on us: only if we signify our approval of Kirkman's repentance by purchasing and profiting from this very book will he obtain the circular proof of his spiritual improvement. This strangely incestuous circle of implication recalls the bad faith of Protestant attempts to rationalize autonomous activity as only a special version of pious subordination to a higher power. Frustrated by the sense of an extreme inconsistency between his efforts and their results, between what he is and what he gets, Kirkman now seems either to be a most cynical Protestant casuist or to have foolishly gotten everything wrong, to have confused means and ends, literal and figurative, so that spiritual grace has been reduced to internal conviction, conviction to community accreditation, and accreditation to sales. And now the picaresque model seems to modulate dangerously from *Guzmán* to *Lazarillo:* from atonement as the absorption of sinful Character by retrospective and repentant Narrator, to atonement as the autodidactic act of self-creation.[35]

This framing vacillation between the abstract passivity of the romance model and the more specified and unstable activity of other modes is opened out, within the body of the work, into a narrative movement from one model to the other. Around the time of his apprenticeship, Francis tells us, he became utterly enchanted with chivalric romances, and "had so firm a belief of the truth of them, that I reckoned them to be Chronicles, and believed them before *Stow, Holingshed,* or *Speed*" (14). But despite this quixotic credulity, the romances are no more directly accessible to his activity than they are to Mary Carleton's. For his fantasies remain undigested daydreams of role models—the knight's squire, the chirurgeon—that he is too passive to attempt to internalize. The most promising of these, because it allows him the role of one who only waits, is that he, too, will be found to be of noble parentage (10–12). And at least as Francis tells it, there is a strong element of family romance in his early life. His father, although not well-born, has been successful; he is apparently a severe and niggardly man, and he apprentices Francis to a scrivener even though his son would prefer to learn the trade of bookselling. His mother's parents, on the other hand, had considerable wealth; Francis adores his mother and is desolated when she suddenly dies early in his apprenticeship. She is quickly replaced by an evil stepmother: Francis's father grows more wealthy and becomes a gentleman, "yet I was miserable and more a Slave than ever" (8–10, 12, 28, 32, 41–42, 49–50). The sense of being imprisoned in the wrong family is reinforced by Francis's ignominious treatment at the hands of his surrogate family, that of the master scrivener, and we overhear the earnest and poignant stories he tells himself about apprentices of better blood than their employers who marry serving maids just to escape their demeaning enslavement (37–41).

Instead of marrying a maid, Francis wanders off into the country, a half-hearted attempt at flight that is taken up with exchanging stories with his fellow travelers and that only ends in his sheepish return to London and to his father's reproach: "Son, whither in God's Name are you going, is not your Ramble done yet?" (140). Now Francis undergoes a thorough reformation of spirit. He absolves his father (and, in effect, his Fortune) of responsibility for his troubles, blaming them instead on "my disobedience and other crimes," which he openly and penitently confesses to us. "And this my disobedience to my Father, I judge to be the cause of those many Misfortunes that have since faln upon me" (152–53). The spell of the family romance has been broken. For his part, the elder Kirkman now prevails on his son's master to give up his claim to Francis, and he finds him another master who, they hope, will be more humanely disposed toward his apprentice (146–47, 150–51, 157). Because the new master is as indolent as the old one was penurious, there is little trade in the shop, and Francis is both obliged and empowered, for the first time, to exercise his industry as extracurricular self-employment (174–75). Indulging his early love of chivalric romance, he now undertakes the self-conscious "Adventure" of translating *Amadis of Gaul* into English with an anticipation that he conveys to us with suggestive insight: "Never did *young Big-belly'd Woman* desire to see the . . . Issue of her Body, as I did

to see my Book finished, and thereby to see my Name in Print; this was
the utmost bounds of my ambition" (175, 178–79). In a further disengagement from the passive and futile imitation of romance, Francis begins to turn romance to his own pragmatic ends, to live it by capitalizing
upon it. Unfortunately this first publication fails as a financial venture,
for "those sort of Romances that treated of old impossible *Knight Errantry*
were out of fashion." Francis's new-found skepticism is part of his new-
found pragmatism, and for his second translation he selects one of the
more modern French romances— *The Loves and Adventures of Clerio and
Lozia*—whose equally "strange impossible Adventures" he thinks will
be more marketable (180–81). With this project Francis learns to be truly
self-creative; for "the Name of the Translator being plac'd on the Title-
page in large Characters, there was also added the honoured Word *Gent.*
to import that the Translator was a Gentleman, that he was every Inch of
him in his own imagination, and did believe that the so printing that word
on the Title of the Book, did as much entitle him to Gentility, as if he had
Letters Patents for it from the *Heralds-Office:* Nay, did suppose this to be
more authentick because more publick" (181–82).

As a means of overcoming his habitual sense of personal displacement
and status inconsistency, Kirkman's second publication has several layers
of significance. Typography ingeniously accommodates the old and passive daydream of the discovery of noble parentage to the vocational
discipline of the young hero who undertakes to "imagine" his own
future, whatever the reality of his past. Princes, the founts of honor,
create knights; industrious apprentices internalize princely absolutism
and create themselves. This has been achieved by persevering in the
calling that Francis has cleaved to all along, and his self-elevation is "more
authentick" than those awarded by the Heralds Office in part because
what it publicizes is also the self-renunciatory and "public" repentance
that we saw in the immediately preceding episode. Having witnessed his
own depravity before the community of his readers, Francis is now, as in
the Puritan version of discovered parentage, renamed and reborn: to his
"Father" (who has enabled this change by finding Francis a "new master") and to himself. Thus self-denial facilitates self-authorship. Kirkman's old and beloved romances cease to be an impossible model of
imitation and become instead a practical means of financial self-improvement. Their place as his major literary model seems to be taken by the
more accessible genre of the picaresque (8, 111, 167–68), whose founding text, like *Don Quixote,* shares with *The Unlucky Citizen* a profound
interest in the self-creative powers of writing and printing.[36]

But the second translation does not make his fortune, and Francis, his
resolution flagging, endures a series of financial setbacks that culminate
in his decision, now symbolically resonant, to travel once more. But
before this can occur, his father not only encourages the project; he also

offers to stake his son to the career that he has always desired, that of a translator-bookseller. And Francis, trying to express to us his pleasure at this turn of events, produces a brief but violent flurry of narrative formulas for the hopeful affirmation of his own authenticity and empowerment. "In fine, I was never on the top of *Fortunes* Wheel till then," he exclaims. But he also plays with the romance role of the solitary hermit, and feels "as if I had been *Dub'd a Knight*." Even more, "I was free from all Commands," and in an apt parallel with Sancho Panza which finally balances autonomy and indebtedness, he observes: "I had the sole Rule and Command of my Shop and Books, and that I thought was equal to the Government of any *Enchanted Island*" (215, 218 [mispaginated 128], 219–20).

But the most effective and lasting formula is the one entailed in the posture of the self-creative author, narrator, and publisher. Travel and bookselling both received the elder Kirkman's easy approval because, despite appearances, one is an adaptive accommodation of the other: the earlier episode of storytelling was dominated by what seemed at the time its necessary occasion, the literal act of physical movement. Young Francis was then indeed like a knight-errant, and once entangled in the polysemous knot of "error," it was hard to dissociate storytelling (including the ongoing narrative itself) from the wandering into disobedience— what his father mildly called "your Ramble"—which those literal travels entailed. But just as Francis has learned to capitalize upon romance, so his travels have become figurative, have become the authorial power to create and control a narrative. Sitting in his London shop, the older Francis spins out plot after plot, challenges us to think "me to be a Rambler indeed," then triumphantly demonstrates that apparent digressions are really integral to the central theme (291). Narrative control, he tells us, is an ethical act, for it ensures that however much we wander, we will not err. At one point Francis remarks on the crucial importance of the dramatic plot, "and how it is managed, so that always *Vice is corrected, and Virtue cherished. How the Poet Creates and Destroys at his pleasure; and still keeps all within the bounds of Justice, giving punishment to Offenders, and reward to the Virtuous*." Ostensibly wandering off now to another topic, he tacitly obliges us to applaud the deeper consistency of apparent error, confirming by his formal activity the substantive claim that "I confine my self to no order in my Writing, but as I think convenient, so I manage my Story; but still keeping to the *Thread* of it" (261).

But does the author's creativity, like the Author's, "keep all within the bounds of justice"? This is of course the great question, for "travel" has now become the authorial power to create and control not only a narrative but also a career. Physical mobility has been transformed into the potential for upward mobility: sitting in his London shop, Francis seeks to "manage" his own career both by making it into a narrative and by ensuring that the result pleases us enough that we will buy this and future books and thereby help him make his fortune. So despite the grandiose fantasy of poetic creation and destruction, Francis is not quite autonomous, for he still must manage his readers. If he were truly godlike in his powers, he would mobilize his engines of social justice to reward his own undoubted virtue. But having only poetic justice in his arsenal, he is obliged to pause, transfixed, in the immobile present of his narrative frame, passively awaiting the judgment of his public as to whether his dream of success will be realized.

Kirkman's dilemma evokes in many ways the early modern crisis of secularization. The dogged internalization of authority and absolute power, the transformation of spiritual creature into aesthetic creator, the liberation of subjective desire and the acquisitive passions—all of these bold projects have their unforeseen consequences. Just as the divine creation of humankind and the princely creation of honors were understood to entail some reciprocal and obligatory service, so typographical publication is not a free gift, but participates in a system of commodity exchange in which the rewards of production and the release from paternalistic patronage are inseparable from an obligation to be consumed with some regularity. We can hear the small businessman's blend of bluff self-confidence and somewhat fretful eagerness to be of service in Kirkman's final account of himself as "a man set up for my self, sole Master of a shop" (292). It would not be wrong to see Kirkman's autobiography as a notable instance of progressive narrative. Certainly in its remarkable play with typography and the Protestant impulse to validate the saint through the accreditation of conscience and community, it is one of the most suggestive experiments in narrative reflexiveness between Kirkman's beloved Cervantes and Samuel Richardson. But herein lies also its ideological instability. For Kirkman shows us what happens when the progressive celebration of industrious virtue, and of the justice of its reward, focuses upon the act of self-creation as its fundamental expression. The spectacle of the individual subject indulgently validating his own virtue so threatens the objectivity of the judgment that the independent reality of that virtue—on whose objective solidity progressive ideology is totally dependent—is thrown into question, and progressive affirmation hovers on the edge of the conservative critique of imaginary value.

All narratives that come under the influence of picaresque and criminal biography are likely to exploit the analogy between physical and social mobility, although perhaps not with the insistence that Kirkman's autobiography does. But there is another form of narrative, the imaginary voyage, which takes the more general relationship between physical and social change as its enabling premise. For only under conditions of radical estrangement from the given, like those created by far-flung foreign travel, does it become possible to conceive a comprehensive and self-sufficient alternative—to discover, that is, or even more to establish, a utopian society. Following in the tradition of their most famous predecessor, Thomas More's *Utopia* (1516), the imaginary voyages of the late seventeenth and early eighteenth centuries often combine a recognizably progressive critique of contemporary social stratification with a nuance of conservative doubt concerning the practicality of attaining utopias through the exercise of industrious virtue. Of course this ideological tension is only more emphatic in the more-or-less admittedly "imaginary" voyages. Under the auspices of scientific empiricism, even the style of travel narratives has explicitly ideological import. Thomas Sprat requires of his "plain, diligent, and laborious observers" the private virtues of "sincere" and objective observation, virtues that are likely to be found among "Artizans, Countrymen, and Merchants," who bring their "eyes uncorrupted" to the recording of reality. By the same token, travel writers who doubted the epistemological claims of the naive empiricists were likely to doubt their progressive ideological implications as well. The transparent persona of the protoanthropological "recorder" is not, however, the only posture available to the narrators of voyages, whether or not imaginary. Travel narratives of this period also mediate problems of status inconsistency through a more active engagement between traveler-protagonist and utopian culture, so that the story and the process of travel itself—the phenomenon of going native, for example, which is a cross-cultural version of social assimilation—become important in the narrative investigation of questions of virtue.[37]

Pastoral and prelapsarian overtones in imaginary voyages emphasize the considerable degree to which their accounts of alien innocence exist to disclose the reciprocal corruptions of European culture. Both conservative and progressive critiques are able to exploit this mechanism, although it is not always easy to discern the ideological character of the resulting narrative. In the French imaginary voyages, the Edenic innocence of discovered utopias is manifested not only by their possession of the universal language, which somehow escaped the confusion of tongues at Babel, but also by social and sexual equality and by the absence of capital accumulation and commodity exchange. Ideological differences may be more pronounced in their English counterparts—the progressive fantasy of status hierarchy obliterated by the universal rule of industrious virtue, for example, and the conservative utopia of an aristocracy authorized by nature itself, with luxury and the lust for money nowhere to be found. But the generalization is vulnerable, as the ideological instability of Aphra Behn's *Oroonoko* (1688) makes abundantly clear.[38]

I have already shown how the ambivalence of Behn's pastoralism contributes to the epistemological instability of *Oroonoko*. Here questions of truth and virtue must intertwine, as Behn's language hints when it assures us that the "Truth" of this "History" "shall come simply into the World, recommended by its own proper Merits." Thus the "soft" primitivism of her approach permits us to see the natural innocence of the Surinam Indians as a reflection on European corruption, while her "hard" primitivism encourages us to read "innocence" as "credulity" and "corruption" as "civilization."[39] Behn's subtitle specifies Oroonoko's mutability to the status inconsistency of a "Royal Slave." As a conservative protagonist, he possesses a nobility of blood sufficiently exotic and alienated from the corrupted standards of contemporary European "honor" (he is not only a heathen but a black man) to seem an archaic remnant of the world before its fall into modern depravity, the vestige of a time when noble birth justly signified inner virtue (10–11, 34–35, 39, 61). Modern depravity is represented here by the invading force of colonialism, which opposes to the true aristocracy of an ancient warrior culture the irresistible corruptions of exchange value. *"Have they won us in Honourable Battle?"* Oroonoko asks his people. *"And are we by the Chance of War become their Slaves? This wou'd not anger a noble Heart; this would not animate a Soldier's Soul: no, but we are bought and sold like Apes or Monkeys . . . And shall we render Obedience to such a degenerate Race, who have no one human Vertue left, to distinguish them from the vilest Creatures?"* Knowing well enough "what he had to do when he dealt with Men of Honour," Oroonoko is nonplussed by the hypocrisy of these white Christians and vows "never to credit one Word they spoke" (61, 66).

So from one perspective, Behn's narrative helps explain the modern phenomena of status inconsistency and the displacement of the deserving, by situating them within the macropastoral context of colonial upstarts and imperialist exploitation. But the narrator's attitude is hardly anticolonialist: she is the proud daughter of the Lieutenant General of a considerable portion of the West Indies, and she bitterly regrets England's failure to exploit the gold of the Amazon (48, 59). As the type of the mobile adventuress, Behn brings to her story a strong dose of progressive faith in modern civilization. It is not just that Oroonoko's physical beauty owes more to Roman than to African nobility (8). His honor and virtue, she thinks, must be characteristics acquired through contact with European merchants, and she seems determined to associate her hero not with the troubling credulity of the Indians but with a scientific and freethinking skepticism that she clearly admires (6–7). In the realm of political activity this intellectual freedom translates easily into the familiar seventeenth-century type of the rebel against unjust authority, the rebel who will lead his followers into liberty or death (61–62). Thus Oroonoko is also able to represent the condition of the new man, who, passively transported from the Old World to the New, shows that he embodies the best principles of progressive ideology more successfully than most of his fellow moderns.

Within progressive utopianism there is a potential conflict between the righteous impulse to overcome status inconsistency by effacing all stratification whatsoever, and the recognition that the progressive ideals of industry and merit depend for their very meaning on the possibility of mobility and relative achievement within some existing system of social rank. These complications tend to be most evident in travel narratives whose protagonists are not simply discoverers of a static realm but actively participate in the establishment of utopia. In the brief travels of George Pine, the problem is wittily resolved almost before it has had time to be raised. When George first arrives at his fateful desert island near Terra Australis Incognita, he is a bookkeeper in the employ of a master merchant—careful, dispassionate, apparently a capable young man eager to make his way in the world. But only four women survive the shipwreck along with him, and George is instantaneously elevated to the head of a makeshift household, "being now all their stay in this lost condition." At first he industriously exercises his ingenuity in salvaging useful supplies from the wreck and beginning to fabricate a new civilization in a hostile environment. But after four months he realizes that hard labor may not be quite so imperative, for the island is a bountiful *locus amoenus*, "so that this place, had it the culture that skilful people might bestow on it, would prove a paradise." After two months more of nuts, fruits, fish, and fowl leaping into their laps, it becomes clear that there is really no need at all for "skillful people" either.[40]

Faced with the prospect of an unmitigated, prelapsarian leisure, George now confides to us that "idleness and a fulness of everything begot in me a desire for enjoying the women" (232). But what appears at first to be a leisure activity quickly proves to be an alternative form of industry. Deprived of the opportunity to manifest his merits through productive labor, the industrious bookkeeper resourcefully turns to reproductive labor, and the rest of the short narrative is filled with the careful quantification of his offspring, which increase by such geometric leaps and bounds that when he undertakes to "number them" in his old age he counts 1,789 contemporaneous "descendants" (234–35). George has indeed "bestowed culture" on his island in the most forthright manner imaginable. The social distinctions of the old world, shaken by his immediate elevation to the head of the family, soon crumble as he happily impregnates master's daughter, maids, and black slave without discrimination. These women become his fixed capital, essential to his productivity, and whatever energy he now devotes to more conventional modes of labor serves this oddly unlaborious discipline— "for having nothing else to do, I had made me several arbors to sleep in with my women in the

heat of the day, in these I and my women passed the time away" (233).
George improves his time by accumulating and accounting not money
but children. His industrious virtue is the cause not simply of social
elevation but of history and society itself, for on the ruins of the old
distinctions he creates a new genealogy. Self-created as its grand patriarch, at the proper moment George apprentices each of his sons in the
business, and at the end of his life he appoints the eldest to be "king and
governor of all the rest" after his own demise (234, 235). So by dissolving
social hierarchy and then re-creating it in his own image, George Pine is
able to have his cake and eat it: to rise to the very pinnacle of a finely
articulated social structure without suffering the guilt attendant on either
idleness or excessive ambition.

The voyages of Edward Coxere, although "real," in another way also
become "imaginary," and they provide a parallel but very different instance of progressive utopianism. Here the recognizable career of the
young man of industrious virtue, the familiar serviceability of physical
toward social mobility, is abruptly terminated by a spiritual conversion.
And afterwards the ideas both of society and of mobility are so thoroughly spiritualized that the ideological character of the narrative is radically thrown into question. Edward's autobiography opens when, at the
age of fourteen, he is sent for a year to live with a French family, a rite of
passage—"the first of my crossing the seas"—that leads him to toy with
the image of himself as a changeling.[41] On his return "care was taken to
put me to a trade" in Zeeland, but "I not settling my mind to a trade, my
lot fell to the sea." Apprenticed briefly to a merchant, Edward becomes
miserably seasick and soon "was gladly received by my mother
again . . . I was not long at home but the old tiresome tone was sounded
in my ears again: 'What trade now?' which grew unpleasant to me, for I
was to seek then as at the first. I could never settle my mind to any
particular trade, so that I was like one that was neither at sea nor ashore"
(4–5). From the first, then, "status inconsistency" is experienced as a
condition of comprehensive instability, and if travel thus falls to his lot as
a mediating stand-in for professional and social identity, it also serves to
figure and signify a more spiritual kind of unsettledness.

Edward ships on a haphazard variety of voyages, discovering in himself a picaresque adaptability to which his linguistic facility is essential: he
learns the special, self-effacing power of the "linguister," whose shadowy
role is suspended between the dominating presences he translates and
interprets to one another (8, 12, 20–21, 22, 34–35, 41, 43, 44, 47, 48, 58).
This effect is reinforced by an impulse toward physical camouflage.
Returning home after an early voyage, Edward looks so much like a
Dutchman that his own mother does not recognize him, so much has his
malleability fulfilled our first intimations of indeterminate parentage
(18–20). Once he marries, however, he becomes conscious of the need to

seek voyages that will provide not just adventure but opportunities for advancement and upward mobility (34, 42, 49, 75), and we are made aware of the steady increase in his salary and shipboard rank (72, 80, 83, 85). This resolve does not preserve him from the sort of mutabilities familiar both to the protagonists of Greek romance and to seventeenth-century merchant seamen, and he is plundered by the French, captured by the Spanish, and enslaved for several months by the Turks (28–29, 43, 54–57, 73–75). Yet after many trials Edward is finally able to stabilize his course and progress through the world. "Now was it a time of prosperity with me, and was gotten beforehand to what I had been, and lived very comfortable and pretty much in favour with such by whom I might a had farther preferment, had not the Lord happily prevented it, Who took me off from the friendship of the world" (85–86).

Edward's conversion to the Quakers is a subtle and comprehensive rebirth in character and behavior. Turning from friendship to Friendship, he loses his old, adaptive concern with the credit of his friends and the approval of his superiors, and undertakes to live instead by a strenuous principle of universal love, which paradoxically militates against an easy adaptability to one's surroundings: "I found a daily cross as to outward behaviours, customs, and manners" (88). His customary techniques of accommodation are now explicitly proscribed. His powers of linguistic mediation become suspect, for he will no longer enter into what seem to him careless and hypocritical shipboard prayer sessions, and his un-willingness to swear oaths rules out an essential stage in mercantile trans-actions (88, 108). So far from exploiting his abilities at adaptive camou-flage, Edward now insists on a Quaker principle—the refusal to doff one's hat—which is calculated not only to offend the powerful but to insult potential customers like "the complimenting Spaniards" (88, 93). And at a time when overseas trade was all but indistinguishable from privateering, the advertised refusal to fight one's fellow-man could only ensure unemployment (87, 88, 89, 90). Moreover, Edward begins now to scruple about fair dealing, with the result that he lacks the spirit to haggle his salary up to the level it had attained before his conversion (91, 98).

The compensation for these setbacks in his upward mobility are fully revealed to us only when Edward and seven other Friends, having refused to take the Oath of Allegiance on the eve of a voyage in which all are to be engaged, begin a term of imprisonment in Yarmouth that will endure for seven months. It proves to be "a sharp trial": they are given nothing but water, and Edward observes the bitter irony that even "when I was a slave under the hands of Turks, such as the Christians call Infidels . . . yet they gave me my bellyful of bread to eat with my water" (100, 101). No longer the conformable young man he used to be, Edward now discovers at home the savagery that once was to be found in exotic travel. Angered by the Quakers' tenacity of will, the bailiffs and jailer impose increasingly difficult conditions on their prisoners; but "the Lord made us able to withstand them in their greatest strength of rage and madness" (100). On earlier occasions Edward had described violent storms in terms of the "raging seas" he had endured (26, 38, 39). As we read now we slowly become aware that like Francis Kirkman, but in a genuinely and explicitly religious fashion, Edward is coming to terms with mobility— and with his ungovernable restlessness for travel and change—by spiritualizing it: "Our enemies seeing it, that in this long storm, in which they thought we would have grown fainthearted for want of provisions, they being, as appeared, weary in their raging tempest, their captain, the Devil, who at first set them to work with promises of a profitable voyage to make a prey on the innocent, but the storm proved so tiresome that they turned back again worse than when they began" (103).

If life itself is a voyage, beset by raging tempests that persecute the innocent, then what is required of the saint is not restless mobility, whether physical or social, but an inner serenity at the eye of the storm, the calm of the traveler whose faith in God's guidance cannot be challenged. Now "having fair weather," the eight prisoners are allowed to send for provisions and to be visited by members of the Yarmouth community of Friends. Like castaways imprisoned on a desert island, they cheerfully begin "to settle ourselves to rights, considering that if we ate upon the main, that little stock some of us had would be spent." The obvious solution is the utopian one of communal food supplies, and to this is added an egalitarian apportionment of the work involved in food preparation, so that each of them—"the merchant and master as well as the mate and seamen"—does all the chores over time, and all social distinctions are dissolved. Thus "settled in order to a long voyage, the next thing was for each man to consider how his proportion of money could be raised towards the stock." Edward and the others (including, he is careful to note, both "master and merchant") with great diligence and ingenuity learn how to spin worsted, and for the first time in his narrative Edward is content to refer to his livelihood as a "trade." The cloth is sold to shops in the town, but "I finding this trade to be of so little profit, my mind inclined to making of shoes," which proceeds so well that Edward is "overjoyed" and sets up as a "master shoemender, for which, by my account, I received for work forty shillings" (103–5).

So at the age of thirty-three, Edward, who "could never settle my mind to any particular trade," learns the spiritual settledness of a material calling that brings his restless mobility of mind to an end. And it is fitting that this particular Puritan should experience his tranquillity as a utopian community of like-minded "friends," bound together in a voyage of discovery—or an island settlement—whose detachment from the vicissitudes of human society, although an incarceration, is also the precondition for their entering into the society of God. Abjuring the Protestant ethic, Edward embraces his Calvinist calling in a spirit that is compatible less with the individualism of progressive ideology than with the communitarian faith of Gerrard Winstanley and the radical sectarians of the Interregnum. In the end Edward's narrative is progressive only in the way that the conviction of personal grace, unimproved by capitalist applications, overturns all the old and socially sanctified ways of designating human virtue and achievement. Admittedly, this is not the end of the story. The Quakers are finally released, and the remaining three pages of the autobiography very briefly recount Edward's further persecutions and imprisonments (one lasting for fifty-one weeks), passing silently over twenty years in which he presumably made a living in the coastal trade, where his religious scruples were not so great an impediment, and at the end of which he records the death of his wife (109). So the seaman remains a literal seaman, and the story ends inconclusively; but its heart lies in those seven months at Yarmouth, where Edward found his prison to be the world, and the world to be a haven from the storms of restless passion for those strong enough to impose the solidity of their own peace upon it.[42]

5
THE GENDERING OF IDEOLOGY

In earlier sections of this study I suggested that romance replaces the stabilizing segregation of nature and culture in mythic narrative with an extended chain of natural-cultural signifiers for transformation.[43] Moreover, in late-medieval English romance there is an increasing preoccupation with the specifically social signifiers of transformation, with the specification of mutability to the realm of the social. This need not entail an abandonment of the amatory signifiers of change, I argued, since love plots always concern, even if only in its ostentatious absence (as in the adulterous love of *fin amor*), the socially significant event of marriage. The major interest of these late-medieval narratives seems to reside at first with the conflict between the social arrogance of aristocrats and the upward mobility of male commoners, whose rise is symbolically if illogically detoxified by the virtuous constancy of the gentlewomen they marry. But over time the profound alliance between the virtuous industry of commoners and the virtuous chastity of women is remarked and exploited by a developing progressive ideology, and interest shifts to the conflict between aristocratic seducers and constant women. Often these women will also be commoners; but since it is the general fate of gentle daughters to suffer the social injustice that is reserved, among gentle sons, for the younger, it is also sufficient liability that they be simply women. And soon virtue in the guise of female chastity becomes powerfully normative in progressive narrative, emblematic of the honor that has been alienated from, and is yet pursued by, a corrupt male aristocracy. As with Protestant thought, then, progressive ideology learns to adapt to its own uses the emotional animus against patriarchal power that has been nourished in other realms of experience, exploiting limited alliances with interests that ultimately diverge from its own. But conservative narrative, too, soon learns to deploy its own version of the struggle between female common virtue and aristocratic male corruption, to regender ideology so that it subverts rather than supports the progressive argument.

A skeletal example of the gendering of progressive ideology can be found in the second of the tales that compose Robert Greene's *Penelopes Web* (1587). Calamus, "a noble man . . . of parentage honorable, as allied to the blood Royall," is possessed by the ruling passion of lust: "his poore tennants groned not under the burden of his couetous desires, but were taxed with the greefe of his voluptuous appetite." But although "the sparkes of lust" are kindled in his heart by the sight of a "countrie huswife" named Cratyna, she resists his efforts to corrupt her and resolves "rather to taste of any miserie, then for lucre to make shipwracke of her chastitie." Finding bribes ineffective, Calamus does not hesitate to use his power in other ways—Cratyna and her rustic husband are his tenants at will—but eviction, abduction, and attempted murder all fail to win the desired result. In the end Cratyna's constancy is so unshakeable that Calamus is reformed by her example. Ashamed of "offering vyolence to so vertuous and chast a mynd," the nobleman instead endows "her with such sufficient lands and possessions, as might very wel maintayne her in the state of a Gentlewoman." Greene's treatment of the problem of mutability in this tale is by no means typical of his procedure. In *Greene's Carde of Fancie* (1584), for example, male rather than female mobility is the central focus; the "change" itself is not actual, but stems from the discovery of elevated parentage; the constancy of the noblewoman ensures the persistence of love until the man's rank can be discovered; but this does not solve the problem, for social mobility is only one of several functions by which mutability is enacted and overcome. In the tale from *Penelopes Web*, however, the problem of mutability has been specified exclusively to the problem of status inconsistency. Chaste love is identified with the true nobility of the rustic housewife, whose constancy to virtue is rewarded by being reconciled with a corresponding wealth and status. Bad love, the inconstancy of lust, is an attribute of the nobleman, "that dishonourable *Calamus,*" whose attempt to corrupt Cratyna's virtue expresses the corruption of aristocratic honor, its incapacity to signify virtue. Only when Calamus is reformed by Cratyna's example is the inconsistency between the aristocrat's outer and inner states, between his status and his virtue, overcome.[44]

It is noteworthy that in this progressive plot chaste love is not the most actively industrious of virtues, for its "work" is to reform the dishonorable nobleman by its example, and thereby to elicit its reward. Yet Cratyna is an extremely vigorous protagonist, despite the necessity of waiting to be raised by another, and in fact the distinctively dynamic quality of the progressive heroine is recognizable even in plots where two seeming requisites—the reformation and the reward—are absent. This can be seen in a manuscript account of a married nobleman's attempt to seduce his sister that was written by Edmund Spenser's friend Gabriel Harvey. The elder Harvey was a successful rope-maker prosperous enough to send his sons to university. Only the daughter, Mercy, has remained at home, but she is more than literate, and the combination in her of a studied pastoral humility and a spirited refinement is important to the quality of pert facility that she shares with a host of later heroines who are greatly overqualified (like overeducated younger sons) for their modest employments. The young nobleman, who remains anonymous, first approaches Mercy through a go-between, who intercepts her one day after milking to say that his master "set more by her than he did by his own ladie." She protests "that she was but a milkmaide, and a plaine cuntrie wench," and proceeds to resist all attempts to corrupt her, provoking the go-between to remark that "you make more straung than most gentlewomen would do of five hundred pounds a yeare." As the suit settles into an epistolary mode Mercy's control is increasingly sure. She reminds the nobleman that what he seeks is "a great dishonor to your lordship. I have hard mie father saie, Virginitie is ye fairist flower in a maides gardin, and chastitie ye ritchist dowrie a pore wench can have." Her figures invite us to contrast her pastoral virtue with his corrupting desire, to measure his shameful prostitution of honor against her own persistence in chastity. And when he sends her a gold ring along with "sugrid words and honysweet offers," the posture of the rude country wench gives her the freedom to taunt his elaborate courtliness as thinly veiled whoring: "Good lord, that you shuld thus seeke after so base and cuntrie stuff abrode, that have so costly and courtlie wares at home." However, Mercy's mastery of the relationship cannot be so secure when it spills over from letters into encounters, and we fear for her when they rendezvous at a neighbor's house and the lord appears in dishabille, kisses her several times, and proceeds to draw her toward the bed. But Mercy has prepared for this eventuality: the neighbor knocks at the door, pretending that Mercy's mother is seeking her, and the young lord, beside himself with rage and frustration, falls to swearing. The whole affair is brought to an abrupt conclusion shortly thereafter when one of the lord's letters is misdirected to brother Gabriel. So the courtship ends having established the fact of status inconsistency by disclosing the depravity of aristocratic honor and the enterprising nobility of chaste virtue, but without having remedied it by the nobleman's moral or Mercy's material elevation.[45]

Despite early examples like these, it was not until the eighteenth century that narrative experiments in the social specification of the love plot began to vie with the sophisticated developments of Restoration drama.[46] And it is therefore not surprising that during that period it was a dramatist, Aphra Behn, who most insistently and inventively raised the problem of mutability within love narratives that are concretely specified to problems of status inconsistency. Behn's progressive heroines are not usually commoners. In one story, the protagonist's father is the discredited type of the fallen aristocrat, "a Man of great Birth, but no Fortune," whose ridiculous vanity is compounded by his tyrannical (and unsuccessful) efforts to force his daughter to marry his best friend, a decayed count who replicates his own status inconsistency. In progressive ideology, the threat of forced marriage to an aristocrat and the threat of aristocratic rape are closely related, violent expressions of corruption; and familial tyranny can be the work not only of parents but also of older brothers. Another Behn story opens with Sir William Wilding succeeding to his father's large estate, inheriting everything "except his Virtues. 'Tis true, he was oblig'd to pay his only Sister a Portion of 6000 l.," but Philadelphia—who, like a younger son, clearly is the true heir of the father's virtue—is denied her material inheritance. Instead, Sir William assumes the role of an aristocratic rake and tries to corrupt his sister's virtue by lodging her in a "naughty-house" run by a "rank Procuress." There she meets and falls in love with Gracelove, who is the antithesis of her brother, a man of honorable character and, being a merchant, common blood. Behn's plot is spiced with romance adventure: in pursuit of business Gracelove becomes a Barbary prisoner; Sir William sinks into dissolution and domestic imprisonment; while Philadelphia, married and quickly widowed, becomes a wealthy and independent woman. And when Gracelove escapes, Philadelphia finds herself in a position to manifest her incorruptible constancy, forgiving and reclaiming Sir William and taking the long-lost Gracelove for her husband. Thus Behn provides two characters to represent the progressive alternative to aristocratic corruption. Industrious virtue is embodied in the honorable merchant, but it also assumes a feminine form in the chaste and successful younger sister, who wins both love and social justice for herself and redeems her noble and filial oppressor.[47]

From these two examples alone it is clear that Behn's ambition is to explore the full potential of progressive narrative rather than to reproduce a single paradigm of it. Another of her stories goes so far as to cast the aristocratic oppressor as a woman. Miranda is heir to "a vast Estate," an older daughter who tries by every means possible to cheat her younger sister out of the rest of the inheritance. She is also "extreamly Inconstant" in her love of men, a vice that is socially specified as a disdain for true nobility and a pathological fixation on aristocratic status as the trigger of sexual desire. Sensing a "Man of Quality" under the habit of a handsome priest she sees in church one day, Miranda is inflamed by his story (he is in fact a prince, a younger son oppressed by familial tyranny) and attempts to entice him through increasingly forward advances. Truly a corrupt aristocrat, at length she tries to take him by force; and when this fails she turns the tables and accuses the priest of attempting to rape her.[48]

But at this point Miranda's attention is suddenly absorbed by a newcomer, Prince Tarquin, whose wealth and physical presence are confirmed by a lineage so exalted—he claims to be of the race of the last kings of Roman antiquity—that Miranda is overcome with desire. And with this match, the ideological function of Behn's inversion of gender becomes clear. In progressive narrative, the aristocrat's sexual desire represents at bottom the longing for his own alienated honor, and when the object of desire is a male and ostentatiously entitled aristocrat, this lust for lineage becomes unmistakable: thus Miranda was "not now so passionately in love with *Tarquin,* as she was with the Prince; not so fond of the Man, as his Titles and of Glory." The reformation of the corrupt aristocrat requires the acknowledgment that honor consists not in lineal rank but in chaste virtue. Miranda's reformation grows out of the discovery, triumphantly announced by the ruling men of quality, that Tarquin has "set up a false Title, only to take place of them; who indeed, was but a Merchant's Son of *Holland.*" This parodic romance discovery of ignoble parentage ironically establishes a consistency of status, confirming Tarquin's true nobility by cleansing him of genealogical nobility. Forced to confront the persistence of her love in the absence of his title, Miranda, chastened and newly chaste, reforms her own heart; and Tarquin retires to his wealthy merchant father's "Country-House; where, with his Princess, he lives as a Private Gentleman."[49]

My final example of Behn's experimentation with the progressive love plot is important because it incorporates, within its critique of aristocratic ideology, a self-conscious defense against the anticipated countercritique of conservative ideology. That this is Behn's strategy is clear from the very first line of the story: "This *Money,* certainly, is a most Devilish thing!" Fighting on two fronts now, the progressive narrator undertakes not only to attack the imaginary value of honor but also to repel the subversive charge of an alliance with the equally imaginary value of money. Behn's strategy is a bold one, for she frankly situates all of her characters within modern, monied, and somewhat cynical culture, but reserves one as her scapegoat progressive, an assimilationist so vulgarly and slavishly devoted to the joint corruptions of title and cash that he makes the others look almost dignified. The scapegoat is Mr. Wou'd be

King. Of vast wealth and pretension, he "had often been told, when he was yet a Stripling, either by one of his *Nurses,* or by his own *Grand-mother,* or by some other *Gypsie,* that he shou'd infallibly be what his Sirname imply'd, a *King,* by *Providence* or *Chance.*" Despite a readiness to spend inexhaustible sums of money, he gets no closer to fulfilling this ambition than to be made King of Twelfth-night by the distribution of lots in the Christmas cake they all share. But King's wealth does facilitate another act of upward mobility. Valentine Goodland, heir to £15,000 a year, would marry the beautiful Philibella, but his father has forbidden it owing to the fact that her portion is only about £500. The problem of inconsistency, in other words, is entirely within the realm of wealth and even then relatively minor; and it is overcome when Philibella's uncle, himself an impoverished younger son who has married upward, con-cocts a scheme to dupe Mr. King into settling £2000 on his niece. But lest we too credulously take fortune as a worthy replacement for Fortune, Behn subjects King to unrelenting ridicule throughout court and city. Word of his Twelfth-night elevation gets out, and in the several epithets applied to him—the fop king, the fantastic monarch, the king in fancy— are conveyed the indistinguishable delusions of aristocratic and monied culture.[50]

Mary Davys, one of Behn's successors, throws into relief the vile lasciviousness of the corrupt aristocrat in one of her own progressive stories by having him reflect at one point that "as an industrious trades-man takes daily care to provide for his family, so will I for my delights." But the conservative mentality perceived that progressive heroes in-dulged their own preferred "delights." As Mary Astell remarked of the male motive in marriage, "There's no great Odds between his marrying for the Love of Money, or for the Love of Beauty; the Man does not act according to Reason in either Case, but is govern'd by irregular Appe-tites." If Behn's scapegoat strategy in the *Memoirs* is inspired, it is also risky, since it broaches the very corruption of progressive value—the reduction of personal merit to financial fortune—that it defends against; and the resulting narrative balances on the edge of an ideological reversal. One of Eliza Haywood's love narratives provides a subtle example of how such a reduction might be more deliberately accomplished.[51]

Philidore embodies the status inconsistency of declining gentility. Although "descended from a very ancient and noble family," he has inherited no wealth; yet he might easily have raised his fortune had he not "labored under the pangs of an unhappy passion which was . . . infinite-ly more grievous to him than all he had to fear from a narrow fortune." This is apparently his hopeless love for Placentia, hopeless because she is "so very much superior in point of fortune" to himself. But Philidore's "unhappy passion" turns out to be more concretely specified than this would suggest, for Haywood's protagonist, ostensibly the traditional romance idealist obsessed with unfulfillable erotic desire, is stealthily indicted as a progressive idealist obsessed with the imaginary powers of money. Placentia for her part quickly falls in love with him. But Philidore, protesting his own "demerits"—which he glosses revealingly as an absence of "fortune"—prohibits the match, fleeing to Persia and generating thereby a maze of romance mutability (shipwreck, pirates, robbers, attempted rape, seraglio intrigues, sale into slavery) which only draws attention to his own very mundane culpability for love's frustration. As luck would have it, Philidore finally inherits a vast estate just when Placentia's has been vastly diminished; and he is astonished now to hear her sadly refuse his ecstatic pledge of marriage because of their disparity in fortunes. "Can wealth be any purchase for perfection such as yours?" he demands. " 'Tis by my love alone that I can hope to merit the glory of being yours." But with these words Philidore refutes his own habitual folly in having accorded money a greater power than merit or status or love. All would be well, says Placentia, "were they on an equality," tacitly chiding her lover for having behaved as though inequality, the problem of status inconsistency, were so critical that all must bow to it. But she is also admonishing him for the vain delusion that the problem may be reduced to a quantitative inequity of fortunes, and solved by an easy, merely monetary equalization. Philidore's love, like his merit, has been subsumed within the material standard of his fortune. It is this fundamental reduction that Placentia protests, because in the guise of an idealistic delicacy of passion it amounts to a morality of the marketplace, where everything can be equalized if the requisite money can be had. Haywood ends her narrative with Placentia persuaded to accept her rich brother's gift of "a fortune on the level with Philidore," and with "these equally enamoured, equally deserving pair" finally agreed on the propriety of marriage. But her plot stands as a gentle critique less of romance idealism than of the new idealism of progressive ideology, which says personal merit when it means cash, and replaces the old idol of status with the new reification of money.[52]

The two destructive passions of love and money are closely associated in Haywood's mind. To appreciate this we need go no further than the opening of another of her narratives, which expediently combines the conventions of the allegorical secret history with those of the imaginary voyage. After much travel, a noble youth arrives at an island famed for its cultural accomplishments, only to find Cupid, like Venus in Apuleius, complaining that his sacred rites go neglected:

My Temples are defaced!—my Altars broke!—and, in my stead, the mistaken Wretches, with sacrilegious Worship, idolize a *Fiend!*—'Tis true, the Demon has usurped my Name! . . . They still revere and call on *Cupid,*— *Cupid* they still adore—but not a *Cupid* accompany'd with Innocence, Virtue, Constancy; but a *Cupid,* ushered in by wild Desires, Impatiencies, Perplexities, and whose ghastly Train are filled with Shame, Disgrace, Remorse, and late Repentance and Despair! Yet this is the Deity to whom they sacrifice—this is the God they invoke, and with *Pecunia* drives from their perverted Souls all Sentiments of Honour, Virtue, Truth, or Gratitude—A blind Gratification of unlicens'd Wishes is all they aim at,—they endeavour not to *merit,* but *obtain* . . . A universal Infatuation seems to have seized the Minds of the Inhabitants of yonder proud *Metropolis.*

We can have little doubt as to the identity of this metropolis, for the evils it worships are those which conservative ideologists of the turn of the century attributed to the English monied interest, whose capital was the City of London. Lust—the carnal degradation of love—and the lust for money have become interchangeable signifiers of corruption. The passions of the flesh and the passions of profit-motive are joint symptoms of the depravity of modern times, which consists in the limitless indulgence of human appetite. While progressive writers were content to commend monetary self-interest as a relatively benign passion useful in countervailing the more malevolent ones, Haywood's response was to show the vanity of that distinction, and her insight into the analogous pathologies of exchange value and sexual libertinage was considerable. Cupid describes the behavior of the devotees of Lust and *Pecunia* in the following terms:

Thus do they spend their days in an eternal Round of Hurry and Confusion— *Pursuit,* which to a Soul truly inspired by me, is full of Fears, Perplexities, and Care, is with them the only Pleasure; and *Enjoyment,* the beginning of a perfect Lover's Happiness, puts an end to the Felicity of these imaginary ones. This is a Humour so near universal, that the few who are of a contrary one, are laugh'd at as Affecters of a Romantick Singularity, and rarely meet with any other return than scorn from the objects of their Constancy.

Here love is sheer inconstancy, like commodity exchange an endless circuit in which the movement toward completion and consumption, a perpetual imagining of an end which must never come, becomes an end in itself. Inconstant love is a figure for the mutability of exchange value, the great motor of social injustice and status inconsistency in the modern age, and for Haywood as for Swift and Bolingbroke, the only alternative to it seemed best conveyed through the self-consciously quaint idealism of "a romantic singularity."[53]

Haywood's Philidore is an essentially agreeable man whose modern vices emerge and are corrected over time. More typically, the protagonists of conservative love narrative are predictable transformations of the progressive hero and heroine: the lascivious aristocrat is replaced by the upstart robe noble, whose lust is the lust for money; and the chaste innocent is replaced by the lubricious and duplicitous little schemer.

(Mary) Delarivière Manley provides examples of both types. What is more perverse and unnatural about Lady Zarah is that her feminine devotion to love does not in the least exclude other sorts of desire. "No Passion, but that of extraordinary Love can fix a Woman's Heart," Manley announces at the outset. "Ambition alone is too weak a Gage for their Fidelity." But Zarah's heart is "fill'd with Love and Ambition; for though she was resolved to gain the Last, she was one who left no Stone unturn'd to secure to her self the First." In Manley's version, the arriviste Marlborough, a self-made man and therefore intimately acquainted with all the corrupting uses of money, is ruled by one lust alone, the acquisitive passion for wealth. Even the Earl of Portland, whose ascent from page to duke is guided throughout by "the wise Maxims of *Machiavel*," also "corrupts" and rapes his young ward according to Machiavellian precept and is prompted in all things by "*Ambition, Desire of Gain, Dissimulation,* [and] *Cunning*." In fact, it might be fair to say that in conservative love plots the most powerful force for mutability and disorder is not bad love but avarice. The inconstancy of love is superseded by the inconstancy of money, a passion so obsessional and destructive that the new aristocrats of conservative ideology are not even capable of reformation. A younger son bred to no useful occupation, Manley's Don Antonio is animated by "*Self-Love*" and "*Self-Interest . . .* yet are his Pleasures always subservient to his *Interest,* and the Delight he takes in *Money;* even *Love,* tho' his Temper is Amorous, can't make him liberal." In the brief compass of an interpolated tale, he succeeds in committing almost every conceivable outrage against the virtuous Elenora, who, despite "this one Inclination, the Love of Money, being alone *conspicuous* in him," is at first charmed by his attentions. The story ends abruptly when Elenora is fortuitously rescued from a count whose imminent rape of her has been arranged by Antonio in exchange for the defrayment of a large debt, and who gallantly assures her that "I will think whatever you will please to have me of that fantastick *Honour* of yours."[54]

I will conclude this discussion of the conservative experimentation with love narratives with an important strain, in which the parodic mode is more sustained and thorough than in the preceding examples. Here the concern is less to unmask the avaricious modern lover of money than to mount a comprehensive critique of that general condition of credulity which is vulnerable first to aristocratic, but also to progressive, fictions of love. This strain's utter self-consciousness makes the distinction between epistemological and social critique more than usually tenuous, and its sensitivity to the pitfalls of belief does not in the least preclude the attempt to rescue some guarded form of faith from the carnage of extreme skepticism. The central example of this strain of conservative love narrative is William Congreve's *Incognita; or, Love and Duty Reconcil'd . . .* (1692).[55] Congreve's fatuous if loveable young noblemen believe everything they have ever heard about the idealism of romantic love. But they are also in revolt against tradition, for Congreve's intricate plot hangs upon the fact that Aurelian is to be a pawn in a patriarchal, arranged marriage aimed at patching up an "ancient quarrel" between two houses, and the young Florentine spends most of the plot convinced that the forced marriage cruelly violates his native liberty and requires an act of filial "disobedience" (257, 269, 272, 273–74, 301). As he exclaims in his most extended outburst: "Cruel father, will nothing else suffice! Am I to be the sacrifice to expiate your offences past; past ere I was born? . . . But oh my soul is free, you have no title to my immortal being, that has existence independent of your power; and must I lose my love, the extract of that being . . . ? No, I'll own my flame, and plead my title too" (282). The progressive resonance of this struggle between the freedom of love and the archaic constraints of tradition is reinforced when Congreve at one point compares Italian family feuds to English primogeniture, since according to harsh Italian law, revenge must "descend lineally like an *English* estate, to all the heirs males of [a] family" (261).

Moreover, Aurelian is not the only one of the young aristocratic principals to be ostentatiously oppressed by familial demands. Since infancy, the life of Juliana (the Incognita of the title) has been clouded by the future specter of forced marriage, resistance to which will entail at the least "perpetually enduring to be baited by my father, brother and other relations" (290). And Congreve deepens our apprehensions of this impending act of aristocratic violence by juxtaposing Juliana's account of it with her thanks to Aurelian for having "saved my life and my honour" from the threat of a rape (291). Even Hippolito and Leonora adopt the posture of progressive rebels, since their fears for the safety of their own love persuade them to undertake a secret marriage that incurs the "most violent passion" of Leonora's father at her "unprosperous choice" (299). So the problem of mutability is securely specified to the battle between amatory constancy and the corruptions of aristocratic arrangement. The inconsistency of personal virtue and familial status—of love and duty— appears comprehensive. But, of course, within Congreve's parodic context these apparent instances of earnest personal merit acquire a very different ideological flavor. This is not simply because the principals are so silly; it is also because their stature as progressive protagonists is ultimately undercut by the same authorial power that subverts their claim to romance heroism. Congreve's epistemological play, which combines a critique of romance truth with a countercritique of the claim to historicity, inevitably invades also the substance of his plot to render all a contrivance. With the final discovery of true parentage, the problem of mutability is indeed "miraculously" suspended, but not in a manner that can satisfy the requirements of romance. For Congreve specifies Authorial to authorial intervention with such ostentatious clumsiness as to destroy any lingering sense we may have that this particular problem exists anywhere but on paper; only the bumbling and manipulated ignorance of the protagonists—and ourselves—has created the illusion of a problem. By the same token, the "personal merit" of the protagonists in resisting aristocratic tyranny evaporates in this effulgence of ignorance, along with the illusion that there ever was a problem of status inconsistency for the constant lovers to overcome.

In short, both the romance problem of mutability and its progressive specification are subjected to ridicule. But Congreve's ridicule is sufficiently indulgent to leave us with the impression that, as with questions of truth, a serious question of virtue has quietly been raised and answered. In a sense we have been offered something like an apology for "forced marriages." As a means of maintaining family unity, arranged marriages replace a code of honor whose method of enforcement is the revenge feud, a practice the bloody consequences of which are kept before our eyes throughout much of Congreve's narrative. *Incognita* does not give us "love and duty reconciled," because here, at least, they are never at variance. But it does "solve" a real problem: it does "compleat the happy reconciliation of two noble families" (273) in a way that is not only a decided improvement over perpetual revenge but that also coincides with personal preference. But what of the modern alternative, the ultimate institutional corollary of the progressive outrage at family tyranny which Congreve so enjoys sending up? Perhaps the conservative ideology of his love plot consists in the advocacy of an increasingly antiquated method of maintaining family unity—the personal authority of the father—against not only the ancient blood feud but also the modern solution, the device of the strict settlement, which conceived of the family as a network of competing interest groups or parcels of property, adjudicated and engineered by the equally impersonal machinery of the legal system.[56]

6

THE CONFLATION OF TRUTH AND VIRTUE

It has been an ongoing assumption of this work that to study the origins of the English novel one must also study the origins of its consciousness as a distinct category. The key to this historical process is the gradual formulation of questions of truth and questions of virtue. I have pursued these questions apart from each other in the preceding chapters for good reason: not only for the sake of organizational and argumentative coherence, but also because they are pursued and propounded by contemporaries as distinct questions. Yet in many instances, especially in the present chapter, questions of truth and questions of virtue have been raised simultaneously by writers of the most diverse aims and formal commitments. At such times we may sense that writers wish to "make something" of the analogous relation between the questions, if only through their tacit juxtaposition. And occasionally the analogy is even asserted explicitly. In this way, questions of truth and virtue begin to seem not so much distinct problems as versions or transformations of each other, distinct ways of formulating and propounding a fundamental problem of what might be called epistemological, social, and ethical signification. And the essential unity of this problem is clear from the fact that progressive and conservative positions on questions of virtue have their obvious corollary positions with respect to questions of truth, even if seventeenth-century writers only sporadically affirm that correlation with real explicitness. The implication is that in the context of early modern narrative, epistemological choices have ideological significance, and a given explanation of the meaning of social mobility is likely to imply a certain epistemological procedure and commitment. Indeed, as we watch writers make these sporadic correlations with increasing confidence, we come to realize what the explicit act of correlation does not so much beget as raise to consciousness—that within this discursive context, questions of truth and their several enactments are inherently ideological. Moreover, we may conceive of these correlations of truth and virtue also in terms of narrative "form" and "content," so that the way the story is told and what it is that is told are implicitly understood to bear an integral relation to each other as separable parts of a greater, dialectical whole. In this respect my argument concurs with the thesis, common to the great novel theorists although diversely articulated by them, that the distinctive feature of novelistic narrative is its internalization or thematization of formal problems on the level of content.[57]

But the conflation of questions of truth and questions of virtue in early modern narrative did not occur easily or quickly. It resulted from much thought and experimentation—some of which we have seen in preceding chapters—expended over time on each set of questions. The conflation begins to occur when writers begin to act—first gingerly, then systematically—upon the insight that the difficulties of one set of questions may be illuminated by the reflection of the other. This insight is the founding premise of the novel genre, whose work it is to engage intellectual and social crisis through a simultaneous and comprehensive mediation. The novel emerges into consciousness when the conflation comes to be made with such mastery that the conflict between naive empiricism and extreme skepticism, between progressive and conservative ideologies, can be embodied in a public controversy between writers who are understood to employ antithetical methods of writing what is nonetheless recognized as the same species of narrative. This occurs in the controversy between Richardson and Fielding—and their respective proponents—

during the early 1740s. But it should be clear enough by now that within the present account of the origins of the English novel—as a long-term historical process that consists both in the experimental conflation of epistemological and social concerns and in the experimental opposition of narrative strategies—there is little sense in seeking the identity of "the first novelist." In the following chapters I will discuss not only the early works of Richardson and Fielding, but also four narratives that predate this confrontation and that exemplify in different ways the systematic and authoritative conflation of truth and virtue. I will juxtapose my readings of *Don Quixote* (1605, 1615) and *The Pilgrim's Progress* (1678, 1684) not because of any crucial intertextual link that subsists between them, but because they are complementary instances of the dialectical transformation—the recapitulation and the negation—of romance. The conjunction of *Robinson Crusoe* (1719) and *Gulliver's Travels* (1726), on the other hand, provides a tacit but fully realized premonition of the dialectical encounter that will become public and institutional two decades later. I have chosen these works for extended discussion because they exemplify most efficiently and profoundly the arguments that are central to my study. But although I have set these readings apart from those made in previous pages, it is not my ambition to provide "comprehensive" interpretations of the narratives they concern, or to treat them as a self-sufficient justification for this study. Instead I have aimed simply to accentuate those features of great works—which are themselves traditionally accorded a central role in the origins of the novel—that confirm the utility of the argument and the evidence that have gone before.

Questions of truth and questions of virtue share a single concern with problems of cultural signification, and the various narrative responses to them follow the fundamental, dialectical pattern of reversal. The pattern is present, first of all, in the dynamic and ongoing progression of secularization and reform. Within these perpetual movements, moreover, two recurrent patterns of "double reversal" can be discerned. Naive empiricism negates the idealist epistemology of romance, and is in turn negated by a more extreme skepticism and a more circumspect approach to truth. Progressive ideology subverts aristocratic ideology, and is in turn subverted by conservative ideology. It is in these double reversals, and in their conflation, that the novel is constituted as a dialectical unity of opposed parts, an achievement that is tacitly acknowledged by the gradual stabilization of "the novel" as a terminological and conceptual category in eighteenth-century usage. But I have also been concerned with a pattern of historical reversal that is of broader dimension than this movement, and from whose more elevated perspective the conflicts that are defined by these double reversals may even appear to dissolve into unity. As we have seen over and over again, the origins of the English novel entail the positing of a "new" generic category as a dialectical negation of a "traditional" dominance—the romance, the aristocracy—whose character still saturates, as an antithetical but formative force, the texture of the category by which it is being both constituted and replaced. The very capacity of seventeenth-century narrative to model itself so self-consciously on established categories bespeaks a detachment sufficient to imagine them *as* categories, to parody and thence to supersede them. And with hindsight we may see that the early development of the novel is our great example of the way the birth of genres results from a momentary negation of the present so intense that it attains the positive status of a new tradition. But at the "first instant" of this broader dialectical reversal, the novel has a definitional volatility, a tendency to dissolve into its antithesis, which encapsulates the dialectical nature of historical process itself at a critical moment in the emergence of the modern world.

To delineate the several dimensions of dialectical reversal that are involved in the origins of the novel is only to give to the general notion of literary "revolution" a certain particularity. When we schematically describe intellectual or social conflict as an opposition between two contending forces, we rightly adopt a schematism that was constructed by seventeenth-century contemporaries to reduce the existent field of indefinite possibility to manageable proportions. One central function of categories like romance and novel, aristocracy and middle class, sword and robe, Whig and Tory, landed and monied interest, is to make conflict—and its mediation—accessible by simplifying and institutionalizing its terms. Indeed, by the end of the eighteenth century, "the novel" and "the middle class" have an institutional and monolithic integrity that would seem to belie even the modest partiality expressed by our epistemological and social conflicts, let alone the broad range of lived diversity which those conflicts make intelligible. The application of reference-group theory to the study of revolution has helped us understand these mysterious currents of historical process because it discloses the multitude of relative perceptions that contribute to an apparently highly singular end like political revolt. Moreover, the tendency of this argument is to enlarge our view of "revolution" itself as a unitary cultural condition or potential that may find expression in a diversity of concurrent or alternative activities—political, social, and intellectual.[58] Early modern English people knew the dialectical truths of reference-group theory. They also ascribed sufficient power and value to literature to regard it as political or social change "by other means." This is nowhere more obvious than in the commonplace insistence that the function of literature, and of satire in particular, is to correct and reform humankind. Troubled by the number of abuses the legal system was impotent to punish, Swift speculated that "it was to supply such defects as these, that Satyr was first introduced into the World." And Fielding's Hercules Vinegar was confident that the utility of his literary "court of judicature" would be evident to anyone who considered "that our laws are not sufficient to restrain or correct half the enormities which spring up in this fruitful soil."[59]

These observations on the status of literary revolutions and the function of literature as a mode of reform suggest a new line of thought concerning a venerable problem in the literary history of the origins of the English novel. Literary scholars have long been troubled by the apparent discontinuity in prose fiction between Deloney and Greene and Defoe—or at least between the late-Elizabethans and mid-Restoration authors like Behn and Kirkman. If the English novel began to rise toward the end of the sixteenth century, why was this literary revolution abruptly curtailed after 1600 and postponed for the better part of a century?[60] As the foregoing chapters make abundantly clear, the first half of the seventeenth century was a comprehensively "revolutionary" period, witnessing not only successful political revolt and unprecedented social mobility but also the establishment of the Baconian revolution, the climax of Puritan radicalism, and the flowering of pamphlet and periodical publications. Is it plausible to regard these striking developments as relatively "materialized" alternatives to the nascent literary revolution in prose fiction, alternatives that did the "work" of revolution "by other means" and with an efficiency and immediacy that temporarily diverted the energies that had begun to be expended on the comparatively mediated activity of specifically literary revolution?

The proposal is an arresting one, for it suggests as a model of historical process a vast and finely equilibrated homeostatic system in which the distribution of "energy" to any given sphere of human activity is proportional to, and entails minute and automatic adjustments in, all other spheres. My disinclination to explore here the subtleties of this model derives not from any obvious defect in it but from the fact that we have at hand a much simpler solution to the problem of discontinuity in the origins of the English novel. For if the previous chapters have done nothing else, they have thoroughly destabilized the epistemological and generic category of "prose fiction." But once the integrity of this category is seen to be highly uncertain, its discontinuity over time becomes not a problem but a tautology. The most valuable discoveries of the preceding pages have depended upon a willingness to recapture an early modern assumption of indeterminacy with respect to the relations of fiction and fact and literature and history. Resisting the more modern, dichotomizing attitude toward these relationships, I have focused instead on transgeneric questions of truth and virtue (questions to which the modern

III

THE DIALECTICAL CONSTITUTION OF THE NOVEL

— Seven —

Romance Transformations (1):
Cervantes and the Disenchantment
of the World

I

Don Quixote (1605, 1615) begins in self-criticism. Profoundly steeped in the romance tradition, Cervantes' masterpiece provided early modern Europe with its most arresting example of antiromance, frozen at the instant of piercing the elastic shell of romance and constituting itself as a distinct and separate form. Yet the transformation was not achieved all at once. In the following chapter I will argue that the text of *Don Quixote* encloses a development from the self-criticism of romance, to the naive empiricism of "true history," to a final orientation of extreme skepticism; and in a correlative movement, from an early and progressive ideology to a late and conservative one. The development can be conceived most easily as a two-stage transformation, for the first and second parts of *Don Quixote* were separated by a ten-year interval. But it is also a good deal more complicated than this schematization would suggest, and the greatness of *Don Quixote* is due in any case to its capacity to efface the tracks of its development and to occupy these several positions simultaneously.

Like *Amadis of Gaul* and *Orlando Furioso* before it, *Don Quixote* criticizes the incredibility of romance in part by criticizing its tendency to authenticate itself through the easy invocation of historical antiquity. Cervantes does this most thoroughly and amusingly by parodying the romance topos of the discovered manuscript. The scene is well known. Early on, in the middle of his hero's battle with the Biscayan, Cervantes suddenly breaks off, deploring "the Abrupt End of this History" that is necessitated by a hiatus in his manuscript source. Incredulous that "the Learned of *La Mancha* were so regardless . . . as not to preserve in their Archives . . . some Memoirs" in addition to these, he suspects that

"Time, the Devourer of all things, had hid or consum'd" them. Yet "I had reason to think, that the History of our Knight could be of no very ancient Date; and that, had it never been continu'd, yet his Neighbours and Friends could not have forgot the most remarkable Passages of his Life." Nonetheless it is indeed "a Parcel of old written Papers," stumbled upon one day in the market at Toledo, that fills the lacuna in the end. Delighted with his discovery, Cervantes quickly hires an obliging Morisco to translate the papers from Arabic, and titles the resulting manuscript "*The History of Don* Quixote de la Mancha; *written by* Cid Hamet Benengeli, *an Arabian Historiographer*."[1]

It is clear that this discovery pokes fun not at the claim to historicity—the claim that these events really happened—but at the more genealogical species of historical authority on which medieval romances often relied. For one thing, the fact of authorship is not repressed but proclaimed. For another, the *"pedantick Garniture"* that Cervantes' friend associates with *"ill-contriv'd Romances"* lives on—for example, in pedantic speculations on the authenticity of Don Quixote's name ("Preface," p. xxiv; I, i, 2, 6). And immediately following a rapt effusion on "Truth, which is the Mother of History," we return to the battle to find it drawn in the purplest colors of chivalric romance (I, ix, 55–56). Most of all, Cervantes modestly compares his own adventure of the discovered manuscript to the adventures of Don Quixote himself (I, ix, 52–53), and he ends Part I with the announcement that he has "met with an ancient Physician" possessed of "a leaden Box . . . found in the Ruins of an old Hermitage," containing "certain Scrolls of Parchment written in *Gothic* Characters" and telling yet more of Don Quixote, to which we are asked to give "as much Credit as judicious Men use to give Books of Knight-Errantry, which are now a-days so generally taking" (I, lii, 439). The worship of ancient manuscripts is of a piece with Don Quixote's worship of ancient romance.

So we end Part I with a parodic apotheosis of the discovered manuscript topos. Yet the epistemology of Part I clearly is not limited to this most primitive and self-reflexive critique of the romance reliance on ancient authority. As Cervantes' friend reminds him with respect to the traditional methods of authentication, *"Your Subject being a Satyr on Knight-Errantry, is so absolutely new, that neither* Aristotle, *St.* Basil, *nor* Cicero *ever dreamt or heard of it* [i.e., of knight-errantry]. *Those fabulous Extravagancies have nothing to do with the impartial Punctuality of true History"* ("Preface," p. xxiii). *Don Quixote* is not simply a sporadically self-critical chivalric romance; it is an autonomous antiromance. And if the fiction of antiquity is quickly and consistently exploded, the aura of circumstantial history that surrounds this preposterous knight, truly "of no very ancient date," deepens with each succeeding chapter. Indeed, even as the claim to antiquity is itself being subjected to ridicule, Cervantes seems rather bemused, even taken, by the fiction's documentary vestiges and by the promise of critical detachment they seem to offer. Over time, even Cid Hamet and the Moorish translator seem unobtrusively to shed their early romance factitiousness and to function more like skeptical historians, exercising a considerable acuity in exposing, on the basis of internal evidence, "Apocryphal" passages that have crept into the text (e.g., II, v, 472, xxiv, 597–98).

In fact, the comparative techniques of textual scholarship assumed a serious and practical weight for Cervantes when, shortly before the printing of Part II, Alonso Fernández de Avellaneda published his spurious continuation of *Don Quixote*.[2] Cervantes is able to forbear from "revengeful Invectives" against Avellaneda in his second "Preface" because he knows that definitive distinctions between true and false histories will be insisted upon by some of his characters (II, 440). Thus Don Quixote is welcomed to Barcelona as "not the Counterfeit and Apocryphal, shewn us lately in false Histories, but the true, legitimate, and identick He, describ'd by *Cid Hamet,* the Flower of Historiographers!" (II, lxi, 859). A bit earlier Sancho Panza and his master had spent some time with the guests at an inn picking out the errors in a copy of Avellaneda's continuation. But their most convincing proof of spuriousness is their own experiential authenticity, and they leave their interlocutors "fully satisfied . . . that these two Persons were the true Don *Quixote* and *Sancho,* and not those obtruded upon the Publick by the *Arragonian* Author." One of the guests goes so far as to wish "that all other Writers whatsoever were forbidden to record the Deeds of the great Don *Quixote,* except *Cid Hamet*" (II, lix, 842–46).

Shortly thereafter Cervantes even has his protagonists meet a character from the spurious continuation. The man is so persuaded that these, and not the others, are the genuine pair that he deposes to their authenticity before the town mayor—as though, adds Cervantes, "their Words and Behaviour had not been enough to make the Distinction" (II, lxxii, 923). Thus Avellaneda's attempt to capitalize on the success of Part I gave Cervantes the opportunity to assert the face-to-face historical truth of his characters by imitating the comparative methods of critical history. Of course the imitation is playful; even so, the informing historicist spirit is earnest enough. But only when it occurs to Cervantes to internalize, within his narrative, the comparison between his now-documentary Part I and the version of it that his characters still hold in their vulnerable memories, are the empiricist and objectivist implications of the comparative method fully realized. It is as if the bogus authentications of the discovered manuscript topos are definitively replaced by the discovery of the printed book. And the significance of that discovery, although resounding, is far from clear; this is also the moment at which empiricism begins its slide into extreme skepticism.

The problem is not simply that both sources—document and memory—lay claim to being genuine, that they present competing versions of true history. The fact that at first the fit between the two seems quite close only raises the question of how anyone could possibly have known all of this, and Don Quixote avers "that the Author of our History must be some Sage Inchanter" possessed of universal knowledge (II, ii, 459). Much earlier Don Quixote had told Sancho Panza that the exemplary knight-errant is obliged to wander the world for many years, "in quest of Adventures" but equally in order that "his Renown may diffuse it self through neighbouring Climes and distant Nations" (I, xxi, 145). This traditional view of fame as the laborious and time-consuming product of word-of-mouth communication is exploded by the discovery that Part I is in print, and Don Quixote now sits "strangely pensive": "He could not be persuaded that there was such a History extant, while yet the Blood of those Enemies he had cut off, had scarce done reeking on the Blade of his Sword; so that they could not have already finish'd and printed the History of his mighty Feats of Arms. However, at last he concluded, that some learned Sage had, by way of Inchantment, been able to commit them to the Press" (II, iii, 459–60). Ultimately, the association of printing with magic will remain only that, for it is a wonderful but human technology that Don Quixote comes to know too well to mystify.[3] Yet it is not only the apparent omnicompetence of the press that makes it seem magical.

It is very common, remarks the knight to Sampson Carrasco, "for Men, who have gain'd a very great Reputation by their Writings, before they printed them, to lose it afterwards quite . . . The Reason's plain, said *Carrasco;* their Faults are more easily discover'd, after their Books are printed, as being then more read, and more narrowly examin'd" (II, iii, 465). Publication secularizes word-of-mouth fame not only by expediting the process but also by objectifying the product. Because the printed book is subject to close examination and exact replication in a way that storytelling and even manuscripts are not, publication tends to suppress standards of judgment that depend heavily on the context and circumstances of presentation, and to encourage criteria that appear appropriate to a discrete and empirically apprehensible thing. The repetition of formulae loses its presentational justification, the problematic status of "details" and "digressions" is intensified by the immediate accessibility of that which they may putatively distract us from, and the dilemma of quantitative completeness becomes correspondingly acute.[4]

Of course, the documentary "objectivity" that is ascribed to Part I by the urgency with which it is examined hot off the press in Part II includes both this self-reflexive sense of discrete objecthood, and the representational sense of a faithful reproduction. By being published, stories become more fully both documents and documentation, and the "objective" reality of Part I is established by the very fact that it can be interrogated, in Part II, as to its "objectivity." But the results of such an examination are not always comforting. Once inconsistencies between document and memory begin to appear, Don Quixote complains that its author has stuffed "his History with foreign Novels and Adventures, not at all to the Purpose; while there was a sufficient Number of my own to have exercis'd his Pen." If it was written "by some Magician who is no Well-wisher to my Glory, he has undoubtedly deliver'd many things with Partiality, misrepresented my Life, inserting a hundred Falshoods for one Truth, and diverting himself with the Relation of idle Stories, foreign to the Purpose, and unsuitable to the Continuation of a true History" (II, iii, 465, viii, 492). So Don Quixote's fame may be ill-served, in the end, by his instantaneous publication. Here the charge of falsehood seems to malign the book's "objectivity" in both senses of the term: it lacks both formal coherence and representational accuracy. The most disturbing issue of this textual criticism of Part I, however, is the stealthy tendency of these two dimensions of objectivity to become separated. The more the question of representational accuracy is pursued, the further it recedes behind the irreducible objecthood of the book as document. The most poignant expression of the problem comes from Sancho Panza.

How is it, Sampson inquires, that Sancho's donkey inexplicably turns up again after disappearing, and what became of the hundred pieces of gold that Sancho found in the Sierra Morena? Many readers have been troubled by these questions (II, iii, 466). At first Sancho rather testily puts off an accounting of details that strangers seem to believe are important. Later he willingly recapitulates his donkey's disappearance in new, circumstantial, and (he believes) very moving detail; but Don Quixote cites a precedent from chivalric romance and Sampson drily observes that the reality in question in any case remains unclarified. "As to that, reply'd *Sancho,* I don't know very well what to say. If the Man [i.e., the author] made a Blunder, who can help it? But mayhap 'twas a Fault of the Printer." On the matter of the gold, Sancho gives a brief and grudging explanation, at the same time wondering "what has any Body to meddle or make whether I found or found not, or spent or spent not?" (II, iv, 468). In different ways, both of Sancho's replies express an apprehension that the reality of his experience has begun to elude him. The details of his life story that he deems integral are disregarded, his private affairs have become disconcertingly public, and responsibility for these matters seems to rest not with himself but with technicians. For Sancho and for us, the book appears to have assumed an independence of the reality it purports to represent.[5] Once the document has been promulgated, in other words, it becomes a ticklish question whether final authority lies with the representational or the self-reflexive dimension of objectivity. And Cervantes' play with the dialectical reversal that is contained in the documentary "objectivity" of print is one sign that the empirical orientation of *Don Quixote* is being incorporated by a more unrelenting skepticism. Taken to its limits, the skeptical claim to historicity becomes an insistence on the factuality not of the representation but of the act of representation: not of the documentation but of the document.

So the critical examination of Part I of *Don Quixote* at the beginning of Part II fulfills Cervantes' real commitment to empiricist epistemology even as it supersedes that commitment. But of course this reversal, deliberately enacted here through the replacement of the discovered manuscript topos by the printed book topos, in a more subtle and suggestive form also haunts the entire narrative. It is instructive to consider the epistemological volatility of *Don Quixote* in terms of the related but more general problem of how one determines that a story is integral. Even more than the esteemed *Tirante the White* (in which "your Knights eat and drink, sleep and die natural Deaths in their Beds, nay, and make their last Wills and Testaments; with a world of other things, of which all the rest of these sort of Books don't say one Syllable" [I, vi, 35–36]), *Don Quixote* takes the general problem of narrative completeness very seriously, and much of the characteristic feeling of the book derives from Cervantes' unending meditation on it. What gives the narrative its peculiar formal complexity is the fact that it draws upon and interweaves a richly divergent range of standards of narrative completeness: the formulaic patterning of nonliterate performance, the mixed parataxis of romance circumlocution, and the quantitative demands of empirical objectivity. The result is a palimpsest of cultural layerings, a laminated cross-section of oral, scribal, and print cultures bonded together in a moment of contradictory coexistence.[6]

A few familiar examples will suffice. As the preceding discussion suggests, the modern, quantitative concern with how many "details" must be included to attain empirical accuracy, and how many may be omitted, tends to arise in self-conscious reflections on the procedure of this present "history of no very ancient date" (e.g., I, xvi, 98–99; II, iii, 462, xviii, 554, xi, 701–2). The oral attention to patterning and performance, on the other hand, is most evident in the endless repetitions peculiar to Sancho Panza's proverbial wisdom, which so irritate Don Quixote. This is especially clear when Sancho tells the story of the fisherman and the goats. Early on, Don Quixote warns his squire that if he persists in his "needless Repetitions, thou'lt not have told thy Story these two Days"; and Sancho defends his narrative style as simply "the Custom" "in our Country." But when Sancho finally gets to the goats and requires his auditor to keep a careful count of them, Don Quixote simply refuses to participate in the ritual and the story comes to an abrupt halt, invalidated by the absence not of a certain quantity of details but of a certain patterning of them (I, xx, 132–34). Finally, while the interpolations of the audience play an integral part in Sancho's folk tale, in Cardenio's romance they "interrupt" and end it. Romance completeness is founded on the strictly authorial manipulation of main story and digressive dilation, as Cardenio knows full well (I, xxvii, 217–18). But although Don Quixote is actually reminded of Sancho's story by Cardenio's plea for silence, he cannot restrain himself and fails to fulfill the conventions of romance as well (I, xxiv, 174, 179–80).

Standards of narrative completeness exist to distinguish the necessary from the contingent. From a distance, all such standards may appear to entail the same basic preoccupation with the status of "details"; but what is considered excrescent by one set of conventions is deemed indispensable by another. Cervantes' exercise in cultural layering historicizes these discrepant standards by confronting each with alternatives that are strong enough to destabilize but not to overthrow its own conventions. The hierarchy of conventional forms is transformed into a dialectical continuum whose walls are solid yet permeable, so that even the same narrative element can be integral and excrescent in turn. Thus Dorothea begins as a minor character in Cardenio's digressive romance; becomes the romance narrator of her own digressive life story; and at last enters the main plot "to act the distressed Lady herself" so as to humor Don Quixote back to his village, an "act" that is scarcely distinguishable from her own "real" existence as a romance heroine (I, xxix, 237). Of course the major butt of these epistemological reversals, at least in Part I, is Don Quixote's romance credulity. "But is it not an amazing Thing," remarks the curate after Dorothea's "act" is concluded, "to see how ready this unfortunate Gentleman is to give Credit to these fictitious Reports, only because they have the Air of the extravagant Stories in Books of Knight-Errantry?" (I, xxx, 254). In fact this is the desiccated core of sanity that lies at the heart of Don Quixote's madness. For in a world where truth is submerged by the interchangeability of competing conventions, belief is the respect we pay to a persuasive consistency of style.

Not that Don Quixote himself can be said to live by this creed of the extreme skeptic. The delicate contingency of his belief is perceptible only to others, like the curate. There is no element of provisionality in Don Quixote's credence; he is simply mad—at least for the most part. But it is precisely his madness that insulates him from the sort of narrative vertigo that we readers experience. His implicit faith in the standards of romance is proof against all competitors; his only real enemy is reality itself. "Whatever our Knight-Errant saw, thought, or imagin'd, was all of a romantick Cast," says our author, "and appear'd to him altogether after the Manner of the Books that had perverted his Imagination" and to

which he continues to have corroborative recourse (I, ii, 9). The reproduction of late-medieval romances and their continuations, which so
preoccupied the European press during its first decades, created for the
first time an objectified corpus of romance that gave to Cervantes the
sense of a tradition, a coherent secular canon. Don Quixote's romances
codify a body of knowledge that tells him both how to read the world and
how to behave within it. They are his standard of narrative completeness,
for with their guidance he is able to know the plot of life a priori, at least
in theory.[7]

In fact some exegetical energy is needed to accommodate his readings
to the minimal demands of real life (I, iii, 15, x, 60–61). This is not to say
that the authority of the canonical texts is ever questioned; but like any
complex code, the texts admit of, even require, some flexibility in their
application to daily experience. If Don Quixote's universe is mystified, it
is also malleable. As he observes at one point, "Knight-Errantry has
ways to conciliate all sorts of Matters" (I, xix, 121). Unfortunately, the fit
between chivalric romance and lived reality is usually so awkward as to
require of Don Quixote a quite radical method of "conciliation." This
method is the theory of enchantments, a sophisticated exegetical technique whose great achievement is to close the gap between the a priori
pronouncements of romance and the phenomenal appearances of daily
life by arguing that things "are" what they appear to be only by virtue of
having been transformed from their true, romance state by an enchanter.
The technique is familiar to all readers of Cervantes—the windmills are
really giants, the sheep are really armies—and in his leveling of the
charge of enchantment against the author of Part I we have already seen a
special application of the theory to the manipulative powers of narration
itself.

Don Quixote's theory of enchantments may be seen as a very rudimentary model for getting along in the modern world of epistemological
incoherence. Its conciliatory method permits its user to believe without
really believing, to behave as though things were different from what
they appear to be, and yet to go on behaving all the same. As such, the
theory is also a rudimentary model for how to tell the truth in narrative.
In order to be made more sophisticated, the theory would have to be
demystified or secularized, and its proponent would have to become
rather less strictly delusional. In two distinguishable ways Cervantes
makes important gestures in this direction, and both are developed most
fully (as we might expect) in Part II of the narrative.

Don Quixote's theory of enchantments is experimentally secularized,
first of all, by Cervantes' several approaches to the notion of aesthetic
distance. The influence of Aristotle's *Poetics* is of course evident in many
parts of *Don Quixote,* but the idea of the aesthetic tends to emerge most
convincingly in Cervantes not discursively but as the momentary solu-

tion to some practical problem the knight's madness has occasioned. This is especially true when, as is the case with Master Peter's Puppet Show, the occasion is representational and artistic in nature. Don Quixote's total investment in the plot represented by the puppet show works here as a model for his total investment in the belief that real life is a romance. Incensed by what he sees, the knight abruptly wades into the scene with sword unsheathed, scattering and mutilating every offending puppet within reach. When he returns to his senses he offers the usual "conciliation":

Well, said Don *Quixote,* now I am thoroughly convinc'd of a Truth, which I have had Reason to believe before, that those cursed Magicians that daily persecute me, do nothing but delude me, first drawing me into dangerous Adventures by the Appearances of them as really they are, and then presently after changing the Face of things as they please. Really and truly Gentlemen, I vow and protest before ye all that hear me, that all that was acted here, seem'd to be really transacted *ipso facto* as it appear'd. (II, xxvi, 616–17)

Perhaps the puppet show did begin as a truly "dangerous adventure." But the aestheticizing language of "as if" defines the event most importantly as a psychological rather than supernatural transformation, in which the metamorphoses of magic have attained the metaphorical status of a convention. Nevertheless, the state of mind that simultaneously entertains the reality of both spheres is still understood to be that of madness, not "aesthetic response."[8]

The second means by which Cervantes experiments with the secularization of the theory of enchantments is through the social process of humoring Don Quixote. It is a frequent phenomenon in Part II of the book, where the energies of many of the characters, from Sancho's "disenchantment" of Dulcinea del Toboso to the several schemes of the Duke and the Duchess, are mainly devoted to reinforcing the delusions of the knight. Like aesthetic experience, the humoring of Don Quixote conciliates difference while dispensing with the metaphysics of enchantment. When the Duke and Duchess welcome Don Quixote to their castle with a riot of chivalric ceremony, Cervantes remarks, "This was indeed the first Day he knew and firmly believ'd himself to be a Real Knight-Errant, and that his Knighthood was more than Fancy; finding himself treated just as he had read the Brothers of the Order were entertain'd in former Ages" (II, xxxi, 642). The humoring of Don Quixote effectively replaces the theory of enchantments because it "disenchants" phenomenal reality according to the standards of romance. And what is particularly emphasized in these scenes is as much the doubleness of the humorers' experience as that of Don Quixote's; a number of skeptical onlookers remark along the way that he who decides to act mad may be crazier than he who has no choice in the matter (II, xiii, 521, xv, 535, lxx,

909). But although Cervantes sees the ironic ramifications of the scenario (to which I will return), he stops considerably short of elaborating a more general theory of the social construction of reality and the social relativity of madness.

One of the prescient implications of *Don Quixote* is that the modern disenchantment of the world entailed not the eradication of enchantment but its transformation, its secularization. But where does this leave the reader on questions of truth? The dense cultural laminations of Cervantes' book divulge no unitary doctrine on how to tell the truth in narrative, but there persists the sense of a lesson on how to negotiate one's way through its various layers. Don Quixote himself can serve as our guide, even though he lacks the necessary skepticism, precisely because he possesses the necessary credulousness. Madness, which is the naive belief in the reality of romance, is the first and indispensable step in the dialectical generation of extreme skepticism, which is the instrumental and saving belief in romance. The epistemological lesson taught by *Don Quixote* is only a generalization of the most characteristic experience of reading it, the vertiginous slippage by which the boundaries between "main story" and "detail" are made to dissolve and to reappear again before our eyes. It is the saving faith of the extreme skeptic, the plausible consistency of the mind itself constantly shifting gears. In this respect the epistemological reversals of *Don Quixote,* and Part I's hypostatization under the self-conscious scrutiny of Part II, constitute an elaborate mechanism for inducing that species of belief-without-really-believing which would become, once the mechanism itself proved unnecessary, the realm of the aesthetic.

2

The transition from questions of truth to questions of virtue may be speeded up by considering an encounter that takes place early in Part I. On the road to Murcia, Don Quixote meets six merchants, whom he proudly insists must confess Dulcinea to be the most beauteous maiden in the world. "Be pleased to let us see her," they reasonably reply, noting that if she is as beautiful as he says, they will be happy to accede to his demand. But Don Quixote does not find this acceptable. "The importance of the thing lies in obliging you to believe it, confess it, affirm it, swear it, and maintain it, without seeing her." Then "for the Discharge of our Consciences, which will not permit us to affirm a thing we never heard or saw," say the merchants, "let us see some Portraiture of that Lady, though 'twere no bigger than a Grain of Wheat." But Don Quixote remains adamant and truculent, the merchants grow impatient, and the affair ends with the knight receiving a painful beating (I, iv, 24–26). The encounter is an almost schematically symbolic one between epistemologically opposed postures (dogmatism versus skepticism, a priori belief versus the evidence of the senses), which also imply a set of oppositions that extend beyond the realm of epistemology: confession of faith versus testimony of conscience, aristocratic feudalism versus mercantile capitalism.

That Sancho is in general terms the epistemological antithesis to Don Quixote, customarily engaged in the setting of materialistic measures against his master's romance idealism, is a point so basic to their characters and to their interaction that it requires no substantiation. That the two men embody also a social opposition is, of course, a major premise of Don Quixote's feudal delusions. As Don Quixote reminds Sancho early on, "There ought to be a Distance kept between the Master and the Man, the Knight and the Squire" (I, xx, 139). But a real social gap lies beneath the feudal fiction. The first thing we know about Don Quixote, after all, is that he is a country gentleman with a small farming estate, a modest household, and a penchant for hunting; and the first thing we learn of Sancho is that he is a neighbor of Don Quixote's and a country laborer (I, i, 1–2, vii, 41). Now, so long as Sancho entertains the hope that Don Quixote will reward him with the governorship of an "isle" won in combat, he also entertains the feudal version of their social differences which supports it. But the fiction tends to wear thin through the constant rough handling of a world that does not conform to it, and from time to time Sancho registers his impatience by frankly broaching a very different system of rewards. At such moments he is likely to counter his master's airy talk of knightly "Favours" bestowed on the deserving squire with the idea of a regular salary of "Wages," paid out of Don Quixote's present estate and recompensed (if it should ever come to that) by the revenues that will flow from the hoped-for isle. To this eminently practical suggestion Don Quixote predictably replies, "I don't think . . . they ever went by the Hire, but rather that they trusted to their Master's Generosity." The romance records are clear enough, at least by omission, to preclude this suspiciously modern expedient of wage labor, by which Don Quixote refuses to alter the terms of Sancho's "Service" and to "break through all the Rules and Customs of Chivalry" (I, xx, 140; II, vii, 486–87).

These conflicts between the socially symbolic standards of favors and wages, custom and contract, suggest that the relationship between Don Quixote and Sancho Panza synoptically mediates the historical transition from feudalism to capitalism. For Don Quixote, what he is pleased to call "the Law of Chivalry" is absolute and prior to all royal and national jurisdictions (I, x, 57–58, xxix, 244, xxx, 245). That it also tends, at least in Part I, ostentatiously to contradict moral law and ethical behavior substantiates Cervantes' general critique of a view of the world that is dangerously "enchanted," deformed by the anachronistic expectations of aristocratic ideology, which encourages discrete, decentralized, and competing authorities in political arrangements and which values personal dependence and customary stratification in social relations. So it is not surprising that when he narrates to Sancho the ideal career of the knight-errant, Don Quixote prefers a plot that best promises to reconcile the real facts of his own background with the requirements of aristocratic ideology. The great triumphs of this ideal knight, Don Quixote says, are capped by his marriage to a beautiful princess,

and in a little Time the King is very well pleas'd with the Match; for now the Knight appears to be the Son of a mighty King . . . [But] suppose we have found out a King and a Princess, and I have fill'd the World with the fame of my unparallel'd Atchievements, yet cannot I tell how to find out that I am of Royal Blood, though it were but Second Cousin to an Emperor: For, 'tis not to be expected that the King will ever consent that I shall wed his Daughter 'till I have made this out by authentick Proofs, tho' my Service deserve it never so much; and thus for want of a Punctilio, I am in danger of losing what my Valour so justly merits. 'Tis true, indeed, I am a Gentleman, and of a Noted ancient Family, and possess'd of an Estate of a hundred and twenty Crowns a Year; nay, perhaps the learned Historiographer who is to write the History of my Life, will so improve and beautify my Genealogy, that he will find me to be the fifth, or sixth at least, in Descent from a King. (I, xxi, 148–49)[9]

In this passage, traditionalistic postures on matters of truth and virtue are united in the image of a romancing "historiographer" confirming knightly merit through the revelation of aristocratic parentage, and our sharp appreciation of the ludicrousness of Don Quixote's ambitions supports the sense that Cervantes is mobilizing not only an empiricist, but also a progressive, critique of his protagonist. In 1605, on the title page of the first part of *Don Quixote*, Cervantes calls his hero *"el ingenioso hidalgo Don Quixote de la Mancha."* The word *hidalgo* ("gentleman") indicates hereditary gentility and denotes the lowest grade of Spanish nobility. Don Quixote belongs to the social type of the impoverished *hidalgo*, whose inherited status is in striking discord with his wealth and social opportunities. Such a type is susceptible, of course, to sympathetic treatment, but Cervantes gives a progressive and satirical edge to the characterization by making his *hidalgo* assume the unmerited title "don." Early in Part I we see Don Quixote soberly submit to a farcical parody of the ceremony of knighthood that would justify such a title (I, iii), the sort of farce that was explicitly condemned by Spanish law and that reveals one important dimension of our hero's "madness" to be the vanity of the nobleman who believes he can prop up his decayed honor with the affectation of a fraudulent rank. But ten years later, on the title page of Part II, the word *hidalgo* is replaced by the word *caballero,* a term which is also equivalent to "gentleman" but literally means "knight," and which therefore erases the intimation of fraudulence and the social slur on the 1605 title page. What might be the ideological significance of this alteration?[10]

As I have suggested with respect to questions of truth, even in Part I Don Quixote's "madness" is not just a hopelessly delusional hallucination. The point is worth making for questions of virtue as well. Early and often it is represented as a belief not that he is actually living in a mystified medieval Spain but that it would be of inestimable benefit if the Golden Age of knight-errantry were "revived" through his offices (I, vii, 41, xi, 64, xx, 129). In Part II, this way of formulating Don Quixote's madness is favored sufficiently to suggest that it is less madness than a conservative interpretation of history. The transformation is by no means total, but the former insistence on the literal existence of the heroes of chivalric romance tends now to modulate subtly into a more reasonable and just assertion that the institution of knight-errantry has had a historical reality (II, i, 452, xviii, 557). The assertion is important to Don Quixote because the ignorance of that real alternative to "this degenerate Age of ours" precludes a crucial perception both of how bad we are by the measure of how far we have fallen, and of how we might inaugurate a movement for social change (II, i, 450). Knighthood has a real, contemporary significance for Don Quixote. At the beginning of Part II, for example, he waxes eloquent on the wisdom of the king's employment of contemporary knights-errant to repulse the current Turkish threat to Christendom (II, i, 446–47, 452).

Once we entertain the view of Don Quixote's madness as a program of social reform, it becomes possible to recognize the connection of this advocacy of an anachronistic military service with the ideology of the *noblesse d'épée*. Certainly he is concerned, in this first chapter, to make an ideologically meaningful distinction between sword and robe nobility: between knighthood as a living institution composed of courageous and adventurous knights dedicated to the cause of virtue and bound to those above and below by complex ties of service and obligation; and knighthood as, at its worst, the effete and bureaucratized institution of modern courtiership, where the administration of royal policy has replaced the defense of virtue, rich damask has replaced the spartan coat of mail, sloth triumphs over vigilance, "Idleness over Industry; Vice over Vertue; Arrogance over Valour, and the Theory of Arms over the Practice" (II, i, 451). In the overall development of *Don Quixote,* the eponymous hero's character deepens from the early, external caricature of a well-known social type—the impoverished *hidalgo*—to a more sympathetic portrait drawn from within. And the change corresponds to a gradual complication of Cervantes' progressive ideology by a more conservative orientation.[11]

In Part I, Don Quixote makes an important distinction between the two basic kinds of lineage: "Some who sprung from mighty Kings and Princes, by little and little have been so lessen'd and obscur'd, that the Estates and Titles of the following Generations have dwindled to nothing, and ended in a Point like a Pyramid; others, who from mean and low Beginnings still rise and rise, till at last they are rais'd to the very Top of human Greatness: So vast the Difference is, that those who were Something are now Nothing, and those that were Nothing are now Something" (I, xxi, 149).[12] Don Quixote hopes (as we have seen) that his own, fantasized marriage to a beautiful princess will be facilitated by the discovery that he is one of the former. From the perspective of my current concern to understand his madness as a conservative historiography, it is not surprising that Don Quixote has been obliged to employ a theory of enchantments, for in this respect, too, the modern world is saturated with illusory appearances—that is, with status inconsistency. On the one hand, there are those whose current social eminence effectively hides their moral depravity; and Don Quixote is well aware that the old as well as the new nobility contributes to this group, that "High-born Knights there are, who seem fond of groveling in the Dust, and being lost in the Crowd of inferior Mortals" (II, vi, 481). On the other hand, there are men like Don Quixote himself, whose status as an impoverished *hidalgo* is treated more sympathetically in the second half of the book in part because his wisdom and virtue are more in evidence there. Thus when Don Quixote inquires into the village gossip about his adventures, Sancho is obliged to report the melancholy facts of his master's social displacement. The other *hidalgos* resent him for assuming the "Don" with no material substance to support it, while the *caballeros* are equally annoyed at what they take to be competition from one who cannot even afford to dress the part. Don Quixote can only lodge a mild protest that "the more eminently Virtue shines, the more 'tis expos'd to the Persecution of Envy" (II, ii, 457–58), a compassionate view of himself that is not challenged by the humorous pathos of Cid Hamet's later apostrophe on the besieged honor of the impoverished *hidalgo* (II, xliv, 732–33).

I have already pointed out the use Cervantes makes of humoring as a kind of secularization of the theory of enchantments which disenchants the world by "conciliating" reality to fantasy. The social phenomenon of status inconsistency is itself a secular manifestation of the enchantment of the modern world, and Don Quixote's project of chivalric reform undertakes the disenchantment of this enchantment, the reconciliation of virtue, wealth, and status. His terse formulation of the difference between the two kinds of lineage—those who were something are now nothing, and those who were nothing are now something—aptly evokes the magical transformation, the metamorphosis of "being" itself, of which radical social alterations seem capable. To see upward and downward mobility as a "social enchantment" helps to identify some of the non-metaphysical sources of Don Quixote's urgency to have Dulcinea "dis-enchanted," by sharpening the social poignancy of his conviction that evil enchanters have "transform'd the Figure and Person of the Beautiful *Dulcinea del Toboso* into the base and sordid Likeness of a Rustic Wench." Many of the metamorphoses that occur in *Don Quixote* have a similarly sociological resonance. When we first encounter Dorothea (of the inter-polated romance) masquerading as a peasant boy, we may take her to be a noble lady engaged in the familiar romance activity of pastoral slumming (I, xxviii, 222), but her status is soon specified much more concretely. For the romance heroine Dorothea has a surprisingly modern social identity. Her father, she says, is the tenant farmer of an Andalusian lord and "but of low degree; but so very rich, that had Fortune equall'd his Birth to his Estate, he cou'd have wanted nothing more." True, her parents "have been Farmers from Father to Son, yet . . . the Antiquity of their Family, together with their large Possessions, and the Port they live in, raises 'em much above their Profession, and has by little and little almost univer-sally gain'd them the Name of Gentlemen" (I, xxviii, 225). Dorothea, in short, is undergoing the transformative social process of becoming one of those who were nothing and are now something, and as her story unfolds we recognize in it the familiar love-plot of problematic upward mobility.

Importuned by Don Ferdinand, the lusty and noble son of her lord, Dorothea reminds him, like Robert Greene's Cratyna,[13] that "I was born your Vassal, but not your Slave." She holds fast to her honor; begs him to "spare your noble Father the Shame and Displeasure of seeing you mar-ry'd to a Person so much below your Birth"; reflects that she would not be the first "whom Marriage has rais'd to unhop'd for Greatness"; and finally succumbs to Ferdinand only to find, when he quickly transfers his desire to Cardenio's Lucinda, that he is an inconstant and dishonorable traitor (I, xxviii, 228–30). The story ends happily with the wonderful reunion at the inn, where the aristocratic rake is reformed by Dorothea's constancy and encouraged by her reminder that "Virtue is the truest Nobility, which if you stain by basely wronging me, you bring a greater Blot upon your Family than Marrying me could cause" (I, xxxvi, 314). So the progressive critique of aristocratic ideology that generally colors Part I is encapsulated by the story of Dorothea's manifestly just social elevation, an enchantment of the reigning aristocratic enchantment, hence a disenchantment of the world. The Dorothea of Part I and the Don Quixote of Part II imply two distinct readings of the past and two antithetical revolutionary programs for future social justice: the pro-gressive utopianism of upward mobility and the career open to talents, and the conservative utopianism of the revival of harmonious "feudal" social relations.

What happens to the progressive plot in Part II of *Don Quixote*? The second half of the book permits us a more sympathetic view not only of Don Quixote's madness but also of Sancho Panza's foolishness. In the chapter that the Moorish translator deems apocryphal owing to Sancho's unaccustomed display of intelligence, Sancho and his wife debate the effect his hoped-for governorship will have upon the family, especially on their daughter. And although the hope derives from the romance fantasy of Don Quixote's early promise to his squire, like the adventures of Dorothea it now becomes specified, in conversation, to the concrete conditions of modern social life; and in this form it extends the consideration of problematic upward mobility that was initiated by Dorothea's love-plot in Part I.[14]

Sancho's ambition is to marry Mary Sancha "so well, that she shall, at least, be call'd my Lady." Teresa's concern, on the other hand, is that her daughter will be caught in the trap of status inconsistency and that she will not know how to play the part. "Let her match with her Match," she advises. "If from clouted Shoes you set her upon high Heels . . . the poor Girl won't know how to behave herself, but will every Foot make a Thousand Blunders, and shew her homespun Country Breeding." But Sancho rejoins that nature is a function of nurture: " 'Twill be but two or three years Prentiship; and then you'll see how strangely she'll alter; your Ladyship and keeping of State will become her, as if they had been made for her" (II, v, 474). As Don Quixote learns through the humorings of the Duke and Duchess, appearance becomes, by the infinitesimal habituations of daily experience, only another word for reality. "When we happen to see a Person well dress'd, richly equipp'd, and with a great Train of Servants," Sancho continues, "we find ourselves mov'd and prompted to pay him Respect, in a manner, in spite of our Teeth, tho' at that very Moment our Memory makes us call to remembrance some low Circumstances, in which we had seen that Person before. Now this Ignominy, be it either by reason of his Poverty, or mean Parentage, as 'tis already pass'd, is no more, and only that which we see before our Eyes remains" (II, v, 477).

What is most striking about this intoxicating vision of the effectual reality of appearances is that it expresses a progressive utopianism so fluid and open-ended that it dissolves, as Teresa intimated, the very basis—the empirical solidity of individual identity and merit—on which progressive ideology is founded. Sancho plans a comparable dissolution for his son: "Be sure you clothe the Boy so, that he may look, not like what he is, but like what he is to be" (II, v, 478). And progressive ideology begins to seem as devoted to externals as the aristocratic ideology its doctrine of inner virtue is designed to replace. This central principle of the conservative critique—the stealthy persistence of the old, imaginary value at the heart of its modern "negation"—is evident even in Sancho's fantasy of how "in the twinkling of an Eye, and while one might toss a

Pancake, I['ll] clap you a Don and a Ladyship upon the Back of her" (II, v, 476). For if the phrase evokes the instantaneous, rags-to-riches transformations of emergent capitalist "magic," it equally recalls the language of romance metamorphosis that dominates the career fantasies of the knight and his squire in Part I of the book (e.g., I, vii, 41, 42, xvi, 97).

Yet when the fantastic governorship finally does arrive, Sancho irritably and surprisingly rejects the effortless assimilationism implicit in his earlier discourse. Addressed as "Lord Don Sancho Panza," he insists "that *Don* does not belong to me, neither was it borne by any of my Family before me . . . Now do I really guess your *Dons* are as thick as Stones in this Island . . . If my Government happens but to last four Days to an end, it shall go hard but I'll clear the Island of those swarms of *Dons* that must needs be as troublesome as so many Flesh-flies" (II, xlv, 738). The repudiation of this external change, moreover, is accompanied by an inner alteration that strikes everyone who sees him. Sancho's principal function as governor is to sit in judgment on the disputes and grievances brought by his subjects, an office he executes with such unexpected wisdom that he appears a changed man (II, xlv, 741, 743, xlix, 766, li, 783). At the end of his first week of governing we find him in "Repose, sated not with Bread and Wine, but cloy'd with hearing Causes, pronouncing Sentences, making Statutes, and putting out Orders and Proclamations," for he has already become a revered Lycurgus whose code survives "to this Day" as "*The Constitutions of the Great Governor Sancho Panza*" (II, liii, 798, li, 791). What began as one of the Duke's exercises in humoring has become serious business, for Sancho has gained, and become, an authority. And the fact that he has refused the crude and implausible garb of an aristocratic title will not keep us from wondering, with his friends, how this extraordinary change could have occurred. Is it simply "that Offices and Places of Trust inspir'd some Men with Understanding, as they stupify'd and confounded others" (II, xlix, 765)? Is the governor a creation of the outward office and its expectations, or have these occasioned the manifesting of an inward virtue that was always "there"?

This question is only sharpened by Sancho's renunciation of his governorship after a week of extraordinary activity. Always up to his tricks, the Duke stages a mock-invasion of the mock-island which succeeds so fully with Sancho that he decides the experiment in upward mobility has failed: "Make way, Gentlemen, said he, and let me return to my former Liberty. Let me go that I may seek my old Course of Life, and rise again from that Death that buries me here alive. I was not born to be a Governor . . . I know better what belongs to Ploughing, Delving, Pruning, and Planting of Vineyards, than how to make Laws, and defend Countries and Kingdoms. St. *Peter* is very well at *Rome:* Which is as much as to say, let every one stick to the Calling he was born to" (II, liii, 801–2). This

final judgment of Sancho's ministry defines his recent state as an enchanted one of inconsistency in which status and virtue, birth and worth, have
been at odds, and the judgment itself operates as a disenchantment, a
negation of a negation, that reestablishes the traditional harmony enjoyed
under a system of aristocratic stratification. But we cannot be so certain.

For the complex logic of conservative ideology, unlike the aristocratic,
seeks somehow to harness the dangerously subjectifying powers of the
imagination by silently acknowledging their necessity. And if Cervantes
would have us concur that Sancho's renunciation makes "good Sense"
(II, liii, 803), he would also have us ponder those unanswerable questions
that conservative ideology, at its most fastidiously self-reflexive, is
obliged to propound. If enchantment entails a disharmony of appearance
and reality, who is the "real" Sancho—that is, who is the one within
whom subsists an accord of inner and outer states? Is he innately a foolish
man of limited capacities whose artificial rise in status temporarily enables him to masquerade as a man of wisdom? Or has he become so
inured to the low expectations he shares with others (we recall the Moorish translator's opinion that the subtlety displayed in II, v branded that
chapter "apocryphal") that his capacity for wisdom can be actualized
only when those expectations alter? Does the beginning of his governorship mark the beginning of his enchantment, or of his (all too brief)
disenchantment?[15]

Don Quixote's old antagonist, Sampson Carrasco, faces a similar
dilemma when, at the end, the fever of incipient death grips the aged
knight and he declares his mind finally to be cleansed of all chivalric
delusions. For such was the passionate investment his long dedication to
the dream had aroused even in the village skeptics that on hearing this
sober renunciation—Don Quixote's counterpart to Sancho's earlier
one—they "concluded some new Frenzy had possess'd him." This is the
final reversal; but Don Quixote, feeling himself close to death, ada-
mantly refuses now to humor them as they have so long humored him.
No one is more grieved and incredulous than Sampson, whose way of
life, like Sancho's, has fused insensibly with the delusions he fought so
hard to dispel. And there is great pathos in his desperate appeal: "What's
all this to the Purpose, Signor Don *Quixote*? We have just had the News
that the Lady *Dulcinea* is dis-inchanted; and now we are upon the point of
turning Shepherds, to sing, and live like Princes, you are dwindl'd down
to a Hermit" (II, lxxiv, 931).

Recent critics of *Don Quixote* have been concerned to correct the
"romantic" reading of it, which tends to idealize Cervantes' protagonist
and to muffle his healthy satire of the ridiculous in a blanket of sentiment.
This revisionism seems to me valuable so long as it does not, in its turn,
obscure the emotional and intellectual depth of Cervantes' concerns and
the deeply problematic nature of his vision. Clearly, my reading of the

work cannot be reconciled with Erich Auerbach's view that "Don Quixote's adventures never reveal any of the basic problems of the society of the time," that "the whole book is a comedy in which well-founded reality holds madness up to ridicule." Once committed to the profound analysis of "enchantment," *Don Quixote* quickly found itself committed also to the secularization of enchantment by specifying it to human comprehension. Caged in an oxcart by the village skeptics toward the end of Part I, Don Quixote is only briefly confused and deflated by this indignity: "[For] perhaps the Inchanters of our Times take a different Method from those in former Ages. Or rather the wise Magicians have invented some Course in their Proceedings for me, being the first Reviver and Restorer of Arms, which have so long been lost in Oblivion, and rusted thro' the Disuse of Chivalry" (I, xlvii, 400). Of course Don Quixote is wrong; he has been preceded in this posture by the Lancelot of Chrétien de Troyes' *Le Chevalier de la Charette*. But while Cervantes thus plays with the question of his own indebtedness to the already self-deflating romance tradition he aims to subvert, he also has a genuine concern to associate enchantment with "a different method from those in former ages," with the strictly sublunary forces of historical process and social change. Indeed, it is these forces—and paradigmatically the invention of typography—that engendered "romance" and "feudalism" as the representation of that which the modern world was not. I have discussed Cervantes' more specifically epistemological sensitivity to the significance of typography. The implications of print for questions of virtue, although less fully elaborated in *Don Quixote* than those for questions of truth, are equally profound.[16]

When the Duchess asks Sancho if his master is the man about whom Part I was written, his poignant reply suggests a confusion as to whether it is his character, or his very being, that may have been altered by the process of objectification through print: "The very same, an't please your Worship, said *Sancho;* and that Squire of his that is, or should be in the Book, *Sancho Panza* by Name, is my own self, if I was not chang'd in my Cradle; I mean, chang'd in the Press" (II, xxx, 639). Printing secularizes the family romance plot of the changeling because it, too, obscures the origins of what must be to some degree a suppositious child, the product both of its author and of the process that has made it an independent and autonomous object. Printing has the power to change what is given. Like upward mobility, it is a species of "magic" that holds out the progressive promise of liberating worth from the narrow and confining channels of birth. But the persuasiveness of Cervantes' conservative ideology requires us to see this act of liberation as equally a creation of imaginary exchange value.

Teresa had feared that in her new social status her daughter might no longer know herself, and Sancho's typographical objectification may look more like a self-alienation, a separation of the private man from the expropriated projections that now seem to lead their independent and profitable lives, quite apart from him, in twelve thousand households.[17] The industrious author of Part I, Sancho knows, already aims to transform the labor of their current adventures into a promised Part II, and he inquires dubiously, "Does he design to do it to get a Penny by it?" (II, iv, 469). Sampson assures him that he does, and at the very end of the book he eagerly joins Don Quixote in the abortive plans to revive the Golden Age of pastoral retirement with words that suggest how Sancho may already be participating in the fetishism of commodities. The great task, Sampson believes, will be to arrive at suitable names for their shepherdesses. And if all else fails, "yet will we give those very Names we find in Books . . . which are to be dispos'd of publickly in the open Market; and when we have purchas'd 'em, they are our own" (II, lxxiii, 928).[18] Already in Part II we have made the acquaintance of the bibliophile student whose profession it is to supply such book markets, and the failed invention of its customers, with the reified creations of others. One of his books is *The Treatise of Liveries and Devices,* by means of which "any Courtier may furnish himself . . . with what may suit his Fancy or Circumstances, without racking his own Invention to find what is agreeable to his Inclination" (II, xxii, 584). So aristocratic honors, no longer subject to exclusively royal creation, join the burgeoning throng of things whose commodification is facilitated by the wonderful invention of the press.

One question remains. I have argued that the two parts of *Don Quixote* enact, albeit over a decade, that schematic movement (from naive empiricism to extreme skepticism, from progressive ideology to conservative ideology) which in the English context is spread over a much greater period and range of works, and which will be embodied, at the end of the English novel's origins, in the intertextual dialectic of competing texts. What is the explanation for this anomaly? Before surrendering to the persuasive but tautological argument of Cervantes' transcendent genius, it may be instructive to recall a similar phenomenon of foreshortening in the picaresque. What unites these cases is of course the shared national culture. And together they encourage the hypothesis that it is because Spain experienced the epistemological and social revolutions of early modern Europe in ways that were significantly different from those of England that the development of prose narrative in the Golden Age looks, to eyes accustomed to the English context, decidedly lopsided. What follows is an attempt to provide for this hypothesis no more than the beginnings of a substantiation.[19]

To say that early modern Spanish culture did not experience an empirical and historicist revolution with anything like the force that English culture did is not to say that the crisis did not occur. Several related influences may be mentioned briefly. First, Cervantes was acutely attuned to the implications of the typographical revolution. While the most radical exploitation of the idea and techniques of typographical objectification took place within a Protestant milieu, the negative tribute to the power of books that was manifested in the institutionalization of the Spanish Inquisition and Index in 1558 still expressed a high degree of sensitivity to the epistemological significance of print. Second, the antiquarianism of Renaissance humanism, perhaps inseparable from the print revolution, was an active phenomenon in Spanish culture, as it was throughout all of Europe, and Cervantes could hardly have been immune to the appeal of its richly ambiguous historicism. In *Don Quixote*'s genuine, but instantaneously circumspect, claim to historicity we see a complex concern with the nature of historical truth that was sharpened by Tridentine dogmatism and by the forgeries and discoveries that fueled the historiographical crisis of his time. In other words, the promise of an objective history and of a transparent narration was a real one in early modern Spanish culture. But largely owing to the force of the Counter Reformation, the empirical revolution remained a potentiality rather than a viable and dynamic force capable of sustaining, as in England, a variety of long-lived intellectual and institutional movements.[20]

With questions of virtue the case is more complicated because early modern Spain felt the full shock of socioeconomic modernity; but its crisis was fundamentally different from England's. The interest in ameliorating poverty and controlling the poor that is evident in the picaresque was stimulated by economic boom, and by the revolution in rising expectations that it fostered. The boom was largely due to the enormous influx of colonial wealth to the Iberian Peninsula, which brought with it some familiar side effects of capitalist development—for example, the complaint that "natural" wealth has been "etherealized in the form of papers, contracts, bonds, letters of exchange and gold or silver coinage." In Quevedo's gloss of a Spanish proverb, "Poderoso caballero es don Dinero": "Sir Money is a powerful Knight."[21] But inflationary prices—which minimized incentives for wage labor performed at fixed rates—along with the absence of ideological arguments for labor discipline and investment, combined to limit the development of capitalist enterprise and activity. After 1550, nascent "middle-class" aspiration became so overwhelmingly assimilationist in character that it was effortlessly absorbed into aristocratic culture without (as in England) either aiding in the internal transformation of that culture or accomplishing a supersessionist divergence from it. Conservative ideology flourished in Spain as early as the sixteenth century because there was no fully developed progressive ideology for it to follow and react against.[22]

Assimilation in early modern Spain was greatly facilitated by the monarchy's creation of new categories of nobility, by its elaboration of complex standards of protocol and precedence, and by the widespread sale of *hidalguía*—honors and patents of nobility—for cash. From this period, on the other hand, dates the social type of the impoverished *hidalgo*, whose noble birth is acutely inconsistent with his destitute circumstances. These familiar instances of status inconsistency with respect to notions of nobility were complicated, moreover, by an additional criterion, "purity" of blood, and the two standards were not the same: nobility descended patrilineally, whereas purity was inherited plurilineally, by both the paternal and the maternal lines. "Old Christians" possessed "cleanliness" of blood; but as with the system of nobility, purity could be bought or counterfeited by upwardly mobile "new Christians" and Jewish *conversos*. Thus we confront the blatant contradiction of a "purity" that was institutionally subject to monetary corruption, and the absence of any creditable standard of achievement between the extremes of the ancient possession of status and the recent purchase of it. It is not surprising, therefore, that a conservative form like the picaresque, at once socially critical and utterly cynical, erupted in sixteenth-century Spain. This context also augments the intelligibility of Cervantes' more inclusive masterpiece, even as it heightens our appreciation for the extraordinary scope of his achievement.[23]

— *Eight* —

Romance Transformations (II):
Bunyan and the Literalization of Allegory

I

Reading *The Pilgrim's Progress* (1678, 1684) is like being Don Quixote: face to face with a reality that has been enchanted by an evil sage, but also privy to a theory by which all may be set right. Our evil sage is Satan leagued with the sinful human heart; our law of chivalry is Holy Scripture; and our theory of enchantments is Christian doctrine, which fitfully disenchants experience by punctuating it with marginal citations, discursive recapitulations, and the didactic applications of Christian and his interlocutors. Just as it is for Don Quixote, life for Christian and his readers is a matter of perpetual and self-conscious interpretation. It entails a responsibility not to "demystify" experience, but on the contrary to disabuse it of its material self-sufficiency—as Help does when he painstakingly explicates the spiritual meaning of the Slough of Despond, or as the shepherds of the Delectable Mountains do when they explain that the Giant Despair has blinded certain pilgrims and "left them to wander to this very day, that the saying of the wise Man might be fulfilled, *He that wandereth out of the way of understanding, shall remain in the Congregation of the dead*" (Proverbs 21:16).[1] The spiritual application of the events in Bunyan's narrative is not always achieved so explicitly as in these episodes, but it often is. And such episodes are generally characteristic of a literal plot in which things and events are to be seen as shadows of their own reality, teleologically taking place in order to fulfill the prior and overarching pattern of spirituality.

But if reading Christian's life is like living Don Quixote's, the author of Christian's plot (unlike Cervantes) is complicit with that evil sage, for it is he who deliberately enchanted the life of the spirit into a physical landscape. In fact, at the end of Part I he explicitly warns us to be careful of the danger he has just created:

> Take heed also, that thou be not extream,
> In playing with the out-side of my Dream:
> Nor let my figure, or similitude,
> Put thee into a laughter or a feud;
> Leave this for Boys and Fools; but as for thee,
> Do thou the substance of my matter see.

("The Conclusion," I, 164)

As we know, Protestant ministers liked to formulate homely rhetorical figures to the express end of "spiritualizing" and "improving" them out of existence. Protestant allegory may plausibly be seen as an extended chain of such figures. But then, as a recent argument has suggestively maintained, the only proper response to Bunyan's literal plot—especially to its central premise that Christian is literally "going somewhere"—is to reject it entirely. Yet this can be only half right, since Bunyan's activity as an evil sage must be seen as one part of a larger plan to mediate truth through falsehood. Confronted with a quite palpable enchantment, the reader is that much more likely to take things into his own hands and wind up with a disenchantment. From this perspective, falsehood stands to truth as fully necessary means stand to ends, a position that Bunyan argues most confidently at the beginning of Part II:

> Things that seem to be hid in words obscure,
> Do but the Godly mind the more alure;
> To study what those Sayings should contain,
> That speak to us in such a Cloudy strain.
>   I also know, a dark Similitude
> Will on the Fancie more it self intrude,
> And will stick faster in the Heart and Head,
> Then things from Similies not borrowed.

("The Authors Way of Sending forth His Second
Part of the Pilgrim," II, 171)[2]

Bunyan's defensiveness is due, of course, to his sensitivity to the problem of mediation, for those dark similitudes are simultaneously a means to resist sin and a temptation to it. The spiritualizing aim is most effectively served just when the reader feels most strongly a sense of concrete, material experience. Yet it is at this very point—when the text is most fully adequate to its task—that the reader is most susceptible to being seduced into a belief in the sufficiency of materialism and an abandonment of the spiritual level of meaning. It must be said, moreover, that readers of The Pilgrim's Progress have been notoriously frank about the ease of this seduction. Recalling a mid-Victorian childhood, Thomas

Burt remarked of Bunyan's narrative: "Not as a dream or allegory, but as solid literal history did it present itself to my boyish mind. I believed every word of it." Perhaps the naiveté of this reader's response may be written off to his youth, but we are uneasily reminded of the Restoration apparition narratives with which Bunyan's work is contemporary, and of their claim to the historicity of the spiritual realm. And although he attributes to Bunyan not historicity but verisimilitude, Samuel Coleridge is in substantial agreement that "with the same illusion as we read any tale known to be fictitious, as a novel, we go on with his characters as real persons, who had been nicknamed by their neighbours." The triumph of Bunyan's immensely compelling plot, in other words, is inseparable from the perpetual possibility of its total failure, for its concreteness threatens to preclude the process of allegorical translation altogether and to become both signifier and signified. In such a case, the reader consents to put up with a story that has foresaken the task of mediation and "disenchantment," a story that must make sense in and of itself, without the intrusion of otherworldly meaning.[3]

But this is perhaps to say no more than that the reader then consents to put up with a "novel." Despite the intrusions, the gaps, the glaring "incompleteness" of the narrative, Bunyan's literal plot makes a powerful imaginative claim on our attention. And its seemingly treacherous pull toward an exclusive self-sufficiency may be seen not simply as a failure, but as a fulfillment of allegorical form so successful that it strains toward a different form entirely—different, but intimately related in spirit and purpose. From the perspective of allegory, literal narrative is defective by definition. But from the perspective of the novel, literal narrative undertakes to reform the tradition by specifying the old problems of sinfulness and mutability to a realm of greater human efficacy. The premise here is that it is possible to succeed in such an enterprise, and it becomes pertinent then to discriminate the successful from the unsuccessful secularization, that which is able to preserve an essential "matter" within an altered form from that which deforms and corrupts its matter out of all recognition. Shortly I will ask what happens when we actually try to read *The Pilgrim's Progress* as though it were a novel. But I will prepare for that experiment by shifting my focus now from the form to the content of Bunyan's allegory, and from questions of truth to questions of virtue.

As I have suggested, the Protestant version of the problem of mediation invades not only narrative form but soteriology and social behavior as well. By Bunyan's Baptist convictions, Christ's reconciliation of the antithesis of manhood and Godhead is a paradoxical act of mediation analogous to that which the allegorist attempts in his leap from the known world of the flesh to the invisible world of the spirit. For since only the divine imputation of Christ's righteousness to the sinner can justify him before God, his earthly works must be, so far as the attain-

ment" of grace is concerned, at best a distraction. In his spiritual autobiography, Bunyan is assaulted by doubts over "whether I was elected
. . . I evidently saw that unless the great God of his infinite grace and
bounty, had voluntarily chosen me to be a vessel of mercy, though I
should desire, and long, and labour until my heart did break, no good
could come of it." In *The Pilgrim's Progress,* he delicately expounds the
implications of the doctrine of election and justification by faith in the
crucial encounters between Christian and the reprobate pilgrims Ignorance and Talkative. [4]

When Christian instructs him in the proper meaning of *"true Justifying
Faith,"* Ignorance is scandalized by the apparent unconcern with the
moral import of our actions in this world: "For what matter how we live
if we may be Justified by Christs personal righteousness from all, when
we believe it?" (I, 148). The question is compelling enough, but it would
be more so had we not already met Talkative a while back. For he, unlike
Ignorance, shows an easy and rather impatient familiarity with "the
insufficiency of our works, the need of Christs righteousness, &c." The
want of talk "is the cause that so few understand the need of faith, and the
necessity of a work of Grace in their Soul, in order to eternal life: but
ignorantly live in the works of the Law . . . All this I know very well. For
a man can receive nothing except it be given him from Heaven; all is of
Grace, not of works: I could give you an hundred Scriptures for the
confirmation of this" (I, 76–77). Talkative's infuriating complacency impels Christian to insist that there is more to religion than pious talk and
professions of faith. As he tells Faithful, "The Soul of Religion is the
practick part . . . at the day of Doom, men shall be judged according to
their fruits. It will not be said then, *Did you believe?* but Were you *Doers,*
or *Talkers* only? and accordingly shall they be judged" (I, 79–80).

Bunyan's fine equilibrium on the matter of works recalls his complexity on the matter of dark similitudes. And if we end this exchange feeling
a bit uneasy about the role of works and outward manifestations in the
great enterprise of salvation, we are really not very different from Christian in this respect. "Not that any thing can be accepted that is not of
Faith," he now adds nervously (I, 80), as if to anticipate and fend off his
own later refutation of Ignorance: "*This faith maketh not Christ a Justifier of
thy person, but of thy actions; and of thy person for thy actions sake, which is
false*" (I, 148). Just as the literal plot of *The Pilgrim's Progress* rivals the
force of its spiritual application, so Bunyan's emphasis there on justification by faith is matched by his stress on the importance of the sanctified
and holy life. For as he argues elsewhere, grace "can no sooner appear to
the soul, but it causeth this blessed fruit in the heart and life." And the
fruit of grace is its correspondent duty or service: "Thou desirest abundance of Grace; thou doest well, and thou shalt have what shall qualifie
and fit thee for the service, that God has for thee to do for him." So if

service is ineffectual in winning grace, it is what we owe God for the gift he has given.[5]

It is, moreover, a principal outward sign by which we signify the fact that we have indeed been justified. "*How doth the saving Grace of God discover it self,*" asks Faithful, "*when it is in the heart of man?*" And after Talkative has talked to no purpose, he himself proceeds to relate how "*A work of grace in the soul discovereth it self, either to him that hath it, or to standers by*" (I, 81, 82). The private conviction of grace is inexpressibly long and arduous, a perpetual round of faith and doubt that may dog the saint to the end of his life. Of his own most bitter period of struggle, Bunyan recalled: "Therefore, this would still stick with me, How can you tell you are Elected? and what if you should not? how then?" The search for certainty and its subjective signs forces Christian to attend as minutely as he does to the individuality of his experience, and it has a great deal to do with the articulated texture and full relief of Bunyan's narrative.[6] The individual saint's signification of his grace to others is depicted most notably, in *The Pilgrim's Progress,* through Christian's entry into the Palace Beautiful soon after his conversion. The palace represents the separatist church of the sort Bunyan belonged to in Bedford, and the professions of faith required of Christian resemble the procedure Bunyan himself had experienced there. "Those who comprised this special society had been required to manifest visible signs of election and participation in the covenant of grace. As far as other believers were concerned, each member had to demonstrate, both initially and continually, visible proof that he had embarked on the soteriological journey of the Christian pilgrim." Unlike the Roman Catholic Church, Bunyan's church did not hold itself infallible at discerning the elect by their outward signs. For the mediation of God's will to human understanding it relied not on hierarchical authority and prescribed ritual but on the subtle and subjective interchange between individual conscience and community accreditation. And crucial to this interchange was an assessment of the words, works, and service of the saint—as Bunyan expressed it, "the Word of Faith, and of good Works, moral Duties Gospelized"—not as the price of grace but as a sign of its presence.[7]

So Christian is entirely committed to a godly discipline and to a constant self-scrutiny for the signs of grace. But he is no less committed to a vigilant defense against the attribution of spiritual significance to manifestations that are merely carnal and profane. In fact, the discrimination between those "works" that signify and those that do not may be seen as the dominating activity of the Protestant saint's lifelong pilgrimage. As we have seen, no articles of Protestant belief were as central to this question or as subject to abuse as labor discipline and the doctrine of the calling. And in *The Pilgrim's Progress,* Bunyan so stoutly resists the reduction of sanctification to worldly success, of service to self-service, of "Puritanism" to "capitalism," that the very notions of labor discipline and the calling may seem to be in jeopardy.[8]

Shortly after escaping his persecutors at Vanity Fair, for example, Christian is joined in his pilgrimage by Hopeful, with whom he renews the "brotherly covenant" that was destroyed with the martyrdom of Faithful ("Thus one died to make Testimony to the Truth, and another rises out of his Ashes to be a Companion with *Christian*") (I, 98). The two pilgrims soon overtake a third, Mr. By-ends of Fair-speech, among whose kin he claims "my Lord *Turn-about*, my Lord *Time-server*, [and] my Lord *Fair-speech*, (from whose Ancestors that town first took its name:) . . . And to tell you the Truth, I am become a Gentleman of good Quality; yet my Great Grand-father was but a Water-man, looking one way, and Rowing another: and I got most of my estate by the same occupation." The remainder of the estate seems to be his by marriage, for his wife "is a very Virtuous woman, the Daughter of a Virtuous woman: She was my Lady *Fainings* Daughter, therefore she came of a very Honourable Family." (I, 99). An assimilationist upstart, By-ends evinces the characteristic tendency to confuse virtue with title. But he is also a professor of religious faith, and shortly after being outdistanced by our scornful protagonists, he meets up with three former schoolfellows who are also gentlemen on pilgrimage. Having studied together under Mr. *Gripe-man*, "a Schoolmaster in *Love-gain*, which is a market town in the County of *Coveting* in the North" (I, 101), all four men are practiced at reconciling religion with self-interest, and By-ends propounds for their diversion the following problem in casuistry.

Suppose that a minister "*should have an advantage lie before him to get the good blessings of this life. Yet so, as that he can by no means come by them, except, in appearance at least, he becomes extraordinary Zealous in some points of Religion, that he medled not with before, he may not use this means to attain his end, and yet be a right honest man?*" (I, 103). Mr. Mony-love eagerly undertakes to expound this appalling case, and we are not surprised to learn that he sees "*no reason but a man may do this (provided he has a call.)*" In fact, "since he is improved in his parts and industry thereby," the minister should really and positively "be counted as one that pursues his call, and the opportunity put into his hand to do good" (I, 103, 104). By-ends's inversion is bad enough, for it is not even a case of the Machiavellian justification of bad means by good ends, but rather a statement that self-interested ends justify hypocritical means. Yet somehow Mr. Mony-love's application makes it worse. For in ostensibly righting the inversion—so that materialistic means are resubordinated to the spiritual ends of "industry," "improvement," and the "calling"—he only underscores how thoroughly materialistic the terminology of labor discipline may become through casuistical manipulation. The exchange is a triumph of "Puritan" hypocrisy, and although Mr. Mony-love is "highly applauded" by his companions, Christian has no difficulty ridiculing the former students of Mr. Gripe-man into silence. By the same token, it is not hard to distinguish the corrupted sycophancy of this mutual admiration society from the "brotherly covenant" of Christian and Hopeful, with whom community accreditation is sufficiently self-critical to be also credible.

But precisely because the example of By-ends and his friends is so deplorable, we are not any wiser on those cases of social ethics which are genuinely problematic and on which we (and Christian) may be truly in need of guidance. And this is generally true of *The Pilgrim's Progress*. In Part II, for example, we are offered a stark contrast between Mercie, Christiana's companion on pilgrimage, and her suitor, Mr. Brisk, "a very busie Young-Man," "a man of some breeding, and that pretended to Religion; but a man that stuck very close to the World." He is attracted to Mercie because she, too, is "always busying of her self in doing," and he imagines that she will make "a good Huswife." But when Mr. Brisk asks Mercie, "And what canst thee *earn* a day?" he finds that she gives all she makes to the poor, and he quickly loses interest in her (II, 226–27). The problem is that between Mr. Brisk, who is a false professor, and Mercie, whose calling is so selfless as to be, however exemplary, quite impractical, there is a vast tract of human behavior inhabited by those real saints of Restoration England who on their earnest pilgrimage toward heaven had also to earn an honest living. What lessons do we draw from the really difficult cases—like Richard Baxter's friend Henry Ashurst, in whom worldly and spiritual success seem to be compatible? Is it possible to seek and enjoy worldly advantage as a sign of election and yet be an honest professor? How, and to what extent? Bunyan himself was no mendicant or ascetic, but a small householder whose family made wills and had owned a cottage for generations. Where might we see a model of how to pursue one's calling modestly and lawfully, but also pragmatically? How can we truly live in this world while journeying with some degree of confidence to the next?[9]

Of course to seek this of Bunyan's allegory may seem to miss the point of my opening words—that it is an allegory. Mony-love and Mercie represent not modes of behavior but states of mind; *The Pilgrim's Progress* aims to teach us not how to conduct our lives but how to have faith. The crucial point, however, is that in Bunyan's soteriology the two cannot be separated: for faith is impossible—indeed, it is contentless—without the psychological and social confirmation provided by discipline and sanctification. In the same way, it is impossible to speak of the figurative "meaning" of Bunyan's allegory divorced from its enabling and embodying plot. If, on the other hand, we seriously entertain the complementary error—if we try to isolate the literal plot of Christian's travels so as to read *The Pilgrim's Progress* as though it were a novel—we may find the model of Christian social behavior that seems to elude us when we seek it, as it were, piecemeal, in selected episodes and spiritualizations of the action.

2

For many years now critics have recognized the indebtedness of Bunyan's plot to the popularized romances he read in his youth and repudiated at his conversion. The central soteriological metaphors of English Protestantism, wayfaring and warfaring, are also central activities of chivalric romance. In certain episodes of *The Pilgrim's Progress* we can see the incidental influence especially of Richard Johnson's *Famous History of the Seven Champions of Christendom* (1596); and the fact that Johnson's work itself has a spiritual dimension, that "the romantic action of the book is often religious even before Bunyan allegorizes it," should modify "our habitual assumption that Bunyan must be struggling to bend a deplorably irreligious medium to his sacred purposes."[10] Even so, it is of some interest that in seeking concrete form for his spiritual argument, Bunyan turned to the literal, if supernatural, plots of chivalric romance, which many of his contemporaries were already attempting to specify, yet further, to the sphere of social agency and mobility. But although adaptation of the established genre of romance is an important aspect of Bunyan's method of "literalization," it should be seen as part of a more general strategy that consists in the conversion and compression of the macroplot of early modern history to the microplot of one commoner's experience of physical and social mobility. Needless to say, the pointed refusal to "disenchant" Bunyan's literal narrative, to translate it to a figurative level of meaning, entails a willful "misreading" of the text, and we cannot expect that it will disclose a coherence and consistency of action that is Aristotelian in its unity. If the following account of Part I's literal plot suggests a more consistent thread of events than the actual reading process of a Burt or a Coleridge could ever provide, it is only because I am purposely avoiding the many discontinuities of discourse and abstraction in order to assess its "material" flavor as immediately as possible.

We first meet Christian as *"a Man cloathed with Raggs,"* walking "solitarily in the Fields," transfixed by the question: *"what shall I do?"* (I, 8, 10). Like his future companions Faithful and Hopeful, he appears to be a "Labouring man" of "base and low estate and condition" (I, 136, 72). But he has left off work, and, oppressed by *"a great burden upon his Back,"* he tells his family and neighbors of his distress and ponders what to do (I, 8). They take his distraction to be madness, and in despair he follows the advice of a man he meets who tells him to flee the city. Later, with Apollyon, we will gain a greater insight into the relation between Christian's labor and his burden, for we learn there that he has fled the hard service of an oppressive taskmaster (I, 57). But for the moment we know only his distress and his solitude.

Yet in this radical wrenching from kindred, friends, and all that is familiar there is also the sense of enablement and opportunity, as though the pain of isolation is a necessary precondition for the reestablishment of unity at a higher level. This equivocal quality of rupture and solitude is a central feature of romance and fairy tale experience, and in his spiritual autobiography Bunyan describes the depredations of despair with an image reminiscent of the family romance: "I often . . . did compare my self in the case of such a Child, whom some Gypsie hath by force took up under her apron, and is carrying from Friend and Country; kick sometimes I did, and also scream and cry; but yet I was as bound in the wings of the temptation, and the wind would carry me away." Here the ambivalence of the romance kidnapping is fully expressed, for it alienates him dangerously from what he knows to be his true self, but thereby facilitates a more profound self-knowledge before he is returned, thus transformed, to his relations.[11] At other times in the autobiography, Bunyan describes the experience of crisis in different terms which yet evoke this same sense of mobility and its doubleness. Thus, several saints he sees "were to me as if they had found a new world, as if they were people that dwelt alone, and were not to be reckoned among their Neighbours, Num. 23.9." But later he exclaims: "O how happy now was every creature over I was! For they stood fast and kept their station, but I was gone and lost." Even Christian's burden has this ambiguity, for once he takes to the road, this symbol of his oppressive service quickly comes to suggest also the liberated vagabondage of the masterless man.[12]

But if Christian is now without a master, he is not eager to prolong this condition of socioeconomic unsettledness. Early on he conceives of his physical mobility not only as a departure but also as an arrival. He seeks "an *Inheritance,*" he hopes to "Inhabit" a "Kingdom" of great plenty where he will be well provided for by the "owner of the place," who is "the Lord, the Governour of that Countrey" (I, 11, 13, 14). The anticipated destination already hints of a feudal noblesse oblige, but its ruler is also sufficiently like Bunyan's in 1678 to manage a national system of highway maintenance, since "by the direction of His Majesties Surveyors" "Labourers" are busily if futilely attempting to fill in the great slough that Christian and Pliable unhappily have fallen into (I, 15). And yet we are soon aware as well that Christian's hoped-for relation to this great "Law-giver" amounts to a choice of one system of laws over alternative and competing jurisdictions: over that of the village of Morality, for example, to which the gentlemen Mr. Worldly-Wiseman and Mr. Legality both are subject; and over the "Custom" by which Formalist and Hypocrisie justify an entrance to the highway which Christian fears is no better than "Trespass, against the Lord of the City" (I, 16, 17–24, 39–40).

Evidently this lord, although powerful, has not fully established his sovereignty over all lesser authorities.[13]

Given the double significance of Christian's burden that has emerged from this reading, when it tumbles off his shoulders at the Cross we may expect him to be at the end both of oppressive service and of masterlessness. And, indeed, at this moment he is also stripped of the rags that bespeak his lowly status, and clothed instead in a "Broidred Coat" which functions as a kind of livery—for Christian understands that "when I come to the Gate of the City, the Lord thereof will know me for good, since I have his Coat on my back" (I, 38, 49, 41). In other words, he has entered into service, and his new master, the Lord of the Hill, is now identified more particularly as a *"great Warriour"* of ancient "Pedigree," who is "such a lover of poor Pilgrims" that in the hospitable spirit of the monasteries before 1540 and of the landed aristocracy thereafter, he indulges in extraordinary acts of charity for them (I, 52, 53). He is the one who erected the Palace Beautiful, at which Christian has now arrived, "for the relief and security of Pilgrims" (I, 46). But it is clear that having now partaken of his plenty and "committed [himself] to [his] Lord for Protection," Christian has done more than simply receive alms (I, 53). Even though he is not precisely doing homage to the Lord of the Hill, insofar as the term itself is not employed, the general spirit of the relationship is surely present, and we seem justified in identifying the developing bond as the familiarly "feudal" one of lord and tenant. Homage was the principal incident of knight service, and knight service was the principal feudal tenure. Accordingly, Christian is shown his lord's "Armory" the next morning, filled with enough equipment "to harness out as many men for the service of their Lord, as there be Stars in the Heaven for multitude." And later, when he resolves to continue his journey, his hosts at the palace lead him back to the armory and "[harness] him from head to foot, with what was of proof, lest perhaps he should meet with assaults in the way" (I, 54, 55).[14]

How has Christian altered his status by entering into knight service with the Lord of the Hill? At the Palace Beautiful he learns that his lord has "made many Pilgrims Princes, though by nature they were Beggars born, and their original had been the Dunghil" (I, 53). Christian's preferment is not quite this dramatic, but it is striking enough, and in a sense he really has been reborn from his former state of indigence. Like Don Quixote, he has received a new name: he tells the palace porter, "My name is, now, *Christian*; but my name at the first was *Graceless:* I came of the Race of *Japhet*" (I, 46). In fact he even has an alternative genealogy: he has entered the "Family" of the Palace Beautiful (I, 46, 47), and in Part II he is given not an Old Testament but a New Testament lineage, for we learn now that his "Ancestors dwelt first at *Antioch*." At this point Gaius reminds Christiana how important it is that her sons be well married, "that the Name of their Father, and the House of his Progenitors may never be forgotten in the World," and Mercie is immediately betrothed to the eldest son, Matthew (II, 260–61). So the "new" family is founded and preserved by the law of primogeniture according to the familiar progressive model. And the rise of this family is justified, of course, first of all by Christian's internal merit; here as elsewhere in seventeenth-century discourse, "grace" and "true nobility" easily operate as metaphors for each other, just as the language of "new birth" and the alternative "aristocracy of grace" have simultaneously a secular and a sacred resonance. In short, Christian's knighting has rectified his previous condition of status inconsistency. His friend Faithful's family also has been redefined. For his haughty "kindred" are mightily offended by his present course of action, which they see as "altogether without *Honour*," and they have "disowned" him as a consequence. But he, to his credit, has "rejected them; and therefore they were to me now no more then if they had never been of my Linage." Faithful does not reject "honor" itself, but he reconceives it radically: "I had rather go through this Valley to the Honour that was so accounted by the wisest" than truckle to his former family's corrupt version of it (I, 71–72).[15]

In exchange for the performance of knight service, Christian may expect not only protection but also that material support of which the groaning board at the Palace Beautiful has provided only a sample. For those whom the Lord of the Hill "had taken into his service . . . he had placed . . . in such Habitations that could neither by length of Days, nor Decaies of Nature, be dissolved" (I, 53). Just before leaving the hill, Christian is given a preview of this land, this "knight's fee," that will be his in exchange for service. From the top of the palace he looks south and beholds the Delectable Mountains, a pastoral *locus amoenus* in the distant country of "*Immanuels Land:* and it is as common . . . as this *Hill* is to, and for all the Pilgrims" (I, 54–55). In a sense, then, the utopian community of the hill works as a geographical prefiguration of the anticipated final reward of land tenure and economic security. The pastoral and communal overtones, clearly biblical, are also reminiscent of recent republican experiments in agrarian communism and of the progress from European corruption to alien innocence in Restoration travel narratives. Asked if he ever thinks of his native country, Christian replies: "Yes, but with much shame and detestation; *Truly, if I had been mindful of that Countrey from whence I came out, I might have had opportunity to have returned; but now I desire a better Countrey*" (I, 49). Actively assimilating himself to the new world, Christian is in the process of going native.[16]

Christian's travels from the Palace Beautiful to the Celestial City cover too much territory to be treated in detail, and for convenience I will concentrate on those three episodes which, central to the journey, are also given the fullest physical realization. These are the battle with Apollyon, the persecution at Vanity Fair, and the imprisonment in Doubting Castle. Recognizably "romance" entanglements, these three adventures also share the quality of being different sort of trials. As Faithful sings at one point,

> *The tryals that those men do meet withal*
> *That are obedient to the Heavenly call,*
> *Are manifold and suited to the flesh,*
> *And come, and come, and come again afresh . . .*

(I, 74)

On the literal level of Bunyan's narrative, these trials have the significance of contesting the legal jurisdiction of Christian's protector—and hence his capacity to reward Christian for service—against the claims of his competitors.

Apollyon, truly a "Monster . . . hidious to behold . . . was cloathed with scales like a Fish . . . had Wings like a Dragon, feet like a Bear, and out of his belly came Fire and Smoak, and his mouth was as the mouth of a Lion." Yet he beholds Christian with the "disdainful countenance" of an arrogant aristocrat, and most of their encounter is in fact a complex verbal trial concerning the technicalities of the knight's prior obligations to the haughty baron (I, 56). These appear at first to be quite daunting. As the "Prince" of the "Countrey" in which the City of Destruction is located, Apollyon claims Christian as "one of my Subjects," and Christian admits that "I was born indeed in your Dominions, but your service was hard, and your wages such as a man could not live on" (I, 56–57). That is, Apollyon addresses Christian as the lord of a manor might address one of his villeins—as a "subject" of his "dominions" who owes him the various labor "services" which, in return for farm holdings, were characteristic of the unfree feudal tenure of villeinage. But Christian's reference to "service" and to "wages" specifies the encounter to a time before the thirteenth century, when the unitary function of the labor services of villein tenure on the lord's demesne began to be replaced by two distinct and alternative functions: that of the copyholder, who held land of the lord in exchange for customary rents, and that of the paid laborer, who was hired to work the lord's demesne in exchange for money payments. Christian now claims the right to have abandoned his obligations to Apollyon when he came of age, an argument which clarifies the circumstances that led to his departure at the opening of the narrative (I, 57). It also directly addresses his former status as a wage laborer, a contractual relation which might plausibly be voided on the attainment of majority.[17]

But what of Christian's obligations of "service" to Apollyon? As the continuing dispute makes clear, Christian is able to refute this argument only by superseding at least the classic political relations of feudalism itself. "But I have let my self to another," he pleads; and if Apollyon is (as he claims) the "Prince" of his dominions, Christian's new lord is "the King of Princes" (I, 57). As Christian now warms to the dispute, he abandons his earlier arguments, which challenged Apollyon's authority over him, and replaces them with language that unmistakably asserts the authority of the Lord of the Hill over Christian and Apollyon alike: "I have given him my faith, and sworn my Allegiance to him; how then can I go back from this, and not be hanged as a Traitor? . . . I count that the Prince under whose Banner now I stand, is able to absolve me; yea, and to pardon also what I did as to my compliance with thee" (I, 57).

By these words, the Lord of the Hill is subtly transformed from one lord among many to the royal lord of lords. The crime of treason and the power of pardon can have meaning here only with reference to monarchy, and Christian's allusion to the swearing of allegiance also emphasizes that the bond he has made is to the royal sovereign. Over the late-feudal and absolutist period, the royal monarch was engaged in exerting the power of the common law in order to oppose his greatest subjects' arbitrary imposition of villeinage on free tenants. And some of the energy of this alliance can be felt in Christian as he now sets aside feudal technicalities by asserting, "To speak truth, I like his Service, his Wages, his Servants, his Government, his Company, and Countrey better then thine: and therefore leave off to persuade me further, I am his Servant, and I will follow him" (I, 57). Apollyon coolly maintains the verbal dispute for a while, but its terms have become so clarified that soon he "[breaks] out into a grievous rage, saying, *I am an enemy to this Prince: I hate his Person, his Laws, and People: I am come out on purpose to withstand thee.*" Christian replies, "Beware what you do, for I am in the kings High-way" (I, 59). He has become not a tenant defined by his vulnerability to baronial oppression but a knight defined by his representation of royal authority, and the real battle is on.[18]

We now leave Christian to repulse Apollyon, but it is important to note in passing how their verbal exchange has sharpened our sense of the character of Christian's knight service and its likely reward. The Lord of the Hill has emerged as an early absolutist monarch engaged in the sapping of baronial autonomy and the establishment of a royal monopoly on violence. In other words, the historical locus, whatever Apollyon's "medieval" monstrosity, is relatively recent, and it is increasingly easy to see Christian, who speaks of "wages" in connection with his new as well as his old lord, as having a contractual relation with the Lord of the Hill. Especially after the Palace Beautiful, it is persuasive to see him as an indentured retainer to the king, to be recompensed not by land tenure but by money or some other form of payment. Indentured retaining was exploited as late as the Tudors (whose monarchs boasted the most retainers in the kingdom), and entailed the wearing of livery and the display of banners of the sort Christian possesses. Indeed, when he first receives his livery, he is also given "a Roll with a Seal upon it" and told to "give it in at the Coelestial Gate" (I, 38). This roll, later called a "Certificate," remains of great importance throughout Christian's journey, and in literal terms it might be viewed as the document by which he is contractually indentured to the Lord of the Hill. On the other hand, the earlier intimations of land tenure cannot be dismissed entirely.[19]

At the town of Vanity, Christian and Faithful are persecuted by a system of legality that is both more rationalized and more barbaric than Apollyon's trial by battle. Vanity Fair is not only a traditional country market for domestic trade of all sorts; it is also a center for international exchange which promotes especially the "Merchandize" of Rome, a convenient and conventional conflation of religious and aristocratic corruption (I, 89).[20] The fair is thrown into chaos by the travelers' total disdain for all its commodities, and they are first examined, then imprisoned, tortured, and finally brought to the bar before Lord Hategood, for their crimes of abstinence. When Faithful speaks out against their indictment, which holds the prisoners *in contempt of the Law of their Prince* Beelzebub, the fury of that law is directed at him in particular (I, 93). In the ensuing trial, commodity, legality, and gentility are inseparably intertwined. Faithful, we recall, has already denounced the false honor of his kinsmen. Now all the witnesses against him are gentlemen.

The first witness reports that Faithful "neither regardeth Prince nor People, Law nor Custom; but doth all that he can to possess all men with certain of his disloyal notions" (I, 93). The testimony of another is yet more damaging:

For he hath railed on our noble Prince *Beelzebub,* and hath spoke contemptibly of his honourable Friends, whose names are the Lord *Old man,* the Lord *Carnal delight,* the Lord *Luxurious,* the Lord *Desire of Vain-glory,* my old Lord *Lechery,* Sir *Having Greedy,* with all the rest of our Nobility; and he hath said moreover, that if all men were of his mind, if possible, there is not one of these Noble-men should have any longer a being in this Town. Besides, he hath not been afraid to rail on you, my Lord, who are now appointed to be his Judge, calling you an ungodly villain, with many other such like vilifying terms, with which he hath bespattered most of the Gentry of our Town. (I, 94–95)

Faithful's trial has come to sound very much like an action for *scandalum magnatum,* which by Bunyan's time was an anachronistically exclusive legal preserve of the aristocracy (later Faithful will be cruelly punished "according to *their* Law" [I, 97], italics mine). Of course Faithful gives as good as he gets, remarking in his defense that "the Prince of this Town, with all the Rablement his Attendants, by this Gentleman named, are more fit for a being in Hell, then in this Town and Countrey" (I, 95). We are reminded of Christian's satirical reflections on his native country after he enters the service of the Lord of the Hill; Samuel Butler's suggestion of a shared genealogy for chivalry and satire helps connect several disparate strands of Bunyan's narrative:

A Satyr is a kinde of Knight Errant that goe's upon Adventures, to Relieve the Distressed Damsel Virtue, and Redeeme Honor out of Inchanted Castles, And opprest Truth, and Reason out of the Captivity of Gyants and Magitians . . . And as those worthys if they Livd in our Days, would hardly be able to Defend themselves against the Laws against vagabonds, so our modern Satyr has enough to do, to secure himselfe against the Penaltys of Scandalum Magnatum, and Libells.[21]

In Vanity more than anywhere else on their journey, our pilgrims are travelers in a foreign country. The "Gentlemen of the Jury" think Faithful a social inferior, a *"Rogue"* and a *"sorry Scrub"* (a mean fellow); like the townspeople, they are ignorant of his lord's livery and mistake its strangeness for insignificance (I, 95, 97, 89–90). But we know, if they do not, that these "Outlandish-men" who speak a strange tongue are undergoing a social elevation that rewards the genuine honor of those who serve the king. At the historical moment captured by Bunyan's fiction, monarchy is sharply separable from aristocracy, and in that fiction's scheme of values, monarchy represents the standard of integrity and authority by which aristocracy stands condemned. So in contrast to the travelers, the nobility and gentry of Vanity possess the spurious and outdated honor of those whose law competes with that of the royal fount of honor. It is under the auspices of their parodic king, Prince Beelzebub, and not those of the Lord of the Hill, that the fair sells, among other commodities, "Places, Honours, Preferments, Titles" (I, 88). In progressive ideology, aristocratic and monetary corruption are indistinguishable. And the status inconsistency of Vanity's antiquated aristocracy, although it is not rectified like that of the "real" king's servants, is nevertheless at least fully exposed for what it is. Thus, when Faithful is accused of libel, Bunyan marks the text with the marginal notation: "*Sins are all Lords and Great ones*" (Faithful has already been warned that the "Mighty" and the "Rich" and the "great" are seldom in accord with the "Religious" [I, 94, 72–73]). The radical disjunction of status, wealth, and virtue among the great is, in fact, the central theme of the Vanity Fair episode, and it balances the dominant movement of the plot, the upward progress of the meritorious, with a complementary castigation of aristocratic luxury and corruption.

In our final episode, at Doubting Castle, Bunyan's emphasis is less on social than on legal status. Finding Christian and Hopeful asleep in the fields into which they have strayed, the Giant Despair rudely informs them they have "trespassed" on his "grounds." The travelers "[know] themselves in a fault," and they are imprisoned by the giant in his castle dungeon (I, 113–14). The imprisonment is cast in terms of a legal trial.

Each day the giant's wife "counsels" him to persuade them to despair and suicide, and each day Christian and Hopeful debate whether or not to take this counsel (I, 114–17). But in the midst of their consultations it occurs to Hopeful *"that all the Law is not in the hand of* Giant Despair: *Others, so far as I can understand, have been taken by him, as well as we; and yet have escaped out of his hand"* (I, 115). And this so works upon the mind of his companion that Christian finally recalls that he himself has a key to the dungeon door, "called *Promise*." It is tried, the door flies open, and the prisoners make good their escape. "Then they went on, and came to the Kings high way again, and so were safe, because they were out of his Jurisdiction" (I, 118).

Like Apollyon, Despair is a monstrous feudal lord who finds himself in competition with the lord of lords. Here the contest pits the seignorial "jurisdiction" of the baron against the king's common law. In the later middle ages, the jurisdiction—personal, territorial, or both—of the old local courts was gradually being undermined by the centralization of royal justice. In their four-day ordeal in the dungeon, the trespassers are convinced of the necessity of submitting to Despair's local law, yet they also have a nagging sense of the possibility of appeal to a higher legality. The conflict between these two jurisdictions—between their conviction of their "fault" and manifest guilt of trespass, and their intuition of a higher law or "promise" by which they may be absolved—is conceived as much in terms of psychological persuasion as of physical force. For what is required of the king's servants is that they resist their customary and habituated deference to seignorial jurisdiction, and instead internalize the authority of royal justice. When this is finally done, Christian internalizes its power as well, and the errant travelers are able to escape— although the fact that they must reach the king's highway before they attain safety may suggest that this local "court" continues to exercise its territorial jurisdiction.[22]

The highway quickly leads the travelers to the Delectable Mountains Christian had seen from the top of the Palace Beautiful. This pleasant place, we are reminded, "belongs" to the Lord of the Hill; from it the final destination itself can be discerned (I, 119). And when the two at last enter "the Country of *Beulah,*" on the very outskirts of the Celestial City, we seem to have arrived at the utopian fulfillment of their service to the lord, the knight's fee of land tenure, for "here they had no want of Corn and Wine; for in this place they met with abundance of what they had sought for in all their Pilgrimage" (I, 155). But we are also obliged to recall the possibility, raised in the battle with Apollyon, that Christian's reward will be rather more "modern" than a knight's fee. For one thing, Beulah, with its "Gardens" and "Kings walks" and "*Arbors,*" looks less like the natural artifice of God's Eden than the artful nature of Hampton Court (I, 155). Furthermore, the Celestial City itself seems, through

Bunyan's biblical imagery ("the Land that flows with Milk and Honey," the "fruits" of the "Tree of Life," the sufferings once sown whose fruit may now be reaped), to be conflated with the countryside (I, 157, 159). These conflations of nature and art, country and city, rural tradition and urban modernity, seem to express a highly synoptic version of the historical mediateness that has characterized Christian's social identity, and they intimate that the final stage of his upward mobility will be other than a feudal land tenure.[23]

This is not to say that a modernized equivalent of the knight's fee was unavailable to Bunyan's imagination. In Part II, Mr. Great-heart tells Christiana's party that "many labouring Men . . . have got good Estates" in the Valley of Humiliation, where "our Lord formerly had his *Countrey-House*" (II, 237, 238). But Christian's—and Bunyan's—attention is now focused on the city. So the king receives the travelers' certificates, and just as Christian had asked at the very beginning of his travels, "What shall I do?" now at the end both men inquire, "What must we do in the holy place?" The answer is that "there also you shall serve him," although now more effectively than before (I, 161, 159). In part this new mode of service to the king consists in administering, from the metropolitan center, the system of royal justice whose consolidation has in the past been so serviceable to Christian himself: "When he shall sit upon the Throne of Judgement, you shall sit by him; yea, and when he shall pass Sentence . . . you also shall have a voice in that Judgement" (I, 160).[24] But to obtain the full flavor of the new position to which Christian has ascended, we must look to the beginning of Part II, where " 'tis confidently affirmed concerning him, that the King of the place where he is, has bestowed upon him already, a very rich and pleasant Dwelling at Court, and that he every day eateth and drinketh, and walketh, and talketh with him, and receiveth of the smiles and favours of him that is Judg of all there" (II, 176). In the end, Christian's progress recapitulates the rise of the new gentility of early modern England: from common laborer or *noblesse d'épée* to *noblesse de robe,* from medieval military knighthood to Restoration administrative bureaucrat, from knight-at-arms to Whitehall courtier.[25]

What conclusions can we draw from the misreading I have now concluded? If in his figurative allegory Bunyan aimed to explain human life according to the overarching pattern of Christian spirituality, it is a remarkable fact that his literal narrative explains life, with some persistence and inventiveness, according to progressive ideology. What this narrative provides is the synoptic history not just of the new gentility but also of the "new Christian": a model of how the average, earnest, modern Protestant may pursue his calling somewhere within the antithetical extremes of utter selfishness and utter selflessness. As Bunyan makes very clear through the episode at Vanity Fair, Christian's career manages to transvalue feudal service and its ethos in a way that does not simply degenerate into individualistic self-interest and capitalist self-service. And to this extent it offers to Bunyan's readers a pragmatic alternative to Mr. Monylove, a successfully preservative secularization of Puritan sainthood. If Christian at court does not look very much like the godly magistrate of high-republican imagination, perhaps we may discern in him at least the earnest, honest, and devoted public servant of the future. Certainly he has avoided the peril that haunts the figure of the courtier throughout Castiglione's efforts to fashion him as a fit and polished purveyor of service, the peril of becoming not a means but an end in itself.[26]

Something similar to this may be concluded with respect to questions of truth. Bunyan's compelling and well-nigh autonomous literal narrative also provides a model for the new Christian teacher, for it suggests that antimaterialist doctrine may be conveyed effectively through a narrative that stubbornly resists the spiritualizing injunction to dematerialize itself. Of course to refuse allegorical translation is, from one perspective, only to conspire in the fetishization of Bunyan's narrative. We agree to objectify the spirit and then to forget the process of objectification, treating the object as an autonomous and noncontingent entity. We thereby mystify an instrumental signifier into a carrier of its own significance. The fetishism of the commodity under capitalism transforms it from a social relation into a mysterious social thing. In an analogous fashion, we might say, the result of the fetishization of Protestant allegory is that mysterious yet familiar thing, the novel. In these terms, the novel is the characteristically modern literary mode because in laying claim to an utter self-sufficiency of meaning, its narrative enacts the drama of a deforming secularization, the imperialistic incorporation of spirit by matter.

But in the early modern period, modes like religious allegory gradually ceased to offer the comfort of a mediating unity and came to propound instead a dualistic and seemingly insoluble problem of mediation. In fact, the early novelists can be seen as struggling toward a form that would defetishize the spirit by freeing it from the realm of the ideal, whence it might descend to inhabit the world of human relations, the material ground on which the real battle against the deadening materialization of the spirit would have to be fought out in future times. And from this perspective, in its putative self-sufficiency Bunyan's literal narrative enacts a positive and preservative secularization and affirms not the destruction, but the greater glory, of the life of the spirit; not the enchantment but the disenchantment of the world.

Bunyan's increasing proximity to the epistemology of the early novelists is suggested by the opening of Part II of *The Pilgrim's Progress*. For here the fiction that the narrative has been dreamed by the first-person narrator, which frames and controls Part I, is complicated by the fuller and more circumstantial participation of the narrator in the early action of the story he dreams. Before lying down to dream again, he tells us that only "the Multiplicity of Business" has kept him from making "further enquiry after whom [Christian] left behind, that I might give you an account of them" (II, 174). Moreover, the transition into the dream mode does not inhibit this oddly literalistic solicitude, since the narrator simply joins the first figure he dreams of, Mr. Sagacity, and pumps him for information. This companion proves to be a man after his own heart, since when the narrator expresses surprise at hearing that Christiana and her sons have embarked on pilgrimage, Mr. Sagacity replies:

> *Sag.* 'Tis true, I can give you an account of the matter, for I was upon the spot at the instant, and was thoroughly acquainted with the whole affair.
>   *Then,* said I, *a man it seems may report it for a truth?*
>   *Sag.* You need not fear to affirm it . . . I will give you an account of the whole of the matter.
>
> (II, 177)

This rather startling claim to historicity—Bunyan in the City of Destruction sounds a bit like Aphra Behn in Surinam—is by no means unprecedented in his fiction, but it may be that the six years between Parts I and II were crucial in forming his taste for empirical epistemology.[27]

For that matter the experience of publishing a second part, and of being preceded in that enterprise by at least one spurious continuation, seems to have affected Bunyan in much the same way (if not at all to the same degree) that it did Cervantes. Bunyan begins the verses prefatory to Part II with the self-conscious conceit that its publication amounts to an act of holy pilgrimage by Christiana and her boys (II, 167). And in order to calm the fears of this personified and objectified volume that people will confuse it with the supposititious continuation, Bunyan points out how it can prove its own authenticity, and he discredits its competitor with an allusive image of counterfeit children and dissembling gypsies (II, 168). Citations from diverse lands and social stations are adduced to confirm the value and universal praise of Part I (II, 169–70), and throughout Part II Bunyan keeps before our eyes not only the exemplary figure of the precedent pilgrim Christian but also the page numbers from his first part where each of Christian's recapitulated adventures can be found and reconfirmed. To this considerable extent, the subject of Part II of *The Pilgrim's Progress* is nothing other than the documentary objectivity of "the first part of the Records of the *Pilgrims Progress*" (II, 285).[28]

In a sense, Part II's indulgence in empirical epistemology and in its characteristic methods of mediating narrative truth seems the logical extension of the forcefully realized literal plot of Part I. Yet despite this apparent consistency in Bunyan's epistemological progress, we are nevertheless struck by the complexity of the following, disarming anticipation of his critics: "But some love not the method of your first, / Romance they count it, throw't away as dust" (II, 171). For in an odd way and despite its ostentatious indebtedness to the materials of chivalric romance, *The Pilgrim's Progress* manages to define itself against romance from the perspective of both Christian and empirical epistemology.[29] To the former, "romance" is a self-sufficient narrative, whereas this is manifestly an allegory. To the latter, "romance" is an imagined fiction, whereas this incorporates its historicity in its own documentary objecthood. Perhaps there is no better sign than this of Bunyan's supremely confident and extraordinary feat of historical mediation.

— Nine —

Parables of the Younger Son (I):
Defoe and the Naturalization of Desire

I

Although the second part of *Robinson Crusoe* followed so quickly upon the first that it successfully prevented all spurious continuations, an unauthorized "abridgement" of Part I nevertheless just managed to precede it into print. In the preface to Part II, Defoe condemns that abridgment and complains that its excision of religious and moral reflections precludes the spiritual improvement that had been a principal feature of the original. The narrative "Invention" of Part II, as well, will be legitimated by the ample opportunity that is provided there for "just Application" and "Improvement." "*The Editor*" of Part I "*believes the thing to be a just History of Fact*." The "Editor" of Part II takes a similar stance: in the spirit of the maxim "strange, therefore true," he asserts that it "contains as strange and surprising Incidents" as its predecessor, of which he adds that "all the Endeavours of envious People to reproach it with being a Romance . . . have proved abortive."[1]

Now, amid such claims to historicity, we might expect the argument against abridgment to be based simply on the complaint that it reduced the narrative to a quantitative incompleteness. But as we know, Defoe's commitment to the claim, although real enough, was decidedly complicated in the later years of his career, and in other contexts as well he emphasizes the spiritual "application" and "improvement" of his work by way of justifying its "invention." The impetus for this reevaluation of the claim did not come entirely from within. Already before the year was over, Charles Gildon was attacking Defoe for having invented the protagonist whose biographical memoirs he was purporting to edit. Gildon is the first in a long line of critics who detect a close relation between the

errancy of Robinson Crusoe and the remarkable vicissitudes and du-
plicities of Daniel Defoe's own career, and he has Defoe tell Crusoe that
"I drew thee from the Consideration of my own Mind; I have been all my
Life that Rambling, Inconsistent Creature, which I have made thee."
"The Fabulous *Proteus* of the Ancient Mythologist," Gildon says of Defoe, "was but a very faint Type of our Hero," and although Defoe would
compare his work with *The Pilgrim's Progress*, Gildon's Crusoe sees a
much closer resemblance to the "Mob" romances of *Guy of Warwick,*
Bevis of Southampton, and *The London Prentice*.[2]

   In fact, the dilemma of quantitative completeness arises within the
plot of *Robinson Crusoe* itself, as a function of that impulse toward materialistic quantification which is so characteristic of empirical epistemology and which is expressed by Defoe (as by other travel narrators)
through a proliferation of times, dates, place names, and nautical terminology. Soon after his arrival on the island and in the spirit both of
Puritan teachings and of the Royal Society's instructions to travelers,
Robinson undertakes a journal that will begin at the beginning. But since
at least the first few weeks of the journal therefore must be a retrospective
re-creation of events, they have the ambiguous power both to confirm
the historicity of those events by referring back to them, and to under-
mine their factuality by providing an alternative version of "what happened." Not that Robinson himself is conscious of this ambiguity, since
he believes simply that "in it will be told all these Particulars over again"
(69). But Defoe was aware of the problem, and in fact many details are
omitted from the journal, while others we learn of for the first time there.
Even more, the two versions seem occasionally to contradict each other
in matters of fact, let alone interpretation. In the narrative, for example,
the storm has abated and the weather cleared when Robinson awakes
after the first night, whereas in the journal the rain continues for the next
few days (47–48, 70–71). And there is a further problem of temporal
sequence. Five weeks after the shipwreck, the journal recounts an event
(the completion of a chair) we first heard of just prior to the journal's
inception, and we may therefore expect all subsequent accounts to be of
uncharted territory (68, 72). Yet very soon after this we are told that
Robinson is excavating a cave which in the narrative clearly had been
made well before the construction of the chair (60, 67, 73). We quickly
find, in other words, that the dilemma of quantitative completeness is
dwarfed by the apparent problem that the journal violates both the substance and the sequence of the narrative's historicity.[3]

   On the other hand, we also begin to be aware, from periodic summarizing and foreshadowing interpolations (e.g., 75, 76), that this is not a
strict journal at all, but one that has been subjected to a kind of secondary
revision by a larger narrative perspective that resumes for good when

Robinson's ink later runs out. Unlike the typical travel journal, which provides rough notes for a later and fuller narrative redaction, Robinson's journal stealthily becomes that redaction even as we read it. Immediately following certain moralizing passages he announces explicitly that now I "return to my Journal" (79, 97)—and at these points the experience is not unlike that of Cervantes' narrative vertigo, in which what we took to be the main thread suddenly is revealed as a digression from it. And yet in the first-person narration of Defoe, the effect is less to throw the historicity of the travels themselves into question than to sensitize us to the personalized veracity of Robinson's experience, which is all the more authentic for having this subjective volatility. Gradually the journal's effort at a temporal ordering of events is subsumed within the larger narrative, and by the time we reach the climactic moment of Robinson's conversion crisis, this formal confusion of "journal" and "narrative" has served as one important guide to the way in which things as usual have come to be suspended on the island.[4]

The peculiar coexistence of historicity and subjectivity in *Robinson Crusoe,* the early dynamic between journal and narrative and the more general one between Character and Narrator—these exemplify the obvious indebtedness of Defoe's work to the formal procedures of spiritual autobiography. The form would of course have been familiar to Defoe, who had been set apart for the nonconformist ministry until his religious crisis at the age of twenty-one. The gap between the sinful young rambler and the repentant convert from whose perspective the story is told is felt very strongly in the first half of *Robinson Crusoe.* "But if I can express at this Distance the Thoughts I had about me at that time," Robinson says at one point, and we are often aware, through retrospective narrative intrusions, of the great divide between this foolish, thoughtless, headstrong, prodigal, sinful youth whose fortunes we attend, and the authoritative, prophetic, but disembodied consciousness that hastens us on into the fateful future (11).[5]

Once on the island, the gap between the two begins to close. The sprouting seeds, the earthquake, his illness and dream, are natural events that we watch Robinson painfully and imperfectly learn to spiritualize, to read as signs of God's presence (78–79, 80–81, 87–91). In order to treat his ague he looks in his seaman's chest for a roll of tobacco, and finds there "a Cure, both for Soul and Body"—not only the roll but a bible as well. Trying "several Experiments" with the tobacco, he listlessly experiments also with bibliomancy for a cure to the spiritual disease of which he is only now, before our eyes, becoming fully conscious (93–94). "Deliverance" is the scriptural word that holds his attention, and he learns to read it in such a way as to release, for the first time, its spiritual application:

Now I began to construe the Words mentioned above, *Call on me, and I will deliver you,* in a different Sense from what I had ever done before; for then I had no Notion of any thing being call'd Deliverance, but my being deliver'd from the Captivity I was in; for tho' I was indeed at large in the Place, yet the Island was certainly a Prison to me, and that in the worst Sense in the World; but now I learn'd to take it in another Sense: . . . [to seek] Deliverance from the Load of Guilt that bore down all my Comfort . . . Deliverance from Sin [is] a much greater Blessing, than Deliverance from Affliction (96–97).

At this point, Robinson's "load," like Christian's, falls from his shoulders because he has learned, like Edward Coxere, to spiritualize his island prison as the prison of the world herebelow. It is the beginning of the movement of narrative "atonement," when Character and Narrator come together, and this can be seen in the ease with which Robinson will shortly distinguish between not aimless past and repentant future but anguished past and contented present: between "Before," when he felt he "was a Prisoner lock'd up with the Eternal Bars and Bolts of the Ocean," and "now," when "I began to exercise my self with new Thoughts" (113). Henceforth he will by no means be immune from backslidings, but they will be ostentatious lapses—his construction of the enormous canoe, his panic over the footprint, his rage against the cannibals—whose rapid moralization will only emphasize how far the Character has internalized the spiritualizing powers of the Narrator.[6]

Thus *Robinson Crusoe* can be seen to be in rather close proximity to the preoccupations of Protestant soteriology in general and of spiritual autobiography in particular. With the spiritualization of "deliverance" Robinson's early urge to "ramble" (3) does not disappear, but it is permanently transvalued for him, as we will see. Physical mobility is reconceived in spiritual terms, as movement both "upward" and "inward": after his dream of the avenging angel he realizes that since leaving home he has had not "one Thought that so much as tended either to looking upwards toward God, or inwards towards a Reflection upon my own Ways" (88). Moreover, the impulse toward introspective veracity that Robinson now evinces is a vital channel for the claim to historicity in spiritual autobiography. But of course the generic status of *Robinson Crusoe* is a good deal more uncertain than this argument would suggest. The dynamic relation between Character and Narrator is, after all, a formal feature of the picaresque as well, and even of that originating strain of picaresque in which the "spiritual" constitution of the protagonist is clearly an "autodidactic" and secular act of self-creation rather than a function of divine creativity. Thus Francis Kirkman, for example, makes more than a gesture toward the language of repentance, confession, and conversion, but we can have no doubt that the instrumental creativity in this narrative is that of the author and not of the Author—and, indeed, that Francis's physical "rambles" are to be converted to "upward mobility" not in the spiritual but in the social sense of the term. By the same token, we are obliged to recall that the interplay between "journal" and "narrative" with which we began is as central to secular travel narrative as to spiritual autobiography.[7]

These fairly random attempts to "place" *Robinson Crusoe* by associating it with one or another established subgenre recapitulate, in different terms, the most important recent controversy concerning its interpretation. The modern tendency to see Defoe's work as essentially an essay in secular materialism is fairly represented by Ian Watt's view that Robinson's religion is the result of a mechanically Puritan "editorial policy." In reaction to this tendency, the traditions of seventeenth-century Puritan allegory and spiritual autobiography have been reviewed by critics, notably George Starr and Paul Hunter, to the end of assimilating *Robinson Crusoe* to something like an ideal type of Protestant narrative religiosity. Both arguments are made with great skill, but both may appear extreme insofar as they seem unnecessarily obliged to imply a mutual exclusion. As the Weber thesis suggests, in the historically transitional territory of early modern Protestantism, spiritual and secular motives are not only "compatible"; they are inseparable, if ultimately contradictory, parts of a complex intellectual and behavioral system.[8]

If, shortly after his conversion, Robinson demonstrates (as in the preface) his ability to use the terms "application" and "improvement" in their spiritual sense (128, 132), throughout the narrative he is far more inclined to use these words as synonyms for material industry (4, 49, 68, 144, 182, 195, 280). Yet both usages are consistent with the unstable strategies of Protestant casuistry—which in any case is only one sphere of discourse in which the instability of secularization and reform is registered during this period. Defoe's pilgrim is the brother of a wide range of progressive travelers to utopian realms: Edward Coxere, George Pine, Francis Kirkman, Capt. Misson, Sancho Panza. And if we wish to appreciate fully the status of *Robinson Crusoe* as a "Protestant narrative," we will need to attend to its filiations not only with *Grace Abounding* but also with the literal plot of *The Pilgrim's Progress*. Of course, Bunyan's entire plot of "romance" adventure exists in order to be spiritualized. In Defoe the balance between spiritualization and the claim to historicity has been reversed, and it is as though he has—not without the spiraling misgivings of the *Serious Reflections*—taken that perilous next step and, in the name of a "positive" secularization, explicitly sanctioned our resistance to allegorical translation. The result is a literal narrative filled with the mutabilities of religion (providence) and romance (pirates, shipwreck), which do not so much undergo in themselves a transformative specification to the mechanics of social mobility, as engineer the conditions under which that mobility is wonderfully enabled to transpire.

2

One focus of the critical controversy to which I have just referred is the question of what Robinson means when he speaks of his "ORIGINAL SIN" in opposing his father's advice that he stay at home and keep to the "middle Station," or "the upper Station of *Low Life*," to which he was born (194, 4–5). Obviously the term ascribes a religious significance to Robinson's physical mobility; but what sort of social significance does it attribute to it? Should we identify Robinson's "original sin" with capitalist industry; or with an anticapitalist impulse to ramble and to evade his capitalist calling; or with an anti-Puritan motive to evade his Puritan calling; or with a general unregenerate waywardness that really has no special social significance at all?[9] In a certain sense, however, this is to begin at the wrong end. For Robinson's mobility gains its religious overtones only with hindsight, through the retrospective viewpoint of the Narrator. In the present tense of narrative action it is primarily a social *rather* than a religious meaning—even the socially charged meaning of Calvinism—that Robinson's mobility possesses when he first leaves home. His father speaks in a general way about the virtues of "Application and Industry," but this is not really the language of labor discipline and the calling (3–6). His appeal is at least as plausibly to what I have been calling "aristocratic ideology": to a very traditionalistic social stratification and to the advisability of maintaining the station of one's birth. How is it, then, that the young Robinson learns to read the social meaning of his wish to ramble through the religious spectacles of Calvinist discipline? And since the Puritan's pursuit of grace might entail either stasis or pilgrimage, either social stability or change, why should his mobility appear so definitively a sign of his sin rather than a token of his election? When does the language of the calling enter Robinson's vocabulary?

On his first sea voyage, Robinson, in mortal fear, bitterly berates himself for "the Breach of my Duty to God and my Father" (7–8). Before this the narration of his early life has been relatively free of religious injunction. Robinson's father is a merchant who became successful through the sort of travel he now forbids his son. One of the older sons is dead; the other has disappeared. Designed now for the law and a "settled" life, Robinson thinks himself at eighteen too old to be set an attorney's clerk or an apprentice, and he seems momentarily to attribute his wanderlust to the marginality of his status in the family: "Being the third Son of the Family, and not bred to any Trade, my Head began to be fill'd very early with rambling Thoughts" (3). But whatever the psychological cause of it, Robinson soon finds a more satisfactory explanation for his unsettledness—more satisfactory because empowered with the ascription of sin—in the idea of a "duty" that has been breached. And this idea he seems to hear first from his friend's father, the master of the ship on which he had made his nearly fatal first voyage. Learning that the youth had sailed with him "only for a Trial in order to go farther Abroad," the master tells Robinson *"to take this for a plain and visible Token that you are not to be a Seafaring Man."* "Why, Sir," says Robinson, "will you go to Sea no more?" *"That is another Case,"* said he, *"it is my Calling, and therefore my Duty"* (14–15). This is Robinson's first lesson in casuistry, at least to our knowledge, and it is an important one. Duty is dictated by calling, and to be out of one's calling is certainly to be in sin. But how do you tell your calling if you have no clear intuition of it and have not been definitively bred to one? Parental authority is one guide. Another is the tokens and signs of divine will that can be read in experience, and it does not require a very subtle interpreter to read God's judgment in this particular case.

At this early stage Robinson is quite blind to providential signs. Yet even so, the narrative voice soon lets us know that returning home is not the only way he might at this point have altered his course for the better. For now Robinson begins to ship on a succession of voyages, and because he has "Money in my Pocket, and good Cloaths upon my Back, I would always go on board in the Habit of a Gentleman" rather than that of a common sailor. Like his creator, he is fond of upwardly mobile masquerade, but the result is that he remains idle and forfeits the opportunity to establish his calling at sea: for "as a Sailor . . . I had learn'd the Duty and Office of a Fore-mast Man; and in time might have quallified my self for a Mate or Lieutenant, if not for a Master" (16). Despite this bad choice, Robinson is lucky enough to be befriended by an honest Guinea captain, who teaches him some of the skills of both sailor and merchant (17). But before we can begin to ask if this employment has the potential of being a redemptive discipline, Robinson is captured by pirates and metamorphosed "from a Merchant to a miserable Slave . . . Now the Hand of Heaven had overtaken me, and I was undone without Redemption" (19).

Nor do his spiritual prospects improve when he escapes from Sallee and gains material prosperity as a planter in Brazil. The problem is more general than the fact of his readiness to sell Xury to the Portuguese captain by whom they are "deliver'd" (in any case Defoe seems to exercise some care in formulating the case so as to make it conscientiously acceptable).[10] It is not that Robinson is specifically and spectacularly sacrilegious, but that he is comprehensively devoid of moral and spiritual constraints. The Portuguese captain himself is a man of such exemplary fair dealing that he would seem to epitomize how the merchant is to pursue his calling; and he treats Robinson so "honourably" and "charitably" that the latter's coarse desire to "gr[o]w rich suddenly" can only suffer by comparison (33–34, 37, 89). Rather than follow the rule of charity or regulate his life by the satisfaction of necessities, Robinson

simply pursues his self-interest in Brazil. When the captain's good advice
leads to his receipt of some valuable goods, Robinson is content to
exploit the market for all he can get, selling them "to a very great Advantage; so that I might say, I had more than four times the Value of my first
Cargo, and was now infinitely beyond my poor Neighbour." In this way
Robinson's overextension and excess are palpably registered by his rapid
advancement over others. It is not the fact of being a trader, but his
"abus'd Prosperity," his unrationalized exploitation of exchange value,
that distinguishes him from those who might be said to pursue their
callings (37). The principles of subsistence and consumption are dominated by the unlimited desire to accumulate, a triumph of excess and
waste that is also expressed in the irony that now Robinson "was coming
into the very Middle Station, or upper Degree of low Life, which my
Father advised me to before; and which if I resolved to go on with, I
might as well ha' staid at Home" (35).[11]

By the same token, the voice of the Narrator makes it clear that despite
past sins, having wandered into this way of life, Robinson might yet have
made a decent calling of it. It is not strictly required, in other words, that
one remain in the station of one's birth. What Robinson fails in for a
second time is the identification of "those Prospects and those measures
of Life, which Nature and Providence concurred to present me with, and
to make my Duty." Our duty and calling are not objective entities, but
conditions in which we find ourselves and which we are able to intuit and
interpret into fulfillment. "As I had once done thus in my breaking away
from my Parents, so I could not be content now, but I must go and leave
the happy View I had of being a rich and thriving Man in my new
Plantation, only to pursue a rash and immoderate Desire of rising faster
than the Nature of the Thing admitted" (38). An incapacity to limit his
desires by sensing the natural and providential limits of his situation is
what makes Robinson successively a prodigal son, an unethical trader,
and now also an imprudent trader: "Now increasing in Business and in
Wealth," says the Narrator, "my Head began to be full of Projects and
Undertakings beyond my Reach" (37–38). When he is offered the chance
to oversee an illegal and highly profitable shipment of African slaves, he
is oblivious to the fact that it would have been "a fair Proposal" only if
made to one who did not already possess a "Settlement" in need of
looking after. For him to accept the offer is to do "the most preposterous
Thing that ever Man in such Circumstances could be guilty of," to
abandon the clear possibility of a settled calling. Nevertheless Robinson
enters into an agreement with his fellow planters and goes "on Board in
an evil Hour" (39–40).

So the prelude to shipwreck is a chronic incapacity to rationalize
worldly activity by the sanctions of a perceived moral duty. The many
years on the island overcome this incapacity by obliging Robinson, de-

void of human society, to experience the society of God. This experience has two crucial dimensions. First, in a state of solitude the greatest impediments to ethical behavior—other people—suddenly disappear. But second, what then remains is the otherness of divinity itself, the absolute moral standard now so inescapable that its very voice may be heard and internalized within one's own desires. Robinson's long isolation schools him in the psychological discipline needed to transform his activity into his calling. In the following pages I will review the central stages in this schooling.

3

I have already suggested that Robinson's island conversion depends upon a new-found ability to spiritualize his situation, to detect and interpret the signs of God's presence in his life on the island. As he explains it, the pleasures of this presence do not only compensate for the absence of human society. They also alter his understanding of his own desires, of what it is he really wants:

Thus I liv'd mighty comfortably, my Mind being entirely composed by resigning to the Will of God, and throwing my self wholly upon the Disposal of his Providence. This made my Life better than sociable, for when I began to regret the want of Conversation, I would ask my self whether thus conversing mutually with my own Thoughts, and, as I hope I may say, with even God himself by Ejaculations, was not better than the utmost Enjoyment of humane Society in the World.

I gave humble and hearty Thanks that God had been pleas'd to discover to me, even that it was possible I might be more happy in this Solitary Condition, than I should have been in a Liberty of Society, and in all the Pleasures of the World. That he could fully make up to me, the Deficiencies of my Solitary State, and the want of Humane Society by his Presence, and the Communications of his Grace to my Soul . . . my very Desires alter'd, my Affections chang'd their Gusts, and my Delights were perfectly new . . .

I look'd now upon the World as a Thing remote, which I had nothing to do with, no Expectation from, and indeed no Desires about: . . . I had neither the *Lust of the Flesh, the Lust of the Eye, or the Pride of Life*. I had nothing to covet; for I had all that I was now capable of enjoying. (135–36, 112–13, 128)

At such moments of radiant contentment, Robinson speaks as though he has shed not only all acquisitive appetites but all "wordly" ambition whatsoever, so that even the language of duty, labor discipline, and the calling has become an irrelevance. Yet we know this is not true. It is not only that he tells us that now "I was very seldom idle; but [had] regularly divided my Time, according to the several daily Employments that were before me, such as, *First,* My Duty to God, and the Reading of Scrip-

tures" (114). It is precisely the enterprising and furiously energetic performance of some of those other employments that dominates our permanent impression of this most industrious of narratives. Robinson does
not give over vocational ambition; on the contrary, he slowly and steadily
makes "all Trades in the World"—farmer, baker, potter, stonecutter,
carpenter, tailor, basketmaker—his calling (122). As he remarks, "By
making the most rational Judgment of things, every Man may be in time
Master of every mechanick Art . . . I improv'd my self in this time in all
the mechanick Exercises which my Necessities put me upon applying
my self to" (68, 144).

It is therefore not so much that Robinson moderates the immoderate
desires that plagued him in his former life, as that their ethical quality has
been altered—limited and therefore detoxified—by the alteration in his
external circumstance: by the substitution, that is, of the society of God
for human society. What this replacement achieves is, first of all, the
transformation of exchange value into value in use. After the shipwreck
but before his conversion, Robinson still believes that things acquire their
value through commodification in the marketplace: although work on
the island is discouragingly primitive, "my Time or Labour was little
worth, and so it was as well employ'd one way as another" (68). But as we
know from his celebrated, King James–version disdain for the found
money—"O Drug! Said I aloud, what art thou good for, Thou art not
worth to me"—Robinson is not slow to realize that there is no marketplace to be found on the island (57). And after a while he is completely
captivated by the distinction between use value and exchange value,
which he seizes many opportunities to rehearse. In the following passage
he pointedly applies it to his former employment, in which exchange
value played such a dominant role:

I might have rais'd Ship Loadings of Corn; but I had no use for it . . . I had
Timber enough to have built a Fleet of Ships. I had Grapes enough to have
made Wine, or to have cur'd into Raisins, to have loaded that Fleet, when they
had been built. But all I could make use of, was, All that was valuable . . . In a
Word, The Nature and Experience of Things dictated to me upon just Reflection, That all the good Things of this World, are no farther good to us, than
they are for our Use . . . I possess'd infinitely more than I knew what to do
with . . . I had, as I hinted before, a Parcel of Money . . . [But] *As it was,* I
had not the least Advantage by it, or Benefit from it. (128–29)

Robinson's tone of cautionary sobriety should not obscure for us the
liberation of being able to "possess infinitely," to accumulate limitless
possessions that cannot entail the risk of becoming commodities in exchange. "*Leaden-hall* Market could not have furnish'd a Table better than
I, in Proportion to the Company"; and the differences that are disclosed
by this analogy are fully as important to Robinson as are the similarities

(109). For here he can lay up great stocks of grain, fully indulging his "Desire of having a good Quantity for Store," without challenging the great end of personal consumption. Indeed, in combining capitalist abstinence with the just belief that "now I work'd for my Bread," Robinson implicitly tempers the danger of attributing an imaginary value to capitalist activity with a labor theory of value, so that all this industry may be confidently sanctified by the biblical conviction "that in time, it wou'd please God to supply me with Bread" (117–18, 123–24).[12]

If the absence of human society prohibits the exchange of goods and the dangerous creation of imaginary value, it also precludes the human register of potentially sinful social advancement and excess. Unlike his sojourn in Brazil, here "there were no Rivals. I had no Competitor, none to dispute Sovereignty or Command with me" (128). Again, this does not prevent Robinson from continuing to behave like a capitalist; it effaces the moral consequences of that behavior. We become aware of this in subtle ways. When he tells us how he first "fenc'd in, and fortify'd," and "enclos'd all my Goods," the voice of the Narrator adds that "there was no need of all this Caution from the Enemies that I apprehended Danger from" (59, 60). But later we see that this is not really so. For once Robinson has again become a farmer in earnest, he finds himself in the position not so much of a Brazilian planter as of an English enclosing landlord. In danger of losing his crop to "Enemies of several Sorts"— goats, hares, and especially birds—he describes his emergency capital improvements in language that is disturbingly evocative of seventeenth- and eighteenth-century agrarian conflicts:[13]

This I saw no Remedy for, but by making an Enclosure about it with a Hedge, which I did with a great deal of Toil; and the more, because it requir'd Speed. However, as my Arable Land was but small, suited to my Crop, I got it totally well fenc'd, in about three Weeks Time; and shooting some of the Creatures in the Day Time, I set my Dog to guard it in the Night . . . I staid by it to load my Gun, and then coming away I could easily see the Thieves sitting upon all the Trees about me, as if they only waited till I was gone away, and the Event proved it to be so . . . I was so provok'd . . . knowing that every Grain that they eat now, was, *as it might be said,* a Peck-loaf to me in the Consequence; but coming up to the Hedge, I fir'd again, and kill'd three of them. This was what I wish'd for; so I took them up, and serv'd them as we serve notorious Thieves in *England, (viz.)* Hang'd them in Chains for a Terror to others. (116–17)

But although Robinson gives vent here to the deep and disquieting emotions of the enclosing landlord, these "enemies," with whom he is indeed in mortal competition, are not expropriated peasants but birds and beasts of the field. The equivocal appetite for elevating oneself over one's neighbors has been slaked even as the categories by which such elevation might be registered—the social "stations" so significant to Robinson's father—

have been erased. And the obscure but pervasive sense of status inconsistency that has all along been expressed in Robinson's persistent desire to "ramble" is quashed under conditions that paradoxically exclude all reference groups whatsoever. There are only himself and God; and the only criteria by which to experience relative deprivation and reward are those dictated by divine justice and mercy.[14]

But as we have just seen in the image of the thieving wildlife, this is only literally true. All readers of *Robinson Crusoe* have been struck by the protagonist's propensity to populate and domesticate his island with figures from home. Unlike many authors of imaginary voyages, Defoe is disinclined to celebrate the reign of use value within the relatively exotic environs of a communist utopia. The passage on the thieving wildlife makes it clear that he is far more attracted by the private property of the landed estate, whose utopian character consists in the "magical extraction," in Raymond Williams's words, of its problematic inhabitants. When Robinson takes his first "Survey of the Island" and comes upon the Edenic valley where he will build the "Bower" that will serve as his "Country-House," he imagines "that this was all my own, that I was King and Lord of all this Country indefeasibly, and had a Right of Possession; and if I could convey it, I might have it in Inheritance, as compleatly as any Lord of a Manor in *England*" (98, 100, 101–2). Later he permits the figure to encompass the entire island: "I was Lord of the whole Mannor; or if I pleas'd, I might call my self King, or Emperor over the whole Country which I had Possession of" (128).[15]

If this fantasy of proprietorship appeals primarily to the impulse toward private ownership and capitalist improvement, there is at least an element here also of contemplative pastoralism and the domestic themes of Horatian retirement. Another way of saying this is that Defoe's island utopia is able to incorporate notions of value that are associated not only with capitalist and laboring industry but also with aristocratic ideology and its location of value in land. Of course, this syncretism can be found in the assimilationist posture of progressive ideology itself. Despite his trenchant attacks on the corruptions of lineage and aristocratic honor, Defoe was obsessed with the illusion of his own gentility, and at various stages in his career he proudly rode in the livery of his merchant's company, outrageously inflated his ancestry, and (going Francis Kirkman one better) employed the medium of print to become armigerous and to aristocratize his name from Foe to De Foe. Marx was certainly right to argue that the utopianism of *Robinson Crusoe* is not nostalgically conservative but progressive, that it is not "merely a reaction against oversophistication and a return to a misunderstood natural life," but "rather, the anticipation of 'civil society'."[16]

What must be added to Marx's view of the function of Defoe's utopia is the crucial and complementary religious element. And Robinson's labor discipline is as successful as it is in confirming his sense of election because the neutralization of its social volatility has been ensured by his utter solitude. This solitude is challenged, of course, when Robinson discovers the print of a man's foot on the shore (an event whose significance I will turn to momentarily). But it is important to recognize the volatility even of Robinson's imaginative figures, which in truth is essential also to the significance of that discovery. As Maximillian Novak has remarked, "If [Robinson's] triumph over the island is mostly an economic conquest, it is an imaginative conquest as well." Like George Pine, Robinson "bestows culture" on his environment, and his creation of mere metaphors for social dominance improves on Pine's procreation of a new population, because it more thoroughly evades the dangers of social ambition and self-aggrandizement. But as we know, Defoe was deeply ambivalent about "the Power of Imagination" and imaginative creativity.[17] Some of its riskiness can be felt in the self-conscious drollery with which Robinson extends the figure of his island lordship: "It would have made a Stoick smile to have seen, me and my little Family sit down to Dinner; there was my Majesty the Prince and Lord of the whole Island; I had the Lives of all my Subjects at my absolute Command. I could hang, draw, give Liberty, and take it away, and no Rebels among all my Subjects" (148). No more than a poignant fiction, of course. But shortly Robinson panics at the thought of being joined by other people, and he is moved not only to reaffirm the old language of social stratification that had been suspended by his utopian solitude but also to remind himself of the *real* sources of absolute sovereignty and creativity: "I consider'd that this was the Station of Life the infinitely wise and good Providence of God had determin'd for me, that . . . I was not to dispute his Sovereignty, who, as I was his Creature, had an undoubted Right by Creation to govern and dispose of me absolutely as he thought fit . . . 'Twas my unquestion'd Duty to resign my self absolutely and entirely to his Will" (157).

Robinson's image of his "little family at dinner" is distracting in part because it suggests the speciousness of a submissive resignation achieved by the brute excision of all opportunities for competitive aggression. Defoe was conscious that his fiction of a desert-island conversion entailed this vulnerability. Still in the voice of Robinson Crusoe he later observed: "It is the Soul's being entangled by outward Objects, that interrupts its Contemplation of divine Objects, which is the Excuse for these Solitudes, and makes the removing the Body from those outward Objects seemingly necessary; but what is there of Religion in all this? . . . a vicious Inclination remov'd from the Object, is still a vicious Inclination." Robinson's imaginative enclosures are more treacherous than his physical ones because they cannot be held accountable to a standard that is clearly distinct from their own. At least part of his island experience, he speculates, was a function of "the brain-sick Fancy, the vapourish Hypochondriack Imagination . . . it was not meer Imagination, but it was the Imagination rais'd up to Disease." Defoe had used similar language— "my brain-begotten faith"—to characterize the nature of his religious doubts during his early crisis over entering the Presbyterian ministry. The Puritan elevation of the private conscience, the saint's injunction to a personal and vigilant spiritualization of all experience, invited simultaneously a rapt sanctification of the world and a nagging uncertainty as to the difference between divine and human spirituality. As we have seen, Robinson's conversion depends on his capacity to look both upward and inward. The lesson of the sprouting seeds, as he tells us pointedly, is not that God works miracles but that he works through us: "For it was really the Work of Providence as to me, that should order or appoint, that 10 or 12 Grains of Corn should remain unspoil'd . . . As also, that I should throw it out in that particular Place" (79). But once the saint has learned to read the presence of God in his own acts and intuitions, he has also become adept at discovering his own intuitions in the world at large. This dialectic is intensified considerably once Robinson finds the human footprint.[18]

4

Remarking on "how many various Shapes affrighted Imagination represented Things to me in," Robinson passes rapidly through several interpretations of the print: that it is his own fancy; the work of the Devil; the mark of a savage from the mainland; even that it "might be a meer Chimera of [his] own; and that this Foot might be the Print of [his] own Foot" (154, 157). This last possibility suggests to him that in his panic he has been like the credulous author of an apparition narrative, that "[he] had play'd the Part of those Fools, who strive to make stories of Spectres, and Apparitions; and then are frighted at them more than any body" (158).[19] But Robinson's relief "to think that there was really nothing in it, but my own Imagination" is short-lived. He cannot resist subjecting the print to empirical measurement, and the disconfirmation "fill'd my Head with new Imaginations, and gave me the Vapours again to the highest Degree" (158, 159). His response to this renewed fear of the presence of other people is basically double. On the one hand, as we have seen, he ostentatiously resubmits himself to God's absolute will and sovereignty. On the other hand he apparently forgets this strategy of submission, and, like Saul, thinks "not only that the *Philistines* were upon him; but that God had forsaken him" (159). That the presence of human society should seem to threaten the absence of God's society is built in, of course, to the utopian mechanism of Robinson's solitude, and he now hits upon a strategy that, ostensibly directed at the putative savages, is also symbolically aimed at a divine audience and in fact only extends his other strategy, that of humble submission: "The first Thing I propos'd to my self, was, to throw down my Enclosures, and turn all my tame Cattle [i.e., his goats] wild into the Woods, that the Enemy might not find them . . . Then to the simple Thing of Digging up my two Corn Fields . . . [and] then to demolish my Bower, and Tent" (159). Physical, like metaphorical, enclosures bespeak a vanity whose traces must be destroyed. Robinson soon thinks better of this wholesale act of decreation, but he does plant a thick grove around his principal fortification so as to ensure that "no Men of what kind soever, would ever imagine that there was any Thing beyond it, much less a Habitation"; and he makes "all Things without look as wild and natural as [he can]" (161, 182).

These frantic oscillations and adjustments suggest in Robinson a fundamental confusion—of self and other, of self and "the enemy," of God and the enemy, of God and self—born of his incomplete internalization of divine righteousness and autonomy. In wishing now to destroy the unnatural signs of his own inventiveness with which he has defaced the landscape, Robinson recurs to the terms of his father, by which he saw himself as a young man bent on rebellion against God and "nature" (5, 38, 194). But the young Robinson was not only unnatural; he was also *too* natural, a "wild" man who "acted like a meer Brute from the Principles of Nature," devoid of revelation, and who had to be ensnared, enclosed, and tamed by God on the island (16, 88). Robinson has learned to internalize this principle of divine cultivation to some degree, for he has trapped, "penn'd," and domesticated the wild beasts of his island, most notably its goats.[20] Now he wavers in his confidence, fearing that his cultured creativity bespeaks only the old wildness and rebellion. But the very cause of his fear ultimately helps solidify his conviction.

Robinson is repelled by the savages, by their "unnatural Custom" of cannibalism and by "the Degeneracy of Humane Nature" that it represents, and for a while his "Invention" and "Imagination" and "Fancy" are completely absorbed with alternative schemes for their efficient massacre (165, 168, 169, 170). But in a satiric movement characteristic of travel narrative, he soon reflects that the culpability of these savages may yet be less than that of corrupted Europeans (his own early prodigality being a case in point), since "they do not know it to be an Offence, and then commit it in Defiance of Divine Justice, as we do in almost all the Sins we commit" (171).[21] Robinson repudiates his bloody imaginings by intuiting that they do not issue from a divine source. Pondering the case at hand, he asks himself: "What Authority, or Call I had, to pretend to be Judge and Executioner upon these Men as Criminals . . . How do I know what God himself judges in this particular Case? . . . I was perfectly out of my Duty, when I was laying all my bloody Schemes . . . I gave most humble Thanks on my Knees to God, that had thus deliver'd me from Blood-Guiltiness; beseeching him . . . that I might not lay my Hands upon them, unless I had a more clear Call from Heaven to do it, in Defence of my own Life" (170–71, 173). As the language of duty and the calling imply, Robinson shows, in the very censoring of his first impulses, that he has learned to read the signs of God's will in his conscience sufficiently well to know how to act upon them. If the savages "have no other Guide than that of their own abominable and vitiated Passions" (170), Robinson is indeed (as he had vainly thought at first) now "distinguish'd from such dreadful Creatures as these" because he has begun to internalize a divine guide whereby to moderate and limit his own abominable passions. And so it becomes "a certain Rule with me, That whenever I found those secret Hints, or pressings of my Mind . . . I never fail'd to obey the secret Dictate; though I knew no other Reason for it, than that such a Pressure, or such a Hint hung upon my Mind." The very persistence of an impulse, in other words, may argue its affiliation with the "secret Intimations of Providence" (175, 176). In the remainder of the narrative, Robinson's increasing exposure to elements of external, human society will proceed alongside his increasingly confident internalization of God's society.

The first test of his capacity to read the marks of God on his own mind comes not from the savages but from a Spanish ship that appears one day on the horizon. Robinson's mind is filled with imaginings, fancies, and conjectures that are violently "rendred present to [his] Mind by the Power of Imagination": "In all the Time of my solitary Life, I never felt so earnest, so strong a Desire after the Society of my Fellow-Creatures, or so deep a Regret at the want of it" (188). Are these "ardent Wishes" the secret hints of providence? It soon appears that the ship has been broken apart by the sea, and the question then becomes whether "there might be yet some living Creature on board, whose Life I might not only save, but might by saving that Life, comfort my own to the last Degree; and . . . I thought the Impression was so strong upon my Mind, that it could not be resisted, that it must come from some invisible Direction" (189). Nothing comes of the rescue mission, but it provides Robinson with experience both in the identification of his desires as heaven-sent and in the way this internalization of providence entails a reciprocal expansion of his own identity as one not only delivered by God but able to deliver others as well. However, the mechanism is still uncertain, and the experiment is not without its costs. Robinson is soon beset with guilt for his preoccupation with a physical deliverance from the island, and it is now that he recalls his "ORIGINAL SIN" of leaving home and its recurrence in Brazil, when he could not be content with the "confin'd Desires" with which providence had blessed him. Here he is once more "fill'd with Projects and Designs . . . for a Ramble" (194). Yet this episode of backsliding does not end, like earlier ones, with a chastening moralization. Or rather it extends that series into new territory.

What happens is that Robinson remains completely oblivious to the "Calm of Mind in my Resignation to Providence" that he had felt earlier, and his obsession with a physical deliverance becomes so palpable that he has "no Power to turn my Thoughts to any thing, but to the Project of a Voyage to the Main[land], which came upon me with such Force, and such an Impetuosity of Desire, that it was not to be resisted" (198). We recognize here, in the distinctive language of God's secret workings on the mind, the logic of inner conviction Robinson has prescribed for himself. A passion that is initially distinguished explicitly from prov- idential directive succeeds, through the sheer force of its persistence, in redefining itself as nothing other than the irresistible dictate of provi- dence. This transvaluation of desire, extraordinary as it is, is given yet more explicit form in what immediately ensues. Agitated beyond de- scription, Robinson falls asleep and dreams that he delivers a savage from the cannibals, who afterward becomes his servant (198–99). And as he had said on an earlier and different occasion, "As I imagin'd, so it was" (51). For a year and a half later the dream materializes before his eyes, and Robinson behaves like nothing so much as the creative author of this drama, dutifully playing his assigned role but sometimes also exercising the playwright's revisionary prerogative when it pleases him to do so.[22]

What of his earlier intuition that the murder of savages is not part of his call or duty? Robinson does indeed recollect now that "I had greatly scrupled the Lawfulness of it to me," and although he knows he might rationalize the breaking of these scruples by arguments of self-preserva- tion and self-defense, the real sanction is simply that "the eager prevailing Desire of Deliverance at length master'd all the rest" (199–200). So when the savages and their escaping prisoner, far down the beach, begin to run toward him, he tells us, in a suggestive choice of words, "I kept my Station." And when it appears that Friday (for it is of course he) will reach Robinson well before the savages do, "It came now very warmly upon my Thoughts, and indeed irresistibly . . . that I was call'd plainly by Providence to save this poor Creature's Life" (202). Providence, rebuffed when it counseled resignation, turns out to have been counseling impas- sioned activity all along. Divine and natural law, abandoning the posture of a moderating and limiting authority over and against human desire, now boldly join forces with it.[23]

When Robinson "saves" Friday from the cannibals, he becomes his deliverer. As God has communicated with Robinson, so Robinson speaks to Friday by "making Signs to him" (203–5). Friday soon learns enough broken English to say, "*You teach wild Mans be good sober tame Mans*": as God tamed Robinson, so Robinson now tames this brute, and he has reason to hope that he has been "made an Instrument under Providence to save" not just the life but "the Soul of a poor Savage" (226, 220). Friday, for his part, makes "all the Signs to me of Subjection, Servitude, and Submission imaginable, to let me know, how he would serve me as long as he liv'd" (206). Thus is this necessarily metaphorical relationship of creator to creature quickly literalized into one of so-ciopolitical subordination, and with this pledge Robinson's dominion on the island ceases to be figurative. Now he names Friday and tells him that his own name will be "*Master*"; but Robinson's new mastery is articulated as much by the mute human presence of what he is not, a slave, and human society is established by the fact of difference (206).[24] At the same time, Friday, like Behn's Oroonoko, is a black man whose "*European*" beauty aids in the further differentiation of cultivated nature from the barbarian. He quickly learns to renounce his cannibalism, and when the master next confronts the savages, he enlists the aid of his civilized slave. Once again Robinson scruples at unsanctioned executions, and although in a "Fit of Fury" at their barbarity, he is if anything even more conscien-tious in his determination not to act without "a Call" (231–33). But the discovery that one of the cannibals' victims is a white European "fir'd all the very Soul within me," and his scruples are countermanded by a higher directive: "Are you ready, *Friday?* said I; yes, says he; let fly then, says I, in the Name of God" (234).

Defoe's aim here is not, of course, to suggest the religious hypocrisy of his protagonist—to make of Robinson what Bunyan makes of Mr. Mony-love—but rather to disclose the exquisitely subtle adjustments that comprise the process of arriving at a firm conviction of moral rec-titude. The inescapable aura of irony that we sense in parts of Robinson's long passage out of sinfulness bespeaks the instability of ideas and institu-tions his author has tried to freeze in the midst of a secularization crisis. And in this respect it is not to the point to show the fidelity of Defoe's contradictory conflations of dependence and independence, of determin-ation and autonomy, to the conventions of spiritual autobiography, for those conventions themselves evince the same overarching instability, and (another way of saying the same thing) Defoe is not writing a spir-itual autobiography. It is not only our hindsight that raises these ques-tions, as previous chapters have sufficiently demonstrated. Defoe himself (not to mention his critics) was as inclined to reprove "entitling a dis-temper'd Brain" to "tacking the awful Name of Providence to every fancy of their own" as he was to rebuke the false claim to historicity. *Robinson Crusoe* at times emits the aura of irony because, like all ideology, it is dedicated to the instrumental disclosure—in Defoe's case with un-paralleled penetration and candor—of a complex of contradictions that it is simultaneously dedicated to mediating and rendering intelligible. The central and recurrent form of this contradiction can be expressed, as we have seen, in the notion of the human internalization of divinity, and it is precisely because Defoe "still" seeks to understand the problem of mediation in the awesome terms of a Christian culture that we, who have long since stopped trying, are sometimes distracted from the profundity to the absurdity of the effort.[25]

5

By now Robinson has become accomplished enough in that internalization to speak, without emotional repercussions, of having "an invincible Impression upon my Thoughts, that my Deliverance was at hand, and that I should not be another Year in this Place" (229). So when the arrival of the English mutineers is preceded by the counsel, "Let no Man despise the secret Hints and Notices of Danger, which sometimes are given him," we are prepared to be asked to view the sequel as a plain interposition of providence (250). Having masterfully trapped these "Brutes" as he once did his wild goats, Robinson remarks "that Providence had ensnar'd them in their own Ways," and he "fences" them in his island "Prison," as God first enclosed him there, on his final deliverance from it (255, 275–76, 269–70). Now Robinson has become, quite insistently, a "Deliverer." But he would not wish this furious activity in delivering others so as to help ensure his own escape to obscure his essential passivity: "For I saw my Deliverance indeed visibly put into my Hands," and "the whole Transaction seemed to be a Chain of Wonders; that such things as these were the Testimonies we had of a secret Hand of Providence governing the World" (273). But as this language of "governing" reminds us, *Robinson Crusoe* is an experiment in the internalization not only of divinity but of sociopolitical authority, and it is in this dimension of experience that Robinson's eventual deliverance from the island depends upon the progressive literalization of relationships that at first were only figurative.[26]

For though he can never be said to "become" God, with the gradual population of his island Robinson does come to exercise absolute sovereignty. This is true not only of his paradigmatic colonial relationship with Friday but also of his rule over other human beings. Once again he is initially inclined to express it as a diverting metaphor, a merely imaginative construct:

> My Island was now peopled, and I thought my self very rich in Subjects; and it was a merry Reflection which I frequently made, How like a King I look'd. First of all, the whole Country was my own meer Property; so that I had an undoubted Right of Dominion. 2dly, My People were perfectly subjected: I was absolute Lord and Law-giver; they all owed their Lives to me, and were ready to lay down their Lives, *if there had been Occasion of it,* for me. It

was remarkable too, we had but three Subjects, and they were of three different Religions . . . However, I allow'd Liberty of Conscience throughout my Dominions. (241)

But so far from feeling guiltily impelled to an implicit retraction of the analogy, Robinson very soon has reason to insist upon its terms. Of the Spaniard he has saved he requires that his companions swear "upon their solemn Oath, That they should be absolutely under my Leading, as their Commander and Captain . . . and to be directed wholly and absolutely by my Orders . . . and that he would bring a Contract from them under their Hands for that Purpose" (245). Of the English captain he demands "that while you stay on this Island with me, you will not pretend to any Authority here; and . . . you will . . . be govern'd by my Orders" (256). And on the climactic victory over the mutineers he conceals his own presence "for Reasons of State" (268). On the basis of a legitimacy no greater than that of settlement and long possession, Robinson has truly come to exercise absolute sovereignty over his territory.[27]

Most important, Robinson is effectively socialized in these authoritative roles by the accreditation of his growing community. He is treated as the "*Generalissimo*" and the "Commander" of the island: "They all call'd me Governour," he says, and as in the case of Sancho Panza, we have good reason to attribute his dignified authority in these roles not simply to the "humoring" of a batty old hermit but to an experience that permits the manifestation of what in some sense was always there in potentiality (267–69). Robinson's consummate control of his environment persuades both the savages and the mutineers that his is an "enchanted Island," but they are degenerations of the race, and, like Sancho's, Robinson's governorship lays claim to being not an enchantment but a disenchantment of the world (243, 266). We have watched him progress, like Bunyan's Christian, through a series of elevations to increasingly authoritative roles, and the end of the series—the reward toward which the progression has always been directed—is the long-awaited deliverance from captivity so as to assume the status of, not robe nobility but private citizen: the self-possessed and enlightened capitalist entrepreneur of the modern age. The suspended time on the island has provided the laboratory conditions for acquiring, slowly and with relative impunity, the psychological equipment needed for possessive individualism. Now Robinson has internalized his utopia, and he is ready to return to society at large.[28]

For these reasons what remains is (as most readers feel) largely anti-climactic; nonetheless there are several points of interest. When Robinson first keeps the money that he ostentatiously scorns, we laugh at him; we know that he is in sin and that he is possessed of "a rash and immoderate desire of rising faster than the nature of the thing admitted" (57, 38). But

when, on his departure from the island, he takes with him the considerable store of money that he has accumulated over the years, he is implicitly in pursuit of his calling; his desire, and the nature of the thing,
have become indistinguishable (278). What this means is that the imaginary value generated by exchange has become lawful because it has become real. Outwardly nothing has changed; the magical time on the
island is immediately replaced by the bewildering but completely characteristic barrage of financial and legal quantifications by which Defoe
generally tends to signify modern experience. But in another sense everything has changed. It is not only the old Portuguese captain who manifests his "honesty," "friendship," "honour," and "trust"; all the capitalists we now encounter are animated by these virtues, and the
atmosphere is thick with fair dealing (280–84).

This is also true of Robinson, who proceeds to exercise his charity not
only on the captain (who had been so charitable years earlier) but on his
two sisters, on the old widow in London, and on the Brazilian monastery
and the poor (285–87). And despite Robinson's return to civilization, an
air of enchantment lingers over Brazil, as though the magic of providence
had effected a merger with that of capitalism. For although Robinson has
become a wealthy man, neither he nor we have experienced any of the
time and exploitation that were presumably expended in that laborious
but invisible creation of exchange value. On the contrary, says Robinson,
"I found all my Wealth about me," of which "I was now Master, all on a
Sudden." Indeed, the event is in full accord with all his recent experiences, for it is an "Estate that Providence . . . put into my Hands" (284–
86). Of course, this painless receipt of God's grace, this unrelieved honor
among merchants, does not provide a "realistic" picture of capitalist
activity, as Defoe well knew it would not. It may be plausible, however,
to see him engaged here in the tangible externalization of Robinson's now
securely internalized utopia, in the representation of the psychological
state of being a principled possessive individualist, fully reconciled to the
naturalness and morality of the pursuit of self-interest.

But in the crossing of the Pyrenees, Defoe clearly acknowledges that
the world remains a treacherous place even for those whose minds are
guided by providence. Robinson's desire to avoid a sea voyage is directly
confirmed, in fact, by the familiar signs: "But let no Man slight the
strong Impulses of his own Thoughts in Cases of such Moment" (288; cf.
250). Despite this, the crossing exposes his traveling party to as dangerous an assault of uncontrolled natural violence—the ravenous mountain wolves—as he has ever encountered, and he concludes that "I would
much rather go a thousand Leagues by Sea, though I were sure to meet
with a Storm once a Week" (302). Their mountain "Guide" had turned
out to be "a Wretched faint-hearted Fellow" (297): had Robinson unaccountably been mistaken in his interpretation of God's secret hints? De-

foe does not answer this question, but immediately after the close escape from the wolves we meet Robinson's "principal Guide . . . my good antient Widow" in London, a "good Gentlewoman" in whom he finds complete "Integrity" and "trust" in the management of his affairs; and the contrast at least confirms the relative moral safety of his financial dealings (303).[29] Admitting with a clear conscience that "I was inur'd to a wandring Life," Robinson has now returned to his earliest scenes of prodigality. At this point, Defoe creates for him a wife, two sons, and a daughter, as though to give this long-lost younger son a second family from which to detach once again; but although we hear nothing more of them, Robinson adopts his two nephews. Between these stepsons he divides his own equivocation between assimilation and supersession, settlement and travel: "The eldest having something of his own, I bred up as a Gentleman, and gave him a Settlement of some addition to his Estate, after my Decease; the other I put out to a Captain of a Ship . . . And this young Fellow afterwards drew me in, as old as I was, to farther Adventures my self" (304–5).

What is crucial about Robinson Crusoe's achievement of social success is not the degree of his elevation but his capacity to justify each station to which he attains as the way of nature and the will of God. As we have seen, this is a learned capacity. The product of his experience first in the society of God and then, gradually, among other people, it represents the hard-won lesson that the metaphysical realm of the Spirit may be accommodated and rendered accessible as the psychological realm of Mind. It is Defoe's remarkable achievement not simply to have provided this psychological access to spiritual crisis but to have specified it, with the mediating guidance of Puritan casuistry and soteriology, to the concrete dimension of material and social ambition. Like Francis Kirkman, Robinson has been able to internalize a creative capacity, and to "spiritualize" his physical mobility—his "rambling"—into social mobility. But unlike Francis (for whom the language of repentance is truly no more than an "editorial policy"), he has mediated this long passage by that other strenuous movement of spiritualization which we see in Edward Coxere, the passage from physical to spiritual mobility. For these reasons he is a great exemplar not only of the Weber thesis but of progressive ideology.

In *Robinson Crusoe,* epistemology is so inextricably embedded in narrative substance that it may feel artificial to separate questions of truth from questions of virtue; but the distinction can be made. It is clear enough that Defoe's claim to historicity oversees the narrative's formal procedures. If it is complicated by the island, the journal, and the temporal dislocations of God's society and the power of imagination, that is because Defoe gives to the notion of the true history of the individual so intimate and introspective a form that it comes close to looking more like self-creation. This applies as well to the dominant, progressive ideology of the narrative, whose account of virtue delivered from early sin and then amply confirmed by the trials and rewards of providence is threatened repeatedly by the never-articulated insight that virtue is nothing but the ability to invoke providence with conviction.

Defoe's narrative hovers on the edge of these dialectical reversals because of the sheer power and perspicuity of his vision. But we should not mistake this crucial element of instability for his central narrative energy, which is generated instead by the figure of the confident entrepreneur whose astonishing descent to the subjective roots of objective and empirical reality has been turned so productively to the stabilizing of that reality that it can be treated as though it had never happened. Defoe's first important work, *An Essay upon Projects* (1697), celebrated the spirit of scientific and technological reform that seemed to contemporaries the capstone of the empirical revolution. But as Jonathan Swift showed with unequaled acerbity, the solid character of the materialistic projector concealed within itself the subversive and subjective heresy of psychological projection. To see the narrative results of a conscious and total dedication to the enactment of those reversals which Defoe has set in motion, we must turn our attention now to Swift.

Ten

Parables of the Younger Son (II):
Swift and the Containment of Desire

I

For a brief time fellow servants of the Tory ministry, Defoe and Swift were never on close, or even cordial, terms. The cultural gulf between the two men, evident enough in their educational and religious differences, can be felt most palpably as a matter of social status. Swift's utter disdain—in 1706 he disingenuously referred to Defoe as "the fellow that was *pilloryed,* I have forgot his name"—elicited an exasperated defensiveness that supports the contention that Defoe "lashed out at Swift less as an individual than as the representative of a social class which treated him and his dearest social aspirations with contempt." Yet Swift hardly saw himself as patrician. To Bolingbroke he said that "my Birth although from a Family not undistinguished in its time is many degrees inferior to Yours . . . I a Younger Son of younger Sons, You born to a great Fortune." Swift had no brothers; the stance of the younger son served as a delicate rebuke of the nobleman for assuming that their material hardships were remotely comparable.[1]

In his panegyric to Sir William Temple many years earlier, Swift had adopted this same stance, complaining that nature unjustly denied to the indifferent poet what she lavished on his esteemed patron:

> Shall I believe a Spirit so divine
> 　　Was cast in the same Mold with mine?
> Why then does Nature so unjustly share
> Among her Elder Sons the whole Estate?
> 　　And all her Jewels and her Plate,
> Poor we *Cadets* of Heav'n, not worth her Care,
> Take up at best with Lumber and the Leavings of a Fate . . .

Here the conceit is that Swift by nature is without deserts and yet deserves more than he gets. The posture of the younger son defined for him a condition of extraordinary instability. Swift believed that the delusions of freethinking were most likely to thrive "amongst the worst Part of the Soldiery, made up of Pages, younger Brothers of obscure Families, and others of desperate Fortunes." But he also wistfully imagined that the "*New-men*" whom the crown was periodically obliged to raise to the pinnacles of state service were "sometimes younger Brothers." It is the distressing spectacle of unrecognized merit that most feeds the conservative psychology of the deprived younger son, and Swift was often inclined to see his own career as a series of missed opportunities for advancement—missed not for a lack of talents in the aspirant but for a lack of gratitude and justice in his masters. Inadequately rewarded for his services to the great, Swift learned a cynicism toward them and their favorites that was consonant with his broader reading of recent English history. On occasion he represented this experience of political and social deprivation in terms of aimless mobility and exile. In the ode to Temple he is "to the Muse's Gallies ty'd," perpetually and vainly struggling to reach shore. To his friends he later described himself, torn between countries and employments, as "a vexed unsettled Vagabond." "I may call my self a stranger in a strange land."[2]

The life of Swift's greatest character shares some of these general features. Lemuel Gulliver begins his travel narrative with the following words:

My Father had a small Estate in *Nottinghamshire;* I was the Third of five Sons. He sent me to *Emanuel-College* in *Cambridge,* at Fourteen Years old, where I resided three Years, and applied my self close to my Studies: But the Charge of maintaining me (although I had a very scanty Allowance) being too great for a narrow Fortune; I was bound Apprentice to Mr. *James Bates,* an eminent Surgeon in *London,* with whom I continued four Years.[3]

Gulliver is one of those younger sons whose "fortunes and employments," in the words of William Sprigge, "are not correspondent to the grandure of their birth and education."[4] Having the foresight to acquire skills "useful in long Voyages," which "I always believed it would be some time or other my Fortune to do," Gulliver studies navigation and physic, and he does make several voyages before resolving "to settle in *London,* to which Mr. *Bates,* my Master, encouraged me" (I, i, 3). So he marries and sets up in practice; but his master soon dies and his business begins to fail. Gulliver goes to sea again, grows "weary" of it, resumes his practice unsuccessfully, and "after three Years Expectation that things would mend," enters employment on the ship that will take him to Lilliput (I, i, 4).

Thus Gulliver's first travels are undertaken in default of a more settled and upward mobility at home. After the voyage to Lilliput, however, the idea of physical travel takes on more of the financial and moral ambiguity it has in other narratives I have discussed, and the change in tone is effected by familiar narrative strategies. The second voyage begins with "my insatiable Desire of seeing foreign Countries," but also "in Hopes to improve my Fortunes." This expectation is not unreasonable, for Gulliver has already "made a considerable Profit by shewing my Cattle to many Persons of Quality" (I, viii, 63–64). But events soon conspire to cast ethical doubts on such "improvements." The tables are turned in Brobdingnag, when the avaricious farmer, "finding how profitable I was like to be, resolved to carry me to the most considerable Cities of the Kingdom" and "to shew me in all the Towns by the Way . . . to any Village or Person of Quality's House where he might expect Custom" (II, ii, 83). The echo is unmistakable: "The more my Master got by me, the more unsatiable he grew" (II, iii, 85). It is no doubt this dangerous connection between physical mobility and the indulgence of unlimited appetite that evokes, as in *Robinson Crusoe,* the retrospective voice of the repentant Narrator. Cornered in the Brobdingnagian cornfield and waiting for the enormous reapers to descend upon him, Gulliver, "wholly overcome by Grief and Despair," "bemoaned my desolate Widow, and Fatherless Children: I lamented my own Folly and Wilfulness in attempting a second Voyage against the Advice of all my Friends and Relations" (II, i, 70). But like Robinson, Gulliver is also able to disown responsibility and to project his desire for a fortune onto Fortune. Part II begins with his "having been condemned by Nature and Fortune to an active and restless Life," and it ends as his "Wife protested I should never go to Sea any more; although my evil Destiny so ordered, that she had not Power to hinder me; as the Reader may know hereafter" (II, i, 67, 133).

The success of the younger son in Defoe's narrative depends on his ability to internalize providence and to naturalize his appetites; less sympathetically, we might say that he learns how to project his desire and then to forget that he has done it. Gulliver never attains that comfort. He undertakes his third voyage because he receives an advantageous proposal, "the Thirst I had of seeing the World, notwithstanding my past Misfortunes, continuing as violent as ever" (III, i, 137–38). His decision to make the fourth interrupts a brief period at home "in a very happy Condition, if I could have learned the Lesson of knowing when I was well" (IV, i, 205). Like Robinson, Gulliver undergoes a decisive island conversion. Inseparable from his conversion experience, however, is the necessity of remaining in the physical presence of the godlike Houyhnhnms and in exile from human society. "But it was decreed by Fortune, my perpetual Enemy, that so great a Felicity should not fall to my Share" (IV, vii, 242). In fact it is a decree of the Grand Council of the Houyhnhnms, "from whence I date all the succeeding Misfortunes of my Life" (IV, ix, 257). Character and Narrator merge at the end, but it is scarcely an act of reconciliation or "atonement." For Gulliver ends radically at odds with himself, violently repudiating his own human nature yet spurned by that other nature with which he has learned to identify so closely. The expectations of the younger son so absolutely and permanently exceed all possibility of reward that status inconsistency becomes a biological condition of existence.

I will return to the land of the Houyhnhnms. For the moment it is enough to see that Swift's narrative both imitates the general movement of the spiritual autobiography and subverts it, by giving us a protagonist whose conviction of depravity issues not in repentance and faith but in the paradoxically prideful mortifications of misanthropy. By the same token, Gulliver's career (and those of several surrogates) both recapitulates that of the progressive, upwardly mobile younger son and parodically negates it in two distinct, and characteristically conservative, trajectories: that of industrious virtue insufficiently rewarded, and that of upstart ambition rewarded beyond all deserts. F. P. Lock is right to compare *Gulliver's Travels* not only to More's *Utopia* but also to Machiavelli's *The Prince,* for Swift's plot is profoundly concerned with questions of state service, and throughout his travels Gulliver repeatedly assumes the role of the "new man," symbolically and unequivocally sundered from any past "inheritance" by his status as a wandering alien who wades ashore willing and eager to serve the reigning prince and receive his due recompense.[5]

The notoriously discontinuous quality of Gulliver's character throughout much of his travels has frequently been cited to confirm the status of *Gulliver's Travels* as a "satire" rather than a "novel." But the retrospective standards by which we judge what is "novelistic" are of problematic relevance to the generically uncertain narratives that are native to the period of the novel's gradual stabilization. It may therefore be more instructive to see the discontinuity of Gulliver's character as a strategy that permits him to reflect satirically upon the serviceable hero of progressive ideology in two very different ways. On the one hand, he is the obsequious sycophant who seems always in the act of "prostrating" himself "at his Majesty's Feet," devoting his "Life to her Majesty's Service," embracing the role of "useful Servant," "most humble Creature and Vassal," and "Favourite," and humbly forbearing to rehearse for us just how honorably he has been treated (I, iii, 28; II, iii, 85–86, 90, iv, 97, viii, 123). Of course, his pride ensures that we will know this very well; a case in point is his vain and insistent allusion to his robe nobility after being honored with the Lilliputian title *Nardac*—"the highest Title of Honour among them"—in reward for the theft of the Blefuscudian fleet (I, v, 37, 39, vi, 49–50). Gulliver's rivalries for court precedence with the Lilliputian High Treasurer and the Brobdingnagian dwarf are equally demeaning, and like the theft of the fleet, his "signal Service" to the enormous king (blandly advising absolute despotism) and to the tiny queen (urinating on her palace) do not speak highly of his virtue and merit (II, iii, 91–92; I, v, 39–40; II, vi, 111, vii, 118). And as we watch Gulliver behaving like a reprehensible upstart, we also hear how this particular career pattern of status inconsistency has come to dominate the modern world. In Lilliput, the "Skills" that earn court preferment are those of the "Rope-Dancer," and honorific "Girdles" are awarded on the basis of "*leaping* and *creeping*" (I, iii, 22–23). To the Brobdingnag king it is evident that despite Gulliver's assurances, it is the great exception "that Men are ennobled on Account of their Virtue" in England (II, vi, 116). Later Gulliver is able to confirm that in modern Europe the most scandalous vices are likely to win "high Titles of Honour, and prodigious Estates," and he goes so far as to admit that even in England, our ancestors' "pure native Virtues [are] prostituted for a Piece of Money by their Grand-children" in pursuit of political interest (III, viii, 184, 185–86). Once in Houyhnhnmland, Gulliver has become quite trenchant on the "three Methods" by which an Englishman "may rise to be Chief Minister," and "Scoundrels [are] raised from the Dust upon the Merit of their Vices" (IV, vi, 239, x, 261).

But Gulliver's example also teaches the equally conservative lesson of, not "vice rewarded" but "merit punished." While his industrious virtue often looks more like obsequious ambition, we also find throughout Part I the thread of a sober and dignified complaint at the "immeasurable . . . Ambition" and "Passions" of princes and their ingratitude to those who serve them well (I, v, 37, 38, vii, 57, viii, 61). Fully "conscious of [his] own Merits and Innocence," Gulliver learns that his enemies at court have secretly obtained his impeachment for treason, and that he has been sentenced to blinding and to starvation by slow degrees. The punishment is deemed lenient; and after all, "it would be sufficient for you to see by the Eyes of the Ministers, since the greatest Princes do no more." "Yet, as to myself," Gulliver reflects, "I must confess, having never been designed for a Courtier, either by my Birth or Education, I was so ill a Judge of Things, that I could not discover the *Lenity* and Favour of this Sentence" (I, vii, 52, 54, 56).

The episode enacts Castiglione's dilemma of the omnicompetent courtier, still nominally in service yet in fact far greater (in this case physically so) than the prince he serves. A rather different deficiency in the established system of state service is reflected in Gulliver's voyage to Laputa and Balnibarbi, for there the ideals of civic humanism have been quite superseded by those of the new philosophy and its modernized conception of reform.[6] By that conception, both the "great Lord at Court" and his retired friend Lord Munodi, although they "had performed many eminent Services for the Crown," are judged men of little utility or understanding. This disregard for affairs of state, however, does not preclude in the king of Laputa a modicum of ambition for absolute power (III, iv, 157, 159, iii, 155). The trip to Luggnagg returns Gulliver to a more traditional political landscape—that of an arbitrary despot and his murderous court—and although he is made some "very honourable Offers" of favor, he prudently avoids entering into service (III, ix, 188–90). Responding, at the end of the narrative, to the suggestion that it was his duty in the several lands he discovered to have taken "Possession in my Sovereign's Name," Gulliver admits to "a few Scruples with relation to the distributive Justice of Princes upon those Occasions," and in the following account of the rapacious founding of "a *modern Colony*," we may recognize writ large the familiar principles of princely ambition (IV, xii, 278–79). But Gulliver's career is not our only source on the failure of princes to reward merit justly. In Glubdubdrib, the survey of dead kings yields the consensus that preferment is never made for "Virtue" or "Merit," and when Gulliver summons up those responsible for truly "Great Services done to Princes and States," he is confronted by people he has never heard of, most of whom "died in Poverty and Disgrace, and the rest on a Scaffold or a Gibbet" (III, viii, 183–84).

2

So the conservative disclosure of status inconsistency is made from two distinct but complementary directions in *Gulliver's Travels*. And because this two-pronged attack on the injustice of the modern, progressive system incorporates the progressive critique of tradition, Swift is characteristically ambivalent with respect to aristocratic ideology. His scorn for the fiction of noble birth is as strong here as anywhere. Thus, Gulliver gives the Brobdingnag king a ludicrously earnest account of the English peers of the realm, "worthy Followers of their most renowned Ancestors, whose Honour had been the Reward of their Virtue; from which their Posterity were never once known to degenerate." And when he calls up the ancestral lineages of royalty and nobility in Glubdubdrib, Gulliver is surprised to find not just that the descendants have decayed from their ancestors, but that the originating ancestors of aristocratic lines are themselves of uncertain status. Everywhere he finds, like Defoe in *The True-Born Englishman*, "an Interruption of Lineages by Pages, Lacqueys, Valets, Coachmen, Gamesters, Fidlers, Players, Captains, and Pickpockets." Later his Houyhnhnm Master, assuming the ideal standard of consistency that obtains in his own country, remarks that Gulliver "must have been born of some Noble Family, because I far exceeded in Shape, Colour, and Cleanliness, all the *Yahoos* of his Nation." And the disillusioned Gulliver ruefully assures him "that, *Nobility* among us was altogether a different Thing from the Idea he had of it . . . That a weak diseased Body, a meager Countenance, and sallow Complexion, are the true Marks of *noble Blood*" (II, vi, 112; III, viii, 182–83; IV, vi, 240–41).

But in the conservative mentality, the absence of noble blood tends also to persist as a conventional sign, never too closely examined, of the absence of merit. Thus when Gulliver reflects that in Houyhnhmnland, unlike England, "no Scoundrels [are] raised from the Dust upon the Merit of their Vices," he adds: "or Nobility thrown into it on account of their Virtues" (IV, x, 261). We have two instances (albeit less drastic) of such a decline in Lord Munodi and his friend, both of whom are manifestly meritorious, have done great service to the Laputan monarch, and are held in utter contempt for their incapacity for abstraction—and whose virtues, we sense, are due at least in part to their ancient and eminent nobility (III, iv, 157, 159). And when Gulliver depicts the type of upstart found in his native England— "where a little contemptible Varlet, without the least Title to Birth, Person, Wit, or common Sense, shall presume to look with Importance, and put himself upon a Foot with the greatest Persons of the Kingdom"—his list of what is lacking here characteristically gives at least a symbolizing precedence to lineage (II, v, 108). This ghostly insinuation of belief in the justice of a traditional, aristocratic stratification is entirely consistent, I have argued, with conservative ideology. It is a socially useful fiction, a cautiously instrumental faith that germinates in the soil left by the flowers of progressive belief once the conservative critique has, to its own satisfaction, quite deracinated them. This fiction is inseparable from the utopian element in conservative ideology. In *Gulliver's Travels* we fleetingly sense its presence in the "*English Yeomen of the old Stamp*" summoned up at Glubdubdrib (III, viii, 185). We hear it articulated more fully in the account of the militia of Brobdingnag, "which is made up of Tradesmen in the several Cities, and Farmers in the Country, whose Commanders are only the Nobility and Gentry, without Pay or Reward . . . Every Farmer is under the Command of his own Landlord, and every Citizen under that of the principal Men in his own City" (II, vii, 122).[7] In Lord Munodi we see an aristocratic landowner, joined by "some few other Persons of Quality and Gentry," who "was content to go on in the old Forms; to live in the Houses his Ancestors had built, and act as they did in every Part of Life without Innovation" (III, iv, 161). Munodi's estate combines, more certainly than those other instances, the conservative utopian elements of a status consistency somehow underwritten by tradition and the stable reality of landed property. But the crucial utopian enclave in *Gulliver's Travels* is, of course, Houyhnhnmland.

On first encountering the oddly equable horses, our serviceable hero naturally expects that it is he, the human, who will be "served" by them (IV, i, 211, ii, 213). He is soon disabused of this error, not by any conventional signs of dominion, as in his earlier voyages, but through the gradual and insensible growth of a natural deference toward the Houyhnhnms. He observes first that the household he is engaged with distinguishes itself into "Master" and "Servants," and after speaking to us for a while of "the Master Horse," he offhandedly refers to "my Master (for so I shall henceforth call him)" (IV, ii, 213, iii, 216, 218). Soon it seems natural to call "my Master" "his Honour," and Gulliver sits in long dialogue with his master about the state of European affairs, much as he had once done with the King of Brobdingnag (IV, v, 229). But although he does indeed come to see himself as in "Service" to his master, the nature of the relationship is very different from those he has experienced in the past: "I did not feel the Treachery or Inconstancy of a Friend, nor the Injuries of a secret or open Enemy. I had no Occasion of bribing, flattering or pimping, to procure the Favour of any great Man, or of his Minion" (IV, x, 264, 265, 260).

This negative model of service is still available in Houyhnhnmland, among the Yahoos, for "in most Herds there was a Sort of ruling *Yahoo*" whose fawning and servile "*Favourite* is hated by the whole Herd" and befouled by it when he comes to be replaced in the affections of the ruler (IV, vii, 246–47). But when Gulliver receives favor now, it is "the Favour of being admitted to several *Houyhnhnms,* who came to visit or dine with my Master," and he is happiest in "the Station of an humble Auditor in such Conversations" (IV, x, 261). If we hear an echo of the old obsequiousness in such statements, we must keep in mind (as Gulliver himself knows) that nothing is to be gained by such arts of the courtier. In Houyhnhnmland, service and its rewards appear indistinguishable; they are something like a religious discipline, the contemplation of virtue. Before his banishment Gulliver had resolved "to pass the rest of my Life among these admirable *Houyhnhnms* in the Contemplation and Practice of every Virtue" (IV, vii, 242). And after it his only ambition is "to discover some small Island uninhabited," where he might "reflect with Delight on the Virtues of those inimitable *Houyhnhnms,*" "which I would have thought a greater Happiness than to be first Minister in the politest Court of *Europe;* so horrible was the Idea I conceived of returning to live in the Society and under the Government of *Yahoos*" (IV, xi, 267).

The very terms of the old dynamic of service and reward are altered by the utopian nature of Houyhnhnm culture because the enabling premise of that dynamic, status inconsistency, has vanished. It is not only their morality that is pervaded, in the apt words of C. J. Rawson, by "an absolute standard of congruity or *fittingness,*" but also their very existence as natural and social beings. When Gulliver assures the Brobdingnag king of the purity of noble lineages in England, he is acting in bad faith. When the Houyhnhnm master assumes Gulliver's nobility, he is simply and truthfully speaking from his own experience, for "among the

Houyhnhnms, the *White*, the *Sorrel*, and the *Iron-grey*, were not so exactly shaped as the *Bay*, the *Dapple-grey*, and the *Black;* nor born with equal Talents of Mind, or a Capacity to improve them; and therefore continued always in the Condition of Servants, without ever aspiring to match out of their own Race, which in that Country would be reckoned monstrous and unnatural" (IV, vi, 240). The appetite for upward mobility— through state service, intermarriage, or whatever means—never arises here, because the very conditions of status inconsistency by which it is generated, the very possibility of expectations that are "relative" to anything but one's own race, are absent. We are reminded of the aristocratic ideal—enforced by the futile stratagem of sumptuary legislation—of a correspondence between internals and externals so absolute that even mind and body are in complete accord. But here the romance convention whereby the noble are instantly recognizable through the purity of their complexions or the fineness of their hair has become a social reality.[8]

True, the smooth running of the social order requires more than the unrationalized operation of a purely natural "instinct." But the Houyhnhnms's recourse to "culture" is a good deal more candidly naturalized to the social order than a stealthy, "convenient fiction" like Socrates' myth of autochthonous origins, for it takes the form of a system of eugenics, which is rationally pursued in order "to preserve the Race from degenerating." It is to this end, and neither for love nor for the consolidation of the estate, that marriages are made, and the young couple is pleased to participate in the system because "it is what they see done every Day; and they look upon it as one of the necessary Actions in a reasonable Being" (IV, viii, 252–53). In such policies we see how socially useful conventions are subtly incorporated within Houyhnhnm social practice and obtain the tacit authority of behavior that is at once socialized and natural. The Houyhnhnm institution of marriage is based neither on the progressive fiction of the freedom of choice of the individual, nor on the aristocratic fiction of sacrifice to the greater end of familial lineage, but on their dialectical mediation.[9]

The Houyhnhnm economy is similarly suffused with a principle of congruity or consistency. In the insatiable avarice of the Brobdingnag farmer, we have already seen an ironic reflection of Gulliver's own insatiable desire for profit and mobility after Lilliput. The rest of the narrative does much to argue that these appetites, and the economic base that permits their unlimited growth, are endemic to English culture. The status inconsistency that nourishes the endless round of service and reward is itself fueled, as the Brobdingnag king discerns, by monetary corruption (II, vi, 113–16; III, viii, 185–86). And in Houyhnhnmland, Gulliver describes to his master how the English economy, unlimited by any principle of necessity or subsistence, thrives on the satisfaction of luxurious appetites, all the while creating fanciful new desires that will in turn need slaking. The key to this, Gulliver explains, is the exchange value of money, with which a European Yahoo "was able to purchase whatever he had a mind to . . . Therefore since *Money* alone, was able to perform all these Feats, our *Yahoos* thought, they could never have enough of it to spend or save," and the result is both conspicuous consumption and avaricious accumulation (IV, vi, 235–37). The only example of this sort of behavior in Houyhnhnmland is found, not surprisingly, among the Yahoos. Although Gulliver's master had long known of their fondness for a certain kind of shining stone, "he could never discover the Reason of this unnatural Appetite, or how these *Stones* could be of any Use to a *Yahoo;* but now he believed it might proceed from the same Principle of *Avarice,* which I had ascribed to Mankind." The same could be said of the principle of luxury and uncontrolled consumption, for there is nothing more odious about the Yahoos "than their undistinguishing Appetite to devour every thing that [comes] in their Way" (IV, vii, 244–45).

Among the Houyhnhnms things are, needless to say, very different. Like the Brobdingnag people, they are committed in general to a limiting principle of utility (II, vii, 120; IV, iv, 226, viii, 252). Just as the Houyhnhnm master could not see the use of the Yahoos' stones, so "I was at much Pains to describe to him the Use of *Money*" (IV, vi, 235). For the use of money lies paradoxically in its alienation, in its exchange, and the Houyhnhnms have no use for exchange, because they have no desire for products that are obtainable only through the circulation of commodities (or indeed for the process of circulation itself, the taste for which is one of the most highly developed in capitalist culture). Theirs is not a "free" but a planned economy, whose principle of privileged communism Swift nicely articulates as the "Supposition that all Animals had a Title to their Share in the Productions of the Earth; and especially those who presided over the rest" (IV, vi, 235). In Houyhnhnmland, the manifest reality of social inequality is seen as quite consistent with economic egalitarianism. The closest the Houyhnhnms come to a system of exchange is a mechanism for the redistribution of goods: every four years, "where-ever there is any Want (which is but seldom) it is immediately supplied by unanimous Consent and Contribution" (IV, viii, 254). And despite his deficient preparation for it, Gulliver learns to practice here his "little Oeconomy"—the account both invites and resists comparison with Robinson Crusoe's ostentatiously noncapitalist improvements—so that the very simple wants of his life are fully satisfied by an equally simple productive regimen (IV, x, 260).

3

Thus the conservative utopia of Houyhnhnmland so successfully dispels the imaginary values and unnatural wants of contemporary English civilization that it seems, finally, to establish a "consistency" between nature and culture. And if this is the achievement of Swift's utopia, the analogy of nature and culture, of biological and social existence, is also, of course, the method by which he has entangled his protagonist in adventure all along. In accord with the tradition of the imaginary voyage, Gulliver's travels are an experience of both sociopolitical and physical transformation, and it is clear that Swift would have us understand and ponder the analogical nature of this relationship. When Gulliver recalls the English variety of the "little contemptible Varlet," for example, it is as "the Moral of my own Behaviour" in Brobdingnag, when he acts the diminutive mock-hero in bombastic defense of his honor against his mortal enemy, the palace monkey (II, v, 107–8). And when he tells us soon after that "I was the Favourite of a great King and Queen, and the Delight of the whole Court; but it was upon such a Foot as ill became the Dignity of human Kind," we are obliged to see that he is describing not just the unique status of a pygmy among giants but the typical indignity of a court favorite (II, viii, 123). As we first know him Gulliver is, of course, much more physically than socially conscious. Like Robinson Crusoe, he is a practical man: a student of "Physick," a pragmatic "Projector," and a "Mechanical Genius," "curious enough to dissect" a Brobdingnag louse, "so curious [as] to weigh and measure" a Brobdingnag hailstone, inclined to wander from his shipmates in order "to entertain [his] Curiosity" (I, i, 3, v, 35; II, i, 69, iv, 97, v, 100, vi, 110; III, iv, 162). Entirely devoted to the evidence of the senses, Gulliver is one of those "plain, diligent, and laborious observers" celebrated by Thomas Sprat, who bring their "eyes uncorrupted" to their work, and he is quite preoccupied with an assortment of instruments—spectacles, pocket perspective, pocket compass—with which he hopes artificially to improve upon "the Weakness of [his] Eyes" (I, ii, 21).[10]

In Gulliver we are confronted with the man of science, a naive empiricist whose modernized version of the old sin of *libido sciendi* consists in the reduction of knowledge to sense impressions. In the problems that plague him in Parts I and II, we first encounter the theme that comes to the center of Swift's narrative in Part III, the critique of scientific empiricism as "the new romance." Already in Brobdingnag we learn that the category of the "*Lusus Naturae*" of "the Modern Philosophy of *Europe*" is, whatever Gulliver believes, no better than "the old Evasion of *occult Causes,* whereby the Followers of *Aristotle* endeavour in vain to disguise their Ignorance" (II, iii, 88). By the time he meets Munodi, Gulliver is content to characterize a projector in terms not of vigorous

skepticism but of "much Curiosity and easy Belief," and the Academy of
Projectors in Lagado in a monument to the ironic reversal by which the
objectivity of scientific projects for reforming the world is shown to
entail a stealthy projection of subjective fancy upon it (III, iv, 162; cf. III,
v–vi).[11]

But the demystification of objectivity is first enacted in the collisions
between Gulliver's quantifying method and the respective standards of
Lilliput and Brobdingnag. At the beginning of Part I, Gulliver's careful
spatial estimates in leagues, degrees, inches, feet, and miles are soon
confounded by phenomena that seem to defy an absolute and unitary
measure ("The great Gate . . . about four Foot high"; leg chains "almost
as large" as "those that hang to a Lady's Watch in *Europe*"; a prince big
enough—"taller by almost the Breadth of my Nail, than any of his
Court"—"to strike an Awe into the Beholders") (I, i, 4–5, 11–12, ii, 14).
At the outset in Part II, we pass quickly from an account of the ship's
movement "by my Computation" to an account of "Trees so lofty that I
could make no Computation of their Altitude" (II, i, 68, 69). And now
the fact of relativity, the reduction of objective quantification to a completely subjective perception, is impressed upon the bewildered Gulliver
with all the force of an ontological theory of relative expectations: "Undoubtedly Philosophers are in the Right when they tell us, that nothing is
great or little otherwise than by Comparison: It might have pleased
Fortune to let the *Lilliputians* find some Nation, where the People were as
diminutive with respect to them, as they were to me. And who knows
but that even this prodigious Race of Mortals might be equally over-
matched in some distant Part of the World, whereof we have yet no
Discovery?" (II, i, 71). But even under these extreme conditions of ontological vertigo, Swift is careful to ensure that physical relativity continues to operate as an analogy for social relativity. Thus Gulliver, although disgusted by the smell of the Brobdingnag "Maids of Honour,"
through an effort of will concedes that they may be "no more disagreeable to their Lovers . . . than People of the same Quality are with us in
England" (II, v, 102). But the appalling sight of a nurse's "monstrous
Breast, which I cannot tell what to compare with," makes him "reflect
upon the fair Skins of our *English* Ladies," and he himself is flatteringly
perceived by the Brobdingnags as having "a Complexion fairer than a
Nobleman's Daughter of Three Years old" (II, i, 75–76, ii, 80).

The relativizing of physical standards of objectivity is an undeniable
accomplishment of the first three voyages, but if we take this to be
irreversibly damaging to the equilibrium of the modern empiricist-trav-
eler, we do him an injustice. In fact, Gulliver's fundamental appetite of
curiosity—the "insatiable Desire of seeing foreign Countries," that "insatiable Desire I had to see the World in every Period of Antiquity"—is
only whetted by the experience of indefinite relativity, for this is after all

precisely what he is seeking: the experience of difference. And like all good travelers, he is well equipped for the experience. Despite his disclaimers, he is very adept at comparison, which permits him, at any single moment, to equilibrate difference, and the result is that he is extraordinarily adaptive to change. If "going native" is a cross-cultural version of social assimilation,[12] Gulliver's assimilative powers are so strong that even Brobdingnag is as much an experience of upward as of downward mobility for him. True, when the English ship comes upon his traveling box in the open sea, he imagines it will be an easy matter for one of the crew to slip his finger through its ring and lift it on board (II, viii, 127). But early on, Gulliver also learns to internalize the standards of what he sees around him and to recall with contempt the affectations of "*English* Lords and Ladies": "My Ideas were wholly taken up with what I saw on every Side of me; and I winked at my own Littleness, as People do at their own Faults" (II, iii, 91, viii, 132; cf. iv, 98, viii, 131, 133).

Gulliver's facility for assimilative comparison depends upon his ability to abstract himself from the fact of difference onto a plane of similarity, to manipulate a kind of epistemological exchange value that accommodates qualitatively dissimilar objects to a more general and equalizing standard. For this reason it is not surprising that like the mobile and serviceable seaman Edward Coxere, Gulliver is a master of languages (like language, "money is," in the words of Anthony Ascham, "an invention onely for the more expedite permutation of things"). Gulliver's facility with languages is so great, and his vanity as translator, purveyor of specialized terminologies, and amateur linguist is so well developed, that he appears to aspire in his own being to fulfill the utopian fantasy of seventeenth-century language projectors, the dream of a universal language. And in the Academy of Projectors at Lagado he is greatly taken with the several schemes by which language would be mechanized, materialized, or allegorized by method so as to render it a universal and transparent medium of exchange (III, v, 166–70, vi, 174–76).[13]

But in Houyhnhnmland this complacent dream is shattered. Here Gulliver is put "to the Pains of many Circumlocutions to give my Master a right Idea of what I spoke" (IV, iv, 226). At first it appears that this is the result of the primitive state of the Houyhnhnms' understanding, reflected in their regrettable paucity of words and expressions. But it soon becomes clear that what they lack is rather the superfluity of vicious desires that make language obscure and complicated and that are symbolized in the confusion of the Tower of Babel (IV, iii, 219, iv, 228). Ironically it is Houyhnhnm speech that approximates most closely, in *Gulliver's Travels,* a universal language. It is employed simply "to make us understand one another, and to receive Information of Facts." The Houyhnhnms have no "Occasion to talk of *Lying,* and *false Representation,*" not only because their wills are not infected, but because in their speech there is a perfect correspondence and consistency of word and thing (IV, iv, 224). In Houyhnhnmland, the absence of a highly elaborated language is directly analogous to the absence of a highly elaborated economy. And Gulliver, frustrated in his attempts to translate between English and Houyhnhnm speech—to equalize them on the linguistic market of exchange—humbly acknowledges, with John Bunyan, the persistence and intractability of the old problem of mediation, and strives "to express [him] self by Similitudes" (IV, iv, 227).[14]

4

As in *Robinson Crusoe,* questions of virtue in *Gulliver's Travels* are never widely separated from questions of truth, and at times Swift is willing to juxtapose them quite directly. When the King of Brobdingnag concludes his attack on the inconsistency of status and virtue in England, for example, Gulliver, despite his "extreme Love of Truth," freely admits to having given the king a more favorable account of the matter "than the strictness of Truth would allow" (II, vi–vii, 116–17). And in Glubdubdrib, immediately after telling us of the remarkable "Interruption of Lineages" among royalty and nobility, he narrates how "disgusted" he was "with modern History" and with "how the World had been misled by prostitute Writers" (III, viii, 183). *Gulliver's Travels* is adorned with all the claims to historicity and all the authenticating devices of "modern history" in general, and of travel narrative in particular. The claim itself is made early, late, and with considerable insistence (pp. xxxv–viii; II, i, 78; IV, xii, 275–76). The narrative is interspersed with documents—letters, maps—that attest to its own documentary objecthood (pp. xxxiii–viii, 2, 66, 136, 204), and it makes reference several times to the "Journal Book" on which, in accordance with the Royal Society's instructions, its own historicity is based (I, ii, 21; IV, iii, 218, xii, 276). The prefatory letter added in 1735 alludes to the spurious continuations and keys that have been published since the first printing, thereby buttressing its founding authenticity, but at the same time it complains of some spelling and other errors in that printing, the most serious of which are editorial deletions and insertions that raise the dilemma of quantitative completeness (pp. xxxiii–xxxvi). We encounter familiar hints that the narrative seems strange and therefore true; that "there is an Air of Truth apparent through the whole"; and that the author has chosen "to relate plain matter of Fact in the simplest Manner and Style" (II, iv, 98–99; p. xxxvii; IV, xii, 275). Finally, we are reminded throughout that what we are reading is indeed a book of travels and may be judged accordingly.[15]

The results of such a judgment are not entirely straightforward. *Gulliver's Travels* is, of course, a satire of the travel narrative, and of the naive empiricism with which it is so closely associated. But just as Swift's critique of progressive ideology shares with that ideology a contempt for the fictions of aristocratic honor, so the subversion of the claim to historicity proceeds from a common, if more relentlessly indulged, skeptical impulse. The conventions of imaginary and "real" voyages were the same, and Swift's wide reading in the form bespeaks (as is so characteristic of his interests) an equivocal fascination composed of attraction as well as repulsion.[16] When Gulliver couples his claim to historicity with the aim of moral "Reformation," he is echoing, to be sure, the sort of statement that preceded not only some of Defoe's works but numerous exercises in quasi-spiritual autobiography and travel as well (p. xxxv). But the coexistence of that aim with his disgusted repudiation of "so absurd a Project as that of reforming the Yahoo Race in this Kingdom" is entirely typical also of Swift's own lifelong ambivalence about the utility of satiric schemes of reformation (p. xxxvi). By the same token, the Swiftian attack upon the incredibility of "true history" would not be as profound as it is if Swift were not deeply committed to some species of historical truth.[17]

What are the implications of Swift's epistemological double reversal for how he would tell the truth in narrative? Obviously he does not underwrite Gulliver's claim to have related "plain matter of fact." The Houyhnhnms can use language to convey and "receive information of facts," but that is because they are Houyhnhnms. Gulliver's commitment to the factual veracity of his factually vulnerable narrative is thus one clear sign of his error. But he is also committed, however fallibly, to the wisdom of the Houyhnhnms, and in his transmission of their wisdom to us he practices another sort of truth-telling in narrative, which he articulates when he says that "a Traveller's chief Aim should be to make Men wiser and better, and to improve their Minds by the bad, as well as good Example of what they deliver concerning foreign Places" (IV, xii, 275). This formulation of how history teaches truth and virtue by example is in fact rather more traditional than Gulliver's—and Swift's—actual practice would warrant, for the texture of circumstantial and authenticating detail is too dense to be dissolved by our somewhat anxious insistence that it is "all ironic."[18]

The epistemology of Gulliver's Travels can be usefully compared with that of the most acute and self-conscious of the spiritual travelers at the end of the previous century, whose plain style and historicity were instruments by which to arrive at a truth that lay through, but not in, the factual.[19] But Swift's parable is noticeably non-Christian, and since we are not asked to acknowledge the Author who lurks behind the author, we are not overly occupied with attributing to an ultimately higher source Swift's creation of the artifice Gulliver has disavowed. As a result, by subverting empirical epistemology, Swift contributes, as fully as Defoe does by sponsoring it, to the growth of modern ideas of realism and the internalized spirituality of the aesthetic. Swift's parabolic pedagogy can tacitly justify its return to an anachronistic attitude toward how to tell the truth in narrative in part because it has, as it were, earned the right to it through a self-conscious evisceration of the more modern alternative, and in part because that modern alternative is learning how to reconcile itself to notions of aesthetic universality through the resuscitation of Aristotelian doctrine. In this respect, as well as in its inevitable dedication to the weapon of perceptual subjectivity, which it employs to attack empirical notions of objectivity, Swift's narrative method is at the forefront of the "modern alternative." The attack would be ineffective if it were based only on the old unsearchability of the divine spirit and its intentions. Yet in substituting for the traditional a modernized critique of materialist sufficiency, Swift participates, as surely as Defoe, in the modern replacement of Spirit by Mind.[20]

But there are also other ways of understanding why *Gulliver's Travels* is non-Christian. In *Robinson Crusoe* Defoe is willing, quasi-metaphorically, to speak of Robinson's "original sin" because in the optimistic spirit of progressive ideology he is willing to conceive that status inconsistency, for which original sin stands as its most irrevocable instance, can be indemnified and overcome. Swift does not speak of original sin because his social vision is too thoroughly infiltrated by a conviction of it, and in the Houyhnhnms he wants to posit a race of mortals—humanoid but necessarily nonhuman—that has no experience of status inconsistency. In Brobdingnag, Gulliver has already shown remarkable powers of resistance to negative socialization. Bestialized at every turn—compared to a weasel, a toad, a spider, a splacknuck, a canary, a frog, a puppy, a diminutive insect, a little odious vermin—it is testimony to his resilience that he is yet able to identify as fully as he does with his enormous human hosts. In Houyhnhnmland the Yahoos confront Gulliver with the similar challenge of an effective theriomorphy, and for a while he fends it off.

When he first encounters the Yahoos they are "Beast[s]," "ugly Monster[s]," deformed "Animals" who bear no relation to the "many Tracks of human Feet" he has earlier observed, a "cursed Brood" that presumably served "the Inhabitants" as "Cattle" (IV, i, 207–8). As the alarming resemblance becomes harder to avoid, he tries to conceal "the Secret of [his] Dress, in order to distinguish [himself] as much as possible" (IV, iii, 220). But at length Gulliver is obliged to acknowledge "that entire Congruity betwixt [himself] and their *Yahoos*," and when a young female, observing him bathe, becomes "inflamed by Desire . . . [he] could no longer deny, that [he] was a real *Yahoo*" (IV, vii, 242, viii, 250–51). Still he entertains some hope that the Houyhnhnms "would condescend to distinguish [him] from the rest of [his] Species," but he is overcome with despair when the General Council exhorts his master "either to employ [him] like the rest of [his] Species, or command [him] to swim back to the Place from whence [he] came" (IV, x, 262, 263).

So Gulliver is obliged against his will to "go native." What is the precise meaning of this assimilation? It is of course in the interest of Gulliver's self-esteem for him to understand himself as the pure form of the species, from whom the "corrupted" Yahoos have "degenerated" (IV, iii, 222, viii, 249). This view receives some support from his master's interpretation of the traditional story of the origins of the Yahoos, "whereof," Gulliver significantly adds, "he had indeed borrowed the Hint from me" (IV, ix, 256).[21] But Gulliver's account of European culture, the impartial observation of the Yahoos, and the wisdom of the Houyhnhnms all point toward the contrary conclusion: that the tincture of reason possessed by the Europeans has aggravated, corrupted, improved, and multiplied the vices and wants that they naturally share with the Yahoos, and made them unquestionably the degenerate and bestial form of the species (IV, v, 232, vii, 243–48, x, 262, xii, 280). The "corruptions" of money, it would appear—its ability to create new and unheard-of desires and vanities—are a subcategory of the "corruptions" of reason. Both are peculiar to that segment of the human race whose vicious appetites have become so unlimited by the constraints of nature and custom as to demand the final and appalling sanction of being, themselves, the standard of what is natural.[22]

One basic argument of the "soft school of interpretation" concerning Part IV of *Gulliver's Travels* is that Swift tacitly and tellingly discredits the Houyhnhnms by making them passionless and cold—an argument which ignores how consistently the containment of the passions operates in Swift's writings as a positive norm. In fact Swift tells us that the language of the Houyhnhnms is well suited to the expression of the passions (IV, i, 210). True, their passions and wants are fewer than ours; but among the appetites they lack is "the Desire of Power and Riches," whereas the detestable type of the first minister of state in England— possessed of rather fewer passions, apparently, than even the Houyhnhnms—"makes use of no other Passions but a violent Desire of Wealth, Power, and Titles" (IV, iv, 226, 228, vi, 239; see also IV, vi, 236, viii, 253, for passions the Houyhnhnms do not know). It is precisely because the passions of the Houyhnhnms are few, and because they place natural and discretionary limits on them—planned marriages, the practice of abstinence, the selective censorship and eventual banishment of Gulliver—that they have avoided the degenerations and corruptions of the human race (IV, v, 231–32, viii, 252–53, x, 263).[23]

For the wisdom of the Houyhnhnms entails not an invulnerability to corruption but the foresight and will to prevent it. And their wisdom in banishing Gulliver is evident in the fact that his assimilationist vanity is in no way limited by his acceptance of his status as a Yahoo, which instead only whets his appetite to become a Houyhnhnm. In what is surely an extreme case of upwardly mobile ambition, Gulliver aspires to the status of a higher species. And when we call up the image of him trotting and whinnying like a Houyhnhnm, we are struck by the justice with which the materialist sufficiency of this man of science is now expressed in the hopelessly physical mode through which he would imitate moral excellence (IV, x, 262–63).[24] Gulliver's impersonation of a horse is his equivalent of Robinson's figures of absolute dominion and divine providence. Both men are engaged in postconversion projects of "improvement"; but whereas Robinson is permitted by his author to project English society upon his island with impunity and to introject a divinity that sanctions his desires, Gulliver's ethnocentric attempts to find an ideal England abroad are consistently frustrated, and the Houyhnhnms absolutely resist introjection.

Although we might be tempted to draw the easy lesson that only this particular conversion has failed, Swift is really reflecting on all suspect conversions that consist in the psychological process of introjection, conversions that succeed if their subjects are complacent enough to be certain that they have. And so he gives us a protagonist whose utopia cannot be internalized, who cannot "make" himself, whose social mobility manifestly cannot signify spiritual achievement, because try as he might, he cannot become what he is not—a truth that is demonstrated most of all in his very willingness to try. Robinson Crusoe's honest old Portuguese captain serves to reflect back to him his heightened spiritual status, to provide the external accreditation of the community. Gulliver's honest Portuguese captain, Don Pedro de Mendez, exists to provide this same assurance, and the fact that Gulliver barely tolerates him bespeaks a fine doubleness. For it supports both a painful truth—even the best of men are only human (and Gulliver has renounced easy confirmations)— and a painful delusion—Gulliver's distaste for Don Pedro is inseparable from his continuing conviction of his own differentness.

So the inwardly divided Gulliver returns to England, makes a "small Purchase of Land," and retires to cultivate "my little Garden." And by that movement he completes, in the double trajectory with which he began, a characteristically circular conservative plot pattern: the embittered return of the disdained country gentleman to his landed enclave (and the type embraces also the retirement of Munodi and Swift himself); and the comic rustication of the unsuccessful younger son, bloated with pride and incomprehendingly indignant at his failure to make it in town or at court (pp. xxxiv, xxxvi; IV, xii, 279). The power of *Gulliver's Travels* as a narrative explanation of status inconsistency cannot be detached from the force of its will to explain, parabolically, our more general condition of mutability and discord. The ironic theme of historical degeneration

and cyclical decay is everywhere: in the testimony of Aristotle at Glubdubdrib when he enunciates the conservative maxim "that new Systems
of Nature [are] but new Fashions," and new truths only recapitulate the
errors of those they replace; in the case of the Struldbruggs, who seem to
Gulliver to promise an "antient Virtue" that may "prevent that continual
Degeneracy of human Nature," but who in fact are a terrible emblem of
physical and mental decay (III, viii, 182, x, 192, 194).[25]

But the generality of the problems Swift investigates in *Gulliver's
Travels* can be overstated. At crucial moments in the critique of ambitious
courtiers and ungrateful princes, we are told that our concern is with the
modern period and the modern world. The familiar-sounding crises that
we hear of in Lilliputian politics began with the present emperor's great-
grandfather and continue to very recent times (I, iv, 32–34, vi, 44). The
present era of Brobdingnag stability dates from the reign of this king's
grandfather, who ended a civil war (II, vii, 122). The virtues of the old
English yeomen have been prostituted by their corrupted grandchildren,
who are even now at large (III, viii, 185–86). The volatile period to which
Swift alludes most insistently, in other words, is the previous century. In
the last analysis it seems important to recognize that *Gulliver's Travels*
intertwines the microplot of Lemuel Gulliver with these allusive invocations of the macroplot of seventeenth-century English history in order to
specify, and explain, a species of error and corruption that, to a very
important degree, Swift saw as a modern phenomenon.

Eleven

The Institutionalization of Conflict (I):
Richardson and the Domestication of Service

I

The claim to historicity in *Pamela* (1740) is inextricable from its epistolary form. At least in the first edition, Richardson appears only as the "editor" of an authentic set of documents that constitute a true "History." Names and places alone have been altered. Nothing else has been done to "disguise the Facts, marr the Reflections, and unnaturalize the Incidents," so that we "have *Pamela* as *Pamela* wrote it; in her own Words, without Amputation, or Addition."[1] Because it is a documentary history, *Pamela* is not a romance, and it is singularly qualified thereby for moral instruction and improvement. The familiar rationale links Richardson not only to the established strain of naive empiricism in narrative but also to the Protestant conviction that concrete and sensible means provide the best mediation to moral and spiritual ends. Later Richardson revealed to friends that although the letters themselves did not possess a literal historicity, there was an "original ground-work of fact, for the general foundation of Pamela's story," in an account he had heard many years earlier. The first version of it appears, in brief but epistolary form, in Richardson's *Familiar Letters* (1741). But before that book was completed he "gave way to enlargement: and so Pamela became as you see her."[2] *Pamela* was quickly published in two volumes, but its astounding success led to yet greater—and unwanted—"enlargements" by spurious imitators and continuers, who were audacious enough to claim that they, and not the person responsible for those volumes, were in possession of the authentic documents. This forced Richardson to publish his own hurried continuation in two more volumes. Unlike Cervantes, he does not have his characters reflect back upon their own documentary objectification in Part I, but he does rather irritably insist, lest anyone "impose new Continuations upon the Publick . . . [that] all the Copies of Mrs. B.'s Observations and Writings, upon every Subject hinted at in the preceding Four Volumes . . . are now in *One Hand Only*."[3]

Epistolary method permits Richardson's characters, unlike Cervantes', to engage in self-reflexive discourse even within Part I of his narrative, an advantage Richardson fully exploits in order to insinuate the documentary objecthood of his material. If the claim to historicity consists in the assertion that the story one is telling really happened, the apotheosis of the convention in Richardson's hands depends on his creation of the sense that it is really happening at this very moment. And the celebrated Richardsonian technique of "writing to the moment"—"the Letters being written under the immediate Impression of every Circumstance which occasioned them" (4)—is closely related to the self-reflexive effect by which the narrative incorporates, as its subject matter, the process of its own production and consumption. The gaps in the text where Pamela "breaks off" in apprehension (26, 40, 53, 78, 317), the tears and the trembling lines that we are told deface the calm surface of the original manuscript (25, 159–60, 171)—these constitute highly emotional "evidence of the senses" that comes very close to the presentational and objective power of the drama while escaping its vulnerability to disconfirmation.[4]

Moreover, throughout the narrative, but especially at the start of the Lincolnshire imprisonment, we watch Pamela husband her supplies of paper, pens, ink, wafers, and sealing wax, the material means of her epistolary and journalistic production (95–96, 105, 113, 134). Several times she minutely recapitulates the contents of the packets she has written and accumulated, and even if we do not take the trouble to positively confirm the accuracy of her reviews, we are left with a subtle and pervasive sense of the objective integrity, the self-consistency, of this collection of objects that are thus so susceptible to systematic collation (197–98, 204–6, 238–39). In attributing authority and objectivity to the narrative, we take our cue not only from its author but also from its other internal readers. When Mr. B. disputes Pamela's account of what passed between her and Parson Williams, she mildly refers him to "the Text" (200). And once they are reconciled, the status of "the text" has become so canonical that Mr. B. can allude to its minor details as though to a scripture which they and we hold in common.[5] For a while he even wanders about the estate correlating events in Pamela's narrative with the tangible factuality of the locales in which they occurred (e.g., 208).

So the epistemological status of *Pamela* is difficult to disentangle from that of Pamela—from her claims to, and her capacity for, credibility. And questions of truth provide one medium for much of the social and sexual conflict in Richardson's narrative. Needless to say, Mr. B. is not always so content to take Pamela's word as authoritative, since what it subserves is a plot of typically progressive ideology (to which I will return). Early on he persistently accuses her of "romancing," of inventing absurdly distorted and fantastic fictions about the absolute moral gulf between her persecuted innocence and his own black intentions (42, 45, 48, 71, 90, 144–45, 162, 181, 201, 202). To B., Pamela is a witch, a sorceress, an enchantress, an artful gypsy who transforms reality like Don Quixote's evil sage (40, 44, 48, 55–56, 62, 146, 155, 156, 162). And like Cervantes' protagonist, he affects to subscribe to the aristocratic maxim that his own credibility is, on the contrary, implicit in his very person: "Pr'ythee, Man," he says to Pamela's father, "consider a little who I am; and if I am not to be believ'd, what signifies talking?" (93). But in fact, B. works hard to reverse the spell of Pamela's progressive plotting with his own inventions, which are characteristically aristocratic in ideology and often even take written form.

Although the rape of Pamela can appear to be Mr. B.'s irreducible and obsessive desire, his real view seems to be that it is a distastefully crude expedient for enacting the venerable aristocratic plot that is his genuine ambition. B.'s friend Sir Simon Darnford gives the most concise and breezy rendition of this plot in dialogue with his wife: "Why, what is all this, my Dear, but that the 'Squire our Neighbour has a mind to his Mother's Waiting-maid? And if he takes care she wants for nothing, I don't see any great Injury will be done her. He hurts no Family by this" (122). The problem is that Pamela's "wants" are at odds with the very premise of this traditional tale of the happily kept commoner. B.'s most elaborate attempt to meet them is the set of written "articles" in which he proposes a life lived in ease and comfort, "as if you was my Wife . . . [and] the foolish Ceremony had passed" (166). Pamela makes clear her contempt for this fiction by refuting each of his proposals in turn. And it is just after reading this document that B. makes his most direct, but oddly equivocal, attempt. For having pinned her to the bed, B. proceeds not to rape her but to exclaim: "I must say one Word to you, *Pamela;* it is this: You see, now you are in my Power! . . . If you resolve not to comply with my Proposals, I will not lose this Opportunity . . . Swear then to me . . . that you will accept my Proposals!" (176). At this crucial moment B. reveals that his dominant motives are not strictly sexual but political, and that he takes power to consist in the ability to make others accept one's version of events as authoritative. B.'s sham-marriage plot is only a less candid variant of the "articles." Since Pamela refuses to give her assent to the basic scenario of luxurious illegitimacy, she must be included in the sham and made to think the foolish ceremony really has passed. She first hears of the plot in an anonymous note left by the gypsy shortly after the failed rape (196). Later B. gives her a fuller account of how they might have lived "very lovingly together" in such a state (230). And before she herself is persuaded to suspend her disbelief, Lady Davers cruelly taunts Pamela for her "credulity" in taking the sham for the real thing (323, 325, 328, 330).[6]

Thus, although B. suggests that both Pamela and her father have had their heads filled with fancies by reading romances (90, 93), the squire has his own fictions to propound. When, on occasion, he is able to neglect the larger plot to concentrate on smaller episodes, he can be even more inventive with aristocratic themes of paternalistic care and forced marriages. In order to pacify Pamela's father, B. maintains that he has sent her temporarily to London to save her from an ill-conceived love match with a destitute clergyman. The chief objection to the match, B. says, is financial. But he intends to provide for the young couple, and he pursues the fantasy long after it is needed to dupe Mr. Andrews—long enough, in fact, to convince poor Parson Williams that the only obstacle to a marriage between himself and Pamela is her consent. B. deceives both men, it should be noted, by letter (90–93, 131–32).[7]

But his most impressive coup is the letter he sends to the farm tenants with whom he lodges Pamela during her kidnapping to the Lincolnshire estate. He tells this honest family that Pamela is a headstrong young gentlewoman who is involved in a ruinous love affair. B. has arranged this redemptive abduction only "*to oblige her Father.*" She, of course, will deny everything. About to throw herself on their mercies, Pamela realizes that she has been outplotted: "I saw all my Plot cut out; and so was forc'd to say the less . . . I saw he was too hard for me, as well in his Contrivances as Riches" (100). Indeed, "the Farmer was so prepossess'd with the Contents of his Letter" that he "made me the Subject of a Lesson for his Daughter's Improvement." So for a brief time Pamela finds herself in a miniature anti-*Pamela*, complete with documentary historicity and moral instructions on the duty of daughters to obey their fathers (100–01). The most grotesque of Mr. B.'s inventions in this general vein may in fact be by Mrs. Jewkes, since it is she who tells Pamela that her master's latest plan is to force Williams to marry Pamela to the dreaded M. Colbrand, who will then sell her to B.! Pamela is torn between skepticism and a justifiably paranoid credulity: "But this, to be sure, is horrid romancing! but abominable as it is, it may possibly serve to introduce some Plot now hatching!" (157).

Yet despite his virtuosity, in the battling of plotters B. is, of course, no match for Pamela. It is her "little History of myself" (173), not his several versions of her, that closely approximates the larger lineaments of *Pamela,* because it is letters written by her, not by him, that overwhelmingly dominate the narrative. She tells his story far more than he tells hers. He even learns to base his retellings of the plot on her version of it (e.g., 267). But there is no reciprocity in this, for when he would "prescribe the Form" of a letter to be sent by her to Mrs. Jervis, insisting that she "not alter one Tittle," Pamela rewrites it with impunity, and Richardson is careful to ensure that we see her version first (93–94, 108–9). Yet Pamela's power as a writer depends entirely on B.'s availability as a reader. And this is paradoxical, because his access to her letters—the fact that he has been reading them, unbeknownst to her, from the beginning—is a major source of his knowledge of and power over her (40, 83, 89, 111). Indeed, this is how Pamela herself sees it. Once imprisoned in Lincolnshire, the fact of her solitude is borne home to her as the absence of an audience, as the fact that even though she can write, she cannot be read (102, 105, 106, 120). And the only consolation is that now, at least, her writings will not be intercepted and read by B. In this crisis of solitude Pamela stops writing letters, and her journal, like Robinson Crusoe's, is born (94). She begins now to divide her time between clandestine writing and trying "to find some way to escape, before this wicked Master comes" (104). But B. arrives, her escape attempts are fruitless, and shortly after the failed rape, Mrs. Jewkes discovers a packet of her writings. This accidental publication strips Pamela of her privacy: "For now he will see all my private Thoughts of him, and all my Secrets, as I may say" (197). When B. asks to see the rest of her journals, she fears a literal undressing as well, for they are sewn into her underclothes; and knowing he will be privy to her future writings, she is sure, will only cause her to deprive them of their freedom and candor (204, 206, 208).

But Pamela is mistaken in these apprehensions. Already B.'s exposure to her had challenged his original expectations of their respective, and sharply distinguished, roles (e.g., 76, 81). Inevitably "putting myself as near as I can in your Place," B. had learned, if only strategically, to sympathize and identify with her (108). Now, confronted with a sustained and continuous narrative, his heart is melted by the "very moving Tale" of Pamela's trials—not just the events themselves, but "the Light you put Things in" (207, 208). He has adopted her viewpoint: "You have too powerful a Pleader for you within me" (200). No longer her adversary, B. has become instead her ideal reader. Before, he had insisted that she reproduce his "prescribed form" unaltered. Now he requires that she change not a word of her own text (204, 237)—not so much because he respects its documentary historicity but because it has acquired the slightly deflected authenticity of the art object. It is this "aesthetic" response to a unified and moving plot that is expressed in B.'s confession that "you have touch'd me sensibly with your mournful Relation, and your sweet Reflections upon it." "I long to see the Particulars of your Plot . . . There is such a pretty Air of Romance, as you relate them, in your Plots, and my Plots, that I shall be better directed in what manner to wind up the Catastrophe of the pretty Novel" (201, 208). Richardson's language balances between the claim to historicity and the doctrine of realism, between plot as deception and plot as aesthetic construct, between literary "acceptance" as an extracted submission to rhetorical force and as a willing suspension of disbelief. And soon its other readers begin to intimate the autonomy and sufficiency of the text, its separability from the reality of which it is the "authentic" record, by experimenting with generic labels by which it might be designated (212–13, 255, 374).[8]

Thus Pamela's private journal, the emblem of her solitude, is providentially revealed to be the medium through which she comes to address her best audience, and her persistence in imprisonment turns out to be her best deliverance from it. Moreover, the words of Pamela herself evoke these echoes of Robinson's paradoxical "divine society": "But see the wonderful Ways of Providence! The very things that I most dreaded his seeing or knowing, the Contents of my Papers, have, as I hope, satisfy'd all his Scruples, and been a means to promote my Happiness . . . For had I made my Escape, which was so often my chief Point of View, and what I had placed my Heart upon, I had escaped the Blessings now before me, and fallen, perhaps headlong, into the Miseries I would have avoided!" (261). Pamela's eagerness to associate this providential power with B. coincides with his own subjugation to the creative power of her journal. Up to that point she is quite firm in associating him rather with Lucifer, the dark angel, the Devil incarnate (45, 61, 65, 86, 100, 175, 181, 196). As soon as he is ready to adopt her terms, however—to give thanks that "your white Angel got the better of my black one" (231)—Pamela is ready to restore Lucifer to his rightful seat beside the Father (e.g., 232, 233, 262, 263). So these instances of an apparently creatural deference on Pamela's part are set in perspective by our knowledge that their strict premise is B.'s acknowledgment that she has in a sense already created him.

Does Pamela also, like Robinson, learn to internalize divinity? One contemporary reader advised Richardson that "if she repeated the Sacred Name much seldomer, it wou'd have so much less the Style of Robinson Crusoe, as wou'd make it much more beneficial to the World." But whatever the excesses of her piety, Pamela does not evince Robinson's willingness to validate the secret workings of the imagination as the voice of God. On the contrary, she is consistently on her guard against the temptation to arrogate to her own ingenuity the praise for "Contrivances" that are truly due only to "the Author of all my Happiness" (120–21, 378). And in her darkest moment of despair, Pamela's conquest of suicide too explicitly and knowingly repudiates the human presumption of a providential power of plotting for us to discover it nonetheless in this very will to survive (153). The most powerful enemy of all, she now learns, is internal: "I mean, the Weakness and Presumption, both in one, of [my] own Mind!" (150). This lesson—the sin of sufficiency—is not an easy one to retain in a world fraught with immediate danger. But if

Pamela's ostensible defenselessness belies an extraordinarily energetic self-reliance (a subject to which I will return), this stealthy empowerment is not ostensibly fueled by the pious internalization of divine creativity—except in the sense that B. becomes a god of Pamela's own creation.[9]

Moreover, Richardson would have us understand that Pamela's creativity, scarcely godlike, is really a rather uncertain faculty of representation and judgment. Mr. B. is right: she is a "romancer," and the more desperate her situation actually becomes, the more it is distorted by her overheated imagination, which "paints" the landscape (a favorite term of B.'s) in the hyperbolic colors of romance. Critics are justified in stressing *Pamela*'s indebtedness to the themes and conventions of popular romance, but to be precise we should assess the major debt less to Richardson than to Pamela herself. For it is of course in her eyes—and therefore in ours—that the Lincolnshire abduction and confinement come to look like episodes of errancy and trial out of *The Pilgrim's Progress* (97–98, 150–54); it is her paranoid fancy that enchants cows into bulls and bulls into Lucifer, Mrs. Jewkes, and the "Monster" Colbrand, whose terrifying presence as a "Giant" out of *Guy of Warwick* owes everything but the proper name itself to Pamela rather than to her creator (136–37, 147–48). This is to say not that Richardson is independent of the romance model, but that it is a rationalized and second-order dependence that is functional primarily in characterizing the volatility of his protagonist's imagination.[10]

Yet it is a mark of Pamela's imaginative powers that, so far from being invalidated in her most unassimilated fantasies of persecuted maidenhood, she gets from others considerable help in their construction. Thus, old Mr. Longman contrives the hoary romance device of the gypsy messenger, and on hearing of that affair, even Mr. B. extracts the moral that "a thousand Dragons" are not enough to keep Pamela from her purpose (230). We are wrong to indict Richardson for naively depending on the fictions of romance. But just as he generally shares with Pamela a primary commitment to the truth of documentary historicity, so he inevitably participates, however tacitly, in the undeniable turn toward extreme skepticism that is implied in her fitful awareness of the projective and constructive powers of her own mind and its "contrivances." In truth, this epistemological reversal has been potential from the start, in an authorial dedication to naive empiricism so intense and uncompromising that it extends the claim to historicity to the extreme frontier of writing to the moment, to the notion of an objectivity so minutely responsive to the very process of recording the truth that it must come to disclose the radically subjective bases of all cognition. And for this most profoundly dialectical reason, *Pamela*, precisely because of its unprecedented power as an antiromance, has the historical status of a great precursor of romanticism. In the space of a page, Mr. B. both condemns and admires Pamela's mind for being "romantick" (208–9), and Richardson could hardly disagree.

2

"You see," says Mr. B., "now you are in my Power!" (176). *Pamela's* central concern is the dilemma of how those without power may be justified in gaining it. In a culture that customarily accords the reigning distribution of power an automatic moral sanction, the only acceptable model for change entails some version of, not winning power but receiving it as a gift. The paradoxical dimensions of the transaction must be fully emphasized: those who gain power must be characterized as far as possible in terms of their powerlessness. The dominant religious version of this model—justification by faith and discipline in the calling—subtly informs Pamela's story even though it does not claim the thematic presence it has in *Robinson Crusoe*. Pamela's essential power is the passive and negative one of being virtuous, of resisting the sexual and social power of others. That she is rewarded for it is a result of her discipline in exemplary self-representation. She writes a "spiritual autobiography" of such persuasive force that she gains the full moral accreditation of the community. In the latter half of the narrative Pamela's story makes her an example and a "Pattern for all the Young Ladies in the County," but it is important that this power be neutralized simultaneously by her reciprocal insistence (to Lady Jones) that "I have been polish'd and improv'd by the Honour of such an Example as yours" (243). B. is reformed and converted as a result of reading her journal, but it is crucial that he then be accorded that "godlike" authority which, some readers have felt, is belied by the very need for reformation. Similarly, if Pamela's reward for virtue is to have meaning, the moral authority of the social order by which it is conferred must remain intact despite the evidence of social injustice manifest in the very need for her reward.

The persistence of Pamela's social deference is essential to justify her acquisition of power: it signifies, paradoxically, that she deserves the elevation by which it is obviated. Thus, a typical show of humility on Pamela's part elicits the observation that "she will adorn . . . her Distinction. Ay . . . she would adorn any Station in Life" (244). Yet once she achieves her distinction, humility also becomes quite shameful. After she is married, Pamela retains her status as the servant girl who deserved social elevation even as she experiences the antithetical consequences of that elevation: "No, *Pamela*," says B., "don't imagine, when you are my Wife, I will suffer you to do any thing unworthy of that Character. I know the Duty of a Husband, and will protect your Gentleness to the utmost, as if you were a Princess by Descent" (277). Because her identity is defined so thoroughly at the outset against what she is not, with her rise it is inevitable that Pamela should be required to be a sign both of herself and of her negation, of power and of its absence. Even the means by which she most longs to exercise her new-found power reflect this contradiction: "O! what a Godlike Power is that of doing Good!—I envy the Rich and the Great for nothing else!" (264; see also 31, 315, 387, 408). For although the gifts of charity and reward are traditional methods of buttressing social divisions (thus B. is the one who instructs her in the techniques of paternalistic largess [296]), they are also the means by which Pamela herself has been enabled to permeate those divisions.

As the ambiguity of charity suggests, to speak of Pamela's highly equivocal possession of power is to acknowledge, from a somewhat different angle, the fact of her status inconsistency and the contradictory readings to which her assimilationism is subject. Until her own conversion, Lady Davers is one gentlewoman who thinks Pamela's example teaches young gentlemen nothing so much as the acceptability of mixed marriages and social chaos. But her brother refutes this reading by arguing that only a girl who is as singular as Pamela will be encouraged by her story. Thus Pamela's case is one of "true nobility," symbolically smoothing over the occasional and inevitable inconsistencies that arise in the social order (349–50). And one of Richardson's readers formulated a cunning defense of the narrative's contribution to social stability rather than social mobility by shifting the focus of the question of its exemplary effects from male to female readers: "So that the *moral Meaning of* PAMELA's Good-fortune, far from tempting young Gentlemen to marry *such* Maids as are found in their Families, is, by teaching Maids, to *deserve to be Mistresses,* to stir up Mistresses *to support their Distinction.*" But how effectively can mistresses be thus stirred up if there is no statistical basis for supposing them any more truly—that is, internally—deserving of social elevation than their maids? For the message that inherited social status is strictly "accidental" and strictly uncorrelated with the "natural" gifts of virtue and merit is central enough to the ideology of *Pamela* to be insisted upon explicitly by characters and prefatory puffers alike (14, 249, 294, 350).[11]

Pamela is not the only case of social mobility in *Pamela.* Mrs. Jervis is "a Gentlewoman born, tho' she has had Misfortunes," and we are reminded on several occasions that Pamela's father has not always been obliged to engage in "hard Labour" (30, 265; see also 27, 328, 375, 387). In other words, it is a world already primed for status inconsistency. Mr. B. himself has an unstable social identity. Not that his is an "upstart Family"; on the contrary, it is, as Lady Davers boasts, "as ancient as the best in the Kingdom" (221). But he is quite decidedly a "modernized" aristocrat: convinced that many "Persons of Title [have] no Honour," contemptuous of "the titled Ape," his brother-in-law, and indifferent to acquiring a title for himself; possessed of "Puritan" ideas (his sister's word) on the relation of birth to worth and the preferability of love to convenience in making the marriage choice; and a monied man who industriously improves his estate, accumulates capital, invests in stock, and enjoys running his household like a "Piece of Clockwork" (278, 307–8, 350, 357, 366, 381). Mr. B. is, in short, as transitional a figure as Pamela is, and they are equally and symmetrically representative of that complex social phenomenon which their posterity learned to call the rise of the middle class. Nevertheless, it is clear that in the broadest ideological movement of the narrative, Pamela and Mr. B. converge and collide from the opposite corners of industrious "virtue" and corrupt, aristocratic "honor." In a quite explicit sense, the battle is over who has the power to define the meaning of these categories and to enforce acceptance of their terms upon the other.[12]

We begin the story with terms apportioned in the traditional manner. As Mrs. Jervis says, Pamela is "virtuous and industrious," whereas her master has "Virtue and Honour" (39). Alternatively, the trait that convention permits commoners to possess in the absence of "honor" is "honesty," a virtue that Pamela knows she can claim since she is "poor and lowly, and am not intitled to call it *Honour*" (41, 187). Mr. B.'s aristocratic honor is closely associated with a pride of "reputation," and he is sensitive to the dangers of public "exposure" (41, 44, 68). But as Pamela is quick to point out, B.'s reputation is most endangered by his own demeaning behavior toward her. However inborn it may be, honor can be lost: as Pamela later puts it, "he professed Honour all the Time with his Mouth, while his Actions did not correspond" (181). She will continue for a time to "call him Gentleman, tho' he has fallen from the Merit of that Title," and it does not take long for her to conclude that he has "forfeited his Honour" (34, 68; see also 36, 69, 72, 95).

Thus far Pamela's words are consistent with contemporary usage, which still indulges, if only as a palpable convention, the idea that there exists some unspecified relation between honor of birth and honor of character. But of course there is an important sense in which Pamela, too, possesses "honor": not gentility as such, but the female capacity to ensure, through chastity, the transmission of gentility and property in the male line.[13] This female honor, reputational by definition, must entail in Pamela as deep a concern for her name as her master evinces (e.g., 44). Furthermore, usage makes a fluid association between this female "honor" and the general category "virtue." "Virtue" of course encompasses much else besides, but it is strictly identified with "honor" in the negative case: failed honor means lost virtue, even though honor preserved cannot guarantee virtue (see 187, where B. limits "virtue" to the meaning of female "honor"). Thus, in its frequent application to Pamela, "virtue" alludes both to her chastity and to her internal moral goodness, and in both senses of the term her virtue ironically bespeaks in her a kind of gentility—as in her observation that "my Virtue is as dear to me, as if I was of the highest Quality" (185–86; see also 39). For the statement reminds us that Pamela's highly developed sense of chastity is entirely inconsistent with the actual opportunities at her social rank for transmitting gentility or even property, but it also tacitly invokes the traditional aristocratic maxim that outward status reflects inward virtue. Moreover, the impression of gentility is ironic not only because Pamela is a commoner but also because the gentle Mr. B., as we have seen, appears to be quite ungentlemanly. In fact, the worse she is treated, the more Pamela is tempted (although with characteristic indirection) to doubt not just Mr. B.'s gentility but the very substance of the category itself (72, 112).

Once in Lincolnshire, the debate over the meaning of "honor" becomes open. "I too much apprehend," says Pamela to Mr. B., "that *your* Notions of Honour and *mine* are very different from one another." Her own "humble" and "just Sense of the Word" is diametrically opposed to his, for as she says to Parson Williams, "The Honour of the Wicked is Disgrace and Shame to the Virtuous." To Mrs. Jewkes's question, "What does [Mr. B.] call Honour, think you?" Pamela replies, "Ruin! Shame! Disgrace!" And several days later she adds: "I shall not at this time dispute with you about the Words *Ruin* or *honourable*. I thank God, we have quite different Notions of both" (114, 124–26). The distillation of conflict into terminological disputes signals the turn it is taking toward Pamela's advantage, for language is her medium. She effortlessly refutes the "Terms" of B.'s written "Proposals" (164–68). And the following rape attempt, which is really also another attempt to make her "accept my Proposals," dramatically advertises that she is "in [his] Power" while stealthily signaling that he is in hers (176). For the attempt, like the kidnapping that enables it, is a theft that symbolically acknowledges not only Pamela's possession of what B. values but also his lack of it. The doubleness of her virtue, its reference both to moral goodness and to chastity, really represents a double threat to his status. Pamela's virtue is both the alien "true nobility" of the progressive individual and the vestigial remnant of aristocratic honor, his own alienated honor that is now lodged unaccountably within her. "Robb'd me!" says B., "why so you have, Hussy; you *have* robb'd me" (63). B.'s lust expresses his will to repossess what his behavior announces he has lost to her, both his honor and his externalized conception of honor, which is now internalized in Pamela's virtue.[14]

This is not to say that B.'s ambition is entirely fantastic; but it cannot be achieved through rape. The only way B. might hope to expropriate Pamela's honor in order to restore his own would be to use it, and its guarantee of genealogical legitimacy, to perpetuate the family line. Yet this would require not rape or concubinage but marriage, which B. has resisted, ironically, as inconsistent with his honor. Indeed, he later maintains it was partly his recognition of this flaw that persuaded him against attempting a sham-marriage, since if any child were born of such a union, "it would be out of my own Power to legitimate it, if I should wish it to inherit my Estate" (230). Pamela's earlier, righteous protest—"How came I to be his Property?" (116)—helps us understand that in seeking so literal a possession of her, B. has mistaken his. "proper" aristocratic purpose, which is not simply to make her his property but to use her in the patrilineal transmission of his estate. Once they are married we might expect this latter purpose to be pursued through the transformation of Pamela into the creative producer not of letters but of heirs. But although we sense that the pathos of Sally Godfrey—and of the adorable bastard Miss Goodwin—exists in part to set off Pamela's virtuous capacity to perpetuate B.'s family honor through offspring, in fact she bears him no children and seems quite content to anticipate taking Sally's daughter under her wing (408).[15]

And this turns out to be consistent with the way Richardson undertakes to resolve the conflict over the meaning of honor. To have stressed children and the perpetuation of lineage would have been to endorse the aristocratic conception of honor and its female transmission. At the end of the narrative B. is still concerned that "my Line is almost extinct; and a great Part of my Estate, in case I die without Issue, will go to another Line." Yet the center of his concern is now not the extinction of the line as such but the consequences this might have for the freedom and security of Pamela herself. So B.'s solution is not to generate heirs, but to rewrite his will and to make "such a Disposition of my Affairs, as will make you independent and happy" (404). This gesture underscores B.'s recognition that Pamela's value is located in her own person, not in her ability to transmit the value of others. Her value to him is exemplary and depends on relations not of contiguity but of similarity: her virtue cannot be repossessed as alienated honor; it can only be imitated. Soon after the Lincolnshire crisis, to be sure, Pamela is speaking again as though the terminological battle had never occurred, and her approaching assimilation to gentility requires that this be so. Occasionally even her customary deference seems to her to be inadequate, and like Gulliver among the Houyhnhnms, she feels linguistically impoverished, begging her master to "learn me some other Language, if there be any, that abounds with more grateful Terms, that I may not thus be choaked with Meanings, for which I can find no adequate Utterance" (305). But we and B. know that it is her terms that have prevailed, that her apparent linguistic assimilation masks a supersession of aristocratic honor. In the end B. simply "resolved, since you would not be mine upon my Terms, you should upon your own: And now I desire you not on any other, I assure you" (254). As he later observes to visiting gentry, "My dear Spouse, there she sits, does

me more Honour in her new Relation, than she receives from me!"
(338).[16]

3

The volatile modernization of feudal conceptions of institutional service
can be said to take two forms and to proceed in two directions: "outward," as the robe nobility and career bureaucracy of the centralized
state; and "inward," as domestic service within the last bastion of feudal
patrimonialism, the family. In eighteenth-century England, the theory
of domestic service continued to be dominated by a "medieval" model of
personal discretion and submission that was increasingly at odds with the
practicalities of wage employment. It is a crucial feature of the love
narrative of Mr. B. and Pamela that it is specified to a conflict not only
between gentry and commoner but also between master and servant. In
fact, the analogy between public and private service—or rather, between
their respective deformations—is an active one in *Pamela*. Much of Pamela's resistance to Mr. B.'s advances he understands not only as insubordination but as a criminal act that gives Pamela the status of a "treasonable" "rebel" against B.'s authority (66, 116, 199, 203). For Pamela, the
conflict entails the struggle of a "free Person" against "lawless Tyranny"
(126, 147). She remains conscious of B.'s very real status as justice of the
peace (63, 64, 156), and his power to subject her to a legal "trial" colors
scenes like that of the attempted rape and contributes to the complex and
shifting significance of the "trial" in their relationship. This period in
England saw the growth of informal friendly societies, "confederacies,"
and proto-union groups among domestic laborers. And B.'s perception
of Pamela's access to the sympathy and support of her fellow servants as a
fomenting of "parties" and "confederacies" among them no doubt owes
something to these developments as well as to forms of political opposition in the analogous, public sphere of service (68, 116, 144, 163, 202,
231).[17]

Pamela's dangerous insubordination as a servant is even related to the
specifically literary mode in which she exercises power. The eighteenth-
century system of domestic service, dependent as it was on the circulation of character references among prospective employers, was ham-
pered by a trade in counterfeit references sufficiently lively to provoke
periodic proposals that servants' characters be subject to mandatory regi-
stration at a centralized agency, and that (in the words of one projector)
"every Servant producing any counterfeit Testimonial, shall, upon Conviction, by Confession, or Oath of one Witness, before Justices of
Peace . . . be committed to the House of Correction." But this is precisely B.'s complaint against Pamela: not only that she is "a great Plotter"

and the author of "treasonable Papers" but that she grossly misrepresents herself, displaying "her own romantick Innocence, at the Price of other People's Characters" (162, 199). In fact Pamela's offensiveness is aggravated by the fact that the idealizations of herself and her "Confederates" that she circulates by letter always entail a reciprocal libel against the "character" of her master (69, 181, 199, 201–2), who does indeed bring her to trial and commit her to his house of correction. Pamela's dignified plea remains that of the naive empiricist: "I have only writ Truth; and I wish he had deserv'd a better Character at my hands, as well for his sake as mine" (206).[18]

The vestigial but resilient ties of eighteenth-century domestic service to the cultural ethos of feudal service made it a particularly unstable social institution, balanced uncertainly between status and class orientations. This can be seen in what happens to the conventions of servants' wearing apparel. Livery remained customary for lower menservants, but a system of signification that once conferred the honor of service was now as likely to suggest a demeaning slavery. "Body servants" received a more subtle "livery," the cast-off clothing of their master or mistress. Although such a custom might aim to advertise the elevation of the employer, it could equally serve a contrary end by blurring the sumptuary distinctions between ranks, so that the servant appeared not as the signifier of his betters but as the self-sufficient signified. In Pamela's case this is true to an extraordinary degree. Early on, Lady Brooks is so impressed by Pamela's "Face and Shape" that she exclaims to Lady Towers, "Why she must be better descended than you have told me!" (59). Richardson is playing with the romance convention preparatory to demystifying it, for Pamela makes it plain that her personal graces can be very well accounted for by the nurture of her deceased mistress, Lady B. As her new master implies and Pamela anticipates, it would not take long for "these fair soft Hands, and that lovely Skin" to become "as red as a Blood-pudden" should she depart for her parents' and "return again to hard Work" (71, 78). Indeed, one of the prefatory letter writers remarks that the fact of Pamela's service to Lady B. is a pragmatically antiromance device without which "it must have carried an Air of Romantick Improbability to account for her polite Education" (20).[19]

From Mr. B.'s mother Pamela learns the more delicate labor of needlework and the gentle arts of singing, dancing, and drawing; and from her she receives the cast-off clothing B. so liberally and alarmingly supplements after his mother's death (30–31, 52, 77). Pamela entertains no romance fantasies about her origins. If she is a foundling, then it is not gypsies but gentry who stole her away; as she tells B., "I have been in Disguise indeed ever since my good Lady, your Mother, took me from my poor Parents . . . and . . . heap'd upon me rich Cloaths, and other Bounties" (62). The disguise is so successful that it amounts to a transformation. Pamela's natural graces, Lady B.'s indulgence, and the customs peculiar to body service have conspired to make Pamela seem not an accomplished lady's maid but a lady. This reality lies behind B.'s insistence that "I will no more consider you as my Servant," and behind Pamela's reproach that she might well "forget that I am your Servant, when you forget what belongs to a Master" (35, 82; see also 71). So although it seems to Pamela a removal of disguise to replace her lady's silks with homespuns preparatory to the trip home, to everyone else—not only B., but all her fellow servants—she is now "metamorphos'd," "a Stranger" whom no one knows because she has assumed the leveling disguise of a country girl (60–62). B.'s speechless confusion at Pamela's witchery in this scene specifies the mutabilities of his growing love to a total discomposure at the status inconsistency of this half-girl half-lady, half-servant half-mistress. "Thou strange Medley of Inconsistence!" he calls her presently, and he does not begin to know how to approach her (76).

This is not so much to say that *Pamela* is an antiromance as to argue that it is a progressive specification of romance to the conditions of eighteenth-century domestic service. As Pamela tells her parents, "You see by my sad Story, and narrow Escapes, what Hardships poor Maidens go thro', whose Lot is to go out to Service" (73). And entailed in this specification is a naturalistic "escape" from the condition of service which is quite alien to the marvelous methods of romance. Socialized to the very top of what J. Jean Hecht has called the "chain of emulation" in Lady B.'s household, Pamela has learned to internalize and to project an expectation of herself for which no accessible social category exists. Like an overeducated younger son, she remarks, "I have been brought up wrong, as Matters stand" (77). Lady B. acted only out of goodness, but as Pamela puts it suggestively, "All her Learning and Education of me . . . will be of little Service to me now" (80). The return to her parents is difficult to contemplate, since her education "will make me but ill Company for my rural Milkmaid Companions that are to be" (77). Yet as far as the household servants are concerned, B. observes that "they had rather serve you than me" (99). B.'s advances trap Pamela between veiled and highly implausible intimations that he might elevate her to the status of gentility (83, 85, 124, 126), and the daily reality of incarceration by a brutal housekeeper whose nominal deference Pamela is obliged to protest candidly: "Pray . . . don't Madam me so . . . for I am a Servant inferior to you, and so much the more as I am turn'd out of Place" (103). The desperate crisis in this "romance" adventure of service is that Pamela, like the courtier whose excellence exceeds not only his peers but even his prince, has no social niche, no place to go.[20]

The solution to the crisis is, of course, marriage. The chief obstacle to it is B.'s consciousness. He must learn to reconceive marriage among the gentry as an institution that, rather than being strictly inconsistent with the institution of domestic service, may under the proper conditions provide the great and culminating link in the chain of emulation. But for this to be possible it is also required, paradoxically, that the theory of marriage be severed from what persists as the theory of domestic service—that marriage cease to be conceived so thoroughly as a form of female service within the patriarchal family. Needless to say, the reconciliation of love and marriage, the reconception of marriage as a public ceremony that is taken primarily to confirm the prior and private fact of love, is a momentous and far-reaching development of the early modern period. For B. it proceeds through several painful stages. As we have seen, his proposals to (in Pamela's words) "make me a vile kept Mistress" are for B. a kind of openly "sham-marriage." Despite her dismay, they are B.'s sincere attempt to invent a status dignified enough to accommodate Pamela's elevated position at the top of the servant hierarchy. If he cannot conceive of marrying her, marriage becomes at least his model for this rather touchingly inadequate invention. Thus the proposals soberly imitate the concerns of a formal contract aimed primarily at the satisfaction of financial convenience, and they even promise Pamela the jewelry that was bought for the gentlewoman whose match with Mr. B. had once been proposed (166). On the night of the attempted rape, when B. tries to force Pamela to accept these proposals, he compounds the offer to clothe her in the jewels of gentility by assuming the leveling disguise of a servant girl, as if by raising her he could simultaneously lower himself to her status, so as somehow to meet her in the middle (175).

In the days that follow this attempt, marriage to Pamela becomes possible for B. And one sign that we have reached this critical point of change is, paradoxically, the explicit and scarcely rationalized absoluteness with which B. now insists on the impossibility of marriage—to Pamela or to anyone else (184, 188). Much later B. will reveal that his violent aversion to marriage was a reaction against a typically aristocratic education, which taught that in the marriage choice, "Convenience, or Birth and Fortune, are the first Motives, Affection the last (if it is at all consulted)" (366). In other words, B. has long been theoretically receptive to a progressive view of the institution (this is one sign that his social identity, too, is fluid). But while the priority of love over convenience seemed a manageable heresy so long as a general consistency of birth and fortune remained the background reality, with Pamela the demand for a radical constancy to internals—to love over convenience, to virtue over birth, fortune, and honor—becomes so overdetermined that the rebellion is inconceivable. B.'s ultimately successful struggle to conceive it, all the same, is inseparable both from the irresistible force of his love for Pamela and from the triumph of her notion of "honor" over his. And these circumstances, in turn, depend entirely on the power of Pamela's mind, on her extraordinary capacity to create a utopian projection of possibility while she is ostensibly and passively contained by the limiting boundaries of domestic service and domestic incarceration at the Lincolnshire estate.

When Pamela is kidnapped she is relieved of her duties as an industrious worker and enters a period of enforced leisure. She had already differed with Mr. B. on the utility of her "scribbling," and had stoutly defended it against the charge of "idleness" (34, 37, 55). Nevertheless, Pamela knows that hard manual labor leaves no opportunity for writing, and she anticipates no "Writing-time" once she returns to her parents—"little thinking it would be my only Employment so soon" (82, 95). In Lincolnshire, writing becomes highly ambiguous. On the one hand, B.'s early judgment that it is idle activity is reinforced by Pamela's recognition that "now it is all the Diversion I have": "I have so much Time upon my Hands, that I must write on to employ myself" (106, 134). On the other hand, Pamela's clandestine self-employment is clearly a subversive activity—subversive not only of her master's "character" but of his right to set the terms of her employment—and she realizes that it is in her interest to compose some inconsequential scribbles in Mrs. Jewkes's presence so that she will "think me usually employ'd to such idle Purposes" and "suppose I employ'd myself . . . to no better Purpose at other times" (113).

A purposeful impersonation of idleness, an act of ostensible leisure that conceals industrious labor, Pamela's writing becomes a self-serving "self-employment" that flourishes only because her service to her master has been formally interrupted. In a way this transformation is a utopian parable of the economic circumstances that accompanied and conditioned the reconception of marriage in the early modern period. More literally even before her marriage than after, Pamela is the type of the "new" woman who is liberated from both the constraints and the freedoms of the old, family-based, domestic system of industry. The institution of marriage becomes humanized at the same time that the scope and significance of domestic activity are narrowed; marriage becomes the exclusive work of women, a realm of enforced leisure, passive consumption, and unpaid labor.[21] What is utopian about Pamela's experience is that with her domestic incarceration comes "self-employment" and the creative labor of writing. The more confined she is, the greater her productivity, the more industrious and ingenious her efforts to circulate and distribute her work (the "sunflower correspondence" is a safer method and accommodates larger packets than the corrupted John Arnold).

The value of Pamela's labor is its capacity to mediate her personal value—her "Person and Mind," "the Merit of your Wit," mental qualities that B. values from the outset and that are not easily distinguished from what various characters mean when they praise her exemplary virtue (54, 202). As a signification of personal value and virtue, Pamela's writings are both parallel and superior to the conventional code of dress. Clothing, after all, is preeminently an instrument of disguise and duplicity (Pamela notes distractedly that B. rushed from her closet "in a rich silk and silver Morning Gown" [66]). Writing provides a less fallible access to the heart. But the positive analogy between words and clothing as modes of self-expression also is insisted on throughout *Pamela:* in the language of the prefatory material (7, 12); in the proximity of Pamela's thoughts on how both her letters and her dress must become less formal (51–52); in the way her division of her clothing into three "parcels," whose contents are then "particulariz'd," is later echoed in her division of the journal into two "parcels" and in the periodic particularization of the journal's contents (78–79, 197–98, 204–8, 238–39, 256–57). But since in Lincolnshire she has taken to wearing her writings "about my Hips," to particularize them she must literally disclose herself: "I must all undress me in a manner to untack them" (198, 204). Thus the modulation from an epistolary to a journalistic mode is further justified by the fact that it confronts B. with an accumulated "corpus," Pamela objectified, which can exercise its creative and aestheticizing powers more effectively than single letters might.[22]

In this subtly figurative sense, the creative labor of Pamela's writings is also that of pregnancy. Earlier, when she first discovers that the sunflower correspondence will be a successful means of publishing herself once again, she exclaims to her parents: "How nobly my Plot succeeds! But I begin to be afraid my Writings may be discover'd; for they grow large! I stitch them hitherto in my Under-coat, next my Linen" (120).[23] And later B. refers to the period of her imprisonment and clandestine journalizing as "the Time of her Confinement" (267). When Pamela learns to clothe herself in her papers, she discovers a method of signifying her value that is far more immediate, efficient, and inalienably "authentic" than those to which women customarily are limited, but that is also an imaginative extension of custom, of bodily decoration and childbirth. Unlike Sally Godfrey, Pamela channels her female "virtue" into the procreative act not of biological generation but of literary persuasion. Her reward is to remain in control of the "issue" of her own plot, and later to find that her "currency" has real value on the marriage market. Ashamed that she does not bring Mr. B. a portion, Pamela exclaims: "But how poor is it to offer nothing but Words for such generous Deeds!" Yet he is now convinced that "you bring me what is infinitely more valuable, an experienc'd Truth, a well-try'd Virtue, and a Wit and Behaviour more than equal to the Station you will be placed in" (283).[24]

4

Thus Richardson seeks to empower his protagonist through behavior whose masquerade as the old powerlessness is convincing enough to evade comprehensive invalidation, and thereby to be truly successful; and it is this assimilationist ambition that has encouraged readers, from B. onward, to see Pamela as a scheming hypocrite. In this respect and in others, the resemblance to Robinson Crusoe's utopia, although discontinuous, is often suggestive. "Beached" at the top of the hierarchy of domestic service, in her very incarceration Pamela finds an unprecedented access to her imprisoner and to the autotelic authority that is his by birth. Her transformation from servant to lady involves an internalization of that authority. It alters her "character" no more than Robinson's is altered on the island, but in facilitating her change in status it reorients her position in the world and changes everything. Pamela too undergoes a species of conversion, although it is not explicitly conceived as such, and it is marked by some familiar signposts. Shortly before their wedding, for example, Mr. B. assures Mr. Andrews that his daughter is as "virtuous" "as the new-born Babe" (248), and the day of the wedding superstitiously commemorates not only Pamela's birthday but also the days of her arrival at Bedfordshire and of her abduction from it, both of which have already been associated with a rebirth (46, 62, 275). Always highly conscious of the need to preserve her "good name" (28, 41, 49, 179), Pamela feels obliged to apologize to her parents for signing herself "PAMELA B——" after the wedding and thereby "glorying in my Change of Name" (301; see also 302–3).

Christian's rebirth entailed an embrace of service; Pamela's requires a repudiation of it, but the lesson is not easy to act upon. Thus her persistence in calling Mr. B. "Master" and herself "servant" is marked enough to be commented on by the local gentry, and she goes so far as to "assist" Mrs. Jewkes in serving them cake (243, 257). Privately she vows "to rise to a softer Epithet" for B. on occasion, and it may only be the later experience of enforced service at the hands of the insufferably haughty Lady Davers that dissuades her from that role in the future (315, 318, 321). And yet, in an odd way, the difficult momentousness of the transition is communicated not only by the gulf between status terms but also by the terms' indistinguishability. B. once sought to make Pamela "a vile kept Mistress" (164), but the word "mistress" is used more often to designate, as a parallel to "master," the lady of the house by reference to her authority over the servants. From time to time we hear speculation that Pamela herself may assume such a position (103, 183, 238, 253), but we can appreciate nonetheless why her father is "grieved" to hear at the local alehouse that the squire had at his estate "a young Creature . . . who *was,* or *was to be,* his Mistress" (247). The word "family" itself is ambiguous. It is still used paternalistically to embrace the domestic staff in a gentle household like B.'s, as well as to refer to the gentle family proper, and it is Pamela's misfortune to be accused of demeaning B. in the eyes of both of these "families" (57, 75, 92, 213, 214, 221, 247, 380). But of course this also implies Pamela's power to redeem B.'s reputation in each of them, a process that is coextensive with her mediation of the families themselves through her successful passage from service to gentility.[25]

This passage is the work of the entire narrative. Like Robinson's conversion, Pamela's marriage marks not the end of struggle but the beginning of a long period of socialization. Marriage and conversion define the essence of the new role, but its practical reality requires the gradual accretion of layers of social experience: not the fundamental, unitary relationship, but multiple group reference and the accreditation of the community. Mr. B.'s perspective on Pamela's future seems almost to demand this sociological sort of language: "For some Company you must keep. My Station will not admit it to be with my common Servants; and the Ladies will fly your Acquaintance; and still, tho' my Wife, will treat you as my Mother's Waiting-maid" (225). Suspended between yahoos and houyhnhnms, Pamela sets out to solidify the nature of her relationship to each of these "families." And to each of these ends her writing continues to be serviceable. In fact, before the wedding, Pamela self-consciously imagines that her powers of "scribbling" will be exercised explicitly in a role of social mediation, that they "will be employ'd in the Family Accounts, between the Servants and me, and me and your good Self" (227). Not only the keeping of accounts, but also the writing of letters, is central to Pamela's longed-for power of doing good by charity and reward (299–303, 387–88). And these modest elevations of the lowly provide a discreet confirmation of her own more permanent ascent (382–84, 387, 400, 403). At the same time, Pamela recognizes that having risen out of the servant hierarchy altogether, it remains her duty, now as mistress, to continue in what Hecht has called "the role of servants as cultural intermediaries."[26]

With gentility, the task of socialization is considerably more difficult. Contemplating her first appearance in "company," Pamela is acutely conscious both of the social significance of her dress and of its treacherous status as an unreliable signifier. If she dresses well, "it would look as if I would be nearer on a Level with him: And yet, should I not, it may be thought a Disgrace to him" (223; cf. 386–87). Soon enough it is clear that for the present task Pamela's literary powers of persuasion will not be appropriate. It is Pamela herself who must be read. B. reports that the ladies beg "to see you just as you are," and now it is Pamela's turn to make the skeptical distinction between things as they are and the interpretative "Light" in which they are read, for she doubts the ladies "will look at me with your favourable Eyes" (233). What follows is a far more elaborate version of those early dramatic "scenes" in which Pamela artlessly charms the closeted Mr. B. (64–66, 78–81). Now the stage is "the longest Gravel Walk in the Garden," and the local gentry study her minutely as she slowly approaches the alcove in which they sit— "They all so gaz'd at me," Pamela says, "that I could not look up" (242–43). Shortly the scene shifts to the parlor, where Mr. B., telling the company that "I would make you all witness to their first Interview," engineers the reunion of Pamela and her father so as to maximize its spectacle and sentiment (249–50). It is as though the act of social accommodation must first be founded on the most ritually powerful and socially engaged—but also most vulnerable—mode of self-representation.

Thereafter Pamela is allowed to perform in the more distanced media of language and narrative. Of course, she is already a subject of narrative: they "have all heard of your uncommon Story" (243). But in the coming days the local gentry will experience the facility of her wit and mind, hear her story from her own mouth, and be conquered by the journal itself, which now begins to circulate among rural gentry whom Pamela has never even met (334–35, 339–41, 374, 377). Both as a servant and as a gentlewoman, in other words, Pamela's power comes from her ability to master the existing means of conferring and creating value. Initially a commodity on the domestic-service market, she appropriates the employer's power by writing her own character references, whose circulation not only governs her own circulation as labor but also effectively transforms her into her own employer. The same method conquers the marriage market. Self-employed, Pamela becomes her own reference, her own signifier: first through her physical presence, but most efficiently by objectifying her character in language and story and dispatching it for publication.

This culminating process of circulation is achieved, ironically, under the auspices of Lady Davers, whose victimization of Pamela before her conversion to her is the most dangerous trial of socialization of all; and it also provides a heightened version of Pamela's initial trials at the hands of Mr. B. Enamored of "ancient and untainted" blood far more than her brother ever was, Lady Davers recapitulates his offenses by keeping Pamela "Prisoner" once again and by even subjecting her to the attenuatedly sexual assault of Jackey's half-unsheathed sword (221, 320–21, 328, 329). Unlike B.'s rape attempt, here aristocratic pride is scarcely displaced by sexual innuendo, and Jackey appears as some foppishly ineffectual *noblesse d'épée* acting out his aunt's apoplectic, obsolescent fury. For her own part, Lady Davers had long sought to act the "domineering" patriarch by arranging, in the absence of the real parents, her brother's marriage to an earl's daughter (224, 341, 367, 374). To her the marriage of Pamela and Mr. B. must appear a sham-marriage most of all if it is legitimate, because "unequal Matches" institutionalize by definition an "utterly in-excusable" and "disgraceful" condition of status inconsistency (221). The onslaughts of Lady Davers spur both Pamela and B. to essentially Chris-tian condemnations of aristocratic vanity (222, 350). Threatened by her with a familial renunciation, B. imitates Bunyan's Faithful by impertur-bably, then passionately, renouncing his family in her person (221, 224, 347). And Pamela is moved to speculate, in a manner worthy of Defoe, on the relativity and circularity of all genealogy (222).

Of course all three are reconciled well before the end of the story, but in a way that is instructive with respect to the larger instability of Rich-ardson's narrative. It is obvious that within this dense texture, questions of virtue cannot be unraveled from questions of truth. To inquire into the morality and social justice of Pamela's upward mobility is necessarily to inquire into the truth of her story, and the thread of epistemological reversal that runs through Richardson's naive empiricism is continuous with a subversive strain in his progressive ideology. In one respect the subversion is self-evident, since we have witnessed it before in other narratives and because it is so much of a piece with its epistemological counterpart. There is an inherent tension between the dynamic form in which Pamela's personal merit is manifested—the plastic powers of her mind—and the progressive ideal of meritocracy, which envisions the replacement of arbitrary aristocratic culture by a rigorous consistency of moral and social success, not by the ethically uncertain force of per-suasive self-creation. It is not just that Pamela the assimilationist seems occasionally inclined, as in contention with Lady Davers, to supersede the traditional system of social status; it is also that the deceptive strength of her character has the potential to convince us both of its own rectitude and of the source of this judgment in an autonomous and external moral order.

There is however another subversive potentiality in Pamela, and it is a function of the fact that her progressive social character is a complex compound composed at the intersection of her two identities as a com-mon servant and a woman. So long as her social rank remains humble, the compound is stable: her subordination as a woman rather unob-trusively deepens what is the more ostensible (and basically analogous) condition, her subordination as a servant. But once Pamela is raised through marriage, the compound becomes volatile: her social rank be-comes superordinate, yet she remains subordinate because she remains a woman. Like Mary Carleton, she encounters a species of status inconsis-tency that is impervious to the reparations of social mobility. On her way home before B.'s final change of heart, Pamela writes in bewilderment, "Lack-a-day, what strange Creatures are Men!"—and then, remember-ing the goodness of her father, "Gentlemen, I should say rather!" (212). In accord with the main thrust of the narrative, the force of the critique is directed at aristocratic, not male, pride. And this tendency is encouraged, even after the wedding, by the aristocratic tyranny Pamela endures at the hands of Lady Davers. Even so, Pamela appeals at one point to her ladyship's sense of solidarity that she, "be the Distance ever so great, is of the same Sex with me" (321). But the appeal must be in vain so long as Lady Davers is incensed enough at the notion of Pamela's claim to be her familial "Sister" to overlook any other sense of the term (323, 329). The only force capable of quelling this aristocratic rage turns out to be that of her brother, not because it is stronger but because it consists more purely, by right of gender, in the patrimonial privilege that is the essence of their shared arrogance. "Leave my House this Instant!" he shouts, the family house being his by inheritance. And with this outburst the lines of conflict are momentarily and suggestively redrawn, for his sister is now obliged to recall that she is a woman first and a lady second.[27]

B. makes the crucial point when he refutes Lady Davers's notion that his marriage to Pamela is no different from the case of her marrying her father's groom: "The Difference is, a Man ennobles the Woman he takes, be she *who* she will; and adopts her into his own Rank, be it *what* it will: But a Woman, tho' ever so nobly born, debases herself by a mean Marriage, and descends from her own Rank, to his she stoops to" (349). The contemporary currency of B.'s rule of thumb is grounded in the patrimonial and patrilineal nature of English property law, and it effectively argues that in the end, gender-based categories are prior even to status-based categories. Indeed it makes sense that if B. really has shed his due share of aristocratic prejudice—the admiration of honor and titles, for example—the distillation of prejudice that remains must be not aristocratic but male. B.'s rage at Lady Davers causes her to relent, Pamela to become her advocate, and B., vastly irritated, to exclaim, "Your Sex is the D——l" (360). The next day the two women are reconciled enough for Lady Davers to tell Pamela, "You deserve the Praises of all our Sex," and to apply to her brother the derogatory term that until now she has applied to Pamela herself: "I believe, if the Truth was known, you lov'd the Wretch not a little" (372).

In this fashion, the very terms of conflict undergo a subtle but arresting modulation toward the end of *Pamela*. As we have seen, B.'s early sexual desire was equivocal, for it masked the more profoundly felt vestiges of aristocratic pride. Now that he is Pamela's husband, that pride has withered and been replaced by the more recognizably gendered passion of patriarchal authority in its relatively liberal, progressive guise. Hoping that he "shan't be a very tyrannical Husband," B. officiously enlarges now on what he expects in a wife. Pamela's response—to us rather than to him—takes the implicitly ironic form of a document interspersed with running editorial comment that she used earlier to refute B.'s "articles" and that Lady Davers has lately employed against her brother's letter (326–27). Pamela's version of "this awful Lecture," and her commentary upon it, have an extraordinary tonal range that permits her to combine several shades of assent with occasional raillery at B.'s masculine presumption (see esp. nos. 22, 24, 30. [pp. 370–71]). So the remarkable utopianism of Pamela's achievement is faintly colored, at the end, by the recognition that there may yet be something more to be achieved. But the problem remains unformulated: for Pamela to aspire to the social status of a man might seem as humanly untenable to the progressive Richardson as Gulliver's aspiration to the condition of a Houyhnhnm does to the conservative Swift. And in fact the emergence of gender conflict here at the end of *Pamela* may work less to supersede the terms of status conflict itself than to afford a venerable vehicle— "the battle of the sexes"—by which to accommodate a supersessionist tension that we can detect from time to time in Pamela's basically assimilationist progressivism. Nevertheless, the volatility of Richardson's ideology has a real significance that is closely analogous to that of his epistemology. Just as Richardson's "objective" claim to historicity is driven so far that it seems at times to unearth its dialectical antithesis, the subjectivity of perception, so the progressive empowerment of individual merit leads in the end to the crucial case of women, a condition of social injustice so deeply rooted that its very disclosure only marks the limits of progressive ideology, the point beyond which it will not venture. Even as it mediates old problems in a new way, *Pamela* reveals these new and analogous ones—the problem of the subject and the problem of women—to which it must remain unresponsive. The revelation should be seen, I think, as testimony not to Richardson's failure but to his success, to the extraordinary power of his conception to carry him further, in the end, than he ever meant to go.

Yet even in its own terms the achievement can be undervalued. Often against the positive backdrop of *Clarissa,* critics have attacked *Pamela*'s denouement as an unconscionable pattern of female fulfillment: freedom as a truckling matrimonial subservience.[28] But the choice between *Pamela* and *Clarissa* is a classic one between two strikingly and reciprocally imperfect alternatives: manifest material and social empowerment, which can be only fitfully acknowledged on the plane of discourse; and manifest discursive and imaginative empowerment, whose material register consists in nothing more substantial than the posthumous requital of one's persecutors. *Pamela* is not an inferior first attempt to achieve what is fulfilled only in *Clarissa;* it successfully achieves an authentic species of fulfillment which *Clarissa,* ambitious of other ends, does not even attempt. Limited to the horizon of contemporary ideology and its view of social possibility, the choice must be recognized as inherently untenable: a choice between not comic repression and tragic freedom but two different kinds of repression. Within these limits, then, what is most remarkable about *Pamela*'s utopian achievement is precisely the image it provides of real empowerment under conditions that seem somehow to be unaltered (as even Lady Davers in the end would agree) by the reconstructive process that is implied in the experience. By this means social change takes on the face of a seamless continuity.

— Twelve —

The Institutionalization of Conflict (II):
Fielding and the Instrumentality of Belief

I

In the Richardson–Fielding rivalry of the 1740s it is easy to be reminded of the more tacit opposition between Defoe and Swift several decades earlier. The similarities are temperamental as well as cultural. Richardson's transparent vanity, masking a persistent sensitivity to his lack of "the very great Advantage of an Academical Education," seems a natural foil to the serene diffidence and careless superiority of the graduate of Eton and Leyden, who counted the Earl of Denbigh among his blood relations. But Fielding's mastery of a certain aristocratic hauteur belies a social background—and social attitudes—of considerable complexity. His father was the younger son of a younger son and a military man under Marlborough. His mother came from a family of established professional standing, and after her death when Henry was eleven, there ensued a custody suit that consumed the remainder of his youth, and enforced on him an alternation between city and country pursuits and between culturally divergent expectations of how his own way was to be made in the world.[1]

Until the Licensing Act of 1737, Fielding made his way most successfully as a playwright, a profession in which many of the narrative preoccupations with which we will be concerned underwent an important development. The highly reflexive quality of much of Fielding's drama suggests that he was both fascinated and impatient with an artistic mode so obligated to the evidence of the senses that its illusions fairly cried out for an easy disconfirmation. In *The Historical Register for the Year 1736*, for example, Fielding toys with the literalistic, pseudo-Aristotelian "unity of time," and its requirement of a strict correspondence between time represented and time elapsed in its representation, in a way that presages his later play with the naive claim to historicity and its pretense to an unselective completeness of narrative detail. These farces are also Fielding's first laboratory for the experimental juxtaposition of questions of truth and virtue. It was not hard to see, in the popular theater of the period, a connection between the epistemological ingratiation of the senses evident in the wholesale reliance on theatrical "spectacle," and the shameless commercial pandering that was entailed in such theatrics. Moreover Fielding often seized the occasion to specify the traditional analogy of the world and the stage to a self-conscious critique of political manipulation and corruption under the Whig "management" of the 1730s. Even the old dramatic device of discovery and reversal takes on (at least with hindsight) a characteristically Fieldingesque exorbitance. Thus, in *The Author's Farce* (1730), we follow the fortunes of a platitudinously progressive hero who, "thrown naked upon the world . . . can make his way through it by his merit and virtuous industry," and who nevertheless turns out, in a riot of romance revelations of parentage, to be heir apparent to royalty.[2]

Given the energy with which he pushed against the conventions of dramatic representation, it is scarcely surprising that, once obliged to turn to narrative, Fielding adopted the skeptical stance of the "historian." His earliest work of this sort, *The History of the Life of the Late Mr. Jonathan Wild the Great* (1743), was substantially complete before *Pamela* appeared at the end of 1740. Its satiric response to the problem of how to tell the truth in narrative therefore owes less to the instigations of Richardson than to Fielding's wide reading in ancient and modern historiography. And the difficult complexity of that response can be explained by the way the parodic mode of his skepticism both does and does not coordinate with the ironic mode of his mock-heroic.[3]

What is shared by these modes is the familiar pattern of "double reversal." Fielding's parodic "history" is first of all a critique of the idealizing, "romancing" method of traditional biographies, with their near-immemorial lineages, premonitions of greatness, frankly supernatural deliverances, fabricated speeches, and the like. Yet the parody of traditional history can also implicitly subvert the modern and rationalizing standard of historicity, from which it is incompletely separated. On this second level of formal satire, Fielding parodies the distinctively modern form of criminal biography, its characteristic devices of authentication, and especially the proliferation of documents on which its claim to historicity depends—ordinary's accounts, authentic letters and journals, convincingly fragmentary shorthand transcriptions, and painstaking ear-witness testimony. Thus the critique of the old, romancing histories is supplemented by a critique of the "new romance" of naive empiricism and its modernized methods of imposing on the credulity of the reader.[4]

By the same token, Fielding's mock-heroic is first of all an ironic reduction of the unheroic rogue by the normative standards of genuine heroism and its conventional panegyric forms; but it is then also an unstable and self-subverting movement against the heroic standard itself. Jonathan Wild is like Alexander and Caesar in evincing the "imperfection" of "a mixture of good and evil in the same character." But Fielding is different from the ancient biographers in knowing—and in letting us know—that these qualities are morally incompatible: that precisely what we call "heroism" is the essence of evil in such figures, and that it entirely overshadows whatever small goodness they may also exhibit (I, i, 3–5; IV, xv, 175–76). Modern heroes are rogues; but so are ancient heroes, and on this recognition Fielding bases his sincere claim "to draw natural, not perfect characters, and to record the truths of history, not the extravagances of romance" (IV, iv, 135). So the critique of modern roguery is supplemented by a critique of ancient roguery and of the romancing historians who call it heroism.[5]

The self-subversive instability of Fielding's mock-heroic, which he shares with his age, is parallel to that of naive empiricism and an expression of the same implacable process. Once launched, the skeptical critique might assume a force of its own and overturn its original premises. What makes Fielding's satire notoriously difficult here is that the same element, traditional historiography, occupies opposed positions in the two parallel reversals. In Fielding's strategy of extreme skepticism, Plutarch and Suetonius are the negative examples that are attacked by the normative standard of empirical history, even as naive empiricism itself is subjected to parody. But in the mock-heroic movement, it is the modern example that is negative; the positive norm by which it is criticized is ancient history, which in turn becomes vulnerable to a similar attack. What is achieved by this remarkable interweaving of satiric strategies that are structurally parallel but asymmetrical in substance? The major effect of the asymmetry—the confusing conflation of terms (positive and negative, ancient and modern, hero and rogue) that have been posited in opposition to each other—is to emphasize what is a dominant feature of each strategy as it operates on its own: the sense of the collapse of categories. At the same time, the structural parallel between the skeptical and mock-heroic strategies is solid enough to suggest that what is at issue here is not only questions of truth. For the latter movement mediates us from the epistemological concerns of the former to an analogous realm of ethical and social concerns, from questions of truth to questions of virtue.

Fielding's central term in the critique of heroism—the slippery notion of "greatness"—bears a close relation to the equally slippery notion of Machiavellian *virtù*. Machiavelli is the modern historian most responsible for extending and transforming the Roman "ideal" of amoral heroism, and Fielding's Jonathan Wild is a classic Machiavellian "new man" who rises by force and fraud and even learns to purvey his own Machiavellian "maxims" (IV, xv, 173–74). Like his epistemology, Fielding's ideology is the issue of a double critique: first of aristocratic ideology by progressive, then of progressive ideology by conservative. The slipperiness of "greatness" is vital to this dialectical movement. To the progressive mentality, the greatness of a newly risen "Great Man" like Sir Robert Walpole is a matter of social stature that implies a correspondent moral elevation. But Fielding shows that progressives are the unconscious and stealthy heirs of ancient aristocratic assumptions about the congruity of inner and outer states. The moral proximity of great men like Walpole and Alexander the Great (who might with justice end their days by hanging), and rogues like Wild (who actually do), argues the conservative truth that status inconsistency yet reigns in the modern world of progressive "social justice" as surely as it did in ancient, aristocratic culture, when "greatness" and "goodness" were taken to be coextensive (IV, xii, 168, xiv, 170, 171).[6]

Yet if Fielding's major purpose in Jonathan Wild is clearly a conservative critique of the progressive upstart, the narrative retains the coherent, if schematic, imprint of its enabling progressive premise, the skeleton of a progressive plot satiric of aristocratic honor. Of course, the progressive foundation is evident elsewhere in Fielding's work as well. Earlier, in the Miscellanies, he is outspoken in his contempt for the way that

the least Pretensions to Pre-eminence in Title, Birth, Riches, Equipage, Dress, &c. constantly overlook the most noble Endowments of Virtue, Honour, Wisdom, Sense, Wit, and every other Quality which can truly dignify and adorn a Man . . . That the fortuitous Accident of Birth, the Acquisition of Wealth, with some outward Ornaments of Dress, should inspire Men with an Insolence capable of treating the rest of Mankind with Disdain, is so preposterous, that nothing less than daily Experience could give it Credit.

And to the "infamous worthless Nobleman" who claims that his inherent worth has descended to him with his title, Fielding makes the empiricist retort "that a Title originally implied Dignity, as it implied the Presence of those Virtues to which Dignity is inseparably annexed; but that no Implication will fly in the Face of downright positive Proof to the contrary."[7]

In Jonathan Wild, the dominant conservative satire is supported by the scaffolding of a progressive satire against aristocratic values. Like Fielding's worthless nobleman, Jonathan Wild is convinced of the genealogical powers of "the blood of the Wilds, which hath run with such uninterrupted purity through so many generations," and he passionately believes honor to be "the essential quality of a gentleman" (IV, x, 156; I, xiii, 37). To appreciate Wild's story as a progressive satire on aristocratic ideology we must isolate that discontinuous but palpable strain of "greatness" which consists in a genealogical gentility distinguished by nothing so much as petty viciousness and bumbling incompetence. We begin with "the fortuitous accident of birth" memorialized in the Wild lineage (I, ii). His father educates "the young gentleman" in "principles of honour and gentility" and sends him on his own version of the Tour (I, iii, 11, vii, 21–22). Wild soon learns to socialize with aristocratic types like Count la Ruse, whose status as "men of honour" is firmly established by their apparent willingness to duel at the drop of a glove (see I, iv, 11–12, viii, 25–26, xi, 31, xiii, 36–37). And his later career is broadly marked by a succession of dupings—generally receiving worse than he gives—that confirm in the "gentleman" an absence both of virtue and of dignity.[8]

In a truly progressive plot, the dominant corollary of this negative example would be the positive story of the rise of industrious virtue.[9] In *Jonathan Wild* we have the problematic shadow of such a corollary in the figure of Heartfree (to whom I will return). But the more fundamental—and characteristically conservative—tendency is to collapse the very distinction between positive and negative, on which progressive plots thrive, by making "industrious virtue" itself a highly suspect category. Thus the "progressive" critique of the "aristocratic" Wild is constantly neutralized by the demonstration that the legitimate and successful man of virtue, against whom he has putatively been judged, is essentially no different from Wild himself. As we are relentlessly compelled to attend to the leveling analogy between rogue and statesman, Fielding's progressive plot dissolves before our eyes. The insistent proximity of Wild and Walpole forces us to identify the trappings of "honor" as the hypocritical aggrandizements of the assimilationist upstart; and the status inconsistency of aristocratic culture, so far from being resolved by the rise of the new men of "virtue," is seen to be aggravated by it.[10]

Echoing his conservative predecessors, Fielding sometimes makes the relation between rogue and statesman intelligible as one not simply of similarity but of contiguity, as the plot of doing well enough in the world to be called no longer the former but the latter:

Can there be a more instructive Lesson against that abominable and pernicious Vice, Ambition, than the Sight of a mean Man, rais'd by fortunate Accidents and execrable Vices to Power, employing the basest Measures and the vilest Instruments to support himself; looked up to only by Sycophants and Slaves and sturdy Beggars, Wretches whom even he must in his Heart despise in all their Tinsel; looked down upon, and scorned and shunned by every Man of Honour . . . without Dignity in his Robes, without Honour from his Titles, without Authority from his Power [?]

Here is the classic conservative reduction. Progressive "virtue" only recapitulates the old arbitrariness of aristocratic "honor": if inherited nobility owes its ascendancy to "the fortuitous accident of birth," the self-made upstart is similarly "raised by fortunate accidents and execrable vices." But in *Jonathan Wild* the rise of rogue to statesman is less crucial than the riveting fact of their similarity. A "great man and a great rogue are synonymous," Fielding writes, and in this conjunction he focuses on the internal quality of "greatness" that is essential to the new aristocracy of upstarts, cutting across the old social categories (in a parody of progressive virtue and Protestant grace) by uniting "high and low life" (IV, xv, 176; I, v, 17). By this means he conflates the several villains of conservative imagination—the scheming rogue of criminal biography, the Whiggish "public servant," the industrious parvenu of improving parables, the enthusiastic convert of spiritual autobiography—into a single resonant figure of corruption.[11]

As the Newgate debtors discover, to be "great" is to be "corrupted in their morals" (IV, xii, 161), a character trait that qualifies the petty London gangleader for legitimate and distinguished professional careers in the (scarcely separable) fields of politics and high finance. As Wild observes at one point, not only robbery but even murder is comfortably carried on "within the law" (III, iii, 91). If fraud is a "courtier's" accomplishment, then the policy of the "statesman" and the "prime minister" elevates petty theft and the betrayal of friends to an engagement with the "public trust" itself (I, vi, 19, v, 16, 18; II, viii, 69). "Greatness," the unifying element in "prigs," "statesmen," and "absolute princes" (I, xiv, 42; II, iv, 58), depends not upon the nature or scope of one's sphere of influence but on one's will to exercise "absolute power" there (III, xiv, 120–22; IV, xv, 175). Fielding's argument resists the customary restriction of "absolutism" to the sphere of princely "authority," radically modernizing it as a psychological and moral capacity to engross power, whose egalitarian servant, willing to work for any man and to corrupt all others, "is indeed the beginning as well as the end of all human devices: I mean money" (I, xiv, 43).

It is not surprising that Fielding propounds the familiar parallel between theft and financial investment, or that Wild passes "for a gentleman of great fortune in the funds" (I, vi, 21; see also I, xiv, 43–44). At the heart of the parallel that ties the absolute politician to the absolute possessive individualist is the unlimited indulgence of the appetites, which here are arranged in a characteristically conservative hierarchy. When Fielding observes that "the truest mark of greatness is insatiability," it is clear at once that he refers most of all to the desire for material goods (II, ii, 51). Wild's "most powerful and predominant passion was ambition . . . His lust was inferior only to his ambition . . . His avarice was immense, but it was of the rapacious, not of the tenacious kind" (IV, xv, 172–73). Avarice and lust are reciprocal signs of corruption, but unlike the case of the progressive villain, here the lust for money predominates. Thus, although Wild is inflamed by the very sight of Mrs. Heartfree, the ruin of Mr. Heartfree has a clear priority over the rape of his wife (II, i, 47, viii, 71). Only when both have been arranged does Wild, "secure . . . of the possession of that lovely woman, together with a rich cargo," anticipate the satisfaction of both appetites in language that renders them well-nigh interchangeable: "In short, he enjoyed in his mind all the happiness which unbridled lust and rapacious avarice could promise him" (II, viii, 74). By the same token, Wild's beloved Laetitia knows that of her "three very predominant passions; to wit, vanity, wantonness, and avarice," she can implicitly rely on Jonathan to satiate the third in particular (II, iii, 55). We, at least, are left in no doubt that theirs is a "Smithfield" match—a marriage for money—and soon after it Laetitia informs her insulted husband that she married him not for love but "because it was convenient, and my parents forced me" (III, vi, 98, viii, 105; see also vi, 99–100, 103).[12]

So despite the intimations that, as in Richardson's progressive ideology, "honor" may be purged of aristocratic poisons and realigned with "virtue," the more compelling argument in *Jonathan Wild* is that the term has been so corrupted by progressive assimilationism as to be completely and unredeemably arbitrary. "A man of honour," says Wild, "is he that is called a man of honour; and while he is so called he so remains, and no longer" (I, xiii, 38). Fielding's "preoccupation with semantic instability"[13] expresses an insight into the analogous relation between linguistic and socioeconomic corruption, an insight he shares with Swift and other utopian travel narrators. The attack on modern cant terms is a microscopic version of the attack on modern narrative, which has only devised, through the pretense of telling an antiromance truth, a more efficient method of imposing on the credulity of the innocent. For corruption to operate successfully in these several spheres it is essential that the two principals, not only the knaves but also the fools, faithfully perform in their respective roles: "Thus while the crafty and designing Part of Mankind, consulting only their own separate Advantage, endeavour to maintain one constant Imposition on others, the whole World becomes a vast Masquerade." "Constant imposition" is crucial both for "*The Art of Politics*" and for "*the Art of thriving.*" In an allegorical satire on the Whig establishment, Fielding depicts monetary corruption not as naked opportunism but as a credulous religious rite, the worship of a deity called MNEY and of its ambitious high priest, whose creed includes the maxim that "All Things Spring from Corruption, so did MNEY, and therefore by Corruption he is most properly come at." As in other conservative writers, the model is of an artfully constructed, quasi-religious social fiction whose greatest power is to impose upon the credulity of the many.[14]

Throughout Fielding's narratives, the law provides an especially persistent example of such a social fiction. Jonathan Wild's main weapon against his enemies is not brute force but the law, which he is able to turn to his own ends only because it depends so fully on procedures of witness, testimony, and evidence that enjoin an earnest empiricist belief and are highly subject to falsification. But Fielding's most explicit articulation of the analogy between sociopolitical and epistemological imposition— between questions of virtue and questions of truth—in *Jonathan Wild* invokes the fictions not of the law but of the stage, and it recalls the analogy of world and stage that had earlier preoccupied him in the farces. Wild is about to enact the supreme betrayal of his friend Heartfree. A great man such as he, Fielding observes, is best compared to a puppet master, for the effectiveness of his manipulations depends entirely upon his inaccessibility to sense perception:

Not that any one is ignorant of his being there, or supposes that the puppets are not mere sticks of wood, and he himself the sole mover; but as this (though every one knows it) doth not appear visibly, i.e. to their eyes, no one is ashamed of consenting to be imposed upon . . .

It would be to suppose thee, gentle reader, one of very little knowledge in this world, to imagine thou has never seen some of these puppet-shows which are so frequently acted on the great stage . . . He must have a very despicable opinion of mankind indeed who can conceive them to be imposed on as often as they appear to be so. The truth is, they are in the same situation with the readers of romances; who, though they know the whole to be one entire fiction, nevertheless agree to be deceived; and, as these find amusement, so do the others find ease and convenience in this concurrence. But, this being a subdigression, I return to my digression. (III, xi, 114)

The passage suggests a three-part analogy of impositions: Wild is to Heartfree as Walpole is to the people, and as the romance writer is to his readers. The willingness of those on the receiving end to be deceived in these relationships is that of the audience at a puppet show. The tenor of the comparison, however, is not art but political exploitation. The effect of the analogy is to oblige us to see the posture of the audience not in the positive light of an "aesthetic response" but in the negative light of political bad faith. And of course the analogy strikes close to home. If we "gentle readers" seek no more than a passive "ease and convenience" in this narration—if we resist Fielding's self-conscious reference to his own digressive manipulations, for example, preferring a comfortable belief in his claims to historicity—then we are really no different from Heartfree.

But what does it mean to be no different from Heartfree? Critics have recognized Heartfree's inadequacy as a positive norm in *Jonathan Wild*, but they have disagreed about Fielding's awareness of this inadequacy and hence about its role in the narrative's moral and social program.[15] Heartfree's several soliloquies on the comforts of a good conscience, the satisfactions of Christian behavior, and the anticipated rewards of the world beyond are indistinguishable from Fielding's "own" precepts, which he occasionally delivers in this homiletic mode, but they also bespeak, in the face of worldly injustice, a comprehensive passivity (III, ii, 88–89, v, 97–98, x, 111). A jeweler by trade, Heartfree is (not surprisingly) a remarkably fair dealer who would never impose on his customers (II, i, 46), and Fielding encourages us to associate the Heartfrees' willingness to "credit" the lies by which Wild and the Count impose upon them with their willingness to extend these villains financial "credit" (e.g., II, iii, 52, viii, 70). There are limits to this credence. When Wild persuades Mrs. Heartfree to flee the country for her husband's sake, Mr. Heartfree soon overcomes his initial doubts about his wife's fidelity (III, i, 85, v, 95–96); but of Wild's account of the affair he cannot help wondering "whether the whole was not a fiction, and Wild . . . had not spirited away, robbed, and murdered his wife" (III, ix, 109). But it is not until Mrs. Heartfree returns from her travels, and is called upon to tell her own story, that Fielding fully illuminates the function of Heartfree in posing the multifaceted problem of imposition and "convenient" fictions.

Even in the absence of the "wonderful chapter" that Fielding deleted after the first edition, Mrs. Heartfree's interpolated tale is replete with events and devices—storm, shipwreck, pirates, attempted rapes, a hermit castaway, a curious native culture—that contemporaries would have associated with the related marvels of romance mutability and travel-narrative historicity. Fielding expressed his contempt for the naive empiricism of romancing travel narratives at several points in his career, most lucidly in his own, posthumously published travel journal. There he distinguishes ancient and modern travel "romances" from the "true history" he himself has composed, "the former being the confounder and corrupter of the latter." Vanity, he claims, leads these travel romancers both to describe things that have never happened and, on the contrary, to record minute trivialities whose only distinction is that they happened to the author. The good traveler must be highly selective. The worth of his character will be reflected not in any spurious, quantitative completeness of detail or observation but in the success of his selection in "diverting or informing" the reader.[16]

Judged by these standards, Mrs. Heartfree's credibility is impugned not only by the conventionalized wonders of her narration but by its patent self-interest. After all, it is the story of how she managed, despite a succession of threats that include the ravenous lust of half a dozen men, not only to preserve her chastity but to miraculously recover the jewels that had been stolen from her husband. Like Robinson Crusoe and Pam-

ela, Mrs. Heartfree attributes all her good fortune to the power of providence, and she ends her narrative with the cheerful lesson that virtue gets
rewarded in the end—"THAT PROVIDENCE WILL SOONER OR LATER PROCURE
THE FELICITY OF THE VIRTUOUS AND INNOCENT" (IV, xi, 161; see also IV,
vii, 145, 146, viii, 147, ix, 153, xi, 160). Yet her self-reliance reminds us of
no one so much as Wild himself. Her adaptive mastery of nautical terminology is striking enough for her husband to comment upon, and she
lingers over the romance compliments of her suitors as though they were
vital to her story rather than to her self-love (IV, vii, 143, ix, 155, xi, 157).
She fends off would-be seducers by pretending to comply with their
desires (e.g., IV, vii, 146), a technique of imposture at which she is so
accomplished that in the crucial exchange—when she obtains the jewels—we experience some doubt as to just how it has been done. To be
sure, Mrs. Heartfree's official story is one of providential repossession
(IV, ix, 153). But it is she herself who plants in her persecutor's mind the
idea that her virtue might be vulnerable to a bribe, and before she is
providentially rescued she energetically attempts "to persuade him of my
venality" (IV, ix, 151). The supposed imposture has the ring of plausibility, for the pragmatic and business-like exchange of one "jewel" for
another may seem by now more likely than the earnest narrator's account
of one more wonderful event. The play on words itself becomes explicit
at the very end of Mrs. Heartfree's narrative, when yet another suitor is
said to give her "a very rich jewel, of less value, he said, than my chastity"
(IV, xi, 160).

Most important, our mounting skepticism at the circumstances of
these windfalls is greatly strengthened by our wish to dissociate ourselves
from the credulity of our surrogate audience, Mr. Heartfree, whose acute
anxiety at the recurrent threats to his wife's virtue during her narration is
exceeded only by the ease with which he credits her persuasions "that
Heaven had preserved her chastity, and again had restored her unsullied
to his arms" (IV, vii, 145; see also IV, vii, 144, ix, 152). And the general
instability of this marital interaction is heightened when it is interrupted
all at once by its mock-heroic reduction. Mrs. Heartfree has been narrating her story in Newgate, and suddenly Wild creates an uproar because he
has caught his wife Laetitia with his confederate Fireblood. For the im-
probably delicate Wild, it is as much his own fastidious "honor" that is
offended as it is hers, and he reiterates the word with a manic insistence
(IV, x, 155–57). Coming as it does in the middle of another tale of
imperiled honor, Wild's absurdly elevated outrage provides a perspective
on both Heartfrees: a reflection of the wife's false idealism, and a foil for
the husband's easy agreement to be deceived. But the episode is also an
artful interpolation within an interpolation, and like Fielding's earlier
"subdigression," it amounts to a formal reminder of the manipulative
and "political" power of the narrator, affording us an opportunity to

distinguish ourselves from the good Mr. Heartfree by doubting the accuracy of his wife's story. In this way Fielding transforms her, if only for the space of her travel narrative, from the constant female lover of romance into the scheming rogue of conservative ideology, whose claim to truth is imposture and whose protestation of inner virtue masks an essential avarice. And her husband, because he will not be a knave like Wild, tends to be his wife's ideal audience—that is, a willing fool.[17]

Thus *Jonathan Wild* reflects, like *Gulliver's Travels* before it, the analogous and interlocked asperities of extreme skepticism and conservative ideology. And like Swift, Fielding is impelled to reverse the implacable momentum of his critique by guardedly reaffirming the old values. As in his predecessors, this amounts not to an unmediated act of faith but to a defense of the instrumentality and utility of belief, a tactic whose repercussions are not easily controlled. Thus, when in other contexts Fielding the latitudinarian refutes deist arguments against the reality of future rewards, his earnest insistence that the "Delusion" (if such it be) affords a "Spring of Pleasure" recalls not only Tillotson and South but also his own rather silly Heartfree. And when he defends the old social forms and titles— "His Grace," "Right Honourable," "Sir"—not because they have any substantial "philosophical" meaning but because, "being imposed by the Laws of Custom," they have become "politically essential," we are reminded as much of Jonathan Wild as of Jonathan Swift.[18]

If the "instrumentality of belief" argument seems even more volatile and contradictory in Fielding's hands than in those of his predecessors, it is partly because his commitment to some of the basic institutions of conservative ideology is less profound than theirs. His family background tied him securely to the "upstart" Marlborough's war, to the system of financial investment by which it was funded, and to the reality of nonlanded property. Moreover Fielding seems to have been sufficiently comfortable with the modern system of political management to have accepted a bribe from Walpole in exchange for delaying publication of *Jonathan Wild*—by Swiftian lights surely an act of "corruption." Because Fielding does not fully share Swift's comprehensive aversion to progressive institutions, he cannot share Swift's circumspect dedication to the utopian idea of a preprogressive culture. As a result, his advocacy of an instrumental belief in institutions whose authority may be fictional—social deference, custom, the law—can sound less like a parabolic intuition of a better dispensation than like a hearty and forward-looking justification of this one. Thus, in *Jonathan Wild* the figure of the "good magistrate" (IV, vi, 141, xv, 176) benevolently beckons our saving faith in a legal system whose viciousness— "politically essential" to the corruptions of great upstarts—Fielding has been at great pains to document from the outset.[19]

Yet the good magistrate is a persistent personage in Fielding's narratives, increasingly a model for the author's own stance as the benevolent narrator. And the example of this dual function—the external institution internalized as an authorial capacity—suggests how Fielding makes the "instrumentality of belief" argument more adequately his own. Whereas in Swift the argument is most explicit in the realm of ideology and sociopolitical institutions, in Fielding the major emphasis modulates to the epistemological "institution" of narrative form, to the reclamation of specifically literary fiction as a mode of telling the truth. Buttressing Fielding's extreme skepticism is a critique of empiricist objectivity (and of the allied belief that the instrument of verification is separable from the object verified) that would make a deist proud. On the basis of this powerful critique, Fielding implicates narrative in the fictionalizing deceptions of the political puppeteer. The question, then, is not how to avoid the inevitable condition of fictionality (of "romance"), but how to avoid the ethical pitfalls that seem to be an inevitable part of it: the impositions of the puppeteer and the bad faith of his audience. What is required is a fiction so palpable, so "evident to the senses," that its power to deceive even a "willing" audience becomes neutralized.[20]

Indeed, Fielding has this requirement in view when, instead of seeking the quantitative completeness of the naive empiricists, he explicitly insists on the necessity of narrative selection and the qualitative discrimination between the virtuous and the vicious, the important and the trivial. In Jonathan Wild we have already seen an example of this insistence in Fielding's advocacy of "mixed characters" and his critique of the notion, among both ancients and moderns, of a perfect "uniformity of character" (I, i, 4). He makes a similar point less explicitly, and with respect to plot rather than character, when he apologizes for the shortness of a chapter that covers eight years in Wild's life. The problem is that the period "contains not one adventure worthy the reader's notice"; and unlike experiential time, narrative time is selective (I, vii, 21–22). Relatively programmatic passages like these should be seen as part of the more general phenomenon of Fielding's highly distinctive self-consciousness, an epistemological strategy that is entirely familiar from his best-known narratives but already effective in Jonathan Wild. Undoubtedly (in the words of the title page of Joseph Andrews) more in "the manner of Cervantes" than of Swift, this narrative reflexiveness aims to enclose its object in a shell of subjective commentary. Its ideal and unstated function is simultaneously to demystify fiction ("romance," "history") as illusion and to detoxify it, to negate its negation, to empower it by ostentatiously enacting, even announcing, its impotence to tell an immediate truth.[21] Two brief examples from Jonathan Wild will help clarify the "theory" of this dialectical technique.

Late in Book II, Jonathan, having cast himself into the sea, is "miraculously within two minutes after replaced in his boat," and the narrator promises to explain how this escape occurred by natural means, without the traditional aid of dolphin or sea horse. Rejecting all "supernatural causes," he personifies Nature, describes her power, depicts her working her purposes on Wild—who obligingly changes his mind and leaps aboard again—and thereby demonstrates the naturalness of his "history" (II, xii, 79–81). Proudly disowning artifice ("romance") at the outset, Fielding makes abundantly clear that what he calls "nature" ("true history") is only art by another name. But to show that all is art is to vindicate its vices by acknowledging their inevitability, and we accept Fielding's manipulations (at least in theory) precisely because they are so ingenuous and obtrusive. In a similar fashion, Fielding's narrator boasts of spurning the romance convention whereby the story ends with a happy marriage, and instead we are treated to Jonathan and Laetitia's marital dispute in the middle of Book III (vii–viii, 103–7).[22] Yet the episode is introduced by conventionalized claims to historicity and then conveyed, in a "dialogue matrimonial," as a page from the script of a bedroom farce. And by the end of the narrative, Fielding is content to close very much according to convention, histrionically rewarding the good and punishing the great (IV, xv, 176–77).

How does this differ, we may ask, from Mrs. Heartfree's dubious invocations of providential reward at the end of her own story? Presumably in the fact that here there is no imposition, because there is no belief: unlike Heartfree, the knowing reader agrees not to be deceived but to be "diverted" (in the language of the *Voyage to Lisbon*) by Fielding's reclamation of fictionality. But we may sense that Fielding would wish to acknowledge this state, too, as a species of belief, if only he could disentangle its mysterious, knowing innocence from the moral opprobrium of the agreed-upon deception. We are close here to the realm of the aesthetic and its own peculiar rationalization of the reader's commitment and response. But the sizable distance yet to be traversed is suggested by the fact that it will entail a rethinking of the other half of the Horatian dictum—not only to be "diverted" but also to be "informed"—which is more fundamental than anything Fielding and his contemporaries are willing to undertake.

2

Thus, by the time *Pamela* was printed in the fall of 1740, Fielding's future course in narrative had already been charted in the unpublished drafts of *Jonathan Wild*. Within the space of a year Fielding wrote *Shamela* and *Joseph Andrews*. In both works it is clear that he is continuing what he had begun and that his target is by no means simply Richardson. But *Pamela* provided an occasion for the emergence into public controversy—for the "institutionalization"—of that characteristically dialectical relation of action and reaction in which the origins of the English novel had thus far less obtrusively consisted. And in this important respect, *Shamela* and *Joseph Andrews* are quite accurately seen as a reactive response to *Pamela*, a negation and a completion of its achievement.[23] In the remainder of this chapter I will attempt to show how the most significant ties of these works both to *Pamela* and to *Jonathan Wild* are also significant for the origins of the novel.

The fact that *Shamela* negates *Pamela* by fully extending its premises can be seen clearly in the way Fielding parodically subverts Richardson's epistolary form. It is not that narrative empiricism is inherently naive, but that, on the contrary, *Pamela*'s claim to historicity is not authentic enough. The events themselves possess a reality, but the documents of which *Pamela* consists (according to Fielding's parodic premise) were fabricated by a hired pen and completely misrepresent her true history. Luckily her mother has communicated the "authentic" "originals" to Parson Oliver. He in turn has sent copies of these to his ingenuous colleague Parson Tickletext, whose former enthusiasm for *Pamela*'s truth and virtue is memorialized in the correspondence that precedes the printing of these truly authentic documents. Tickletext's name itself ties him to the vanity and credulousness of Protestant self-documentation. But having read Oliver's "authentic copies," he is much abashed at having endured so easily the "imposition" of *Pamela*, and it is he who is responsible for publishing (in the words of the title page) these "exact Copies of authentick Papers delivered to the Editor."[24]

Tickletext is like a Heartfree who has ceased to agree to be deceived. And it is easy to see why, since everything is altered, in this truer history, by the candor of the narrator. It is not entirely clear whether the name change—Shamela's parodic rebirth into the romance gentility of a Pamela—is due to the ingenuity of the protagonist or to that of the hack author of *Pamela* (cf. 308, 309, 337). But the restoration of the authentic name aptly encapsulates Fielding's central strategy, which is to restore the crucial access to Pamela's inner motives, whose absence rendered the historicity of *Pamela* (we can now appreciate) fatally incomplete. Even Richardson's Pamela is obliged to engage in the occasional subterfuge, to counterplot against Mr. B.'s plotting. And Mrs. Heartfree carries this extenuated duplicity further. But Shamela's character consists in nothing but the will to impose herself upon Mr. Booby, to misrepresent herself as what she is not. Fielding makes good use of those episodes in *Pamela*, like the pretended drowning (321), in which Shamela's deceit can be seen to have a basis in Pamela's. But he also makes Shamela a complete "Politician" (299), as Pamela never was. Thus her master's excitement at seeing her dressed like a farmer's daughter clearly becomes, as Mr. B. had charged, the result of a deliberate "stratagem" on Shamela's part (315). Yet even here, the barely plausible effect is that of, not a different person but the same person unbowdlerized, carelessly and candidly reporting the whole truth back home to her mother. And the whole truth requires not a greater quantity of details but a critical selection of the most vital ones concerning her own conniving state of mind. In this context, "writing to the moment" can only appear suspect, one more instance of supposedly "innocent" activity hilariously betrayed by the intimately self-conscious reflex of reporting (e.g., 313). Pamela's "virtue" becomes Shamela's "vartue," like Machiavelli's *virtù* a corrupted term that embodies its own contradictory negation. Moving from *Pamela* to *Shamela* is like hearing Mary Carleton's story retold as a rogue's tale by her husband John and posterity—except that here the transformation is achieved simply by letting the protagonist speak in her own person.[25]

Shamela is a rogue because she is a scheming, ambitious upstart. Fielding leaves us in no doubt as to the moral both of his own work and of its model. *Pamela* teaches "young gentlemen . . . to marry their mother's chambermaids" and "servant-maids . . . to look out for their masters as sharp as they can" (338, 307). By disclosing the real Pamela in action, *Shamela* reverses this moral. We see her profiting from the subversive loyalty of the "family of servants"; we observe her "betraying the secrets of families"; we watch her plot her progress from one family to the other; and we end up convinced of Parson Oliver's prediction that "the character of Shamela will make young gentlemen wary how they take the most fatal step both to themselves and families, by youthful, hasty and improper matches" (316, 338, 337). Six years after the publication of *Shamela* Fielding himself was content to marry his first wife's maid. But for the moment this kind of social mobility, at least in Richardson's rendition of it, could resonate for Fielding with the culturally fraught effrontery of the rise of the undeserving. Fielding's ostensible target in *Shamela* is not only the anonymous author of *Pamela* but also Colley Cibber's autobiographical *Apology* of 1740 and Conyers Middleton's *Life of Cicero* (1741). And as Hugh Amory has observed, the attack is unified by the fact that all three works "explain the success of *parvenus* by their superior moral merit and all three substantiate this contention from the very mouths of their *parvenus,* whose naive candor seems unquestionable."[26]

Shamela's status as a conservative villainess is solidified by the predominance of her avarice. Of course her lubricity is never in doubt either, at least when Parson Williams is around. But her first lust is the lust for money. Like her mother and Mrs. Jervis, Shamela is at heart a whore (308–9). Advised by the former early on to make "a good market" with her "rich fool" of a master (311), she is pleased to find in Lincolnshire that Mrs. Jewkes also will help "sell me to my master" (317). But as in all such roguery, the success of the transaction depends upon the hypocritical disguise of financial ambition as the outer mark of inner virtue. Shamela tells Booby that "I value my vartue more than all the world, and I had rather be the poorest man's wife, than the richest man's whore" (324). And in a certain sense she is quite sincere. Presented with the possibility of being a whore—of a sham-marriage "settlement" as Mr. Booby's "mistress"—Shamela, like Pamela, rejects the offer (313, 321). But her reasons are rather different. Whereas Pamela fears the loss of (what is admittedly a complex entity) her virtue, Shamela simply fears the loss of the more lucrative settlement of a genuine marriage. "No, Mrs. Jervis," she insists, "nothing under a regular taking into keeping, a settled settlement, for me, and all my heirs, all my whole lifetime, shall do the business" (313). To be a wife is a financial improvement on being a whore; "virtue" is eminently profitable. Indeed, this is the meaning of Shamela's famous Machiavellian maxim: "I thought once of making a little fortune by my person. I now intend to make a great one by my vartue" (325). The corruption of virtue culminates in the corruption of marriage.

After the wedding Shamela allows the mask to slip somewhat. She engages in a bit of desultory charity. But unlike Pamela, who exults, "Oh how I long to be doing some Good!" Shamela only complains: "I long to be in London that I may have an opportunity of laying some out, as well as giving away. What signifies having money if one doth not spend it." "It would be hard indeed," she adds, "that a woman who marries a man only for his money, should be debarred from spending it" (331, 332). In the presence of such consummate presumption, even the fatuous Booby takes on some dignity, and in the final scenes of the narrative he affords us fleeting glimpses of a normative type in conservative ideology: the Tory squire, natural ruler of the besieged English countryside. To Shamela he vents his just irritation at Parson Williams, "whose family hath been raised from the dunghill by ours; and who hath received from me twenty kindnesses, and yet is not contented to destroy the game in all other places, which I freely give him leave to do; but hath the impudence to pursue a few hares, which I am desirous to preserve, round about this little coppice" (333). That night Booby rails against the ignorant politics of Williams and the rest of the company that presumes upon his hospitality until all hours, "a parcel of scoundrels roaring forth the principles of honest men over their cups" (335).[27]

As we might expect, the opportunistic parson is of "the court-side," holding that "every Christian ought to be on the same with the bishops" (336). But Williams becomes a rather complicated satirical butt in Fielding's conservative treatment. As a proponent of "what we believe" over "what we do" (319), Williams represents for Fielding the Methodist reawakening of the old Puritan individualism and self-indulgence. The historical continuity had a real basis, and Fielding's association of the renovated doctrine of faith not only with progressive notions of "virtue" but also with empirical standards of truth is clear in the deep appreciation expressed by the credulous Parson Tickletext for "the useful and truly religious doctrine of *grace*" that Williams preaches (304). But Williams advocates at least a certain species of "works" as well, contending "that to go to church, and to pray, and to sing psalms, and to honour the clergy, and to repent, is true religion" (319). Fielding's additional target here is, in part, the nominal observance promoted by complacent Anglican opponents of the Methodist revival. Yet much else about Shamela's favorite clergyman—doctrinal points like the conviction that a multitude of sins can "be purged away by frequent and sincere repentance," but also the haughty ease of his general manner and address—carries the cavalier associations of High Church Laudian and crypto-Jacobite culture (317–18).[28]

In this respect there is a Swiftian economy to Williams's overdetermination as a satiric butt, for he demonstrates, like Jack in *A Tale of a Tub,* how the radical subversion of Anglican orthodoxy involuntarily and stealthily recapitulates the original Roman enemy. But Fielding's Anglicanism is not Swift's, and it is not entirely clear that his two-pronged attack through the serviceable figure of Williams leaves any room for his own middle way. Like the latitudinarian divines he admired, Fielding is eloquent on the preferability of actions to words as a guide in ethical judgments. But so is the Puritan Bunyan, who excoriates Talkative for ignoring that "the soul of religion is the practice part." Whatever Fielding's contemporaries wished to believe, Puritanism and latitudinarianism are not simply antagonists; they are closely parallel Protestant strategies for confronting the problem of mediation, and they necessarily reflect a similar instability. No less than Puritan discipline, Fielding's hearty and no-nonsense embrace of good works places a large instrumental faith in the power of worldly institutions and achievements to make a moral signification, an investment whose ideological implications could only be uncertain. The greatest commitment of this sort in *Joseph Andrews* is to the institutional practice of charity.[29]

3

As Martin Battestin has shown most fully, *Joseph Andrews* is dedicated to promulgating the two Christian virtues that are embodied in its two principal characters, Joseph and Abraham Adams. Chastity and charity may be understood, respectively, as analogous private and public modes of moral restraint, the Christian capacity to limit the power of the selfish and destructive human passions. Joseph's early resistance to Lady Booby, which is the narrative's most declaratory reaction against Richardsonian example, broadly represents to us the triumph of chastity as such. If *Shamela* is Pamela as she really is, stripped of her feigned innocence, Joseph is Pamela as she should have been, stripped of her self-indulgence. Joseph is a reproach to Richardson's progressive protagonist because, unlike her, he masters both his sexual and his social appetites. Although he deferentially models his behavior on his older sister's, we are made to sense the unwitting and ironic contrast when he writes to her, "I never loved to tell the Secrets of my Master's Family," instantly reconciling himself to leaving Lady Booby's service so as to "maintain my Virtue against all Temptations."[30] But despite Fielding's easily insinuated parallel between the social servitude of Joseph the footman and that of Pamela the lady's maid, the sexual difference is all-important. It is not just that, as Fielding admits, a man's "Chastity is always in his own power" (I, xviii, 87). By making the issue one of male chastity, he slyly avoids all the social ramifications of female chastity.

For Richardson's Pamela, the "religious" injunction to remain chaste is overlaid by a complex "political" requirement, and she has both more to lose and more to gain—a social transformation—as the potential consequence of a liaison with her better. For Fielding's Joseph the situation is, despite appearances, much simpler. Already in love with Fanny, he must do no more than control his momentary sexual desire (I, x, 46–47). Although to Lady Booby he implies that he is chaste by virtue of being "the Brother of *Pamela,*" to Pamela he writes that it is as much from Parson Adams's religious instruction as from her that he has learned "that Chastity is as great a virtue in a Man as in a Woman" (I, viii, 41, x, 46; see also xii, 53). And for Adams the principle of chastity, devoid of any social complexities, has the simple moral purpose of guarding against "the Indulgence of carnal Appetites" (IV, viii, 307). Of course succumbing to Lady Booby would bring some material reward. Adams knows that with the proper encouragement and education, Joseph might rise up the ladder of domestic service as his sister did (I, iii, 26). But the final great elevation, from service to gentility, is not within the power of Lady Booby to engineer. This is the lesson Mr. B. teaches his sister, Lady Davers, in *Pamela*. In *Joseph Andrews* Lady Booby ends up the counterpart, in this respect, of Lady Davers rather than of Mr. B., prevented from doing what Mr. Booby has done with Pamela not only by Joseph's resistance but also by her own obsessive fear that so far from raising him to her level, she has the power only "to sacrifice my Reputation, my Character, my Rank in Life, to the Indulgence of a mean and vile Appetite" (IV, xiii, 328). Lady Booby's echo of Parson Adams's religious teachings here clearly is not a sign that she, too, believes in chastity. Instead it suggests how effectively Fielding has managed, not to refute Richardson's progressive social ethics in the great contest between "industrious virtue" and "aristocratic corruption," but to defuse its social volatility through

the stealthy reversal of sexes. Adrift from its moorings in female experience, Joseph's heroically passive resistance soon becomes rather silly;[31]
and in a characteristically conservative turn, neither "virtue" nor "corruption" comes off very well in the contest. In fact, so far from occupying
the center stage that it has in *Pamela,* in *Joseph Andrews* the encounter
quickly shrinks into an attenuated frame within which questions of virtue are most efficiently propounded in terms of the problem not of
chastity but of charity.

An English Quixote obsessed with the rule of Apostolic charity, not
of romance chivalry,[32] Abraham Adams reminds us of both the madness
of the *hidalgo* estranged from reality and the conservative wisdom of the
utopian social reformer. Traversing the circuit to London and back again,
he upholds the standard of good works against a cross-section of humanity whose complacency, hypocrisy, and downright viciousness announce, again and again, the absence of charity in the modern world.
The traditional proponents of charity—clergymen like Barnabas and
Trulliber—abhore Methodist reform for the wrong reasons and jeal-
ously defend their own material comforts against the needs of the poor (I,
xvii; II, xiv). The inheritors of the feudal obligation of charity, the country gentry, are, if possible, even worse. One squire specializes in en-
trapping the needy with false promises of munificence. Having been
tricked himself by this man, Adams then listens in horror to "true Stories" of how the squire has ruined several local youths, among them a
Pamela figure and a hopeful younger son, by feeding their expectations of
upward mobility and withdrawing his support only after they have become fully dependent upon it (II, xvi–xvii). Another squire is so corrupted in sensibility and education that he has become addicted to victimizing
those who have come into his care. Adams protests that "I am your
Guest, and by the Laws of Hospitality entitled to your Protection" (III,
vii, 247), but the practical jokes culminate in a serious attack upon his
traveling party and the abduction of Fanny as a prospective "Sacrifice to
the Lust of a Ravisher." The rape is foiled by Lady Booby's steward, Peter
Pounce, a "Gentleman" and burlesque progressive "gallant"—the chivalric protector as monied man—who "loved a pretty Girl better than any
thing, besides his own Money, or the Money of other People" (III, xii,
268–69). But needless to say, the monied man soon evinces his own
species of corruption, and the adventure ends on a conservative note with
Pounce replicating the sins of the selfish gentry, reviling the poor laws
and asserting that charity "does not so much consist in the Act as in the
Disposition" to relieve the distressed (III, xiii, 274).

The paradigmatic instance of failed charity in *Joseph Andrews* is the
early stagecoach episode, in which an entire social spectrum of respect-
able passengers refuses to relieve Joseph's distress until the lowest of them
all, the postilion, gives him his greatcoat (I, xii). Later confirmed by the

humble goodness of Betty the chambermaid and the mysterious pedlar (I, xii, 55; II, xv, 170; IV, viii, 309–10), this episode establishes the basic paradox that if charity involves giving something for nothing, only those with nothing are likely to be charitable. And the traveling lawyer is of course no more compassionate than anyone else. Throughout *Joseph Andrews* the law is seen as the secularizer of traditional institutions, possessed of at least the potential to civilize their social functions for the modern world. In the progressively oriented "History of Leonora," for example, the symbolic supplanting of sword by robe nobility is intimated by the rivalry between the dishonorable fop Bellarmine, an accomplished "Cavalier," and the sober Horatio, who, "being a Lawyer . . . would seek Revenge in his own way" (II, iv, 115). Most often, however, the authority of the law in the settlement of modern disputes works only to aggravate the old thirst for "revenge" by making it financially profitable. This Adams learns when the interpolated tale of Leonora is itself interrupted by the fistfight at the inn, and a litigious bystander advises the parson's antagonist that "was I in your Circumstances, every Drop of my Blood should convey an Ounce of Gold into my Pocket" (II, v, 121). Later on Mrs. Trulliber, seeing that her husband is about to strike Adams for calling him uncharitable and un-Christian, advises him instead to "shew himself a true Christian, and take the Law of him" (II, xiv, 168).

It is a typically conservative reversal that in *Joseph Andrews* the modern institution of the law tends not to civilize the bloody passions of anger and revenge but to corrupt them, to replace physical with financial violence. And in this respect the law is a distinct deterioration from the traditional peacekeeping institutions—like Christianity—that it is quickly displacing in the modern world. When Adams delivers Fanny from her highway ravisher, he does it in the chivalric spirit of a stout "Champion" in defense of an innocent "Damsel" (II, ix, 139). But when the case is brought before the justice it is quickly corrupted by the ambitions of everyone involved for some portion of the reward. The innocents are libeled as "Robbers," "Highwaymen," and "Rogues," and they escape only through the chance intervention of a local squire and the justice's extreme obsequiousness to gentility (II, x–xi, 142–43, 145, 148–49). And when Lady Booby wishes to foil the match between Joseph and Fanny, she has no trouble persuading Lawyer Scout and Justice Frolick to help her in circumventing the settlement laws. As Scout puts it, "The Laws of this Land are not so vulgar, to permit a mean Fellow to contend with one of your Ladyship's Fortune" (IV, iii, 285).

But if the modern purveyors of charity and justice are riddled with corruption, we are also justified in being skeptical about the efficacy of Adams's anachronistic ideals, and not simply because the parson's own means of fulfilling them are severely limited. As a comprehensive moral imperative, the rule of charity does not readily admit of fine ethical distinctions as to relative obligations and deserts, a problem of which the growing popularity of benevolist philosophies was making contemporaries aware.[33] The innkeeper Mrs. Tow-wouse is surely discredited when she exclaims to her husband, "Common Charity, a F——t!" (I, xii, 56). But her real point here is suggestively echoed later on by Adams's wife and daughter. Book IV opens with a sharp contrast between the reception of Lady Booby and that of Parson Adams on their return to their respective country seats. We are well aware of the total absence of feudal care in her ladyship, and Fielding's ironic portrait of her entry into "the Parish amidst the ringing of Bells, and the Acclamations of the Poor" is quickly followed by a sincere account of how the parson's parishioners "flocked about" him "like dutiful Children round an indulgent Parent, and vyed with each other in Demonstrations of Duty and Love" (IV, i, 277). As Mrs. Adams tells Lady Booby, her husband does indeed say "that the whole Parish are his Children," but there are children of his own on whose career prospects the parson has exercised less patriarchal care than on those of Joseph and Fanny. "It behoved every Man to take the first Care of his Family," she complains to her husband. However, Adams is oblivious, Fielding adds, persisting "in doing his Duty without regarding the Consequence it might have on his worldly Interest" (IV, xi, 321, viii, 307). There is certainly no calculation on the part of the parson, but is his virtue always untainted by his interest? Even the innocent Joseph knows how "an Ambition to be respected" can inspire acts of goodness, and Fielding has allowed us to observe how Adams's vanity can be manifested in the very denunciation of vanity (III, vi, 233, iii, 214–15). Fielding's latitudinarian beliefs are very close to the Mandevillian argument that the autonomous purity of virtue is a pleasing fiction. And although we clearly are not encouraged to see the parson's undiscriminating love of his neighbor as a stealthy self-love, nevertheless, to a real degree, the Apostolic and feudal rule of charity is itself demystified in *Joseph Andrews* as a Quixotic social fiction.

By the same token, although Fielding surely strips modern institutions like the law and the gentry of their authority, at times the assault is moderated and the reigning fictions are allowed a certain instrumental utility. We have already seen this to be true of the law in *Jonathan Wild* and of gentility in *Shamela*. When Mr. Booby discovers that his brother-in-law has been ordered to Bridewell for, in Justice Frolick's sage words, "a kind of felonious larcenous thing," he is shocked by the triviality and brutality of the law. But the justice is happy to commit Joseph and Fanny to Booby's benevolent custody instead, easily discerning now, with the kindly lechery that often distinguishes Fielding's basically good-natured men, that Fanny's beauty deserves better than Bridewell (IV, v, 289–91). And at the end of the narrative, Booby calls to mind his own briefly normative incarnation in *Shamela,* becoming the true representative of feudal gentility by dispensing gifts of "unprecedented Generosity" and by entertaining the assembled company "in the most splendid manner, after the Custom of the old *English* Hospitality, which is still preserved in some very few Families in the remote Parts of *England*" (IV, xvi, 343, 341).

At such moments of affirmation, customary noblesse oblige and the hallowed system of the English law seem able to redeem themselves as the best scheme of social justice available, if also the only one. But this is not to say that they are also able to counter the endemic condition of status inconsistency—perhaps the more precise term for Fielding would be "status indeterminacy." In a central chapter of *Joseph Andrews,* Fielding characteristically affirms that social distinctions are merely formal, being determined neither by birth nor by accomplishments but by fashion (II, xiii, 156–58). "*High* People" are distinguished from "*Low* People" by the way they dress, and the great "Ladder of Dependance," of which social hierarchy consists, is a closely articulated chain of employments, each of which attends upon its next-highest neighbor and is attended upon, in turn, by the next-lowest one. The function of attendance is essentially the same; what differs is the level at which it is done. Thus social station is arbitrary: the relative placement of a Walpole or a Wild—of a Booby or a Slipslop (I, vii, 34)—is quite accidental. But if the ladder is a fiction in that its rungs are placed arbitrarily, the ladder itself is systematic and functional. And if there is no basis for affirming the justice of the present arrangement, there is no reason to suppose that any systematic alteration would be an improvement. To be sure, there are exceptions to the rule of status inconsistency. Fielding "could name a Commoner raised higher above the Multitude by superior Talents, than is in the Power of his Prince to exalt him," but he also "could name a Peer no less elevated by Nature than by Fortune" (III, i, 190–91; cf. III, vi, 235). The very ease with which exceptions to all rules can be enumerated seems to strengthen the implacability of the system itself, which continues remorselessly to grind out the present dispensation, certainly no better, but probably no worse, than any replacement for it might do.

Something akin to this quiet desperation must be the issue of any direct attempt to distill Fielding's stance on matters of social justice and reform—on questions of virtue—in *Joseph Andrews.* And it is strikingly discordant with the genial and confident exuberance of the voice that self-consciously suffuses so much of the narrative. How does his stance on questions of truth help palliate Fielding's social vision? Calling itself, on the title page and at various points throughout the narrative, a true and authentic history, *Joseph Andrews* deploys the range of authenticating devices and claims to historicity with which we have become familiar not only in Fielding's predecessors but also in his own earlier efforts.[34] His extreme skepticism is never really in doubt, but it is conveyed to us through a characteristic combination of parodic impersonation and self-subversive definition that undertakes the positing of a form by a series of contradictory negations. In Chapter I, for example, Fielding specifies his "History" as a biographical life; yet after a brief allusion to ancient Roman biographies, his chief instances of this form are several late-medieval redactions of chivalric romance (I, i, 17–18).[35] Moreover, two eminent modern examples are autobiographies that work, "as the common Method is, from authentic Papers and Records"; but these are none other than Cibber's *Apology* and *Pamela* (I, i, 18).

In the first chapter of Book III (185–91) Fielding picks up, where this early discussion left off, the account of what he means by "history," and now he is prepared to be more explicit in his epistemological reversals. Whatever "Authority" they may be accorded by the vulgar, books that bear the title "the History of *England,* the History of *France,* of *Spain,* &c." are really the work of "Romance-Writers." The skeptical reader is correct to judge them "as no other than a Romance, in which the Writer hath indulged a happy and fertile Invention," for it is in biography "that Truth only is to be found." Of course no one would deny that the aforementioned "histories" can be relied upon for the quantitative and topographical recording of isolated "Facts." "But as to the Actions and Characters of Men," the very same facts can be "set forth in a different Light." Biography is concerned with this more qualitative sort of truth. The "Facts we deliver may be relied on" because their truth is understood to be fully dependent upon the interpretive "light" in which they are "set forth." Biography aims at the truth of general nature and of universal types. A good example is the "true History" of Gil Blas or Don Quixote: the "Time and Place" of Cervantes' characters may well be questioned, but "is there in the World such a Sceptic as to disbelieve the Madness of *Cardenio,* the Perfidy of *Ferdinand . . . ?*"

It is clear enough that Fielding is seeking here to distinguish between a naively empiricist and a more "imaginative" species of belief. But he is also at pains to emphasize the crucial degree to which he is in accord with the empiricist perspective, and to distinguish his preferred sort of belief also from the sheer creativity of romance.[36] For he quickly adds, "I would by no means be thought to comprehend" in this preferred category "the Authors of immense Romances" or of *chroniques scandaleuses,* "who without any Assistance from Nature or History, record Persons who never were, or will be, and Facts which never did nor possibly can happen: Whose Heroes are of their own Creation." Both romancers and romancing historians, in other words, rely too much on a "happy and fertile invention." As a biographer, Fielding is "contented to copy Nature" and to write "little more than I have seen," aiming not at all to repudiate the evidence of the senses but to do full justice to its complexity. And the category "true History," in which he places *Joseph Andrews* at the conclusion of the chapter, provides a positive term for the complicated dance of double negation—neither romance nor history—in which his extreme skepticism has thus far consisted.

Another such category, of course, is "comic romance." Fielding's "Preface" to *Joseph Andrews* is as celebrated as it is in part because it so explicitly announces the fact that this is a project in epistemological and generic categorization, an effort to describe a "kind of Writing, which I do not remember to have seen hitherto attempted in our Language," and which "no Critic hath thought proper to . . . assign . . . a particular Name to itself" (3). Fielding's taxonomic procedure in the "Preface" is self-consciously imitative of Aristotle's, but only up to a point. For given the normative meaning of "history" in Fielding's redefinition of the term, the invidious Aristotelian distinction between "history" and "poetry" can hold no attraction for him. So despite its crucial importance in most of his other generic considerations, in what has become the most famous of all the term "history" makes no appearance whatsoever. Even so, "comic romance" is an appropriate substitute for "true history." Together these terms resuscitate the two generic categories Fielding's extreme skepticism has decisively discredited, and the adjectival addition in each case signifies that the naiveté of the original category has been corrected by (a Cervantic procedure) conjoining it more closely with its supposed antithesis.[37]

How does "romance" correct "history" in the body of *Joseph Andrews?* Most obviously, in the parodic and self-subversive deployment of the claim to historicity that I have already noted. But as in *Jonathan Wild,* all modes of self-conscious narration work here to subjectify the objective historicity of the narrative line. On the micronarrative level these reflexive intrusions are everywhere, and they are most amusing when Fielding's ostensible purpose is not to frankly advertise his control of the plot but on the contrary to underwrite a self-effacing authenticity.[38] On the macronarrative level, authorial intrusion amounts to a quite palpable interruption of the main action by apparently unrelated episodes. On such occasions, the challenge to the historical criterion of truth involves replacing the linear coherence of contiguity by—not chaos, but the alternative coherence of relations of similarity, which are simply too neat to be "natural." The most complex instance of this in *Joseph Andrews* occurs in Book III, when the "authentic History" of Fanny's rape (ix, 255) is interrupted by two successive chapters of static dialogue, first between the poet and the player and then between Joseph and Adams (x, xi). The first discourse, disclaimed as "of no other Use in this History, but to divert the Reader" (x, 259), concerns the power of actors to affect for good or ill the material that authors give them to work with. The second discourse, acknowledged as "a sort of Counterpart of this" (x, 264),

debates the proper degree of human submission to "the Dispensations of
Providence." And when at last we irritably return to Fanny's plight, we
find that the "main plot" has really been continued rather than suspended
by these analogous "episodes," since she was destined all along to be
delivered by Peter Pounce (had we only had patience enough to submit
ourselves to Fielding's narrative dispensations).[39]

Because *Joseph Andrews* is periodically punctuated by coincidental
meetings that increasingly seem too neat to be natural—Joseph with
Adams (I, xiv, 64), Adams with Fanny (II, x, 143), Joseph with Fanny (II,
xii, 154–55), Fanny with Peter Pounce (III, xii, 269)—its entire plot
gradually takes on the air of a "historical" line that has been charmed, by
the magical intrusions of "romance," into a circle. Yet there is one coincidental discovery, Joseph's meeting with Mr. Wilson, that is different from
these in that our intrusive author denies us the crucial knowledge needed
to distinguish it from the random ongoingness of everyday history—the
knowledge that Mr. Wilson is Joseph's father. (Thus our ignorance of our
hero's lineal descent at this point preserves the impression of linear contingency.) We cannot say that we have not been warned—although the
early clues are rather ambiguous. True, there have been "romance" intimations of Joseph's genealogical gentility in what we have heard of his
external appearance (I, viii, 38–39, xiv, 61). But readers have long since
become used to hearing such things said of progressive protagonists who
possess "true," as distinct from inherited, gentility, especially in narratives that progressively insist, as here, that their heroes are capable "of
acquiring Honour" even in the total absence of ancestry (I, ii, 21). In other
words, Fielding's "romance" conventions are equally parodic, antiromance conventions, and they create in us the erroneous expectation of an
empiricist and a progressive ending.[40]

So as his long-lost child, innocently returned to his place of birth, sits
listening, Mr. Wilson concludes the history of his life with the only
episode for which he cannot gratefully thank "the great Author," the
theft of his eldest son by gypsies. Shortly thereafter the three travelers
renew their journey. Joseph and Adams are soon lost in discourse about
the rival claims of nature and nurture, until they find themselves all at
once in "a kind of natural Amphitheatre," nature reworked by art, whose
trees "seemed to have been disposed by the Design of the most skillful
Planter . . . [And] the whole Place might have raised romantic Ideas in
elder Minds than those of *Joseph* and *Fanny,* without the Assistance of
Love" (III, iii, 224, v, 232). Here the travelers rest, and here our own
author, as though encouraging us to rest in his analogous design, informs
us that Mr. Wilson plans to pass through Parson Adams's parish in a
week's time, "a Circumstance which we thought too immaterial to mention before." And as a pledge of his good will Fielding ends this chapter
by letting the reader in on what the next contains, "for we scorn to betray

him into any such Reading, without first giving him Warning" (III, v, 233). Thus the narrative power of imposition is defused by being made explicit, and the incredibility of "romance" coincidence is gently softened into a benign and watchful disposition of the author. When Mr. Wilson's visit later turns out to coincide remarkably with other events to which it is intimately related, Fielding will remind us that we knew it was going to happen (IV, xv, 338), as though now encouraging us toward an instrumental belief in a palpable fiction in which, after all, we are already to this degree knowingly invested. The last chapter heading—"In which this true History is brought to a happy Conclusion"—finely balances the claims of history and romance contrivance, and its closing words pleasantly insist upon the present historicity of Fielding's characters, as if counting on us to know the sort of belief with which to honor that claim (IV, xvi, 339, 343–44).

It is tempting to say that questions of truth and virtue merge with the climactic discovery of Joseph's parentage. Certainly it is a scene of contrivance calculated enough to permit the ghosts of romance idealism and aristocratic ideology to be raised simultaneously. But the effect depends so fully on the delicate balance of our liaison with our author that the relation is most accurately seen not as a merging but as a subsumption of questions of virtue by questions of truth. Not that Fielding does anything now to discourage our (highly provisional) belief in the benevolent authority of the gentry and the law. Thus far he has led us to associate Joseph's social elevation—the overcoming of his status inconsistency— with the interested goodness of Mr. Booby, who not only improves the law of Justice Frolick but immediately thereafter has Joseph "drest like a Gentleman" (IV, v, 292). If anything, Mr. Booby's charity increases in the last episodes of the narrative. But of course the real agent of Joseph's upward mobility, Fielding's narrative procedure insists, is not noblesse oblige at all; it is the good will of our benevolent author. Social justice and the rule of charity are most dependably institutionalized not in the law or the gentry but in the patriarchal care of the narrator, who internalizes the charity of an imagined "old English hospitality."

The representatives of the archaic feudal order that one finds among Fielding's characters are plentiful enough, but they are hedged about with a suppositional aura that we detect also in the power of providence—in some respects analogous to the power of the old gentry in Fielding—largely because of the perpetual association of providence with the more manifest power of the author. Not that he would have us doubt for a moment the reality of divine justice. But the belief in it that Fielding argues for most energetically tends to be a well-rationalized and instrumental one. And meanwhile we are able to experience the palpable poetic justice of the narrator—why not call it providence?—who periodically intrudes into the daily life of story so as to ensure there what divine and human justice manifestly do not ensure in the world out-side.[41] Fielding's subsumption of questions of virtue by questions of truth transfers the major challenge of utopian projection from the sub-stantive to the formal realm. And a central reason for this, we may speculate, is the relative uncertainty of his commitment to the utopian institutions and communities envisioned by conservative ideology. At-tracted, on the other hand, to the energy of the career open to talents, Fielding was appalled by the vanity and pretension of those who enacted that career with any success or conviction. Accordingly, what "happens" at the end of *Joseph Andrews* (and *Tom Jones*) is less a social than an epistemological event; not upward mobility but—as in the invoked model of *Oedipus* (IV, xv, 336)—the acquisition of knowledge.

The subsumption is anticipated in *Joseph Andrews* in its two most extended discussions of formal strategy, the "Preface" and the first chap-ter of Book III. In both discussions Fielding's extreme sensitivity to the analogous relation between questions of truth and questions of virtue leads him to exemplify the former by the latter. Thus we are told in the "Preface" that comic romance works through the discovery of affecta-tion, as when we find someone "to be the exact Reverse of what he affects." And the exemplary cases of affectation are also cases of status inconsistency: a "dirty Fellow" who "descend[s] from his Coach and Six, or bolt[s] from his Chair with his Hat under his Arm"; or a "wretched Family" in whose presence we find an "Affectation of Riches and Finery either on their Persons or in their Furniture" (9). Later on Fielding qualifies his technique of representing universal types in biography by acknowledging that life admits of exceptions to the rule. And the excep-tions singled out for comment are those elevated individuals whose social status is, surprisingly enough, consistent with their "superior Talents" and "Mind" (III, i, 190). The ease with which formal argument com-prehends the substantive social problem in both of these passages, by treating it as an exemplary case, prefigures the increasing facility with which Fielding's charitable narrator will tacitly compensate for the failure of social—and providential—mechanisms to justify our provisional cre-dence, by mobilizing narrative's own more perfect versions of them. Fielding's reflexive narration permits the discursive argument of the in-strumentality of a belief in what cannot be shown to be credible to infiltrate narrative form itself. And once acclimatized, it becomes an automatic and all-purpose gesture of reconciliation, an invisible thread of affirmation that is as unconditional as the fact of the narrative form into which it has been woven. Approaching it from a very different direction, Fielding meets Richardson at the nexus where moral and social pedagogy hesitate on the edge of their transformation into something else entirely, aesthetic pleasure.

To suggest that epistemological and social conflict were "institutionalized" by the encounter between Richardson and Fielding is of course not to say that contemporaries registered that encounter in the explanatory terms that have been most useful and recurrent in this study. In the Conclusion I will argue the basic compatibility, despite terminological differences, of my account with their perceptions of the relationship between Richardson and Fielding during the decade that followed the publication of *Jonathan Wild*. But I will also observe how the entire framework of conflict, so long in the construction, now quickly seems to alter its shape as the new genre emerges into the light of historical consciousness.

Conclusion

The argument of this study has been that the origins of the English novel, whose climax is signaled by the Richardson-Fielding rivalry of the 1740s, consist in the establishment of a form sufficient for the joint inquiry into analogous epistemological and social problems which themselves had a long prehistory of intense and diversified public debate. Rivalry does not preclude agreement: the real fact of conflict only facilitated the recognition that the two writers were engaged in what was also a common enterprise. The emergence of a distinct new form was affirmed first of all by the authors themselves. Richardson believed he had introduced a new "species" of writing; Fielding claimed a new "kind" or "province." These affirmations were echoed enthusiastically by their respective admirers. And after 1750 it was increasingly easy to speak of them, as exemplary and founding figures, in the same breath. As early as *Clarissa*'s publication, moreover, the two men were able to exchange generous and apparently sincere appreciations of each other's work. But the modern critical impulse to minimize the conflict, both theoretical and personal, between Richardson and Fielding is not entirely convincing. If Richardson waited until the publication of *Tom Jones* to complain of *Shamela* and *Joseph Andrews,* he did so then with some acerbity. *Pamela*'s creator could not have been ignorant of Fielding's contribution to the anti-*Pamela* campaign, or insensitive to the trenchant attacks of the early 1740s. Friendly contact seems still to have been possible even after the success of *Tom Jones* and *Amelia*. But the tenor of Richardson's extant allusions to Fielding after 1748 is bitter and narrowly critical, and Fielding's posthumous bow to Richardson's pedagogic method successfully calls to the reader's mind an image less of authority than of hypocrisy.[1]

More significant than the two writers' personal antipathy is the articulated conflict, between them and between their supporters, on matters of principle. Much of this I have already documented through Fielding's narratives, in which the critique of Richardsonian principle plays a central role. His final critique, in the *Voyage to Lisbon,* recalls those early ones. Richardson is here "the great man" who requires authors "to convey instruction in the vehicle of entertainment," but who himself undertakes to reform "a whole people, by making use of a vehicular story, to wheel in among them worse manners than their own." This is to some degree the old problem of mediation—means become ends, signifiers become signifieds, vehicles become tenors—but Richardson's piety tended to provoke his critics into charging that the story was gratuitously seductive and that its displacement of an improving moral was somehow intentional. This is the burden, for example, of *Pamela Censured: in a Letter to the Editor: Shewing That under the Specious Pretence of Cultivating the Principles of Virtue in the Minds of the Youth of both Sexes, the* MOST ARTFUL and ALLURING AMOROUS IDEAS *are convey'd* . . . (1741). "Thus you act the part of the serpent," Richardson was later reproached, "and not only throw out to men the tempting suggestions of lust and pleasure, but likewise instruct the weak head and the corrupt heart in the methods how to proceed to their gratification."[2]

This perversion of pedagogy is closely related to another problem in Richardson, the inadequacy of his supposedly exemplary characters. The "secret," with which he appears to be "intirely unacquainted," is "to blend vices and virtues of a similar quality so together, as to render them all uniformly consistent." Paradoxically, consistency is the product of a proper mixture. And the anonymous critic contrasts the improbable "inconsistencies" in Sir Charles Grandison with the judiciously mixed and therefore more imitable Squire Allworthy. Elizabeth Carter gives this problem a rather different formulation. *Tom Jones,* she thinks, "is the most natural representation of what passes in the world, and of the bizarreries which arise from the mixture of good and bad which makes up the composition of most folks." Carter is untroubled by Richardson's examples of virtue, "but there is a strange awkwardness and extravagance in his vicious characters" (e.g., Lovelace). For "being totally ignorant in what manner . . . wickedness operates upon the human heart, and what checks and restraints it meets with to prevent its ever being perfectly uniform and consistent in any one character, he has drawn . . . a monster." Here the criticism is not of the virtuous but of the vicious, and Richardson's uniformity is chastized not for inconsistency but for too great a consistency; nevertheless, the underlying complaint is much the same.[3]

From these cases it is clear that the problem of character inconsistency in Richardson is one not only of "immorality" but also of "unnaturalness." For some of his critics the problem takes on a familiar social coloring as well. One of the imitators of *Pamela,* for example, accused his predecessor of having Pamela "talking like a *Philosopher* in one Page and like a *Changling* the next: As we hope her Master will be found to talk a little more like a Gentleman." The treatment of Lord Davers, he adds, "plainly betrays the Mechanick; for such, knowing nothing of the Behaviour and Conversation of the Nobility, imagine every LORD is a FOOL." Lady Mary Wortley Montagu told her daughter that

even that model of Perfection, Clarissa, is so faulty in her behaviour as to deserve little Compassion . . . I look upon [*Clarissa*] and Pamela to be two Books that will do more general mischeif than the Works of Lord Rochester . . . Richardson is as ignorant in Morality as he is in Anatomy . . . His Anna How[e] and Charlotte Grandison are recommended as Patterns of charming Pleasantry . . . Charlotte acts with an Ingratitude that I think too black for Human Nature, with such coarse Jokes and low expressions as are only to be heard amongst the Lowest Class of People . . . I believe this Author was never admitted into higher Company, and should Confine his Pen to the Amours of Housemaids and the conversation at the Steward's Table, where I imagine he has sometimes intruded, thô oftner in the Servants' Hall.

Here character inconsistency is comfortably specified to status inconsistency, which in turn is conveyed as the linguistic incompetence of an author who clownishly confounds the language of servants with that of their masters. The social sneer recalls Fielding's play with Shamela's linguistic duplicity in his attack upon her upstart upward mobility, an effrontery that others as well "allowed to be the general bad Tendency" of *Pamela.*[4]

Richardson and his supporters defended him against the charge of Pamela's status inconsistency and its incitement to social chaos by asserting not just the reality but the uniqueness of her virtue, and the power of her story to support rather than subvert the social order. Yet the social dynamics of *Clarissa* already reveal a subtle shift in focus. One obvious sign of this shift is Richardson's new-found contempt for the poetic justice of a "happy Issue." Now "*sudden Conversions*" and reformations— perhaps even the reformation of Mr. B.—are implicitly suspect on grounds of both "naturalness" and "morality," and poetic justice is impugned as potentially anti-Christian. "A Writer who follows Nature and pretends to keep the Christian System in his Eye, cannot make a Heaven in this World for his Favourites . . . Clarissa I once more averr could not be rewarded in this World." Thus morality is preserved by denying not only easy conversions to the vicious but even upward mobility to the virtuous.[5]

So the wonderfully happy ending of *Pamela* made Richardson feel vulnerable on the issue of naturalness as well as on that of morality. Generally speaking, of course, a ready defense against the charge that *Pamela*'s characters or narrative procedure were unnatural was to be found in the assertion of the documentary historicity of the epistolary form. But Richardson's claim to historicity soon became troublesome. The standard of quantitative completeness which it seemed to enforce quickly drew the fire of his imitators. "Nor shall we load our Readers," said one, "with a Heap of trivial Circumstances, which, tho' they may be true, it is very idle to trouble the Public with." The criticism reveals a Fieldingesque unwillingness to equate truth with exhaustive factuality; the truth of *Shamela* depends not on more details but on a different principle of selection. Of course the obvious reply was in a certain sense unanswerable: historical documents are what they are; if you want artifice, go to a romancer. That Richardson did not avail himself of this sort of refutation may be due to the fact that the claim to historicity presented other, even more immediate, problems.[6]

One of these was once again his imitators. For so far from establishing his unassailable access to truth, the fiction of authentic documents was eagerly exploited by them to assert that they, and *not* he, had material possession of the truth. A second problem was occasioned equally by Richardson's vanity. The disavowal of authorship seemed to give him an impunity in self-praise, but the breathtaking conceit of *Pamela*'s prefatory material only encouraged Richardson's critics to explode the fiction of editorship, which was itself conventional enough to have escaped comment under less odious circumstances. In the view of one critic, the fact "that you could not otherwise be acquitted of intolerable Vanity in applauding yourself as you have done, has induced you to stile yourself only *Editor*." And late in 1741 Richardson ingenuously admitted that "the Praises in those Pieces are carried so high, that since I cou'd not pass as the Editor only, as I once hoped to do, I wish they had never been Inserted."[7]

Nevertheless Richardson continued, with some ambivalence, to associate naturalness with the claim to historicity. And his tenacity in this association testifies to the influence the empiricist assumptions of the claim continued to exercise over him even as its real meaning was obliged to undergo a subtle transformation. In the preface he contributed to the first edition of volumes III and IV of *Clarissa* (1748), William Warburton confesses that the author has "told his Tale in a Series of Letters, supposed to be written by the Parties concerned, as the Circumstances related, passed." Although grateful to his friend, Richardson nonetheless remarked that "I could wish that the *Air* of Genuineness had been kept up, tho' I want not the letters to be *thought* genuine; only so far kept up, I mean, as that they should not prefatically be owned *not* to be genuine: and this for fear of weakening their Influence where any of them are aimed to be exemplary: as well as to avoid hurting that kind of Historical Faith which Fiction itself is generally read with, tho' we know it to be Fiction." In his own preface to volume I (1747), Richardson self-consciously preserves the editorial fiction while defending the length of the work on the grounds of its naturalness—meaning, however, not explicitly its historicity so much as its representation of hearts fully and affectingly "engaged in their Subjects." By 1751 he is pleased to announce the restoration of passages that had earlier been omitted, and the length is now eclectically justified, by Richardson and his supporters, as the consequence of a close attention to historicity, probability, and subjectivity. The convention of the claim to historicity is becoming increasingly vestigial.[8]

As early as *Pamela*, Richardson's epistolary method had suggested to some of his supporters a generic model different from the historical document and fundamentally alien to its empirical mode of naturalness, the model of drama. And ten years after *Pamela* Richardson was expressing his own uncertainty by referring to "the History (or rather Dramatic Narrative) of Clarissa." The attractions of the dramatic model were considerable, among them the legitimating authority of a classical literary tradition and of established criteria of stylistic propriety. But to the extent that Richardson embraced that model for his epistolary dialogue, he also inevitably distanced himself from the epistemological premises of documentary historicity. This can be seen in what we are probably right to take as his response to Fielding's urbane dismissal of "the epistolary Style" as unsuitable "to the Novel or Story-Writer." A series of letters, Richardson says, offers "the only natural Opportunity . . . of representing with any Grace those lively and delicate Impressions, which *Things present* are known to make upon the Minds of those affected by them," and which lead "us farther into the Recesses of the human Mind, than the colder and more general Reflections suited to a continued and more contracted Narrative." Thus the letter becomes a passport not to the objectivity of sense impressions but to the subjectivity of mind. And the exhaustiveness of the protagonist's reflections is justified not by the fact that she really made them, but because they are her very own. Which is not to say that the length and circumstantiality of Richardson's narratives have ceased to be a vulnerability, but only that the terms of the critique must be altered. This is recognized by Lady Mary when she complains of Harriet Byron that "she follows the Maxim of Clarissa, of declaring all she thinks to all the people she sees, without refflecting [*sic*] that in this Mortal state of Imperfection Fig leaves are as necessary for our Minds as our Bodies, and tis as indecent to shew all we think as all we have."[9]

2

It will be clear by now that when contemporaries concern themselves with problems of "naturalness" and "morality" in narrative, they address something closely related to what I have been calling questions of truth and virtue. These criteria were thought to be as pertinent to Fielding's works as to Richardson's. Stung by the popular reception of *Tom Jones,* Richardson demanded of Lady Bradshaigh: "Has not the world shewn me, that it is much better pleased to receive and applaud the character that shews us what we are (little of novelty as one would think there is in that) than what we ought to be? Are there not who think Clarissa's an unnatural character?" Richardson was right. Fielding's supporters did praise him for showing readers "that pure Nature could furnish out as agreeable Entertainment, as those airy non-entical Forms they had long ador'd," and for disclosing "Characters which really existed." But by the same token, Fielding's detractors criticized him for a technique so "natural" that it inevitably deviated, unlike Richardson's, into "immorality."[10]

The criticism was made, of course, by Richardson himself: for example, in his peevish comparisons between Clarissa Harlowe's ideal goodness and Sophia Western's easy and vulgar capacity to please undiscriminating audiences. But he was not alone in this judgment. Displeased by the absence of "a moral design" in *Joseph Andrews* and *Tom Jones,* one of Richardson's supporters found *Amelia* little better, and eagerly awaited the appearance of the *"good man"* Sir Charles Grandison. Her friend agreed: "Poor Fielding, I believe, designed to be good [in *Amelia*], but did not know how, and in the attempt lost his genius, low humour." She expects *Grandison*'s morality to "rescue us." And after Richardson's last novel was published, he corresponded with another reader who "much preferred his pure characters to those in certain recent novels, which seem to think all men a mixture of virtue and vice." After *Pamela,* at least, Richardson believed that this kind of immorality was only aggravated by happy endings in which vicious characters, suddenly reformed, are rewarded for their wickedness. He told his correspondents that he had resisted Fielding's advice that he give *Clarissa* a happy issue, and he concluded *Grandison* by making a strong case against such immorality:

It has been said in behalf of many modern fictitious pieces, in which authors have given success (and *happiness,* as it is called) to their heroes of vicious, if not of profligate, characters, that they have exhibited Human Nature as it *is.* Its corruption may, indeed, be exhibited in the faulty character; but need pictures of this be held out in books? Is not vice crowned with success, triumphant, and rewarded, and perhaps set off with wit and spirit, a dangerous representation? And is it not made even *more* dangerous by the hasty reformation, introduced, in contradiction to all probability, for the sake of patching up what is called a happy ending?

Here Richardson is able to indict Fielding (at least by innuendo) not only of immorality but also of improbability—that is, unnaturalness.[11]

Of course Fielding has a pedagogic rationale for his preference of "mixed characters" that justifies them on grounds of both naturalness and morality. Nevertheless it was a common charge against him that in his pursuit of the natural, Fielding courted the immoral, and in this argument Richardson was able to count among his allies the powerful voice of Samuel Johnson. Johnson's famous paper on the fiction of the present age deserves to be quoted at some length on this subject:

It is justly considered as the greatest excellency of art, to imitate nature; but it is necessary to distinguish those parts of nature, which are most proper for imitation: greater care is still required in representing life, which is so often discoloured by passion, or deformed by wickedness. If the world be promiscuously described, I cannot see of what use it can be to read the account; or why it may not be as safe to turn the eye immediately upon mankind, as upon a mirror which shews all that presents itself without discrimination.

It is therefore not a sufficient vindication of a character, that it is drawn as it appears, for many characters ought never to be drawn; nor of a narrative, that the train of events is agreeable to observation and experience, for that observation which is called knowledge of the world, will be found much more frequently to make men cunning than good . . .

Many writers, for the sake of following nature, so mingle good and bad qualities in their principal personages, that they are both equally conspicuous; and as we accompany them through their adventures with delight, and are led by degrees to interest ourselves in their favour, we lose the abhorrence of their faults, because they do not hinder our pleasure, or, perhaps, regard them with some kindness for being united with so much merit.

Eighteen years later Johnson approvingly quoted Richardson to the effect "that the virtues of Fielding's heroes were the vices of a truly good man." Indeed, Johnson here implies that Richardson's heroes are not only more virtuous but also more natural. Fielding draws entertaining "characters of manners." But with Richardson's "characters of nature . . . a man must dive into the recesses of the human heart."[12]

As in the attacks upon Richardson, criticism of Fielding for a naturalness that entails a regrettable moral lowness tends to include the failing of social lowness as well.

BOSWELL. Will you not allow, Sir, that [Fielding] draws very natural pictures of human life?

JOHNSON. Why, Sir, it is of very low life. Richardson used to say, that had he not known who Fielding was, he should have believed he was an ostler.

Shortly after its publication, George Cheyne told Richardson that *Joseph Andrews* "will entertain none but Porters or Watermen," and six years later Fielding was scorned anonymously for writing, in *Joseph Andrews* and *Jonathan Wild*, "the Adventures of Footmen, and the Lives of Thief-Catchers":

> *Low Humour*, like *his own*, he once exprest,
> In *Footman*, *Country Wench*, and Country *Priest*.

The extended exercise in social invalidation that was carried out so effectively against Richardson by Lady Mary Wortley Montagu was accomplished, in Fielding's case, by Richardson himself. Having read the first volume of *Amelia*, he wrote:

[I] had intended to go through with it; but I found the characters and situations so wretchedly low and dirty, that I imagined I could not be interested for any one of them . . . His brawls, his jarrs, his gaols, his spunging-houses, are all drawn from what he has seen and known. As I said . . . he has little or no invention . . .

Poor Fielding! I could not help telling his sister, that I was equally surprised at and concerned for his continued lowness. Had your brother, said I, been born in a stable, or been a runner at a sponging-house, we should have thought him a genius, and wished he had had the advantage of a liberal education, and of being admitted into good company; but it is beyond my conception, that a man of family, and who had some learning, and who really is a writer, should descend so excessively low, in all his pieces. Who can care for any of his people?

Social lowness seems here to interfere with Richardson's moral sympathy—a mechanism, incidentally, he would have hotly contested a decade earlier with respect to his own *Pamela*. While Fielding's novels cannot be accused of inculcating status inconsistency, they may be fairly charged with teaching a morality of the gutter.[13]

3

One of the arresting features of this controversy is that although it reflects a strong sense of conflict between Richardson and Fielding, often enough the two men seem to be praised and blamed for the same things. This impression may well vindicate the view of them as, if in conflict, also at work on a common enterprise; but it is possible to be somewhat more precise. What is arresting is that in certain respects Richardson and Fielding seem, by 1750, to have reversed positions. Now it is Richardson, the naive empiricist, who prides himself on disclosing "what ought to be," not "what is," and who disdains his rival for a lack not of historicity but of "invention." Now it is Fielding, skeptical demystifier of a quantitative completeness in narrative and staunch proponent of a principled selection, who is associated with "promiscuous description" and with a belief in the sufficiency of "observation and experience" alone in the construction of narrative.[14] Although it is by no means a complete reversal, this phenomenon is not an optical illusion. The emergence of the origins of the novel into public consciousness and controversy marks the point at which the genre is both identified as such, as a "new species," and redirected into new territory.

Readers have long recognized that after their initial collision at the beginning of the 1740s, Fielding and Richardson spent the next decade edging closer to each other. Fielding's entanglement of the micronarrative of *Tom Jones* with the macronarrative of the '45 Rising provides the most intricate vindication in his work of the view that novelistic "invention" is consistent with a painstaking truth to "history." If the plot of Tom the bastard bears a subtle relation to the conservative career of the Young Pretender, wandering in search of his patrimony, it is less an imitation than a parody fueled by Fielding's anti-Jacobite contempt for the hereditary claims of the Stuarts. Unlike Joseph Andrews, Tom, although of gentle lineage, is truly a bastard. Born to be hanged, he is industrious and active where Joseph is passive, yet basically virtuous where Jonathan Wild is vicious. A rogue figure who makes good, Tom is much closer to the model of the progressive protagonist than anything Fielding had previously attempted. Clarissa Harlowe, on the other hand, resists assimilation to the progressive model of her predecessor Pamela Andrews. She is a conservative heroine, torn between the monetary and material corruption of her upwardly mobile family and the libertine corruption of the aristocratic rake Lovelace. The progressive ambition of the Harlowes is to "raise the family" through an arranged marriage with the vile and monied Mr. Solmes. If Lovelace is for his part a vile aristocrat, he is at least the real thing. A paternalistic protector of his tenants, rightly contemptuous of the upstart Harlowes, his vice is not the lust of avarice but lust itself. And in reserving this heroine's reward for heaven, Richardson evinces the darker, conservative apprehension that the essence of utopia is that it is not to be found in this world.

If we distance ourselves from the details of this *rapprochement* between Richardson and Fielding, we may catch a glimpse of where the novel goes after its origins. The capacity of both of these authors to reconcile, within the movement of their respective careers, naive empiricism and extreme skepticism, progressive and conservative ideologies, attests not only to their supreme virtuosity but also to the fact that these oppositions are losing their intellectual and social significance. Of course the claim to historicity continues to be serviceable, in various ways, to future generations of novelists. But in a more general sense, both the claim and its subversion end in the triumph of the creative human mind, a triumph already prefigured at the moment of the novel's emergence: in Richardson the triumphant mind is that of the protagonist; in Fielding it is that of the author. The implications of the formal breakthrough of the 1740s are pursued with such feverish intensity over the next two decades that after *Tristram Shandy,* it may be said, the young genre settles down to a more deliberate and studied recapitulation of the same ground, this time for the next two centuries. By the end of the eighteenth century, romance idealism will have emerged from the long process of positive revaluation that issues in the romantic movement and in the ascendancy of the secularized, human spirituality of the aesthetic.[15] In the realm of prose fiction, questions of truth will be addressed by reference to a notion of "history" that is now sufficiently separated from "literature" to be "realistically" represented by it. In this sense, the questions of truth that have thus far organized the origins of the English novel are not so much solved now as drastically reformulated.

This can be said also of questions of virtue. By the end of the eighteenth century, the status orientation toward social relations has become so dominated—or incorporated—by a class orientation that the problem of status inconsistency is very difficult to conceive in the old way. The individual, and the idea of the individual, have risen decisively. The question of whether particular elevations are merited is neither academic nor passé, but the problem of inconsistency to which modern attention is most exquisitely attuned is the more abstract one of "self" and "society." Hypostatized over against the individual, "society" slowly separates from "self" as "history" does from "literature," a ponderous and alienated structure whose massive impingement on the individual paradoxically signifies the latter's autonomy, the very fact of the individual's "rise," as well as the subjection of self to this greater power. The autonomy of the self consists in its capacity to enter into largely negative relation with the society it vainly conceives itself to have created, to resist its encroachments and to be constructed by them. The work of the novel after 1820 is increasingly to record this struggle.

4

At the outset of this study I suggested that the function of literary genres is to mediate and explain intractable problems, and the study itself has proceeded on that understanding. The problem the novel was formulated to mediate is, on the most general level of all, not questions of truth and questions of virtue in themselves so much as their division, their separation from each other. And the fact that the novel originates when it does signifies that it is in this period that the separation of these two realms of thought and experience comes to be felt most acutely. The relative absence of this apprehension before the modern age can be seen in the long

ascendancy and authority of the idea of lineage. From Hesiod to Chrétien, lineage existed to resolve questions of virtue and truth with a tacit
simultaneity, making both a causal claim of genealogical descent attesting to an eminence of birth, hence worth, and a logical claim of testimonial precedent validating all present claims as true. The origins of the
novel's mediatory project mark the discovery not of the relation between
these realms but of an increasing division between them that is too great
to ignore. In this respect the novel, although "new," is the explicit com-
memoration of a previous and tacit knowledge, as well as of its fragility
and dissolution. We need not evoke the elegiac nostalgia of archetypalist
thought to recognize the contradictory complexity of this historical moment. Henceforth the very ground of the novel, like that of the world it
inhabits and explains, is the fact of division—the division of labor, the
division of knowledge—and the technical powers of the novel as a literary form are augmented in proportion to the impassability of the gulfs it
now undertakes to subtend.

With these remarks I bring my long account of the origins of the English
novel to a close. Readers who have persisted through it will have become
habituated to the recurrence, in varied contexts and at several levels of
analysis, of a fundamental pattern of dialectical movement, a structure of
"reversal" in which change takes place as the generation of difference
from similarity, of opposition from identity. And it may have occurred
more than once to readers that there is something rather "too" dialectical
about this method, that it never can be tested or "falsified," because its
indulgent flexibility allows all apparent exceptions to be reconciled, with
only a slight adjustment of focus, to its explanatory mechanism. Any
plausible protest—for example, "That sounds more like conservative
than progressive ideology"—can always be met (it may be objected) by
the plausible retort, "But progressive ideology has an inherent tendency
toward the conservative." Under these conditions, "categorial instability" may come to seem a far too automatic and comprehensive answer
to all possible questions. The charge of unfalsifiability is a fair one, and it
cannot be refuted; at least, not on its own terms. For the only reply that
can be made is that the problem lies not with the method but with the
subject matter to whose features it seeks to be adequate. It is first of all not
method but history that is dialectical and that resists the dichotomous
fixity that a rigorously "scientific" method might impose upon its categories. Early modern culture exhibited in an aggravated form the categorial instability that inhabits all historical experience. But once this is
said, it must also be affirmed that anyone who would seek to disclose the
dialectical process of historical experience must be in some committed (if
skeptical) way an empiricist, responsible to the evidence at hand lest it

appear that by "history" one means finally that realm where everything can be found to equal everything else.

In the very recent criticism of the eighteenth-century English novel there is a final, pertinent example of how dialectical thought may aid in uncovering the complex movement of historical process. There has been considerable interest of late in the way *Clarissa* underscores, and is "about," the subjective powers of language and the letter form to render meaning radically indeterminate.[16] The interest would appear to direct our attention to a double innovation: the subversive subjectivity of the Richardsonian deployment of "epistolarity" is revealed by the subversive deconstructions of poststructuralist criticism. But to acknowledge only this parallel is to freeze the categories of which it consists apart from their respective historical movements. As we have seen, Richardson's "writing to the moment" not only subverted the empiricist claim to historicity and its naive belief in "objective" truth; it was also the fullest extension of naive empiricism. The extreme skepticism of Richardson's later epistemology was an unrationalized consequence, and an inseparable expression, of having set in motion the naive-empiricist machine of documentary historicity. By the same token, poststructuralist skepticism is not only a "reaction against" the long ascendancy of the New Criticism and of the structuralist orthodoxy with which it has some affinities. It is also a dialectical extension of these critical doctrines, a negation born of their most extreme application. And in the gleefully earnest energy that it invests in the deconstruction of empiricism, poststructuralism stealthily betrays the kind of negative commitment that is most characteristic of the recent convert. In other words, the parallel is between not isolated instances of radical innovation but ongoing processes by which ideas unfold in time. The current critical rediscovery of *Clarissa* thus helps vindicate, both as intellectual structure and as transhistorical echo, the fundamental logic of the great historical movement that occasioned the origins of the English novel.

Notes

Cross-references to endnote numbers in a given chapter demarcate particular passages in the text. Place of publication of pre-eighteenth-century works is London unless otherwise specified.

INTRODUCTION: DIALECTICAL METHOD IN LITERARY HISTORY

1. Ian Watt, *The Rise of the Novel: Studies in Defoe, Richardson, and Fielding* (Berkeley and Los Angeles: University of California Press, [1957] 1964); all parenthetical citations in the text are to the 1964 edition.

2. A third criticism, that Watt's study tacitly defines "the novel" as "the English novel," is equally important but susceptible to strategies that are perhaps less in need of theoretical articulation. The present study undertakes the more limited subject of the origins of the English novel, at the same time aiming to acknowledge the most obvious and crucial interactions between this English phenomenon and other national cultures.

3. Romance in the three novelists: see Sheridan Baker, "The Idea of Romance in the Eighteenth-Century Novel," *Papers of the Michigan Academy of Science, Arts, and Letters*, 49 (1964), 507–22; Margaret Dalziel, "Richardson and Romance," *Journal of Australasian Universities Language and Literature Assn.*, 33 (May, 1970), 5–24; Henry Knight Miller, *Henry Fielding's Tom Jones and the Romance Tradition*, English Literary Studies no. 6 (Victoria, B.C.: University of Victoria, 1976), passim. Defoe's spirituality: see Maximillian E. Novak, *Economics and the Fiction of Daniel Defoe* (Berkeley and Los Angeles: University of California Press, 1962), 32–48; George A. Starr, *Defoe and Spiritual Autobiography* (Princeton: Princeton University Press, 1965), chap. 3; J. Paul Hunter, *The Reluctant Pilgrim: Defoe's Emblematic Method and Quest for Form in Robinson Crusoe* (Baltimore: Johns Hopkins Press, 1966), passim. Romance outpouring in the period: see Maximillian E. Novak, "Fiction and Society in the Early Eighteenth Century," in *England in the Restoration and Early Eighteenth Century: Essays on Culture and Society*, ed. H. T. Swedenberg, Jr. (Berkeley and Los Angeles: Univer-

sity of California Press, 1972), 51–70. Much of John J. Richetti's argument and evidence also might be seen to support a view of the period as dominated not only by "formal realism" but also by "romance"; see Richetti's *Popular Fiction before Richardson: Narrative Patterns, 1700–1739* (Oxford: Clarendon Press, 1969). Formal realism in romance: see Paul Turner, "Novels, Ancient and Modern," *Novel,* 2 (1968), 15–24; Diana Spearman, *The Novel and Society* (London: Routledge and Kegan Paul, 1966), chap. 2.

4. See Watt, *Rise of the Novel,* 25, 27, 30; and idem, "Serious Reflections on *The Rise of the Novel,*" *Novel,* 1, no. 3 (1968), 207, 213. The cuts in the manuscript were made, Watt says, owing to editorial constraints.

5. See Watt, "Serious Reflections," 216–18.

6. Early eighteenth century dominance: see Spearman, *Novel and Society,* chap. 1. Thirteenth-century middle class: see most recently Alan Macfarlane, *The Origins of English Individualism: The Family, Property, and Social Transition* (New York: Cambridge University Press, 1979). Fielding and declining gentry: see Swingewood's argument in Diana Laurenson and Alan Swingewood, *The Sociology of Literature* (London: Paladin, 1972), chap. 8.

7. *The Myth of the Eternal Return; or, Cosmos and History,* trans. Willard R. Trask, Bollingen Series XLVI (Princeton: Princeton University Press, [1949] 1974), 35, 86.

8. Bracketing "content": e.g., see Claude Lévi-Strauss, *The Savage Mind* (Chicago: University of Chicago Press, [1962] 1966), 13, 75–76, 95, 115–16, 126, 129; idem, "Postscript to Chapter XV" (1953), in Lévi-Strauss, *Structural Anthropology,* vol. I, trans. Claire Jacobson and Brooke G. Schoepf (Garden City, N.Y.: Doubleday, 1967), 330; for a fuller consideration of these matters see my article "The 'Marxism' of Claude Lévi-Strauss," *Dialectical Anthropology,* 6 (1981), 123–50. Oedipus myth: see Claude Lévi-Strauss, "The Structural Study of Myth" (1955), in *Structural Anthropology,* I, 202–28.

9. Claude Lévi-Strauss, *The Origin of Table Manners: Introduction to a Science of Mythology: 3,* trans. John and Doreen Weightman (London: Jonathan Cape, [1968] 1978), 129, 130–131. Cf. idem, *The Naked Man: Introduction to a Science of Mythology: 4,* trans. John and Doreen Weightman (New York: Harper and Row, [1971] 1981), 652–53.

10. Claude Lévi-Strauss, "How Myths Die" (1971), in *Structural Anthropology,* vol. II, trans. Monique Layton (New York: Basic Books, 1976), 256, 266, 268. Lévi-Strauss does not appear to use the words *roman* and *romanesque* with the intention of designating clearly either romance or novel.

11. Northrop Frye, *The Secular Scripture: A Study of the Structure of Romance* (Cambridge: Harvard University Press, 1976), 36.

12. Northrop Frye, "Myth, Fiction, and Displacement," in *Fables of Identity: Studies in Poetic Mythology* (New York: Harbinger Books, 1963), 36; idem, *Anatomy of Criticism: Four Essays* (New York: Atheneum, [1957] 1966), 137, 63, 51 (all parenthetical citations in the text are to the 1966 edition).

13. Frye, *Secular Scripture,* 38.

14. Sigmund Freud, *The Interpretations of Dreams,* trans. James Strachey (New York: Avon, [1900] 1965), 343.

15. E.g., see the comments of Fredric Jameson, *The Political Unconscious: Narrative as a Socially Symbolic Act* (Ithaca: Cornell University Press, 1981), 106–7, 141–44, 151–52.

16. Mikhail M. Bakhtin, *The Dialogic Imagination: Four Essays by M. M. Bakhtin,* trans. Caryl Emerson and Michael Holquist, ed. Holquist (Austin: University of Texas Press, 1981), 3; all parenthetical citations in the text are to this edition.

17. Defamiliarization: e.g., see Viktor Shklovsky, "Art as Technique" (1917) and "Sterne's *Tristram Shandy:* Stylistic Commentary" (1921), in *Russian Formalist Criticism: Four Essays,* trans. and ed. Lee T. Lemon and Marion J. Reis (Lincoln: University of Nebraska Press, 1965), 3–57. As contextualization: see Tony Bennett, *Formalism and Marxism* (New York: Methuen, 1979), 56–57, 59–60; see, generally, several of the essays in Claudio Guillén, *Literature as System: Essays toward the Theory of Literary History* (Princeton: Princeton University Press, 1971). Fossilization: see Viktor Shklovsky, "The Resurrection of the Word" (1914), in *Russian Formalism: A Collection of Articles and Texts in Translation,* ed. Stephen Bann and John E. Bowlt (New York: Barnes and Noble, 1973), 41–47. On the temporal potential of Shklovsky's category see Bennett, *Formalism and Marxism,* 22–23, 55; and Fredric Jameson, *The Prison-House of Language: A Critical Account of Structuralism and Russian Formalism* (Princeton: Princeton University Press, 1972), 52–53 (Jameson [p. 58] points out the relationship between Shklovsky's "defamiliarization" and Brecht's "estrangement-effect"). Parody: see the discussion of Margaret A. Rose, *Parody/Meta-Fiction: An Analysis of Parody as a Critical Mirror to the Writing and Reception of Fiction* (London: Croom Helm, 1979), 33–35; compare the view of "realism" as parodic disillusion in Harry Levin, *The Gates of Horn: A Study of Five French Realists* (New York: Oxford University Press, 1966), chap. 2.

18. "Mode" is Frye's chosen term for elaborating a method of "historical criticism"; see his *Anatomy of Criticism,* First Essay. His "theory of genres" (Fourth Essay) is a good deal less attentive to the historicity of literary forms than is his "theory of modes." I am not speaking here of the "presentational" modes—dramatic, narrative, etc.

19. Jameson, *Political Unconscious,* 109; see also idem, "Magical Narratives: Romance as Genre," *NLH,* 7, no. 1 (Autumn, 1975), 135–63, an earlier version of this argument, which takes a different attitude toward the fact of mutual exclusion (see 137–38).

20. Karl Marx, *Grundrisse* (composed 1857–58), trans. and ed. Martin Nicolaus (Harmondsworth: Penguin, 1973); all parenthetical citations in the text are to this edition. In fact Marx very briefly turns his attention here to the problem of the historical existence of specifically literary categories (see 109–11). For a discussion of this passage and its utility in the historicizing of the idea of aesthetic value, see my article "The Origins of Aesthetic Value," *Telos,* no. 57 (Fall, 1983), 63–82.

21. Louis Althusser, *For Marx,* trans. Ben Brewster (New York: Vintage, 1970), 198–99.

CHAPTER ONE: THE DESTABILIZATION OF GENERIC CATEGORIES

1. E.g., see Charlotte E. Morgan, *The Rise of the Novel of Manners: A Study of English Prose Fiction between 1600 and 1740* (New York: Columbia University Press, 1911); Arthur J. Tieje, "The Expressed Aim of the Long Prose Fiction from 1579 to 1740," *Journal of English and Germanic Philology,* 11, no. 3 (July, 1912), 402–32; and idem, *The Theory of Characterization in Prose Fiction Prior to 1740,* University of Minnesota Studies in Language and Literature no. 5 (Minneapolis: Bulletin of the University of Minnesota, 1916).

2. For John Starkey's catalog see *Annals of Love . . .* (1672), sig. Dd7ᵛ–Ee4ᵛ; Robert Clavell, *A Catalogue of all the Books printed in England since the Dreadful Fire of London, in 1666, to the End of Michaelmas Term, 1672 . . .* (1673). For Thackeray see Margaret Spufford, *Small Books and Pleasant Histories: Popular Fiction and Its Readership in Seventeenth-Century England* (Athens: University of Georgia Press,

1982), 262–67 (Thackeray's willingness to combine conceptual and format criteria in distinguishing categories of narrative is not unusual during this period); Francis Kirkman, *The Famous and Delectable History of Don Bellianis of Greece; or, The Honour of Chivalry* . . . (1673), "To the Reader," sig. A2^{r-v}; idem, *The History of Prince Erastus . . . And those famous Philosophers Called the Seven Wise Masters of Rome* . . . (1674), sig. A3^r (see also A2^v). Clavell also includes Kirkman's translation of the *History of Don Bellianis* under the category "History"; see his *General Catalogue of Books . . . to the End of Trinity term, 1674* (1675).

3. William London, *A Catalogve of The most vendible Books in England* . . . (1657); Peter Motteux, *The Gentleman's Journal,* Jan., 1692, 1ff.; ibid., March, 1692, 3.

4. John Nalson, *An Impartial Collection of the Great Affairs of State* . . . (1682–83), I, i; Thomas Shadwell, "To Sir Charles Sedley," prefixed to *A True Widow. A Comedy* (1679), in *The Complete Works of Thomas Shadwell,* ed. Montague Summers (London: Fortune Press, 1927), III, 283; Aphra Behn, *The Unfortunate Bride; or, The Blind Lady a Beauty. A Novel* (1698), in *Histories, Novels, and Translations, Written by the most Ingenious Mrs. Behn* . . . , II (1700), 9; Joseph Glanvill, *The Vanity of Dogmatizing* . . . (1661), sig. A8^r; Marchamont Nedham, *News from Brussels In A Letter from a Near Attendant on His Majesties Person* . . . (1660), 5; John Dryden, *Sir Martin Mar-all* (1668), II, ii, 16–17; *Poor Robin's Memoirs; or, The Life, Travels and Adventures of S. Mendacio* (1677–78), no. 4, Jan. 7, 1678 (verso); Samuel Butler, *Prose Observations,* ed. Hugh de Quehen (Oxford: Oxford University Press, 1979), 179. Throughout this study I will emphasize the dominant, epistemological dimension of the early modern critique of romance rather than its moral dimension, which is nonetheless also important.

5. Karl Marx, *Grundrisse,* trans. Martin Nicolaus (Harmondsworth: Penguin, 1973), 105, 106; see above, Introduction, nn. 20–21.

6. Eric A. Havelock, "The Character and Content of the Code" (1973), in *The Literate Revolution in Greece and Its Cultural Consequences* (Princeton: Princeton University Press, 1982), 141; idem, *Preface to Plato* (Cambridge: Harvard University Press, 1963), 121; idem, "Transcription of the Code of a Non-Literate Culture" (1973), in *Literate Revolution,* 116; Jack Goody and Ian Watt, "The Consequences of Literacy," *Comparative Studies in Society and History,* 5 (1963), 310–11. On this feature of nonliterate lineages see also M. T. Clanchy, "Remembering the Past and the Good Old Law," *History,* 55 (1970), 168–70.

7. See Havelock, *Literate Revolution,* pp. 13–14 and chap. 8; Hugh Lloyd-Jones, "Remarks on the Homeric Question," in *History and Imagination: Essays in Honor of H. R. Trevor-Roper,* ed. Hugh Lloyd-Jones, Valerie Pearl, and Blair Worden (New York: Holmes and Meier, 1981), 15–29.

8. Eric A. Havelock, "The Preliteracy of the Greeks" (1977), in *Literate Revolution,* 187; see also idem, "The Oral Composition of Greek Drama" (1980), ibid., 261–62. For a recent and balanced argument against the dichotomous opposition of literate and nonliterate modes that also insists upon the importance of the distinction, see Jack Goody, *The Domestication of the Savage Mind* (Cambridge: Cambridge University Press, 1977).

9. See Havelock, *Preface to Plato,* 104–5; Charles R. Beye, *Ancient Greek Literature and Society* (Garden City, N.Y.: Anchor Books, 1975), 101, 188–89; Goody and Watt, "Consequences of Literacy," 322–24.

10. See Gerald A. Press, "History and the Development of the Idea of History in Antiquity," *History and Theory,* 16, no. 3 (1977), 285; Arnaldo Momigliano, "Greek Historiography," ibid., 17, no. 1 (1978), 9; Timothy P. Wiseman, *Clio's Cosmetics: Three Studies in Greco-Roman Literature* (Leicester: Leicester University Press, 1979), 48–49.

11. See Momigliano, "Greek Historiography," 5; and idem, "Historiography on Written Tradition and Historiography on Oral Tradition" (1961–62), in *Studies in Historiography* (New York: Harper Torchbooks, 1966), 214–16. On the tests for veracity and eyewitness testimony see Thucydides, *The Peloponnesian War,* trans. Richard Crawley (New York: Modern Library, 1951), I, 20–22 (pp. 13–14). The significance of a preference for eyewitness testimony is ambiguous, however, since it may also express the skeptical criteria of empirical science (see above, chap. 2).

12. See F. M. Cornford, *Thucydides Mythistoricus* (London: Edward Arnold, 1907); Kieran Egan, "Thucydides, Tragedian," in *The Writing of History: Literary Form and Historical Understanding,* ed. Robert H. Canary and Henry Kozicki (Madison: University of Wisconsin Press, 1978), 63–92.

13. See Michael McKeon, "The Origins of Aesthetic Value," *Telos,* no. 83 (Fall, 1983), 73–80.

14. See Wiseman, *Clio's Cosmetics,* chap. 9.

15. Plato, *Phaedrus,* 275a, trans. R. Hackforth, in *The Collected Dialogues of Plato,* ed. Edith Hamilton and Huntington Cairns, Bollingen Series LXXI (New York: Pantheon, 1961), 520; idem, Letter II, 314c, trans. L. A. Post, in ed. cit., 1567; idem, *Theaetetus,* 143a–c, trans. F. M. Cornford, in ed. cit., 847–48.

16. Havelock, *Preface to Plato,* 209. Cf. Sigmund Freud, *The Interpretation of Dreams,* trans. James Strachey (New York: Avon Books [1900] 1965), 216: "An intelligent and cultivated young woman, reserved and undemonstrative in her behaviour, reported as follows: *I dreamt that I arrived too late at the market and could get nothing either from the butcher or from the woman who sells vegetables.* An innocent dream, no doubt; but dreams are not as simple as that, so I asked to be told it in greater detail. She thereupon gave me the following account . . . The dream's connection with the previous day was [after retelling] quite straightforward."

17. Plato, *Phaedrus,* 246a, ed. cit., 493.

18. Havelock, *Preface to Plato,* 200.

19. See above, Introduction, nn. 12–13.

20. See Aristotle's *Poetics,* 1452a–b, 1454b–1455a, trans. Ingram Bywater, in *Introduction to Aristotle,* ed. Richard McKeon, 2nd ed. (Chicago: University of Chicago Press, 1973), 683–84, 690–92.

21. For a brief discussion of the Latin tale of Cupid and Psyche see above, chap. 4, n. 12.

22. See Sophie Trenkner, *The Greek Novella in the Classical Period* (Cambridge: Cambridge University Press, 1958), chap. 9; Ben E. Perry, *The Ancient Romances: A Literary-Historical Account of Their Origins* (Berkeley and Los Angeles: University of California Press, 1967), chap. 2; and Tomas Hägg, *The Novel in Antiquity* (Berkeley and Los Angeles: University of California Press, 1983), chap. 3. For discussions of terminology see Perry, *Ancient Romances,* 3; Hägg, *Novel in Antiquity,* 2–4; Gareth L. Schmeling, *Chariton* (New York: Twayne, 1974), 26–27, 37–42; and Arthur Heiserman, *The Novel before the Novel: Essays and Discussions about the Beginnings of Prose Fiction in the West* (Chicago: University of Chicago Press, 1977), 3–5, 41, 75.

23. Noting that no term exists for "the ancient novel," Hägg, *Novel in Antiquity,* 3, quotes Julian the Apostate's warning against "fictions [*plasmata*] . . . in the form of history, love subjects, and—in short—everything of that kind." On the relationship between ancient romance and historiography, see the discussion in Schmeling, *Chariton,* 51–56.

24. See Mircea Eliade, *The Myth of the Eternal Return, or, Cosmos and History,* trans. Willard R. Trask, Bollingen Series XLVI (Princeton: Princeton University Press, [1949] 1971), 104–7; Erich Auerbach, *Mimesis: The Representation of Reality*

in Western Literature, trans. Willard R. Trask (Garden City, N.Y.: Anchor Books, [1946] 1957), 11–14; Herbert N. Schneidau, *Sacred Discontent: The Bible and Western Tradition* (Baton Rouge: Louisiana State University Press, 1976), pp. 10, 25, 178, 202, 213 and passim.

25. Northrop Frye, *The Secular Scripture: A Study of the Structure of Romance* (Cambridge: Harvard University Press, 1976), 18.

26. See Mircea Eliade, *Myth and Reality,* trans. Willard R. Trask (New York: Harper Torchbooks, 1968), chap. 9; William Nelson, *Fact or Fiction: The Dilemma of the Renaissance Storyteller* (Cambridge: Harvard University Press, 1973), 19–23, cites examples.

27. Gershom Scholem, *The Messianic Idea in Judaism* (New York: Schocken, 1974), 2; Augustine, *On Christian Doctrine,* trans. D. W. Robertson, Jr. (Indianapolis: Bobbs-Merrill, 1958), I, iv, 9–10.

28. See S. G. Nichols, Jr., "The Interaction of Life and Literature in the Peregrinationes ad Loca Sancta and the Chansons de Geste," *Speculum,* 44 (Jan., 1969), 51–77.

29. On the centrality of relic veneration to early medieval—and especially popular—belief, and on its relation to contiguous magic and "archaic" regeneration, see R. W. Southern, *Western Society and the Church in the Middle Ages* (Harmondsworth: Penguin, 1970), 30; Patrick J. Geary, "The Ninth-Century Relic Trade: A Response to Popular Piety?," in *Religion and the People, 800–1700,* ed. James Obelkevich (Chapel Hill: University of North Carolina Press, 1979), 8–19. Cf. the discussion of "medieval realism" in Johan Huizinga, *The Waning of the Middle Ages* (Garden City, N.Y.: Anchor Books, [1924] 1954), chaps. 15 and 16.

30. See Giles Constable, "Opposition to Pilgrimage in the Middle Ages," *Studia Gratiana,* 19 (1976), 123–46.

31. See Jonathan Sumption, *Pilgrimage: An Image of Medieval Religion* (London: Faber and Faber, 1975), 257–60. See, generally, Christian K. Zacher, *Curiosity and Pilgrimage: The Literature of Discovery in Fourteenth-Century England* (Baltimore: Johns Hopkins University Press, 1976); Donald R. Howard, *Writers and Pilgrims: Medieval Pilgrimage Narratives and Their Posterity* (Berkeley and Los Angeles: University of California Press, 1980).

32. Huizinga, *Waning of the Middle Ages,* 152, 156. Cf. Auerbach, *Mimesis,* 42–43, 64–65; and idem, "Figura" (1944), in *Scenes from the Drama of European Literature* (New York: Meridian Books, 1959), 28–76.

33. See Charles H. Haskins, *The Renaissance of the Twelfth Century* (Cambridge: Harvard University Press, 1928), esp. chaps 10 and 11.

34. M. T. Clanchy, *From Memory to Written Record, England, 1066–1307* (Cambridge: Harvard University Press, 1979), 1; Brian Stock, *The Implications of Literacy: Written Language and Models of Interpretation in the Eleventh and Twelfth Centuries* (Princeton: Princeton University Press, 1982), chap. 3.

35. See Clanchy, "Remembering the Past," 173; R. Howard Bloch, *Medieval French Literature and Law* (Berkeley and Los Angeles: University of California Press, 1977), 18–21, 32–33, 48, 120, 130, 131, 137, 162. On the coexistence of the two modes see also Clanchy, "Remembering the Past," 175; idem, *From Memory,* chaps. 8, 9; Stock, *Implications of Literacy,* chap. 1; and below, nn. 81–84. On the controversy concerning the "individualism" of the twelfth century see also above, chap. 4, nn. 16–17, 21.

36. See Walter Ullmann, *The Individual and Society in the Middle Ages* (Baltimore: Johns Hopkins Press, 1966), 6, 45, 110–11; Colin Morris, *The Discovery of the Individual, 1050–1200* (New York: Harper and Row, 1972), 79–86 and passim. For the argument that the medieval notion of "the individual" is distinct from the modern notion of the "individual subject," see Timothy J. Reiss, *The Discourse of*

Modernism (Ithaca: Cornell University Press, 1982), chap. 2; see, generally, chap. 1, on the passage from premodern "patterning" to a modern discourse of "analytico-referentiality."

37. E.g., see Haskins, *Renaissance of the Twelfth Century*, 236.

38. See Erwin Panofsky, *Renaissance and Renascences in Western Art* (London: Paladin, 1970), 55–81, 108–10; Amos Funkenstein, "Periodization and Self-Understanding in the Middle Ages and Early Modern Times," *Medievalia et Humanistica*, n.s., 5 (1974), 8, 10–12, 14. On post-Conquest England and the Anglo-Saxon past, see R. W. Southern, "The Place of England in the Twelfth-Century Renaissance," *History*, 45 (Oct., 1960), 208; Antonia Gransden, "Realistic Observation in Twelfth-Century England," *Speculum*, 47, no. 1 (Jan., 1972), 33. See the observations of Donald R. Kelley, "Clio and the Lawyers: Forms of Historical Consciousness in Medieval Jurisprudence," *Medievalia et Humanistica*, n.s., 5 (1974), 25–49.

39. See R. W. Southern, "Aspects of the European Tradition of Historical Writing," *Trans. Roy. Hist. Soc.*, ser. 5, 20 (1970), 180–82; Jeanette M. A. Beer, *Narrative Conventions of Truth in the Middle Ages* (Geneva: Librairie Droz, 1981), 10, 29, 33, 48–49; Nancy F. Partner, *Serious Entertainments: The Writing of History in Twelfth-Century England* (Chicago: University of Chicago Press, 1977), 195.

40. See Auerbach, *Mimesis*, pp. 106–7; Nichols, "Life and Literature," 68; Peter Haidu, "Introduction," *Yale French Studies*, 51 (1974), 5–6; Dieter Mehl, *The Middle English Romances of the Thirteenth and Fourteenth Centuries* (London: Routledge and Kegan Paul, 1968), 20–22; Donald R. Kelly, "*Matière* and *genera dicendi* in Medieval Romance," *Yale French Studies*, 51 (1974), 147. On the origins of the term "romance" and its application to medieval narrative, see Edith Kern, "The Romance of Novel/Novella," in *The Disciplines of Criticism*, ed. Peter Demetz, Thomas Green, and Lowry Nelson, Jr. (New Haven: Yale University Press, 1968), 512–13.

41. See Heiserman, *Novel before the Novel*, 221n.2; Southern, "Aspects," 190–94; Denys Hay, *Annalists and Historians: Western Historiography from the Eighth to the Eighteenth Centuries* (London: Methuen, 1977), 59–60; Nelson, *Fact or Fiction*, 24; Kelly, "*Matière*," 147. On the importance of the eyewitness convention see Beer, *Narrative Conventions*, chaps. 2 and 3.

42. See *The 'Gest Hystoriale' of the Destruction of Troy*, ed. D. Donaldson and G. A. Panton (London: Early English Texts Society, 1869, 1874), "Prologue," 1–4; *Partonope of Blois, the Middle English Versions*, ed. A. T. Bödtker (London: Early English Texts Society, 1912). On the genre of the *Gest* cf. *The 'Gest Hystoriale*,' lxiii; Lee C. Ramsay, *Chivalric Romances: Popular Literature in Medieval England* (Bloomington: Indiana University Press, 1983), 72; and Mehl, *Middle English Romances*, 267n.56.

43. See Chrétien de Troyes, *Cligés*, ed. Alexandre Micha (Paris: Librairie Champion, 1965), "Prologue," ll. 8–13, 18–27; idem, *Erec et Enide*, ed. Mario Roques (Paris: Librairie Champion, 1963), ll. 19–26, 6674–82. See also the discussion of Marie-Louis Ollier, "The Author in the Text: The Prologues of Chrétien de Troyes," *Yale French Studies*, 51 (1974), 26–41.

44. *Boeve de Haumtone* (13th century; 12th-century text postulated) opens with the promise that it will be "sung" but is said at the end to have been "read" aloud; see M. Dominica Legge, *Anglo-Norman Literature and Its Background* (Oxford: Clarendon Press, 1963), 156–57. Components of the Lancelot Prose Cycle incorporate accounts of the royal commissioning, according to inquest formula, of their own transcription; see Bloch, *Medieval French Literature and Law*, 203–7.

45. E.g., see Peter Haidu, "Realism, Convention, Fictionality, and the Theory of Genres in *Le Bel Inconnu*," *L'Esprit créatur*, 12 (1972), 60; Robert W. Han-

ning, *The Individual in Twelfth-Century Romance* (New Haven: Yale University Press, 1977), 62, 155–56, 171–72, 193, and passim.

46. See Chaucer, *Troilus and Criseyde* (14th century), I, 393–99; V, 1044–50. On the "indeterminacy" of twelfth-century romance see Haidu, "Introduction," 5. It is only on the basis of these later associations that W. P. Ker can propound the paradox that twelfth-century romance contains far less of the "Pure Romance"— which is "the name for the sort of imagination that possesses the mystery and the spell of everything remote and unattainable"—than do the old northern epics and the *chansons de geste;* see his *Epic and Romance: Essays on Medieval Literature* (London: Macmillan, [1896] 1922), 325, 321.

47. See the discussions of Morton W. Bloomfield, "Authenticating Realism and the Realism of Chaucer," in *Essays and Explorations: Studies in Ideas, Language, and Literature* (Cambridge: Harvard University Press, 1970), 175–98; John Stevens, *Medieval Romance: Themes and Approaches* (London: Hutchinson University Library, 1973), 212–14; Kelly, "*Matière,*" 148–49; Ramsay, *Chivalric Romances,* 77–81; and Auerbach, *Mimesis,* 115–16.

48. See Morton W. Bloomfield, "Episodic Motivation and Marvels in Epic and Romance," in *Essays and Explorations,* 97–128. On the flowering of collections of *Miracles of the Virgin* around the beginning of the twelfth century see R. W. Southern, *The Making of the Middle Ages* (New Haven: Yale University Press, 1964), 246–50. On the Christianity and the parataxis of the *chanson de geste* see Auerbach, *Mimesis,* chap. 5.

49. E.g., cf. Eugene Vinaver, *The Rise of Romance* (Oxford: Oxford University Press, 1971); William W. Ryding, *Structure in Medieval Narrative* (The Hague: Mouton, 1971); and Robert M. Jordan, *Chaucer and the Shape of Creation: The Aesthetic Possibilities of Inorganic Structure* (Cambridge: Harvard University Press, 1967).

50. See Leo Spitzer, "Linguistic Perspectivism in the *Don Quijote,*" in *Linguistics and Literary History* (Princeton: Princeton University Press, 1948), 47–50; F. Borchardt, "Etymology in Tradition and in the Northern Renaissance," *Journal of the History of Ideas,* 29 (July–Sept., 1968), 415–29; Chrétien, *Erec et Enide,* ed. cit., ll. 1040–42.

51. See Spitzer, "Linguistic Perspectivism," 74n.2; Lionel J. Friedman, "Occulta Cordis," *Romance Philology,* 11 (1957–58), 109–19; Fredric Jameson, "Magical Narratives: Romance as Genre," *NLH,* 7, no. 1 (Autumn, 1975), 139, 161; Clanchy, "Remembering the Past," 174–75; idem, *From Memory,* 2, 184; Mikhail Bakhtin, *The Dialogic Imagination,* trans. Caryl Emerson and Michael Holquist, ed. Holquist (Austin: University of Texas Press, 1981), 31.

52. Panofsky, *Renaissance and Renascences,* 113.

53. John Aubrey, *Essay Towards the Description of the North Division of Wiltshire* (composed 1659), Introduction, in *Brief Lives and Other Selected Writings of John Aubrey,* ed. Anthony Powell (London: Cresset Press, 1949), 2; Sir Henry Spelman, *Of the Ancient Government of England* (1727), quoted in Arthur B. Ferguson, *Clio Unbound: Perception of the Social and Cultural Past in Renaissance England* (Durham: Duke University Press, 1980), 308; Margaret T. Hodgen, *Early Anthropology in the Sixteenth and Seventeenth Centuries* (Philadelphia: University of Pennsylvania Press, 1964), 194–201 and, generally, chaps. 6 and 8. On the use of the "negative formula" by Montaigne and Swift, see below, chap. 10, n. 24. On the Renaissance assimilation of exotics to ancient pagans, see Michael T. Ryan, "Assimilating New Worlds in the Sixteenth and Seventeenth Centuries," *Comparative Studies in Society and History,* 23 (1981), 519–38. On the Ten Lost Tribes see Cecil Roth, ed., *Magna Bibliotheca Anglo-Judaica* (London: Jewish Historical

Society of England, 1937), 279–80. On these matters generally, see also Steven Mullaney, "Strange Things, Gross Terms, Curious Customs: The Rehearsal of Cultures in the Late Renaissance," *Representations,* no. 3 (Summer, 1983), 40–67.

54. See William von Leyden, "Antiquity and Authority," *Journal of the History of Ideas,* 19 (1958), 478; Alan G. Chester, "The New Learning: A Semantic Note," *Studies in the Renaissance,* 2 (1955), 139–47.

55. By Sir Henry Spelman, *De Non Temerandis Ecclesiis* (1613), in *English Works,* ed. Edmund Gibson (1727), I, 26; see Philip Styles, "Politics and Historical Research in the Early Seventeenth Century," in *English Historical Scholarship in the Sixteenth and Seventeenth Centuries,* ed. Levi Fox (London: Oxford University Press, 1956), 64. On the Reformation and the apocalypse see Ernest L. Tuveson, *Millennium and Utopia: A Study in the Background of the Idea of Progress* (New York: Harper Torchbooks, [1949] 1964), 25–26.

56. The first (and eccentric) usage may be associated most closely with Karl Popper.

57. E.g., see Joseph Preston, "Was There an Historical Revolution?," *Journal of the History of Ideas,* 38, no. 2 (April–June, 1977), 362. For three general treatments of this subject as it forms part of the larger topic of the history of skeptical thought, see Herschel Baker, *The Wars of Truth: Studies in the Decay of Christian Humanism in the Earlier Seventeenth Century* (Cambridge: Harvard University Press, 1952); Richard H. Popkin, *The History of Scepticism from Erasmus to Descartes,* rev. ed. (New York: Humanities Press, 1964); Don Cameron Allen, *Doubt's Boundless Sea: Skepticism and Faith in the Renaissance* (Baltimore: Johns Hopkins Press, 1964). For the argument of a "historical revolution" in late sixteenth- and early seventeenth-century England, see F. Smith Fussner, *The Historical Revolution: English Historical Writing and Thought, 1580–1640* (New York: Columbia University Press, 1962), esp. chap. 12.

58. J. G. A. Pocock, *The Ancient Constitution and the Feudal Law: English Historical Thought in the Seventeenth Century* (New York: Norton, [1957] 1967), 36, 46. Pocock's is the central text on the historiographical influence of the English common law. See also Herbert Butterfield, *The Englishman and His History* (Cambridge: Cambridge University Press, 1944); and idem, *Magna Carta in the Historiography of the Sixteenth and Seventeenth Centuries,* The Stenton Lecture, 1968 (Reading: University of Reading, 1969); Ferguson, *Clio Unbound,* 115–25 and chap. 8. On French law see Donald R. Kelley, *Foundations of Modern Historical Scholarship: Language, Law, and History in the French Renaissance* (New York: Columbia University Press, 1970), chap. 7 and passim.

59. See Fussner, *Historical Revolution,* 30–32; Styles, "Politics and Historical Research," 63; Ferguson, *Clio Unbound,* 273–74.

60. See Pocock, *Ancient Constitution,* 92; see also 36–37, 235. On the two societies see Fussner, *Historical Revolution,* chap. 5; Ferguson, *Clio Unbound,* chap. 4.

61. See Pocock, *Ancient Constitution,* chaps. 2, 8; Christopher Brooks and Kevin Sharpe, "History, English Law, and the Renaissance," *Past and Present,* 72 (Aug., 1976), 133–42; Christopher Hill, *The World Turned Upside Down: Radical Ideas during the English Revolution* (New York: Viking, 1972), chap. 12; idem, "The Norman Yoke," in *Puritanism and Revolution: Studies in Interpretation of the English Revolution of the Seventeenth Century* (London: Panther, 1965), 68, 70–77.

62. See Hill, "Norman Yoke," 67–68. On the critique of "the British History" see Herschel Baker, *The Race of Time: Three Lectures on Renaissance Historiography* (Toronto: University of Toronto Press, 1967), 90–96; Ferguson, *Clio Unbound,* 104–15.

63. See Arnaldo Momigliano, "Ancient History and the Antiquarian" (1950), in *Studies in Historiography*, 8–15; Stuart Piggott, "Antiquarian Thought in the Sixteenth and Seventeenth Centuries," in *English Historical Scholarship*, ed. Fox, 94–95, 112–13; Barbara J. Shapiro, *Probability and Certainty in Seventeenth-Century England* (Princeton: Princeton University Press, 1983), chaps. 4 and 5 (see pp. 141–44 on the dispute concerning the relative accuracy of firsthand observation and time-attested documentation). On collections see Hodgen, *Early Anthropology*, chap. 4; Mullaney, "Strange Things." On the growth of collections of records and documents see Fussner, *Historical Revolution*, 32–37, 60–91. There was a large overlap among members of the scientific community and the practitioners of one or another sort of history: see Piggott, "Antiquarian Thought," 106–7; Shapiro, *Probability and Certainty*, chap. 4. The degree of institutional and public support given to English antiquarian research at this time "was unique in Europe": David C. Douglas, *English Scholars, 1660–1730*, 2nd ed. (London: Eyre and Spottiswoode, 1951), 270. But the antiquary was an ambiguous figure, and less commonly symbolized the modern investment in empirical science than an old-fashioned dedication to the dead past; for a typical portrait see Samuel Butler, "An Antiquary," in *Characters* (written 1667–69), ed. Charles W. Daves (Cleveland: Case Western University Press, 1970), 76–78.

64. See Elizabeth L. Eisenstein, *The Printing Press as an Agent of Change: Communications and Cultural Transformations in Early Modern Europe* (Cambridge: Cambridge University Press, 1979), chap. 2 and passim; Joseph Addison, *Dialogues upon the Usefulness of Ancient Medals* . . . (Glasgow, 1751), 20–21.

65. On the Renaissance see Eisenstein, *Printing Press*, 200 and chap. 3 passim; on the scientific revolution see ibid., pt. 3.

66. Andrew Marvell, *The Rehearsal Transpros'd* (1672), ed. D. I. B. Smith (Oxford: Clarendon Press, 1971), 4; William Haller, *The Elect Nation: The Meaning and Relevance of Foxe's Book of Martyrs* (New York: Harper and Row, 1963), 52; Eisenstein, *Printing Press*, 311, 330–35, 415–17, 421–26, and chap. 4 passim. On the Christian preoccupation see above, nn. 24–26.

67. Sensitive to the determinisms of other historians, Eisenstein nonetheless seems too often to be propounding her own species of technological determinism, in which conceptual change, and all other instances of "material" change, became relatively epiphenomenal elements in the early modern secularization process. By the same token, the invention of print becomes *sui generis:* for Eisenstein, typography had many consequences, but it itself tends to be seen as the consequence of nothing.

68. See Eisenstein, *Printing Press*, 168–70, 510.

69. See above, n. 8.

70. William Winstanley, *Histories and Observations Domestick and Foreign* . . . (1683), "Preface to the Reader," sig. A5ʳ⁻ᵛ, A6ʳ. On Don Quixote see below, chap. 7, n. 7. Cf. also Shakespeare's Mopsa in *The Winter's Tale* (1611), IV, iv, 261–62. For an argument that the genre of the novel is occasioned by the ambiguity introduced into reading and writing "by the technology of the printed book," see Walter L. Reed, *An Exemplary History of the Novel: The Quixotic versus the Picaresque* (Chicago: University of Chicago Press, 1981), 25 and chap. 2 passim.

71. See Eisenstein, *Printing Press*, 124, 131. On pulpit and press see the diverse observations of Marvell, *Rehearsal Transpros'd*, 5; Richard Baxter, *A Christian Directory* . . . (1673), 60; J[ohn] C[ollinges], *The Weavers Pocket-Book; or, Weaving Spiritualized* . . . (1675), "Epistle to the Reader," sig. A8ʳ; and Daniel Defoe, *The Storm* . . . (1704), sig. A2ʳ⁻ᵛ.

72. See above, nn. 23, 35, 63. Compare the reassurances of Autolycus in *The Winter's Tale* (1611), IV, iv, 284–85: "Five justices' hands at it, and witnesses more than my pack will hold." See W. K., *News from Hereford; or, A Wonderful and Terrible Earthquake* (1661), which is filled with circumstantial detail and ends with "a list of the names of the [nine] persons that witnesseth the truth of this . . . And divers others, too many to be here inserted"; and *The Disturbed Ghost . . .* (1674), whose truth many men have "justified . . . Before the Magistrates of *Marlborough* town," in *The Pack of Autolycus*, ed. Hyder E. Rollins (Cambridge: Harvard University Press, [1927] 1969), no. 14:86 and no. 29:175; see also no. 22:138 and no. 23:145.

73. The reversal is at least intimated in *Truth brought to Light; or, Wonderful strange and true news from Gloucester shire . . .* (1662): "Let not this seem incredible to any, / Because it is a thing affirmed by many, / This is no feigned story, though tis new, / But as tis very strange tis very true" (*Pack of Autolycus*, no. 16:100). Cf. *The Euing Collection of English Broadside Ballads in the Library of the University of Glasgow*, intro. John Holloway (Glasgow: University of Glasgow Publications, 1971), no. 56:78 and nos. 225–27:363–68. For a discussion of the epistemological stance of seventeenth-century ballads see Lennard J. Davis, *Factual Fictions: The Origins of the English Novel* (New York: Columbia University Press, 1983), 47–56.

74. *Pace* John J. Richetti, *Popular Fiction before Richardson: Narrative Patterns, 1700–1739* (Oxford: Clarendon Press, 1969), 168–69. This is true even of ballads that do not purport to tell "news," like Martin Parker's updating of Robin Hood; see the title and sts. 117–19 of *A True Tale of Robbin [Hood] . . .* (1632), no. 154 in *The English and Scottish Popular Ballads*, ed. Francis J. Child (New York: Dover, [1882–98] 1965), III, 227–33.

75. Richard Brathwaite, *The Whimzies; or, A New Cast of Characters . . .* (1631), ed. James O. Halliwell (London: Thomas Richards, 1859), 22, 20; Ben Jonson, *The Staple of Newes* (1631), end of second "intermeane," in *Works*, ed. C. H. Herford and Percy and Evelyn Simpson (Oxford: Clarendon Press, 1938), VI, 325 (with Jonson's drama compare Brathwaite's *The English Gentleman . . .* [1630], 139). Compare Samuel Butler's claim that "true or false is all one to" the newsmonger, "for Novelty being the Grace of both, a truth grows stale as soon as a Lye": *Characters*, 177. Contemporaries knew the etymological relationship of "news" and "novel." John Florio translated the Italian "*novella*" both as "*a tale, a nouell*" and as "*a noveltie, a discourse, a newes, a message*"; see his *A World of Wordes* (1598), 241, quoted in Dale B. Randall, *The Golden Tapestry: A Critical Survey of Non-chivalric Spanish Fiction in English Translation (1543–1657)* (Durham: Duke University Press, 1963), 126.

76. *A Presse full of Pamphlets . . .* (1642), sig. A2ᵛ, A3ᵛ–A4ʳ; *Britanicus Vapulans; or, The Whipping of poore British Mercury, set out in a Letter directed to him from Mercurius Urbanus, younger Brother to Aulicus* (1643), 2 (the reference is no doubt to Lucan's *Pharsalia*, a "historical" epic poem on the Roman Civil Wars; the first battle of Newbury was fought in Sept., 1643); J[ohn] C[leveland], *A Character of a Diurnal-Maker* (1654), 3, 5, 11–12; idem, *The Character of a London-Diurnall* (1653), 90 (a Solyfidian is one who believes in justification by faith alone; see above, chap. 5, n. 26). The association of naive empiricism with Calvinist Protestantism will be an important one in the argument of this study. For other attacks on news reporting see Ernest Bernbaum, *The Mary Carleton Narratives, 1663–1673: A Missing Chapter in the History of the English Novel* (Cambridge: Harvard University Press, 1914), 79–83; Joseph Frank, *The Beginnings of the English Newspaper, 1620–60* (Cambridge: Harvard University Press, 1961), 275–77.

77. See above, n. 56.

78. John Rushworth, *Historical Collections* . . . , I (1659), "The Preface," sig. b2ᵛ–b3ʳ, b3ᵛ–b4ʳ, c1ʳ.

79. John Nalson, *An Impartial Collection of the Great Affairs of State* . . . , I (1682), "The Introduction," ii.

80. *Tatler*, no. 178, May 27–30, 1710. On the "Romantick" circumstantiality of "*Historians*" see also Steele's *Spectator*, no. 136, Aug. 6, 1711. For Brathwaite's irritation see also *Whimzies*, 20–21, 23–24.

81. But the growing anachronism of the manuscript newsletter is also heightened by the appearance, late in the century, of printed "newsletters" that use script type fonts; see Stanley Morison, *Ichabod Dawks and his News-Letter, with an Account of the Dawks Family of Booksellers and Stationers, 1635–1731* (Cambridge: Cambridge University Press, 1931). On both manuscript and oral circulation in the early part of the century, see F. J. Levy, "How Information Spread among the Gentry, 1550–1640," *Journal of British Studies*, 21, no. 2 (Spring, 1982), 20–25. In 1665 Henry Newcome, a Presbyterian minister of Manchester, took his turn in the oral recitation of news reports to a group of auditors. He "recᵈ & read a letter, mistakeing yᶜ *Duke* for yᶜ *Du[t]ch;* wᶜʰ vexed me ill, yᵗ I shˡᵈ cause ill newes to be spread yᵗ is not so" (Chetham's Library [Manchester] MS. Mun. A. 6.95[1], 191). In a literate culture, errors even in oral transmission are likely to retain the status of error, rather than silently to alter the tradition, because of the availability of fixed written records against which they may be invalidated (thus Newcome's vexation with himself). From examples like this it is not hard to see why people were tempted to identify the very criterion of truth with the fact of typographical documentation. The resonance of Steele's remarks about newspaper styles in *Tatler* no. 178 is deepened by our knowledge that the setting is a coffeehouse, where newspapers are (as is the custom) being read aloud, and that the negative example of journalistic style, which Steele takes to be typical, is one of the counterfeit script "letters" of Ichabod Dawks. "His Style is a Dialect between the Familiarity of Talking and Writing," Steele says, "and his Letter such as you cannot distinguish whether Print or Manuscript." It is a moment, uncommonly sharp in its articulation, in which oral, scribal, and typographical modes achieve a volatile coexistence.

82. See Bernbaum, *Mary Carleton Narratives;* Davis, *Factual Fictions.* For a fuller refutation of Davis's argument, see Michael McKeon, "The Origins of the English Novel," *Modern Philology,* 82, no. 1 (Aug., 1984), 76–86.

83. See Victor E. Neuburg, *Popular Education in Eighteenth-Century England* (London: Woburn Press, 1971), 106–11, 122; Margaret Spufford, *Small Books and Pleasant Histories: Popular Fiction and Its Readership in Seventeenth-Century England* (Athens: University of Georgia Press, 1982), 9–10, 13, 32, 68.

84. See Eisenstein, *Printing Press,* 60–63 and n. 61. For what is still a good survey of the subject's general outlines and pitfalls, see Ian Watt, *The Rise of the Novel: Studies in Defoe, Richardson, and Fielding* (Berkeley and Los Angeles: University of California Press, 1957), chap. 2.

85. See Ian Watt, "Publishers and Sinners: The Augustan View," *Studies in Bibliography,* 12 (1959), 4–5, 7–8; idem, *Rise of the Novel,* 53–59; Terry Belanger, "Publishers and Writers in Eighteenth-Century England," in *Books and Their Readers in Eighteenth-Century England,* ed. Isabel Rivers (New York: St. Martin's, 1982), 5–25. On print legislation see Frederick S. Siebert, *Freedom of the Press in England, 1476–1776: The Rise and Decline of Government Control* (Urbana: University of Illinois Press, 1965). On the development of the idea of literary property and the first copyright act of 1710, see Harry Ransom, *The First Copyright Statute:*

An Essay on An Act for the Encouragement of Learning, 1710 (Austin: University of Texas Press, 1956).

86. Marx, *Grundrisse,* ed. cit., 91; see above, Introduction, nn. 20–21. On the importance of elementary education see Neuburg, *Popular Education,* chap. 3; Spufford, *Small Books,* 19, 26–27; and idem, "First Steps in Literacy: The Reading and Writing Experiences of the Humblest Seventeenth-Century Spiritual Auto-biographers," *Social History,* 4, no. 3 (Oct., 1979), 407–35. See, in general, Law-rence Stone, "The Educational Revolution in England, 1540–1640," *Past and Present,* no. 28 (1964), 41–80; and idem, "Literacy and Education in England, 1640–1900," ibid., no. 42 (1969), 69–139.

87. See David Cressy, *Literacy and the Social Order: Reading and Writing in Tudor and Stuart England* (Cambridge: Cambridge University Press, 1980), 186. For example, around 1700, 25 percent of women in country districts could write their own names; by 1760 this figure had risen to 33 percent. Around 1650, 10 percent of all women in England could sign; one hundred years later the figure was 36 percent. The rate of increase is more dramatic for London women: in the 1680s, 36 percent could sign; in the 1690s, 48 percent; in the 1720s, 56 percent. (Ibid., 59, 145–47.) According to Stone ("Literacy and Education"), the overall rate of increase in literacy slowed considerably in the century after 1670. Literacy could be taken for granted among English gentlemen over this period.

88. According to R. S. Schofield, "A measure based on the ability to sign probably overestimates the number able to write, underestimates the number able to read at an elementary level, and gives a fair indication of the number able to read fluently"; see his "The Measurement of Literacy in Pre-Industrial England," in *Literacy in Traditional Societies,* ed. Jack Goody (Cambridge: Cambridge Uni-versity Press, 1968), 324. Reading predominated over writing skills because read-ing was taught before writing, and could be acquired before children were old enough to have their education interrupted for the purpose of profitable labor. See Spufford, *Small Books,* 26–27; idem, "First Steps in Literacy," 414; Cressy, *Literacy and the Social Order,* 55.

89. On increased leisure see Watt, *Rise of the Novel,* 43–47, 189–90; on women and reading see Alban K. Forcione, *Cervantes, Aristotle, and the Persiles* (Princeton: Princeton University Press, 1970), 15–16.

90. For an optimistic assessment of a wide range of evidence regarding popu-lar literacy in this period, see Neuburg, *Popular Education,* chap. 4. For a similar overview of the eighteenth century which includes an account of the newspaper influence, see Roy M. Wiles, "Middle-Class Literacy in Eighteenth-Century England: Fresh Evidence," in *Studies in the Eighteenth Century,* ed. R. F. Bris-senden (Canberra: Australian National University Press, 1968), 49–65. On chap-books see Spufford, *Small Books,* chaps. 4 and 5; Neuburg, *Popular Education,* chap. 5 (see also app. II for an annotated list of chapbook booksellers and their publications in London and the provinces). On serials see Roy M. Wiles, *Serial Publication in England before 1750* (Cambridge: Cambridge University Press, 1957); and idem, "The Relish for Reading in Provincial England Two Centuries Ago," in *The Widening Circle: Essays in the Circulation of Literature in Eighteenth-Century Europe,* ed. Paul J. Korshin (Philadelphia: University of Pennsylvania Press, 1976), 85–115. For a short-title list of serial publications before 1750 see Wiles, *Serial Publication,* app. B.

91. On subscription lists see Pat Rogers, *Robinson Crusoe* (London: Allen and Unwin, 1979), 102–3; W. A. Speck, "Politicians, Peers, and Publication by Sub-scription, 1700–50," in *Books and Their Readers,* ed. Rivers, 64–66. Subscription lists are no more dependable as a guide to total or typical readership than is

signing to writing or reading skills, but according to Speck, "at least subscription lists document a precise readership" (65). On chapbook redactions see Spufford, *Small Books*, 14, 46–47; Bakhtin, *Dialogic Imagination*, 379; Maximillian E. Novak, "Fiction and Society in the Early Eighteenth Century," in *England in the Restoration and Early Eighteenth Century: Essays on Culture and Society*, ed. H. T. Swedenberg, Jr. (Berkeley and Los Angeles: University of California Press, 1972), 61–62 (on the well-known transformation of *Guy of Warwick* see above, chap. 4, n. 28). Contrast Pat Rogers, "Classics and Chapbooks," in *Books and Their Readers*, ed. Rivers, 28.

92. On which see above, chap. 4.

93. Lionardo Salviati, *Risposta all' Apologia di Torquato Tasso* (1585), 15, translated by and quoted in Bernard Weinberg, *A History of Literary Criticism in the Italian Renaissance* (Chicago: University of Chicago Press, 1961), 1017. See Aristotle, *Poetics*, 1451^{a-b}, 1447^b, ed. cit., 681–82, 671. The printed text of the *Poetics* became available in Latin and Greek in 1498 and 1508, respectively; see, generally, Weinberg, *History of Literary Criticism*, chap. 9. For a somewhat fuller attempt than the following to situate the rediscovery of the *Poetics* within early modern discourse see Michael McKeon, "Politics of Discourses and the Rise of the Aesthetic in Seventeenth-Century England," in *Politics of Discourse: The Literature and History of Seventeenth-Century England*, ed. Kevin Sharpe and Steven Zwicker (Berkeley and Los Angeles: University of California Press, 1987), 35–51.

94. See above, chap. 3, sec. 6.

95. Meric Casaubon, *Of Credulity and Incredulity, In things Natural, Civil, and Divine* . . . (1668), 155; Père le Moyne, *De l'histoire* (Paris, 1670), 85, translated by and quoted in Erica Harth, *Ideology and Culture in Seventeenth-Century France* (Ithaca: Cornell University Press, 1983), 145; Margaret Cavendish, Duchess of Newcastle, *The Life of . . . William Cavendishe, Duke, Marquess, and Earl of Newcastle* . . . (1667), "The Preface," sig. b2^v, c2^r.

96. Pierre Daniel Huet, Bishop of Avranches, *The History of Romances* . . . (1670), trans. Stephen Lewis (1715), in *Novel and Romance, 1700–1800: A Documentary Record*, ed. Ioan Williams (New York: Barnes and Noble, 1970), 46. In the following discussion I have relied, as far as possible, on quotations from foreign works in their contemporary English translations.

97. See, in general, Frederick C. Green, "The Critic of the Seventeenth Century and His Attitude towards the French Novel," *Modern Philology*, 24 (1926–27), 285–95; Mark Bannister, *Privileged Mortals: The French Heroic Novel, 1630–1660* (Oxford: Oxford University Press, 1983), chap. 6. Cf. [Madeleine de Scudéry], *Ibrahim; or, The Illustrious Bassa. An Excellent new Romance* . . . (1641), trans. Henry Cogan (1652), "The Preface," sig. A3^v–A4^r; idem, *Artamenes; or, The Grand Cyrus. An Excellent New Romance* (1649), trans. F. G. (1653), "To the Reader," sig. A4^r.

98. Cf. Scudéry, *Ibrahim*, II, ii, 29, iv, 73–74, quoted in Helga Drougge, *The Significance of Congreve's Incognita* (Stockholm: Almqvist and Wiskell, 1976), 67. On the combination of *vraisemblance* and the allusion to "real" personages, see the discussion of Honoré d'Urfé's *L'Astrée* (1607–27) in Harth, *Ideology and Culture*, chap. 2. For examples of the coexistence of *vraisemblance* and the claim to historicity, see Scudéry, *Ibrahim*, sig. A4^r; idem, *Artamenes*, I, ii, 60.

99. E.g., see Marie, comtesse de La Fayette, *The Princess of Monpensier* . . . (1666), "The Translator to the Reader," sig. A3^{r-v}, and "The French Bookseller to the Reader," sig. A4^r–A5^r (first published anonymously); [Gatien de Courtilz, sieur de Sandras], *The Memoirs of the count de Rochefort* . . . (1696), "The French Publishers Preface," sig. A2^v; idem, *The French Spy; or, The Memoirs of John*

Baptist De La Fontaine . . . (1700), "The Preface." sig. A2^r, A3^{r-v}. On the *nouvelles* and the relationship between generic categorization and absolutist politics see especially Harth, *Ideology and Culture,* chaps. 4 and 5. On the French claim to historicity, even the research by English-speaking scholars has been extensive: see the pioneering article by Arthur J. Tieje, "A Peculiar Phase of the Theory of Realism in Pre-Richardsonian Fiction," *PMLA,* 28, n.s., 21 (1913), 213–52; Vivienne Mylne, *The Eighteenth-Century French Novel: Techniques of Illusion* (Manchester: Manchester University Press, 1965); Philip Stewart, *Imitation and Illusion in the French Memoir-Novel, 1700–1750: The Art of Make-Believe,* Yale Romantic Studies, 2nd ser., 20 (New Haven: Yale University Press, 1969); and English Showalter, Jr., *The Evolution of the French Novel, 1641–1782* (Princeton: Princeton University Press, 1972), 169–76.

100. [Marie, comtesse d'Aulnoy], *The Ingenious and Diverting Letters of the Lady —— Travels into Spain* . . . (1691), "To the Reader," sig. A4^{r-v}. (In fact, d'Aulnoy's Spanish travels were plagiarized; see Percy G. Adams, *Travelers and Travel Liars, 1660–1800* [Berkeley and Los Angeles: University of California Press, 1962], 97–99.) Cf. [Gatien de Courtilz, sieur de Sandras?], *The Amorous Conquests Of the Great Alcander* . . . (1685), "The Preface," sig. A2^r; *The Cabinet Open'd, or the Secret History of the Amours of Madam de Maintenon, With the French King* . . . (1690), "The Author's Preface to the Reader," sig. A4^v–A5^r.

101. *The Dictionary Historical and Critical of Mr Peter Bayle* (1697), 2nd ed. (1734–38), IV, "Nidhard," n. C, 365–66. Cf. [Mary Davys], *The Accomplished Rake; or, Modern Fine Gentleman* . . . (1727), "The Preface" (the French, "where they pretend to write true history, give themselves the utmost liberty of feigning"), quoted in William H. McBurney, ed., *Four before Richardson: Selected English Novels, 1720–1727* (Lincoln: University of Nebraska Press, 1964), 235.

102. Garci Rodríguez de Montalvo, *Amadis of Gaul,* bks. I and II, trans. Edward B. Place and Herbert C. Behn (Lexington: University Press of Kentucky, 1974), "Prológo," 19, 20. On antiromance sentiment see John J. O'Connor, *Amadis de Gaule and Its Influence on Elizabethan Literature* (New Brunswick, N.J.: Rutgers University Press, 1970), 216.

103. E.g., see Scudéry, *Artamenes,* preface. See the discussions of Ariosto in Robert M. Durling, *The Figure of the Poet in Renaissance Epic* (Cambridge: Harvard University Press, 1965), 112–32; and Patricia A. Parker, *Inescapable Romance: Studies in the Poetics of a Mode* (Princeton: Princeton University Press, 1979), 25–53. Of course the parody is not confined to works that we would call romances; e.g., see François Rabelais, *The First Book of . . . Gargantua and his Sonne Pantagruel* . . . (1535), trans. Thomas Urquhart (1653), I, i, which compounds the parody by making the discovered ancient manuscript a copy of Gargantua's ancient genealogy.

104. See Eisenstein, *Printing Press,* 291, 572.

105. Butler, "An Antiquary," in *Characters,* 77. On the history of the topos see Tieje, "Peculiar Phase," 220–27; Nelson, *Fact or Fiction,* 23.

106. [Simon Tyssot de Patot], *The Travels and Adventures of James Massey* (1710), trans. Stephen Whatley (1733), 287; [Giovanni Paolo Marana], *The First Volume of Letters Writ by a Turkish Spy* . . . [1684–86,] *Written Originally in Arabick, first Translated into Italian, afterwards into French, and now into English, The Sixth Edition* (1694), "To the Reader," sig. A3^{r-v}, A4^r, A5^v, A6^v–A7^v.

107. For a separate discussion of *Don Quixote* see above, chap. 7.

108. [Charles Sorel], *The Extravagant Shepherd; or, The History Of the Shepherd Lysis. An Anti-Romance* . . . (1627–28, 1633–34), trans. John Davies (1654), "The Author to the Reader," sig. e2^r; XIII, 68; XIV, 96. Compare the account of

how the novel both opposes and "encloses" or "absorbs" romance in José Ortega y Gasset, *Meditations on Quixote,* trans. Evelyn Rugg and Diego Marín (New York: Norton, 1961), 137, 139.

109. Compare Sorel's *De la Connoissance des Bons Livres* (Paris, 1671), 115–17, where he points out the bad faith of romancers who claim *vraisemblance* for having eschewed the supernatural effects of chivalric romance while depending heavily on the manipulations of Fortune (quoted in Drougge, *Significance of Congreve's Incognita,* 53).

110. E.g., see Paul Scarron, *The Comical Romance,* trans. Tom Brown et al. (1700), intro. Benjamin Boyce (New York: Benjamin Blom, 1968), I, viii, 28, ix, 35–36; II, vii, 212.

111. [Antoine Furetière], *Scarron's City Romance . . .* (actually an anonymous translation of Furetière's *Roman Bourgeois*) (1671), sig. A4ʳ, pp. 19, 40–41, 46, 159, 160.

112. For the misconception see especially Henry K. Miller, "Augustan Prose Fiction and the Romance Tradition," in *Studies in the Eighteenth Century, III,* ed. R. F. Brissenden and J. C. Eade (Canberra: Australian National University Press, 1976), 244n.7, 246–47 (quotation, 246); and idem, *Henry Fielding's Tom Jones and the Romance Tradition,* English Literary Studies no. 6 (Victoria, B.C.: University of Victoria, 1976), 11. Miller is generalizing from a misreading of Fielding in particular, whom he would reconcile with an "older romance tradition" (ibid.). (On Fielding see above, chap. 12, nn. 35–37.) But see also McBurney, *Four before Richardson,* xii; Kern, "Romance of Novel/Novella," 530; Davis, *Factual Fictions,* 104; Dieter Schulz, " 'Novel,' 'Romance,' and Popular Fiction in the First Half of the Eighteenth Century," *Studies in Philology,* 70, no. 1 (1973), 91; and Jerry C. Beasley, *Novels of the 1740s* (Athens: University of Georgia Press, 1982), 216–17 n. 15. The latter two scholars would expand the category not backward but forward, to include certain subgenres that flourished after the French heroic romance. On the humanists' assault see Robert P. Adams, "Bold Bawdry and Open Manslaughter: The English New Humanist Attack on Medieval Romance," *Huntington Library Quarterly,* 23, no. 1 (1959–60), 33–48 (for the epistemological critique see 44–45).

113. *John Barclay His Argenis, Translated ovt of Latine into English . . . With a Clauis annexed to it for the satisfaction of the Reader, and helping him to vnderstand, what persons were by the Author intended, vnder the fained Names imposed by him vpon them . . . ,* trans. Sir Robert Le Grys (1628), 485, 131–32. On *roman-à-clef* censorship in Barclay, the French romance, and the English "royal romance," see the discussion of Annabel M. Patterson, *Censorship and Interpretation: The Conditions of Writing and Reading in Early Modern England* (Madison: University of Wisconsin Press, 1984), 180–202. The standard work on English imitations of the French romance remains Thomas P. Haviland, *The Roman de Longue Haleine on English Soil* (Philadelphia: University of Pennsylvania Press, 1931).

114. [Roger Boyle, Lord Broghill], *Parthenissa, A Romance . . . ,* pt. 1 (1655), "The Preface," sig. A2ᵛ, B1ᵛ; [Sir George Mackenzie], *Aretina; or, The Serious Romance . . . ,* pt. 1 (Edinburgh, 1660), "An Apologie for ROMANCES," 6–7: in *Prefaces to Four Seventeenth-Century Romances,* ed. Charles Davies, Augustan Reprint Society, no. 42 (1953). By the time he arrives at part 6 of *Parthenissa,* Boyle is claiming to give *"the Truth of the History"* as opposed to "romance"; see Haviland, *The Roman de Longue Haleine,* 118. For a continuation of the political-allegorical mode see [Richard Brathwaite], *Panthalia; or, The Royal Romance . . .* (1659).

115. The most successful are Richard Bentley's *Modern Novels,* 12 vols. (1692), and Samuel Croxall's *A Select Collection of Novels . . . ,* 6 vols. (1720–22).

Twenty-nine of Croxall's thirty-three "novels" are translations; thirty-seven of Bentley's forty-eight have French originals; see McBurney, *Four before Richardson*, xiii. For useful discussions of some of this material, see Maximillian E. Novak, "Fiction and Society," and "Some Notes toward a History of Fictional Forms: From Aphra Behn to Daniel Defoe," *Novel*, 6 (1973), 120–33.

116. E.g., see *The Obliging Mistress; or, The Fashionable Gallant. A Novel* (1678), Bentley vol. 7, "Epistle Dedicatory," sig. A4^v; *Ottoman Gallantries; or, The Life of the Bassa of Buda*, trans. B. Berenclow (1687), Bentley vol. 6, pp. 1–2; S. Bremond, *Gallant Memoirs; or, The Adventures of a Person of Quality*, trans. P. Belou (1681), Bentley vol. 9, pp. 1–2; *Ethelinda. An English Novel, Done from the Italian of Flaminiani* (1721), Croxall vol. 5, "Advertisement," 93. Cf. *Vertue Rewarded; or, The Irish Princess. A new Novel* (1693), "The Preface to the Ill-Natur'd Reader," sig. A4^{r-v}.

117. *The Annals of Love, Containing Select Histories of the Amours of divers Princes Courts, Pleasantly Related* (1672), "The Preface," sig. A2^{r-v}; for the table see sig. A3^v–A4^v. For another appeal to probability see *Three Ingenious Spanish Novels . . .* (1709), "To the Reader," sig. A3^r. The bookseller Nathaniel Crouch printed several collections of short exemplary narratives which are abridged from more voluminous histories and accompanied by citations "that they may thereby obtain the more Credit with the Reader": R. B., *Wonderful Prodigies of Judgment and Mercy . . .* (1685), "To the Reader," sig. A2^v. See also R. B., *Admirable Curiosities Rarities, & Wonders in England, Scotland and Ireland . . .* (1682); idem, *The Extraordinary Adventures and Discoveries Of Several Famous Men . . .* (1683); idem, *Unparallel'd Varieties; or, The Matchless Actions and Passions of Mankind . . .*, "3rd ed." (1699). Their titles suggest that these volumes should be seen as a narrative equivalent of the antiquarian "collection" of rare and wonderful curiosities (see above, n. 63). It may also be useful to understand these "historical" collections as the hybrid counterpart of the "romance" collections under discussion, the mirror image not only of an epochal separation of "history" from "romance" but also of its incompleteness.

118. E.g., see Rousseau de la Valette, *Casimer, King of Poland . . .* (1681), Bentley vol. 8, sig. A3^r; *Cynthia: with the Tragical Account of the Unfortunate Loves of Almerin and Desdemona . . .*, "5th ed." (1709), "To the Reader," sig. A4^v.

119. E.g., see Eliza Haywood, *The Fair Hebrew; or, A True, but Secret History of Two Jewish Ladies, who lately resided in London* (1729), "Preface," in *Criticism of Henry Fielding*, ed. I. Williams, 85. The lucidity of Haywood's claim may owe to the fact that she is really transferring the notion of the "secret history" to domestic contexts, thereby avoiding the complications created by the publicness of state affairs and the specter of censorship. Compare Aphra Behn, who heightens the earwitness claim to historicity not by calling her narratives secret histories but by remarking that the real names of the characters have been concealed by pseudonyms: *The Fair Jilt; or, The History of Prince Tarquin, and Miranda* (1696), in *Histories and Novels*, I, 4; idem, *The Unfortunate Happy Lady. A True History* (1698), in *Histories, Novels, and Translations, Written by the Most Ingenious Mrs. Behn . . .*, II (1700), 21.

120. [Mary Delarivière Manley], *The Secret History of Queen Zarah, and the Zarazians; being a Looking-glass for ——— ——— In the Kingdom of Albigion. Faithfully Translated from the Italian Copy now lodg'd in the Vatican at Rome, and never before Printed in any Language* (Albigion, 1705), I, "To the Reader," sig. A2^{r-v} A4^{r-v}; II, "The Preface," sig. A2^r–A4^r. Compare Manley's *Secret Memoirs and Manners Of several Persons of Quality, of Both Sexes. From the New Atalantis . . .*, 2nd ed. (1709), "Dedication," ii–iii, which purports to be translated from the

Italian by way of the French. Manley's practice of calling her works translations is usually associated with her fear of prosecution for libel. See her autobiographical *Adventures of Rivella . . .* (1714), intro. Malcolm J. Bosse (New York: Garland, 1972), 113; Introduction, 6. (This work, as well, is said to be a translation; see "The Translator's Preface," i–iii.) It is a motive that presumably was shared by many secret historians on both sides of the Channel and that only deepens the epistemological concerns that are my central subject. With Manley's procedure in the *Secret History* compare George Lyttleton, *The Court Secret: A Melancholy Truth: Now first translated from the Original Arabic* (1741), 1, 2, 49–50. On the flowering of these allusive "secret histories," which he calls "didactic romances," in the 1730s and 1740s, see Jerry Beasley, *Novels of the 1740s,* chaps. 2 and 3; and idem, "Romance and the 'New' Novels of Richardson, Fielding, and Smollett," *Studies in English Literature,* 16, no. 3 (1976), 437–50.

121. *Tatler,* no. 84, Oct. 22, 1709. Cf. Daniel Defoe, *A Collection of Miscellany Letters out of Mist's Weekly Journal* (1722–27), IV, 124–25, quoted in Maximillian E. Novak, "Defoe's Theory of Fiction," *Studies in Philology,* 61, no. 4 (Oct., 1964), 657.

122. Jonathan Swift, *A Tale of a Tub, To which is added The Battle of the Books and the Mechanical Operation of the Spirit,* ed. A. C. Guthkelch and D. Nichol Smith, 2nd ed. (Oxford: Clarendon Press, 1958), 66, 133. For the fairy-tale frame and the burlesque of chivalric conventions, see the beginning of sec. II, pp. 73–74. The *Tale* was composed during the 1690s.

123. William Congreve, *Incognita; or, Love and Duty Reconcil'd. A Novel,* in *Shorter Novels: Seventeenth Century,* ed. Philip Henderson (London: J. M. Dent, 1962), 241, 270, 264, 277.

124. See ibid., 271, 251, 264, 274, 289, 274–275, 285–86, 287, 260, 261. Scarron's interpolated "History of the Invisible Mistress" provides the closest single model for the plot and method of *Incognita;* see *Comical Romance,* ed. cit., I, ix, 32–49, especially 35–36. Another major influence on Congreve's self-conscious narration is, of course, Restoration comedy.

125. Congreve, *Incognita,* 291–92. For the bookseller's ploy see Charles Wilson, *Memoirs of the Life, Writings, and Amours of William Congreve Esq.* (1730), 125, quoted in Maximillian E. Novak, "Congreve's 'Incognita' and the Art of the Novella," *Criticism,* 11, no. 4 (Fall, 1969), 329–30, and in Drougge, *Significance of Congreve's Incognita,* 91. For the recognition that Congreve's antiromance method entails a double movement—that it also parodies the antiromance "realism" of writers like Aphra Behn—see Novak, "Congreve's *Incognita,*" 342; Drougge, *Significance of Congreve's Incognita,* 34–35. My reading of *Incognita* as an expression of "extreme skepticism" is not compatible with the view that it is an affirmation of the workings of Providence; see Aubrey L. Williams, *An Approach to Congreve* (New Haven: Yale University Press, 1979), chap. 5. On the providential argument see above, chap. 3, sec. 7.

CHAPTER TWO: THE EVIDENCE OF THE SENSES: SECULARIZATION
AND EPISTEMOLOGICAL CRISIS

1. Francis Bacon, *The New Organon* (1620), *The Great Instauration* (1620), and *A Description of the Intellectual Globe* (n.d.), in *The Works of Francis Bacon,* ed. James Spedding, Robert L. Ellis, and Douglas D. Heath (London: Longmans, 1870), IV, 26, 40, 51, 54, 58, 110; V, 511.

2. Bacon, *New Organon,* ed. cit., IV, 65–66.

3. Ibid., 43, 79, 81, 98, 104, 113, 115.

4. Ibid., 42; Francis Bacon, *The Wisdom of the Ancients* (1609), in *Works of Francis Bacon,* ed. cit., VI, 695, 696, 729.

5. Bacon, *New Organon,* ed. cit., IV, 113; idem, *Of the Dignity and Advancement of Learning* (1623), in *Works,* ed. cit., IV, 292, 301, 315–16. On Aristotle's distinction, see above, chap. 1, n. 93. Bacon was not alone in effecting this reversal; see Herschel Baker, *The Race of Time: Three Lectures on Renaissance Historiography* (Toronto: University of Toronto Press, 1967), 84–89.

6. For related accounts of the two movements, and of the emerging standard of probability, in early modern scientific epistemology, see Margaret J. Osler, "Certainty, Scepticism, and Scientific Optimism: The Roots of Eighteenth-Century Attitudes toward Scientific Knowledge," in *Probability, Time, and Space in Eighteenth-Century Literature,* ed. Paula R. Backscheider (New York: AMS Press, 1979), 3–28; M. M. Slaughter, *Universal Languages and Scientific Taxonomy in the Seventeenth Century* (Cambridge: Cambridge University Press, 1982); Barbara J. Shapiro, *Probability and Certainty in Seventeenth-Century England* (Princeton: Princeton University Press, 1983). On Renaissance historicism see above, chap. 1, n. 56.

7. Thomas Sprat, *The History of the Royal-Society of London, For the Improving of Natural Knowledge* (1667), 90–91, 340; Joseph Glanvill, *Plus Ultra; or, The Progress and Advancement of Knowledge Since the Days of Aristotle . . .* (1668), 109; idem, *The Vanity of Dogmatizing . . .* (1661), 173.

8. Glanvill, *Vanity,* 114–15; idem, *Plus Ultra,* 89; Thomas Molyneux, *Philosophical Transactions of the Royal Society,* 20 (1700–1701), 507–8, quoted in *Memoirs of the Extraordinary Life, Works, and Discoveries of Martinus Scriblerus,* ed. Charles Kirby-Miller (New York: Russell and Russell, 1966), 265; John Spencer, *A Discourse concerning Prodigies . . .* (Cambridge, 2nd ed., 1665), 398.

9. Glanvill, *Vanity,* 182, 181, 239–40; idem, *Scepsis Scientifica . . .* (1665), "An Address to the Royal Society," sig. C1^v, b4^r (the *Scepsis* is a rewriting of the *Vanity*); idem, *Plus Ultra,* 55; Sprat, *History of the Royal-Society,* 392, 397.

10. Sprat, *History of the Royal-Society,* 214–15.

11. On the "strange, therefore true" formula see above, chap. 1, nn. 73, 100. On the incompatibility of verisimilitude and the claim to historicity see above, chap. 1, nn. 94–95.

12. Henry Stubbe, *The Plus Ultra reduced to a Non Plus . . .* (1670), 11. See also his refutation of Glanvill's criticism of this passage: *A Reply unto the Letter written to Mr Henry Stubbe in Defense of the History of the Royal Society . . .* (Oxford, 1671), 50. Compare Stubbe's *Legends no Histories; or, A Specimen Of some Animadversions Upon the History of the Royal Society . . .* (1670), sig. t3^r, where he says that the "credit" of writers like Sprat and Glanvill "cannot equal that of *Amadis* de *Gaule,* King *Arthur, Timaeus,* or *Schioppius.*"

13. Stubbe, *Legends,* sig. *1^v; idem, *Campanella Revived; or, An Enquiry into the History of the Royal Society . . .* (1670), 22; idem, *Plus Ultra reduced,* 12. Stubbe uses the term "novellist" more or less synonymously with "new philosopher," "virtuoso," and "modern"; see his *Reply,* 49, and *Plus Ultra reduced,* 73, 93, 96.

14. Stubbe, *Reply,* 56–57; idem, *Plus Ultra reduced,* 40, 41. For Steele and Bayle see above, chap. 1, nn. 80, 101, 121. For a recent portrait of Stubbe as a radical thinker, critical not of the new philosophy but of some of its tendencies and proponents, see James R. Jacob, *Henry Stubbe: Radical Protestantism in the Early Enlightenment* (Cambridge: Cambridge University Press, 1983).

15. Samuel Butler, "The Elephant in the Moon" (written ca. 1676, printed 1759), ed. Alexander C. Spence, *Augustan Reprint Society,* no. 88 (1961), ll. 235–40, 509–20 (pp. 13–14, 25); idem, *Characters* (written 1667–69), ed. Charles W.

Daves (Cleveland: Case Western University Press, 1970), 122–23. The "account" of the elephant is to be published in the serial *Transactions* or *"Gazette"* of the Royal Society. For a similar usage see Thomas Hobbes, *Behemoth; or, The Long Parliament* (1678), ed. Ferdinand Tönnies (1889); 2nd ed. M. M. Goldsmith (New York: Barnes and Noble, 1969), 148. For recent confirmations of Butler's support for the new philosophy, see Ken Robinson, "The Skepticism of Butler's Satire on Science: Optimistic or Pessimistic?," *Restoration*, 7, no. 1 (Spring, 1983), 1–7; and William C. Horne, "Curiosity and Ridicule in Samuel Butler's Satire on Science," ibid., 8–18.

16. Galileo Galilei, letters to the Grand Duchess and Foscarini, 1615, in *Discoveries and Opinions of Galileo*, trans. and ed. Stillman Drake (Garden City, N.Y.: Anchor Books, 1957), 166, 181, 182, 197.

17. E.g., see Thomas Burnet, *The Sacred Theory of the Earth . . .* (1684), "Preface to the Reader," sig. a2^r.

18. [Daniel Defoe], *Serious Reflections During the Life And Surprising Adventures of Robinson Crusoe: with his Vision of the Angelick World* (1720), 46 (new pagination); John Milton, *Of Education. To Master Samuel Hartlib* (1644), 2. For the doctrine see, e.g., idem, *Of Christian Doctrine* (written ca. 1658), in *Complete Prose Works of John Milton*, trans. John Carey, ed. Maurice Kelley (New Haven: Yale University Press, 1973), VI, 133–34; Benjamin Keach, *Tropologia: A Key to Open Scripture-Metaphors . . .* (1682), "To the Reader" preceding bk. I, sig. A2^r, and "Epistle to the Reader" preceding bk. IV, sig. A2^v–A3^r. Cf. Milton's *Paradise Lost* (1667), V, 563–76. On the problem of mediation see above, chap. 1, n. 27. In the broadest sense the problem is of course not exclusively Christian; cf. Plato, *Meno*, 80e.

19. Henry Stubbe, *A Censure upon Certaine Passages Contained in the History of the Royal Society . . .* (Oxford, 1670), 56, 62. The contemporary interest in language reform, artificial languages, and the mediation of word and thing provides another avenue to this common ground. See, in general, Slaughter, *Universal Languages*; Michel Foucault, *The Order of Things: An Archaeology of the Human Sciences* (New York: Vintage, 1973), esp. chap. 5; James Knowlson, *Universal Language Schemes in England and France, 1600–1800* (Toronto: University of Toronto Press, 1975); and Murray Cohen, *Sensible Words: Linguistic Practice in England, 1640–1785* (Baltimore: Johns Hopkins University Press, 1977).

20. For arguments that diversely contribute to this revision see Russell Fraser, *The War Against Poetry* (Princeton: Princeton University Press, 1970), chap. 7 and passim; Margot Heinemann, *Puritanism and Theatre: Thomas Middleton and Opposition Drama under the Early Stuarts* (Cambridge: Cambridge University Press, 1980), chap. 2; Timothy J. Reiss, *The Discourse of Modernism* (Ithaca: Cornell University Press, 1982), 304; James R. Siemon, *Shakespearean Iconoclasm* (Berkeley and Los Angeles: University of California Press, 1984), chap. 1.

21. Robert Ferguson, *The Interest of Reason in Religion; With the Import and Use of Scripture-Metaphors* (1675), 322, 325, quoted in Barbara K. Lewalski, *Protestant Poetics and the Seventeenth-Century Religious Lyric* (Princeton: Princeton University Press, 1979), 224. The analogy between scientific and religious "experiment" is a related avenue by which contemporaries made explicit their understanding of this basic connection. See, e.g., John Rogers, *Ohel or Beth-shemesh . . .* (1653), 354; Jonathan Edwards, *A Treatise Concerning Religious Affections* (1746), III, 452. The idea of "experiment" as it is used in these works also broaches another sort of analogy that is central to the present study, that between Protestant rhetoric and Protestant soteriology, questions of truth and questions of virtue; see above, chap. 5, sec. 3.

22. William Whitaker, *Disputatio Sacra Scriptura* (Cambridge, 1588), trans.

Fitzgerald, and William Perkins, *A Commentarie or Exposition upon the Five First Chapters of the Epistle to the Galatians* (Cambridge, 1604), 346, quoted in Lewalski, *Protestant Poetics,* 120–21. For discussions of scriptural figures as the foundation of the highly figurative rhetoric of Protestantism, see William Haller, *The Rise of Puritanism* (New York: Harper Torchbooks, [1938] 1957), chap. 4; Lewalski, *Protestant Poetics,* chap. 3; John R. Knott, Jr., *The Sword of the Spirit: Puritan Responses to the Bible* (Chicago: University of Chicago Press, 1980).

23. John Flavell, *Navigation Spiritualized; or, A New Compass for Seamen . . .* (Newburyport, Mass., [1664] 1796), "Epistle Dedicatory," 7. On Protestant typology see Lewalski, *Protestant Poetics,* 116–19, 129–40; Hans W. Frei, *The Eclipse of Biblical Narrative: A Study in Eighteenth- and Nineteenth-Century Hermeneutics* (New Haven: Yale University Press, 1974), 31, 36–37, 40 (see also, above, chap. 1, n. 32). On plain speaking see Haller, *Rise of Puritanism,* 140–41.

24. On visual epistemology see Forrest G. Robinson, *The Shape of Things Known: Sidney's Apology in Its Philosophical Tradition* (Cambridge: Harvard University Press, 1972). In any case Protestantism exploited the printed image no less than the printed word; see Elizabeth L. Eisenstein, *The Printing Press as an Agent of Change: Communications and Cultural Transformations in Early Modern Europe* (Cambridge: Cambridge University Press, 1979), 67–70. On Protestantism and print see above, chap. 1, n. 66.

25. Richard Overton, *The Araignment of Mr. Persecution* (1645), in *Tracts on Liberty in the Puritan Revolution,* ed. William Haller (New York: Columbia University Press, 1934), III, 230; *The Autobiography of Richard Baxter,* abridged by J. M. Lloyd Thomas from the posthumous *Reliquiae Baxterianae* (1697), ed. N. H. Keeble (London: J. M. Dent, [1931] 1974), 127, 126, 111; *The Princess Cloria; or, The Royal Romance . . .* (1661), quoted in Annabel M. Patterson, *Censorship and Interpretation: The Conditions of Writing and Reading in Early Modern England* (Madison: University of Wisconsin Press, 1984), 196; Samuel Mather, *The Figures or Types of the Old Testament* (Dublin, 1683), p. 162, quoted in Lewalski, *Protestant Poetics,* 124.

26. Gerrard Winstanley, *Truth lifting up its head above scandals . . .* (1649) and *The law of freedom in a platform . . .* (1652), in *The Works of Gerrard Winstanley,* ed. George H. Sabine (Ithaca: Cornell University Press, 1941), 100, 523; Samuel Fisher, *The Testimony of Truth Exalted* (1679, a reprint of earlier tracts), 435, quoted in Christopher Hill, *The World Turned Upside Down: Radical Ideas during the English Revolution* (New York: Viking, 1973), 214; Lawrence Clarkson, *A Single Eye All Light, No Darkness . . .* (1650), 16, quoted in Hill, *World Turned Upside Down,* 211. On the English radicals' critique of Scripture see, generally, Hill, *World Turned Upside Down,* chap. 11.

27. William Dell, *The Trial of Spirits* (1653), quoted in Hill, *World Turned Upside Down,* 208; John Bunyan, *Grace Abounding to the Chief of Sinners . . .* (1666), ed. Roger Sharrock (Oxford: Clarendon Press, 1962), 31; idem, *The Life and Death of Mr. Badman . . .* (1680), 255; Defoe, *Serious Reflections,* 101; [Simon Tyssot de Patot], *The Travels and Adventures of James Massey* (1710), trans. Stephen Watley (1733), 15; *Remarks upon Dr. Sherlock's Book* (1690), 15, in reference to *The Case of the Allegiance Due to Soveraign Powers . . .* (1690), by William Sherlock, Dean of St. Paul's, quoted in Gerald M. Straka, *Anglican Reaction to the Revolution of 1688,* State Historical Society of Wisconsin (Madison: University of Wisconsin Press, 1962), 124.

28. George Swinnock, *The Christian mans calling . . . the second part* (1663), 22, quoted in David Cressy, *Literacy and the Social Order: Reading and Writing in Tudor and Stuart England* (Cambridge: Cambridge University Press, 1980), 3; the

words of a Brownist pastor quoted in ibid., 206 n. 37; Thomas Bambridge, *An Answer to a Book Entituled, Reason and Authority* (1687), 1, in reference to Joshua Bassett's *Reason and Authority; or, The Motives of a late Protestants Reconciliation to the Catholic Church* (1687), quoted in Louis I. Bredvold, *The Intellectual Milieu of John Dryden* (Ann Arbor: University of Michigan Press, [1934] 1962), 96.

29. John Dryden, *Religio Laici* (1682), ll. 270–71, and *The Hind and the Panther* (1687), I, ll. 91–92, III, l. 2, in *The Poems and Fables of John Dryden*, ed. James Kinsley (London: Oxford University Press, 1962), 289, 357, 388.

30. John Craig, *Theologiae Christianae Principia Mathematica* (1690), trans. (as *Mathematical Principles of Christian Theology*) and excerpted in *History and Theory*, Beiheft 4 (1963), pp. 3, 27, 23 (the 1699 edition was used). Craig's ambition to mathematize skepticism and prophecy is placed in its immediate context by Louis I. Bredvold, "The Invention of the Ethical Calculus," in *The Seventeenth Century: Studies in the History of English Thought and Literature from Bacon to Pope by Richard F. Jones and Others Writing in His Honor* (Stanford: Stanford University Press, 1951), 173.

31. John Locke, *An Essay Concerning Human Understanding* (1690), ed. Alexander C. Fraser (New York: Dover, [1894] 1959), IV, xix, 4, xviii, 5, xix, 3, xviii, 5, 7, 5 (II, 431, 421, 430, 436, 421, 423, 421). "If there be nothing but the strength of our persuasions, whereby to judge of our persuasions: if reason must not examine their truth by something extrinsical to the persuasions themselves, inspirations and delusions, truth and falsehood, will have the same measure, and will not be possible to be distinguished" (ibid., IV, xix, 14 [II, 439]).

32. Ibid., IV, xix, 9, 10, 15–16 (II, 434, 435, 439–40). Compare the more skeptical language of IV, xviii, 4 (II, 419).

33. Frei, *Eclipse of Biblical Narrative*, 67, 138, 77, 78. See also Victor Harris, "Allegory to Analogy in Interpretation of Scriptures," *Philological Quarterly*, 45 (1966), 1–23.

34. [Thomas Sherlock], *The Tryal of the Witnesses of the Resurrection of Jesus* (1729), 9, 9–10, 107–8. On the common-law mentality and the distinction between appeals to historicity and to antiquity see above, chap. 1, nn. 58–60, 103–6. On the seventeenth-century replacement of reliance on the verbal oath by reliance on empirical evidence and interest, see Christopher Hill, *Society and Puritanism in Pre-Revolutionary England* (London: Panther, 1969), chap. 11; Susan Staves, *Players' Scepters: Fictions of Authority in the Restoration* (Lincoln: University of Nebraska Press, 1979), chap. 4.

35. [Daniel Defoe], *A New Family Instructor; in Familiar Discourses between a Father and his Children, On the most Essential Points of the Christian Religion . . .* (1727), 253, 256, 257, 258; Jonathan Swift, "On the Trinity" (1744; date of delivery unknown), in Jonathan Swift, *Irish Tracts, 1720–1723, And Sermons*, ed. Louis Landa (Oxford: Basil Blackwell, 1948), 164, 167–68 (for the creed see Hebrews 11:1). Cf. David Hume, *An Enquiry Concerning Human Understanding* (1748), ed. L. A. Selby-Bigge, 2nd ed. (Oxford: Clarendon Press, 1966), X, 86, 90, 98, 100 (pp. 109, 115, 127, 130).

36. Frei, *Eclipse of Biblical Narrative*, 138; see George A. Starr, *Defoe and Casuistry* (Princeton: Princeton University Press, 1971). On the rise of epistemology in the seventeenth century see Richard Rorty, *Philosophy and the Mirror of Nature* (Princeton: Princeton University Press, 1979), chap. 3.

37. Spencer, *Discourse concerning Prodigies*, 226; Meric Casaubon, *Of Credulity and Incredulity, In things Natural, Civil, and Divine . . .* (1668), 159, 312. For obviously partisan accounts of this sort see, e.g., *A Wonder in Stafford-shire . . .* (1661); *ENIAYTOS TERASTIOS. Mirabilis Annus . . .* (1661); *Mirabilis Annus Secun-*

dus . . . (1662). For other accounts see *Strange News from the West, being a true and perfect Account of several miraculous Sights* . . . (1661) and the following ballads reprinted in *The Pack of Autolycus*, ed. Hyder E. Rollins (Cambridge: Harvard University Press, [1927] 1969): no. 16, *Truth brought to Light, or, Wonderful strange and true news from Gloucester shire* . . . (1662); no. 29, *The Disturbed Ghost* . . . (1674); no. 35, T. L., *The wonder of wonders; or, The strange Birth in Hampshire* . . . (1675?); no. 38, *Man's Amazement* . . . (1684).

38. William Turner, *A Compleat History Of the Most Remarkable Providences, both of Judgment and Mercy, Which have Hapned in this Present Age* . . . (1697), sig. b1ᵛ; Moses Pitt, *An Account of one Ann Jefferies, Now Living in the County of Cornwall* . . . (1696), 6, in *Seventeenth-Century Tales of the Supernatural*, ed. Isabel M. Westcott, *Augustan Reprint Society*, no. 74 (1958); [Daniel Defoe], *The Storm; or, A Collection of the most Remarkable Casualties and Disasters Which happen'd in the Late Dreadful Tempest, Both By Sea and Land* (1704), sig. A5ᵛ–A6ʳ; Richard Baxter, *The Certainty of the Worlds of Spirits* . . . *Fully evinced by the unquestionable Histories of Apparitions, Operations, Witchcrafts, Voices, &c.* . . . (1691), sig. A3ᵛ–A4ʳ.

39. [John Dunton], *The Christians Gazette; or, Nice and curious speculations Chiefly respecting The Invisible World. Being a Pacquet For the Pious Virtuosi, (Or Lovers of Novelty.)* . . . , 2nd ed. (1713); Joseph Glanvill, *Saducismus Triumphatus; or, Full and Plain Evidence Concerning Witches and Apparitions* . . . (1681), 4, 111, 3, 5. On the testimony of Glanvill and other Fellows of the Royal Society to the miraculous efficacy of Valentine Greatrakes, the Irish stroker, see Michael McKeon, *Politics and Poetry in Restoration England: The Case of Dryden's Annus Mirabilis* (Cambridge: Harvard University Press, 1975), 213–14.

40. Defoe, *The Storm*, "Preface," sig. A6ʳ⁻ᵛ, A3ʳ, A7ʳ, p. 193 (on stylistic authenticity see also Glanvill, *Saducismus*, 306); [Daniel Defoe], *A True Relation Of the Apparition of one Mrs. Veal* . . . (1706), in *Robinson Crusoe and Other Writings*, ed. James Sutherland (Boston: Houghton Mifflin, 1968), 294, 303.

41. Defoe, *The Storm*, sig. A5ʳ⁻ᵛ (see also idem, *True Relation*, 301); Glanvill, *Saducismus*, 10.

42. Defoe, *New Family Instructor*, 55–57.

CHAPTER THREE: HISTORIES OF THE INDIVIDUAL

1. George Cavendish, *The Life and Death of Cardinal Wolsey*, and William Roper, *The Life of Sir Thomas More*, in *Two Early Tudor Lives*, ed. Richard S. Sylvester and Davis P. Harding (New Haven: Yale University Press, 1964), 11. See also 6, 11, 13, 45, 192 (intrusions); and 3, 4, 11 (claims to historicity).

2. John Foxe, *Acts and Monuments* (1563, expanded 1570), ed. S. R. Cattley, 8 vols. (London: Seeley and Burnside, 1839). Seventeenth-century Puritans regarded Foxe's *Book of Martyrs* as a classic of their faith; editions based on the text of 1570 were printed in 1583, 1596, 1610, 1631–32, 1641, and 1684.

3. See William Haller, *The Elect Nation: The Meaning and Relevance of Foxe's Book of Martyrs* (New York: Harper and Row, 1963), 122, 159–60, 198, 213–14.

4. Foxe, *Acts and Monuments*, VIII, 739–40.

5. Ibid., 233. On standards of narrative completeness, see above, chap. 1, nn. 49–51, 79–80.

6. Foxe, *Acts and Monuments*, VIII, 233–34. The fact that Foxe actually includes Harding's accusation in his book nicely captures the doubleness of the quantitative standard, its omnivorous power to incorporate and reconcile all diversity as well as the infinite regress of its vulnerability to the charge of in-

completeness. Compare René Descartes' observation that "even the most faithfull Histories, if they neither change or augment the value of things, to render them the more worthy to be read, at least, they always omit the basest and less remarkable circumstances; whence it is . . . that those who form their Manners by the examples they thence derive, are subject to fall into the extravagancies of the *Paladins* of our Romances, and to conceive designes beyond their abilities": *A Discourse of a Method For the well guiding of Reason, And the Discovery of Truth in the Sciences* (1637), Eng. trans. (1649), 10–11.

7. On the rise of realism as dependent on separating history-likeness from history see Hans W. Frei, *The Eclipse of Biblical Narrative: A Study in Eighteenth- and Nineteenth-Century Hermeneutics* (New Haven: Yale University Press, 1974), 11–14.

8. Samuel Clarke, *The Lives Of sundry Eminent Persons in this Later Age* . . . (1683), Baxter's "To the Reader," sig. a3^v, a4^r. Thus Baxter says of Clarke himself: "The Author was well known to be a man of great sincerity, a hater of lying, and great lover of truth" (sig. a3^v). On Clarke's voluminous publications see William Haller, *The Rise of Puritanism* (New York: Harper Torchbooks, [1938] 1957), 102–8.

9. John Bunyan, *The Life and Death of Mr. Badman* . . . (1680), "The Author to the Reader," sig. A4^v, pp. 23–25, 152, 272, 326. With Bunyan's finger compare Madeleine de Scudéry's notification that if we come upon Turkish words in her heroic romance, "I have done it of purpose, Reader, and have left them as Historicall marks": *Ibrahim; or, The Illustrious Bassa* . . . , trans. Henry Cogan (1652), "The Preface," sig. A4^r. On Scudéry see above, chap. 1, nn. 97–98.

10. Preface to Robert Boyle's *The Martyrdom of Theodora, And of Didymus* (1687), sig. A3^v–A6^r, A8^v, in *Prefaces to Four Seventeenth-Century Romances,* ed. Charles Davies, *Augustan Reprint Society,* no. 42 (1953). Boyle defends the historicity of one of the details in his expanded story of Theodora by observing that "possibly her Action would not appear very strange, if we were not too enclinable to estimate the Affairs of Past Times, and Remote Regions, by the Opinions and Customes of our own Age and Countrys" (sig. a4^v). Thus Boyle the narrator justifies his activity according to the historicizing principle dear to him also as a new philosopher (see above, chap. 2, sec. 2; on Boyle see also below, n. 28).

11. On the maintenance of this balance in spiritual autobiography see George A. Starr, *Defoe and Spiritual Autobiography* (Princeton: Princeton University Press, 1965), 50, 162; and J. Paul Hunter, *The Reluctant Pilgrim: Defoe's Emblematic Method and Quest for Form in Robinson Crusoe* (Baltimore: Johns Hopkins Press, 1966), 89–90.

12. *The Works of John Milton,* vol. IV, ed. William Haller (New York: Columbia University Press, 1931), pp. 310–11. This argument flourished at the end of the century among authors eager to refute Jeremy Collier's charge of the immorality of the stage; see Aubrey L. Williams, *An Approach to Congreve* (New Haven: Yale University Press, 1979), 53, 71.

13. *The Diary of Ralph Thoresby, FRS, Author of the Topography of Leeds (1677–1724),* ed. Rev. Joseph Hunter (1830), I, xv, quoted in Starr, *Defoe and Spiritual Autobiography,* 10; *The Diary of the Rev. Henry Newcome, from . . . 1661 to . . . 1663,* ed. Thomas Heywood (Manchester: Chetham Society, 1849), 45. On the Protestant requirement of a full and circumstantial documentation of the self see, generally, Haller, *Rise of Puritanism,* 95–100.

14. For other discussions of this question see Alexander A. Parker, *Literature and the Delinquent: The Picaresque Novel in Spain and Europe, 1599–1753* (Edin-

burgh: Edinburgh University Press, 1967), 6; Claudio Guillén, *Literature as System: Essays toward the Theory of Literary History* (Princeton: Princeton University Press, 1971), 137–44; Harry Sieber, *The Picaresque* (London: Methuen, 1977), 10–12. On the religious context of *Lazarillo* see Parker, *Literature and the Delinquent*, 20–25.

15. E.g., see J. A. Jones, "The Duality and Complexity of *Guzmán de Alfarache*: Some Thoughts on the Structure and Interpretation of Alemán's Novel," in *Knaves and Swindlers: Essays on the Picaresque Novel in Europe*, ed. Christine J. Whitbourn (London: Oxford University Press, for the University of Hull, 1974), 30–31, 35; Christine J. Whitbourn, "Moral Ambiguity in the Spanish Picaresque Tradition," ibid., 1–24; Parker, *Literature and the Delinquent*, 32–36; Sieber, *The Picaresque*, 18–29. Whitbourn ("Moral Ambiguity," 13) and Parker (*Literature and the Delinquent*, 70, 102–3) also discuss Quevedo's *El buscón* (1626). For readings that would dispute the internalization of Narrator in Character in *Lazarillo*, see A. D. Deyermond, *Lazarillo de Tormes: A Critical Guide* (London: Grant and Cutler, 1975), chap. 7. On the notion of autodidacticism in spiritual autobiography see Starr, *Defoe and Spiritual Autobiography*, 27–29. For an account of *Lazarillo's* "hidden discourse" concerning the individualizing powers of language and the act of writing, see Harry Sieber, *Language and Society in La vida de Lazarillo de Tormes* (Baltimore: Johns Hopkins University Press, 1978). The argument might be given greater historical depth by considering the self-objectifying powers of the newly invented printing press (see above, chap. 1, secs. 4 and 5). On picaresque and the seventeenth-century disjunction between traditional belief and individual behavior see Guillén, *Literature as System*, 102. It is interesting to observe that from a Counter-Reformation perspective, the absorption of unregenerate Character by moralizing Narrator in *Guzmán* (not to mention spiritual autobiography) also appeared to sanction a materialist sufficiency, since the protagonist is able to see the necessity of conversion without benefit of priestly mediation. For this reason, a 1615 German version of *Guzmán* by the Jesuit Aegidius Albertinus definitively divides the narrative into two unconnected sequences. The first follows the episodic adventures of the entirely unreflective *pícaro*. At the beginning of the second he has already experienced first remorse, and the substance of the narrative consists in his conversion through the offices of a sermonizing religious hermit. See the discussion by Richard Bjornson, "The Picaresque Novel in France, England, and Germany," *Comparative Literature*, 29 (Spring, 1977), 129–31.

16. Thus Parker, *Literature and the Delinquent*, 102, argues that Bunyan's *Life and Death of Mr. Badman* should be classed as a picaresque novel of the *Guzmán* type. On Mabbe's *The Rogue* see Dale B. Randall, *The Golden Tapestry: A Critical Survey of Non-Chivalric Spanish Fiction in English Translation (1543–1657)* (Durham: Duke University Press, 1963), pp. 177–79. On the late sixteenth-century picaresque influence see Margaret Schlaunch, *Antecedents of the English Novel, 1400–1600* (Warsaw and London: Polish Scientific Publishers, Oxford University Press, 1963), 206–19.

17. For thoughtful discussions of some of these aspects of criminal biography see John J. Richetti, *Popular Fiction before Richardson: Narrative Patterns, 1700–1739* (Oxford: Clarendon Press, 1969), 30–32, 35; Lennard J. Davis, "Wicked Actions and Feigned Words: Criminals, Criminality, and the Early English Novel," *Yale French Studies*, 59 (1980), 108–12; and Maximillian E. Novak, *Realism, Myth, and History in Defoe's Fiction* (Lincoln: University of Nebraska Press, 1983), chap. 6.

18. Criminal biographers often waited to publish their narratives until they

could include passages from the "Accounts" of the Ordinary of Newgate, which were printed the day after executions; see Robert Singleton, "English Criminal Biography, 1651–1722," *Harvard Library Bulletin*, 18 (1970), 65.

19. Thomas Dangerfield, *Dangerfield's Memoires, Digested into Adventures, Receits, and Expences. By his Own Hand* (1685), "To the Reader," sig. A2ʳ. On Dangerfield see David Ogg, *England in the Reign of Charles II*, 2nd ed. (Oxford: Oxford University Press, 1963), II, 592, 598.

20. E.g., see *The English Rogue Described, in the Life of Meriton Latroon, A Witty Extravagant*, 2nd ed. (1666), "The Preface," sig. A5ᵛ; *Jackson's Recantation* (1674), in *The Counterfeit Lady Unveiled and Other Criminal Fiction of Seventeenth Century England*, ed. Spiro Peterson (Garden City, N.Y.: Doubleday Anchor, 1961), "Postscript," 174. Cf. Richard Head, *The Life and Death of Mother Shipton* (1687), sheet preceding A1.

21. See *The Case of Madam Mary Carleton* . . . (1663), 11–12, 70–71, 81–82, 75–76, 80, 100–03. These devices of documentary historicity do not prevent Mary from appealing to more traditional and idealist standards of narrative truth as well; cf. sig. A4ʳ⁻ᵛ, and see above, chap. 6, nn. 32–34. See, generally, Ernest Bernbaum, *The Mary Carleton Narratives, 1663–1673: A Missing Chapter in the History of the English Novel* (Cambridge: Harvard University Press, 1914); Charles F. Main, "The German Princess: Or, Mary Carleton in Fact and Fiction," *Harvard Library Bulletin*, 10 (1956), 166–85.

22. *The Ultimum Vale of John Carleton* . . . (1663), 7, 37; Francis Kirkman, *The Counterfeit Lady Unveiled* . . . (1673), 12. On Kirkman's work see the exhaustive analysis in Bernbaum, *Mary Carleton Narratives*, chaps. 4–6; and the commentary in *Counterfeit Lady Unveiled*, ed. Peterson.

23. A. O. Exquemelin, *The History of the Bucaniers of America* (1678), trans. A. B. (1684), translator's "Epistle to the Reader," sig. A5ᵛ. For convenient collections of both sorts of narrative see *The complete Newgate calendar; being Captain Charles Johnson's General history of the lives and adventures of the most famous highwaymen [1724]* . . . *Captain Alexander Smith's Compleat history of the lives and robberies of the most notorious highwaymen [1714]* . . . , ed. J. L. Rayner and G. T. Crook, 5 vols. (London: Navarre Society, 1926).

24. "Capt. Charles Johnson" [Daniel Defoe], *A General History of the Pyrates* . . . , "2nd ed." (1724), sig. A4ᵛ, A5ʳ⁻ᵛ, A6ᵛ, p. 46; Exquemelin, *History of the Bucaniers*, A. B.'s "Epistle to the Reader," sig. A3ᵛ–A4ʳ. See Richetti, *Popular Fiction before Richardson*, 84–85, 89–90, 118, for a discussion of both the biographical and the autobiographical form of the narrative tension in pirate narratives. The narrator of the story of "Capt. Bartho. Roberts" moralizes the examples both of the repentant and of the unrepentant at their executions; see Defoe, *General History*, I, 326–29. On Defoe's attractive and imaginary Captain Misson see above, chap. 6, n. 31.

25. H[enry] T[imberlake], *A strange and true Account of the Travels of two English pilgrims* . . . *to Jerusalem* . . . (1603), in *Two Journeys to Jerusalem* . . . (1683), 19; [Mary Davys], *The Accomplished Rake; or, Modern Fine Gentleman* . . . (1727), "The Preface," in William H. McBurney, ed. *Four before Richardson: Selected English Novels, 1720–1727* (Lincoln: University of Nebraska Press, 1963), 235. On the epistemological status of travel literature before and during this period see, generally, Percy G. Adams, *Travelers and Travel Liars, 1660–1800* (Berkeley and Los Angeles: University of California Press, 1962); and idem, *Travel Literature and the Evolution of the Novel* (Lexington: University Press of Kentucky, 1983), chaps. 2–4. On the medieval pilgrimage narrative see above, chap. 1, nn. 28–31.

26. Thomas Sprat, *The History of the Royal-Society of London, For the Improving*

of Natural Knowledge (1667), 86, 129–30. With Sprat's enthusiasm contrast the skeptical critique of the commodification of "news," above, chap. 1, n. 75. For a sense of the variety and extent of the Society's correspondence see that of its first secretary, still being published, with eleven volumes already in print: *The Correspondence of Henry Oldenburg*, ed. A. R. Hall and M. B. Hall (Madison: University of Wisconsin Press, 1965–73; London: Mansell, 1975–).

27. On the reform of prose style see the groundbreaking articles of Richard F. Jones, "Science and English Prose Style in the Third Quarter of the Seventeenth Century," "The Attack on Pulpit Eloquence in the Restoration: An Episode in the Development of the Neo-Classical Standard for Prose," and "Science and Language in England of the Mid-Seventeenth Century," reprinted in *The Seventeenth Century: Studies in the History of English Thought and Literature from Bacon to Pope by Richard F. Jones and Others Writing in His Honor* (Stanford: Stanford University Press, [1951] 1969), 75–160. For earlier instructions see Adams, *Travel Literature*, 78 (Ferdinand to Columbus, Hakluyt to Frobisher); Margaret T. Hodgen, *Early Anthropology in the Sixteenth and Seventeenth Centuries* (Philadelphia: University of Pennsylvania Press, 1964), 187; Francis Bacon, *Essayes* (1625), XVIII, "Of Travel." On the success of the Society's campaign see the figures and estimates given by George B. Parks in "Travel as Education," in Jones et al., *The Seventeenth Century*, 286. See, in general, the important work of R. W. Frantz, *The English Traveler and the Movement of Ideas, 1660–1732* (Lincoln: University of Nebraska Press, [1934] 1967), 48–71.

28. *Philosophical Transactions*, 11 (1676), 552; Robert Hooke, "The Preface" to Robert Knox's *An Historical Relation Of the Island Ceylon, in the East-Indies . . .* (1681), ed. James Ryan (Glasgow: James MacLehose, 1911), xliv; *Philosophical Transactions*, 1 (1665–66), 141–43, 186–89. See Robert Boyle, *General Heads for the Natural History of a Country . . . for the Use of Travellers and Navigators* (1692). Boyle's original instructions are excerpted from his *Some Considerations of the Usefulness of Experimental Natural Philosophy* (1663).

29. *Philosophical Transactions*, 1 (1665–66), 141; Awnsham Churchill and John Churchill, eds., *A Collection of Voyages and Travels . . .* (1704), I, lxxv; William Dampier, *A New Voyage round the World . . .* (1697), "Preface," sig. A3ʳ; John Braithwaite, *The History of the Revolutions in the Empire of Morocco . . .* (1729), "Preface," v. Lionel Wafer "was but Young when I was abroad, and I kept no *Journal* . . . Yet I have not trusted altogether to my *own Memory;* but some Things I committed to *Writing,* long before I return'd to *England": A New Voyage and Description of the Isthmus of America . . .* (1699), sig. A4ʳ.

30. Hooke's "Preface" to Knox, *Historical Relation*, xliv. For critiques of past, and of some contemporary, narratives for their idealistic partiality and intrusions see Braithwaite, *History of the Revolutions*, vi; and Jean Frederic Bernard, *Recueil de Voyages au Nord* (1715–24), 3rd ed. (Amsterdam, 1731–37), "Dissertation Contenant des Instructions pour voyager utilement," I, cl–clxxi. On the French travel narrative during this period see Erica Harth, *Ideology and Culture in Seventeenth-Century France* (Ithaca: Cornell University Press, 1983), chap. 6.

31. Sprat, *History of the Royal-Society,* 72; *Essays of Michael seigneur de Montaigne . . . ,* I (1580), trans. Charles Cotton (1685), chap. 30, "Of Canniballs," 364–65. Cf. Bernard, *Recueil de Voyages,* I, "Dissertation," cxlvii; and the commendation of John Fryer's style in *Philosophical Transactions,* 20 (1698), 338–39 (see Fryer, *A New Account of East-India and Persia . . .* [1698], sig. A4ᵛ). On the appeal of the plain style in travel narratives before 1660 see Adams, *Travel Literature,* 247–49. On the plain style in "mechanick preaching" see above, chap. 2, n. 23.

32. *The Travels of Don Francisco De Quevedo Through Terra Australis Incognita . . . A Novel. Originally in Spanish,* trans. John Healey (1684), "To the Reader," sig. A3ᵛ; *The Voiage and Travaile of Sir John Maundevile, Kt . . .* (1725), "The Editor's Preface," v–vi; Joshua Barnes, *Gerania: A New Discovery of a Little sort of People Anciently Discoursed of, called Pygmies . . .* (1675), "The Preface to the Reader," sig. A3ʳ: "There is such an innate principle in the Hearts of most Men, that they are able to admit nothing for currant, but what is obvious, nor reckon any thing credible, unless it be visible"; [Gabriel Daniel], *A Voyage to The World of Cartesius. Written Originally in French, and now Translated into English* (1692), "A General View Of the whole Work." On the imaginary voyage, especially during the seventeenth and early eighteenth centuries, see Geoffroy Atkinson, *The Extraordinary Voyage in French Literature before 1700* (New York: Columbia University Press, 1920); idem, *The Extraordinary Voyage in French Literature from 1700 to 1720* (Paris: Honoré Champion, 1922); Philip P. Gove, *The Imaginary Voyage in Prose Fiction: A History of Its Criticism and a Guide for Its Study, with an Annotated Check List of 215 Imaginary Voyages from 1700 to 1800* (New York: Columbia University Press, 1941); Marjorie H. Nicolson, *Voyages to the Moon* (New York: Macmillan, 1948); Paul Cornelius, *Languages in Seventeenth- and Early Eighteenth-Century Imaginary Voyages* (Geneva: Librarie Droz, 1965).

33. See Nicolson, *Voyages to the Moon,* 41, 56; Atkinson, *Extraordinary Voyage from 1700 to 1720,* 111; Gove, *Imaginary Voyage in Prose Fiction,* 97–98, 104–9.

34. Michael Hunter, *Science and Society in Restoration England* (Cambridge: Cambridge University Press, 1981), 17 (see also 15, 18); Churchill and Churchill, *Collection of Voyages,* I, ii; Dampier, *New Voyage,* "Preface," sig. A3ᵛ; Edward Cooke, *A Voyage to the South Sea, and Round the World . . .* (1712), I, "The Introduction," sig. c3ᵛ–c4ʳ; II, ii.

35. Cooke, *Voyage to the South Sea,* I, 36–37; II, xviii–xix, xxiv.

36. Nicholas del Techo, *The History of the Provinces of Paraguay, Tucuman . . . ,* translator's "Preface," quoted in Churchill and Churchill, *Collection of Voyages,* IV, 681; Churchill and Churchill, *Collection of Voyages,* I, lxxxiv–lxxxv, concerning *Relation nouvelle & exacte d'un Voyage de la Terre Sainte . . .* (1688); Simon Patrick, *The Parable of the Pilgrim: Written to a Friend* (1665), 434–35, 436–37, 442; see *Adventures by Sea of Edward Coxere,* ed. E. H. W. Meyerstein (Oxford: Clarendon Press, 1945), 27, 29–30, 43, 85–86.

37. Churchill and Churchill, *Collection of Voyages,* I, v, xciii; see also I, xcv. Other travelers: ibid., I, iii, vii; [A. Roberts], *The Adventures of (Mʳ T. S.) An English Merchant . . .* (1670), epistle dedicatory, sig. A3ʳ⁻ᵛ, p. 242; George Psalmanaazaar [sic], *An Historical and Geographical Description of Formosa . . .* (1704), "Preface," i–ii. Eyewitness: see Churchill and Churchill, *Collection of Voyages,* I, lxxxviii, xcix; William Lithgow, *Lithgow's Nineteen Years Travels through The most Eminent Places in the Habitable World . . .* (1682; according to a flyleaf notation, composed before 1639), "The Prologue to the Reader," sig. A3ᵛ; Knox, *Historical Relation,* "Epistle Dedicatory," 1; Gabriel Dellon, *A Voyage to the East-Indies . . .* (1698), translator's "Preface to the Reader" paraphrasing the author, sig. A7ʳ⁻ᵛ.

38. Fernandez Navarette, *An Account of the Empire of China . . . ,* translated for and printed in Churchill and Churchill, *Collection of Voyages,* I, "The Author to the Reader," sig. Aᵛ; I, xcix. The effect of Navarette's resolve is vitiated by his liberal citations of Isidore, Jerome, Diogenes Laertius, Scripture, and other traditional sources as part of his reading. According to William Biddulph, "One eie witnesse is more worth then ten eare witnesses: for they which heare, report what

they haue heard: but they which see, know plainely, and report by sight": *The Travels of certaine Englishmen . . .* (1609), "The Preface to the Reader," sig. A3ʳ.

39. See Churchill and Churchill, *Collection of Voyages,* I, iii, iv, v, vii, xcix, 612; Navarrete, *Empire of China,* in Churchill and Churchill, *Collection of Voyages,* I, "The Author to the Reader," sig. Aᵛ; Knox, *Historical Relation,* commendatory letters from East India Company Court of Committees and Christopher Wren, xxxvii, and Hooke's "Preface," xlvii.

40. Psalmanaazaar, *Description of Formosa,* ii. For Locke see above, chap. 2, n. 31.

41. Churchill and Churchill, *Collection of Voyages,* I, viii. On the social component in this stylistic capability compare ibid., I, v: "The Method is plain, and such as might be expected from Sailors" and Dampier, *New Voyages,* "Preface," sig. A3ᵛ: "As to my Stile, it cannot be expected, that a Seaman should affect Politeness." On the "air of truth" see Churchill and Churchill, *Collection of Voyages,* I, vii; Christopher Borri, *An Account of Cochin-China . . .* , translator's "To the Reader," in Churchill and Churchill, *Collection of Voyages,* II, 787.

42. E.g., see Ellis Veryard, *An Account of divers Choice Remarks . . . Taken in a Journey through the Low-Countries, France, Italy, and Part of Spain . . .* (1701), "The Preface," sig. b2ᵛ.

43. See Churchill and Churchill, *Collection of Voyages,* I, xcix, cxix; I, xcix, on John Josselyn's *An Account of two Voyages to New-England . . .* (1674) (cf. Josselyn, 34, beginning of the second voyage); I, lxxxviii; I, xcix.

44. [Denis Vairasse d'Allais], *The History of the Sevarites or Sevarambi: A Nation inhabiting part of the third Continent, Commonly called, Terrae Australes Incognitae . . .* (1675); idem, *The History of The Sevarites . . . The Second Part more wonderful and delightful than the First* (1679); [Gabriel de Foigny], *A New Discovery of Terra Incognita Australis, or the Southern World. By James Sadeur a Frenchman . . . These Memoirs were thought so curious, that they were kept Secret in the Closet of a late Great Minister of State, and never Published till now since his Death . . .* (1693). The Churchills' notice (*Collection of Voyages,* I, lxxxiii) is taken at least in part from the review of a 1692 French reprint of Foigny's book in *Journal des Sçavans* (1693), XX, 526–32. On the parodic element of these works see Harth, *Ideology and Culture,* 295–99.

45. *The Memoirs of Sigr Gaudentio di Lucca. Taken from his Confession and Examination before the Fathers of the Inquisition at Bologna in Italy. Making a Discovery of an unknown Country . . . Copied from the original Manuscript kept in St. Mark's Library at Venice: With Critical Notes of the Lerned Signor Rhedi, late Library-Keeper of the said Library. To which is prefix'd, a Letter of the Secretary of the Inquisition, to the same Signor Rhedi, giving an Account of the Manner and Causes of his being seized. Faithfully Translated from the Italian, by E. T. Gent* (1737). In fact the memoirs are original in English. Traditionally attributed to Bishop Berkeley, they are now generally accepted as the work of the Reverend Simon Berington. See *Notes & Queries,* 2 (1850), 327–28; and Lee M. Ellison, " 'Gaudentio di Lucca': A Forgotten Utopia," *PMLA,* 50, no. 2 (June, 1935), 494–509.

46. *Memoirs of Sigr Gaudentio di Lucca,* "The Publisher to the Reader," iii–xiii (a gap in these sheets owing to rough handling by Marseilles customs officials attests to the artless imperfection and authenticity of the document; the hiatus is acknowledged, when it occurs, at 282 of the *Memoirs*); ibid., "Introduction," 1–24. See also 335, where the Secretary of the Inquisitors acknowledges that they believe di Lucca to be what he professes.

47. E.g., see Spenser's defense of his "voyage" to "Faerie lond" in *The Faerie*

Queene (1590), II, proem. On the paradox see above, chap. 1, nn. 73, 100, and chap. 2, nn. 11, 41.

48. Vairasse d'Allais, *History* (1675), sig. A4ʳ; idem, *History* (1679), sig. A3ʳ⁻ᵛ; Dellon, *Voyage to the East-Indies,* translator's "Preface to the Reader," sig. A6ᵛ; Heliogenes de L'Epy, *A Voyage into Tartary . . .* (1689), "The Preface," sig. A7ʳ–A8ᵛ, A9ᵛ; Father Louis Hennepin, *A New Discovery of a Vast Country in America . . .* (1698), 4.

49. Aphra Behn, *The Fair Jilt; or, The History of Prince Tarquin, and Miranda,* in *The Histories and Novels Of the Late Ingenious Mrs Behn . . .* (1696), 4. Compare Behn's dedication to Henry Pain: "This little History . . . is Truth; Truth, which you so much admire . . . This is Reality, and Matter of Fact, and acted in this our latter Age . . . [Part of it] I had from the Mouth of this unhappy Great Man [Tarquin], and was an Eye-Witness to the rest" (sig. A2ᵛ, A3ʳ). For other claims to historicity see 19, 24, 35, 161. Cf. Behn, *Oroonoko,* ed. Lore Metzger (New York, Norton, 1973), 1; subsequent citations will be to this edition and will appear in the text. For a summary of the scholarship arguing the fictionality of Behn's experiences in Surinam as recounted in these writings, see George Guffey, "Aphra Behn's *Oroonoko:* Occasion and Accomplishment," in *Two English Novelists: Aphra Behn and Anthony Trollope,* William Andrews Clark Memorial Library (Berkeley and Los Angeles: University of California Press, 1975), 5–8.

50. *Histories and Novels Of . . . Mrs Behn,* "Epistle Dedicatory," sig. A5ᵛ–A6ᵛ.

51. Contrast Congreve's teasing invitation that we discover a "force, or a whim of the author's"; see above, chap. 1, n. 124.

52. [Richard Head], *O-Brazile, or the Inchanted Island: being A perfect Relation of the late Discovery and Wonderful Dis-Inchantment of an Island On the North of Ireland . . .* (1675), in *Seventeenth-Century Tales of the Supernatural,* ed. Isabel M. Westcott, *Augustan Reprint Society,* no. 74 (1958); John Macky, *A Journey through England . . .* (1724), II, iii, quoted in Adams, *Travel Literature,* 106. For Jean Chapelain it is not Scudéry but la Calprenède who represents the old romance that is replaced by the new romance of travel; see letter of 1663 quoted in Atkinson, *Extraordinary Voyage from 1700 to 1720,* 10. For a critique of the French memoir as the new romance see above, chap. 1, nn. 101, 121.

53. Henry Stubbe, *The Plus Ultra reduced to a Non Plus . . .* (1670), 21.

54. François Misson, *A New Voyage to the East-Indies, by Francis Leguat and His Companions . . .* (London and Amsterdam, 1708), "The Author's Preface," iii–iv. The "Preface" especially is saturated with claims to historicity, sincerity, and stylistic simplicity. Cf. Misson, *New Voyage,* ed. Capt. Pasfield Oliver (London: Publications of the Hakluyt Society, 1891), preface, ix: "The chief modern scientific interest, however, in Leguat's description undoubtedly hinges upon the circumstantial detail which he gives of the curious bird-fauna then extant in the Mascarene Islands, the subsequent destruction of which has rendered the personal observations of the philosophic Huguenot invaluable to naturalists, marked as they are by such evident simplicity and veracity" (quoted in Atkinson, *Extraordinary Voyage from 1700 to 1720,* 44). The work was accepted as by Leguat (a real person) until Atkinson (35–65) showed it to be a tissue of borrowings and argued that certainly the preface, and probably the voyage itself, was by Misson. For the object of Misson's travel-narrative parody see [François Timoléon], *Journal du voyage de Siam fait en 1685 et 1686, par M. l'abbé de Choisy* (1687), intro. Maurice Garçon (Paris: Ducharte, 1930). The form is that of a verbatim journal; for examples of stylistic self-consciousness and the claim to historicity, see 1, 7. With Misson's parody compare G. H. Bougeant, *Voyage merveilleux du Prince Fan-*

Férédin dans la Romancie . . . (1735), whose first-person, eponymous hero claims the historicity of his travels to Romancie, the land of his beloved *romans* (see Adams, *Travel Literature,* 272–73).

55. E.g., see John Ryther, *A Plat for Mariners* . . . (1672), sig. A3, and Josiah Woodward, *The Seaman's Monitor* . . . (1703), 40, quoted in J. P. Hunter, *Reluctant Pilgrim,* 83–84, 71n.55. On the other hand, Aphra Behn seems to have distinguished sharply between the seriousness of journalistic documentation as she herself claimed to practice it in her histories, and its particularly Protestant employment. See *The Feign'd Curtezans; or, A Night's Intrigue* (1679), III, i, where the Puritan divine Mr. Tickletext, traveling on the Continent as tutor to Sir Signal Buffoon, is asked the nature of the book he carries with him: "A small Volume, Sir, into which I transcribe the most memorable and remarkable Transactions of the Day . . . [A passage is read aloud]: *April* the twentieth, arose a very great Storm of Wind, Thunder, Lightning and Rain,—which was a shrewd sign of foul Weather. The 22th 9 of our 12 Chickens getting loose, flew over-board, the other three miraculously escaping, by being eaten by me that Morning for Breakfast." Later Tickletext says: "At my return, Sir, for the good of the Nation, I will print it, and I think it will deserve it."

56. William Okeley, *Eben-Ezer; or, A Small Monument of Great Mercy. Appearing in the Miraculous Deliverance of William Okeley* [et al.] *From the Miserable Slavery of Algiers* . . . (1764). First published in 1675 and again in 1678 (see sig. A2ᵛ), Okeley's narrative recounts an expedition of 1639, capture by Turkish pirates, enslavement in Algiers, enforced privateering, escape in 1644, and return to an England embroiled in civil war. Okeley's adherence to the conventions of spiritual autobiography increases as the narrative progresses. For a discussion of *Eben-Ezer* and of other travel narratives that share some of its features, see George A. Starr, "Escape from Barbary: A Seventeenth-Century Genre," *Huntington Library Quarterly,* 29 (1965), 35–52. Citations of Okeley's work are made parenthetically in the text. For Augustine see above, chap. 1, n. 27.

57. I.e., Thomas Shelton's *Tachygraphy* . . . (1638), a system of shorthand; compare Sir Richard Steele's skepticism regarding eyewitness military memoirs, above, chap. 1, n. 121.

58. Anthony Ashley Cooper, Third Earl of Shaftesbury, "*Soliloquy; or, Advice to an Author*" (1710), in *Characteristicks of Men, Manners, Opinions, Times,* 2nd ed. (1714), I, 344–47.

59. E.g., see Ian Watt, *The Rise of the Novel: Studies in Defoe, Richardson, and Fielding* (Berkeley and Los Angeles: University of California Press, 1964), 17; Mikhail M. Bakhtin, *The Dialogic Imagination: Four Essays by M. M. Bakhtin,* trans. Caryl Emerson and Michael Holquist, ed. Holquist (Austin: University of Texas Press, 1981), 41. Contrast Renato Poggioli's notion of an unofficial and "unwritten" poetics that exists "within or alongside the written or articulate poetics" of a given period: "Poetics and Metrics," in Poggioli, *The Spirit of the Letter: Essays in European Literature* (Cambridge: Harvard University Press, 1965), 346.

60. On spiritual autobiography see the works cited above in nn. 10 and 14. On the familiar letter see, among other works, Katherine G. Hornbeak, *The Complete Letter Writer in English, 1568–1800,* Smith College Studies in Modern Languages, 15, nos. 3–4 (April–July, 1934) (Northampton, Mass., 1934); idem, *Richardson's Familiar Letters and the Domestic Conduct Books,* Smith College Studies in Modern Languages, 19, no. 2 (Jan., 1938) (Northampton, Mass., 1937); Sister Mary Humiliata, "Standards of Taste Advocated for Feminine Letter Writing, 1640–1797," *Huntington Library Quarterly,* 13 (1950), 261–77; Howard Anderson,

Philip B. Daghlian, and Irvin Ehrenpreis, eds., *The Familiar Letter in the Eighteenth Century* (Lawrence: University of Kansas Press, 1966); and Ruth Perry, *Women, Letters, and the Novel,* AMS Studies in the Eighteenth Century, no. 4 (New York: AMS Press, 1980), chap. 3. Contemporaries knew that letters have the double status of private articulation and documentary object, that "in the very Notion of them [they] carry something of Secrecy; Though after all, the *Reader* cannot but observe an Air of History to run, in a manner, through the whole composition": *The Secret History of White-Hall* (1697), sig. A6ʳ, quoted in Robert A. Day, *Told in Letters: Epistolary Fiction before Richardson* (Ann Arbor: University of Michigan Press, 1966), 94–95. Day (chap. 6) shows how seventeenth-century epistolary fiction learned to exploit, with great subtlety, both the personal and the historical methods of authentication inherent in its form. For a discussion of this epistemological doubleness in both the traditional and the seventeenth-century familiar letter, see Annabel M. Patterson, *Censorship and Interpretation: The Conditions of Writing and Reading in Early Modern England* (Madison: University of Wisconsin Press, 1984), chap. 5.

61. On Bakhtin see above, Introduction, nn. 16–17. He comes closer to recognizing the outlines of the dialectic that I have argued in his notion of the First and Second Stylistic Lines of the novel; see Bakhtin, *Dialogic Imagination,* 398–99, 409, 414. To a limited extent, of course, parody is an active ingredient in the posture of naive empiricism as well (e.g., see above, chap. 1, sec. 7, on the emergence of antiromance).

62. See above, chap. 1, n. 93.

63. Daniel Defoe, *The Storm* . . . (1704), sig. A3ʳ. Defoe even discountenances "that Men shou'd invent a Story . . . to preserve the Remembrance of Divine Vengeance" (83).

64. Daniel Defoe, *Serious Reflections During the Life And Surprising Adventures of Robinson Crusoe: with his Vision of the Angelick World* (1720), 117, 116. Further citations are made parenthetically in the text. For the charges see [Charles Gildon], *The Life And Strange Surprizing Adventures of Mr. D—— De F——* . . . (1719), 33.

65. J. P. Hunter, *Reluctant Pilgrim,* 117–18, provides contemporary arguments of improvement which seem to establish the immediate exegetical tradition within which Defoe took himself to be working. For comparable accounts of his immediate casuistical context see George A. Starr, *Defoe and Casuistry* (Princeton: Princeton University Press, 1971), 197–201; and James Thompson, "Lying and Dissembling in the Restoration," *Restoration,* 6, no. 1 (Spring, 1982), 11–19. Neither sort of argument appears to bear the weight that Defoe wishes to exert.

66. See, especially, Defoe, *Serious Reflections,* "Preface," sig. A2ʳ–A7ʳ; idem, *A New Family Instructor; in Familiar Discourses between a Father and his Children* . . . (1727), 51–55.

67. Cf. the prefaces to *Robinson Crusoe* (1719), *The Farther Adventures of Robinson Crusoe* (1719), *Colonel Jack* (1722), *Moll Flanders* (1722), and *Roxana* (1724), in Ioan Williams, ed., *Novel and Romance, 1700–1800: A Documentary Record* (New York: Barnes and Noble, 1970), 56, 64–65, 73–74, 75–78, 80–81.

68. E.g., see "Preface" to *Colonel Jack,* in I. Williams, *Novel and Romance,* 74.

69. E.g., see prefaces to *Moll Flanders* and *Roxana,* ibid., 75–76, 81.

70. See Ernst H. Kantorowicz, "The Sovereignty of the Artist: A Note on Legal Maxims and Renaissance Theories of Art," in *Selected Studies* (Locust Valley, N.Y.: J. J. Augustin, 1965), 352–65; Martin Kemp, "From 'Mimesis' to 'Fantasia': The Quattrocento Vocabulary of Creation, Inspiration, and Genius in the Visual Arts," *Viator,* 8 (1977), 382–84, 393–95; Elizabeth L. Eisenstein, *The*

Printing Press as an Agent of Change: Communications and Cultural Transformations in Early Modern Europe (Cambridge: Cambridge University Press, 1979), 120–22, 229, 240.

71. On the Weber thesis see above, chap. 5, sec. 3.

72. The fundamental analogy between religious and capitalist impulses is present in Marx's notion of "commodity fetishism." See Karl Marx, *Economic and Philosophical Manuscripts,* in *Early Writings,* trans. and ed. T. B. Bottomore (New York: McGraw-Hill, 1964), 125; idem, *Capital,* trans. Samuel Moore and Edward Aveling (New York: International Publishers, 1967), I, i, i, 71–83.

73. See the discussion by Eisenstein, *Printing Press,* 116, 552.

74. See above, sec. 1; chap. 1, n. 24.

75. See A. Williams, *Approach to Congreve,* passim; idem, "Interpositions of Providence and the Design of Fielding's Novels," *South Atlantic Quarterly,* 70, no. 1 (Spring, 1971), 265–86; Martin Battestin, *The Providence of Wit: Aspects of Form in Augustan Literature and the Arts* (Oxford: Clarendon Press, 1974).

76. See Keith Thomas, *Religion and the Decline of Magic: Studies in Popular Beliefs in Sixteenth- and Seventeenth-Century England* (Harmondsworth: Penguin, 1973), 129–31.

77. A. Williams, *Approach to Congreve,* 40. For the doctrine see Thomas Rymer, *The Tragedies of the Last Age Consider'd and Examin'd . . .* (1677), in *The Critical Works of Thomas Rymer,* ed. Curt A. Zimansky (New Haven: Yale University Press, 1956), 22.

78. Francis Bacon, *Of the Proficience and Advancement of Learning Divine and Humane* (1605), in *The Works of Francis Bacon,* ed. James Spedding et al. (Boston: Taggard and Thompson, 1863), VI, ii, 203. Also during the Restoration and in a similar fashion, the invocation of providence in political contexts became unprecedentedly popular in justification of an act that was manifestly the work neither of divine nor of hereditary right but of human expediency—the Hanoverian Settlement. See Gerald M. Straka, *Anglican Reaction to the Revolution of 1688,* State Historical Society of Wisconsin (Madison: University of Wisconsin Press, 1962), 66; and below, chap. 5, nn. 10–11.

79. Samuel Butler, *Prose Observations,* ed. Hugh de Quehen (Oxford: Oxford University Press, 1979), 71–72; A[braham] J[enings], *Miraculum basilicon; or, The Royal Miracle . . .* (1664), sig. B4^v; D. P. Walker, *The Decline of Hell: Seventeenth-Century Discussions of Eternal Torment* (Chicago: University of Chicago Press, 1964), 4–5, 69; "Postscript" to *Clarissa* (4th ed., 1751), VII, 350–51, in Samuel Richardson, *Clarissa: Preface, Hints of Prefaces, and Postscript,* ed. R. F. Brissenden, Augustan Reprint Society, no. 103 (1964). Cf. Samuel Richardson to Lady Bradshaigh, Dec. 15, 1748, in *Selected Letters of Samuel Richardson,* ed. John Carroll (Oxford: Clarendon Press, 1964), 108; and [Sarah Fielding], *Remarks on Clarissa, Addressed to the Author . . .* (1749), who agrees that "poetical Justice" is really "anti-providential Justice" (49).

80. John and Anna Laetitia Aikin (Barbauld), *Miscellaneous Pieces in Prose and Verse* (1773); Henry Mackenzie, *The Lounger,* no. 20, June 18, 1785; and Thomas Monroe, *Olla Podrida,* no. 15, June 23, 1787: all quoted in I. Williams, *Novel and Romance,* 289, 330, 350. On the defenders of *catharsis* against Jeremy Collier see A. Williams, *Approach to Congreve,* 71–72.

81. On the use of the figure of the human dramatist as an improving divinity, see A. Williams, *Approach to Congreve,* chaps. 2 and 3; and Battestin, *Providence of Wit,* chap. 5. Both believe that this figure is no more volatile than the conventional figure of God as a dramatist, which it reverses. On Congreve and Fielding see above, chap. 1, nn. 123–25, and chap. 12.

82. For recent attempts to explain the replacement of drama by the novel in the eighteenth century, see Laura Brown, *English Dramatic Form, 1660–1760: An Essay in Generic History* (New Haven: Yale University Press, 1981), chaps. 5 and 6 (see 229 n. 59 for citations of earlier attempts); and J. Paul Hunter, "The World as Stage and Closet," in *British Theater and Other Arts, 1660–1800,* ed. Shirley S. Kenney (Washington, D.C.: Folger Shakespeare Library, 1984), 271–87. See also the interesting discussion by Georg Lukács, *The Historical Novel,* trans. Hannah and Stanley Mitchell (London: Merlin Press, 1962), chap. 2. Unlike Brown, I take the crucial formal "replacement" that stands in need of explanation to be that of dramatic presentation by literary narration. The formal similarities between letters and printed dialogue, as well as Samuel Richardson's ruminations on his own narrative method (see below, Conclusion, nn. 31–32), have stimulated the related view that drama is the chief source for the eighteenth-century epistolary novel. See, especially, Day, *Told in Letters,* 194–200; and Mark Kinkead-Weekes, *Samuel Richardson: Dramatic Novelist* (Ithaca: Cornell University Press, 1973), chap. 10.

To argue that narrative "replaced" drama as the dominant mode during the eighteenth century is not, of course, to say that drama now loses either its vitality or its audience; see Paula R. Backscheider, gen. ed., *Eighteenth-Century English Drama,* 69 vols. (New York: Garland, 1983).

83. See William Congreve, *Incognita . . .* (1692), "Preface to the Reader," in *Shorter Novels: Seventeenth Century,* ed. Philip Henderson (London: J. M. Dent, 1962), 242–43.

84. Ibid., 242; Aristotle, *Poetics,* 1460a, trans. Ingram Bywater, in *Introduction to Aristotle,* ed. Richard McKeon, 2nd ed. (Chicago: University of Chicago Press, 1973), 706; John Dryden, *Of Dramatic Poesy: An Essay* (1668), in Dryden, *Of Dramatic Poesy and Other Critical Essays,* ed. George Watson (London: J. M. Dent, 1962), I, 51.

85. See Dryden, *Of Dramatic Poesy,* I, 62–64 (cf. "A Defence of *An Essay of Dramatic Poesy . . .*" [1668], ibid., I, 126–28); "Preface" to *The Plays of William Shakespeare* (1765), in *The Works of Samuel Johnson,* ed. Arthur Sherbo (New Haven: Yale University Press, 1968), VII, 74–79.

86. Samuel Taylor Coleridge, *Biographia Literaria* (1817), ed. George Watson (London: J. M. Dent, 1965), II, xiv (p. 169).

CHAPTER FOUR: THE DESTABILIZATION OF SOCIAL CATEGORIES

1. See Julian Pitt-Rivers, "Honour and Social Status," in *Honour and Shame: The Values of Mediterranean Society,* ed. J. G. Peristiany (London: Weidenfeld and Nicolson, 1965), 37; Ruth Kelso, *The Doctrine of the English Gentleman in the Sixteenth Century,* University of Illinois Studies in Language and Literature, 14, nos. 1–2 (Urbana, Feb.–May, 1929), 18–19. Cf. Friedrich Nietzsche, *Beyond Good and Evil: Prelude to a Philosophy of the Future,* trans. Walter Kaufmann (New York: Vintage, 1966), 204–5.

2. Aristotle, *Politics,* 1283a, trans. Benjamin Jowett, in *The Basic Works of Aristotle,* ed. Richard McKeon (New York: Random House, 1941), 1194; James I, *Basilikon Doron* (1599), quoted in John E. Mason, *Gentlefolk in the Making: Studies in the History of English Courtesy Literature and Related Topics from 1531 to 1774* (New York: Octagon Books, [1935] 1971), 33; [Mary Delarivière Manley], *The Secret History of Queen Zarah, and the Zarazians . . .* (1711), II, 126; Thomas Elyot, *The Boke Named the Gouvernour* (1531), ed. H. H. S. Croft (New York: Burt Franklin, [1883] 1967), II, 198–99; Edmund Bolton, *Elements of Armories* (1610), 5, quoted in Michael Walzer, *The Revolution of the Saints: A Study in the*

Origins of Radical Politics (Cambridge: Harvard University Press, 1965), 249; William London, *A Catalogve of the most vendible Books in England* . . . (1657), sig. I1ʳ. For the heritability of virtue through aristocratic lineage see the sixteenth-century sources cited in Mason, *Gentlefolk*, 46; and Kelso, *English Gentleman*, 23 n. 21. On the physical distinction of the privileged see Peter Laslett, *The World We Have Lost Further Explored*, 3rd ed. (New York: Charles Scribner's, 1984), 89. On the College of Heralds see Anthony R. Wagner, *English Genealogy* (London: Clarendon Press, 1960), 313–14.

3. See Laslett, *The World We Have Lost*, 239–41; Jack Goody, *The Development of the Family and Marriage in Europe* (Cambridge: Cambridge University Press, 1983), 44; Lawrence Stone and Jeanne C. F. Stone, *An Open Elite? England, 1540–1880* (Oxford: Clarendon Press, 1984), 397. On true nobility see G. M. Vogt, "Gleanings for the History of a Sentiment: Generositas Virtus, non Sanguis," *Journal of English and Germanic Philology*, 24 (1925), 102–24. On romance discovery see the observations of Christopher Hill, *Reformation to Industrial Revolution, 1530–1780*, Pelican Economic History of England, vol. 2 (Harmondsworth: Penguin, 1971), 59. On romance naming and the transmutation of oral lineages see above, chap. 1, nn. 6, 50.

4. Claude Lévi-Strauss, *The Savage Mind* (Chicago: University of Chicago Press, 1966), 115–16, 233.

5. Ibid., 116; see also Claude Lévi-Strauss, "The Structural Study of Myth," in Lévi-Strauss, *Structural Anthropology*, trans. Claire Jacobson and Brooke G. Schoepf (Garden City, N.Y.: Anchor Books, 1967), 202–28.

6. Theognis of Megara, in *Greek Lyrics*, trans. Richmond Lattimore, 2nd ed. (Chicago: University of Chicago Press, 1960), 30 (also quoted in Alvin W. Gouldner, *Enter Plato: Classical Greece and the Origins of Social Theory* [New York: Basic Books, 1965], 17); Moses Finley, "Views and Controversies," in *Slavery in Classical Antiquity*, ed. M. I. Finley (Cambridge: Heffer, 1960), 69, quoted in Gouldner, *Enter Plato*, 25. See also Gouldner, *Enter Plato*, 14, 17, 18–20, and pt. 1 passim; and Perry Anderson, *Passages from Antiquity to Feudalism* (London: New Left Books, 1974), 31–32.

7. Sophocles, *Oedipus the King*, trans. David Grene, in *The Complete Greek Tragedies: Sophocles I* (Chicago: University of Chicago Press, 1954), ll. 1061–63, 1078–82; Nietzsche, *Beyond Good and Evil*, ed. cit., 43–44.

8. Plato, *Republic*, trans. Francis M. Cornford (New York: Oxford University Press, 1959), II, 370C, II, 374E, III, 414B–415C (pp. 57, 62, 106–7).

9. On justice and the functional notion of virtue see ibid., I, 353B, IV, 433A (pp. 38, 127). For the medieval use of the functional view see Ruth Mohl, *The Three Estates in Medieval and Renaissance Literature* (New York: Columbia University Press, 1933); and R. H. Tawney, *Religion and the Rise of Capitalism: A Historical Study* (New York: Mentor, [1926] 1958), chap. 1, sec. 1.

10. Hannah Arendt, *Between Past and Future: Six Exercises in Political Thought* (New York: Meridian Books, 1961), 122. On Roman *virtus* see Bernard Mandeville, *An Enquiry into the Origins of Honour and the Usefulness of Christianity in War* (1732), ed. M. M. Goldsmith (London: Frank Cass, 1971), "The Preface." On Cicero and the *novus homo* see H. H. Scullard, "The Political Career of a *Novus Homo*," in *Cicero*, ed. T. A. Dorey (London: Routledge, 1965), 1–5, 17; and Timothy P. Wiseman, *New Men in the Roman Senate, 139 B.C.–A.D. 14* (Oxford: Oxford University Press, 1971), 107, 109–10, and annotated list, 209–83.

11. Madeleine de Scudéry, Preface to *Ibrahim: or, The Illustrious Bassa*, trans. Henry Cogan (1652), sig. A4ᵛ, quoted in Annabel M. Patterson, *Censorship and Interpretation: The Conditions of Writing and Reading in Early Modern England*

(Madison: University of Wisconsin Press, 1984), 186. For explicit comparisons see, e.g., Xenophon of Ephesus, *An Ephesian Tale,* and Longus, *Daphnis and Chloe,* in *Three Greek Romances,* trans. Moses Hadas, Library of Liberal Arts (Indianapolis: Bobbs-Merrill, 1964), 73, 17–18. On the social context of the Greek romances see Ben E. Perry, *The Ancient Romances: A Literary-Historical Account of Their Origins* (Berkeley and Los Angeles: University of California Press, 1967), chap. 2; Tomas Hägg, *The Novel in Antiquity* (Berkeley and Los Angeles: University of California Press, 1983), chap. 3.

12. Longus, *Daphnis and Chloe,* ed. cit.; Apuleius, *The Golden Ass,* trans. Jack Lindsay (Bloomington: Indiana University Press, 1973), 133–34, 141–42 (Apuleius wrote in the second century A.D.).

13. On the Jewish experience see Herbert N. Schneidau, *Sacred Discontent: The Bible and Western Tradition* (Baton Rouge: Louisiana State University Press, 1976), 106, 241. The Gospel: see Matthew 12:50; 19:29. On Church prohibitions and the spiritualization of kinship, see Goody, *Family and Marriage in Europe,* 44–82, 194–204. On the social ambiguity of the Incarnation and Passion within the context of the development of a Christian *sermo humilis,* see Erich Auerbach, *Mimesis: The Representation of Reality in Western Literature,* trans. Willard Trask (Garden City, N.Y.: Anchor Books, 1957), 63; and idem, *Literary Language and Its Public in Late Latin Antiquity and in the Middle Ages,* trans. Ralph Manheim, Bollingen Series LXXIV (New York: Pantheon, 1965), chaps. 1 and 2.

14. See F. L. Ganshof, *Feudalism,* trans. Philip Grierson, 3rd Eng. ed. (New York: Harper Torchbooks, 1964), 139–40; David Herlihy, "Three Patterns of Social Mobility in Medieval History," *Journal of Interdisciplinary History,* 3, no. 4 (Spring, 1973), 625, 626, 632; R. Howard Bloch, *Medieval French Literature and Law* (Berkeley and Los Angeles: University of California Press, 1977), 98–99; Georges Duby, "Northwest France: The 'Young' in Twelfth-Century Aristocratic Society," in *Social Historians in Contemporary France: Essays from Annales* (New York: Harper Torchbooks, 1972), 87–99; idem, *Medieval Marriage: Two Models from Twelfth-Century France* (Baltimore: Johns Hopkins University Press, 1978), 14; Herbert Moller, "The Social Causation of the Courtly Love Complex," *Comparative Studies in Society and History,* 1 (1959), 146–57; Lionel Rothkrug, "Popular Religion and Holy Shrines: Their Influence on the Origins of the German Reformation and Their Role in German Cultural Development," in *Religion and the People, 800–1700,* ed. James Obelkevich (Chapel Hill: University of North Carolina Press, 1979), 26, 57. On these various social conflicts see also Colin Morris, *The Discovery of the Individual, 1050–1200* (New York: Harper and Row, 1972), 37–48 and chap. 6. Needless to say, these generalizations coordinate an enormous national and cultural diversity.

15. *The Poem of the Cid,* trans. Lesley B. Simpson (Berkeley and Los Angeles: University of California Press, 1962), 139 (on the "entrepreneurial" career of the Cid see Herlihy, "Social Mobility in Medieval History," 639, Pitt-Rivers, "Honour and Social Status," 23); Peter Haidu, "Introduction," and W. T. H. Jackson, "The Nature of Romance," *Yale French Studies,* 51 (1974), 3, 19; Bloch, *Medieval French Literature and Law,* 46, 140, 196–97, and, summarizing a thesis of Erich Köhler, 220–21. On the replacement of ordeal by inquest see above, chap. 1, n. 35.

16. See Robert W. Hanning, *The Individual in Twelfth-Century Romance* (New Haven: Yale University Press, 1977), 3, 4, 5, 53, 148, 208, 287n.49; Bloch, *Medieval French Literature and Law,* 141, 143–44, 158, 163–64, 190–92, 231–36, 250; John Stevens, *Medieval Romance: Themes and Approaches* (London: Hutchinson University Library, 1973), 166n.3. On the Church's consistent obstruction of

kinship ties through the encouragement of inheritance by direct descent, see Goody, *Family and Marriage in Europe,* 152–56 and chaps. 5 and 6 passim.

17. See Duby, "Northwest France," 97–98; Moller, "Courtly Love Complex," 160; Andreas Capellanus, *The Art of Courtly Love,* trans. and ed. John J. Parry (New York: Norton, 1969), 33–141. On the disparity between the courtly images of adultery and marriage and their reality, see John F. Benton, "Clio and Venus: An Historical View of Medieval Love," in *The Meaning of Courtly Love,* ed. F. X. Newman (Albany: State University of New York Press, 1968), 19–42.

18. See Chrétien de Troyes, *Le Chevalier au Lion,* ed. Mario Roques (Paris: Librairie Champion, 1965), ll. 4703–6437, 2763–4612, 6629–723. On the role of true nobility in the courtly fictions see Moller, "Courtly Love Complex," 161; Johan Huizinga, *The Waning of the Middle Ages* (Garden City, N.Y.: Anchor Books, [1924] 1954), 63–64.

19. W. P. Ker, *Epic and Romance: Essays on Medieval Literature* (London: Macmillan, [1896] 1922), 323. For a recent analysis of the counterromance element in twelfth-century romance see Jackson, "Nature of Romance," 22–25. Huizinga's memorable account of this "unstable equilibrium between sentimentality and mockery" (*Waning of the Middle Ages,* 80) is generally concerned with the culture of the Continent in the fourteenth and fifteenth centuries. On the emergence of antiromance with respect to questions of truth see above, chap. 1, nn. 101–11, 122–25.

20. See F. W. Maitland, *The Constitutional History of England* (Cambridge: Cambridge University Press, [1908] 1965), 37, 151, 156–57; G. O. Sayles, *The Medieval Foundations of England* (New York: A. S. Barnes, 1961), 211, 238, 240, 241.

21. See Alan Macfarlane, *The Origins of English Individualism: The Family, Property, and Social Transition* (New York: Cambridge University Press, 1979), 85–88, 163, 197; on this preexistent behavior see also below, nn. 48–49. The sources that Macfarlane cites to show the extremity of the English application of primogeniture are from the sixteenth century (see 87).

22. See M. Dominica Legge, *Anglo-Norman Literature and Its Background* (Oxford: Clarendon Press, 1963), 139–48, 174 (quotation, 148). For versions of *Guy* see Laura H. Loomis, *Medieval Romance in English* (New York: Burt Franklin, [1924] 1960), 127–28; Legge, *Anglo-Norman Literature,* 162–65; *Gesta Romanorum; or, Entertaining Moral Stories,* trans. Charles Swan, rev. Wynnard Hooper (New York: Dover, 1959), 325–33; William J. Thoms, ed., *Early English Prose Romances* (London: Routledge and Kegan Paul, 1907), 331–407. On *Amis and Amiloun* see Loomis, *Medieval Romance in English,* 65–68.

23. Thomas Warton, *History of English Poetry* (1774), quoted in *Gesta Romanorum,* ed. cit., 419. See Lee C. Ramsey, *Chivalric Romances: Popular Literature in Medieval England* (Bloomington: Indiana University Press, 1983), 83–93, 97, and chap. 2. On the English tendency toward "homiletic romance" see Dieter Mehl, *The Middle English Romances of the Thirteenth and Fourteenth Centuries* (London: Routledge and Kegan Paul, 1968), 17, 19, 121.

24. On the peerage see Maitland, *Constitutional History of England,* 166–71; the peerage was composed of earls and barons, along with the new ranks of duke, marquess, and viscount. For John Ball's question see Vogt, "History of a Sentiment," 116.

25. On the Gawain stories see Ramsey, *Chivalric Romances,* 200–208. On Chaucer see Jill Mann, *Chaucer and Medieval Estates Satire: The Literature of Social Classes and the General Prologue to the Canterbury Tales* (Cambridge: Cambridge University Press, 1973); Michael Stroud, "Chivalric Terminology in Late Medi-

eval Literature," *Journal of the History of Ideas,* 37 (1976), 323–34; Anne Middleton,
"Chaucher's 'New Men' and the Good of Literature in the *Canterbury Tales,*" in
Literature and Society: Selected Papers from the English Institute, 1978, ed. Edward W.
Said (Baltimore: Johns Hopkins University Press, 1980), 15–56; Terry Jones,
Chaucer's Knight: The Portrait of a Medieval Mercenary (London: Weidenfeld and
Nicolson, 1980). On William of Palerne see *William of Palerne: A New Edition,* ed.
Norman T. Simms (n.p.: Norwood Editions, 1973); Loomis, *Medieval Romance in
English,* 214–22; Ramsay, *Chivalric Romances,* 123–27 (the fourteenth-century
ME version is preceded by a twelfth-century French original).

    26. "Lord of Learne," l. 316, "The Nutt browne mayd," ll. 135–37, 199–200,
in *Bishop Percy's Folio Manuscript. Ballads and Romances,* ed. J. W. Hales and F. J.
Furnivall (London: N. Trübner, 1868), I, 193; III, 182, 184. "Lord of Learne" is a
ballad version of the fifteenth-century romance *Roswall and Lillian,* in which
knowledge of the boy's origins remains of greater importance; see parallel texts
edited by O. Lengert, *Englische Studien* (Leipzig), 16, no. 3 (1892), 321–56.

    27. "Thomas of Potte," ll. 22, 381, 384–89, in *Bishop Percy's Folio Manuscript,*
ed. cit., III, 135–50. As a boy, Samuel Richardson composed romances for his
schoolmates, one of whom requested that he write a "History" on the model of
"Tommy Potts": see Richardson to Stinstra, June 2, 1753, in *Selected Letters of
Samuel Richardson,* ed. John Carroll (Oxford: Clarendon Press, 1964), 231–32.

    28. *The Squyr of Lowe Degre, A Middle English Metrical Romance,* ed. W. E.
Mead (Boston: Ginn, 1904), ll. 69–70, 73–74, 79–80, 373–74, 377–80, 1085–88. I
have quoted from the most elaborate version. Mead notes many parallels with
Guy of Warwick (see pp. xxxvii, xlv), whose enormous popularity throughout this
period was maintained by frequent redactions, which themselves reflect the process of social specification I have been documenting. Thus by the seventeenth
century there existed a chapbook version for humble readers in which the gentle
origins of Guy's father are omitted and Guy becomes simply the industrious and
upwardly mobile son of a steward; see Margaret Spufford, *Small Books and Pleasant Histories: Popular Fiction and Its Readership in Seventeenth-Century England* (Athens: University of Georgia Press, 1982), 225, 227. On the redactions of *Guy of
Warwick* see also Ronald S. Crane, "The Vogue of *Guy of Warwick* from the Close
of the Middle Ages to the Romantic Revival," *PMLA,* 30 (1915), 125–94. With
these relatively slight romances compare *The Faerie Queene* (1590), in which
Britomart is both the ideal embodiment and the chivalric champion of chastity,
questing for a beloved of uncertain birth with whom, as Merlin foretells (III, iii),
she eventually will found the lineage of British royalty.

    29. Edward Waterhouse, *The Gentleman's Monitor; or, A Sober Inspection into
the Vertues, Vices, and Ordinary Means, Of the Rise and Decay of Men and Families*
(1665), 261–62. On the Heralds' Visitations and sumptuary legislation see Hill,
Reformation to Industrial Revolution, 49, 51; and N. B. Harte, "State Control of
Dress and Social Change in Pre-Industrial England," in *Trade, Government, and
Economy in Pre-Industrial England: Essays Presented to F. J. Fisher,* ed. D. C. Cole-
man and A. H. John (London: Weidenfeld and Nicolson, 1976), 132–65. On
scandalum magnatum see John C. Lassiter, "Defamation of Peers: The Rise and
Decline of the Action for *Scandalum Magnatum,* 1497–1773," *American Journal of
Legal History,* 22 (July, 1978), 219–20, 236. On the providential argument see
above, chap. 3, nn. 74–79.

    30. For the sixteenth-century argument on nobility and status hierarchy see
C. A. Patrides, "The Scale of Nature and Renaissance Treatises on Nobility,"
Studia Neophilologica, 36 (1964), 63–68; and Mohl, *Three Estates,* 332–40. On the

primogeniture debate see Joan Thirsk, "The European Debate on Customs of Inheritance, 1500–1700," in *Family and Inheritance: Rural Society in Western Europe, 1200–1800,* ed. Jack Goody, Joan Thirsk, and E. P. Thompson (Cambridge: Cambridge University Press, 1976), 177–91; see 183 on the question of how the emergence of debate itself is to be interpreted. For the degree speech see Shakespeare, *Troilus and Cressida* (1609), I, iii, 75–137. On the transformation of the doctrine of honor in the Elizabethan age see Mervyn James, *English Politics and the Concept of Honour, 1485–1642, Past and Present,* suppl. 3 (1978), 58–92.

31. See Lawrence Stone, *The Crisis of the Aristocracy, 1558–1641* (Oxford: Clarendon Press, 1965), 65 and chap. 3 passim (comparative figures are given for grants and creations at the ranks of gentleman, knight, baronet, baron, viscount, earl, marquis, and duke; the hereditary title 'baronet' was created in 1611); *The Institution of a Gentleman* (1586), bk. III, quoted in Mildred Campbell, *The English Yeoman under Elizabeth and the Early Stuarts* (New Haven: Yale University Press, 1942), 44–45; Edward Walker, *Observations upon the Inconveniencies that have attended the frequent Promotions to Titles of Honour and Dignity, since King James I. came to the Crown of England* (written 1653), in *Historical Discourses, upon Several Occasions . . .* (1705), 291, 300, 303 (Walker was Garter, Principal King of Arms); Thomas Scott, *The Belgick Pismire . . .* (1622), 30; John Rushworth, *Historical Collections* (1721), I, 334, 336, 337, quoted in Stone, *Crisis of the Aristocracy,* 113–14, 120; Lassiter, "Defamation of Peers," 222, 223.

32. Bod. Wood MSS. F21, quoted in Stone, *Crisis of the Aristocracy,* 77; Samuel Butler, *Prose Observations,* ed. Hugh de Quehen (Oxford: Oxford University Press, 1979), 122–23; idem, *Hudibras . . .* (1663), II, iii; idem, *Hudibras . . .* (1663), ed. Zachary Grey (1764), II, 63–64; Francis Bacon, *The New Organon* (1620), in *The Works of Francis Bacon,* ed. James Spedding, Robert L. Ellis, and Douglas D. Heath (London: Longmans, 1870), IV, 108–9.

33. See E. A. Wrigley and R. Schofield, *The Population History of England, 1541–1871: A Reconstruction* (Cambridge: Harvard University Press, 1982), 162, 402, and pullout 1, endpaper; J. P. Cooper, "Patterns of Inheritance and Settlement by Great Landowners from the Fifteenth to the Eighteenth Centuries," in *Family and Inheritance,* ed. Goody et al., 229–30; Stone and Stone, *An Open Elite?* 82–83, 100–09, 126–42, 276–77. On the meaning of the category "landed elite" employed by Stone and Stone see below, n. 45.

34. Among recent contributions to the controversy see Eileen Spring, "The Family, Strict Settlement, and Historians," *Canadian Journal of History,* 18 (Dec., 1983), 379–98; Lloyd Bonfield, "Marriage Settlements, 1660–1740: The Adoption of the Strict Settlement in Kent and Northamptonshire," in *Marriage and Society: Studies in the Social History of Marriage,* ed. R. B. Outhwaite (New York: St. Martin's, 1981), 103, 106, 114; idem, *Marriage Settlements, 1601–1740: The Adoption of the Strict Settlement* (Cambridge: Cambridge University Press, 1983), 119, 120, 122; Barbara English and John Saville, *Strict Settlement: A Guide for Historians,* Occasional Papers in Economic and Social History, no. 10 (Hull: Hull University Press, 1983), 11, 114; Randolph Trumbach, *The Rise of the Egalitarian Family: Aristocratic Kinship and Domestic Relations in Eighteenth-Century England* (New York: Academic Press, 1978), 70–71, 76, 116.

35. Daniel Defoe: *A Plan of the English Commerce . . . ,* 2nd ed. (1730) (New York: Augustus M. Kelley, 1967), 11; *Review,* III, no. 10 (Jan. 22, 1706); *The True-Born Englishman. A Satyr* (1700), 15, 20, 22; *The Compleat English Gentleman* (written 1728–29), ed. Karl D. Bülbring (London: David Nutt, 1890), 16–17.

36. Richard Allestree, *The Gentleman's Calling* ([1660] 1672), 132–34; Man-

deville, *Enquiry into the Origins of Honour,* ed. cit., 48, 86; idem, *The Fable of the Bees* (1714), ed. Phillip Harth (Harmondsworth: Penguin, 1970), "Remark (R)," 212–13; Richard Steele, *Tatler,* no. 25 (June 4–7, 1709).

37. Samuel Butler, *Characters* (written 1667–69), ed. Charles W. Daves (Cleveland: Case Western University Press, 1970), 69; William Sprigge, *A Modest Plea for an Equal Common-wealth Against Monarchy* . . . (1659), 77–78; Defoe, *Compleat Gentleman,* 21, 24, 28, 171; idem, *True-Born Englishman,* 70–71; Mandeville, *Fable,* "Remark (R)," 212. For the disengagement of "true nobility" from its strict service to aristocratic ideology, see Richard Brathwaite, *The English Gentleman* . . . (1630), sig. 2^{r-v}; and George MacKenzie, *Moral Gallantry* . . . (1669), sig. A5^r. See also the examples cited in Mason, *Gentlefolk,* 122, 124, 128, 156; W. L. Ustick, "Changing Ideals of Aristocratic Character and Conduct in Seventeenth Century England," *Modern Philology,* 30, no. 2 (1932), 152–53; Walzer, *Revolution of the Saints,* 250; and Jerrilyn G. Marston, "Gentry Honor and Royalism in Early Stuart England," *Journal of British Studies,* 13, no. 1 (1973), 21–43. Generalizations on the meaning of "honor" are based on usage in seventeenth-century drama; see C. L. Barber, *The Idea of Honour in the English Drama, 1591–1700,* Gothenburg Studies in English, 6 (Gothenburg: Elanders, 1957), 330–31. On the detachment of "history" from "romance" see above, chap. 1, nn. 69–70, 102.

38. For the anthropological account of marriage see Claude Lévi-Strauss, *The Elementary Structures of Kinship* (1949, 1967), especially as expounded by Randall Collins, "A Conflict Theory of Sexual Stratification," *Social Problems,* 19, no. 1 (Summer, 1971), 3–21, and Gayle Rubin, "The Traffic in Women: Notes on the 'Political Economy' of Sex," in *Toward an Anthropology of Women,* ed. Rayna R. Reiter (New York: Monthly Review Press, 1975), 157–210. For the common wisdom see, e.g., Mary Astell, *Some Reflections upon Marriage,* 4th ed. (1730) (New York: Source Book Press, 1970), 44; and below, chap. 11, n. 26. On the peculiarly English custom and on surrogate heirs see Stone and Stone, *An Open Elite?* 126–27.

39. *Critical Remarks on Sir Charles Grandison, Clarissa, and Pamela* (1754), intro. Alan D. McKillop, *Augustan Reprint Society,* no. 21, ser. IV, no. 3 (1950), 29–30, 32–33. On the medieval Church's interest in weakening kinship ties see above, nn. 13, 16.

40. On the intersexual double standard see Keith Thomas, "The Double Standard," *Journal of the History of Ideas,* 20, no. 2 (April, 1959), 203–4 and passim; Lawrence Stone, *The Family, Sex, and Marriage in England, 1500–1800* (New York: Harper and Row, 1977), 501–7, 636–37. On the intrasexual double standard see Thomas, "Double Standard," 206; Stone, *Family,* 191–93, 292–97; *Critical Remarks on Sir Charles Grandison,* 30, 33; Spufford, *Small Books,* 157–58, 162, 164–65, 187 n. 26. On the comical treatment of male chastity see Barber, *Honour,* 121, 309–10; and above, chap. 12, n. 31. For some well-known evidence that the genealogical explanation of the rule of female chastity was current in the eighteenth century, see James Boswell, *Life of Johnson,* ed. George Birkbeck Hill and L. F. Powell (Oxford: Clarendon Press, 1934), II, 55–56, 456–57; III, 406; V, 209. Johnson distinguishes the genealogical from the religious rationale by the former's inapplicability to men.

41. Butler, *Prose Observations,* 74; Astell, *Marriage,* 91–92. On the increased designation of "chastity" as "honor" during the seventeenth century see Barber, *Honour,* tables 4–6, pp. 91–93. The great example of this sort of progressive critique is, of course, Richardson's *Pamela* (1740): see above, chap. 11, sec. 2.

42. See E. A. Wrigley, "Marriage, Fertility and Population Growth in Eigh-

teenth-Century England," in *Marriage and Society,* ed. Outhwaite, 146, 162, 183; Stone, *Family,* 629–30, 637–38. For an interesting account of the novel which distinguishes the Freudian family romance into the paradigmatic careers of the foundling and the bastard, see Marthe Robert, *Origins of the Novel,* trans. Sacha Rabinovitch (Bloomington: Indiana University Press, 1980). Tony Tanner's restriction of "category-confusion" to the act of adultery also restricts his important discussion to what he calls the nineteenth-century "bourgeois" novel: see *Adultery in the Novel* (Baltimore: Johns Hopkins University Press, 1979), 12.

43. See R. H. Tawney, "The Rise of the Gentry, 1558–1640," *Economic History Review,* 11 (1941), 3 n. 1, 4; idem, "Rise of the Gentry: A Postscript," ibid., 2nd ser., 7 (1954), 93, 97; Stone, *Crisis of the Aristocracy,* chap. 2; idem, *The Causes of the English Revolution, 1529–1642* (London: Routledge and Kegan Paul, 1972), 33–34; Laslett, *The World We Have Lost,* chap. 2; Wagner, *English Genealogy,* 89–96; J. H. Hexter, "Storm over the Gentry," in *Reappraisals in History: New Views on History and Society in Early Modern Europe,* 2nd ed. (Chicago: University of Chicago Press, [1961] 1979), 128–29; Christopher Hill, *Puritanism and Revolution: Studies in Interpretation of the English Revolution of the Seventeenth Century* (London: Panther, 1968), 17–18; Perez Zagorin, *The Court and the Country: The Beginning of the English Revolution of the Mid-Seventeenth Century* (New York: Atheneum, 1970), 19–30; G. E. Mingay, *The Gentry: The Rise and Fall of a Ruling Class* (London: Longman, 1976), 2–4. For a recent review of the gentry controversy see R. C. Richardson, *The Debate on the English Revolution* (New York: St. Martin's, 1977). Throughout this discussion of the fruits of the gentry controversy my predominant concern with problems of definition should not be taken to discount the reality and force of disagreements that have arisen over empirical findings.

44. H. R. Trevor-Roper, "The Gentry, 1540–1640," *Economic History Review,* suppl. 1 (1953), 5 (see Hexter's quotation and discussion of this passage in "Storm over the Gentry," 127); Hill, *Puritanism and Revolution,* 18.

45. Hexter, "Storm over the Gentry," 128–29; idem, "The Myth of the Middle Class in Tudor England," in *Reappraisals in History,* 75, 95, 96–97 (see also 91); Stone, *Crisis of the Aristocracy,* 39, 13. For the use of the absorption model with reference to seventeenth-century Holland see Ivo Schöffer, "Did Holland's Golden Age Coincide with a Period of Crisis?" in *The General Crisis of the Seventeenth Century,* ed. Geoffrey Parker and Lesley M. Smith (London: Routledge and Kegan Paul, 1978), pp. 100–01. Stone has recently reversed his position on this subject, advancing findings which argue that the English aristocracy has been, if anything, unabsorptive of outsiders. But the criterion of upward mobility into the "aristocracy" on which this research is based—the purchase of a country seat and estate and the permanent establishment of a "county family"—is very precise, and Stone also acknowledges here the reality of varieties of *cultural* assimilation which by earlier and looser criteria might have qualified as absorption as such (see Stone and Stone, *An Open Elite?* 406–12). The revisionist picture of an unabsorptive English aristocracy has been supported by John Cannon, *Aristocratic Century: The Peerage of Eighteenth-Century England* (Cambridge: Cambridge University Press, 1985), whose equally precise criterion of upward mobility into the aristocracy is entry into the peerage. But Cannon's argument is vulnerable to the familiar accusation of categorial slippage, since in order to accommodate considerable evidence of upward mobility, "intra-peerage creation" expands to admit all those who had some sort of "connection" with the peerage, and "endogamous marriage" to include marriage to "close connections," landed gentry, etc. (see 20–25, 86). The kinds of connections upon which Cannon places considerable weight here are the political connections that facilitated the power of an aristocrat

in the eighteenth century; but these were not closely based upon "connections" in the kinship sense of the term (see Trumbach, *Egalitarian Family,* 62–63).

46. R. H. Tawney, "Harrington's Interpretation of His Age," Ralegh Lecture, *Proceedings of the British Academy,* 27 (1941), 207, quoted in Hexter, "Storm over the Gentry," 117. On the centrality of land and landownership in the discrimination of status during this period see, e.g., Stone, *Crisis of the Aristocracy,* 41.

47. Max Weber, "Class, Status, Party," in *From Max Weber: Essays in Sociology,* ed. H. H. Gerth and C. Wright Mills (New York: Oxford University Press, 1958), 186–87; Thomas Hobbes, *Leviathan* . . . (1651), I, x, 42, 44.

48. For the argument of a twelfth- or thirteenth-century rise, see Macfarlane, *English Individualism,* 196 and passim; and Hexter, "Myth of the Middle Class," 80–81. On the simple abstraction see above, Introduction, nn. 20–21.

49. On the meaning of Marx's dual usage see E. J. Hobsbawn, "Class Consciousness in History," in *Aspects of History and Class Consciousness,* ed. István Mészáros (New York: Herder and Herder, 1972), 5–8; E. P. Thompson, "Eighteenth-Century English Society: Class Struggle without Class?" *Social History,* 3 (1978), 146–50; see also idem, *The Making of the English Working Class* (New York: Vintage, 1966), chap. 16. For the argument of a nineteenth-century rise see Harold Perkin, *The Origins of Modern English Society, 1780–1880* (London: Routledge and Kegan Paul, 1969), chaps. 6–7 (for the absorption model see pp. 56–62); see also Diana Spearman, *The Novel and Society* (London: Routledge and Kegan Paul, 1966), chap. 1. For attempts to discuss these problems from a perspective more compatible with my own, see Rodney Hilton, "Capitalism—What's in a Name?" in *The Transition from Feudalism to Capitalism,* ed. Hilton (London: New Left Books, 1976), 145–58; R. S. Neale, "The Bourgeoisie, Historically, Has Played a Most Revolutionary Part," in *Feudalism, Capitalism, and Beyond,* ed. Eugene Kamenka and Neale (London: St. Martin's, 1975), 84–102; and idem, *Class in English History, 1680–1850* (Totowa, N.J.: Barnes and Noble, 1981), chaps. 1 and 3. For the social terminology of "class" before mid-century see especially Defoe, *Review,* no. 96 (Oct. 13, 1705); *The Great Law of Subordination consider'd* . . . (1724), 12, 14, 16, 287; *Conjugal Lewdness; or, Matrimonial Whoredom* . . . (1727), 257; and *The Compleat English Gentleman,* ed. cit., 18. On the later usage, see Asa Briggs, "The Language of 'Class' in early Nineteenth-Century England," in *Essays in Labour History,* ed. Briggs and John Saville (New York: St. Martin's, 1960), 43–73; and idem, "Middle-Class Consciousness in English Politics, 1780–1846," *Past and Present,* no. 9 (1956), 65–74.

50. Two versions of Gregory King's table exist: see *Natural and Political Observations and Conclusions upon the State and Condition of England, 1696,* app. to George Chalmers, *Estimate of the Comparative Strength of Great Britain* . . . (1804); and Charles Davenant, *An Essay upon the Probable Methods of making a People Gainers in the Balance of Trade* (1699), in *The Political and Commercial Works of . . . Charles D'Avenant* . . . , ed. Charles Whitworth (London: R. Horsfield, 1771), vol. II. On the significance of King's table see David Cressy, "Describing the Social Order of Elizabethan and Stuart England," *Literature and History,* no. 3 (March, 1976), 29–44; and G. S. Holmes, "Gregory King and the Social Structure of Preindustrial England," *Trans. Roy. Hist. Soc.,* 5th ser., 27 (1977), 52–54, 64–65. On Joseph Massie, *A Computation* . . . (1760), see Peter Matthias, "The Social Structure in the Eighteenth Century: A Calculation by Joseph Massie," in *The Transformation of England: Essays in the Economic and Social History of England in the Eighteenth Century* (New York: Columbia University Press, 1979), 171–89 (see 176, 186, and 188 for a comparison of Massie and King).

51. On the controversy over primogeniture and the fate of younger sons see

Joan Thirsk, "Younger Sons in the Seventeenth Century," *History,* 54 (1969), 358–77; and idem, "European Debate," 177–78, 183–85, 190. Conduct books and social commentary: see Helen S. Hughes, "The Middle-Class Reader and the English Novel," *Journal of English and Germanic Philology,* 25 (1926), 366–69; Walzer, *Revolution of the Saints,* 248–49; Lawrence Stone, "Social Mobility in England, 1500–1700," *Past and Present,* no. 33 (1966), 27–28, 52–53. Some recent empirical studies of the interpenetration of land and trade: Alan Everitt (the idea of the urban "pseudogentry"), "Social Mobility in Early Modern England," ibid., 70–72; idem, *Change in the Provinces: The Seventeenth Century,* Leicester University Department of English Local History Occasional Papers, 2nd ser., no. 1 (Leicester: Leicester University Press, 1972), 43–46 (see also Stone, "Social Mobility," 53); R. G. Lang, "Social Origins and Social Aspirations of Jacobean London Merchants," *Economic History Review,* 27 (1974), 40, 45 (sample of 140 London aldermen, 1600–1624); Nicholas Rogers, "Money, Land, and Lineage: The Big Bourgeoisie of Hanoverian London," *Social History,* 4 (1979), 444–45, 452–53 (also London aldermen); B. A. Holderness, "The English Land Market in the Eighteenth Century: The Case of Lincolnshire," *Economic History Review,* 2nd ser., 27, no. 4 (Nov., 1974), 557–76; Richard Grassby, "Social Mobility and Business Enterprise in Seventeenth-Century England," in *Puritans and Revolutionaries: Essays in Seventeenth-Century History Presented to Christopher Hill,* ed. Donald Pennington and Keith Thomas (Oxford: Clarendon Press, 1978), 356–57; Stone and Stone, *An Open Elite?* 154, 180, 211–12, 234, 237, 287–89, 406.

52. See, especially, W. A. Speck, "Social Status in Late Stuart England," *Past and Present,* no. 34 (1966), 127–29; idem, "Conflict in Society," in *Britain after the Glorious Revolution,* ed. Geoffrey Holmes (London: Macmillan, 1969), 145. See also J. G. A. Pocock, *The Machiavellian Moment: Florentine Political Thought and the Atlantic Republican Tradition* (Princeton: Princeton University Press, 1975), chap. 13; Marvin Rosen, "The Dictatorship of the Bourgeoisie: England, 1688–1721," *Science and Society,* 45, no. 1 (Spring, 1981), 24–51.

53. For the orthodox view see J. H. Plumb, *The Growth of Political Stability in England, 1675–1725* (Harmondsworth: Peregrine Books, 1969); Daniel A. Baugh, "Introduction: The Social Basis of Stability," in *Aristocratic Government and Society in Eighteenth-Century England: The Foundations of Stability,* ed. Baugh (New York: Franklin Watts, 1975), 1–23.

54. J. G. A. Pocock, "Introduction" to *Three British Revolutions: 1641, 1688, 1776,* ed. Pocock (Princeton: Princeton University Press, 1980), 6, 12, 14, 17; Christopher Hill, "A Bourgeois Revolution?" ibid., 121. On the early modern history of romance, see above, chap. 1, sec. 7. Following the gentry controversy it has become fairly common to suggest that the hypothetical rise of a "new" social group in early modern England (or Europe) be reconceived as the "transformation" or "reconstruction" of an old one: e.g., see Hexter, "Education of the Aristocracy in the Renaissance," 70; Walzer, *Revolution of the Saints,* 236 n. 12; Trumbach, *Egalitarian Family,* 11; Elizabeth L. Eisenstein, *The Printing Press as an Agent of Change: Communications and Cultural Transformations in Early Modern Europe* (Cambridge: Cambridge University Press, 1979), 396.

55. See Pocock, "Introduction," *Three British Revolutions,* ed. Pocock, 5, 7–9; see also Pocock, *Machiavellian Moment,* 432, 448, 460–461. For Hexter see above, n. 45. Marx's own inconsistent usage is partly responsible for the confusing equation of "bourgeois" with "middle class" or "capitalist." For an illuminating discussion see Neale, "The Bourgeoisie," in *Feudalism, Capitalism, and Beyond,* ed. Kamenka and Neale, 85–89.

56. C. B. Macpherson, *The Political Theory of Possessive Individualism: Hobbes*

to Locke (Oxford: Oxford University Press, 1962), 193. On enclosure see most recently J. R. Wordie, "The Chronology of English Enclosure, 1500–1914," *Economic History Review,* 2nd ser., 36, no. 4 (Nov., 1983), 502 and passim. On agrarian capitalist improvement see also Stone, *Crisis of the Aristocracy,* chaps. 6 and 7; Hexter, "Myth of the Middle Class," 86–90; Stone and Stone, *An Open Elite?* 282–86, 419–20; Perkin, *Modern English Society,* 63–67, 73–80; Joyce O. Appleby, *Economic Thought and Ideology in Seventeenth-Century England* (Princeton: Princeton University Press, 1978), 275. On the unity of rural and urban capitalist enterprise see Tawney, "Rise of the Gentry," 17–18; Richard Grassby, "English Merchant Capitalism in the Late Seventeenth Century: The Composition of Business Fortunes," *Past and Present,* no. 46 (1970), 106. In general, see John Merrington, "Town and Country in the Transition to Capitalism," in *Transition from Feudalism to Capitalism,* ed. Hilton, 170–95.

57. For suggestive summary discussions of these fifteenth- and sixteenth-century developments, see Perry Anderson, *Lineages of the Absolutist State* (London: New Left Books, 1974), 124–27; Stone and Stone, *An Open Elite?* 256–58, in explanation of a "new" terminology of "the landed elite." On twelfth-century romance see above, n. 17. On the word "aristocracy" see the *OED.*

58. On "social theater" in eighteenth-century England, see E. P. Thompson, "Patrician Society, Plebeian Culture," *Journal of Social History,* 7 (1974), 382–405. On the antithetical and the thetical simple abstraction see above, chap. 1, n. 70.

59. Jonathan Swift, *An Enquiry into the Behaviour of the Queen's last Ministry . . .* (1715), in *The Prose Works of Jonathan Swift,* vol. VIII: *Political Tracts, 1713–19,* ed. Herbert Davis and Irvin Ehrenpreis (Oxford: Blackwell, 1953), 135; Swift to Charles Ford, Dec. 8, 1719, *The Correspondence of Jonathan Swift,* ed. Harold Williams (Oxford: Clarendon Press, 1963), II, 331; Jonathan Swift, "The Foolish Methods of Education among the Nobility," (Irish) *Intelligencer,* no. 9 (1728), in *Prose Works,* vol. XII: *Irish Tracts, 1728–1733,* ed. Herbert Davis (Oxford: Blackwell, 1964), 53.

60. Jonathan Swift, *Examiner,* no. 40 (May 10, 1711), in *Prose Works,* vol. III: *The Examiner and Other Pieces Written in 1710–11,* ed. Herbert Davis (Oxford: Blackwell, 1940), 150–51 (see also idem, "Foolish Methods of Education," ed. cit., 48); Davenant, *Essay upon the Probable Methods,* ed. cit., II, 367–68.

61. See Christopher Hill, *The Century of Revolution, 1603–1714* (New York: Norton, 1966), 280–85; idem, *Reformation to Industrial Revolution,* 196, 213–14, 267; Isaac Kramnick, *Bolingbroke and His Circle: The Politics of Nostalgia in the Age of Walpole* (Cambridge: Harvard University Press, 1968), 171–72. See also Thompson, "Eighteenth-Century English Society," 144.

62. Walker, *Observations,* in *Historical Discourses,* 305; Henry St. John, Viscount Bolingbroke, *A Dissertation Upon Parties* (1733–34), in *The Works of Lord Bolingbroke* (Philadelphia: Carey and Hart, 1841), II, 165; Sprigge, *A Modest Plea* 61; Champianus Northtonus, *The Younger Brother's Advocate . . .* (1655), 4; David Hume, *A Treatise of Human Nature* (1739–40), 2nd ed., ed. L. A. Selby-Bigge and P. H. Nidditch (Oxford: Clarendon Press, 1978), II, i, 323.

63. Walter G. Runciman, *Relative Deprivation and Social Justice: A Study of Attitudes to Social Inequality in Twentieth-Century England* (Berkeley and Los Angeles: University of California Press, 1966), 9 (see also 10–11); Robert K. Merton, *Social Theory and Social Structure,* rev. ed. (Glencoe, Ill.: Free Press, 1957), 235, 240–41 (Alice Rossi collaborated on chap. 8). See also John Urry, *Reference Groups and the Theory of Revolution* (London: Routledge and Kegan Paul, 1973), 13, 17. For a very useful discussion of the literature see Stone, *Causes of the English Revolution,* chap. 1. Compare Peter Laslett's odd presumption "that neither yeo-

man, husbandman, pauper nor craftsman, nor even a gentleman, in the pre-industrial world would be likely to change his reference group in such a way as to feel aware of what is called relative deprivation" (*The World We Have Lost*, 215).

64. For examples of the criticism and the response see Theda Skocpol, *States and Social Revolutions: A Comparative Analysis of France, Russia, and China* (Cambridge: Cambridge University Press, 1979), 9, 296–97 n. 19; and Isaac Kramnick, "Reflections on Revolution: Definition and Explanation in Recent Scholarship," *History and Theory*, 11 (1972), 41–44. Skocpol also criticizes modern Marxists for a similar failing consequent on overemphasizing the importance of class-consciousness in revolutionary behavior. And she quotes Eric Hobsbawn to the effect that "theories which overstress the voluntarist or subjective elements in revolution, are to be treated with caution" ("Revolution," paper presented at 14th International Congress of Historical Sciences, San Francisco, Aug., 1975, 10; quote on 18). But there is an important distinction to be made between *voluntarist* elements—which assume conscious will and may even imply a fit between revolutionary aims and achievements—and *subjective* elements, which do neither, instead only making the crucial addition of subjective to objective forces in the determination of revolutionary behavior. For Marx's own articulation of reference-group principles, see *Wage Labour and Capital* (1849), in Karl Marx and Friedrich Engels, *Selected Works* (Moscow: Foreign Language Publishing House, 1962), I, 94. On the dialectical theory of genre see above, Introduction.

65. For the extension of revolutionary behavior to cultural activity, see Kramnick, "Reflections on Revolution," 31–32; Stone, *Causes of the English Revolution*, 14; Paul Schrecker, "Revolution as a Problem in the Philosophy of History," *Nomos* VIII, *Revolution*, ed. Carl J. Friedrich (New York: Atherton, 1966), 34–53; Perez Zagorin, "Prolegomena to the Comparative History of Revolution in Early Modern Europe," *Comparative Studies in Society and History*, 18 (1976), 166–67, 173–74. Kramnick and Zagorin both instance the influential extensions of "revolution" to the realm of "knowledge production" by Thomas S. Kuhn, *The Structure of Scientific Revolutions*, 2nd ed. (Chicago: University of Chicago Press, 1970). Schrecker discusses "revolutions" in literary or artistic style. Laslett (*The World We Have Lost*, chap. 8) lodges a wholesale protest against the understanding of seventeenth-century England as "revolutionary."

66. Aegremont Ratcliffe, trans., *Politique Discourses* . . . (1578), sig. A3b, quoted in Kelso, *English Gentleman*, 32.

CHAPTER FIVE: ABSOLUTISM AND CAPITALIST IDEOLOGY:
THE VOLATILITY OF REFORM

1. See Christopher Hill, *Reformation to Industrial Revolution, 1530–1780*, Pelican Economic History of Britain, vol. 2 (Harmondsworth: Penguin, 1971), 135, 146–48, 155, 169, 180, 184; Alan Macfarlane, *The Origins of English Individualism: The Family, Property, and Social Transition* (New York: Cambridge University Press, 1979), 184, 203, and passim. On the discovery of feudalism see above, chap. 1, nn. 57–61.

2. Fiscal feudalism: see Joel Hurstfield, "The Revival of Feudalism in Early Tudor England," *History*, n.s., 37 (1952), 131–45; idem, "The Profits of Fiscal Feudalism, 1541–1602," *Economic History Review*, 2nd ser., 8 (1955–56), 53; Christopher Hill, *The Century of Revolution, 1603–1714* (New York: Norton, 1966), 49–50, 55; see also Peter Roebuck, "Post-Restoration Landownership: The Impact of the Abolition of Wardship," *Journal of British Studies*, 18 (Fall, 1978), 67–

85. Bastard feudalism: see W. H. Dunham, "Lord Hastings' Indentured Retainers, 1461–1483: The Lawfulness of Livery and Retaining under the Yorkists and Tudors," *Transactions of the Connecticut Academy of Arts and Sciences*, 39 (1957), 7; Helen Cam, "The Decline and Fall of English Feudalism," *History*, 25 (1940), 223–26, 232; K. B. MacFarlane, "Bastard Feudalism," *Bull. Inst. Hist. Rsch.*, 20 (1943–45), 161–80; idem, "Parliament and Bastard Feudalism," *Trans. Roy. Hist. Soc.*, 4th ser., 26 (1944), 53–79; J. H. Hexter, "Storm over the Gentry," in *Reappraisals in History: New Views on Society and History in Early Modern Europe*, 2nd ed. (Chicago: University of Chicago Press, [1961] 1979), 144–48; V. J. Scattergood, *Politics and Poetry in the Fifteenth Century* (New York: Barnes and Noble, 1972), 308. Irrational capitalism: Max Weber, *General Economic History*, trans. Frank H. Knight (London: Allen and Unwin, 1927), 350; see also idem, *The Protestant Ethic and the Spirit of Capitalism*, trans. Talcott Parsons (New York: Charles Scribner's [1904–5] 1958), 152; A. D. Lublinskaya, *French Absolutism: The Crucial Phase, 1620–29*, trans. Brian Pearce (Cambridge: Cambridge University Press, 1968), 7–8.

3. See the discussions by Brian Manning, "The Nobles, the People, and the Constitution," in *Crisis in Europe, 1560–1660*, ed. Trevor Aston (New York: Anchor Books, 1967), 261–71; and Perry Anderson, *Lineages of the Absolutist State* (London: New Left Books, 1974), 18, 429.

4. Daniel Defoe, *The Compleat English Gentleman* (written 1728–29), ed. Karl D. Bülbring (London: David Nutt, 1890), 62–63; J. H. Hexter, "The Myth of the Middle Class in Tudor England," in *Reappraisals in History*, 114. See also Anderson, *Lineages*, 429–30.

5. Ernst H. Kantorowicz, *The King's Two Bodies: A Study in Medieval Political Theology* (Princeton: Princeton University Press, 1957), 235. See G. R. Elton, Introduction to *The Divine Right of Kings*, by John N. Figgis (New York: Harper Torchbooks, [1896] 1965); Gordon J. Schochet, *Patriarchalism in Political Thought: The Authoritarian Family and Political Speculation and Attitudes Especially in Seventeenth-Century England* (New York: Basic Books, 1975), 54–55, 86; and Ernst H. Kantorowicz, "Mysteries of State: An Absolutist Concept and Its Late Medieval Origins," in *Selected Studies* (Locust Valley, N.Y.: J. J. Augustin, 1965), 381–98 (see also idem, *The King's Two Bodies*, 93; chap. 4, sec. 3; and chap. 5, secs. 1 and 2).

6. Peter Heylyn, *Aerius redivivus; or, The History of the Presbyterians* (Oxford: 1670), 447, quoted in Corinne C. Weston and Janelle R. Greenberg, *Subjects and Sovereigns: The Grand Controversy over Legal Sovereignty in Stuart England* (Cambridge: Cambridge University Press, 1981), 47; *Remonstrance of both Houses . . .*, printed in J. P. Kenyon, ed., *The Stuart Constitution, 1603–1688: Documents and Commentary* (Cambridge: Cambridge University Press, 1966), 243; *Declaration of the Lords and Commons . . .*, quoted in Kantorowicz, *The King's Two Bodies*, 21; Anthony Ascham, *Of the Confusions and Revolutions of Goverments* [sic] *. . .* (1649), 4.

7. Christopher Hill, "The Norman Yoke," in *Puritanism and Revolution: Studies in Interpretation of the English Revolution of the Seventeenth Century* (London: Panther, 1968), 81. On the common-law argument and its place in the historical revolution see above, chap. 1, nn. 58–61. On its role in the attempt to formulate a nonmonarchal theory of sovereignty see Hill, *Century of Revolution*, 53–55, 60–68.

8. Charles I, "Answer to the Nineteen Propositions," June 18, 1642, in Kenyon, *Stuart Constitution*, 22–23. On the principle of the coordinate powers see Weston and Greenberg, *Subjects and Sovereigns*, 34–49 and chaps. 3 and 4 passim.

9. See Christopher Hill, *The World Turned Upside Down: Radical Ideas during the English Revolution* (New York: Viking, 1972), 11–13; idem, *Century of Revolution*, 130–33. On the Engagement Controversy see the discussion by John M. Wallace, *Destiny His Choice: The Loyalism of Andrew Marvell* (Cambridge: Cambridge University Press, 1968), 43–68. For antiaristocratic sentiments see, besides Hill, *World Turned Upside Down*, Brian Manning, *The English People and the English Revolution, 1640–1649* (New York: Holmes and Meier, 1976), 254–61.

10. William Sherlock, *The Case of the Allegiance due to Sovereign Powers* (1691); Edward Stillingfleet, *A Discourse Concerning the Unreasonableness of a New Separation* (1689), 32, and idem, "An Answer to the Paper delivered by Mr. Ashton," in *A Collection of State Tracts for the Reign of William III* (1705–11), II, 106; all quoted in Gerald M. Straka, *Anglican Reaction to the Revolution of 1688*, State Historical Society of Wisconsin (Madison: University of Wisconsin Press, 1962), 71, 55, 33. For the Act of Settlement see E. Neville Williams, ed., *The Eighteenth-Century Constitution, 1688–1815: Documents and Commentary* (Cambridge: Cambridge University Press, 1960), 56; see the discussion in Straka, *Anglican Reaction*, 105.

11. *A Discourse on Hereditary Right, Written in the year 1712, By a Celebrated Clergyman* (n.d.), 8, quoted in Margaret Steele, "Anti-Jacobite Pamphleteering, 1701–1720," *Scottish Historical Review*, 60, no. 2 (Oct., 1981), 146. On assimilation and supersession see above, chap. 4, nn. 46, 66. On the discovered manuscript topos and the claim to historicity see above, chap. 1, nn. 102–6. On the doctrine of providence see above, chap. 3, nn. 75–80. In some respects, the revolution in the laws of settlement and inheritance was more radical on the public scale of kingship than on the private scale of landed property: by the device of the strict settlement, a younger son could not displace his older brother as sole heir of the estate even if the latter was a Roman Catholic. See Barbara English and John Saville, *Strict Settlement: A Guide for Historians* (Hull: University of Hull Press, 1983), 24.

12. See Ruth Kelso, *The Doctrine of the English Gentleman in the Sixteenth Century*, University of Illinois Studies in Language and Literature, 14, nos. 1–2 (Feb.–May, 1929), 29–30, 40–41; Arthur B. Ferguson, *The Indian Summer of English Chivalry* (Durham: Duke University Press, 1960), 76–78, 119, 127, 135, 195, 204–5; Anderson, *Lineages*, 37–39; J. H. Hexter, "The Education of the Aristocracy in the Renaissance," in *Reappraisals in History*, 66–67, 69–70; Joel Hurstfield, "Tradition and Change in the English Renaissance," in *Freedom, Corruption, and Government in Elizabethan England* (Cambridge: Harvard University Press, 1973), 216–17; J. G. A. Pocock, *The Machiavellian Moment: Florentine Political Thought and the Atlantic Republican Tradition* (Princeton: Princeton University Press, 1975), 338–40; Michael Walzer, *The Revolution of the Saints: A Study in the Origins of Radical Politics* (Cambridge: Harvard University Press, 1965), 237. For an extended treatment of some of these themes see Arthur B. Ferguson, *The Articulate Citizen and the English Renaissance* (Durham: Duke University Press, 1965).

13. Lawrence Stone: see *The Crisis of the Aristocracy, 1558–1641* (Oxford: Clarendon Press, 1965), chaps. 5, 8; see also Anderson, *Lineages*, 32–33, 125, 127; and Mervyn James, *English Politics and the Concept of Honour, 1485–1642, Past and Present*, suppl. 3 (1978), 18–19, 22–23. Arthur B. Ferguson: *Indian Summer*, 10; cf. Johan Huizinga, *The Waning of the Middle Ages* (Garden City, N.Y.: Anchor Books, [1924] 1954), 39, 72: "The essence of chivalry is the imitation of the ideal hero, just as the imitation of the ancient sage is the essence of humanism . . . Thus the aspiration to the splendour of antique life, which is the characteristic of the Renaissance, has its roots in the chivalrous ideal." On the "recovery" of

chivalric literature see also above, chap. 1, nn. 68–69. "Letters" over "arms": see
Kelso, *English Gentleman,* 43–49. "Carpet knight": e.g., see Robert Greene, *Carde of Fancie* (1584), title page, in *Shorter Novels: Elizabethan,* ed. Philip Henderson
(London: J. M. Dent, 1972), 157; Thomas Nashe, *The Unfortunate Traveller*
(1594), ibid., 336; and the chapbook version of *Don Flores of Greece,* quoted in
Margaret Spufford, *Small Books and Pleasant Histories: Popular Fiction and Its Readership in Seventeenth-Century England* (Athens: University of Georgia Press, 1982),
234; see also above, chap. 7, n. 11. On the two nobilities, status inconsistency, and
the problematic role of the bourgeoisie see P. J. Coveney, ed., *France in Crisis,
1620–1675* (Totawa, N.J.: Rowman and Littlefield, 1977), 16–20 and chap. 4; see
also J. H. M. Salmon, "Storm over the Noblesse," *Journal of Modern History,* 53,
no. 2 (June, 1981), 242–57.

14. Baldesar Castiglione, *The Book of the Courtier,* trans. Charles S. Singleton
(Garden City, N.Y.: Anchor Books, 1959), I, 28–32. All parenthetical citations in
the text are to this edition.

15. On the social utility of courtly love in the twelfth century see above, chap.
4, nn. 16–18.

16. Niccolò Machiavelli, *The Prince,* in *The Prince and the Discourses,* trans.
Luigi Ricci and E. R. P. Vincent (New York: Modern Library, 1950), II, 5–6; all
parenthetical citations in the text are to this edition.

17. For Bacon see above, chap. 2, n. 2. On Mandeville and the latitudinarians
see below, nn. 42–43, 49.

18. See also *Discourses on the First Ten Books of Titus Livius* (1531), trans.
Christian E. Detmold, in Machiavelli, *The Prince and the Discourses,* ed. cit., II,
xxix, 380–83.

19. British Library Harleian MS. 6918, fol. 34, quoted in Alan Everitt,
Change in the Provinces: the Seventeenth Century, Leicester University Department
of English Local History Occasional Papers, 2nd ser., no. 1 (Leicester: Leicester
University Press, 1972), 49; see also Walzer, *Revolution of the Saints,* 253. "Court
versus Country": see the discussion by H. R. Trevor-Roper, "The Gentry, 1540–
1640," *Economic History Review,* suppl. 1 (1953), 26–30; and idem, "The General
Crisis of the Seventeenth Century," in *Crisis in Europe,* ed. Aston, 63–102
(Trevor-Roper rejects "absolutism" as a historical category, instead using "Renaissance state"); and Perez Zagorin, *The Court and the Country: The Beginning of
the English Revolution of the Mid-Seventeenth Century* (New York: Atheneum,
1970). Interregnum officeholding: see G. E. Aylmer, *The State's Servants: The
Civil Service of the English Republic, 1649–1660* (London: Routledge and Kegan
Paul, 1973).

20. Oliver Cromwell to Suffolk County committee, Aug. 29 and Sept. 28,
1643, in *The Writings and Speeches of Oliver Cromwell,* ed. Wilbur C. Abbott
(Cambridge: Harvard University Press, 1937), I, 256, 262; Andrew Marvell,
"The First Anniversary of the Government under His Highness the Lord Protector, 1655," ll. 387–88, in *Andrew Marvell: The Complete Poems,* ed. Elizabeth S.
Donno (Harmondsworth: Penguin, 1978), 136. On the New Model Army see
Mark Kishlansky, "The Case of the Army Truly Stated: The Creation of the New
Model Army," *Past and Present,* no. 81 (Nov., 1978), 58; see also idem, *The Rise of
the New Model Army* (Cambridge: Cambridge University Press, 1979). On mas-
terless men and the Army see Hill, *World Turned Upside Down,* chaps. 3 and 4. For
the ordinance see S. R. Gardiner, ed., *The Constitutional Documents of the Puritan
Revolution, 1625–1660* (Oxford: Clarendon Press, 1899), 287–88.

21. Earl of Clarendon, *The Parliamentary History of England* (London: Han-
sard, 1806–20), IV, 206; idem, *The History of the Rebellion,* ed. W. D. Macray

(Oxford: Clarendon Press, 1888), VI, 176; Hill, *Century of Revolution*, 189. On the development of the opposition to standing armies see Lois G. Schwoerer, *"No Standing Armies!" The Antiarmy Ideology in Seventeenth-Century England* (Baltimore: Johns Hopkins University Press, 1974). On the landed and monied interests see above, chap. 4, n. 52. On the connection between the early-century country interest and the late-century landed interest see Trevor-Roper, "Gentry," 52–53.

22. Joseph Glanvill, *Scepsis Scientifica* . . . (1665), "An Address to the Royal Society," sig. b2^v, b3^v–b4^r; Thomas Sprat, *The History of the Royal-Society of London* . . . (1667), 404–5; Henry Stubbe, *Legends no Histories* . . , (1670), sig. *2^{r-v}. Compare the civic humanist argument of [William London], *A Catalogve of The most vendible Books in England* . . . (1657), "Epistle Dedicatory," sig. A3^v–A4^v. On these matters I part company with Pocock, *Machiavellian Moment*, whose formulation of the split between what he calls the "Country" and the "Court ideology" (486–87) reflects his far greater emphasis on the influence of a Machiavellian tradition of civic humanism, his neglect of the contribution of economic discourse to the ideological conflict, and his belief that seventeenth-century Protestant thought played a negligible role in the justification of capitalist activity (see 423, 440, 445–46, 464). Unlike Pocock, moreover, I take both ideologies to possess a theory of virtue. In fact it is in order to provide rival accounts of the relationship between virtue, status, and action in the modern world that they are principally designed. Finally, I take the formation of capitalist ideology in the seventeenth century to provide a major impetus for the formation of progressive and conservative ideology—again unlike Pocock, who sees capitalist ideology as an eighteenth-century reaction to country ideology.

23. Christopher Hill, "Social and Economic Consequences of the Henrician Reformation," in *Puritanism and Revolution*, 47. On the English Reformation as an "absolutist" act of state see also Hill, *Reformation*, pt. II, chap. 1.

24. *Corpus Reformatorum*, ed. G. Baum et al. (Brunswick, W. Germany, 1863–97), 46, 136, quoted in David Little, *Religion, Order, and Law: A Study in Pre-Revolutionary England* (New York: Harper, 1969), 61; and see chap. 3 passim. See also R. H. Tawney, *Religion and the Rise of Capitalism: A Historical Study* (New York: Mentor Books, [1926] 1958), 83–84, 90–91.

25. Conflict between Elizabethan Puritans and Anglicans on political theory: see, generally, Little, *Religion, Order, and Law*, chaps. 4 and 5. Recent work: cf. Tawney, *Religion and the Rise of Capitalism*, chap. 2; Charles H. George and Katherine George, *The Protestant Mind of the English Reformation, 1570–1640* (Princeton: Princeton University Press, 1961), 128–29, 134–35, 163–72; Michael Walzer, "Puritanism as a Revolutionary Ideology," *History and Theory*, 3 (1963–64), 66–68; Timothy H. Breen, "The Non-existent Controversy: Puritan and Anglican Attitudes on Work and Wealth, 1600–1640," *Church History*, 35 (1966), 273–87; Paul Seaver, "The Puritan Work Ethic Revisited," *Journal of British Studies*, 19, no. 2 (Spring, 1980), 35–53.

26. See Weber, *Protestant Ethic*, 112–16; Tawney, *Religion and the Rise of Capitalism*, 96; and William Haller, *The Rise of Puritanism* (New York: Harper Torchbooks, 1957), 86–88. For useful collections of documents relating to the Weber thesis controversy, see M. J. Kitch, ed., *Capitalism and the Reformation*, Problems and Perspectives in History (London: Longman, 1967), and Robert W. Green, ed., *Protestantism, Capitalism, and Social Science: The Weber Thesis Controversy*, 2nd ed., Problems in European Civilization (Lexington, Mass.: D. C. Heath, 1973).

27. Hill, *World Turned Upside Down*, 126; Samuel Hieron, *Sermons* (1624), 373

(quoted in ibid., 330); Haller, *Rise of Puritanism*, 89. On the problem of mediation see above, chap. 2, sec. 3.

28. Edmund Calamy, *The Noblemans Pattern of true and real Thankfulness* (1643), quoted in Manning, *The English People*, 259; Thomas Edwards, "The Holy Choice," in *Three Sermons* (1625), 63–64, quoted in Walzer, *Revolution of the Saints*, 235; Thomas Hooker, *The Christians Two Chiefe Lessons* . . . (1640), 288, quoted in David Leverenz, *The Language of Puritan Feeling: An Exploration in Literature, Psychology, and Social History* (New Brunswick, N.J.: Rutgers University Press, 1980), 119 (on the language of the family romance see, generally, chap. 4); Oliver Cromwell, *The Letters and Speeches of Oliver Cromwell*, ed. Thomas Carlyle (London, 1893), III, 52, quoted in Walzer, *Revolution of the Saints*, 266. Although prohibited from bearing heraldic arms, common people traditionally made "marks" or "notes" that represented the implements of their trade and were in some sense analogous to armorial bearings. See the discussions by Andrew Favyn, *The Theater of Honour and Knight-hood* . . . (1623, trans. from French of 1620), 16; and David Cressy, *Literacy and the Social Order: Reading and Writing in Tudor and Stuart England* (Cambridge: Cambridge University Press, 1980), 55 (examples are reproduced on 60). Edmund Bolton, *The Cities Advocate* . . . (1629), 5–8, discusses and depicts the heraldic arms that have traditionally represented the honor of the City of London and its guilds. With Cromwell's Puritan alternative to the armorial bearings of the nobility, compare Thomas Sprat's "new-philosophical" advice that the armigerous devote more serious attention to the natural creatures that "are the chief *Instruments* of *Heraldry* . . . If they value the *Antiquity* of *Families*, and long race of *Pedigrees*: What can be more worthy their consideration than all the divers lineages of *Nature?*" (*History of the Royal-Society*, 411).

29. Tawney, *Religion and the Rise of Capitalism*, 200–201; John Ward, *God Judging Among the Gods* (1645), 16, quoted in Walzer, *Revolution of the Saints*, 235.

30. Denis Greenville, *Counsel and Directions Divine and Moral* (1685), 112–13, quoted in W. L. Ustick, "Changing Ideals of Aristocratic Character and Conduct in Seventeenth-Century England," *Modern Philology*, 30, no. 2 (1932), 160; Walzer, *Revolution of the Saints*, 253–54, 252. On the amalgamation of sainthood and gentility compare Bernard Mandeville, *An Enquiry into the Origins of Honour and the Usefulness of Christianity in War* (1732), ed. M. M. Goldsmith (London: Frank Cass, 1971), 232. The most important of the seventeenth-century conduct books is Richard Brathwaite's *The English Gentleman* . . . (1630): see Ustick, "Ideals of Aristocratic Character," 155; and Kelso, *English Gentleman*, 107.

31. Weber, *Protestant Ethic*, 110–11, 115, 129; Tawney, *Religion and the Rise of Capitalism*, 96; Weber, *Protestant Ethic*, 115.

32. Mary Astell, *Some Reflections upon Marriage* . . . , 4th ed. (1730) (New York: Source Book Press, 1970), 99.

33. Richard Hooker, *Works*, ed. John Keble (London, 1888), II, 342–43, quoted in Little, *Religion, Order, and Law*, 152; Hill, *World Turned Upside Down*, 124; Haller, *Rise of Puritanism*, 90–91. On Calvinist individualization and internalization see, especially, the acute analyses by Hill, *World Turned Upside Down*, 76–77, 121–24, 128, 300–301. On individualism and collectivism in Weber's reading of Calvin's thought, see Little, *Religion, Order, and Law*, 76n.173, 110–11 n.112, 235.

34. Walzer, *Revolution of the Saints*, 252; on Puritanism as a response to social mobility see idem, "Puritanism as a Revolutionary Ideology," 86, 88. On the dialectical relationship of Puritan doctrine and social and physical mobility, see Lawrence Stone, "Social Mobility in England, 1500–1700," *Past and Present*, no.

33 (1966), 43–44, 49–50; and Hill, *World Turned Upside Down,* chap. 3. Of the antithetical ideal types, Walzer tends to concentrate on the negative response, to the neglect of the positive alternative. On the transvaluation of honor see, generally, chap. 4, sec. 4, above.

35. Richard B. Schlatter, *The Social Ideas of Religious Leaders, 1660–1688* (Oxford: Oxford University Press, 1940), 188, 197; cf. Tawney, *Religion and the Rise of Capitalism,* 202–4. Collinges: J. C., *The Weavers Pocket-Book; or, Weaving Spiritualized . . .* (1675), 133. On the Lutheran accusation see Weber, *Protestant Ethic,* 115. On the pedagogy of spiritualization see above, chap. 2, n. 23. On "visible saints" see Christopher Hill, *Society and Puritanism in Pre-Revolutionary England* (London: Panther, 1969), 248–50.

36. Jonathan Swift, *A Tale of a Tub, To which is added The Battle of the Books and the Mechanical Operation of the Spirit,* ed. A. C. Guthkelch and D. Nichol Smith, 2nd ed. (Oxford: Clarendon Press, 1958), sec. XI, p. 200; see also "A Discourse Concerning the Mechanical Operation of the Spirit, &c.," ibid., pp. 259–89. The argument that papists and Protestant sectarians were extremes that met was a commonplace, particularly in consideration of their common political interests after the Restoration: see Michael McKeon, *Politics and Poetry in Restoration England: The Case of Dryden's Annus Mirabilis* (Cambridge: Harvard University Press, 1975), 132–33.

37. On Weber's treatment of the Reformation as a positive secularization see Little, *Religion, Order, and Law,* 1, 235.

38. Richard Steele, *The Trades-man's Calling . . .* (1684), 204; Joseph Lee, *A Vindication of the Considerations Concerning Common-Fields and Inclosures* (1656), 41, quoted in Hill, *Reformation,* 152; Richard Baxter, *A Christian Directory; or, A Summ of Practical Theologie and Cases of Conscience . . . ,* 2nd ed. (1678), IV, 212. On the popularity of problems of fair dealing in the casuistical literature, see George A. Starr, *Defoe and Casuistry* (Princeton: Princeton University Press, 1971), e.g., 16.

39. John Bunyan, *The Life and Death of Mr. Badman . . .* (1680), 221; John Cook, *Unum Necessarium . . .* (1648), 13, quoted in Joyce O. Appleby, *Economic Thought and Ideology in Seventeenth-Century England* (Princeton: Princeton University Press, 1978), 56; R. Steele, *Trades-man's Calling,* 107; *The Grounds of Sovereignty and Greatness* (1675), 19–20, quoted in J. A. W. Gunn, *Politics and the Public Interest in the Seventeenth Century* (London: Routledge and Kegan Paul, 1969), 213. For the general rule of thumb see George and George, *Protestant Mind,* 172; Walzer, "Puritanism as a Revolutionary Ideology," 66–67; Breen, "Nonexistent Controversy," 284; Seaver, "Puritan Work Ethic Revisited," 49. On the eclipse of the rules of charity and necessity during the Restoration period see Schlatter, *Social Ideas of Religious Leaders,* 189, 204n.2, 209–11.

40. Andrew Marvell, *The Character of Holland* (1653?), ll. 71–74, in *Complete Poems,* ed. cit., 113. After the Restoration, Marvell was to extend the analogy, and the critique, to the field of intellectual controversy, where absolute freedom of invective threatened to institutionalize a system of free enterprise whose first principle was that no one shall be free of his neighbor's competitive aggression. " 'Tis better that evil men should be left in an undisturbed possession of their repute, how unjustly soever they may have acquired it, then that the Exchange and Credit of mankind should be universally shaken, wherein the best too will suffer and be involved": *The Rehearsal Transpros'd* (1672–73), ed. D. I. B. Smith (Oxford, Clarendon Press, 1971), 161. On the radical sectarians see Hill, *World Turned Upside Down,* chaps. 6 and 8; and on Winstanley, in particular, see ibid., chap. 7 and app. 1.

41. On the commonplace association of freedom of trade and freedom of conscience, see Schlatter, *Social Ideal of Religious Leaders,* pt. 3; Gunn, *Politics and the Public Interest,* chap. 4. The radical solvent of Puritan activism: see Christopher Hill, "Protestantism and the Rise of Capitalism," in *Essays in the Economic and Social History of Tudor and Stuart England in Honour of R. H. Tawney,* ed. F. J. Fisher (Cambridge: Cambridge University Press, 1961), 37; idem, *Society and Puritanism,* 490–94. Poor laws and the reformation of manners: see W. K. Jordan, *Philanthropy in England, 1480–1660: A Study of the Changing Pattern of English Social Aspirations* (London: Allen and Unwin, 1959), 143–44, 150–54; Dudley W. R. Bahlman, *The Moral Revolution of 1688* (New Haven: Yale University Press, 1957); T. C. Curtis and W. A. Speck, "The Societies for the Reformation of Manners: A Case Study in the Theory and Practice of Moral Reform," *Literature and History,* no. 3 (1976), 45–64. Anglican work ethic: C. John Sommerville, "The Anti-Puritan Work Ethic," *Journal of British Studies,* 20, no. 2 (Spring, 1981), 70–81.

42. Schlatter, *Social Ideals of Religious Leaders,* 200, 203; Margaret C. Jacob, *The Newtonians and the English Revolution, 1689–1720* (Ithaca: Cornell University Press, 1976), 56 (see chap. 1 passim); Humphrey Mackworth, *A Discourse by way of Dialogue Concerning Providence . . . ,* 2nd ed. (1705), 23, quoted in Richard Harvey, "English Poverty and God's Providence, 1675–1725," *Historian,* 4 (May, 1979), 505 n. 23; *The History of Religion* (1694), xiv, quoted in Straka, *Anglican Reaction,* 123.

43. Jacob, *Newtonians,* 51; Richard Allestree, *The Causes of the Decay of Christian Piety . . .* (1667), 351–52.

44. On Tawney's thesis see above, chap. 4, sec. 5.

45. Industrial feudalism: see Hill, *Reformation,* 107. Irrational capitalism: see above, n. 2. Late-Restoration pamphleteer: *The Linnen and Woolen Manufactory Discoursed* (1691), 3, quoted in Appleby, *Economic Thought and Ideology,* 111. On Tudor protectionism see Lawrence Stone, "State Control in Sixteenth Century England," *Economic History Review,* 17 (1947), 103–20. On the mediatory status of mercantilism see Anderson, *Lineages,* 36; Manning, "The Nobles," 267; Hill, *Reformation,* 53–54, 96.

46. Adam Smith, *An Inquiry into the Nature and Causes of the Wealth of Nations* (1776), ed. Edwin Cannan (New York: Modern Library, 1937), IV, ii, 423; Lewes Roberts, *The Treasure of Traffike* (1641), 1–2, quoted in Gunn, *Politics and the Public Interest,* 212. On the familiarity of this argument in the seventeenth century see Gunn, *Politics and the Public Interest,* 210–13. On the replacement of divine order by the market system see Appleby, *Economic Thought and Ideology,* 41, 242–45, 255. For the view that capitalist ideology is a product of eighteenth-century political debate see above, n. 22.

47. Thomas Scott, *The Belgick Pismire . . .* (1622), 32, 34; John Denham, *Coopers Hill* (1642), ll. 28–34, in *Expans'd Hieroglyphicks: A Critical Edition of John Denham's Coopers Hill,* ed. Brendan O'Hehir (Berkeley and Los Angeles: University of California Press, 1969), 111–12; Gunn, *Politics and the Public Interest,* 138; Tawney, *Religion and the Rise of Capitalism,* 153; Thomas Taylor, *A Sermon Preach'd . . . on the Second Day of December, 1697* (1697), quoted in Straka, *Anglican Reaction,* 111.

48. Appleby, *Economic Thought and Ideology,* 184 (see also 7, 94–95, 97, 183–85, 193, 247–48); Albert Hirschman, *The Passions and the Interests: Political Arguments for Capitalism before Its Triumph* (Princeton: Princeton University Press, 1977), 43–44 and pt. 1 passim.

49. Bernard Mandeville, "An Enquiry into the Origin of Moral Virtue"

(1714), in *The Fable of the Bees,* ed. Phillip Harth (Harmondsworth: Penguin, 1970), 81. For Defoe's version, and fascinated discussion, of the Mandevillian paradox see *Review,* III, no. 10 (Jan. 22, 1706); idem, *The Complete English Tradesman, in Familiar Letters . . . ,* 2nd ed. (1727), II, pt. 2, chaps. 4 and 5. Compare *Review,* III, no. 11 (Jan. 24, 1706), where Defoe says that tradesmen "plead for Luxury, not as a Vice in Manners, but as a Vertue in Trade . . . What a mighty Prospect of Reformation must this shew us, that whenever we come to reform our Manners, we shall ruin our Manufactures."

50. William Petty, *Political Anatomy of Ireland* (1691), 63–64, quoted in Appleby, *Economic Thought and Ideology,* 84; Ascham, *Confusions and Revolutions,* 27, 30. On the monied interest see above, chap. 4, n. 52.

51. Nicholas Barbon, *A Discourse concerning Coining the New Money Lighter* (1696), 43, and idem, *A Discourse of Trade* (1690), 15, quoted in Appleby, *Economic Thought and Ideology,* 229, 169; Hill, *Society and Puritanism,* 405; Appleby, *Economic Thought and Ideology,* 188; *Grand Concern of England Explained* (1673), 51, and *The Brief Observations of J. C. . . . Briefly Examined* (1668), 63, quoted in Appleby, *Economic Thought and Ideology,* 189, 92. On the institution of the trust in the later seventeenth century see R. S. Neale, "The Bourgeoisie, Historically, Has Played a Most Revolutionary Part," in *Feudalism, Capitalism, and Beyond,* ed. Eugene Kamenka and R. S. Neale (New York: St. Martin's, 1975), 99–101.

52. Defoe, *Review,* III, no. 126 (Oct. 22, 1706), no. 5 (Jan. 10, 1706) (see also idem, *Complete English Tradesman,* I, letter 24, esp. p. 344), no. 7 (Jan. 15, 1706), no. 9 (Jan. 18, 1706) (cf. no. 2 [Jan. 3, 1706]); VII, no. 130 (Jan. 23, 1711). On the "imaginary honor" of aristocratic ideology see above, chap. 4, n. 37. On women and exchange see above, chap. 4, n. 38. On Defoe and the false claim to historicity see above, chap. 3, nn. 63–69.

53. Charles Davenant, "Discourses on the Public Revenues" (1698), in *The Political and Commercial Works of . . . Charles D'Avenant . . . ,* ed. Charles Whitworth (London: R. Horsfield, 1771), I, 151.

54. Swift: *Examiner,* no. 13 (Nov. 2, 1710) and no. 34 (Mar. 29, 1711), in *The Prose Works of Jonathan Swift,* vol. III: *The Examiner and Other Pieces Written in 1710–11,* ed. Herbert Davis (Oxford: Blackwell, 1940), 6–7, 119; idem, "The Run upon the Bankers" (1720), ll. 33–36, in *The Poems of Jonathan Swift,* ed. Harold Williams, 2nd ed. (Oxford: Clarendon Press, 1958), I, 238 (see also "The Bubble" [1720], ibid., I, 248–59); idem, *The Conduct of the Allies . . .* (1711), 87, 70. Bolingbroke: Henry St. John to Lord Orrery, July 9, 1709, in Bod. MS. Eng. Misc. e. 180, fols. 4–5, quoted in W. A. Speck, "Social Status in Late Stuart England," *Past and Present,* no. 34 (1966), 129. Swift thought that the law should be determined only by those with property in land: see his "Thoughts on Various Subjects," in *Prose Works,* vol. IV: *A Proposal for Correcting the English Tongue, Polite Conversation, Etc.,* ed. Herbert Davis and Louis Landa (Oxford: Blackwell, 1957), 245; idem, *An Humble Address . . .* (1735), in *Prose Works,* vol. X: *The Drapier's Letters and Other Works 1724–1725,* ed. Herbert Davis (Oxford: Blackwell, 1959), 134. For Swift on aristocratic ideology see above, chap. 4, n. 60.

55. Allestree, *Decay of Christian Piety,* 238; Swift: *Examiner,* no. 13 (Nov. 2, 1710), in *Prose Works,* III, 5; M. B. Drapier, *A Letter to the . . . Common-People of Ireland . . .* (Dublin, 1724), in *Prose Works,* X, 4, 7, 12.

56. Swift: "The Character of Sir Robert Walpole" (1631), ll. 7–10, in *Poems,* II, 540. Bolingbroke: *Some Reflections on the Present State of the Nation* (1749), and *A Dissertation Upon Parties* (1733–34), in *The Works of Lord Bolingbroke* (Philadelphia: Carey and Hart, 1841), II, 455, 152; and *Craftsman,* no. 184 (Jan. 10, 1730). Davenant: *Tom Double Return'd out of the Country . . . a Second Dialogue*

between Mr. Whiglove & Mr. Double . . . , 2nd ed. (1702), 63. On Tory radicalism
see above, chap. 4, n. 61.

57. Swift, *Examiner*, no. 13 (Nov. 2, 1710), in *Prose Works*, III, 5; Swift to
Pope, Jan. 10, 1721, in *The Correspondence of Jonathan Swift*, ed. Harold Williams
(Oxford: Clarendon Press, 1963), II, 372. On the dangers and attractions of
political co-optation see Bertrand A. Goldgar, *Walpole and the Wits: The Relation of
Politics to Literature, 1722–1742* (Lincoln: University of Nebraska Press, 1976).
Pope's ambivalence is most evident in his vacillation between the role of amateur
and that of professional poet, between the elitist coterie and the literary marketplace. See, especially, his "Preface" to the *Works* (1717); *Peri Bathous; or, Of the
Art of Sinking in Poetry* (1728); "Epistle to Dr. Arbuthnot" (1735); and *The Dun-
ciad* (1728–43). On Swift's ambivalent attempts to associate himself with a "country seat" see Carole Fabricant, *Swift's Landscape* (Baltimore: Johns Hopkins University Press, 1983), 70–71, 166–69.

58. James Boswell, *Life of Johnson*, ed. George B. Hill and L. F. Powell (Oxford: Clarendon Press, 1934), I, 442, 447–48; Edmund Burke, *Reflections on the
Revolution in France* (1790), ed. Thomas H. D. Mahoney and Oskar Piest (Indianapolis: Bobbs-Merrill, 1955), 87.

59. Bolingbroke: *The Idea of a Patriot King* (1739), in *Works*, II, 397; (cf. *Crafts-
man*, no. 456 [Mar. 29, 1735], where Bolingbroke tacitly compares the period of
the rise of the *novi homines* with contemporary England); *Craftsman*, no. 9 (Jan. 2,
1727). Walpole's supporter: *Daily Gazeteer*, no. 24 (July 26, 1735), quoted in Isaac
Kramnick, "Augustan Politics and English Historiography: The Debate on the
English Past, 1730–35," *History and Theory*, 6, no. 1 (1967), 41. Swift: "Ode to the
Honble Sir William Temple" (1692), ll. 59–61, in *Poems*, I, 28. Harrington: *The
Commonwealth of Oceana* (1656), in *The Political Works of James Harrington*, ed. J. G.
A. Pocock (Cambridge: Cambridge University Press, 1977), 173. On the Tory
reappropriation of the myth of the ancient constitution see Kramnick, "Augustan
Politics." On Roman *auctoritas* and the figure of the *novus homo* see above, chap. 4,
n. 10. Walpole was understood by his opponents to be the model of the "great
man" who was therefore by definition not also "good"; see above, chap. 12, n. 6.

CHAPTER SIX: STORIES OF VIRTUE

1. James I to Prince Charles and the Duke of Buckingham, Feb., 1623,
British Library Harleian MS. 6987, fol. 13, quoted in Annabel M. Patterson,
*Censorship and Interpretation: The Conditions of Writing and Reading in Early Modern
England* (Madison: University of Wisconsin Press, 1984), 167; on the Rubens
portrait see 168. Charles II's escape: "An Account of His Majesty's Escape from
Worcester, Dictated to Mr. Pepys, by the King himselfe" (1680); *An Exact Narrative and Relation* . . . (1660); Father Huddleston, "A Brief Account of his Majesties Escape from Worcester . . ."; and Col. George Gounter, "The last act in the
miraculous storie of his Majestie's escape . . ."; all reprinted in *Charles II's Escape
from Worcester: A Collection of Narratives Assembled by Samuel Pepys*, ed. William
Matthews (Berkeley and Los Angeles: University of California Press, 1966), 40,
50, 88, 94, 96, 107, 160. On the utility of walnut skins to disguise gentle birth see,
e.g., Aphra Behn, *The Wandring Beauty. A Novel* (1698), in *Histories, Novels, and
Translations, Written by the most Ingenious Mrs. Behn* . . . , vol. II (1700), 10; and
Eliza Haywood, *Philidore and Placentia; or, L'Amour trop Delicat* (1727), in *Four
before Richardson: Selected English Novels, 1720–1727*, ed. William H. McBurney
(Lincoln: University of Nebraska Press, 1963), 159. For an argument parallel to

the following one, concerning the suitability of narrative with respect not to questions of virtue but to questions of truth, see above, chap. 3, nn. 81–86.

2. On emplacement and specification see above, Introduction, nn. 14–15.

3. Henry Spelman, *The History and Fate of Sacrilege* (1698; written ca. 1630) (London: Joseph Masters, 1846), 167–68; Edward Walker, *Observations . . .* (written 1653), in *Historical Discourses, upon Several Occasions . . .* (1705), 299; Thomas Fuller, *The History of the Worthies of England* (1662), 44; Jonathan Swift, *A Discourse of the Contests and Dissensions between the Nobles and the Commons in Athens and Rome . . .* (1701), in *The Prose Works of Jonathan Swift*, vol. I: *A Tale of a Tub with Other Early Works, 1696–1707*, ed. Herbert Davis (Oxford: Blackwell, 1957), 230–31; Daniel Defoe, *A Plan of the English Commerce . . .* , 2nd ed. (1730) (New York: Augustus M. Kelley, 1967), 49–50 (see also *Review*, III, nos. 7, 10, 11 [Jan. 15, 22, 24, 1706]). For contemporary explanations of the decline of the gentry by reference to sin or mutability see, e.g., [Richard Allestree], *The Gentleman's Calling* ([1660] 1672), sig. A5ʳ, A6ʳ; Edward Waterhouse, *The Gentlemans Monitor . . .* (1665), 28–30, 440–55.

4. John Foxe, *Acts and Monuments* (1563; expanded 1570), ed. S. R. Cattley (London: Seeley and Burnside, 1839), VIII, 473–74.

5. Andrew Marvell, "Upon Appleton House" (written ca. 1652), ll. 90, 269–74, in *Andrew Marvell: The Complete Poems*, ed. Elizabeth S. Donno (Harmondsworth: Penguin, 1972), 78, 83–84. On Protestant typology see above, chap. 2, n. 23.

6. Jonathan Swift, *A Tale of a Tub, To which is added The Battle of the Books and the Mechanical Operation of the Spirit*, ed. A. C. Guthkelch and D. Nichol Smith, 2nd ed. (Oxford: Clarendon Press, 1958), secs. II, IV, VI, pp. 73, 105, 122, 136, 138–39. At one point Swift, apparently inadvertently, distinguishes the two reforming brothers as "The Elder" and "the younger" (sec. IV, p. 117). The macrofamilial revolt against the papal father (or the bogus older brother) is alluded to on the microfamilial level in the fact that the English Reformation was also a revolt against the paternal prohibition of divorce, remarriage, and the production of a legitimate heir: see Jack Goody, *The Development of the Family and Marriage in Europe* (Cambridge: Cambridge University Press, 1983), 168, 172.

7. Aphra Behn, *The Younger Brother; or, The Amorous Jilt* (1696), I, i, in *The Works of Aphra Behn*, ed. Montague Summers (New York: Benjamin Blom, [1915] 1967), IV, 327; William Sprigge, *A Modest Plea for an Equal Common-wealth Against Monarchy . . .* (1659), 62–63, 68–69.

8. Shakespeare, *As You Like It* (1599), I, i, 18, 55–58 (also 39–41); Thomas Wilson, *The State of England Anno Dom. 1600*, ed. F. J. Fisher, Camden Society Miscellany, XVI (London: Offices of the Society, 1936), 24; Sprigge, *Modest Plea*, 59.

9. Edmund Bolton, *The Cities Advocate, in this case or question of Honor and Armes; whether Apprentiship extinguisheth Gentry? . . .* (1629), p. 51, sig. a4ᵛ, p. 52; Waterhouse, *Gentlemans Monitor*, 70; Daniel Defoe, *The Complete English Tradesman, in Familiar Letters . . .* , 2nd ed. (1727), I, 310; idem, *Plan of English Commerce*, 12 (cf. *Review*, III, no. 10 [Jan. 22, 1706]); John Corbet, *A Discourse of the Religion of England . . .* (1667?), 47.

10. Richard Baxter, *Faithful Souls shall be with Christ . . . Exemplified in the truly-Christian Life and Death of that excellent amiable Saint, Henry Ashhurst Esq; Citizen of London . . .* (1681), 38. On the explanatory powers of temporal ordering see Kenneth Burke's discussion of the "temporizing of essence," in *A Grammar of Motives* (Berkeley and Los Angeles: University of California Press, 1969), 430–40.

11. Defoe, *Review*, III, no. 9 (Jan. 18, 1706), and no. 7 (Jan. 15, 1706). Cf. idem, *The Compleat English Gentleman* (written 1728–29), ed. Karl D. Bülbring (London: David Nutt, 1890), 246–50.

12. Defoe, *Complete English Tradesman*, I, 311; idem, *Compleat English Gentleman*, 257, 258, 262, 275; Richard Brathwaite, *Panthalia; or, The Royal Romance . . .* (1659), 272–73. Many thought that lowly origins could be purified in as little time as a single generation, at least in England: see Lawrence Stone and Jeanne C. F. Stone, *An Open Elite? England, 1540–1880* (Oxford: Clarendon Press, 1984), 239, 290.

13. Defoe, *Compleat English Gentleman*, 18, 145, 177; idem, *Complete English Tradesman*, I, 308; Bernard Mandeville, *The Fable of the Bees* (1714), ed. Phillip Harth (Harmondsworth: Penguin, 1970), "Remark (R)," 232. Cf. Samuel Butler's character of "A Degenerate Noble; or, One that is proud of his Birth," in *Characters* (written 1667–69), ed. Charles W. Daves (Cleveland: Case Western University Press, 1970), 67–69. Mandeville's observation is an example of what Judith N. Shklar calls "subversive genealogy," a kind of critique which, at least in its progressive form, must also become subversive of genealogy itself; see Shklar's "Subversive Genealogies," in *Myth, Symbol, and Culture*, ed. Clifford Geertz (New York: Norton, 1971), 129–54. For a comparably supersessionist spirit among upwardly mobile yeomen, see Mildred Campbell, *The English Yeoman under Elizabeth and the Early Stuarts* (New Haven: Yale University Press, 1942), 50–53.

14. Thomas Deloney, *The Pleasant History of John Winchcomb, in his Younger Yeares called Jack of Newbery* (1597), in *Shorter Novels: Elizabethan*, ed. George Saintsbury and Philip Henderson (London: J. M. Dent, 1972), 6, 11, 20; all parenthetical citations in the text are to this edition. For discussions of the Elizabethan form exemplified by *Jack of Newbery*, see Walter R. Davis, *Idea and Act in Elizabethan Fiction* (Princeton: Princeton University Press, 1969), 261–68; and Laura S. O'Connell, "The Elizabethan Bourgeois Hero Tale: Aspects of an Adolescent Social Consciousness," in *After the Reformation: Essays in Honor of J. H. Hexter*, ed. Barbara C. Malament (Philadelphia: University of Pennsylvania Press, 1980), 267–90. Davis sees the work as a doctrinaire and unproblematic idealization of "middle-class" values (see 250, 252, 260–61, 283). For a more considered view see O'Connell, "Elizabethan Bourgeois Hero Tale"; and idem, "Anti-Entrepreneurial Attitudes in Elizabethan Sermons and Popular Literature," *Journal of British Studies*, 15 (Spring, 1976), 1–20.

15. On bastard feudalism and social theater see above, chap. 5, n. 2; chap. 4, n. 58.

16. Yelverton: A. F. Pollard and Marjorie Blatcher, "Hayward Townshend's Journals," *Bulletin of the Institute of Historical Research*, 12 (1934–35), 7, quoted in Joan Thirsk, "Younger Sons in the Seventeenth Century," *History*, 54 (1969), 363; prefatory letter in Bolton, *Cities Advocate*, sig. B1v; John Vanbrugh, *The Relapse* (1696), I, ii, 86–87; Stephen Penton, *New Instructions to the Guardian . . .* (1696), 135–36.

17. Sprigge, *Modest Plea*, pp. 66–67, sig. A3v–A4r, p. 65, sig. A4v.

18. Ibid., 64–65, 61–62 (see above, chap. 4, n. 62); Edward Hyde, *The History of the Rebellion*, ed. W. D. Macray (Oxford: Clarendon Press, 1888), II, 296; John Oglander, *A Royalist's Notebook*, ed. Francis Bamford (London: Constable, 1936), 109; Jonathan Swift, "The Foolish Methods of Education among the Nobility," (Irish) *Intelligencer*, no. 9 (1728), in *Prose Works*, vol. XII: *Irish Tracts, 1728–1733*, ed. Herbert Davis (Oxford: Blackwell, 1964), 47. Both the Levellers and the Diggers concerned themselves with the plight of younger sons. William

Walwyn and John Lilburne were younger sons of modest gentry families. In 1649 the Levellers sought the modification of primogeniture; the Diggers advocated the abolition of private property altogether. On the political debate over these issues during the late 1640s and the 1650s, see Thirsk, "Younger Sons," 369–71 (on the connection between the radical sectarians and conservative ideology see above, chap. 5, n. 40). On the political volatility of young men whose status inconsistency was due to overeducation see Thirsk, "Younger Sons," 366–67; and Mark Curtis, "The Alienated Intellectuals of Early Stuart England," in *Crisis in Europe, 1560–1660*, ed. Trevor Aston (Garden City, N.Y.: Anchor Books, 1967), 309–31. Cf. above, chap. 4, n. 14, on twelfth-century *juventes*. In fact more heirs than younger sons received higher educations at university during the seventeenth century, and the gap increased after 1650; see Stone and Stone, *An Open Elite?* 231.

19. Jonathan Swift, *The Conduct of the Allies* . . . (1711), 12–13; Bod. Carte MS. 117, fol. 177, and Henry St. John to Lord Orrery, July 9, 1709, in Bod. MS. Eng. Misc. e. 180, folls. 4–5, quoted in W. A. Speck, "Social Status in Late Stuart England," *Past and Present*, no. 34 (1966), 129. Compare Swift, *Examiner*, no. 13 (Nov. 2, 1710), in *Prose Works*, vol. III: *The Examiner and Other Pieces Written in 1710–11*, ed. Herbert Davis (Oxford: Blackwell, 1940), 5–6, where the "Set of Upstarts" is called "an under Sett of Men."

20. Jonathan Swift to Alexander Pope, Jan. 21, 1721, in *The Correspondence of Jonathan Swift*, ed. Harold Williams (Oxford: Clarendon Press, 1963), II, 372–73; Swift, *Conduct of the Allies*, 82–83; Jonathan Swift to Bolingbroke, Dec. 19, 1719, in *Correspondence*, II, 332. Compare Swift's concentration of the Irish economic crisis into the microplot of a landowner compelled to reduce his estate expenditures by half: *A Proposal that All the Ladies and Women of Ireland should appear constantly in Irish Manufactures* (1729), in *Prose Works*, XII, 123–24.

21. James Heath, *A Brief Chronicle Of the Late Intestine Warr* . . . , 2nd impression (1663), frontispiece, reproduced in Michael McKeon, *Politics and Poetry in Restoration England: The Case of Dryden's Annus Mirabilis* (Cambridge: Harvard University Press, 1975), 265 (see also Thomas Hobbes, *Behemoth; or, The Long Parliament* [1681], ed. Ferdinand Tönnies [London: Simpkin, Marshall, 1889], 204); John Earle, *Micro-cosmographie* . . . , 6th ed. (1633), no. 28, sig. F5ʳ–F6ᵛ; Swift, "Foolish Methods," in *Prose Works*, XII, 83–84.

22. The major figure in this modulation is Henry Fielding; see above, chap. 12.

23. Charles Davenant, *The True Picture of a Modern Whig, Set forth in a Dialogue between Mr. Whiglove & Mr. Double* . . . , "6th ed." (1701), 14–32.

24. [Mary Delarivière Manley], *The Secret History of Queen Zarah, and the Sarazians* . . . (1711), I, 9, 36–37, 40, 53, 65, 100–01, 101–2, 104; II, 94–95. The idea of having in effect been given the crown with neither entitlement nor the traditional obligations of authority expresses for Manley the essence of the undeserving upstart; see also II, 43–44. For Swift see above, chap. 5, n. 55.

25. [Mary Delarivière Manley], *Secret Memoirs and Manners Of several Persons of Quality, of Both Sexes. From the New Atalantis, An Island in the Mediterranean*, 2nd ed. (1709), I, 21, 27. The Earl of Portland is characterized by Manley on a similar model; see I, 44–52.

26. Thomas Deloney, *Thomas of Reading; or, The sixe worthie Yeomen of the West*, in *Shorter Novels: Elizabethan*, ed. Saintsbury and Henderson; all parenthetical citations in the text are to this edition.

27. On *ministeriales* in the twelfth century see above, chap. 4, n. 14.

28. See Merritt E. Lawlis, *Apology for the Middle Class: The Dramatic Novels of*

Thomas Deloney (Bloomington: Indiana University Press, 1960), 61; Davis, *Idea and Act*, 278–79.

29. For a brief consideration of the Spanish social context during this period, see above, chap. 7, nn. 21–23.

30. *The Pleasant History of Lazarillo de Tormes* . . . , trans. David Rowland, 3rd ed. (1639), sig. A8^v, B6^{r-v}, F3^v–I4^v; R. W. Truman, "Lazaro de Tormes and the *Novus Homo* Tradition," *MLR*, 64 (1969), 66 (see also idem, "*Lazarillo de Tormes*, Petrarch's *De remediis adversae fortunae*, and Erasmus's *Praise of Folly*," *Bulletin of Hispanic Studies*, 52 [Jan., 1975], 38–39, 53). See Claudio Guillén, *Literature as System: Essays toward the Theory of Literary History* (Princeton: Princeton University Press, 1971), 79–80, 88; Harry Sieber, *The Picaresque* (London: Methuen, 1977), 14–15; Alexander A. Parker, *Literature and the Delinquent: The Picaresque Novel in Spain and Europe, 1599–1753* (Edinburgh: Edinburgh University Press, 1967), 27; A. D. Deyermond, *Lazarillo de Tormes: A Critical Guide* (London: Grant and Cutler, 1975), 29, 72; Richard Bjornson, "The Picaresque Novel in France, England, and Germany," *Comparative Literature*, 29 (Spring, 1977), 142. On picaresque and pastoral see Parker, *Literature and the Delinquent*, 16–19; and Guillén, *Literature as System*, 97. For the terms "alternative" and "oppositional," see Raymond Williams, "Base and Superstructure in Marxist Cultural Theory," *New Left Review*, no. 82 (Nov.–Dec., 1973), 10–11. On the turn inaugurated by *Guzmán* see the discussion by Richard Bjornson, "*Guzmán de Alfarache:* Apologia for a 'Converso,' " *Romanische Forschungen*, 85 (1973), 314–29. The ideological instability of the form is closely analogous to its epistemological instability; see above, chap. 3, nn. 14–19.

31. Davenant: *True Picture*, 15, 31; *An Essay upon the Probable Methods of making a People Gainers in the Balance of Trade* (1699), in *The Political and Commercial Works of . . . Charles D'Avenant . . .* , ed. Charles Whitworth (London: R. Horsfield, 1771), II, 369. Defoe: *Weekly Journal or Saturday's Post*, Sept. 16, 1721, quoted in Maximillian E. Novak, *Realism, Myth, and History in Defoe's Fiction* (Lincoln: University of Nebraska Press, 1983), 129; *Of Captain Misson* (1728), ed. Maximillian E. Novak, *Augustan Reprint Society*, no. 87 (1961), 2, 12, 31; for the parallel see also ibid., i, and Maximillian E. Novak, *Economics and the Fiction of Daniel Defoe*, University of California English Studies, no. 24 (Berkeley and Los Angeles: University of California Press, 1962), chap. 5. Holles: *Memorials of the Holles Family, 1493–1656*, ed. A. C. Wood, Camden Society, 3rd ser., 55 (London: Offices of the Society, 1937), 3, 4, 18–19, 34–35 (for the claim to historicity see 3, 9); further citations in the text are to this work.

32. *The Case of Madam Mary Carleton, Lately stiled The German Princess, Truely Stated: With an Historical Relation of her Birth, Education, and Fortunes; in an Appeal to His Illustrious Highness Prince Rupert* (1663), 10, 30–31; additional citations of the *Case* appear parenthetically in the text.

33. Modern biographers: see Ernest Bernbaum, *The Mary Carleton Narratives, 1663–1673: A Missing Chapter in the History of the English Novel* (Cambridge: Harvard University Press, 1914); Charles F. Main, "The German Princess: or, Mary Carleton in Fact and Fiction," *Harvard Library Bulletin*, 10 (1956), 166–85. On claims to historicity in the Mary Carleton literature see above, chap. 3, nn. 21–22.

34. Bernbaum, *Mary Carleton Narratives*, chaps. 3 and 4, and Main, "German Princess," 175–78, describe these publications. For Mary's address to the ladies and gentlewomen see *Case*, dedication; and idem, *An Historicall Narrative of the German Princess . . .* (1663), dedication and p. 4. In a final gesture of careless appropriation, Main (173) contends, without evidence, that Mary's works are

really by a male "hack" ghost writer—perhaps following Bernbaum (12, 20–25), who argues one or more "press-agents" on the assumption that Mary herself would have lacked the requisite erudition and narrative invention. Daniel Defoe's *The Fortunate Mistress; or, . . . Roxana . . .* (1724), whose narrator at one point compares herself to "the *German Princess,*" is a profound and disturbing investigation of the themes of transgression with which Mary Carleton's own telling of her story is concerned.

35. See Francis Kirkman, *The Unlucky Citizen Experimentally Described in the Various Misfortunes Of an Unlucky Londoner . . .* (1673), frontispiece; "Preface," sig. A3ʳ–A6ʳ; second "Preface," sig. A7ʳ–A8ʳ; and "To the Reader instead of the Errata," sig. A8ᵛ (here and elsewhere Kirkman plays on the relationship between physical, moral, and typographical "errancy"), pp. 295–96. For the quotation see sig. A6ʳ. Further citations appear parenthetically in the text. On Kirkman's life see Strickland Gibson, *A Bibliography of Francis Kirkman,* Oxford Bibliographical Society, n.s., I, fasc. ii (1947) (Oxford: Oxford University Press, 1949), 51–68. On repentance and atonement in picaresque and spiritual autobiography, see above, chap. 3, nn. 11–15.

36. *Lazarillo* focuses on the writing rather than the printing process; see above, chap. 3, n. 15. On *Don Quixote* and print see above, chap. 7, nn. 3–5, 16–18. Kirkman's title alludes to the best-known work of the English picaresque, Thomas Nashe's *The Unfortunate Traveller* (1594). On Puritan rebirth and the family romance see above, chap. 5, n. 28.

37. Thomas Sprat, *The History of the Royal-Society of London . . .* (1667), 72, 113; see above, chap. 3, n. 31.

38. See [Denis Vairasse d'Allais], *The History of the Sevarites . . . The Second Part . . .* (1679), 19, 20–21, 37, 38; [Gabriel de Foigny], *A New Discovery of Terra Incognita Australis . . .* (1693), 21–22, 71–72, 74, 76–78; [Simon Berington], *The Memoirs of Sigr Gaudentio di Lucca . . .* (1737), 207–19, 229; Joshua Barnes, *Gerania: A New Discovery of a Little sort of People Anciently Discoursed of, called Pygmies . . .* (1675), 9, 51–52, 80, 85–86. The social utopianism of Vairasse and Foigny has a quite specific political target in the corruptions of absolutist politics under Louis XIV; see Erica Harth, *Ideology and Culture in Seventeenth-Century France* (Ithaca: Cornell University Press, 1983), 278–309. On the universal language see Paul Cornelius, *Languages in Seventeenth- and Early Eighteenth-Century Imaginary Voyages* (Geneva: Librarie Droz, 1965); and James Knowlson, *Universal Language Schemes in England and France, 1600–1800* (Toronto: University of Toronto Press, 1975).

39. Aphra Behn, *Oroonoko; or, The Royal Slave. A True History* (1688), ed. Lore Metzger (New York: Norton, 1973), 1; all parenthetical citations in the text are to this edition. On the epistemological instability of *Oroonoko* see above, chap. 3, nn. 50–51. For the distinction between hard and soft primitivism see Arthur O. Lovejoy and George Boas, *Primitivism and Related Ideas in Antiquity* (Baltimore: Johns Hopkins Press, 1935), 9–11.

40. [Henry Neville], *The Isle of Pines; or, A late Discovery of a fourth Island near Terra Australis, Incognita by Henry Cornelius Van Sloetten . . .* (1668), in *Shorter Novels: Seventeenth Century,* ed. Philip Henderson (London: J. M. Dent, 1962), 229–31; all parenthetical citations in the text are to this edition. Neville is best known as a Harringtonian republican. *The Isle of Pines* makes a fairly earnest claim to historicity and documentary objectivity; see its title page, ibid., 225.

41. *Adventures by Sea of Edward Coxere* (written ca. 1690), ed. E. H. W. Meyerstein (Oxford: Clarendon Press, 1945), 3; all parenthetical citations in the text are to this edition.

42. On the radical sectarians see above, chap. 5, n. 40. See also the Christian mariner William Okeley, above, chap. 3, n. 56.

43. For the arguments this paragraph summarizes see above, chap. 4, nn. 11–13, 23–28, 38–41.

44. Robert Greene, *Penelopes Web,* in *Life and Complete Works in Prose and Verse of Robert Greene, M.A.,* ed. Alexander B. Grosart (New York: Russell and Russell, [1881–86] 1964), V, 203, 204, 215, 216, 219; cf. *Greene's Carde of Fancie* (1584), in *Shorter Novels: Elizabethan,* ed. Saintsbury and Henderson, 157–260. The analogy between the progressive exploitation of Protestant and female virtue is suggested by Defoe's variation on Greene's plot, in which the lord of the manor is literally converted by the pious discourse of one of his lowly (male) cottagers, whom he then rewards with land and offices; see Daniel Defoe, *Religious Courtship: being Historical Discourses . . .* (1722), 60, 80n.

45. Gabriel Harvey, "A Noble Mans Sute to a Cuntrie Maide," in *Letter-Book of Gabriel Harvey, 1573–1580,* ed. Edward J. L. Scott, Camden Society, n.s., 33 (London: Nichols and Sons, 1884), 144, 145, 147, 149–50.

46. Some of the social specifications of Restoration comedy were of course anticipated by Jacobean "City Comedy". See L. C. Knights, *Drama and Society in the Age of Jonson* (London: Chatto and Windus, 1951); Brian Gibbons, *Jacobean City Comedy: A Study of Satiric Plays by Jonson, Marston, and Middleton* (Cambridge: Harvard University Press, 1968); and Susan Wells, "Jacobean City Comedy and the Ideology of the City," *ELH,* 48, no. 1 (Spring, 1981), 37–60.

47. Aphra Behn, *The Lucky Mistake. A New Novel* (1696), in *The Histories and Novels Of the Late Ingenious Mrs Behn . . .* (1696), 354; idem, *The Unfortunate Happy Lady. A True History* (1698), in *Histories, Novels, and Translations, Written by the most Ingenious Mrs. Behn . . . ,* vol. II (1700), 21, 38. Behn's narratives often explore the justice and limits of rebellion against parental control of the marriage choice; cf. *The Wandering Beauty. A Novel* (1698) and *The Unhappy Mistake; or, The Impious Vow Punish'd* (1698), ibid.

48. Aphra Behn, *The Fair Jilt; or, The History of Prince Tarquin, and Miranda* (1696), in *Histories and Novels Of . . . Mrs. Behn,* 6, 8, 9.

49. Ibid., 162, 171, 178.

50. Aphra Behn, *Memoirs of the Court of the King of Bantam* (n.d.), in *All the Histories and Novels Written by the Late Ingenious Mrs. Behn . . . ,* "5th ed." (1705), 401, 442 (pagination skips 402–41), 452, 453, 462.

51. Mary Davys, *The Accomplished Rake; or, Modern Fine Gentleman . . .* (1727), in *Four before Richardson,* ed. McBurney, 300; Mary Astell, *Some Reflections upon Marriage . . . ,* 4th ed. (1730) (New York: Source Book Press, 1970), 25.

52. Eliza Haywood, *Philidore and Placentia; or, L'Amour trop Delicat* (1727), in *Four before Richardson,* ed. McBurney, 157, 158, 178, 182, 226, 230–31. Exhibiting one aspect of the obsessiveness Haywood criticizes, Defoe distinguishes "inequality" or "unsuitability" in marriage into five categories: age, quality or blood, estates, temper, and religious principles; see Daniel Defoe, *Conjugal Lewdness; or, Matrimonial Whoredom . . .* (1727), 227.

53. Eliza Haywood, *Memoirs Of a Certain Island Adjacent to the Kingdom of Utopia . . .* (1725), 4–5, 202. For Apuleius see above, chap. 4, n. 12. For the idea of the countervailing passion see above, chap. 5, n. 48. Compare the famous description of commodity exchange in Karl Marx, *Capital,* trans. Samuel Moore and Edward Aveling (New York: International Publishers, 1967), I, II, iv (pp. 146–55). For Swift and Bolingbroke see above, chap. 5, n. 59. John J. Richetti has noted the importance of the connection between lust and avarice in the work of

Haywood and Mary Manley; see his *Popular Fiction before Richardson: Narrative Patterns, 1700–1739* (Oxford: Clarendon Press, 1969), 133, 152, 156, and chap. 4 passim.

54. Manley, *Secret History of Queen Zarah*, I, 9, 41; idem, *New Atalantis*, I, 45, 49, 52, 61; II, 62, 63, 65, 108. On Marlborough's passion for wealth see above, n. 25. The dangers of John Richetti's generally illuminating method are evident in his treatment of conservative villains like Portland, whom he sees simply as "the male villain, the archetypal aristocratic seducer" (*Popular Fiction before Richardson*, 146). The structural reduction of characters to a few "mythical types"—here, the persecuted maiden and the aristocratic seducer—may entail an "ideological simplification" so extreme that it obscures a vital distinction between types of aristocratic seducer, and types of ideology, which the authors themselves would insist upon (see ibid., 124–25). For a concentration of macropolitics—the colonial rape of Ireland by England—into a Manleyesque micronarrative of seduction, exploitation, and abandonment, see Jonathan Swift, *The Story of the Injured Lady. Being a true Picture of Scotch Perfidy, Irish Poverty, and Egnlish Partiality . . .* (1746), in *Prose Works*, vol. IX: *Irish Tracts 1720–1723 And Sermons*, ed. Louis Landa (Oxford: Blackwell, 1948), 3–12.

55. William Congreve, *Incognita; or, Love and Duty Reconcil'd . . .* (1692), in *Shorter Novels: Seventeenth Century*, ed. Henderson; all parenthetical citations in the text are to this edition.

56. On the strict settlement see above, chap. 4, n. 34.

57. See Georg Lukács, *The Theory of the Novel*, trans. Anna Bostock (Cambridge: MIT Press, 1973), 60–62, 71–73; José Ortega y Gasset, *Meditations on Quixote*, trans. Evelyn Rugg and Diego Marín (New York: Norton, 1961), 143–44; and Mikhail M. Bakhtin, *The Dialogic Imagination: Four Essays*, trans. Caryl Emerson and Michael Holquist, ed. Holquist (Austin: University of Texas Press, 1981), 45–49.

58. On these matters see above, chap. 4, sec. 9.

59. Swift, *Examiner*, no. 38 (April 26, 1711), in *Prose Works*, III, 141; Henry Fielding, *The Champion*, 2 vols. (1741), Dec. 22, 1739, I, 112. Cf. Richard Steele, *Tatler*, no. 84 (Oct. 22, 1709).

60. For recent examples see Charles C. Mish, "English Short Fiction in the Seventeenth Century," *Studies in Short Fiction*, 6 (1969), 233; Charles C. Mish, ed., *Restoration Prose Fiction, 1666–1700: An Anthology of Representative Pieces* (Lincoln: University of Nebraska Press, 1970), introduction, vii; Frederick R. Karl, *A Reader's Guide to the Development of the English Novel in the Eighteenth Century* (London: Thames and Hudson, 1975), 45–48. See also Mish's chronological checklist, *English Prose Fiction, 1600–1700* (Charlottesville: Bibliographical Society of the University of Virginia, 1952). Some scholars have argued that Restoration criminal biography provides the "missing link" between Deloney and Defoe; see Bernbaum, *Mary Carleton Narratives*, 2–4, 90; Spiro Peterson, ed., *The Counterfeit Lady Unveiled and Other Criminal Fiction of Seventeenth-Century England* (Garden City, N.J.: Anchor Books, 1961), introduction.

CHAPTER SEVEN: ROMANCE TRANSFORMATIONS (I): CERVANTES
AND THE DISENCHANTMENT OF THE WORLD

1. Miguel de Cervantes Saavedra, *The Life and Atchievements of the Renown'd Don Quixote de la Mancha*, trans. Peter Motteux (1712), rev. John Ozell (New York: Modern Library, 1930), I, viii–ix, 51–53 (hereafter cited as *Don Quixote*); all parenthetical citations in the text and in subsequent notes are to this translation

and consist of part and chapter numbers as well as page references to this edition (the author's division of chapters into separate books in Part I has been ignored and the chapters have been numbered consecutively). On the romance topos of the discovered manuscript see above, chap. 1, nn. 102–7.

2. For excerpts from Avellaneda's continuation, see Miguel de Cervantes Saavedra, *Don Quixote,* ed. Joseph R. Jones and Kenneth Douglas, trans. John Ormsby, rev. ed. (New York: Norton, 1981) (hereafter cited as Norton *Don Quixote*), 885–92. See the discussion by Stephen Gilman, "The *Apocryphal Quixote,*" in *Cervantes across the Centuries,* ed. Angel Flores and J. J. Bernadete (New York: Dryden Press, 1947), 247–53, reprinted in Norton *Don Quixote,* 994–1001.

3. See *Don Quixote,* II, lxii, for Don Quixote's visit to a printing house in Barcelona.

4. On the dilemma of quantitative completeness see above, chap. 1, nn. 49–51; chap. 3, nn. 6–7.

5. See the discussion by Walter L. Reed, *An Exemplary History of the Novel: The Quixotic versus the Picaresque* (Chicago: University of Chicago Press, 1981), 84–85. For another work of criticism that recognizes the importance of the typographical revolution to the epistemology of *Don Quixote,* see Robert B. Alter, *Partial Magic: The Novel as a Self-conscious Genre* (Berkeley and Los Angeles: University of California Press, 1975), chap. 1.

6. For a classic account of this effect as a specifically linguistic phenomenon, see Leo Spitzer, "Linguistic Perspectivism in the *Don Quijote,*" in *Linguistics and Literary History* (Princeton: Princeton University Press, 1948), 41–86. The sense of cultural multiplicity is somewhat vitiated in Spitzer's account, however, by his tendency to ignore the difference between the specifically empirical attitudes of humanist book culture and the general reverence for ancient manuscripts and antiquity (see 51–52 and nn. 16–18). For thoughtful formulations of the epistemological parody in *Don Quixote* as a "double-edged" "reversal," as a parody first of romance fantasy but then of its critique, see Reed, *History of the Novel,* 30; and Alban K. Forcione, *Cervantes, Aristotle, and the Persiles* (Princeton: Princeton University Press, 1970), 140–41. Cf. Ronald Paulson, *Satire and the Novel in Eighteenth-Century England* (New Haven: Yale University Press, 1967), 36.

7. On the typographical fixing of "romance" see above, chap. 1, nn. 68–70.

8. In *Cervantes, Aristotle, and the Persiles,* Forcione argues that Cervantes' parody of the claim to historicity represents a critique specifically of the Neo-Aristotelian interpretations of the newly rediscovered *Poetics,* which imposed an empiricist bias on the Aristotelian doctrines of imitation and probability. But often enough it would seem to be Forcione himself, as much as the Neo-Aristotelians, who confuses the requirement of verisimilitude with the claim to historicity (see, e.g., 35, 41, 47, 96–97, 112, 127). On the importance of the distinction see above, chap. 1, nn. 93–95.

9. Motteux' specification of Don Quixote's income here is not supported by the Spanish text; see Norton *Don Quixote,* 149n.4.

10. For a comparison of the two title pages see Norton *Don Quixote,* 2. The comparison is also suggestive for questions of truth. The 1605 title page says that Cervantes "composed" (*compuesto*) the work, implying "compilation" and "arrangement" as much as authorship. The 1615 title page says simply, "by Miguel de Cervantes Saavedra, author of the first part," implying at the least an altered attitude toward the serviceability of the documentary fiction (ibid.). On Don Quixote as an impoverished *hidalgo* see A. Morel-Fatio, "Social and Historical Background," in *Cervantes across the Centuries,* ed. Flores and Bernadete, 112; and Erich Auerbach, *Mimesis: The Representation of Reality in Western Literature,* trans.

Willard Trask (Garden City, N.Y.: Anchor Books, 1957), 120. Morel-Fatio (113) goes so far as to say that the critique of *hidalguism* "is the principal intention of the book." See also the discussion in Martín de Riquer, "Cervantes and the Romances of Chivalry," in *Suma Cervantina,* ed. J. B. Avalle-Arce and E. C. Riley (London: Tamesis Books, 1973), 273–92, trans. J. R. Jones in Norton *Don Quixote,* 909–10.

11. Compare *Don Quixote,* I, xx, 131, where Don Quixote repudiates the role of the slothful "Carpet-Knight" (on the term see above, chap. 5, n. 13). At times he is willing to accord modern courtiership its own very modest legitimacy; see ibid., II, vi, 479, xvii, 552. On the ideology of the *noblesse d'épée* see above, chap. 5, sec. 2. Riquer, "Cervantes," 899, 910, points out that "real" knights-errant still wandered the roads of Europe a scant century before Cervantes published his book, and that Don Quixote's armor, inherited from his great-grandfather, would have dated from the same period.

12. In Part II Don Quixote expands the number of basic kinds to four in order to include those two groups, the high and the low, that undergo no change and persist as they began (*Don Quixote,* II, vi, 481–82). Sancho's version of the two lineages is, as we might expect, a good deal more quantitative than his master's: "My old Grannum (rest her Soul) was wont to say, there were but two Families in the World, *Have-much* and *Have-little*" (ibid., xx, 574).

13. See above, chap. 6, n. 44.

14. Throughout *Don Quixote,* Sancho periodically protests his "Old Christian" purity, a condition of birth which considerably complicates the consideration of his social status, and indeed, of all questions of virtue in *Don Quixote.* Space limitations preclude treating this complication in the following discussion of Sancho's status inconsistency, but on the general subject see below, n. 23.

15. The difficulty involved in distinguishing nature from nurture in the episode of Sancho's wise governorship recalls the plot of the most famous of Cervantes' interpolated stories in *Don Quixote,* "The Novel of the Curious Impertinent" (I, xxxiii–xxxv, 269–310). Not content to believe implicitly in his wife Camilla's virtue so long as it remains untested, Anselmo tempts her to betray him with such subtlety and persistence that he ends up an unwitting cuckold, deluded by everyone involved. Behind the tale is a more general version of the questions of truth and virtue: Did the substitution of experience for faith reveal Camilla's "true" nature, or did it simply socialize her into a faithlessness that she came to know was expected of her?

16. Auerbach, *Mimesis,* 303, 305. For critiques of the "romantic" reading of *Don Quixote,* see ibid., 301–2, 305, 311; and, most recently, Anthony Close, *The Romantic Approach to 'Don Quixote': A Critical History of the Romantic Tradition in 'Quixote' Criticism* (Cambridge: Cambridge University Press, 1978).

17. See *Don Quixote,* II, iii, 461 (the estimate of copies currently in print is Sampson's).

18. Don Quixote's terminal sanity requires that the essential aura of his own romance name be obliterated, and in the final chapter he becomes simply Alonso Quixano once more (ibid., lxxiv, 931, 932, 933).

19. On the picaresque see above, chap. 3, nn. 14–15; chap. 6, nn. 29–30. *Lazarillo de Tormes* seems less to enclose the full intertextual movement than to concentrate—but in response to no evident antithetical counterforce—on the end of it.

20. On the response to print in Roman Catholic culture see the discussion by Reed, *History of the Novel,* 32–39; see also Elizabeth L. Eisenstein, *The Printing Press as an Agent of Change: Communications and Cultural Transformations in Early*

Modern Europe (Cambridge: Cambridge University Press, 1979), 326, 343–48. On humanist historicism see Spitzer, "Linguistic Perspectivism," 78n.18 (but see above, n. 6). On historiographical crisis see Bruce W. Wardropper, " 'Don Quixote': Story or History?" *Modern Philology*, 63, no. 1 (1965), 1–11.

21. Martin Gonzâles de Cellorigo (ca. 1600), quoted in Pierre Vilar, "The Age of Don Quixote," *New Left Review*, no. 68 (July–Aug., 1971), 67; Francisco Gómez de Quevedo y Villegas, quoted in Julio Caro Baroja, "Honour and Shame: A Historical Account of Several Conflicts," in *Honour and Shame: The Values of Mediterranean Society*, ed. J. G. Peristiany (London: Weidenfeld and Nicolson, 1965), 106. On economic boom and its consequences see Derek W. Lomax, "On Re-reading the *Lazarillo de Tormes*," *Studia Iberica: Festschrift für Hans Flasche* (Bern: Francke, 1973), 375–76. The Poor Law of 1540, like the successive English Settlement Acts before that of 1697, sought to limit the physical mobility of the poor; see Javier Herrero, "Renaissance Poverty and Lazarillo's Family: The Birth of the Picaresque Genre," *PMLA*, 94, no. 5 (Oct., 1979), 879.

22. See Vilar, "Age of Don Quixote," 65, 68, 69; Fernand Braudel, *The Mediterranean and the Mediterranean World in the Age of Philip II*, trans. Siân Reynolds (New York: Harper and Row, [1949] 1973), 726–27, 729, 732, 734. J. H. Elliott, "The Decline of Spain," in *Crisis in Europe, 1560–1600*, ed. Trevor Aston (Garden City, N.Y.: Anchor Books, 1967), 196, wonders if assimilation to aristocratic culture can fully explain the decline in industrious activity.

23. See Baroja, "Honour and Shame," 98–99, 100–103, 105–6; Braudel, *The Mediterranean*, 715, 731–32. Elliot, "Decline of Spain," 181, compares the impoverished *hidalgos* of Spain to the (presumbly "lesser") gentry of England.

CHAPTER EIGHT: ROMANCE TRANSFORMATIONS (II): BUNYAN AND THE LITERALIZATION OF ALLEGORY

1. John Bunyan, *The Pilgrim's Progress from this World to That which is to Come*, ed. James B. Wharey; 2nd ed. rev. Roger Sharrock (Oxford: Clarendon Press, 1960), I, 121. All parenthetical citations in the text are to the Sharrock edition.

2. On Protestant figures see above, chap. 2, n. 23; chap. 5, n. 35. For the recent argument see Stanley E. Fish, "Progress in *The Pilgrim's Progress*," in *Self-consuming Artifacts: The Experience of Seventeenth-Century Literature* (Berkeley and Los Angeles: University of California Press, 1972), chap. 4.

3. *Thomas Burt, M.P., D.C.L., Pitman and Privy Councillor: An Autobiography* (1924), p. 115, quoted in Richard D. Altick, *The English Common Reader: A Social History of the Mass Reading Public, 1800–1900* (Chicago: University of Chicago Press, 1963), 255–56; T. M. Raysor, ed., *Coleridge's Miscellaneous Criticism* (London: Constable, 1936), 31. On the tension between linear movement and stasis in Bunyan's plot, see U. Milo Kaufmann, *The Pilgrim's Progress and Traditions in Puritan Meditation* (New Haven: Yale University Press, 1966), 107, 112, 116. On the apparition narratives see above, chap. 2, sec. 5.

4. John Bunyan, *Grace Abounding to the Chief of Sinners . . .* (1666), ed. Roger Sharrock (Oxford: Clarendon Press, 1962), 20–21. For Bunyan's theology I have relied on Richard L. Greaves, *John Bunyan*, Courtenay Studies in Reformation Theology, no. 2 (Grand Rapids, Mich.: Wm. B. Eerdmans, 1969). On Protestant soteriology and social teachings see also above, chap. 5, sec. 3.

5. John Bunyan, *Saved by Grace* and *The Desire of the Righteous Granted*, in *The Works of That Eminent Servant of Christ, Mr. John Bunyan*, ed. Charles Doe (1692), 573, 253, quoted in Greaves, *Bunyan*, 146, 147; see also 114.

6. See Bunyan, *Grace Abounding*, 21. On this point see the observations of

Wolfgang Iser, *The Implied Reader: Patterns of Communication in Prose Fiction from Bunyan to Beckett* (Baltimore: Johns Hopkins University Press, 1974), 23–24, 27–28; and Brian Nellist, "*The Pilgrim's Progress* and Allegory," in *The Pilgrim's Progress: Critical and Historical Views,* ed. Vincent Newey (Totowa, N.J.: Barnes and Noble, 1980), 132–53.

7. Greaves, *Bunyan,* 123; John Bunyan, *A Confession of My Faith,* in *The Works . . . of John Bunyan,* ed. John Wilson (1736–37), II, 61, quoted in Greaves, *Bunyan,* 132. On Bunyan's Bedford church see Greaves, *Bunyan,* 123–27; and Gordon Campbell, "The Theology of *The Pilgrim's Progress,*" in *The Pilgrim's Progress,* ed. Newey, 252.

8. See the comments of Michael Walzer, "Puritanism as a Revolutionary Ideology," *History and Theory,* 3 (1963–64), 73.

9. For Henry Ashurst see above, chap. 6, n. 10. On Bunyan's family see Christopher Hill, "John Bunyan and the English Revolution," *Marxist Perspectives,* 2, no. 3 (Fall, 1979), 16.

10. Nick Shrimpton, "Bunyan's Military Metaphor," in *The Pilgrim's Progress,* ed. Newey, 214; see, generally, 212–15. Johnson's romance had been reprinted as recently as 1670. But it is not as exceptional in possessing a religious dimension as Shrimpton implies; see Thomas Warton's remark above, chap. 4, n. 23. On Bunyan's indebtedness to romance see the sources cited and discussed in Nick Davis, "The Problem of Misfortune in *The Pilgrim's Progress,*" and Shrimpton, "Bunyan's Military Metaphor," in *The Pilgrim's Progress,* ed. Newey, p. 202, nn. 12 and 16, and pp. 210–12. On wayfaring and warfaring see ibid., pp. 209–10.

11. In *The Pilgrim's Progress,* Christian is returned both to God (at the end of Part I) and to Christiana and the children (who follow Christian to the Celestial City in Part II). Christian is distraught that his family has "left me to wander in this manner alone" (I, 51), but as Bunyan painfully concluded of his own isolating imprisonment, the flight from the family only abandoned them, like himself, to divine care. See Bunyan, *Grace Abounding,* 99; and the discussion in N. H. Keeble, "Christiana's Key: The Unity of *The Pilgrim's Progress,*" in *The Pilgrim's Progress,* ed. Newey, 11–13. In Part II, Christiana's guide, Mr. Great-heart, is accused by an enemy of practicing "the craft of a *Kidnapper,*" since he "gatherest up Women and Children, and carriest them into a strange Countrey, to the weakning of my Masters Kingdom" (II, 244). For the gypsy passage see Bunyan, *Grace Abounding,* 32. Davis, "Problem of Misfortune, 203 n. 25, quotes Max Lüthi, *Once Upon a Time: On the Nature of Fairy Tales* (Bloomington: University of Indiana Press, 1976), 68: "This is *the* image of man which somehow shines forth in every fairytale: outwardly isolated, but just for this reason free to establish essential contacts." See also Davis, "Problem of Misfortune," 192–93.

12. Bunyan, *Grace Abounding,* 15, 59. On Christian as a masterless man see Christopher Hill, *The World Turned Upside Down: Radical Ideas during the English Revolution* (New York: Viking, 1972), 329. On masterless men see above, chap. 5, n. 20.

13. On the centrality of lawmaking to the idea of political sovereignty, see above, chap. 5, n. 8. Royal responsibility for highway maintenance seems to have been formalized only in the sixteenth century, when Philip and Mary created local parish machinery for the appointment of surveyors and for their liaison with royal authority via justices of the peace. Seventeenth-century royal proclamations and statutes testify to the established centralization of this responsibility; see W. S. Holdsworth, *A History of English Law,* 3rd ed. (London: Methuen, 1923), IV, 139, 156, 157; VI, 310 and n. 3. Richard Baxter, *A Christian Directory* (1673), IV, xxi,

speaks of God as the "Chief Owner," while Richard Steele, *The Husbandmans Calling* (1672), chap. X, sec. 9, compares the payment of rent to paying dues to the "Great Landlord" on high; both quoted in Richard B. Schlatter, *The Social Ideas of Religious Leaders, 1660–1688* (Oxford: Oxford University Press, 1940), 191, 195.

14. The act of homage signified, on the lord's side, protection, defense, and warranty, and on the tenant's side, reverence and subjection; see Bracton, quoted in Theodore F. T. Plucknett, *A Concise History of the Common Law,* 5th ed. (Boston: Little Brown, 1956), 533.

15. For the progressive model see, e.g., above, chap. 6, nn. 9–13, on the rise of new families. On the reciprocity of sacred and secular language see above, chap. 5, nn. 28–30. Predictably, Talkative knows all about "the necessity of the New-birth" (I, 76).

16. In 1650 the communist Digger movement was active not far from Bunyan's Bedford; see Hill, "John Bunyan," 14. On knight's fee see Plucknett, *History of the Common Law,* 532.

17. See Holdsworth, *History of English Law,* III, 518–19 and 519n.1. According to Holdsworth, the law on personal contracts of this sort is ill-developed even in the early seventeenth century. On villeinage and its transformation see ibid., III, 198–209; and G. O. Sayles, *The Medieval Foundations of England* (New York: A. S. Barnes, 1961), 434. For a recent account of the "monetization" of landholding during this period, see Alan Macfarlane, *The Origins of English Individualism: The Family, Property, and Social Transition* (New York: Cambridge University Press, 1979).

18. See Holdsworth, *History of English Law,* III, 56, 503. Petit treason against someone other than the king was, even at the time treason first attained to a statutory offense (1352), "merely an archaic survival"; see ibid., 287–89.

19. On retaining under the Tudors, see W. H. Dunham, "Lord Hastings' Indentured Retainers, 1461–1483: The Lawfulness of Livery and Retaining under the Yorkists and Tudors," *Transactions of the Connecticut Academy of Arts and Sciences,* 39 (1957), chap. 5. In 1628 the House of Commons repealed statutes concerning the giving of liveries (see ibid., p. 112). See also above, chap. 5, n. 2.

20. E.g., see above, chap. 6, n. 4 (Foxe's *Book of Martyrs*) and n. 15. For his account of Faithful's martyrdom, Bunyan may be indebted to Foxe; see *The Pilgrim's Progress,* I, 97n (p. 328).

21. Samuel Butler, *Prose Observations,* ed. Hugh de Quehen (Oxford: Oxford University Press, 1979), 215–16. On *scandalum magnatum* see above, chap. 4, n. 29.

22. Holdsworth, *History of English Law,* I, 64–65, distinguishes the old local courts into four categories: (1) communal (county and hundred); (2) franchise (private persons); (3) feudal (lords holding courts for tenants); (4) manorial (jurisdiction relating specifically to tenants of land). See, more generally, ibid., I, 64–193; and III, 206–8. According to Plucknett, *History of the Common Law,* 99, around 1300 manorial law was still vigorous and flexible in areas where the king's courts gave no remedy; see, more generally, ibid., 95–100, 105, 169, 509.

23. The conflation occurs more strikingly in *The Pilgrim's Progress,* II, 303–4, where Beulah, with its orchards and vineyards, blends imperceptibly into the bells and streets of the Celestial City.

24. Compare ibid., 176, where it is anticipated that the king will go on progress into the provinces in order to administer justice directly to Christian's former oppressors.

25. In 1664, Clement Ellis wrote that a gentleman's "highest ambition is to be

a favourite in the Court of Heaven" (quoted in Lawrence Stone, *The Crisis of the Aristocracy, 1558–1641* [Oxford: Clarendon Press, 1965], 265). On the similar impulse to public service and reform in Calvinist discipline and robe nobility, see above, chap. 5, nn. 29–32. Among other protagonists who rose from the lower orders to robe nobility are Cardinal Wolsey and Thomas of Reading; see above, chap. 6, nn. 15, 26.

26. See above, chap. 5, n. 14.

27. On Bunyan's claim to historicity in *The Life and Death of Mr. Badman* . . . (1680), see above, chap. 3, n. 9. Cf. Bunyan's *Holy War* . . . (1682), ed. Roger Sharrock and James J. Forrest (Oxford: Clarendon Press, 1980), "To the Reader," 1 (ll. 23–30), 2 (ll. 4–11, 18–21).

28. On the matter of the continuation(s) see *The Pilgrim's Progress,* II, 168n (pp. 338–39).

29. On these matters see the discussions above, chap. 2, n. 42, and chap. 3, n. 72.

CHAPTER NINE: PARABLES OF THE YOUNGER SON (I): DEFOE AND THE NATURALIZATION OF DESIRE

1. Daniel Defoe, *The Farther Adventures of Robinson Crusoe* . . . (1719), "Preface," in *Novel and Romance, 1700–1800: A Documentary Record,* ed. Ioan Williams (New York: Barnes and Noble, 1970), 64–65 (hereafter cited as *Farther Adventures*); and idem, *The Life and Strange Surprizing Adventures of Robinson Crusoe* . . . (1719), ed. J. Donald Crowley, Oxford English Novels (London: Oxford University Press, 1972), "Preface," I (hereafter cited as *Robinson Crusoe*). All parenthetical citations in the text are to the Crowley edition. Part II appeared 117 days before Part I. In fact the complaint itself may have been written by Defoe's publisher, William Taylor. Not surprisingly, abridgments of Part I—a dozen or more were published between 1720 and 1830—tended to give priority to the literal events of Robinson's shipwreck and early life on the island; see Pat Rogers, "Classics and Chapbooks," in *Books and Their Readers in Eighteenth-Century England,* ed. Isabel Rivers (New York: St. Martin's, 1982), 30–31. Defoe compares this sort of pirating of printed works to "Robbing on the Highway" (*Farther Adventures,* "Preface," 65). On piracies of Part I see Pat Rogers, *Robinson Crusoe* (London: Allen and Unwin, 1979), 7–8.

2. [Charles Gildon], *The Life and Strange Surprizing Adventures of Mr. D——— De F——* . . . (1719), x, iii. Defoe's own *Serious Reflections During the Life And Surprising Adventures of Robinson Crusoe: with his Vision of the Angelick World* (1720) has played a central role in making the autobiographical interpretation of *Robinson Crusoe* seem plausible and attractive. On the progress of Defoe's commitment to the claim to historicity see above, chap. 3, nn. 63–69.

3. Rogers, *Robinson Crusoe,* 122–23, interestingly discusses a related but more general feature of Defoe's style, which he calls "approximating" and "alternative" figures (e.g., "about a mile," "two or three"). "The effect is often to suggest compulsive mensuration even where accurate counting is not possible." On the interest of Puritans and the Royal Society in keeping autobiographical journals, see above, chap. 3, secs. 1, 3.

4. On Robinson's journal and its destabilization of objective recording and chronology, see Homer O. Brown, "The Displaced Self in the Novels of Daniel Defoe," *ELH,* 38, no. 4 (Dec., 1971), 584–85; and Timothy J. Reiss, *The Discourse of Modernism* (Ithaca: Cornell University Press, 1982), 323–24. J. Paul Hunter, *The Reluctant Pilgrim: Defoe's Emblematic Method and Quest for Form in Robinson*

Crusoe (Baltimore: Johns Hopkins University Press, 1966), 144–45, notes that the journal has been edited. On the disruption of temporality in *Robinson Crusoe* see, more generally, Paul Alkon, *Defoe and Fictional Time* (Athens: University of Georgia Press, 1979); and Elizabeth D. Ermarth, *Realism and Consensus in the English Novel* (Princeton: Princeton University Press, 1983), chap. 4. The ambiguous significance of the journal is well conveyed by the fact that its documentary objectivity permits Robinson, "by casting up Times past," to discover the "strange Concurrence of Days" in the typological pattern of his life crises, and its very medium of definitiveness has, through successive dilutions, become so ghostly and "pale it scarce left any Appearance of black upon the Paper" (133). Rather than tax Defoe for discrepancies between narrative and journal, Gildon, 31 (*Adventures of Mr. D—— De F——*, prefers to criticize his lack of inventiveness: "You have been forc'd to give us the same Reflections over and over again, as well as repeat the same Fact afterwards in a Journal, which you had told us before in a plain Narration."

5. See, e.g., *Robinson Crusoe*, 3, 5–6, 7–8, 9–10, 14–15, 16, 17, 19, 35–36, 38, 40. On Defoe's religious upbringing see Michael Shinagel, *Defoe and Middle-Class Gentility* (Cambridge: Harvard University Press, 1968), chap. 1.

6. See *Robinson Crusoe*, 124–28, 153–57, 168–73. On the conventionality of postconversion lapses in spiritual autobiography, see George A. Starr, *Defoe and Spiritual Autobiography* (Princeton: Princeton University Press, 1965), 160; Hunter, *Reluctant Pilgrim*, 187. On Coxere see above, chap. 6, nn. 41–42. For William Okeley's spiritualization of travel and captivity see above, chap. 3, n. 56.

7. On the picaresque see above, chap. 3, sec. 2. On Kirkman see above, chap. 6, nn. 35–36.

8. See Ian Watt, *The Rise of the Novel: Studies in Defoe, Richardson, and Fielding* (Berkeley and Los Angeles: University of California Press, 1957), 81 (but Watt's position is not as extreme as it has sometimes been taken to be; see 82–83); Starr, *Defoe and Spiritual Autobiography;* and Hunter, *Reluctant Pilgrim.* Among more recent critics, John J. Richetti has gone furthest in arguing against this mutual exclusion: see his thoughtful discussions in *Popular Fiction before Richardson: Narrative Patterns, 1700–1739* (Oxford: Clarendon Press, 1969), 13–18, 92–96; and *Defoe's Narratives: Situations and Structures* (Oxford: Clarendon Press, 1975), 23 and chap. 2 passim.

9. See Watt, *Rise of the Novel*, 65; Starr, *Defoe and Spiritual Autobiography*, 74–81; Hunter, *Reluctant Pilgrim*, 38–39; Shinagel, *Defoe and Middle-Class Gentility*, 126–27 and 268–69n. 5; Rogers, *Robinson Crusoe*, 76–77; Maximillian E. Novak, *Economics and the Fiction of Daniel Defoe*, University of California English Studies, no. 24 (Berkeley and Los Angeles: University of California Press, 1962), chap. 2; C. N. Manlove, *Literature and Reality, 1600–1800* (New York: St. Martin's, 1978), chap. 7. Cf. Gildon, *Adventures of Mr. D—— De F——*, 5–6.

10. See, e.g., Richard Baxter's handling of the question, "*Is it lawful to buy and use men as Slaves?*" in *The Catechizing of Families . . .* (1683), 311.

11. On the rule of charity and the limiting standard of the satisfaction of necessities, see above, chap. 5, n. 39. On the persistence of a secularized conception of "honor" as "credit" and "trust" in business dealings, see above, chap. 5, nn. 51–53.

12. On theories of value see above, chap. 5, sec. 4. On capitalist abstinence see, e.g., Eric Roll, *A History of Economic Thought*, 4th ed. rev. (London: Faber and Faber, 1973), 344–46. When Robinson attributes the preservation of the shipwrecked commodities to providence, he associates them with the gift of God's grace and achieves a similar sanctification (*Robinson Crusoe*, 130–31). See also Ian

Watt's discussion of the mystique of the dignity of labor in relation to *Robinson Crusoe* in "Robinson Crusoe as a Myth," in *Eighteenth-Century English Literature: Modern Essays in Criticism*, ed. James L. Clifford (New York: Oxford University Press, 1959), 163–67. For Robinson's fascination with use and exchange value, see *Robinson Crusoe*, 50, 64, 189, 193, 195, 278.

13. For useful treatments of several aspects of the subject see Raymond Williams, *The Country and the City* (New York: Oxford University Press, 1973), chap. 10; Douglas Hay, "Poaching and the Game Laws on Cannock Chase," in *Albion's Fatal Tree: Crime and Society in Eighteenth-Century England* (New York: Pantheon, 1975), 189–253. For a discussion that has bearing on mine here, see Richetti, *Popular Fiction before Richardson*, 95–96.

14. Compare the following passages from *Robinson Crusoe*: "All our Discontents about what we want, appear'd to me, to spring from the Want of Thankfulness for what we have" (130); and "Thus we never see the true State of our Condition, till it is illustrated to us by its Contraries; nor know how to value what we enjoy, but by the want of it" (139).

15. Defoe was fond of comparing a landowner's absolute possession to a monarch's; see above, chap. 5, n. 4. Later, on his return to the island, Robinson "reserv'd to [him] self the Property of the whole" (*Robinson Crusoe*, 305). For Williams's argument see *Country and City*, 32; his subject is the country-house poems of Jonson and Carew.

16. Karl Marx, *Grundrisse*, trans. Martin Nicolaus (Harmondsworth: Penguin, 1973), 83. On Defoe's assimilationism see Shinagel, *Defoe and Middle-Class Gentility*, 29–30, 47–48, 73–74, 103–4. On the retirement themes see Pat Rogers, "Crusoe's Home," *Essays in Criticism*, 24 (1974), 375–90.

17. See above, chap. 3, nn. 63–69; chap. 4, n. 37; chap. 5, n. 52. On Pine see above, chap. 6, n. 40. See Maximillian E. Novak, *Realism, Myth, and History in Defoe's Fiction* (Lincoln: University of Nebraska Press, 1983), 45. On the utility of Robinson's imaginative figures see also Michael Seidel, "Crusoe in Exile," *PMLA*, 96, no. 3 (May, 1981), 363–74.

18. Defoe, *Serious Reflections*, 8; idem, *A Vision of the Angelick World*, 12, 11 (ibid., new pagination); idem, *Meditations* (written 1681), 5, quoted in Shinagel, *Defoe and Middle-Class Gentility*, 16.

19. On Defoe's apparition narratives see above, chap. 2, nn. 40–41.

20. See, e.g., *Robinson Crusoe*, 111–12, 145–46. For this point see Richetti, *Defoe's Narratives*, 50.

21. Compare the passage on 251, where Friday suspects the English mutineers are going to eat their prisoners: "*No, no, says I, Friday, I am afraid they will murther them indeed, but you may be sure they will not eat them*" (an irony that takes in Robinson's own, initial, murderous desires with respect to the savages).

22. See the following passages: "I could not depend by any means upon my Dream for the rest of it" (202); and "I did not let my Dream come to pass in that Part" (205).

23. On Defoe's conception of natural law see Maximillian E. Novak, *Defoe and the Nature of Man* (Oxford: Oxford University Press, 1963), chap. 2. On the naturalization of human desire during this period, see above, chap. 5, nn. 46–48.

24. The scene is prefigured in terms that are both more and less explicit when Robinson, having named and talked to his tame parrot, returns home after an unusually long absence and is startled to hear Poll repeat Robinson's own name back to him (*Robinson Crusoe*, 119, 142–43). On the dialectical constitution of colonizer and colonized see Albert Memmi, *The Colonizer and the Colonized* (Boston: Beacon Press, 1967).

25. For Defoe's reproof see *Serious Reflections*, 226. Gildon (*Adventures of Mr. D—— De F——*, 8, 5) speaks of Robinson's "Coining of Providences," and points out that the adventures themselves commence with his "Secret Impulse to a Seafaring Life, to which Impulse you so often recommend a blind Obedience, whether grounded on Reason or not, and would perswade us that it proceeds from the secret Inspiration either of Providence, or some good Spirit" (see also ibid., 14, 37). For a useful formulation of *Robinson Crusoe's* ideological function see the comments in Richetti, *Defoe's Narratives*, 30–32; see also Reiss, *Discourse of Modernism*, 322. On the conventions of spiritual autobiography see, e.g., Starr, *Defoe and Spiritual Autobiography*, 123, 185–97.

26. For Robinson as a deliverer see, e.g., *Robinson Crusoe*, 235, 238, 248, 254, 255, 258, 272.

27. Now Robinson extends to human malefactors the policy he earlier practiced on the thieving birds, by hanging the rebel captain as a sign to his confederates; cf. ibid., 117, 276. On settlement and possession as criteria of sovereignty see above, chap. 5, n. 10 (Robinson also has "the concurrent consent of the nation," as I am about to argue).

28. Woodes Rogers reports that Alexander Selkirk's rescuers called him "Governour," and he himself refers to the castaway as "absolute Monarch" of the island; see Percy G. Adams, *Travel Literature and the Evolution of the Novel* (Lexington: University Press of Kentucky, 1983), 131. In *A Vision of the Angelick World*, 11 (in *Serious Reflections*, new pagination), Defoe admits that in the midst of one of his vapourish states "it had been easy to have possess'd me, if I had continued so much longer, that it was an enchanted Island, that there was a Million of evil Spirits in it, and that the Devil was Lord of the Manor."

29. Drawing on the coventions of Puritan metaphor, Hunter (*Reluctant Pilgrim*, 198–99) understands the episode of the wolves as Robinson's final allegorical victory over bestiality.

CHAPTER TEN: PARABLES OF THE YOUNGER SON (II): SWIFT
AND THE CONTAINMENT OF DESIRE

1. Michael Shinagel, *Defoe and Middle-Class Gentility* (Cambridge: Harvard University Press, 1968), 81, 86; Jonathan Swift to Viscount Bolingbroke, Oct. 31, 1729, in *The Correspondence of Jonathan Swift*, ed. Harold Williams (Oxford: Clarendon Press, 1963), III, 354.

2. Jonathan Swift: "Ode to the Honble Sir William Temple" (1692), ll. 178–84, in *The Poems of Jonathan Swift*, ed. Harold Williams, 2nd ed. (Oxford: Clarendon Press, 1958), I, 32; (Irish) *Intelligencer*, no. 9 (1728), in *The Prose Works of Jonathan Swift*, vol. 12: *Irish Tracts, 1728–1733*, ed. Herbert Davis (Oxford: Blackwell, 1964), 47; *A Letter to a Young Gentleman, Lately enter'd into Holy Orders . . .* (1721), in *Prose Works*, vol. 9: *Irish Tracts, 1720–1723 and Sermons*, ed. Louis Landa (Oxford: Blackwell, 1948), 78; "Ode to Temple," l. 191, in *Poems*, I, 32; Swift to John Arbuthnot, July 3, 1714, and Swift to Alexander Pope, Aug. 11, 1729, in *Correspondence*, II, 46, and III, 341. On Swift's sense of physical alienation, and on his profound attachment to Ireland, see Carole Fabricant, *Swift's Landscape* (Baltimore: Johns Hopkins University Press, 1983), chap. 6. On the conservative reading of recent English history and the psychology of the younger son, see above, chap. 6, sec. 3.

3. Jonathan Swift, *Travels into several Remote Nations of the World. In Four Parts. By Lemuel Gulliver . . .* (1726), vol. 11 of *Prose Works*, ed. Herbert Davis (Oxford: Basil Blackwell, 1941), I, i, 3 (hereafter cited as *Travels*); all parenthetical

citations in the text are to this edition, and consist of part, chapter, and page number.

4. See above chap. 4, n. 62.

5. F. P. Lock, *The Politics of Gulliver's Travels* (Oxford: Clarendon Press, 1980), 22. Machiavelli was of fundamental importance to both progressive and conservative ideology; for a discussion primarily of the former influence, see above, chap. 5, nn. 16–18.

6. See above, chap. 5, n. 22. On Castiglione see above, chap. 5, n. 14.

7. Swift's immediate model here is less the old Cavalier army (see above, chap. 5, n. 19), than the Machiavellian republican tradition.

8. C. J. Rawson, *Gulliver and the Gentle Reader: Studies in Swift and Our Time* (London: Routledge and Kegan Paul, 1973), 19. On sumptuary legislation see above, chap. 4, nn. 2, 29.

9. But while status distinctions are thereby reinforced, like many utopian communities, the Houyhnhnms (and the Lilliputians) are opposed to the extreme socialization of sex difference; see *Travels*, I, vi, 46; IV, viii, 253. For other utopian practices in this regard, see above, chap. 6, n. 38. On Socrates see above, chap. 4, nn. 8–9.

10. See also *Travels*, I, v, 35–36, viii, 62, and, for the utility of the magnifying glass and the looking glass in Brobdingnag, II, i, 76, iii, 88, 91, viii, 131. For Sprat see above, chap. 3, n. 31. Gulliver likes to keep his instruments of sight in his most private and secret pockets, and he tells us of his gratitude when the pirates of Part III and the mutineers of Part IV refrain from a pocket search: *Travels*, III, i, 139; IV, i, 206. Given this empiricist investment in his eyesight, it is particularly disturbing that the punishment with which Gulliver is threatened in Lilliput is blinding: ibid., I, vii, 54, 56. On the potential "corruptions" of the telescope see the comments of Swift's skeptical predecessors in the critique of the new philosophy, Henry Stubbe and Samuel Butler, above, chap. 2, nn. 14–15.

11. David Renaker has argued that only the science of Lagado represents Newtonianism and the experimental method of the Royal Society, and that the abstracted speculators of Laputa represent Cartesian rationalism: "Swift's Laputians as a Caricature of the Cartesians," *PMLA*, 94, no. 5 (Oct., 1979), 936–44.

12. See above, chap. 6, n. 37.

13. Gulliver's facility with languages and translation: *Travels*, I, i, 4, ii, 15, 18–20; II, i, 73; IV, ii, 216. Nautical terminology: ibid., p. xxxv, II, i, 68. Gulliver as a linguist: ibid., II, ii, 79; III, ii, 145–46. On the concern of imaginary voyages with the universal language see above, chap. 6, n. 38. For Ascham see above, chap. 5, n. 50. For Coxere see above, chap. 6, nn. 41–42.

14. Compare Hosea 12:10: "I have used . . . similitudes," which provides the epigraph for *The Pilgrim's Progress*. In his account of the Brazilian Indians, Michel de Montaigne similarly associates economic with linguistic simplicity: "It is a Nation wherein there is no manner of Traffick . . . no use of Service, Riches or Poverty, no Contracts, no Successions, no Dividents . . . no Agriculture, no Mettal, no use of Corn or Wine, and where so much as the very words that signifie, Lying, Treachery, Dissimulation, Avarice, Envy, Detraction and Pardon, were never heard of" (*Essays of Michael seigneur de Montaigne . . .*, trans. Charles Cotton [1685], "Of Canniballs," I, 368–69).

15. See *Travels*, II, i, 78, iv, 98–99, viii, 131; III, xi, 198; IV, ii, 216–17, viii, 251, x, 266, xii, 275–77. Documentation: Part I also contains Gulliver's "Word for Word" translations of several official Lilliputian documents; ibid., I, ii, 18–20, iii, 27–28, vii, 52–53. Gulliver makes clear his intellectual affiliation with the Royal Society by telling us that he has donated several Brobdingnag wasp stings

to that institution; ibid., II, iii, 94. Printing errors: The printer has erroneously transformed "Brobdingrag" into "Brobdingnag"; compare Edward Cooke, *A Voyage to the South Sea, and Round the World* . . . (1712), II, vi, where "Selkirk" is corrected to Selcrag." On quantitative completeness see also *Travels*, II, i, 78, vii, 117.

16. Many narrators of travels, both real and imaginary, made the plausible argument that our doubts concerning the existence of things—lands, peoples, extraordinary animals—we do not know may reflect only our skepticism, not their unreality; e.g., see above, chap. 3, nn. 48–50. John Arbuthnot told Swift of readers who behaved as though *Gulliver's Travels* was authentic; see Arbuthnot to Swift, Nov. 5, 1726, in *Correspondence*, III, 180. On the complexity of Swift's attitude toward travel narratives see also Percy G. Adams, *Travel Literature and the Evolution of the Novel* (Lexington: University Press of Kentucky, 1983), 142–44.

17. Lock has made an important objection to the common and uncritical assumption that much of the political allegory that has been attributed to *Gulliver's Travels* was intended by Swift. But he is wrong to suggest that reference to particular historical cases was foreign to Swift's aim in that work, and to maintain that "to bury the meanings so deeply that the allegory could neither be recognized nor certainly interpreted if discovered was self-defeating" (*Politics of Gulliver's Travels*, 106). I have earlier argued that the uncertainty of allegorical interpretation provides Swift and his contemporaries with a crucial focus for investigating the problem of mediation, especially as that problem was trivialized and aggravated (for people like Swift) by naive empiricist or enthusiastic beliefs in the possibility of an immediate access to truth. This is nowhere more clear than in *A Tale of a Tub* (1704), where Swift attacks simultaneously the opposed but complementary errors of deep and superficial reading. In the episode of the political allegorizers in *Gulliver's Travels* (III, vi, 175), Swift creates a similar sort of double-bind for his readers by calling them "the Natives called *Langden*" "in the Kingdom of *Tribnia*." Lock thinks these are "crudely intrusive anagrams that make the satire . . . needlessly specific" (*Politics of Gulliver's Travels*, 82). But the effect of the names is to implicate us inextricably in the problem of interpretation, for by automatically deciphering them as "England" and "Britain," we replicate the behavior of the projectors whom Swift obliges us to scorn. (Another way of saying this is to suggest that Swift here employs a second-order satire whose principal target is not really "the English" at all, but overly elaborate interpreta-tion—like that required to read the currently popular secret histories and *romans à clef* [see above, chap. 1, nn. 99–100].) Here Swift has a little joke at our expense. But the critical problem of interpretive indeterminacy, although it may feel self-defeating, is a serious one that ramifies into many areas of his thought.

18. See the intelligent discussion of how we are to take Gulliver's claim to historicity in Rawson, *Gulliver and the Gentle Reader*, 9–10.

19. E.g., cf. William Okeley, above, chap. 3, n. 56.

20. On these matters see above, chap. 3, sec. 6.

21. In the first edition, Gulliver elaborates this interpretation to suggest that the Yahoos are the "very much defaced" descendants of specifically English people; see *Travels*, "Textual Notes," 306.

22. See above, chap. 5, sec. 4. The idea that human reason works to corrupt rather than to enhance human nature was a familiar one in political and utopian literature; e.g., in [Gabriel de Foigny], *A New Discovery of Terra Incognita Aus-tralis* . . . (1693), 75–76, the wise old man tells Sadeur that his countrymen "have

some *Sparks of Reason,* but they are so weak, that instead of enlightning them, they only serve to conduct 'em more surely in their Error."

23. Like other conservative writers, Swift thus implicitly mocks the progressive claim that the indulgence of the avaricious passions may help countervail more destructive ones; see above, chap. 6, nn. 25, 53. On the soft and hard schools of interpretation see James L. Clifford, "Gulliver's Fourth Voyage: Hard and Soft Schools of Interpretation," in *Quick Springs of Sense: Studies in the Eighteenth Century,* ed. Larry S. Champion (Athens: University of Georgia Press, 1974), 33–49.

24. The amusing silliness of a Houyhnhnm threading a needle, on the other hand, is Swift's mild self-mockery of the inadequacy of his own efforts (a very minor version of his hero's failings) to mediate Houyhnhnm to human nature by way of physical resemblance. But note that even here it is Gulliver who creates the incongruity by lending the mare a needle: *Travels,* IV, ix, 258. With Gulliver's vain ambition compare the desperate and self-censored aspiration of Mary Carleton to be a different sex (above, chap. 6, nn. 32–34). It is easy to sympathize with her ambition, as it is not in the case of Gulliver's, because hers amounts to a just desire to obtain the power she merits rather than a vain emulation of a status that is beyond her internal capacities.

25. On the circular patterns of conservative plots see above, chap. 6, nn. 21–22.

CHAPTER ELEVEN: THE INSTITUTIONALIZATION OF CONFLICT (I):
RICHARDSON AND THE DOMESTICATION OF SERVICE

1. Samuel Richardson, *Pamela; or, Virtue Rewarded,* ed. T. C. Duncan Eaves and Ben D. Kimpel (Boston: Houghton Mifflin, 1971), 7, prefatory letter attributed to the Reverend William Webster; see also 5, letter of Jean Baptiste de Freval. All parenthetical references in the text are to this edition (hereafter cited as *Pamela*). *Pamela* as a "History": 5, 409. Richardson as "Editor": 3, 4, 6, 9, 412; the editorial voice intrudes on 89–94, 109n, 142, and 408–12. Some of the introductory material added to the second edition refers to the "author" of *Pamela;* see 10, 17, 22.

2. Samuel Richardson to Aaron Hill, Jan. 1741, in *Selected Letters of Samuel Richardson,* ed. John Carroll (Oxford: Clarendon Press, 1964), 39–41. The "real" story is told here (39–40), and is alluded to again in Richardson to Johannes Stinstra, June 2, 1753, ibid., 232. See Samuel Richardson, *Letters Written to and for Particular Friends On the most Important Occasions . . . ,* ed. Brian Downs as *Familiar Letters on Important Occasions* (London: Routledge, 1928), nos. 138 and 139. On the relation of history to moral instruction see de Freval's letter, *Pamela,* 4: "For, as it borrows none of its Excellencies from the romantic Flights of unnatural Fancy, its being founded in Truth and Nature, and built upon Experience, will be a lasting Recommendation to the Discerning and Judicious." For the Protestant rationale, compare Richardson's Bunyanesque explanation: "I am endeavouring to write a Story, which shall catch young and airy Minds, and when Passions run high in them, to shew how they may be directed to laudable Meanings and Purposes, in order to decry such Novels and Romances, as have a Tendency to inflame and corrupt . . . If we can properly mingle Instruction with Entertainment, so as to make the latter *seemingly* the *View,* while the former is *really* the End, I imagine it will be doing a great deal" (Richardson to George Cheyne, Aug. 31, 1741, in *Selected Letters,* 46–47). Richardson was of course aware of the danger

that entertaining means might usurp instructive ends; see, e.g., *Clarissa* (1747–48), I, xv. Richardson was the printer of several works that were important in the propagation of the naive empiricist strain, e.g., Defoe's *A New Family Instructor . . .* (1727), and an expansion of the Churchills' *A Collection of Voyages and Travels . . .* (1732); see William M. Sale, Jr., *Samuel Richardson: Master Printer* (Ithaca: Cornell University Press, 1950), 94, 160, 162.

3. Quoted in T. C. Duncan Eaves and Ben D. Kimpel, *Samuel Richardson: A Biography* (Oxford: Clarendon Press, 1971), 148. (The circumstantial resemblance to Cervantes' dilemma was noted by one of Richardson's anonymous correspondents; see ibid., 138.) Thus Richardson's attempt to capitalize on the impersonal authority of "real events" was partly compromised by his need to claim personal authority over, in any case, the documents themselves. If he was not the inventor, he was at least the proprietor: when his own continuation was printed he copyrighted the two new volumes entirely in his own name, and with his collaborating booksellers he "took further pains to protect his interest from abridgement as well as piracy by obtaining a Royal License for the sole printing, publishing, and sale of the four volumes" (ibid., 145). Spurious continuations: The author of *The Life of Pamela . . .* (1741) has access to "the original Papers now in the Hands of the Reverend Mr. *Perkins* of *Shendisford Abbey*" and berates "whoever put together the other Account that has been published of *Pamela,*" which includes details "supply'd by the Compiler's Invention, when he knew not the real Facts" (2n). See also *Pamela in High Life: or, Virtue Rewarded. In a Series of Familiar Letters from Pamela to her Parents. Carefully Extracted from Original Manuscripts, communicated to the Editor by her Son . . .* (1741). The advertisement for John Kelly's vol. I of *Pamela's Conduct in High Life* (1741) disdainfully boasts that it is "published from original Papers, *without the Consent, or even Knowledge,* of the *pretended* Author of Pamela, or Virtue rewarded" (quoted in Eaves and Kimpel, *Samuel Richardson,* 138). Of course the claim is also made, although from the calculatedly parodic viewpoint of extreme skepticism, by Fielding in *Shamela* (1741); see above, chap. 12, n. 24. For a discussion of *Pamela*'s imitations, continuations, and parodies see Bernard Kriessman, *Pamela-Shamela: A Study of the Criticisms, Burlesques, Parodies, and Adaptations of Richardson's Pamela,* University of Nebraska Studies, n.s., no. 22 (Lincoln: University of Nebraska Press, 1960). For the best account of Richardson's hurried continuation, see Alan D. McKillop, *Samuel Richardson, Printer and Novelist* (Chapel Hill: University of North Carolina Press, [1936] 1960), 51–59. The present discussion is concerned only with Part I of *Pamela.*

4. On which see above, chap. 3, nn. 81–86. Interruption and discontinuity as signs of documentary authenticity were themselves conventional in epistolary discourse; see Robert A. Day, *Told in Letters: Epistolary Fiction before Richardson* (Ann Arbor: University of Michigan Press, 1966), 50–51, 91–93, 225n.20.

5. See *Pamela,* 266, which self-consciously alludes to an earlier passage that is itself concerned with scriptural allusion, Pamela's alteration of the 137th Psalm (127–28). Written in a time of adversity, Pamela's version of sacred writ has been incorporated into her own, and a textual comparison now explicitly juxtaposes it, verse by verse, with the original (267–71). And with this act it is as though Pamela's writ earns the right to an autonomous canonicity, for it is immediately afterward that Mr. B. makes the wholly "secular" allusion to the sunflower (272, alluding to 120).

6. Recent critics have recognized that B. is not essentially motivated by sexual desire: see, especially, Mark Kinkead-Weekes, *Samuel Richardson: Dramatic Novelist* (Ithaca: Cornell University Press, 1973), 22–23, 50–51, 108–9; and Mar-

garet A. Doody, *A Natural Passion: A Study of the Novels of Samuel Richardson* (Oxford: Clarendon Press, 1974), 47–48. See the suggestive contrast between Mr. B.'s and Pamela's "sense of story" in Patricia M. Spacks, *Imagining a Self: Autobiography and Novel in Eighteenth-Century England* (Cambridge: Harvard University Press, 1976), 197.

7. In his own eyes, Williams is the hero of a tentative progressive plot in which he saves Pamela from libertine corruption by a daring marriage proposal (*Pamela*, 129–30); but this scenario is co-opted by B.'s plot of the benevolent arranged marriage. For B.'s first broaching of it see 85–86. For Pamela's predictable view on forced marriages, see 291–92. As we might expect, her father gives her complete freedom in the marriage choice (142). Compare Pamela's plight with that of Mary Carleton, who is called a romancer by her romancing husband (above, chap. 6, n. 22; see also chap. 6, nn. 32–33).

8. Thus Pamela's modulation from discontinuous letters to sustained journal is essential to the rhetorical logic and emotional development of the narrative, and critics are wrong to see it as a "breakdown" of the epistolary method and as evidence of *Pamela*'s formal inferiority to *Clarissa*. See Ian Watt, *The Rise of the Novel: Studies in Defoe, Richardson, and Fielding* (Berkeley and Los Angeles: University of California Press, 1964), 208–9; Donald L. Ball, "*Pamela II:* A Primary Link in Richardson's Development as a Novelist," *Modern Philology*, 65, no. 4 (May, 1968), 341; Eaves and Kimpel, *Samuel Richardson*, 149.

9. For the comparison to *Robinson Crusoe*, see letter of Nov. 15, 1740, to Richardson's publisher, Charles Rivington, partially printed in the second edition of *Pamela*, 12–13 (the quoted passage is omitted by Richardson but printed by his modern editors [12n.8]).

10. Many critics have observed Richardson's debt to *Guy of Warwick* for the account of Colbrand; but recall B.'s claim, in this respect plausible, that "the Girl's Head's turn'd by Romances" (90). Kinkead-Weekes, *Samuel Richardson*, 431, rightly points out (with B.) the "pronounced exaggerations, the vivid blacks and whites" of Pamela's judgment, but he slights the very real degree to which her "paranoia" is justified and her prudence not a weakness but a virtue (55–57). On *Pamela* and popular romance, see D. C. Muecke, "Beauty and Mr. B.," *Studies in English Literature*, 7, no. 3 (1967), 467–74; Margaret Dalziel, "Richardson and Romance," *Journal of Australasian Universities Language and Literature Association*, 33 (May, 1970), 5–24; Carol H. Flynn, *Samuel Richardson: Man of Letters* (Princeton: Princeton University Press, 1982), chap. 4.

11. The author of the defense is unknown; it was printed in the second edition of *Pamela*, 21. Lady Davers's view of the effect of Pamela's example is supported by Fielding in *Shamela* (see above, chap. 12), and by the author of *Pamela Censured . . .* (1741), ed. Charles Batten, Jr., *Augustan Reprint Society*, no. 175 (1976), 18–19. Cf. *The Ladies Calling* (1673), quoted in Katherine Hornbeak, "Richardson's *Familiar Letters* and the Domestic Conduct Books," *Smith College Studies in Modern Languages*, 19, no. 2 (Jan., 1938), 25. For discussions of contemporary models of radically mixed marriages in narrative and drama as well as in historical experience, see McKillop, *Samuel Richardson*, 29–35; Ira Konigsberg, *Samuel Richardson and the Dramatic Novel* (Lexington: University Press of Kentucky, 1968), 17–28; Doody, *A Natural Passion*, 36–40. See also above, chap. 6, sec. 5.

12. On this terminological battle see Spacks, *Imagining a Self*, 210–11, 212–13. Pamela's protestation of her father's more elevated past leads the incensed Lady Davers to wonder if soon there will be "a Search at the Herald's-office, to set out thy wretched Obscurity" (*Pamela*, 328). But when Mr. Andrews is persuaded to borrow Mr. B.'s coat and waistcoat, "they fitted him very well" (ibid., 264; the

social significance of clothing in *Pamela* is discussed later in this chapter). Of course Lady Davers herself has married into the aristocracy. In Part II, chap. xxix, Mr. B.'s modernity is expressed by his rejection of the idea of seeking a baronetcy.

13. For a fuller discussion of these matters see above, chap. 4, nn. 38–41.

14. Compare Aphra Behn's instructive variation on this progressive pattern in *The Fair Jilt* (1696): above, chap. 6, nn. 48–49. Compare Terry Eagleton, *The Rape of Clarissa: Writing, Sexuality, and Class Struggle in Samuel Richardson* (Oxford: Blackwell, 1982), 57–60, where the rapist's (in this case, Lovelace's) desire for repossession is conceived in the psychoanalytic terms of the search for the lost phallus.

15. In Part II Pamela bears Mr. B. seven children, but Richardson evidently did not see motherhood as necessary to his original conception of her fulfillment, which was to have been accomplished in Part I.

16. In *Pamela*, Part II, letter xcviii, B. says that he "must look out for a *better* Guide to conduct me, than the proud Word *Honour* can be, in the general Acceptation of it among us lively young Gentlemen."

17. On the tension between the theory and practice of domestic service, see J. Jean Hecht, *The Domestic Servant Class in Eighteenth-Century England* (London: Routledge and Kegan Paul, 1956), chap. 3; on servants' "confederacies" see ibid., pp. 85–87. On the powers of the justice of the peace see David Ogg, *England in the Reign of Charles II,* 2nd ed. (London: Oxford University Press, [1934] 1963), 487–90; Christopher Hill, *Reformation to Industrial Revolution, 1530–1780,* Pelican Economic History of England, vol. 2 (Harmondsworth: Penguin, 1971), 140–42. After Pamela escapes from Lady Davers, Sir Simon Darnford domesticates the political office he shares with Mr. B. by telling her that had she not a good excuse for being late, "your Spouse and I should have sat in Judgment upon you, and condemned you to a fearful Punishment for your first Crime of *Laesae Majestatis* (I had this explained to me afterwards, as a sort of Treason against my Liege Lord and Husband)" (*Pamela,* 334). On the meaning of "trial" in *Pamela,* see Albert M. Lyles, "Pamela's Trials," *College Language Association Journal,* 8, no. 3 (March, 1965), 290–92. Pamela briefly "hopes to get a Party among" the farm tenants with whom she stays during her kidnapping to the Lincolnshire estate (*Pamela,* 100).

18. The projector is Christopher Tancred, *A Scheme for an Act of Parliament for the Better Regulating Servants, and Ascertaining Their Wages* (1724), 19–20, quoted in Hecht, *Domestic Servant Class,* 92; see also ibid., 83–85.

19. On livery as resonant of enslavement see Hecht, *Domestic Servant Class,* 35, 179. On the dangers of cast-off clothing see ibid., 120–23, 209–11.

20. On the "chain of emulation" see ibid., 204.

21. For useful discussions see Robert P. Utter and Gwendolyn B. Needham, *Pamela's Daughters* (New York: Macmillan, 1936), chap. 2; Watt, *Rise of the Novel,* 135–51. Needless to say, there is no single "parable" that can describe the experience of both upper- and lower-rank women.

22. See above, n. 8.

23. Cf. Richardson's use of the word "enlargement" to describe his own creation of *Pamela,* above, n. 2.

24. On these matters Pamela has important predecessors: compare the epistolary powers of Mercy Harvey, the creative ambitions of Mary Carleton, and the self-publication of Francis Kirkman (above, chap. 6, nn. 45, 32–36). See, in general, Ruth Perry, *Women, Letters, and the Novel* (New York: AMS Press, 1980), chap. 5.

25. On the "little" and the "great" family in the gentle household, see Randolph Trumbach, *The Rise of the Egalitarian Family: Aristocratic Kinship and Domes-*

tic Relations in Eighteenth-Century England (New York: Academic Press, 1978), 129.

26. Hecht, *Domestic Servant Class,* 223. Compare *Pamela,* 280, where Pamela enunciates her hope to incite respectively in the good, the indifferent, and the bad servant encouragement, emulation, and reform. For the role of charity in confirming the protagonist's ascent see Deloney's *Jack of Newbery,* above, chap. 6, nn. 14–15.

27. On Mary Carleton see above, chap. 6, nn. 32–34.

28. See, most recently, Eagleton, *The Rape of Clarissa,* 37, 39, who concedes that *Pamela* "contains, grotesque though it may sound, a utopian element," but derides it nonetheless as "a cynical displacement of women's sufferings into consolatory myth" and sharply opposes its comic "celebration of male ruling-class power" to the "devastating demystification" and "tragic reality" of *Clarissa.*

CHAPTER TWELVE: THE INSTITUTIONALIZATION OF CONFLICT (II):
FIELDING AND THE INSTRUMENTALITY OF BELIEF

1. During Henry Fielding's lifetime the family was thought to derive from the Hapsburgs, a spurious genealogy that was concocted once Denbigh's main line had been raised to the peerage after his marriage to the Duke of Buckingham's sister in 1622. On Fielding's lineage and on the custody suit, see Wilber L. Cross, *The History of Henry Fielding,* 3 vols. (New Haven: Yale University Press, 1918), vol. I, chap. 1. On the inflation of honors under Buckingham and James I, see above, chap. 4, n. 31. For Richardson's sensitivity see Samuel Richardson to David Graham, May 3, 1750, in *Selected Letters of Samuel Richardson,* ed. John Carroll (Oxford: Clarendon Press, 1964), 158.

2. Henry Fielding, *The Author's Farce,* ed. Charles B. Woods, Regents Restoration Drama Series (Lincoln: University of Nebraska Press, 1966), II, x, 15–17 (the speaker is the hero's beloved). For the unity of time see idem, *Historical Register,* ed. William W. Appleton, Regents Restoration Drama Series (Lincoln: University of Nebraska Press, 1967), I, 58–59, 66–69, where Sourwit wonders "how you can bring the actions of a whole year into the circumference of four-and-twenty hours," and Medley replies, "My register is not to be filled like those of vulgar news-writers with trash for want of news, and therefore if I say little or nothing, you may thank those who have done little or nothing." See Fielding's *Jonathan Wild* (1743), I, vii, and *Tom Jones* (1749), II, i, for a similar comparison and argument. Ronald Paulson, *Satire and the Novel in Eighteenth-Century England* (New Haven: Yale University Press, 1967), 52–53, observes the affinity between Pope's and Fielding's satire on the spectacles of "the Smithfield Muses." On the analogy of world and stage see J. Paul Hunter, *Occasional Form: Henry Fielding and the Chains of Circumstance* (Baltimore: Johns Hopkins University Press, 1975), 57–67; see also Hunter's suggestive discussion of reflexiveness in Fielding's drama (69–74). On the formal relations between drama and narrative see above, chap. 3, nn. 81–86.

3. *Jonathan Wild* was published in 1743 as Volume III of the *Miscellanies.* On its composition see F. Homes Dudden, *Henry Fielding: His Life, Works, and Times* (Oxford: Clarendon Press, 1952), I, 480–483; Bertrand A. Goldgar, *Walpole and the Wits: The Relation of Politics to Literature, 1722–1742* (Lincoln: University of Nebraska Press, 1976), 197–98. On the extent and character of Fielding's historiographical reading see Robert M. Wallace, "Fielding's Knowledge of History and Biography," *Studies in Philology,* 44, no. 1 (Jan., 1947), 89–107.

4. For the primary critique of traditional biography see Henry Fielding,

Jonathan Wild, ed. A. R. Humphreys and Douglas Brooks (London: Everyman's Library, 1973), I, ii–iii, 5–9; II, xii, 79–81; III, vi, 100–01 (hereafter cited as *Jonathan Wild* [Everyman's ed.]). All parenthetical references in the text are to this edition and include book, chapter, and page numbers. In these examples, the second-level critique occurs where the supernatural intrusion of dolphins and sea horses is disowned only to be replaced by the ostentatiously "natural" intrusion of authorial rationales, and the eloquence of modern heroes also is shown to be an invention. For parody of the authenticating devices of criminal biography see ibid., I, vii, 22, xiii, 36; II, vii, 67–68; III, vi, 100, vii, 103; IV, xii–xiii, 163–65, xiv, 169. On the form of criminal biography see above, chap. 3, nn. 16–24. Among the several models available to Fielding for the writing of this particular life was Daniel Defoe's *True and Genuine Account of the Life and Actions of the late Jonathan Wild; not Made up out of Fiction & Fable, but Taken from his own Mouth, and Collected from Papers of his own Writing* (1725). On Wild's contemporary notoriety see William R. Irwin, *The Making of Jonathan Wild: A Study in the Literary Method of Henry Fielding* (New York: Columbia University Press, 1941), chap. 1. Maximillian Novak observes in Fielding and Swift a similar distrust of the materials of criminal biography as conducive to a "wrong kind of art"; see his *Realism, Myth, and History in Defoe's Fiction* (Lincoln: University of Nebraska Press, 1983), 122.

5. For *Jonathan Wild* as a normatively stable mock-heroic, see William J. Farrell, "The Mock-Heroic Form of *Jonathan Wild,*" *Modern Philology,* 63, no. 3 (Feb., 1966), 216–26. On its formal instability see John M. Steadman, *Milton and the Renaissance Hero* (Oxford: Clarendon Press, 1967), 173; and C. J. Rawson, *Henry Fielding and the Augustan Ideal under Stress* (London: Routledge and Kegan Paul, 1972), 158. On the relation between the critique of ancient heroes and that of ancient historians in *Jonathan Wild,* see ibid., 148–55.

6. On the Machiavellian connection see, generally, Bernard Shea, "Machiavelli and Fielding's *Jonathan Wild,*" *PMLA,* 72, no. 1 (March, 1957), 54–73. Shea argues that Fielding was indebted to the 1695 translation of Machiavelli by the republican Henry Neville, and he sees an especially close parallel between Fielding's version of Wild's career and the *Life of Castruccio Castracani of Lucca* (ibid., 66–73). On Machiavellian *virtù* see above, chap. 5, nn. 16–18. On the common application of the term "great man" to Walpole for purposes of both praise and blame, see John E. Wells, "Fielding's Political Purpose in *Jonathan Wild,*" *PMLA,* 28, no. 1 (1913), 14–19.

7. Henry Fielding, "An Essay on Conversation," in *Miscellanies by Henry Fielding, Esq;* (1743), vol. I, ed. Henry K. Miller (Oxford: Clarendon Press, 1972), 138, 140; Henry Fielding, "An Essay on Nothing," ibid., 186. In his imaginary voyages of Job Vinegar, Fielding satirizes the belief of the Ptfghsiumgski or "Inconstants" that the virtues of the nobility "descend in a perpetual Line to their Posterity"; see *Champion,* no. 106 (July 17, 1740), in "The Voyages of Mr. Job Vinegar," ed. S. J. Sackett, *Augustan Reprint Society,* no. 67 (1958), 7.

8. Compare Henry Fielding, *The Covent-Garden Journal,* ed. Gerard E. Jensen (New Haven: Yale University Press, 1915), no. 4 (Jan. 14, 1752), I, 156, where Fielding defines "Honour" simply as "Duelling." For other instances of Fielding's ironic subversion of gentility and aristocratic honor see Glenn W. Hatfield, *Henry Fielding and the Language of Irony* (Chicago: University of Chicago Press, 1968), 19–20, 117–18, 163–65, 168–73. Rawson is particularly sensitive to the comic oafishness of Fielding's protagonist; see his *Henry Fielding,* especially chap. 4.

9. The corollary is explicit in Fielding's diatribes against hereditary honor.

E.g., see Henry Fielding, *The Champion*, 2 vols (1741), Nov. 17, 1739, I, 8, 10–11: "This Esteem for hereditary Honour was at so high a Pitch among [the ancient Romans], that they looked on the *Plebians* as Persons of almost a different Species, which may, I think, be collected from the Appelation they gave to what we call an Upstart, namely, *Novus Homo, a new Man* . . . I have often wondered how such Words as *Upstart, First of his Family,* &c. crept into a Nation, whose Strength and Support is Trade . . . For my Part, I am at a Loss to see why a Man, who has brought 100,000 *l.* into his Country by a beneficial Trade, is not as worthy and honourable a Member of the Community, as he who hath spent that Sum abroad, or sent it thither after *French* Wines and *French* Foppery."

10. Paulson, *Satire and the Novel*, 75, argues that John Gay's *The Beggar's Opera* (1728) "was Fielding's most important source for the use of the heroic level as a parallel instead of a contrast to his subject." Fielding's own *Don Quixote in England* (1734) uses the wise madness of the Cervantic protagonist to discern the rogue in the statesman or vice versa; see Paulson, *Satire and the Novel*, 89. On the assimilationism of rogues and statesmen compare Fielding's account of *Jonathan Wild* in the "Preface" to the *Miscellanies*, ed. cit., I, 13: "This Bombast Greatness then is the Character I intend to expose . . . [which takes] to itself not only Riches and Power, but often Honour, or at least the Shadow of it." In his *Brief and true History of Robert Walpole and his Family From Their Original to the Present Time* . . . (1738), William Musgrave spends thirty-eight pages tracing Walpole's lineage up from the Norman Conquest. Among his sources are "several ancient Charters in the Custody of the Right Honourable Sir *Robert Walpole,* who out of Regard to Literature, and the Memory of his Ancestors, favoured me with the Perusal of them" (2).

11. Fielding is not the only writer to see the possibilities of this sort of generic conflation. *The Statesman's Progress* . . . (1741), an anonymous parodic fusion of *The Pilgrim's Progress* and *The Life and Death of Mr. Badman*, narrates the allegorical journey of a rogue figure toward "Greatness Hill"; see Irwin's discussion in *The Making of Jonathan Wild*, 46–47. For the classic conservative reduction see *Champion*, June 10, 1740, II, 318. On the fortuitous accident of birth see above, n. 7. Compare *Champion*, Dec. 6, 1739, I, 66, 67, where Fielding gives a characteristically conservative account of Oliver Cromwell's career as exemplifying the Juvenalian maxim that *"Fortune often picks a great Man, in Jest, out of the lowest of People."* Cromwell is the Machiavellian "new prince" who owes his power "principally to Chance; namely, to the Death of those great Men whom the long Continuance of the Civil War had exhausted; those who begun [*sic*] that War would have disdained to have seen the Nation enslaved to the absolute Will of a Subject, in Rank very little above the common Level." For related conservative accounts of the macronarrative of the English Revolution see above, chap. 6, n. 18.

12. Conservative ideologues were able to understand marriages of convenience as an institution of aristocratic culture given new life by the culture's supposed, progressive antagonist. For another context in which Fielding clearly associates such marriages with the new monied culture, see *Champion*, no. 114 (Aug. 5, 1740), in "Voyages of Mr. Job Vinegar," ed. cit., 15–17. Paulson, *Satire and the Novel*, 80, remarks on the characteristic inadequacy of Fielding's "great" villains as lovers, in contrast to their political and financial success; cf. Justice Squeezum in Fielding's *Rape upon Rape; or, The Coffee-House Politician* (1730). For the parallel between theft and financial investment, and for the conservative hierarchy of appetites, see above, chap. 6, nn. 31, 53–54.

13. Hatfield, *Henry Fielding*, 40.

14. Henry Fielding, "An Essay on the Knowledge of the Characters of Men," in *Miscellanies,* ed. cit., I, 154–55; *Champion,* no. 98 (June 28, 1740), in "Voyages of Mr. Job Vinegar," ed. cit., 5. In a parody of the Royal Society's *Philosophical Transactions,* Fielding combines the critique of naive empiricism with the critique of the naive progressive enchantment with money; see "Some Papers Proper to be Read before the R——l Society, Concerning the Terrestrial Chrysipus, Golden-Foot or Guinea," in *Miscellanies,* ed. cit., I, 191–204. (For other satirical allusions to the Royal Society by Fielding see ibid., p. xl, n. 1; and Hatfield, *Henry Fielding,* pp. 30–31 and n. 8.). With Fielding's cult of MNEY compare Eliza Haywood's cult of Lust and Pecunia in her *Memoirs of a Certain Island* (1725), above, chap. 6, n. 53.

15. E.g., cf. Allan Wendt, "The Moral Allegory of *Jonathan Wild,*" *ELH,* 24 (1970), 302–20; and Rawson, *Henry Fielding,* chap. 7.

16. Henry Fielding, *The Journal of a Voyage to Lisbon* (1755), printed with *Jonathan Wild* (Everyman's ed.), "Author's Preface," I, 187; see, generally, 183–88. The deleted chapter is IV, ix of the 1743 edition. Its subtitle invokes the maxim "strange, therefore true": "A very wonderful chapter indeed; which, to those who have not read many voyages, may seem incredible; and which the reader may believe or not, as he pleases" (*The Life of Mr Jonathan Wild the Great* [London: Shakespeare Head, n.d.], IV, ix, 196). For a parody of the self-advertising mode in travel narratives see *Champion,* no. 112 (July 31, 1740), in "Voyages of Mr. Job Vinegar," ed. cit., 12–15. Fielding precedes this parodic political allegory by complaining that "there are a sort of Men so sceptical in their Opinions, that they are unwilling to believe any Thing which they do not see . . . Several excellent Accounts of *Asia* and *Africa* have been look'd on as little better than fabulous Romances. But if a Traveller hath the good Fortune to satisfy his Curiosity by the Discovery of any new Countries, any Islands never before known, his Reader allows him no more Credit than is given to the Adventures of *Cassandra,* or the celebrated Countess *Danois's Fairy Tales.* To omit *Robinson Cruso,* and other grave Writers, the facetious Capt. *Gulliver* is more admired, I believe, for his Wit than his Truth" (*Champion,* no. 55 [March 20, 1740], in "Voyages of Mr. Job Vinegar," ed. cit. 1). See also Fielding's imaginary voyage, which opens with the discovered manuscript topos and has been refused by the Royal Society (according to its discoverer) because "there was nothing in it wonderful enough for them": *A Journey from This World to the Next* (1743), ed. C. J. Rawson (London: Everyman's Library, 1973), 2. As Rawson observes (viii–xiii), the formal self-consciousness of the *Journey* seems to be aimed both at a Lucianic or Scriblerian satire of "learned" works and at a parody of the modern claim to historicity. Fielding much admired the works of Lucian, among them the *True History;* see the discussion in Henry K. Miller, *Essays on Fielding's Miscellanies: A Commentary on Volume One* (Princeton: Princeton University Press, 1961), 366–86.

17. With Mrs. Heartfree's tale compare the first account of Bavia's adventures in W. P., *The Jamaica Lady; or, The Life of Bavia* (1720), in which Bavia refuses the advances of the ship's captain on the grounds "that her honor was dearer to her than her life," but promises him, in exchange for her deliverance, "one rich jewel of a very great value, which she brought with her by accident." The skeptical audience to this account, Captain Fustian, "believed it (as he afterwards found it) all a romance." See William H. McBurney, ed., *Four before Richardson: Selected English Novels, 1720–1727* (Lincoln: University of Nebraska Press, 1963), 100, 102. For the common "jewel/jewel" metaphor see, e.g., Samuel Richardson, *Pamela* (1740), ed. T. C. Duncan Eaves and Ben D. Kimpel (Boston: Houghton Mifflin, 1971), 166.

18. See *Champion*, Jan. 22, 1740, I, 208–9 (cf. Heartfree on the same subject, *Jonathan Wild* (Everyman's ed.), III, ii, 88–89); Fielding, "An Essay on Conversation," in *Miscellanies*, ed. cit., I, 127–28.

19. On the political significance of Fielding's family background see Brian McCrea, *Henry Fielding and the Politics of Mid-Eighteenth Century England* (Athens: University of Georgia Press, 1981), chap. 2. For documentation of Fielding's great admiration for Marlborough see ibid., 217n.19. Contrast Swift and other conservative authors, above, chap. 5, n. 55; chap. 6, nn. 24–25. McCrea's useful argument nevertheless ignores some important evidence of Fielding's profound distaste for monied culture. For a review of the evidence for the general proposition that Fielding took money from Walpole, and for the particular role of *Jonathan Wild* in this relationship, see Martin C. Battestin, "Fielding's Changing Politics and *Joseph Andrews*," *Philological Quarterly*, 39, no. 1 (Jan., 1960), 39–55; Goldgar, *Walpole and the Wits*, 197–98, 205–7. Goldgar (219) summarizes how most of the men of letters contemporary with Fielding "sought some accommodation with the administration." Fielding later defended a writer's changing sides for money; see *The Jacobite's Journal*, ed. W. B. Coley (Oxford: Oxford University Press, for Wesleyan University Press, 1975), no. 17 (March 26, 1748), 215.

20. For Fielding's extreme skepticism, compare *Champion*, March 1, 1740, I, 322: "Writing seems to be understood as arrogating to yourself a Superiority (which of all others will be granted with the greatest Reluctance) of the Understanding . . . *The Understanding, like the Eye* (says Mr. *Lock) whilst it makes us see and perceive all other Things, takes no Notice of itself; and it requires Art and Pains to set it at a Distance and make it its own Object.* This Comparison, fine as it is, is inadequate: For the Eye can contemplate itself in a Glass, but no *Narcissus* hath hitherto discovered any Mirrour for the Understanding, no Knowledge of which is to be obtained but by the Means Mr. *Lock* prescribes, which as it requires Art and Pains, or in other Words, a very good Understanding to execute, it generally happens that the Superiority in it, is a Cause tried on every dark and presumptive Evidence, and a Verdict commonly found by self Love for ourselves." On Lockean epistemology and the analogy between knowledge and visual sense perception see above, chap. 2, nn. 31–32, 36. On the parallel between magistrate and narrator see the discussion in Paulson, *Satire and the Novel*, 96.

21. For a related argument concerning what he calls Fielding's "language of irony" see Hatfield, *Henry Fielding*, esp. chap. 6.

22. The device was common in the French antiromance: cf. [Charles Sorel], *The Extravagant Shepherd* . . . (1654), trans. John Davies, 193; and [Antoine Furetière], *Scarron's City Romance* . . . (1671) (a translation of Furetière's *Roman Bourgeois*), 19. See also Samuel Richardson, "Hints of Prefaces for Clarissa," 2, in *Clarissa: Preface, Hints of Prefaces, and Postscript*, ed. R. F. Brissenden, *Augustan Reprint Society*, no. 103 (1964).

23. The unity is artificial, however, if limited to this interchange. Part II of *Pamela*, which was begun two weeks after the publication of *Shamela* in April, 1741, may be at least in part a counterdefense against it; see Owen Jenkins, "Richardson's *Pamela* and Fielding's 'Vile Forgeries,'" *Philological Quarterly*, 44 (Oct., 1965), 200–210.

24. Henry Fielding, *An Apology for the Life of Mrs. Shamela Andrews* . . . (1741), in *Joseph Andrews and Shamela*, ed. Martin C. Battestin (Boston: Houghton Mifflin, 1961), 299, 306–8, 337, 339; all parenthetical citations to *Shamela* in the text are to this edition. A source for Fielding's credulous clergyman may be found in the Mr. Tickletext of Aphra Behn's *The Feign'd*

504 Notes to Pages 396–399

Curtezans; or, A Night's Intrigue (1679) (see above, chap. 3, n. 55). Fielding refers to Behn's character in discussing the absurdities of the claim to historicity in travel journals; see "Author's Preface," *Voyage to Lisbon*, 187–88. Behn's Tickletext as a source for Fielding's has been overlooked by editors of *Shamela;* see, e.g., Fielding, *Joseph Andrews and Shamela*, ed. Sheridan Baker (New York: Thomas Y. Crowell, 1972), 9–10n.9. Fielding was not the only critic of *Pamela* who used the strategy of claiming to possess the truly authentic papers; see above, chap. 11, n. 3.

25. See above, chap. 6, nn. 32–34.

26. Hugh Amory, "*Shamela* as Aesopic Satire," *ELH*, 38, no. 2 (June, 1971), 241. On Fielding's second marriage see Cross, *History of Henry Fielding*, II, 60; his first wife had died three years earlier. The parallel with Mr. B. and Pamela did not escape the notice of Fielding's critics (ibid., II, 61).

27. With Fielding's Booby compare Swift's Lord Munodi, above, chap. 10, n. 7. For Pamela's exultation see *Pamela*, 315.

28. On Fielding's satire of complacent, and of High Church, Anglicanism see, respectively, Hunter, *Occasional Form*, 78–80, and Amory, "*Shamela* as Aesopic Satire," 245–46. On Methodist satire—and the relation of Methodism to Puritanism—see Eric Rothstein, "The Framework of *Shamela*," *ELH*, 35, no. 3 (1968), 389–95. On the continuity between seventeenth-century radical Protestantism and eighteenth-century Methodism see, generally, Umphrey Lee, *The Historical Backgrounds of Early Methodist Enthusiasm* (New York: Columbia University Press, 1931). For a discussion of pious, and specifically Methodist, journals, lives, and spiritual autobiographies of the 1730s and 1740s that reflect many features of their seventeenth-century predecessors, see Jerry C. Beasley, *Novels of the 1740s* (Athens: University of Georgia Press, 1982), 128–34. On the provenance of Tickletext's credulity see above, n. 24.

29. On the relationship between "latitudinarian" liberal Anglicanism and capitalist ideology see above, chap. 5, nn. 42–43. Compare *Champion*, Jan. 24, 1740, I, 213: "Virtue is not . . . of that morose and rigid Nature, which some mistake her to be . . . she has been known to raise some to the highest Dignities in the State, in the Army, and in the Law. So that we find Virtue and Interest are not . . . as repugnant as Fire and Water." For the defense of actions over words see *Champion*, Dec. 11, 1739, I, 79; and Fielding, "An Essay on the Knowledge of the Characters of Men," in *Miscellanies*, ed. cit., I, 162–63 (cf. *Jonathan Wild* [Everyman's ed.], IV, xv, 174). On the stealthy recapitulation in Swift's *Tale*, and its relation to the double reversal of extreme skepticism, see above, chap. 5, n. 36.

30. Henry Fielding, *The History of the Adventures of Joseph Andrews And of his Friend Mr. Abraham Adams. Written in Imitation of The Manner of Cervantes, Author of Don Quixote* (1742), ed. Martin C. Battestin (Oxford: Clarendon Press, 1967), I, v, 29–30, x, 47 (hereafter cited as *Joseph Andrews*). All parenthetical citations in the text and in the notes of this chapter are to this edition, and include book, chapter, and page numbers. While still in her service, Joseph hopes "your Ladyship can't tax me with ever betraying the Secrets of the Family, and I hope, if you was to turn me away, I might have the Character of you" (ibid., I, v, 29). When he later learns that Lady Booby "would not give him a Character," Joseph says that he will nonetheless always give her "a good Character where-ever he went" (ibid., IV, i, 279). On the importance of these matters of "character" in *Pamela*, see above, chap. 11. n. 18. On Joseph and Abraham as embodiments of chastity and charity, see Martin C. Battestin, *The Moral Basis of Fielding's Art: A Study of Joseph Andrews* (Middletown, Ct.: Wesleyan University Press, 1959), chaps. 2, 3, and passim.

31. Many critics have observed this. However, it is worth noting that what is ludicrous is not male chastity itself but the spuriously social resonance it acquires in this particular encounter. On male chastity see above, chap. 4, n. 40.

32. See the observations of Paulson, *Satire and the Novel*, 120.

33. E.g., see Samuel Johnson, *Rambler,* no. 99 (Feb. 26, 1751), in *The Rambler,* ed. W. J. Bate and Albrecht B. Strauss, Yale Edition of the Works of Samuel Johnson (New Haven: Yale University Press, 1969), II, 164–69.

34. E.g., see *Joseph Andrews,* I, ii, 20, xvi, 71–72; II, xv, 168; III, vi, 235, vii, 246, ix, 255; IV, v, 289, xvi, 339.

35. In *Jacobite's Journal,* ed. cit., no. 13 (Feb. 27, 1748), 177–78, Fielding attacks Thomas Carte's *General History of England* as a "great Romance," compares it to these same popular romances, and advises that if published serially as they are, it should have as good a sale as "the inimitable Adventures of *Robinson Crusoe.*"

36. The difficulty of the exercise is suggested by the fact that in another context Fielding used the story of Cardenio, Ferdinand, Dorothea, and Lucinda as an example of how Cervantes "in many Instances, approaches very near to the Romances which he ridicules": *Covent-Garden Journal,* ed. cit., no. 24 (March 24, 1752), I, 281. In the absence of a stable critical theory, to reject naive empiricism inevitably risks a return to its antagonist, romance idealism.

37. Thus, just as Fielding distinguishes his own "true history" from the naive claim to historicity that he discredits, so here he distinguishes the "comic Romance" from the serious "Romance." And we would seem to be justified in identifying the latter with "those voluminous Works commonly called *Romances*" (*Joseph Andrews,* "Preface," 3–4), that is, with the French heroic romances that he later alludes to as those "immense Romances" and that he discredits for their idealist detachment from both nature and history (see above). As Sheridan Baker has argued, and despite modern critical practice, the significant generic term in the "Preface" is "comic Romance" and not the pedantically exhaustive synonym "comic Epic-Poem in Prose"; see Baker's "Henry Fielding's Comic Romances," *Papers of the Michigan Academy of Science, Arts, and Letters,* 45 (1960), 441.

38. Contrast the following passages from *Joseph Andrews:* "to which likewise he had some other Inducements which the Reader, without being a Conjurer, cannot possibly guess; 'till we have given him those hints, which it may be now proper to open" (I, x, 47); and "Indeed, I have been often assured by both, that they spent these Hours in a most delightful Conversation: but as I never could prevail on either to relate it, so I cannot communicate it to the Reader" (II, xv, 168).

39. Compare the technique of Cervantes (above, chap. 7, sec. 1). The invasion of "historical" contiguity by "romance" similarity is especially pleasing when it occurs within an interpolated tale, which is already itself an interruption of the linear plot and which nonetheless may lay claim to being integral with it. A good example of this in *Jonathan Wild* is the disruption of Mrs. Heartfree's travel narrative by Wild's marital outrage. The best instance in *Joseph Andrews* is the progressive plot of Leonora (II, iv–vi), which is accompanied by claims to historicity but interrupted by the conservative themes that arise during Adams's fistfight at the inn.

40. In *Joseph Andrews* Fanny also has a "natural Gentility" (II, xii, 153), so much so that once on the road she is more than once taken to be a young lady of quality either run or stolen away from her parents (III, ii, 199–200, ix, 257).

41. Thus the status of Fielding's narratives as expressions of a belief in a providentially ordered universe seems to me far more problematic—or, at its

simplest level, far less interesting—than it does to Aubrey Williams, "Interpositions of Providence and the Design of Fielding's Novels," *South Atlantic Quarterly,* 70, no. 1 (Spring, 1971), 265–86; see also Martin C. Battestin, *The Providence of Wit: Aspects of Form in Augustan Literature and the Arts* (Oxford: Clarendon Press, 1974), chap. 5. See above, chap. 3, nn. 75–80. For Fielding's instrumental belief in divine justice see, e.g., above, n. 18.

CONCLUSION

1. A new form: Samuel Richardson to Aaron Hill, 1741 and Jan. 5 and 26, 1747, and Richardson to Lady Echlin, Oct. 10, 1754, in *Selected Letters of Samuel Richardson,* ed. John Carroll (Oxford: Clarendon Press, 1964), 41, 76, 78, 316; Henry Fielding, *Joseph Andrews* (1742), "Author's Preface," and *Tom Jones* (1748), II, i. Affirmed by others: on Richardson see Aaron Hill to Richardson, May, 1743, and May, 1748, in *The Works of the Late Aaron Hill . . .* (1753), II, 228, 269; comments of Philip Skelton and Joseph Spence, ca. 1750, in Richardson's "Hints of Prefaces for Clarissa," *Clarissa: Preface, Hints of Prefaces, and Postscript,* ed. R. F. Brissenden, *Augustan Reprint Society,* no. 103 (1964), 7, 8; [Edward Young], *Conjectures on Original Composition. In a Letter to the Author of Sir Charles Grandison* (1759), 77–78; on Fielding see comments of P. F. G. Desfontaines (1743), William Warburton (1751), and Dr. John Hill (1751), in Ronald Paulson and Thomas Lockwood, eds., *Henry Fielding: The Critical Heritage* (London: Routledge and Kegan Paul, 1969), 126–27, 282, 283; [Francis Coventry], *An Essay on the New Species of Writing Founded by Mr Fielding . . .* (1751), ed. Alan D. McKillop, *Augustan Reprint Society,* no. 95 (1962). In the same breath: e.g., see *The History of Charlotte Summers . . .* (1750), "Preface" to *The Adventures of a Valet* (1752), and William Whitehead, *The World,* no. 19 (May 10, 1753), in Paulson and Lockwood, *Fielding: Critical Heritage,* 221–22, 337, 362. Mutual appreciation: see Fielding, *Jacobite's Journal,* no. 5 (Dec. 26, 1747), and letter to Richardson, Oct. 15, 1748, in Ioan Williams, ed., *The Criticism of Henry Fielding* (New York: Barnes and Noble, 1970), 201–2, 188–90; Richardson to Edward Moore, Oct. 3, 1748, quoted in T. C. Duncan Eaves and Ben D. Kimpel, *Samuel Richardson: A Biography* (Oxford: Clarendon Press, 1971), 294. Modern impulse: William Park has argued with some plausibility the common pursuit rather than the conflict of Richardson and Fielding: see his "Fielding *and* Richardson," *PMLA,* 81, no. 5 (Oct., 1966), 381–88; and "What Was New about the 'New Species of Writing'?" *Studies in the Novel,* 2, no. 2 (Summer, 1970), 112–30. Richardson's resentment: see Richardson to Lady Bradshaigh, late 1749, in *Selected Letters,* 133–34; Alan D. McKillop, "The Personal Relations between Fielding and Richardson," *Modern Philology,* 28 (1931), 423–25, 433; and idem, *Samuel Richardson, Printer and Novelist* (Chapel Hill: University of North Carolina Press, [1936] 1960), 73. An authoritative scholar, McKillop nonetheless tends here to understate matters of conflict. Friendly contact: Richardson told several correspondents that Fielding was among those who advised him to give *Clarissa* a happy ending, and Fielding is said to have received aid from Richardson in obtaining accommodations in Lisbon shortly before his death: see Eaves and Kimpel, *Samuel Richardson,* 295, 305. Continuing acrimony: see Richardson to Aaron Hill, July 12 and Aug. 18, 1749, Astraea and Minerva Hill, Aug. 4, 1749, Frances Grainger, Jan. 22, 1750, J. B. de Freval, Jan. 21, 1751, Thomas Edwards, Feb. 21, 1752, Anne Donnellan, Feb. 22, 1752, and Lady Bradshaigh, Feb. 23, 1752, in *Selected Letters,* 126–30, 143–44, 175, 195–97, 198–99; and Henry Fielding, *The Journal of a Voyage to*

Lisbon (1755), ed. A. R. Humphreys and Douglas Brooks (London: Everyman's Library, 1973), "Author's Preface," 189.

2. Fielding, *Voyage to Lisbon,* 189 (cf. *Clarissa,* 4th ed. [1751], I, "Preface," vi); *Pamela Censured,* ed. Charles Batten, Jr., *Augustan Reprint Society,* no. 175 (1976); *Critical Remarks on Sir Charles Grandison, Clarissa, and Pamela . . .* (1754), ed. Alan D. McKillop, *Augustan Reprint Society,* no. 21, ser. 4, no. 3 (1950), 43.

3. See *Critical Remarks,* 18–20; Elizabeth Carter to Catherine Talbot, June 20, 1749, in Ioan Williams, ed., *Novel and Romance, 1700–1800: A Documentary Record* (New York: Barnes and Noble, 1970), 125.

4. *The Life of Pamela . . .* (1741), 185n, 249n (on "monstrous Inconsistencies" see also 340n); Lady Mary to Lady Bute, March, 1752, and Oct., 1755, in *Complete Letters of Lady Mary Wortley Montagu,* ed. Robert Halsband (Oxford: Clarendon Press, 1965–67), III, 9, 96; *Pamela Censured,* 18. In October, 1750, Lady Mary told her daughter that *Pamela* "was all the Fashion at Paris and Versailles, and is still the Joy of the Chambermaids of all Nations": *Complete Letters,* II, 470.

5. Richardson, *Clarissa: Preface,* "Postscript," 349–51, and "Hints," 2; Richardson to Lady Bradshaigh, Dec. 15, 1748, in *Selected Letters,* 108. Contrast not only the narrative practice of *Pamela* but the explicit doctrine of its protagonist, at least in Part II; see *Pamela,* Part II (1741), letter xci. On the spiritual implications of poetic justice see above, chap. 3, nn. 77–79. For the Richardsonian defense see above, chap. 11, n. 11.

6. *Life of Pamela,* 185–86n. For imitations of *Pamela* (especially one by William Shenstone) that parody its wealth of circumstantial detail more thoroughly than Fielding does, see Bernard Kriessman, *Pamela-Shamela: A Study of the Criticisms, Burlesques, Parodies, and Adaptations of Richardson's Pamela,* University of Nebraska Studies, n.s., no. 22 (Lincoln: University of Nebraska Press, 1960), 69–71. Pierre Marivaux makes the "obvious reply" in *Marianne* (1731–41), trans. John Lockman (1736), I, 1–2: "The Truth is, that, was this History a meer Fiction, very likely the Form of it would have been different. *Marianne's* Reflections would be neither so long nor so frequent . . . But *Marianne* . . . pleased herself in setting down indifferently the whole Compass of her Reflections on every Incident of her Life. They are long or short, according as the Subject of them pleased her" (quoted in McKillop, *Samuel Richardson,* 37).

7. *Pamela Censured,* 9; Richardson to Ralph Allen, Oct. 8, 1741, in *Selected Letters,* 52. Compare Henry Fielding, *Shamela* (1741), whose prefatory "Letters to the Editor" include one from John Puff, Esq., and one from "the Editor to Himself." In *Voyage to Lisbon,* 189, Fielding alludes to "the conduct of authors, who often fill a whole sheet with their own praises, to which they sometimes set their own real names, and sometimes a fictitious one."

The explosion of Richardson's claim to historicity in *Pamela* is one central aim of the author of *Pamela Censured,* and he achieves it elsewhere in the tract by less circumstantial means than in this passage. *Pamela's* prefatory material, and its self-praise, were conceived around the same time a letter was planted in the *Weekly Miscellany* for Oct. 11, 1739, urging on "the Author of Pamela" to publication; see McKillop, *Samuel Richardson,* 42–43. But there is no basis for McKillop's inference, similar to that of *Pamela Censured,* that therefore the fiction of the editor was also an afterthought, "planned at the last moment to help the cause along" by facilitating the self-praise. On the imitators' exploitation of the fiction of authentic documents see above, chap. 11, n. 3.

8. Williams, *Novel and Romance,* 124; Richardson to William Warburton,

April 19, 1748, in *Selected Letters*, 85; Williams, *Novel and Romance*, 117–18. On the restorations see the preface to the second edition of vol. I of *Clarissa*, in Williams, *Novel and Romance*, 167; and Richardson, *Clarissa: Preface*, "Hints," 12. In the words of Joseph Spence, "The Author of Clarissa has attempted to give a plain and natural Account of an Affair that happened in a private Family, just in the manner that it did happen. He has aimed solely at following Nature; and giving the Sentiments of the Persons concerned, just as they flowed warm from their Hearts" (ibid., "Hints," 8; see also Philip Skelton's discussion, ibid., "Hints," 7). In Richardson's words, "There was frequently a necessity to be very circumstantial and minute, in order to preserve and maintain that Air of Probability, which is necessary to be maintained in a Story designed to represent real Life" (ibid., "Postscript," 368).

9. See letter from Aaron Hill, Dec. 17, 1740, printed in "Introduction to this Second Edition," *Pamela*, ed. T. C. Duncan Eaves and Ben D. Kimpel (Boston: Houghton Mifflin, 1971), 10, where the narrative is compared to "a Kind of Dramatical Representation"; Richardson, *Clarissa: Preface*, "Postscript," 351; Fielding, "Preface" to [Sarah Fielding], *Familiar Letters between the Principal Characters in David Simple, And Some Others* (1747), I, ix–xii; Richardson, *Clarissa: Preface*, "Hints," 6 (a later passage suggests more obviously that Richardson is defending himself against Fielding: "We need not insist on the evident Superiority of this Method to the dry Narrative; where the *Novelist* moves on, his own dull Pace, to the End of his Chapter and Book interweaving impertinent Digressions, for fear the Reader's Patience should be exhausted by his tedious Dwelling on one Subject, in the same Style" [ibid., 13]); Lady Mary to Lady Bute, Oct., 1755, in *Complete Letters*, III, 97.

10. Richardson to Lady Bradshaigh, late 1749, in *Selected Letters*, 133; Coventry, *New Species of Writing*, ed. cit., 15, 16.

11. Mary Granville (Pendarves) Delaney to Mrs. Dewes, Jan. 18, 1752, and Anne Donnellan to Richardson, Feb. 11, 1752, in Paulson and Lockwood, *Fielding: Critical Heritage*, 313, 319 (cf. Elizabeth Carter, who thought that Richardson did not know how to depict vice, above, n. 3); anonymous letter of 1754 paraphrased by Eaves and Kimpel, *Samuel Richardson*, 305; Richardson, *The History of Sir Charles Grandison . . .* (1753), VII, 303 (it is probably this passage that occasioned Fielding's allusion to Richardson in the preface to the *Voyage to Lisbon;* see above, n. 2). For the comparison of Clarissa and Sophia see Richardson to Astraea and Minerva Hill, Aug. 4, 1749, Frances Grainger, Jan. 22, 1750, and Lady Bradshaigh, early 1751, in *Selected Letters*, 127–28, 143–44, 178. Resisting Fielding's advice: e.g., see Richardson to Aaron Hill, Nov. 7, 1748, ibid., 99.

12. Samuel Johnson, *Rambler*, no. 4 (March 31, 1750), in *The Rambler*, ed. W. J. Bate and Albrecht B. Strauss, Yale Edition of the Works of Samuel Johnson (New Haven: Yale University Press, 1969), III, 22–23 (now widely accepted, the suggestion that this paper was occasioned by the popularity of *Tom Jones* and *Roderick Random* was first made by Alexander Chalmers, *The Works of Samuel Johnson* [1816], IV, 24); James Boswell, *Life of Johnson*, ed. George Birkbeck Hill and L. F. Powell, 2nd ed. (Oxford: Clarendon Press, 1964), II, 49. See also the invidious comparison reported by Hannah More in 1780, in Paulson and Lockwood, *Fielding: Critical Heritage*, 443. But to both Boswell and Hester Thrale, Johnson praised Amelia over all other "romance heroines." See Boswell, *Life of Johnson*, III, 43n.2; and Paulson and Lockwood, *Fielding: Critical Heritage*, 445. Thomas Edwards believed that Richardson's ability to depict virtue better than Fielding was due to his close acquaintance with it in his own breast: see Edwards to Charles Yorke, Jan. 15, 1749, quoted in McKillop, "Personal Relations," 430;

and Edwards to the Reverend Mr. Lawry, Feb. 12, 1752, in *Fielding: Critical Heritage*, 320. For Fielding's pedagogic rationale see above, chap. 12, n. 5, on the "mixture of good and evil in the same character" as an expression of the aim "to draw natural, not perfect characters, and to record the truths of history, not the extravagances of romance." See also *The Champion*, 2 vols. (1741), June 10, 1740, II, 316–17, where Fielding argues that "we are much better and easier taught by the Examples of what we are to shun, than by those which would instruct us what to pursue."

13. Boswell, *Life of Johnson*, April, 1772, II, 174; George Cheyne to Richardson, March 9, 1742, in Paulson and Lockwood, *Fielding: Critical Heritage*, 118; *Old England*, March, 1748, quoted in Frederic T. Blanchard, *Fielding the Novelist* (New Haven: Yale University Press, 1927), 22, 23; Richardson to Anne Donnellan, Feb. 22, 1752, and Lady Bradshaigh, Feb. 23, 1752, in *Selected Letters*, 196–97, 198–99.

14. See above, nn. 10, 11, 13, 12.

15. For one sort of guide to this process of positive revaluation see Hans Eichner, ed., *"Romantic" and Its Cognates: The European History of a Word* (Toronto: University of Toronto Press, 1972).

16. See William B. Warner, *Reading Clarissa: The Struggles of Interpretation* (New Haven: Yale University Press, 1979); Terry Castle, *Clarissa's Ciphers: Meaning and Disruption in Richardson's "Clarissa"* (Ithaca: Cornell University Press, 1982); Terry Eagleton, *The Rape of Clarissa: Writing, Sexuality, and the Class Struggle in Samuel Richardson* (Oxford: Blackwell, 1982).

Index

Abraham, 76

Absolutism: and absolute private property, 177–78, 326, 327, 333; in Bunyan,
307; and Calvinism, 192, 193; and
capitalist activity, 204–5, 206, 226, 236;
and centralization of state power, 177,
234; and civic service, 182–88, 224; and
doctrines of sovereignty, 177–82, 184–
86; in the family, 227; in Fielding, 387;
as mediation of feudalism and capitalism, 177, 201; and Protestant reform,
189–200; in Swift, 343; Tudor, 178,
179, 183, 189, 199, 224, 226

Achilles, 134–35

Addison, Joseph, 43

Aelianus, Claudius, 68

Aeneas, 36, 138

Aesthetic, realm of the, 63, 119–20, 125–
26, 128, 248, 419; in Cervantes, 280,
281, 282; in Fielding, 389, 394, 408; in
Richardson, 361, 374; in Swift, 353

Agamemnon, 134

Agrarian revolution, 168

Albigenses, 77

Alemán, Mateo: *Guzmán de Alfarache,* 97,
98, 238, 242, 244

Alexander the Great, 201, 384, 385

Allegory: Christian, 34; Hesiodic, 137; of
love, 147; and novelistic narrative, 312;
pilgrimage, 107, 115, 295–314; political, 54, 59, 60, 232, 261, 494n.17,
502n.16; Protestant, 115–16, 254, 296,
297, 312, 319; *Robinson Crusoe* as, 121;
A Tale of a Tub as, 61; in travel narrative, 105

Allestree, Richard, 155, 200, 207

Althusser, Louis, 19

Amadis of Gaul, 56, 245, 273

American Indians, 40, 111, 113, 116, 117,
250; in Defoe, 328, 329, 331–32

Amis and Amiloun, 146

Amory, Hugh, 399

Anabaptists, 77

Ancient constitution, doctrine of the, 41–
42, 179

Ancients and moderns, quarrel of, 40, 68–
73, 153

Anglicanism: and biblical exegesis, 79,
81–82, 88; Calvinist element in, 190,
198–99, 398; and conservative ideology, 218; and Hanoverian succession,
181. *See also* Latitudinarianism

Annals of Love, The, 26

Anne (queen of England), 171, 233

Antiquarianism, 42–43, 49, 293

Antiquaries, Society of, 42

Apollo, 139

Apparition narratives, 83–87, 98, 99, 116,
124, 297, 328